THE QUARTERMASTER CORPS:

ORGANIZATION,

SUPPLY, AND SERVICES

Volume I

LT. GEN. EDMUND B. GREGORY, *The Quartermaster General During World War II.*

UNITED STATES ARMY IN WORLD WAR II

The Technical Services

THE QUARTERMASTER CORPS: ORGANIZATION, SUPPLY, AND SERVICES

Volume I

by

Erna Risch

MILITARY INSTRVCTION

CENTER OF MILITARY HISTORY
UNITED STATES ARMY
WASHINGTON, D.C., 2014

First Printed 1953—CMH Pub 10–12–1

For sale by the Superintendent of Documents, U.S. Government Printing Office
Internet: bookstore.gpo.gov   Phone: toll free (866) 512-1800;   DC area (202) 512-1800
Fax: (202) 512-2104 Mail: Stop IDCC, Washington, DC 20402-0001

ISBN 978-0-16-092513-9

UNITED STATES ARMY IN WORLD WAR II

Kent Roberts Greenfield, General Editor

Advisory Committee

Office of the Chief of Military History

Maj. Gen. Orlando Ward, Chief

. . . to Those Who Served

Foreword

This volume is the first in a series which will record the experiences of the Quartermaster Corps in World War II. It should serve to impress students of military affairs, particularly those in staff and command positions, with the vastness and complexity of the activity involved in equipping and maintaining troops in the field. It tells a story of rapid expansion to meet the needs of a growing Army, of organizational readjustment in the midst of operations, of supply programs scrapped or modified in the face of unexpected demands, of improvisation and production under pressure when plans were inadequate or lacking. It clearly demonstrates the necessity in time of peace for a flexible organization, vision and care in planning, and a program of continuous military research and development to meet the sudden impact of war.

ORLANDO WARD

Washington, D. C.   Maj. Gen., U. S. A.
15 March 1952   Chief of Military History

Note on the History of the Quartermaster Corps

This is the first volume of a group of four narrating the operation of the Quartermaster Corps in World War II. *Organization, Supply, and Services*, Volume I, and its companion volume of the same title, Volume II, analyze activities in the zone of interior. Two other volumes, in preparation, describe Quartermaster operations in the war against Germany and the war against Japan.

Primarily this volume relates the story of Quartermaster supply during World War II, a phase of the broader subject of military supply which has been much neglected in the past in favor of the more colorful and dramatic combat history. As the main function of the Corps, supply operations included the development of Quartermaster items, the estimation of requirements, the procurement of clothing, equipment, subsistence, and general supplies, and their storage and distribution. These aspects of the supply process are analyzed in this volume and set against the background of organizational changes in the Office of The Quartermaster General and in the field.

The author, Dr. Erna Risch, received her Ph. D. degree from the University of Chicago. After extensive teaching experience, she joined the staff of the Historical Section, Office of The Quartermaster General, in 1943. She has prepared a number of historical studies that have been published by the Quartermaster Corps, in addition to writing the present volume.

THOMAS M. PITKIN
Chief, Historical Section
Office of The Quartermaster General

Washington, D. C.
1 January 1952

Preface

Some three centuries ago Lion Gardener, in his *Relation of the Pequot Warres*, sagely observed that "war is like a three-footed Stool, want one foot and down comes all; and these three feet are men, victuals, and munitions." Nevertheless, until quite recently, military history has almost completely neglected problems of supply. The allocation of volumes for the series, UNITED STATES ARMY IN WORLD WAR II, promises a more balanced approach to the subject. There has been a generous assignment of volumes to the supply agencies of the Army, and among these are four covering the activities of the Quartermaster Corps. Two of these, of which the present volume is the first, will be devoted to operations of the Corps in the zone of interior.

One of the oldest of all War Department agencies, the Quartermaster Corps, in spite of the loss of some of its traditional functions, remained throughout World War II one of the most important of the supply, or technical, services. In addition to its main mission of supplying broad categories of items needed by the Army, the Corps had, in the course of its long existence, become responsible for a variety of services to troops in the field. The multiplicity of its activities made a chronological treatment of the war period practically impossible. It was considered more advantageous to project a narrative which would first develop completely the supply operation of the Corps as its major function, then analyze personnel and training problems, and finally discuss the special services performed by the Corps for the Army.

This volume begins but does not complete the analysis of Quartermaster supply, which is envisaged in broad terms as a continuous process starting with the development of military items and moving through the estimating of requirements, the procurement of supplies, their storage and distribution, the reclamation and salvage of items to ease supply, and the final process of industrial demobilization. This approach permitted a functional treatment, although not all activities—notably the supply of subsistence and of fuels and lubricants—were organized functionally in the Office of The Quartermaster General. Within the limits of each function a chronological development is followed.

A history of Quartermaster activities in World War II could not begin with the attack on Pearl Harbor nor even with the declaration of the national emergency in 1939, for many of the Corps' policies were rooted in the years immediately following World War I. Primary emphasis is placed upon developments after December 1941, but, in summary at least, the period covered extends from 1920 to August 1945.

The historical program initiated by the Historical Section of the Office of The Quartermaster General in the summer of 1942 laid the groundwork for a thorough and detailed analysis of the supply function of the Corps. A vast amount of source material was examined and selections were, for the most part, photostated currently with the operations being described and analyzed in the monographic series published by the Historical Section during the war years. This collection of material and published monographs, as well as the historical reports and monographs from historical units established at Quartermaster field installations and supervised by the Historical Section, provided an invaluable body of material for the more general treatment of supply in this volume. It was supplemented by additional research to provide more continuous coverage of the supply program of the Corps.

Limitation of time has precluded any search into the records of other governmental agencies with which the Quartermaster Corps co-operated during the war, as, for example, the War Production Board. As a rule, however, sufficient interdepartmental correspondence has been available in Quartermaster files to permit objective treatment.

Over-all supply of the Army was directed and co-ordinated by the Services of Supply, later renamed the Army Service Forces as a result of the reorganization of the War Department in March 1942. While relationships with this higher echelon have been explored, the point of view throughout this volume remains that of the Quartermaster Corps.

The material obtained from the official records maintained in the central files of the Office of The Quartermaster General has been supplemented by a wide use of interviews. Operating personnel were interviewed during the war years as a means of eking out the written record, which in many instances was meager, since transactions frequently were completed by telephone, and transcriptions of such conversations were not necessarily available. Correspondence and interviews, in the years since the war ended, with some of the directors of Quartermaster wartime operations have also added to the record. The memories of these directors may not always be precise as to their motives in a given action or with regard to the exact sequence of events. With due allowances made, their comments were nevertheless fruitful in directing research into neglected areas, or in providing explanations nowhere else obtainable.

This volume was circulated in manuscript form before final editing and was greatly benefited by the frank criticism accorded it by the wartime directors of the principal divisions concerned with supply in the Office of The Quartermaster General and their key operators. They were most generous in reading relevant portions of the text and in commenting by letter or in personal interviews. These comments enabled the author to correct errors of fact, to include developments that had been inadvertently omitted, and to make such revisions as were warranted by re-examination of the record in the light of the criticism offered.

Throughout the preparation of this volume the author could and did rely heavily upon the scholarly advice and assistance offered by the Chief of the Historical Section, Dr. Thomas M. Pitkin. Under his general direction work has been in progress since 1947 not only on this volume and its companion, which cover Quartermaster activities in the zone of interior, but also on two volumes dealing with Quartermaster overseas operations. Throughout the years of her association with the program, the author has also been indebted to her colleagues for their unfailing co-operation and help with problems relevant to their specialized fields. No acknowledgment would be complete without a large vote of thanks to the assistants who toiled in the central and storage files of the Office.

Thanks are also due the Editorial and Photographic Sections, Office of the Chief of Military History. Final editing of the volume was carried out by Mr. W. Brooks Phillips, senior editor, assisted by Mrs. Loretto Stevens. Miss Margaret E. Tackley, photographic editor, was most helpful in selecting the photographs and preparing them for the printer.

Washington, D. C.
1 January 1952

ERNA RISCH

xii

Contents

Part One: Administration

Chapter   *Page*

INTRODUCTORY   3
   Historical Background   3
   Status of QMC in 1939   7
   Effect of World War II   7

I. ADMINISTRATIVE ORGANIZATION   11
   Expansion of the Organization   11
   Transfer of Functions   16
   General Reorganization after Pearl Harbor   22
   Problems of Adjustment Under Office Order 84   26
   Readjustments in 1942   28
   Evolution of Functional-Commodity-Type Organization, 1943–45   34
   Field Organization   38
   Relations with Other Agencies   45

Part Two: Supply

II. FACTORS SHAPING RESEARCH ACTIVITIES   51
   Influence of World War I Surplus Property   52
   Lack of Integrated Research Program   54
   Financial Restrictions   55
   Influence of Procurement Planning   56
   Impact of Global War   57
   Effect of Materials Shortages on Design   58

III. THE DEVELOPMENT OF ARMY CLOTHING   75
   Organization for Product Development   75
   Development and Standardization Procedure   86
   Winter Combat Clothing   88
   Summer Combat Clothing   97
   Jungle Combat Clothing   99
   Combat Headgear   101
   Combat Footgear   102
   Clothing for Women in the Army   110
   Textile and Leather Problems   117
   Summary   121

Chapter   *Page*

IV. THE DEVELOPMENT OF PERSONAL AND ORGANIZATIONAL
      EQUIPMENT 123
      Personal Equipment 123
      Organizational Equipment 138
      Summary 172

V. THE DEVELOPMENT OF SUBSISTENCE 174
      Administrative Background 175
      The Development of Special Rations 177
      Development of Components of A and B Rations 192
      Development of Packaging and Packing 201
      Summary 206

VI. FORECASTING WAR REQUIREMENTS FOR QUARTERMASTER
      SUPPLIES 208
      Administrative Background 209
      Theory of Forecasting Requirements 212
      Elements in the Determination of Requirements 212
      Evolution of the Army Supply Program 221
      Quartermaster Contributions to Improved Techniques . . . 224
      Development of Supply Control System 226
      Computation of Task Force Requirements 229
      Overseas Requirements Tables 230
      Subsistence Requirements 231
      Elements in Subsistence Forecasting 233
      Petroleum Requirements 238
      Summary 242

VII. PROCUREMENT POLICIES AND PROCEDURES 243
      The Quartermaster Supply System in 1939 243
      War Procurement Plans 246
      Developments in Procurement Organization 247
      Expansion of Centralized Procurement 249
      Experimentation with Decentralized Procurement Operations 251
      Streamlining Procurement Methods 252
      Contract Placement Policies and Problems 265
      Special Procurement Responsibilities 279

VIII. PRODUCTION CONTROL 283
      Organization for Production Control 283
      Causes of Contract Delinquency 285
      Expediting Efforts of Contractors and Depots 287
      Flow of Materials and Equipment 288
      Production Planning and Scheduling 301
      Other Aids for Expediting Production 303
      Inspection of Quartermaster Procurements 308

Chapter *Page*

IX. QUARTERMASTER STORAGE OPERATIONS 323
    Administrative Background 323
    Depot Storage Operations 326
    Expansion of Depot Storage Facilities 329
    Use of Commercial Storage Space 334
    Space Control 342
    Materials Handling 347
    Packing Operations 355

X. STOCK CONTROL OPERATIONS 360
    Supply Administration Prior to 1942 360
    Establishment of New Methods of Stock Control 364
    Stock Control System in Operation 372
    Administrative Developments 376
    Excess Stocks 379
    Disposal of Surplus Property 384

BIBLIOGRAPHICAL NOTE 392

LIST OF ABBREVIATIONS 396

INDEX 400

Charts

No.

1. The Quartermaster Corps in the War Department: 1941 13
2. The Quartermaster Corps in the War Department: March 1942 25
3. Office of The Quartermaster General: 31 July 1942 32
4. Office of The Quartermaster General: 15 July 1944 37
5. Research and Development Branch, OQMG: 16 June 1944 78
6. Quartermaster Board Shoe Test Track 82
7. Quartermaster Board Combat Course (1,700 Feet) 83
8. Principal Changes in K Ration Components 187
9. Supply Pipeline (Quartermaster Items) 220
10. Quartermaster Corps Depot System: 1939 331
11. Quartermaster Corps Depot System: 1 December 1944 335

Illustrations

Lt. Gen. Edmund B. Gregory . . . . *Frontispiece*
Service Uniforms of 1918 and 1941 89
Utilization of the Layering Principle 91

	Page
Field Jacket M–1943	92
Combat Uniform with Hood	93
Footwear Developed by the Quartermaster Corps	105
Shoepacs and Wool Ski Socks	108
The Original WAAC Uniform	112
Army Nurse Corps Uniforms	114
Nurse's Seersucker Uniform	115
Jungle Pack	125
Barracks Bag	128
Duffel Bag	129
Intrenching Shovel M–1943	135
Combination Intrenching Tool	137
Filling Blitz Cans from Railroad Tank Car	145
Field Range M–1937	147
Gasoline Cooking Stoves	148
Small Detachment Cooking Outfit	152
20-Man Cooking Outfit	153
Army Field Bake Oven No. 1	154
Portable Repair Units	162
Ten-in-One Army Field Ration	190
Dehydrated Food Products	198
Fork-Lift Truck	348

All illustrations in this volume are from U. S. Department of Defense files.

PART ONE

ADMINISTRATION

Introductory

Historical Background

The Quartermaster Corps (QMC) is one of the oldest supply agencies of the War Department. Its origin can be traced to 16 June 1775, when the Continental Congress passed a resolution providing "that there be one quarter master general for the grand army, and a deputy, under him, for the separate army." [1] Known as the Quartermaster's Department during its early existence, it suffered many tribulations, including temporary extinction on more than one occasion, but the importance of its functions compelled its re-establishment.

The mission of the Quartermaster organization has always been one of broad and varied service to combat troops. From Revolutionary days it was responsible until recent years for all transportation and most construction, as well as for the storage and issue of many types of supplies for the support of armies in the field, though at first it did not always procure its own items.

In the post-Revolutionary period, when the Quartermaster's Department was temporarily abolished, the Secretary of War purchased supplies for the tiny peacetime army through civilian contractors. During the twenty years and more following the adoption of the Constitution, procurement of supplies was handled by a kaleidoscopic succession of quartermasters, contractors, and agents variously named, under the direction, sometimes of the Treasury, sometimes of the War Department.

The approach of war with England brought about the re-establishment of the department early in the spring of 1812. [2] While the Quartermaster General was given broad procurement responsibilities, being authorized "to purchase military stores, camp equipage and other articles requisite for the troops, and generally to procure and provide means of transport for the army, its stores, artillery, and camp equipage," at the same time Congress established a Commissary General of Purchases whose duty it was "to conduct the procuring and providing of all arms, military stores, clothing, and generally all articles of supply requisite for the military service of the United States."

Under the stress of war the overlapping jurisdictions thus created, together with the absence of specific provision for a subsistence department, soon brought confusion forcing remedial legislation. Congress authorized the Secretary of War to define more precisely the responsibilities of the two agencies. Furthermore, when contracting failures occurred and such action was deemed expedient by the President, the Quartermaster's Department might be authorized to procure and issue subsistence directly in the field. [3]

In the overhauling of the supply system that followed the War of 1812, the responsibilities of the office of the Commissary General of Purchases were further delimited and reduced. The Ordnance Department acquired the right of procurement in its own field in 1815. A separate Subsistence Department was created under its own Commissary General in 1818. Although the office of the Commissary General of Pur-

---

[1] *Journals of the Continental Congress,* edited by Worthington C. Ford *et al.* (34 vols, Washington: GPO, 1904–37), II, 94.

[2] *U.S. Statutes at Large,* II, 696–99, act approved 28 Mar 1812.

[3] *Ibid.,* II, 816–18, act approved 3 Mar 1813.

chases remained in existence until 1842, its remaining functions were gradually absorbed by the Quartermaster's Department. In 1826 the Department acquired the additional responsibility of receiving from the purchasing department and distributing to the Army "all clothing and camp and garrison equipage required for the use of the troops." By 1842, just before the Mexican War, the Quartermaster organization had taken over complete responsibility for procurement and distribution to the field forces of all noncombat supplies, except subsistence.[4]

The duties of the Quartermaster General were traditionally performed with the Army in the field and had been generally considered to exist only in time of war. With the appointment of Lt. Col. Thomas S. Jesup in 1818, however, it was understood that the new Quartermaster General would establish his headquarters in Washington. Under his guidance the Department emerged as a permanent supply staff agency of the Secretary of War.[5]

During the long administration of Quartermaster General Jesup, which lasted until the summer of 1860, central and regional organization and facilities developed slowly. Field facilities were largely improvised during the early years of the country's history, although the importance of established depots to the movement and distribution of supplies over long distances, as during the Indian campaigns, was recognized on several occasions. In 1842, with the abolition of the office of the Commissary General of Purchases, the Quartermaster's Department acquired its principal depot, the Schuylkill Arsenal. Under the name of the Philadelphia Quartermaster Depot, it became the cornerstone of the great system of Quartermaster depots. There, for more than a hundred years army clothing was procured and manufactured in peace and war. A system of reserve and field depots was established during the Civil War,[6] and a number of these were retained at its close.

In a sense, the modern development of the Quartermaster organization began during the Civil War, with the problems incident to this first experience of mobilization and war that absorbed a large part of the energy of the nation. To supervise and handle the expanding procurement and distribution operations, among other activities, and to direct the efforts of the many newly established field installations, a commodity-type organization was eventually established in the Quartermaster General's office wherein designated branches handled the purchase and distribution of one or more specific types of supplies provided for the troops.[7] All functions expanded enormously in the course of the war, and new facilities and programs of lasting importance were set up in many fields. In 1862, for example, responsibility was assumed for the management of national cemeteries and the interment of the bodies of war dead in these permanent locations.[8]

In the thirty years following the Civil War there were no large-scale operations to provide incentive for maintaining an alert, progressive agency and the Quartermaster's Department merely drifted. With the outbreak of the Spanish-American War, however, the Department was suddenly called upon to clothe and equip more than a quarter of a million men in contrast to the peacetime force of only 26,000. Under the strain of mobilization, supply broke down. Troops were sent to the tropics in winter uniforms, and congestion of men and supplies at Port Tampa, the port of embarkation for oper-

---

[4] *Ibid.*, III, 203, act approved 8 Feb 1815. *Ibid.*, III, 426–27, act approved 14 Apr 1818. *Ibid.*, IV, 173–74, act approved 18 May 1826. *Ibid.*, V, 513, act approved 23 Aug 1842.

[5] Thomas M. Pitkin, "Evolution of the Quartermaster Corps, 1775–1950," *Quartermaster Review*, XXX (May–June 1950), 104ff. *Quartermaster Review* is hereafter cited as *QMR*.

[6] *U.S. Statutes at Large*, XIII, 394–98, act approved 4 Jul 1864.

[7] *Ibid.*, XIII, 394–95.

[8] *Ibid.*, XII, 596, act approved 17 Jul 1862. *Ibid.*, XIII, 394–98, act approved 4 Jul 1864.

ations in Cuba, defied description. The Subsistence Department, responsible for feeding the Army, was equally unprepared for the task confronting it.

The investigations and recommendations that followed the war resulted in the enactment in 1912 of legislation [9] consolidating the Army Subsistence, Pay, and Quartermaster's Departments. Prior to 1912 the Quartermaster's Department had acquired responsibility for the supply of clothing, camp and garrison equipment, individual equipment, and general supplies for the Army, the transportation of the Army, the handling of construction and real estate activities, the operation of utilities at camps and stations, and certain miscellaneous activities, including the administration of national cemeteries. As a result of the merger of the three supply organizations, the newly designated Quartermaster Corps also acquired responsibility for feeding and paying the Army. The period from the summer of 1912 to early 1917 probably was the high-water mark in the history of the Corps with respect to the mere number of important supply and service functions for which it had general responsibility throughout the War Department.

Impact of World War I

When World War I began, the Office of the Quartermaster General (OQMG) was still organized on a commodity basis. The office consisted of five divisions—Administrative, Finance and Accounting, Construction and Repair, Transportation, and Supplies—whose functions were largely administrative and supervisory. The operations of procurement and distribution were decentralized to the field. The actual distribution of supplies was accomplished by the post and camp quartermasters who submitted requisitions to the quartermasters of the territorial departments into which the country was divided for administrative purposes. They, in turn, approved and forwarded the requisitions to the depot quartermasters who procured, stored, and issued supplies on the basis of these requisitions. There were seven general depots and certain other specialized depots designated as points of supply. The procurement of certain classes of supplies was centralized in specific depots, as, for example, clothing at the Philadelphia Depot and wagons and harness at the Jeffersonville Depot. Thus a degree of "centralized decentralization" prevailed in this supply system. Most of the depots acted independently of each other because of the policy of decentralization. The purchase of subsistence was even more decentralized since it was carried on "as near to the points of consumption as was consistent with advantage to the Government." [10]

There was nothing wrong with this organization itself, but decentralization of purchase could not continue under the economic strain of manufacturing for the Allies, for the government, and for the civilian population. Furthermore, in the absence of effective co-ordination, the QMC, as well as every other supply bureau, sought to accomplish its task independently of all other agencies. In the ensuing competition occasioned by shortages of materials, facilities, and transportation, supply difficulties increased and the need for a centralized control to direct the war effort became evident.

Moreover, as the Army grew in size, the tendency was to multiply the number of separate bureaus to carry out expanded functions. Responsibility for construction was transferred from the Corps to a new and separate Cantonment Division. Similarly, the duties of water transportation were taken over by the Embarkation Service.

In an effort to secure greater efficiency and co-ordination, the War Department reorganized

---

[9] *Ibid.*, XXXVII, 591, act approved 24 Aug 1912.
[10] *Report of the Quartermaster General to the Secretary of War, 1919* (Washington: GPO, 1920), pp. 9–10.

the supply bureaus. These agencies, including the QMC, were temporarily absorbed by the General Staff in special divisions that were organized along functional lines. At the end of the war, the QMC was a part of the Purchase, Storage and Traffic Division.

Once again the shortcomings revealed by war, and particularly the failure to plan in advance for mobilization, led to the enactment of remedial legislation. Under one of the provisions of the National Defense Act of 1920, the QMC was re-established as a separate supply service, and the functions of transportation and construction were restored to the Corps. On the other hand, the pay function of the Corps was transferred permanently to a separate jurisdiction.[11]

Administrative Developments, 1920–39

When the National Defense Act of 1920 abolished the Purchase, Storage and Traffic Division and restored the functions of procurement, storage, and issue to the supply arms and services, the OQMG was again organized along commodity lines.[12] The major units of its organization were variously known as "services" or as "divisions" during the next few years. As the office gradually consolidated its many activities for peacetime operation, four divisions emerged to handle most Quartermaster activities. These were the Administrative Division, under which, in general, functions of a staff character were combined; the Supply Division composed of several commodity branches, such as the Subsistence Branch, the Clothing and Equipage Branch, and the General Supplies Branch, among others; and the self-contained Construction and Transportation Divisions.[13] The functions of construction and transportation were lodged in divisions, each of which was established as an integrated agency with plenary operating powers, for it was intended that the organization set up in the OQMG should be

potentially adaptable to the exigencies of a national emergency. A ready framework was to exist for adaptation and expansion.

World War I experience with the Purchase, Storage and Traffic Division, which had combined staff and operating functions in the same agency, had emphasized the desirability of separating staff agencies, which developed plans and policies and specified procedures for their execution, from operating units, which carried them out. As a consequence, the OQMG in 1920 sought to place all staff or planning activities pertaining to supply in a Control Service. Operating activities lay within the province of the Supply Division. The Control Service exercised general administrative, procedural, and functional supervision. It was charged with formulating war plans, controlling all fiscal matters, preparing statistical data, consolidating requirements, and maintaining liaison with higher authority on these matters. Incidentally, during the twenties and thirties the OQMG set up planning and staff controls as directed by higher authority, but the staff units were often skeleton or mere paper organizations.

While the OQMG organization attempted to separate staff and operating functions, the lesson of World War I was neglected more often than not. There was a steady tendency for current operations to absorb staff functions. Within a comparatively short time the majority of the control functions were delegated to the operating branches.[14] This change resulted from the developing self-sufficiency of the operating agencies and the dwindling of supervisory duties and personnel in the OQMG. As a consequence, it proved more feasible to lodge staff functions in operating branches during a peacetime period

---

[11] U.S. Statutes at Large, XLI, 766, act approved 4 Jun 20.

[12] OQMG Cir 11, 28 Jul 20, sub: Orgn of QMC.

[13] OQMG OO 4, 7 Jan 37, sub: Office Orgn.

[14] OQMG Office Memo 119, 30 Aug 21, sub: Orgn of OQMG.

when the scope of Quartermaster activities was sharply reduced.

Congress had been highly critical of the lack of planning revealed by World War I, and in legislating for national defense in 1920 it had created the position of Assistant Secretary of War, making him responsible for procurement planning and the supervision of the procurement of all military supplies. Hence The Quartermaster General was under the supervision of the Assistant Secretary of War in all these matters, while directly responsible to the General Staff on all others. During this period the OQMG established units with varying names to carry on its war-planning functions. For example, it created the War Plans and Training Division in the Administrative Service in 1926 directly as a result of the need for meeting the emphasis of the Assistant Secretary of War on planning activities.[15] But the inevitable tendency was to divorce planning for a distant emergency from the organization for current peacetime operations. This was to have important repercussions in World War II.

The OQMG organization during these years was not disturbed by the participation of the QMC in the Civilian Conservation Corps (CCC) and other New Deal activities of the thirties. The impact was felt primarily at the field installations. If it had no important effect on headquarters organization, participation in government relief and other emergency economic activities of the period proved an experience of tremendous significance in other ways.[16] By contributing to the improvement and crystallization of operating methods, it undoubtedly smoothed the way for the intensification of purely military preparations.

Status of QMC in 1939

In September 1939, when war began in Europe, the QMC was a small supply agency of the War Department which had potentialities for expansion, in case of an emergency, into a large organization. It consisted of less than 12,000 military personnel and approximately 37,000 civilians,[17] who trained Quartermaster personnel and provided supplies and services for an Army of not far from 200,000 men stationed at posts, camps, and stations in the United States and at such outposts as Alaska, Hawaii, and the Panama Canal Zone. These activities were accomplished through a Washington headquarters, organized on a commodity basis as it had been since Civil War days, through field installations, such as depots, engaged in procuring and distributing supplies, and through certain schools operated by the Corps—the Quartermaster School and the Motor Transport School—which trained the military personnel needed by the QMC. For the most part, the depots were located in the eastern half of the United States, a significant fact in view of the necessity of mounting a war in the Pacific.

Effect of World War II

The outbreak of war in Europe was felt at once in the United States Army. The presidential proclamation of limited emergency increased the size of the Army to 227,000 men from the 210,000 provided by earlier legislative action on the Army appropriation bill. The QMC and other supply services took this limited increase in the military establishment more or less in stride. The fall of France in June 1940, however, brought a more dramatic enlargement of the Army. Congressional action added to the size of the Regular Army, the National Guard was inducted into the Federal service, and Congress

---

[15] OQMG OO 19, 12 May 26, no sub.

[16] For a summary view of these trends and developments see the annual *Report of the Secretary of War to the President,* Fiscal Years 1930–35.

[17] More than half of this civilian personnel was employed in the Civilian Conservation Corps, Public Works Administration (PWA), and Works Progress Administration (WPA) working on QMC projects.

passed the Selective Service Act in September providing for an Army of 1,400,000 men.[18] Because of its broad and varied supply responsibilities, the QMC was greatly and immediately affected by this tremendous expansion.

More than any other supply service, the Corps had to anticipate the needs of the Army that was to be mobilized by having in readiness housing for the troops and the increased amounts of supplies needed to clothe, equip, and feed them. Such supply was carried out through the familiar system of depots which procured and distributed supplies requisitioned by quartermasters at posts, camps, and stations.

Purchase responsibility for the basic classes of items became even more concentrated than heretofore at designated key depots: for example, footwear at the Boston Quartermaster Depot, clothing still at the Philadelphia Depot, and tentage at the Jeffersonville Depot. This centralized purchase of specialty items by the depots was a fundamental feature of the field purchasing system that had been developing even before World War I. However, co-ordination was not neglected as it had been at the beginning of World War I, for the Supply Division and later the Procurement Division guided and directed these centralized purchase operations and acted as the procurement control agency of the OQMG.

Supply of the troops was the primary mission of the Corps, and this included the procurement of horses and mules and the purchase of automotive equipment. But the Corps had other functions to perform. It operated remount depots where horses were conditioned and trained, and it repaired automotive equipment at its motor-transport bases and depots. It built camps, hospitals, and other facilities to accommodate the expanding Army; it transported troops; and it provided and operated laundries for them. By the end of the emergency period it was also operating repair shops for shoes, clothing, and equipment. Furthermore, it continued to be re-

sponsible for the maintenance of national cemeteries and the care of the dead.

To accomplish these tasks and to meet new responsibilities imposed on the Corps during the war, the QMC expanded its personnel and its organization in the field and in Washington. It enlarged its headquarters organization from four to thirteen divisions before the war ended. Its military personnel increased from less than 12,000 to more than 500,000. In sharp contrast to the continued rise in military personnel during the war, civilian personnel tended to become stabilized at about 75,000, after construction and transportation functions and the personnel connected with the execution of these responsibilities had been transferred from the Corps to other agencies early in the war.

The commodity organization was simply expanded during the emergency period to handle the increased Quartermaster burden. After Pearl Harbor, however, more fundamental changes occurred. The organization of the OQMG was radically shifted from a commodity to a functional basis. Instead of commodity branches responsible for the procurement and distribution of specific items of supply, single divisions were established which were responsible solely for the procurement of most Quartermaster supplies or for the storage and distribution of them. This was a change that occurred in the midst of war as a part of the drastic and fundamental reorganization of the War Department in March 1942. As might be expected, it posed many problems and entailed numerous adjustments.

The field organization of the Corps was also expanded and altered. During the emergency and early war years, the depot system was greatly expanded and new facilities were established in the south and in the western part of the United States to back up the war in the Pacific. The use

---

[18] (1) *Biennial Report of the Chief of Staff of the United States Army, July 1, 1939, to June 30, 1941, to the Secretary of War* (Washington: GPO, 1941), p. 2. (2) 54 *U.S. Statutes* 885–97, act approved 16 Sep 40.

of dogs in war resulted in the establishment of centers for their training. The necessity to co-ordinate the military procurement of subsistence led to the creation of a nationwide market center system by the QMC. Other new facilities, such as repair subdepots and a great expansion of Quartermaster repair shops followed from the urgent need to conserve materials and decrease the burden placed upon industry for the production of new goods.

Of tremendous significance was the development of Quartermaster laboratories, for in World War II as never before an increasing emphasis was placed on exploiting and applying scientific knowledge and technological skills to the problems posed by military supplies. For the first time in Quartermaster history, a large and integrated research program was directed by the OQMG, and results were so impressive that it seems unlikely to be omitted from any future operations. Instead, the importance of a continuous program of research in peace as well as in war has been underscored.

Finally the war not only brought far-reaching administrative changes and expansion in personnel, but it modified supply procedures by streamlining procurement methods as well as those for storage and distribution. This was a war of mechanization and motorization not only in the combat areas but in the zone of interior as well. The use of IBM machines and teletypes speeded supply operations at depots and in the OQMG, while the use of fork-lift trucks and other mechanical equipment enabled the Corps to handle the tremendous volume of tonnage required for a global war.

CHAPTER I

Administrative Organization

Traditionally, the OQMG had been organized along commodity lines, and the outbreak of war in Europe in September 1939 brought no significant departure from this basic principle of commodity administration. The OQMG was then operating under a simple plan of organization which, except for minor variations, had been in effect since 1920. Of the four divisions handling Quartermaster activities, the Administrative Division combined within its province functions which were of a staff character. The Supply Division, consisting of a number of commodity branches, handled the procurement and distribution of Quartermaster supplies. The functions of construction and transportation were vested in two self-contained divisions.

The extended period of the emergency, which lasted from the presidential proclamation of limited emergency in September 1939 until 7 December 1941, provided an opportunity for orderly administrative development and expansion. However, the great expansion of Quartermaster activity did not begin until mid-1940, after the fall of France had increased the apprehensions of the United States and defense preparations were accelerated. On the eve of that expansion the QMC acquired a new Quartermaster General, who was to guide its activities throughout World War II. Maj. Gen. (later Lt. Gen.) Edmund B. Gregory was first appointed for a four-year period beginning 1 April 1940, and upon the expiration of this term he was reappointed acting The Quartermaster General, relinquishing the office on 31 January 1946. Having spent the greater part of his thirty-six

years in the Army in the service of the Corps, he brought a well-rounded knowledge to bear upon Quartermaster problems.[1]

Expansion of the Organization

In order to handle its increasing activities, the OQMG for the most part multiplied its administrative units by expanding sections into branches and by separating branches and establishing them as independent divisions. Nearly all this subdivision occurred within the Administrative Division. The one exception was the creation of the important Motor Transport Division in the summer of 1940 by separating it from the Transportation Division.[2] Fiscal and personnel activities were separated from the Administrative Division and given divisional status.[3] Within a few weeks, the expansion of numerous activities of the Administrative Division was recognized by the addition of a Statistical and Public Relations Branch and a Storage Control Branch to the already existing Production Control, and War Plans and Training Branches. All four handled important planning and staff activities.[4] By the close of the year the Memorial Branch was raised to a division.[5]

More significant than this increase in administrative units was the important realignment of

[1] (1) GO 5, 1 May 40, no sub. (2) "The New Quartermaster General," *QMR*, XIX (March–April 1940), 21ff.
[2] OQMG OO 49, 26 Jul 40, no sub.
[3] *Ibid.*
[4] OQMG OO 71, 24 Aug 40, no sub.
[5] OQMG OO 144, 27 Dec 40, sub: Office Orgn.

staff and operating phases of Quartermaster organization which occurred during this period. For example, the activities of the War Plans and Training Branch were separated. Its military training functions were transferred to the Personnel Division. Its planning functions, along with the activities of the Contracts and Claims Branch of the Supply Division, were vested in a new War Procurement and Requirements Branch in the Administrative Division.[6] This furthered the concentration of planning and policy functions on the staff level. Unfortunately this development made the Administrative Division unwieldy; the need for reorganizing certain of its important activities became apparent.

The most important basic reorganization in the OQMG before Pearl Harbor was initiated in a series of orders early in 1941. These were formalized and integrated later in the year by a revision of the basic organizational directive of the OQMG.[7] Separation of the Administrative Division's functions of administrative service from those of policy control constituted the most obvious need. Some of the former functions, namely those pertaining to departmental or headquarters activities, had a tendency to gravitate toward the executive office; hence a separate supervisory Executive Office was established as a formal agency under The Quartermaster General. To this office were transferred the activities of communications and central records, the OQMG library, a welfare service, and other miscellaneous office services. Attached directly to the Executive Office was an Executive Officer for Civilian Conservation Corps Affairs, charged with the control and supervision of all duties of the Corps pertaining to its participation in CCC matters. An Executive Officer for Civilian Personnel Affairs was responsible, under the direction and supervision of The Quartermaster General, for formulating and administering all policy matters relating to civilian employees of the Corps.[8]

The remaining administrative service functions were retained in the Administrative Division, which was renamed the General Service Division. It supervised those services of an administrative nature which pertained primarily to field activities and handled all administrative matters of general concern not assigned elsewhere.[9] In the basic chart[10] drawn to prescribe OQMG organization at this time, this division and the Executive Office as well as the Fiscal, Civilian Personnel, Military Personnel and Training, and Planning and Control Divisions were placed in theoretically close association in a group of "Executive Divisions."

The establishment of the Planning and Control Division early in 1941 resulted from the need to co-ordinate basic operating functions scattered throughout the commodity branches. As problems relating to procurement and other functional aspects of supply activity increased with the developing emergency, the necessity for a control agency became increasingly more compelling. After administrative and policy phases of control had been separated, the necessity to consolidate, reorganize, and refine the latter phase under a single agency became basic in the reorganization of OQMG activities. In establishing the Planning and Control Division, the procurement control, storage control, and war planning and requirements functions of the former Administrative Division were transferred to it as well as that division's activities in reference to statistics, claims, and contracts. In addition, the war planning activities of the Personnel Division were transferred to it.

Staff-operating relations between the Planning and Control Division and the Supply Division during the emergency period developed consid-

---

[6] OQMG OO 99, 10 Oct 40, no sub.

[7] OQMG OO 25, 3 Feb 41, sub: Office Orgn, and Supplements A–G, published from March to December, covering the organization of most of the separate divisions.

[8] OQMG OO 25, 3 Feb 41, sub: Office Orgn.

[9] OQMG OO 14, 23 Jan 41, no sub.

[10] See Chart 1.

CHART 1—THE QUARTERMASTER CORPS IN THE WAR DEPARTMENT: 1941

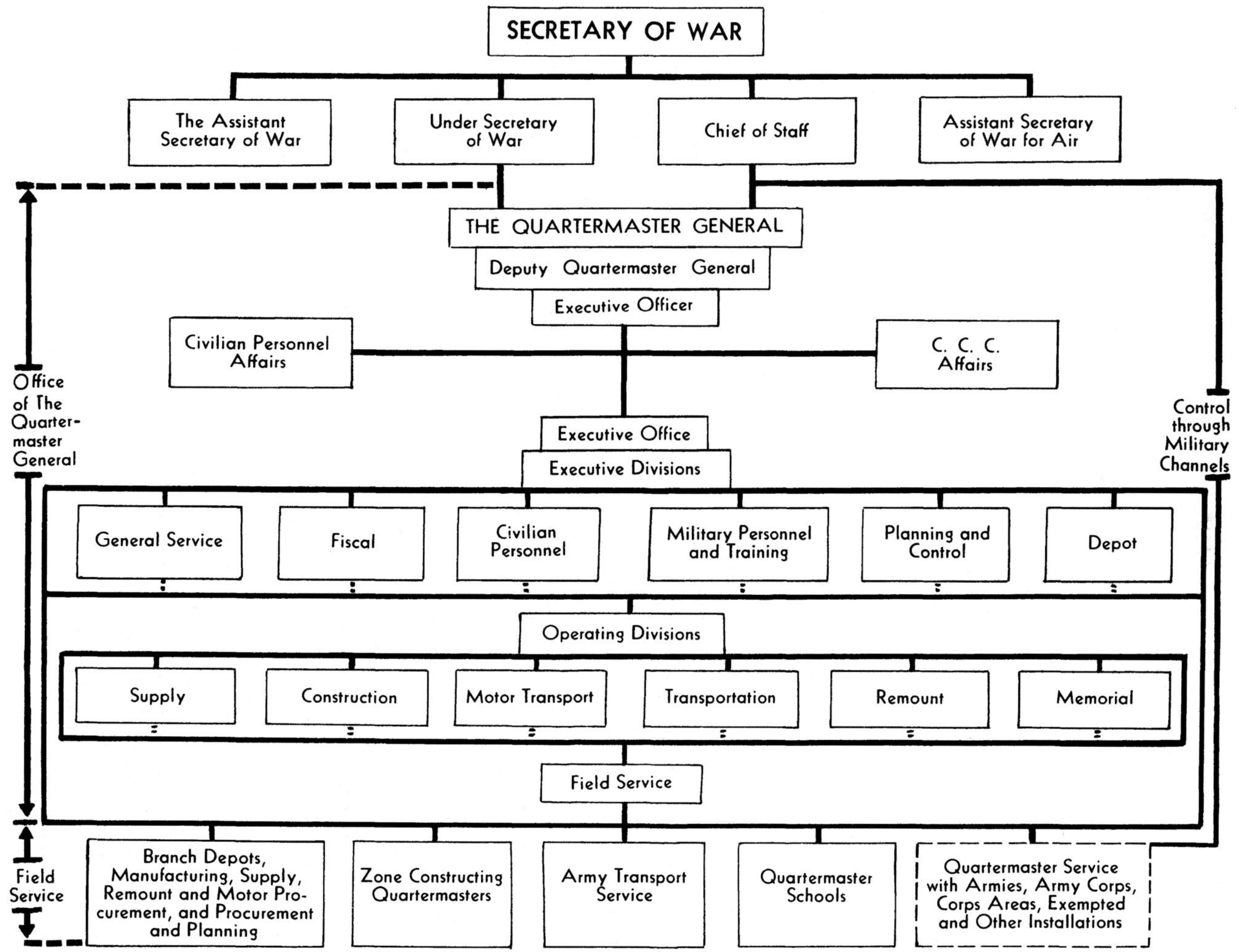

SECRETARY OF WAR

The Assistant Secretary of War

Under Secretary of War

Chief of Staff

Assistant Secretary of War for Air

THE QUARTERMASTER GENERAL

Deputy Quartermaster General

Executive Officer

Civilian Personnel Affairs

C. C. C. Affairs

Executive Office

Executive Divisions

General Service

Fiscal

Civilian Personnel

Military Personnel and Training

Planning and Control

Depot

Operating Divisions

Supply

Construction

Motor Transport

Transportation

Remount

Memorial

Field Service

Branch Depots, Manufacturing, Supply, Remount and Motor Procurement, and Procurement and Planning

Zone Constructing Quartermasters

Army Transport Service

Quartermaster Schools

Quartermaster Service with Armies, Army Corps, Corps Areas, Exempted and Other Installations

Control through Military Channels

Office of The Quartermaster General

Field Service

erable friction. There were present, of course, the normal irritations and difficulties incident to expansion of personnel and perfection of organization. Furthermore, the personalities and policies of certain of the key staff and operating officials inevitably played a part, while the reluctance of the operating units to accept direction and "interference" was undoubtedly a contributing factor.

As to the general resistance of the operating divisions to control, it is significant that a formal attempt was made to minimize this factor through designation of the staff units as "Executive Divisions." The chief of the Planning and Control Division was intended to have general powers of direction over the activities of the OQMG, but these were translated with difficulty into binding orders on procurement, distribution, and other activities. The operating divisions were encouraged in their independence by the relative unfamiliarity of the staff agencies with operating problems and their uncertainty as to the scope of their jurisdiction and power. In any event, commodity branches and divisions had long been accustomed to having complete and integrated responsibility for their operations.

Conflict and confusion in policies were even more basic causes of the difficulties. These developed out of the uncertainties which stemmed from the fact that the country was drifting along through a period of partial or limited mobilization, whereas the procurement planners had based their plans on abrupt and complete industrial mobilization for war.

For twenty years following the passage of the National Defense Act, the procurement planners in the OQMG under the guidance of the Assistant Secretary of War had been formulating war procurement plans to meet a future emergency. Such planning had been separated from current peacetime operations in the commodity branches of the Supply Division, and it had followed a radically different line from that of the operators in the commodity branches

who were developing a centralized procurement system. Regional self-sufficiency and decentralization of procurement to districts that were roughly coterminous with the corps areas constituted the heart of the procurement plans that were drafted. Policies stemming from such a decentralized system were obviously at sharp variance with those of centralized operations which carried over into the emergency period. The planners were further handicapped in carrying out their policies since procurement plans were intended to be put into effect on an M Day (Mobilization Day) which never came. Instead a wholly unanticipated, prolonged emergency period occurred, with the result that the plans were held in abeyance and operating personnel met the day-to-day problems by using established peacetime procedures. By the time war was declared, the momentum was too great to permit a resort to the plans that had been prepared.

Because the emergency period was primarily one of procurement effort, administrative adjustments naturally revolved around this activity, and staff-operating relationships must be considered first in reference to it. The production control agencies were somewhat intolerant of concessions which had to be made as a result of the actual course of emergency transition. They were opposed to alternative systems and methods which negated the economic and industrial benefits long planned through controlled mobilization and production. On the other hand, the approach of the current procurement agencies to this matter was more expedient. They recognized the difficulty under the circumstances of securing an ideal distribution of orders and allocation and full utilization of industrial facilities. They were interested primarily in pushing those policies which seemed acceptable and practicable in meeting procurement objectives.[11]

Both production and purchasing policies relat-

---

[11] See below, Ch. VII.

ing to selection of contractors and facilities were affected by various complex factors—profit and competitive motives, business pressures, indecision on the part of higher planning agencies in the government, and other elements which tended to interfere with the procedures of mobilization developed by the procurement planners. The latter had formulated programs for allocating contracts to industrial facilities, but depot personnel ignored their advice in carrying out current operations. Most depot officers and many officers in the Supply Division were also extremely timorous about abandoning peacetime purchasing policies and adopting the method of negotiation advocated by the planners. The Supply Division, for the most part, pursued a legalistic and hesitant approach to emergency purchasing and production. Commodity organizations on all levels resisted or resented the pressure exerted by the staff units for the application of new and more radical policies and methods.

Such differences probably acted as the greatest single deterrent to extension and perfection of administrative controls on the part of the staff agencies of the Planning and Control Division. But while the heritage of a ready-made set of controls would have been of inestimable value after Pearl Harbor, it must be emphasized that relatively loose supervision could be tolerated before that time. Insofar as the supervision of procurement policies by the Planning and Control Division was concerned, the situation could even be rationalized as consisting merely of a necessary, if troublesome, stage in the process of transition to war.

Considerations of administrative control and orientation were highly interdependent in all phases of procurement. One more illustration emphasizes this point. There was considerable pressure for expediting procurement, but production scheduling could still be viewed primarily as a fiscal matter and accomplished in the course of distributing appropriations and funds.

The need had not yet developed for tight scheduling and therefore for welding the computation of requirements, based on distribution and other field data, and the issuance of procurement directives into a single, co-ordinated process. OQMG staff-operating conflicts over this phase of procurement control, however, were already present.

If administrative adjustments thus far had centered particularly on procurement activities, developments were looming nonetheless in other fields, especially with respect to the distribution of supplies. The former Storage Control Branch of the Administrative Division had remained for a time with the Planning and Control Division, but by May 1941 it was transferred to the Executive Office as a staff unit and renamed the Depot Division.[12] This division functioned as the agency dealing with Quartermaster depots and Quartermaster sections of general depots on all general matters of depot administration in which the various OQMG divisions had an interest. It also served as the supply agency for warehouse equipment of all kinds, kept records bearing on the allocation and utilization of storage space, and initiated the procurement and training of personnel to meet the requirements of new depots. In the summer of 1941 Quartermaster depots and Quartermaster sections of general depots tended to operate as separate autonomies rather than as parts of the depot system. Each installation was using various methods and systems for doing business with little regard for the existence of similar supply organizations. It was the mission of the Depot Division to standardize and co-ordinate the activities of these installations and to insure the efficient operation of the individual depot.[13]

---

[12] (1) OQMG OO 25A, 24 Mar 41, no sub. (2) OQMG OO 92, 14 May 41, no sub.
[13] (1) Chief of Depot Opns Div to Exec Off, S&D Sv, 28 Jul 42, sub: Material to be Included in Annual Rpt of SW. (2) See below, Ch. IX, *passim*, for elaboration of activities.

A weakness in the position of the Depot Division lay partly in the looseness of its responsibility for the administrative servicing and planning on the field level of a variety of activities for which other divisions often claimed primary responsibility. It was enjoined specifically from interfering with the "prerogatives of Chiefs of Operating Divisions" in supervising the procurement, storage, and issue of supplies. At the same time it was made the main channel of contact with the depots on those matters of administration in which it dealt, a function normally assigned to an operating agency at headquarters. Because it was difficult to distinguish activities of general concern from those which were prerogatives of the operating units, there was ample ground for friction to develop with the commodity branches of the Supply Division.

As in the case of procurement, so in distribution there was no need during these months for rigid control. Just as the tight scheduling of requirements depended upon influences developing later in the war, so inventory and stock control were hardly required at this time, and the Depot Division concerned itself, insofar as its administrative functions were involved, only with standard organization and procedures in depots. The placing of stock accounting and reporting activities on a machine basis in 1941, however, superseding the old manual system, presaged the emergence of control problems as well as the need for functional realignment of distribution activities.[14]

Although a number of other changes, including the setting up of a lend-lease agency in the OQMG, occurred in the last few months before Pearl Harbor, the administrative adjustments involved in the staff-operating relationships on procurement and distribution constituted the main lines of development. In the pre-Pearl Harbor period, despite the development of functional controls and services and a general tendency to concentrate them in staff units, the OQMG remained organized fundamentally on

the commodity principle. Subject to directions from higher authority and to varying degrees of functional supervision and aid from agencies within the OQMG, each commodity branch retained fairly complete responsibility for the handling of a group of supply items, from determining requirements to seeing that such items reached points of issue.

Transfer of Functions

War was to bring further changes in the administrative organization of the OQMG and in the mission assigned to the Corps. Within a few months after Pearl Harbor, a number of important functions were lost to the QMC. As in World War I, construction, transportation, and motor transport activities were again either transferred to other technical services or established as separate organizations.

Construction

In the case of construction, action to remove this function from the QMC was actually begun in the fall of 1941 and completed a few days before Pearl Harbor. In September the War Department submitted a bill to the House of Representatives, providing for the transfer of new construction for the Army and the maintenance and repair of buildings from The Quartermaster General to the Chief of Engineers. To justify this transfer the Secretary of War urged that it would eliminate a large amount of duplication of effort, cost, and administrative personnel. A more efficient long-range program of construction could be set up. The proposed bill placed the construction work of the War Department under the Corps of Engineers because, even in peacetime, with its river and harbor and flood-control projects, the Corps of Engineers, unlike the QMC, had a

---

[14] See below, Ch. X.

large construction program. It was argued that it also had a long-established organization to handle such work, whereas the organization of the QMC for these activities was of much more recent creation. Finally, it was urged that the construction activities of the War Department during the emergency were more closely related to the other functions of the Corps of Engineers and to the training of combat engineer forces than they were to the other functions of the QMC.[15]

The Quartermaster General, General Gregory, took exception to the reasons advanced for this transfer. He observed that if housing for the Civilian Conservation Corps were included the Quartermaster expenditures for construction for the past ten years would be larger than those of the Engineer Corps. This program had been carried out in an economical and satisfactory manner. Moreover, a small, continuous, permanent housing construction program had been handled by the Construction Division, OQMG. In any case, neither the peacetime construction program of the Corps of Engineers nor that of the QMC was comparable to the load of construction in an emergency. In addition, the type of work done by the Engineer Corps was quite different from that involved in the construction of troop housing. Except for a period during World War I when a separate Construction Division was formed, the QMC had handled construction at military posts for more than one hundred years. In The Quartermaster General's opinion the training of combat engineering forces had very little in common with the construction work involved in the zone of interior. He objected to the transfer of maintenance activities and the repair of buildings and utilities, for these were intimately involved with the functions of the Corps at all military posts.

In short, the Quartermaster Corps is already on the job. It is in intimate touch with every phase of Army life. There is a Quartermaster Officer wherever a group of soldiers can be found. The Engineer Corps, on the other hand, handles specialized work usually completely aloof from the rest of the Army and entirely out of touch with the day to day life of military organizations.[16]

Although The Quartermaster General objected to losing the construction function, the War Department and the Construction Division, OQMG, had been much criticized by the Truman Committee for the excessive cost of the construction program for camps and cantonments. The committee had recommended that the Secretary of War be granted authority to assign additional construction work to the Corps of Engineers. Air Corps construction had already been assigned to the Engineers by Congress in 1940.[17]

Under these circumstances there was little doubt that the bill offered by the Secretary of War would be enacted into law. The Quartermaster General was therefore directed to collaborate with the Chief of Engineers in developing a plan for the transfer of construction activities. Such a plan was submitted in November.[18] On 1 December 1941 Congress passed the law transferring construction, real estate, and repairs and utilities activities to the Corps of Engineers, a transfer that was made effective on 16 December 1941.[19]

The QMC had borne the major burden of construction during the emergency period. Although it had been very critical of this program, the Truman Committee observed:

---

[15] Ltr, Robert P. Patterson, Actg SW, to Speaker of HR, 2 Sep 41, no sub.

[16] Memo, TQMG for CofS, 4 Sep 41, no sub.

[17] S Rpt 480, Part 2, 77th Cong, 1st Sess, "Camp and Cantonment Investigation," p. 35.

[18] (1) Ltr, TAG to TQMG, 21 Oct 41, sub: Transfer of Const Activities from QMC to CE, AG 600.12 (10–20–41) MO-D. (2) Ltr, TQMG and CofEngrs to TAG, 10 Nov 41, same sub. (3) Memo, ACofS for CofS, 19 Nov 41, sub: Transfer of Const and Real Estate Activities from QMC to CE.

[19] (1) 66 U.S. Statutes 787–88. (2) Ltr, TAG to TQMG, 3 Dec 41, sub: Transfer of Const Activities from QMC to CE, AG 600.12 (11–10–41) MO-D.

By making such criticism the committee does not wish to detract in any way from the very important fact that housing, training, and recreational facilities for 1,216,459 men were provided in the space of a few short months and in most instances were finished and ready for occupancy before the troops arrived. The Construction Division of the Quartermaster General's Office supervised the construction of projects which . . . due to their size and the necessity of speed, presented some of the greatest problems ever encountered by any construction agency in this country and the facilities so provided are better than the troop facilities possessed by any other country. Adequate provision has been made for the comfort and health of the soldiers. Furthermore, the facilities are better than those provided for the troops in the last World War.[20]

Transportation

Three months after the transfer of construction, as part of the general reorganization of the Army in March 1942, responsibility for transportation and traffic control was centralized in the Services of Supply (SOS), and the Transportation Division, OQMG, was separated from that office.[21] In the years since 1920, when Congress by legislative action had returned transportation activities to the QMC despite recommendations for the establishment of a permanent transportation corps, decentralized operating responsibilities had developed. The Quartermaster General was responsible for the movement of troops and supplies by common carriers in the zone of interior and by Army transports and commercial vessels between the United States and its overseas bases. Commanders of ports of embarkation, however, reported directly to the War Department General Staff. Their functions in regard to Army transports were not clearly differentiated from those of The Quartermaster General. The chiefs of other supply services maintained separate traffic organizations to look after their transportation interests such as shipping and procuring agencies. The Supply Division, G-4, of the General Staff exercised over-all supervision of transportation activities.[22]

This decentralization was the real weakness of the transportation organization. In the period of the emergency, when overseas bases were being strengthened and transportation difficulties were multiplying, the Transportation Branch of G-4 promoted the co-ordination of Army transportation activities. Its activities expanded even more rapidly after Pearl Harbor. But this co-ordination offered no real solution to the problem, which stemmed from the fact that no one operating organization was directly responsible for inland, terminal, and overseas transportation.[23] This was provided in March 1942 by consolidating all War Department transportation and traffic control under SOS. A Transportation Division, in charge of a Chief of Transportation, was established in the SOS. By 31 July 1942 it emerged as the Transportation Corps.[24]

---

[20] (1) S Rpt 480, Part 2, 77th Cong, 1st Sess, "Camp and Cantonment Investigation," p. 34. (2) This work was done under Lt. Col. Brehon B. Somervell, Corps of Engineers, who was detailed for duty in the QMC and assigned as chief of the Construction Division. OQMG OO 130, 11 Dec 40, no sub. (3) For a detailed discussion of construction, see Remington, Coll, and Fine, Corps of Engineers: Zone of Interior Construction, a volume in preparation for the series UNITED STATES ARMY IN WORLD WAR II.

[21] WD Cir 59, 2 Mar 42, sub: WD Reorgn. Three commands were established: the Army Ground Forces (AGF), the Army Air Forces (AAF), and the SOS, renamed a year later the Army Service Forces (ASF).

[22] (1) AR 30-1190, 12 Dec 41, sub: Oversea Mvmt of Orgns and Casuals. (2) AR 30-930, 6 Nov 30, sub: Trans of Troops. (3) Rpt, 30 Nov 45, sub: Rpt of

[23] Memo, Col T. N. Dillon, OQMG, for Brig Gen CofT ASF WW II, pp. 17-18. Brehon B. Somervell, ACofS G-4, 4 Feb 42, sub: Trans Orgn.

[24] (1) Maj Gen C. P. Gross, CofT, "The Transportation Corps—Its Organization and Major Functions," QMR, XXIII (January–February 1944), 19ff. (2) Chester Wardlow, The Transportation Corps: Responsibilities, Organization, and Operations (Washington, 1951), in the series UNITED STATES ARMY IN WORLD WAR II.

Motor Transport

The last important change made in Quartermaster activities during the war was the transfer of motor transport activities in the summer of 1942. Long before this there had been rumors of impending changes. The Under Secretary of War was concerned with the problem of utilizing industrial capacity to the best advantage. He directed John D. Hertz, an authority on motor transportation, to make a special study of the subject, primarily from the viewpoint of effective use and conservation of automotive equipment already on hand. The scope of this survey was restricted to vehicles of Quartermaster responsibility, and consequently tanks and other combat vehicles, which were procured by the Ordnance Department, were excluded from consideration in this investigation. The report of the Hertz committee, submitted in November 1941, recommended that one service be made completely responsible for all automotive maintenance. This control agency was to be established in General Headquarters inasmuch as the committee had found the activation of a Headquarters Motor Transport approved in a Table of Organization, 1 November 1940. The Hertz report recommended no change in jurisdiction over procurement of motor equipment.[25]

A month earlier the General Staff had considered the reorganization of the armored division, one aspect of which had involved the delegation of all third echelon vehicle maintenance to the divisional ordnance battalion.[26] At that time both Ordnance and Quartermaster personnel maintained such third echelon activities. While acknowledging that this led to duplication of overhead, equipment, and effort and that this responsibility should rest with one agency, The Quartermaster General had urged that it be placed with the QMC because about two thirds of the 3,300 motor-propelled vehicles provided for an armored division were procured by the Corps. All but about four hundred of the vehicles used commercial-type motors.[27] In January 1942 Brig. Gen. Brehon B. Somervell, then Assistant Chief of Staff, G-4, informed The Quartermaster General that orders were being issued to the Army directing the pooling of third and fourth echelon shops of the QMC and the Ordnance Department.[28]

Many officers of the Motor Transport Division, OQMG, hoped that a separate corps would be established. General Somervell also favored a separate automotive corps, which would be responsible not only for maintenance but also for design and procurement of tanks and other combat, as well as noncombat, cars.[29] In an analysis of the Hertz report submitted to the Chief of Staff, he emphasized that "the reconditioning of the present automotive fleet, the proper instruction of the present personnel, the provision of the necessary training of maintenance units for the increased automotive fleet laid down in the program provide a tremendous problem which must be solved within the year 1942 if our field armies are to wage successful

---

[25] (1) Ltr, John D. Hertz to Robert P. Patterson, 18 Nov 41, no sub, enclosing rpt. (2) Memo, USW for CofS, 24 Nov 41, sub: Mr. John Hertz, Rpt on Mtr Veh Maint. (3) Memo, Hertz for USW, 15 Jan 42, sub: Criticisms on Rpt of Mtr Veh Maint. (4) Ltr, Hertz et al., to USW, 28 Jan 42, no sub.

[26] Memo, Brig Gen H. L. Twaddle, ACofS, for TQMG, 21 Oct 41, sub: Reorgn of Armd Div.

[27] Memo, TQMG for ACofS G-3, 3 Nov 41, Reorg of Armd Div.

[28] Memo, Gen Somervell for TQMG, 17 Jan 42, sub: Autmv Tng and Maint.

[29] In a study he prepared to be submitted to the Chief of Staff, General Somervell had the assistance of Col. R. P. Shugg, Chief of Staff, 3d Armored Division. The latter heartily endorsed the Hertz report but recommended one change, namely, that command control of all automotive equipment be exercised by one authority. He had long been an advocate of a separate motor transport corps. See (1) Ltr, Col Shugg to John Hertz, 8 Dec 41, no sub; (2) Ltr, Shugg to Hertz, 18 Nov 41, no sub, enclosing rpt on Third Army maneuvers, by Shugg, 10 Jun 40; (3) Ltr, Shugg to Hertz, 9 Dec 41, no sub, enclosing rpt to Gen Somervell commenting on Hertz rpt.

mechanized or motorized warfare." [30] In his opinion, however, the existing division of motor transport responsibilities among the QMC, the Ordnance Department, the Corps of Engineers, the corps areas, the General Staff, General Headquarters, and the field armies would prevent the accomplishment of this program.

Insofar as maintenance was concerned the Hertz report had found existing procedures clearly defined and adequate for a satisfactory maintenance program. This led the Assistant Chief of Staff, G-4, to conclude that the fault rested in the controls established and the lack of attention given to this vital problem by the high command. Maintenance companies had been authorized months after equipment had been put in service, spare parts had not been ordered with vehicles, and efforts of The Quartermaster General to create an organization at General Headquarters to supervise maintenance had been disapproved on the recommendation of that agency. The latter's failure to provide adequate training had stemmed from the view of the Chief of Staff, General Headquarters, that "maintenance of modern commercial vehicles is not a serious problem, provided sufficient spare parts are available promptly." [31]

The Chief of the Armored Force and the Chief of Field Artillery were strongly in favor of the organization of a separate automotive corps as proposed by the Assistant Chief of Staff, G-4. The advocates of such a separate service urged that it would heighten combat efficiency, give access to the high command, promote economy of material and personnel, and provide a vitalized service with no other interests. In opposition was the weight of tradition, of "vested rights and privileges." [32] The opponents of a separate service objected to reorganization in the midst of war, claiming that confusion would result even if advantages did accrue at a later date. In the opinion of the Under Secretary of War the transfer of responsibility for the design and procurement of tanks and other combat cars from the Ordnance Department to an automotive corps would be unfortunate. The Deputy Chief of Staff concurred. He felt that the resulting confusion would cause delay in procurement and development of tanks, self-propelled antitank guns and artillery, and other automotive equipment of the Ordnance Department. [33] The Chief of Ordnance and The Quartermaster General strongly opposed the establishment of a separate automotive corps. The idea was discarded for the time being. Instead, both the QMC and the Ordnance Department made efforts to improve their field services, and the OQMG strengthened its Motor Transport Division. [34]

In May 1942 General Somervell, as Commanding General, SOS, visited the European Theater of Operations (ETO). While there he became interested in the unified maintenance organization of the British Army. Upon his return he was more than ever convinced of the desirability of combining maintenance for Ordnance and Quartermaster automotive and tank equipment under a single head.

Developments which culminated in the transfer of motor transport functions from the QMC to the Ordnance Department now moved rapidly. On 22 June 1942 General Somervell sent a memorandum to Lt. Gen. Dwight D. Eisenhower, discussing some of the difficulties encountered in World War I because the organization of the American Expeditionary Forces (AEF) differed from that of the War Depart-

[30] Memo, Gen Somervell for CofS, 7 Jan 42, sub: Rpt on Mtr Veh Maint by Mr. John Hertz.

[31] Ibid.

[32] Ibid.

[33] (1) Memo, Robert P. Patterson, USW, for Maj Gen R. C. Moore, Deputy CofS, 6 Jan 42, sub: MT. (2) Memo, Patterson for Moore, 12 Jan 42, sub: Mtr Maint. (3) Memo, Deputy CofS for CofS, 10 Jan 42, sub: Mtr Veh Maint.

[34] (1) Memo, Gen Somervell for CofS, 7 Jan 42, sub: Rpt on Mtr Veh Maint by Mr. John Hertz. (2) Memo, Gen Moore, Deputy CofS, for CofS, 10 Jan 42, sub: Mtr Veh Maint. (3) Memo, Moore for USW, 12 Jan 42, no sub.

ment. In this connection he asked whether a separate motor transport corps, entirely divorced from the QMC, were desirable. Within a week an affirmative message was received from General Eisenhower's headquarters. On 3 July SOS informed The Quartermaster General that the establishment of a separate automotive corps was under consideration and invited him to submit his views on the matter.[35]

General Gregory vigorously opposed the move. He outlined the current duties of the Motor Transport Service to show that it was not a transportation service but a supply organization which purchased, stored, and distributed general-purpose vehicles, parts, and equipment. The Army commands were responsible for the operation of the vehicles assigned to them. He urged that the distinction between the activities of the Motor Transport Service and a transportation service should not be lost. He asserted that the establishment of a separate motor transport corps would create many new problems.

While he conceded that there might be certain advantages in creating an automotive corps to carry out the functions now performed by the QMC, General Gregory declared that it was his belief that "the activities involving design, procurement, storage and distribution, and the operation of base shops are now being administered and controlled effectively." The procedures under which these activities were operating were understood by all, and constantly increasing effectiveness could be expected as field commanders came to realize more keenly the importance of "strict command supervision over the operation and maintenance of motor vehicles." He felt that it was inadvisable to increase the number of organizations under the Commanding General, SOS, and that future improvements in the organization could be made within the existing structure as effectively as under any new organization operating under a different name.

Any change from the present organization, he believed, could be justified only if the efficiency of the Army as a whole would thereby be increased, and he could find nothing in the proposal that promised this result. Furthermore, he argued that, if the new corps were created without change in management and operating personnel, the only result would be a change of insignia; if personnel were also changed, it would mean the elimination of people who had worked intensively on motor transport problems for the past two years. He concluded with the declaration that he did not feel the present organization had failed, and therefore he could not approve plans to create a separate motor transport corps. Two days later, having reflected further on the matter, General Gregory sent another memorandum to the Commanding General, SOS, emphasizing the duplication of overhead that would result from the establishment of a new service.[36]

Whether the arguments of The Quartermaster General were persuasive, or whether a counterproposal was presented to focus attention of the SOS elsewhere, interest shifted once more from the creation of a separate motor transport corps to the transfer of maintenance responsibility. This had been discussed for some time, and there had been occasional talk about concentrating full responsibility for motor procurement either in the Ordnance Department or the QMC. Each service naturally felt that, if procurement and other responsibilities for motors were combined, it should perform the work because it was best organized and qualified to do so. At any rate, less than a week after General Gregory had submitted his second memorandum opposing creation of a separate motor

---

[35] (1) Memo, Somervell for Eisenhower, 22 Jun 42, no sub. (2) Cable 2398, London to AGWAR, 29 Jun 42. (3) Memo, Brig Gen W. D. Styer for TQMG, 3 Jul 42, sub: Creation of a Separate Autmv Corps.

[36] (1) Memo, Gen Gregory for CG SOS, 6 Jul 42, sub: Creation of a Separate Autmv Corps. (2) Memo, Gregory for CG SOS, 8 July 42, same sub.

corps, SOS asked him to submit his reasons for believing that the Motor Transport Service should not be separated from the QMC and attached to the Ordnance Department.

General Gregory called attention to his two earlier memoranda on the subject and declared that it was his understanding that the principal reason for the proposal was "that the Ordnance repair activities and the Quartermaster Corps repair activities may be combined." This he conceded might have some advantages, particularly in the armored divisions, but in the ordinary triangular division Quartermaster vehicles predominated. Moreover, transfer of the motor activities to the Ordnance Department, he felt, would result in the establishment at every post of another overhead organization, and "confusion already exists at a great many posts because of the change in the Quartermasters' duties." This change would add to the confusion. He insisted that a change at this time would require an undesirable period of adjustment. If, however, maintenance of vehicles were to be transferred, he advocated that the procurement and distribution of motor vehicles be left as a function of the QMC.[37]

The arguments of General Gregory did not prevail. The desirability of centralizing procurement as well as maintenance of automotive equipment was emphasized by a study being made by the Control Division, SOS. It surveyed the problems of the Tank and Combat Vehicles Division of the Ordnance Department and recommended centralization of all tank and automotive procurement in Detroit, a suggestion that was carried out immediately following the transfer of motor transport activities.[38] On 17 July 1942, three days after General Gregory had presented his case, Headquarters, SOS, issued an order transferring motor transport activities to the Ordnance Department. The regulation which put the transfer into effect designated 1 August as the effective date.[39]

Despite the loss of functions to the Corps of Engineers, the Transportation Corps, and the Ordnance Department, the QMC ranked next to the Ordnance Department as the most important procurement service of the ASF. The Quartermaster General remained responsible for the procurement, storage, and issue of subsistence, petroleum and lubricants, clothing, broad categories of equipment, and all general supplies. These functions constituted the basis of a mission unusually broad for any single operating agency and involved many complex administrative problems.

General Reorganization After Pearl Harbor

When the United States entered the war, the supply mission of the QMC was administered by a headquarters office in Washington, which for a short time continued to be organized on a commodity basis, and a field organization, the most important components of which consisted of depots and market centers. The Quartermaster General was still under the direct supervision of the General Staff and, insofar as procurement matters were concerned, the Assistant Secretary of War, whose title by this time had been changed to Under Secretary of War. Because of pressures both within and without the office, the OQMG was soon to undergo a general reorganization.

Early in March 1942 the War Department was reorganized, and as a result the QMC came under the direct supervisory control of the Commanding General, SOS. Apparently no particular change was contemplated, however, in

---

[37] Memo, Gen Gregory for Brig Gen LeRoy Lutes, SOS, 14 Jul 42, sub: Transfer of MT Activities.
[38] Hist Rpt, Hist Sec, Control Div, ASF, History of Control Division, ASF, 1942–1945 (Apr 46), p. 53. On file in the Office of the Chief of Military History (OCMH), Department of the Army.
[39] (1) Ltr, Gen Somervell to TQMG, 17 Jul 42, sub: Transfer of Certain Functions and Activities in Connection with MT from QMC to Ord Dept. (2) WD Cir 245, 24 Jul 42, sub: Transfer of MT Activities.

the responsibilities and functions of the QMC and the other supply arms and services.[40] While a change occurred in the top structure of the War Department, it did not directly affect the internal organization or operations of the supply services. Indirectly and powerfully, however, the functional organization of the SOS influenced the internal organization of the QMC.

The functional type of organization was diametrically opposed to the commodity principle. Instead of a vertical organization it offered a horizontal type wherein one function was assigned to a single unit of that organization. Thus, instead of a group of branches in a supply division, each concerned with one type of commodity from procurement to issue, a single procurement division would purchase all supplies bought by the agency, while a distribution division would distribute and issue such supplies. Such clear-cut delineation of responsibilities could be projected in an ideal, theoretical organization to prevent overlapping responsibilities which contributed to confusion and delay. In actual practice, however, the OQMG never achieved a purely functional organization.

To anticipate developments within the OQMG, the functional principle was frequently compromised. Divisions, such as the Subsistence and the Fuels and Lubricants Divisions, were frankly organized on a commodity basis. Even within functionally organized divisions, branches were established on commodity lines. The reorganization within the OQMG after Pearl Harbor resulted in the development of a hybrid functional-commodity type organization. Because of the speed with which the OQMG was reorganized, as well as misunderstandings of the functional principle, precise definitions of the responsibilities of divisions were not established. This resulted in considerable internal conflict which was further aggravated by clashing personalities.

Similarly, in theory, a sharp distinction was drawn between staff agencies, which developed

plans and policies and specified procedures for their execution, and operating units, which carried them out. In the reorganization of the OQMG in March 1942, an attempt was made to differentiate between staff and operating divisions, but analysis of their functions reveals that responsibility for staff functions was often vested in operating units so that confusion resulted. Theory and practice were frequently in conflict. Despite the fact that the OQMG was undergoing a major reorganization, however, the QMC successfully achieved its part in mounting the campaign in North Africa in 1942 and subsequent campaigns.

The Control Division, SOS, exerted vigorous pressure from the beginning to promote a policy of conformity in organization throughout the supply services, primarily to facilitate control and liaison. Since the organization of staff activities immediately under the commanding general was logically functional, the main pressure was designed to force into line with SOS organization the activities of the technical headquarters as well as those of regional and field organizations. The correlation of functions between agencies on the two levels was designed to create well-defined channels through which SOS instructions on policy and procedure could be circulated and enforced, and to make possible more effective liaison on functional problems between units of the OQMG and the other supply services.

Within the OQMG a control group under Col. Harold A. Barnes worked closely with representatives of the Control Division, SOS. Several civilian experts who came from commercial organizations employing the functional principle were added about this time to the group. In general, they were advocates of

---

[40] (1) WD Cir 59, 2 Mar 42, sub: WD Reorgn. (2) Ltr, CG SOS to Chiefs of All Sup Arms and Svs et al., 9 Mar 42, sub: Initial Directive for Orgn of SOS.

immediate and fundamental change in Quartermaster organization.[41]

On the other hand, criticism of the functional principle was usually voiced by commodity operators and executives who naturally defended a system to which they were accustomed. But the trend of developments was against the continuation of a purely commodity organization. Other government agencies with which the Corps had relations were organized functionally, and ease of communication would be promoted by a similar organizational arrangement in the OQMG. The business world, too, generally made use of the functional principle. According to The Quartermaster General, the OQMG would therefore have been reorganized gradually along functional lines even if pressure had not been exerted from the SOS.[42]

As a result of these pressures, the OQMG suddenly abandoned its traditional commodity-type organization. Within three weeks after the formation of the SOS, the OQMG was reorganized on a functional basis. There was little time for prolonged discussion. On 26 March General Gregory informed his division chiefs of the proposed changes and the allocation of office space in accordance with a planned move of the OQMG to new quarters in Washington.[43] On 31 March the OQMG issued Office Order 84, which became the blueprint for organization and responsibilities throughout the war. In the five-day interval division chiefs had prepared organization charts and functional statements for their respective divisions, including each branch and section involved. This mass of data was turned over to the newly formed administrative control staff to be drafted into Office Order 84. As a consequence, some matters involving controversy were included, while others requiring further deliberation for their settlement, such as the establishment of deputies for administration and operations, were omitted.

The new organization provided for an administrative and advisory staff.[44] Under this staff were grouped an Administrative Assistant to The Quartermaster General and the "staff" divisions of Budget and Accounting, Civilian Personnel Affairs, Military Personnel and Training, Defense Aid, Inspection, and Organization Planning and Control. A seventh staff division, General Administrative Services, was mentioned only in the specific statement of functions. Activities of this division—the successor to the former General Service Division—were not fully determined at this time, but most of the former activities of the Executive Office were shortly transferred to it, making the division responsible in general for administrative service activities in both the OQMG and the field.

Six "operating services" were provided for under the titles of Military Planning, Production, Procurement, Storage and Distribution, Service Installations, and Motor Transport. Except for obscurity on certain matters of common interest, the functions of the basic purchasing and distributing services were outlined as might be expected for services with their general missions. The title "Service Installations" was used to designate the agency supervising a number of special field installations or activities in the nature of services to the Army which had long been identified with the QMC. Actually it was a catch-all agency for this purpose, since it handled a group of miscellaneous activities, such as remount, memorial, field printing, and laundry, while at the same time it was a functional operating service, administering the activities of conservation, reclamation, and salvage, which were the final stages in the supply process. The

---

[41] Based on interviews with a number of the members of this group and upon their points of view as later expressed and revealed in documentary evidence.

[42] Interv, OQMG historian with Gen Gregory, 21 Feb 51.

[43] Memo, TQMG for Chiefs of Proposed Divs & Svs, 26 Mar 42, sub: Modification of Orgn, OQMG. The quarters referred to were Temporary Buildings "B" and "C," in which, together with Temporary Building "A," the OQMG remained for the rest of the war.

[44] See Chart 2.

CHART 2—THE QUARTERMASTER CORPS IN THE WAR DEPARTMENT: MARCH 1942

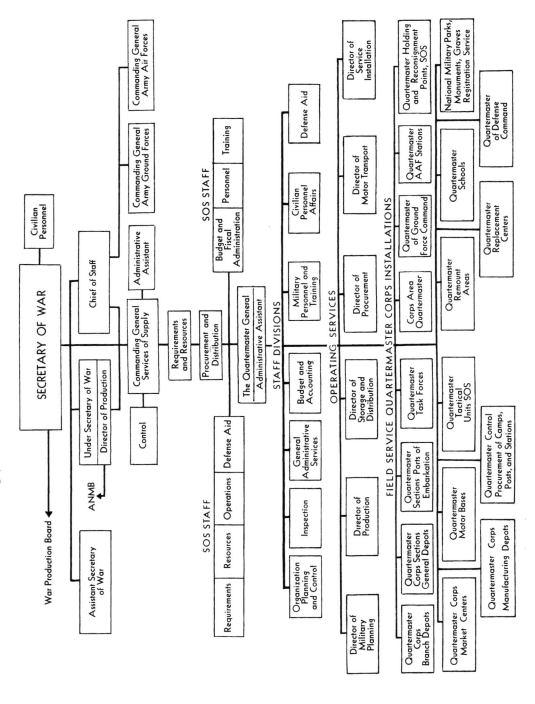

interrelation of many of these activities, especially salvage, with functions of the other basic services was to constitute a problem that eventually demanded definition. Divisional supervision of the heterogeneous activities of Service Installations was necessarily rather loose and was never completely satisfactory.

Problems of Adjustment Under Office Order 84

The broad, functional responsibilities of the new staff divisions and operating services as outlined in Office Order 84 conformed, insofar as possible, to those of corresponding staff units. Although the statements defining these responsibilities were relatively clear-cut and distinct, they did not agree in all cases with those of specific functions allocated to divisions. These, in many instances, had been incorporated verbatim from the functional statements submitted by officers who were interested in the broadest possible statement of their responsibilities. The chiefs of many divisional and branch units were naturally reluctant to surrender traditional responsibilities, yet they were eager to obtain others. The resultant overlapping of responsibilities provided fertile ground for conflict because the functional statements could often, with justification, be used to prevent the transfer of activities and personnel or to dispute the jurisdiction and policies of other chiefs with similar responsibilities.

Within a few days of the announcement of the reorganization it was evident that an impasse existed. Most of the areas of co-operative or overlapping responsibility between divisions were the subject of protracted discussion, and few if any of the suggested transfers of units were taking place. By the second week in April this situation had progressed to the point where The Quartermaster General felt constrained to address the directors of the several functional agencies, calling attention to the need for full

co-operation between all units and individuals and the necessity for resisting "the tendency to build up autonomous organizations" within the OQMG.[45] He re-emphasized that the functional plan was in his opinion necessary to "meet the organization" of the SOS. The organization being installed was by no means perfect and would require many adjustments. Such duplications of effort as could be tolerated, he added, would be mainly "in the nature of a double check," as, for example, on the validity of requirements data. It was several months, however, before the problem of extensive duplication of activities resulting from the failure to transfer and consolidate units came to a head.

Although General Gregory was well aware of the duplications that existed, he preferred to restrain the organization planners in the Organization Planning and Control Division who were eager to carry out their theories at once and eliminate all maladjustments immediately. He felt that he had to exercise patience and to tolerate duplications in the interest of maintaining continuity of operations in the Corps, for these changes were being made at a time when the QMC was under heavy and increasing pressure to supply the troops. The Quartermaster General observed that where two groups were vested with the same responsibility, they frequently prodded each other into action. When the opportune moment presented itself, he could and did direct the necessary adjustments.[46]

Among the many individual maladjustments arising from the wording of Office Order 84 or from the organizational alignments created by it, the most immediately critical were those relating to the organization and conduct of the procurement and production functions of the Corps. Ambiguities in responsibilities for the estimation of requirements, purchasing, and

[45] Memo, TQMG for Dirs of Svs, OQMG, 11 Apr 42, no sub.
[46] Interv, OQMG historian with Gen Gregory, 21 Feb 51.

production controls were typical of the general indefiniteness regarding activities of common interest to two or more functional units. The details of the procurement and production organization and purchasing procedure, as well as consideration of methods and organization for requirements, came immediately under examination and criticism. While decisive action on requirements was held in abeyance pending the development of a need for rigid scheduling and control of supply, a number of surveys reviewing the Quartermaster procurement organization were made by the OQMG, the Control Division, SOS, and other government agencies.

Production expediting was one of the areas of conflicting jurisdiction. The production-expediting functions of the former Production Branch in the Planning and Control Division were turned over to the Procurement Service ostensibly in recognition of the necessity for blending this phase of production control with the purchasing program. Actually, very few of the officials and employees of the Production Expediting Section were relinquished when this transfer occurred. They remained with the Production Branch and became a part of the Production Service when it was created, in part by absorption of most of the Requirements and Production Branches of the former Planning and Control Division. The Production Service therefore had the only sizable and qualified group available for expediting duties. It was charged with providing a consulting service for the Procurement Service on production problems. As a result, depot personnel continued to call directly upon it for help in solving production problems. There were ample grounds for the view of some executives that the Production Service constituted in reality the agency responsible for expediting production. There was equally good reason for the Procurement Service to resent interference with its supervision of field activities and encroachment upon what it considered its proper functional sphere granted by specific order.[47]

Procurement functions offered another fruitful source of conflict between the Procurement Service and the Storage and Distribution Service. When the old Supply Division was broken up as a result of the functional reorganization of the OQMG, the purchasing sections of its commodity branches formed the basis of the newly created Procurement Service. The remnants of these commodity branches were absorbed by the Storage and Distribution Service. In addition, the Subsistence Branch of the former Supply Division and the Fuel and Utilities Branch of the Executive Office also became part of that service. It was only natural that resistance to the transfer of procurement activities should come from units of the former Supply Division lodged in the Storage and Distribution Service. Office Order 84 made the Procurement Service responsible for the purchase of all supplies for the Quartermaster Corps except those for motor transport. A survey in the fall of 1942 disclosed, however, that the Storage and Distribution Service was still supervising purchase in several major categories,[48] such as subsistence, and gasoline and lubricants purchased under Treasury or Quartermaster contracts.[49]

Adjustments between the Procurement Service and the Storage and Distribution Service were also hampered by the very broad view of

---

[47] For elaboration see below, Ch. VIII.

[48] Hist Rpt, Hist Sec, OQMG, to Control Div, SOS, Dec 42, Rpt on Administrative Developments, 7 Dec 41–1 Dec 42.

[49] Although motor transport activities had been transferred to Ordnance on 1 August, certain functions relating to motor transport supplies were subsequently returned to the QMC and assigned to the Storage and Distribution Division. Oddly enough the purchase of all motor transport supplies was also assigned to the Director of Procurement. (1) OQMG OO 25–9, 30 Sep 42, sub: Reasgmt of QMC Functions. (2) S&D Sv O 16, 29 Sep 42, sub: Establishment of Gasoline & Oil Br.

the latter's mission entertained by its director. He considered that the service was intended to be the real control agency and summarized his views as follows:

The Storage and Distribution Service *computes the requirements of the Army in Quartermaster items* and transmits these requirements to the Director of the Procurement Service who *does the actual* purchasing. The Storage and Distribution Service also furnishes the Director of Procurement with the desired distribution of the items to be purchased. *Once the items have been procured and accepted, the Procurement Service has no further responsibility.* From this point on the Storage and Distribution Service is responsible for the receipt of these items at depots, their storage, classification, and safeguarding, and their subsequent issue to troops.[50]

The computation of requirements and supply control furnished still another area of disputed jurisdiction. Under Office Order 84 the Storage and Distribution Service computed the requirements actually used as the basis of Quartermaster procurement. On the other hand, the Requirements Division of the Production Service arrived at independent calculations for inclusion in the long-range Army Supply Program, since it was responsible for calculating all long-term requirements and translating these into terms of raw materials and production facilities. The two sets of figures thus derived proved mutually unacceptable to the services concerned. In effect, the conflict present under the earlier OQMG organization, in which there had been repeated difficulty in reconciling data submitted by the Planning and Control Division with that of the commodity branches, and in persuading the staff and operating agencies to accept each other's figures, was thus preserved.[51]

Readjustments in 1942

These maladjustments provoked a re-evaluation of the basic organization of the OQMG in the summer of 1942. The first definite recommendation for modification of the Quartermaster procurement organization was offered in May by the Control Division, SOS. At the request of The Quartermaster General this division had attempted to appraise the efficacy of the reorganization of the OQMG which occurred in March. For this purpose it employed the services of Mr. R. R. Stevens of Montgomery Ward and Company [52] who proposed certain organizational changes.

His general conclusion was that the reorganization had been in the right direction but had not gone far enough in co-ordinating related activities and in decentralizing procurement operations. He asserted that there was no justification for the existence of separate Production and Procurement Services, since the production problem confronting the Corps was a relatively minor one.[53] He further recommended that planning, production, and the programming of requirements be consolidated with the procurement organization in a supply division and that such general planning and controls as were needed be placed on a staff basis within that organization. Distribution functions were also to be included in the proposed supply division as were research and developmental activities. Actual procurement and distribution was to be decentralized to commodity branches in the field, the chiefs of which would be in no way responsible to the commanding officers of the depots but would be responsible to the director of the supply division.

---

[50] Transcript of Speech, Brig Gen F. F. Scowden, 18 Jun 42, Conf with OP&C Div Staff to Acquaint Members with Pers and Opns of Corps.

[51] (1) Memo, Lawrence I. Peak, OP&C Div, 17 Apr 42, sub: Comments on OO 84. (2) See below, Ch. VI, for elaboration.

[52] A representative of the Procurement and Distribution Division, SOS, and members of the regular staff of the Control Division, SOS, collaborated with Mr. Stevens in this study of Quartermaster procurement organization.

[53] Memo, Col C. F. Robinson for CG SOS, 6 May 42, no sub, enclosing R. R. Stevens memo, n.d., sub: Notes on Suggested Reorgn of OQMG.

Obviously a large part of these recommendations ran counter to Quartermaster experience and particularly to the centralized procurement system that the Corps had been developing since World War I. Although the proposal for field commodity branches was not accepted, there was nevertheless a trend toward decentralizing procurement. Decentralization was persistently advocated by the ASF during the war and some steps were taken in that direction by the Corps.[54] Generally speaking, however, centralization remained the characteristic of Quartermaster procurement operations.

The proposal to unite research and procurement activities was rejected, although the character of Quartermaster research naturally demanded that it be correlated closely with current procurement and industrial management activities of the Corps as well as with production planning. During World War I, developmental activities had been thoroughly submerged in various commodity branches of the office, a mistake that those who were aware of the growing importance of research in the QMC were determined not to repeat. On the other hand, the recommendation to unite production and procurement in one division was accepted by the OQMG.

Immediate action, however, was not taken on these matters. In part the delay in settling the outline of procurement organization was due to consideration of a number of comprehensive surveys of procurement administration and policies which were being conducted by or in conjunction with higher authority. Two of these surveys, the so-called Cincinnati and the New York Field Surveys, were studies of regional activities in the areas indicated. Concerned mainly with integration of War Department procurement operations, they produced only incidental observations on the organization of purchasing and production in the technical services.

In the meantime, the basic steps in Quartermaster procurement became the subject of another study with primary emphasis placed on the process rather than the organizational structure. It was undertaken during the summer of 1942 by a representative of the Bureau of the Budget, Spencer Platt, with the aid of members of the OQMG and SOS control staffs and did make thoroughgoing recommendations directly applicable to Quartermaster activities.[55] This survey undertook a complete analysis of all OQMG functions relating to procurement. A work-flow study was submitted which showed how a commodity item was handled through the various stages of work, including product development, computation of long-term requirements, procurement planning (scheduling of purchases and production), resources analysis (computation of the availability and requirements of raw materials and plant facilities), purchasing, and production expediting. Urging recognition of their control or staff nature, the Platt Report called for the transfer of all production planning and resources-analysis activities either to the Procurement Service as a staff branch or to the Military Planning Service. This was the only specific proposal for realignment of organization growing out of the survey.

Primarily the Platt Report was concerned with the consolidation of functional activities in several important fields relating to procurement and the adjustment of responsibilities between divisions in order to promote better control and more effective operations, particularly in relation to the vital matter of requirements. It recommended that all research and developmental work at the OQMG be centralized in the Product Development Branch of the Production Service. While Office Order 84 had

---

[54] See below, Ch. VII.

[55] Chief of OP&C to Dirs of Divs, OQMG, 10 Sep 42, no sub, with two attachments prepared by survey teams, subs: Memo of Recommendations—OQMG Procurement, and Memo on Basic QMC Procurement Functions. This report is hereafter referred to as the Platt Report.

placed general functional responsibility for research in this service, it had failed to provide for the transfer to it of the research units established in the commodity branches of the former Supply Division. Duplication and conflict resulted. For example, when the Clothing and Equipage Branch was transferred to the Storage and Distribution Division, it retained intact its own research organization.[56]

The Platt Report specifically called for the transfer of all fiscal activities to the Fiscal Division. Virtually no change in the status of these activities had taken place, though a recent order had provided for the progressive consolidation of the fiscal accounting units under the Fiscal Division. It did not touch directly the work of the fiscal estimating units in the commodity branches though it emphasized that "the Chief of the Fiscal Division represents the Quartermaster Corps in securing the necessary funds to carry out the plans, programs, and operations of the Corps."[57]

After noting the reluctance of units of the former Supply Division to relinquish their procurement functions, the Platt Report recommended that all purchasing be placed forthwith in the Procurement Service. It further recommended that the Requirements Division take over the translation of the supply program into monthly requirements and that these be used directly by the Procurement Service for purposes of procurement planning, thereby eliminating the processing of a separate request or "plan" for purchase. It suggested, however, that to make the procedure effective the Requirements Division should be encouraged to develop closer liaison with the Storage and Distribution Service, thus avoiding the acceptance of unrealistic figures. The Platt Report was emphatic in its insistence that the current separation of procurement planning and procurement was a definite impediment to proper purchasing operations.

By the middle of the summer of 1942 it was evident that a more or less fundamental reorganization of OQMG activities was in the offing. Among the surveys made, only one[58] had raised the question of the desirability of returning to a commodity-type organization. When reorganization of the OQMG came up for definite consideration in June, the majority of the Quartermaster organization planning staff was convinced that the functional plan of organization was basically sound, but that some of the existing functional responsibilities needed clarification.[59] The need for developing adequate co-ordination between the several functional activities was recognized as imperative, for it was clear that the clash of personalities and competition for functions among certain of the division and branch chiefs was actually imperiling the successful execution of the supply program.

A further important factor dictating against reconsideration of the decision to perfect a functional system was the determination on the part of The Quartermaster General and others to merge the activities of motor transport, subsistence, and other large self-contained commodity units into the functional organization or at least subject them to a high degree of functional supervision. This determination seems to have been due in part to the desire to present an integrated Quartermaster organization in answer to proposals for the transfer of certain functions to other jurisdictions. The creation of a separate motor transport service was then under consideration and the QMC was also confronted at this time by agitation

---

[56] See below, Ch. III.

[57] OQMG OO 130, 6 Jun 42, sub: Centralization of Fiscal Accounting. It was at this time that the name of the Budget and Accounting Division was changed to Fiscal Division.

[58] Memo, Col Robinson for CG SOS, 6 May 42, no sub, enclosing R. R. Stevens memo, n.d., sub: Notes on Suggested Reorgn of OQMG.

[59] Transcript of Conf of Key Pers of OP&C with OQMG, 18 Jun 42.

for the assumption of all government food procurement by the Department of Agriculture.[60]

The arguments for a return to a commodity basis were definitely rejected and this form of organization was never officially under consideration again during the remainder of the war period.[61] As time went on, the further disadvantage of risking fundamental change in the midst of intensified military activities had to be considered. The reconsideration of OQMG organization begun in May was resolved in favor of retention of the functional system.

The OQMG issued Office Order 184 on 31 July 1942. It attempted to solve the problems that had arisen within the general framework of the functional organization established in March. It sought first of all to correct the most obvious deficiency of the earlier order by recognizing that the supply planning and control functions were in theory as well as in fact "staff" in nature. An effort was therefore made to group all of the existing activities relating to control of supply into a single agency, a new Military Planning Division, which was expressly designated a staff agency.[62] This division combined the functions of the former Military Planning Service and of the Production Service, except for a residue transferred to the Procurement Division.

Office Order 184 also combined production control and procurement. As late as the summer of 1942, however, this question had not been settled. At a staff conference in June many Quartermaster officials urged the continued maintenance of production control as a separate staff activity rather than its consolidation with the purchasing organization.[63] The fact that procurement activities were tending to be decentralized more and more to the field ruled out their administration by a staff agency. They could be handled more appropriately by the agency directly supervising depot activities. The order therefore transferred the Facilities Section and the supervision of the regional procurement planning districts from the Production Service to the Procurement Division. Thereafter technical control and co-ordination of field purchasing and production activities remained a responsibility of the Procurement Division. It developed its own production service program, which was not limited to the survey of facilities and production expediting but included activities in reference to priorities, the handling of labor questions, and financial aid to contractors, all of which were important in overcoming production difficulties.

One other important change in the reassignment of functions was made in July. This involved a more extensive consolidation of procurement activities than had taken place in March. Thus, the responsibility for the procurement of all pier, warehouse, and materials-handling equipment assigned to the Corps was vested in the Procurement Division. Its responsibility for the purchase of all general supplies was reaffirmed, and all procurement functions of the Service Installations Division were transferred to it. Furthermore, it became responsible for the procurement of gasoline and lubricants. On the other hand, the transfer of all subsistence procurement to the division as directed by the order was never accomplished.[64]

[60] *Ibid.*
[61] Memo, Col E. W. Reilley to Col H. A. Barnes, OQMG, 17 Oct 42, enclosing staff memo of Howard C. Adams, asst chief of OP&C Div, 10 Oct 42, sub: Recommended Changes in Office Layout to Effect Closer Co-ordination and Increase Effectiveness. This memorandum summarized the attitude of the group of administrative specialists on the subject of basic organization.
[62] (1) All of the principal subdivisions of the OQMG were designated "divisions" by Office Order 184, the next lower unit being the "branch." This was done primarily as a result of instructions received from Headquarters, SOS, requiring the use of uniform designations of organizational units throughout the SOS. Ltr, Gen Styer, SOS, to OQMG, 23 Jul 42, no sub. (2) See Chart 3.
[63] Transcript of Conf of Key Pers of OP&C Div with TQMG, 18 Jun 42.
[64] See below, p. 36.

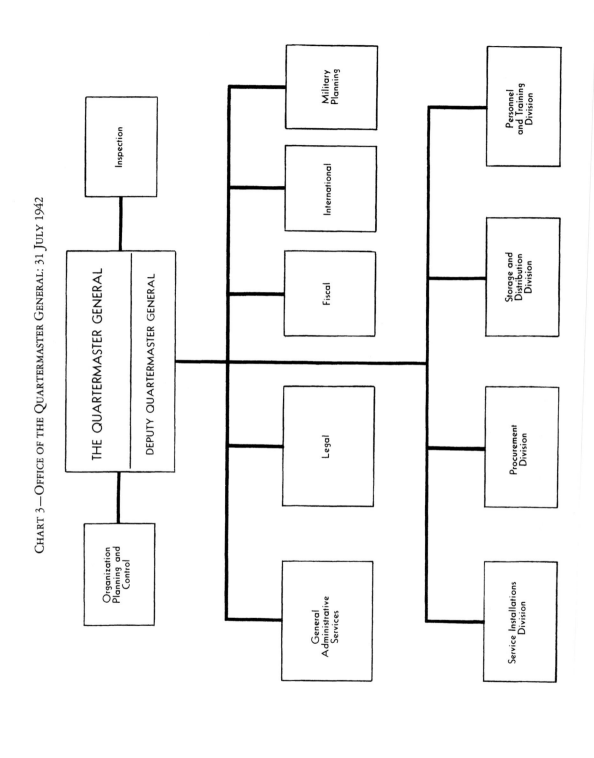

CHART 3—OFFICE OF THE QUARTERMASTER GENERAL: 31 JULY 1942

THE QUARTERMASTER GENERAL

DEPUTY QUARTERMASTER GENERAL

Inspection

Organization Planning and Control

Military Planning

International

Fiscal

Legal

General Administrative Services

Personnel and Training Division

Storage and Distribution Division

Procurement Division

Service Installations Division

The changes instituted in OQMG organization in the summer of 1942 represented the last major reorganization affecting functions during the war. Later changes were largely in the nature of refinement, and administrative planning was occupied primarily with improving co-ordination between divisions and creating a better organization for management of OQMG activities from the top. The functions and responsibilities of divisions, particularly with reference to the co-operative responsibilities of several of them in handling specific phases of supply activity, were defined more exactly in basic office orders in an effort to make lines of authority clear and to prevent duplication of activities and confusion in command relationships with the field. In addition, the divisions in co-operation with the Organization Planning and Control Division drafted more specific statements of functions. Specific instructions were also drawn up, covering basic procedures and allocations of responsibility on general and special phases of work. Thus, procedures governing the co-operative handling of lend-lease transactions by the International Division and the operating divisions were precisely defined. Illustrative of this same trend was the clarification of procedures and the exact allocation of responsibilities for handling various phases of the Controlled Materials Plan.[65]

The functional reorganization imposed a severe burden upon The Quartermaster General, in that chiefs of twelve separate divisions were reporting directly to him and taking up time he needed for more important matters of general policy. He solved this problem in the fall of 1942 by delegating supervisory responsibility to two deputies, each with responsibility for directing and co-ordinating the activities of six divisions.[66] Generally speaking, functions of a staff character were placed under the Deputy Quartermaster General for Administration and Management,[67] while those most closely associated with actual supply activities came under the Deputy Quartermaster General for Supply Planning and Operations.[68]

Each Deputy Quartermaster General had definite authority to make decisions concerning the activities of the divisions under his supervision. However, the Deputy Quartermaster General for Administration and Management was also given authority to co-ordinate important matters of administration in all echelons by the provision that division heads take up with him all questions involving administrative activities and personnel requiring the decision of The Quartermaster General.

To help him discharge his responsibilities, a small staff of specialists was organized, the members of which were designated "Executive Assistants to the Deputy Quartermaster General for Administration and Management." Attached for administrative purposes to the Organization Planning and Control Division, they were selected particularly for their ability to solve problems resulting from the recent changes in the organization and distribution of functions. For example, the transfer of motor transportation to the Ordnance Department on 1 August 1942 required an expert in this field to assist in the redistribution of functions between the two agencies. Similarly, relationships between the Corps and the newly organized service commands[69] required that an expert be appointed to help co-ordinate policies and procedures of the OQMG with functions of service commands as established by Headquarters, SOS. The executive assistants conducted studies and investigations of matters assigned to them by the Deputy Quartermaster General and prepared

---

[65] See below, Ch. VIII.

[66] OQMG OO 25–10, 10 Oct 42, sub: Apmt and Reasgmt of Key Pers.

[67] OP&C, Gen Admin Svs, Legal, Fiscal, Pers, and Mil Tng Divs.

[68] Procurement, S&D, Mil Plng, International, Sv Instls, and Insp Divs.

[69] See below, pp. 40–41.

recommendations for action to insure the proper determination, interpretation, and administration of new policies and procedures.

Evolution of Functional-Commodity-Type Organization, 1943–45

Despite the efforts made in 1942 to transform the Quartermaster administrative organization from a commodity to a functional system, the OQMG was never organized along purely functional lines. Instead it was an organization that consisted of both functional and commodity divisions. The commodity divisions handling the procurement and distribution of subsistence and petroleum products were outstanding exceptions to the general pattern of functional organization.

Fuels and Lubricants Division

A commodity unit, ostensibly responsible for the procurement, storage, and distribution of petroleum supplies, had existed since 1920 within the Supply Division. While in theory it was responsible for the control of petroleum products, in actual practice such operating divisions as Transportation and Construction performed almost all petroleum functions except the co-ordination of requirements. In March 1942 an attempt was made to divide petroleum responsibilities along functional lines between the Director of Procurement and the Director of Storage and Distribution. The latter was reluctant, however, to transfer the Fuel and Heavy Equipment Branch, as the unit was then called, to the Procurement Division despite the recommendations of the Organization Planning and Control Division in its survey of the problem.[70] The survey contended that the branch was a procuring organization with no storage or distribution function.

Although Office Order 184 lodged responsibility for the purchase of fuels with the Director of Procurement, the petroleum-procurement situation remained confused in the fall of 1942. The Storage and Distribution Division was issuing directives to the Procurement Division for the purchase of petroleum products for task forces. All supply services in the SOS, many of them in direct competition with one another, were procuring various petroleum products. The Navy also was purchasing petroleum products for the Army, and practically all the ports of embarkation were individually directing procurement of petroleum products in which they were interested. Such diversity of procurement might be permitted in peacetime, but it was not feasible when the country was faced by the exigencies of wartime markets.

The necessity for consolidating and centralizing petroleum procurement led to the establishment of a Petroleum Branch in the Procurement Division in December 1942.[71] By the following summer growing military needs, including unprecedented demands for packaged fuels and lubricants, resulting from the invasion of North Africa, required integrated staff work on the part of the services. Petroleum had become so important that it aroused the active interest and co-operation of the Commanding General, ASF, who proceeded to reconstitute the entire Army petroleum organization by creating in the OQMG a new Fuels and Lubricants Division.[72] It was a thoroughly integrated commodity organization which handled the procurement, storage, and issue of petroleum products as well

---

[70] William A. McCormack to Col G. F. Doriot, OQMG, 22 Aug 42, sub: Personal and Confidential Rpt on Fuel & Heavy Equip Div.

[71] OQMG OO 25-22, 3 Dec 42, sub: Reasgmt of QMC Functions Relating to Petrl and Petrl Products, Fuel Containers and Drums.

[72] (1) OQMG OO 25-37, 29 May 43, sub: Establishment of F&L Div. (2) For an analysis of the work of this division during the war see Erna Risch, *Fuels for Global Conflict* QMC Historical Studies 9, rev ed (Washington, 1952).

as research and developmental work in reference to containers and equipment. Since the Director, Military Planning Division, contended that all research on Quartermaster items should be concentrated in the Research and Development Branch of that division, considerable friction developed initially in this field.[73]

The Fuels and Lubricants Division was unique in that it not only retained all the operating responsibility it had had prior to that time as the Petroleum Branch in the OQMG, but it also acquired staff activities; that is, with certain specified exceptions, The Quartermaster General became responsible for the performance of all staff functions necessary to the discharge of the operating responsibilities either assigned or subsequently delegated by Headquarters, ASF, to the OQMG.[74] In addition, the director of the division acted as deputy to the Commanding General, ASF, in his capacity as a member of the Army-Navy Petroleum Board (ANPB), so that in this instance the division operated on the level of the Joint Chiefs of Staff.

Subsistence Division

The Subsistence Division constituted another exception to the general pattern of functional organization. Until 1912 the Commissary General of Subsistence had always been independent of The Quartermaster General. Although the Subsistence Department was merged with the QMC in that year, its tradition of independence lingered. Subsistence had for many years been organized as a commodity branch, and its personnel insisted that it could function efficiently only on a commodity basis. At the time of Pearl Harbor it was located in the Supply Division. When the OQMG was reorganized functionally, it was transferred intact as a commodity branch to the Storage and Distribution Service (later Division). It refused to adopt an internal organization which would lend itself to the

functional system, and it resisted all attempts to transfer the functions of subsistence procurement or research to the appropriate functional divisions.[75]

In the summer of 1942, for example, responsibility for the research, development, standardization, and adaptation of all types of Quartermaster equipment, except those utilized for petroleum products, was vested in the Research and Development Branch of the Military Planning Division. Despite this assignment of responsibility, subsistence research continued to be conducted by the Subsistence Branch and the Subsistence Research Laboratory,[76] which was formally connected with the OQMG only through the commanding officer of the Chicago Quartermaster Depot. In the past there had been some lack of co-ordination and some duplication of activity, but on the whole the two units had worked in harmony and with good results. Subsistence research continued to be handled by these units until the close of 1942.

At that time the OQMG attempted to clarify this situation by reaffirming the responsibility of the Military Planning Division for all research.[77] This division was responsible thereafter for assigning projects to, and directing the technical activities of, the Subsistence Research Laboratory. The chief of the laboratory remained under the authority of the command-

[73] (1) Dir of Mil Plng Div to Deputy QMG, 4 Aug 43, no sub. (2) OQMG OO 25-37B, 25 Aug 43, sub: Responsibility for Spec, Design, R&D of Containers for Petrl Products. (3) OQMG OO 25-70, 25 Mar 44, sub: Asgmt of Responsibility for Equip.

[74] (1) ASF Cir 33, 26 May 43, sub: Procurement, S&D of Petrl Products, Fuels (Liquid and Solid) and Lubricants. (2) Rescinded by ASF Cir 151, 15 Dec 43, same sub.

[75] Based on intervs, author with Lt Col Cecil G. Dunn, Subs Br, 5 Jan 43, and Loyola M. Coyne, Mil Plng Div, 6 Jan 43.

[76] See Walter Porges, The Subsistence Research Laboratory (OQMG historical monograph, May 1943). On file in Hist Sec, OQMG.

[77] OQMG OO 25-24, 14 Dec 42, sub: Subs R&D Activities.

ing general of the Chicago Quartermaster Depot
with respect to all activities, except those relating to the technical aspects of subsistence research. A Subsistence Research Project Board
was also created at this time. One of its duties
was to "initiate projects for research and development on any subject which it deems of benefit to Army subsistence." The vice chairman and
one other of the members appointed to this
board were from the Subsistence Branch. Thus,
although the actual responsibility for research
and development in this field rested with the
Military Planning Division, it was possible for
the Subsistence Branch through its representation on the new board to maintain an active
interest in subsistence research.

In pursuance of the functional plan of organization, Office Order 184 directed the transfer to
the Procurement Division of all functions of
the Subsistence Branch related to procurement
and all personnel engaged in procurement activities. At the same time, however, the order
also provided that "no physical movement of
personnel of the Subsistence Division will be
made without further approval of The Quartermaster General." Several problems were involved in this projected move. At the outset
there was the question of the feasibility of split-
ting purchase from distribution of subsistence.
The entire operation, at least for perishable
items, was a highly synchronized one, performed
through the specialized machinery of the market
center system. Secondly, the operation was recognized as primarily one of commodity procurement, with distribution accomplished more or
less incidentally and directly from the markets
where the food was purchased to using components of the Army, without the use of depot or
other permanent storage in transit. Certainly
the projected division of responsibilities would
have meant the transfer of virtually the entire
Subsistence Branch organization to the Procurement Division. Such a transfer had in fact been
under consideration earlier, but was rejected be-

cause, in the opinion of The Quartermaster
General, the move would have been of doubtful
effectiveness in promoting co-operation among
personnel within the OQMG.[78]

The major part of Quartermaster activities
relating to the handling of subsistence in the
Army and its special problems continued to be
centralized under the Subsistence Branch of the
Storage and Distribution Division until the
summer of 1944. Since subsistence always accounted for the major portion of Quartermaster
procurement, the Subsistence Branch was actually doing more purchasing than the Procurement Division. In May the branch was established as a separate division[79] under a director
who represented The Quartermaster General in
all interagency contacts pertaining to the purchase, supply, and preparation of food. He also
directed all Army programs connected with
preparation and service of food. Thus the Subsistence Division continued as a commodity
organization within the generally functionalized
organization of the OQMG.

Creation of the Subsistence Division represented the last important modification in the
organization of the OQMG during the war
years. From May 1944 until the end of the war
there were thirteen divisions carrying out the
duties assigned to the QMC.[80] The pattern of
commodity-functional organization was set. Debate on the advantage of commodity versus
functional organization was not reopened after
the summer of 1942. Earlier conflicts, resulting
from overlapping responsibilities, had been adjusted by 1944, and the QMC accomplished its
mission during the remainder of the war period
with a relatively smooth-functioning, harmonious organization.

[78] Transcript of Conf of Key Pers of OP&C Div with
OQMG, 18 Jun 42.
[79] OQMG OO 25-80, 17 May 44, sub: Establishment of Subs Div.
[80] See Chart 4.

CHART 4—OFFICE OF THE QUARTERMASTER GENERAL: 15 JULY 1944

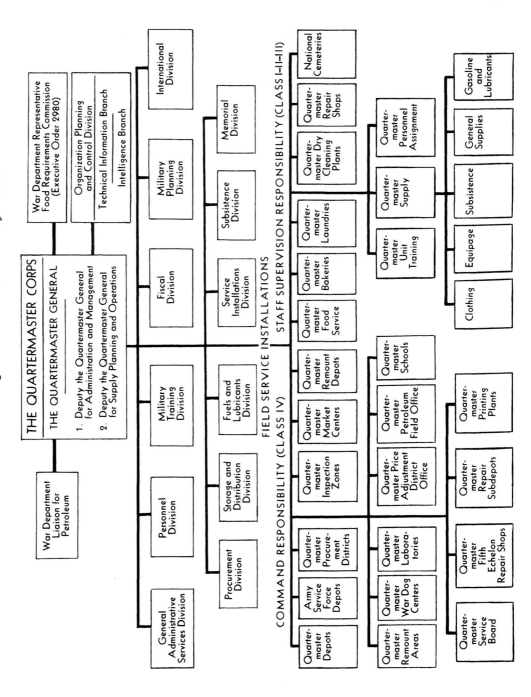

Field Organization

In 1939 the basic field installations of the QMC were the depots, with most Quartermaster field activities either administered through the depots or physically located at these installations. Some of the depots were of a specialized type known as Remount depots, which conditioned and provided limited training of animals and issued horses and mules to troop units.[81] The most important depots were those engaged in the procurement and distribution of Quartermaster supplies. When the emergency began there were twelve of these supply depots, but some of them were relatively inactive, being used almost exclusively to store war reserve and other slow moving stocks. They exercised a large degree of autonomy in conducting their operations, for the OQMG provided little centralized control or co-ordination of their activities. Instead, each of the commodity branches of the Supply Division dealt with the depots, making for a multiplicity of contacts between depots and the OQMG.

Depot quartermasters procured and issued supplies on the basis of requisitions forwarded to them by corps area quartermasters. In 1939 the United States was divided for administrative purposes into nine geographical units called corps areas, with The Quartermaster General exercising direct supervision over the quartermasters who represented him on the headquarters staff of the corps area commanders. Quartermaster activities at the posts, camps, and stations located in the corps areas were administered by the local quartermasters. They requisitioned and issued supplies needed by the troops stationed at the posts and operated for them such Quartermaster services as laundries. These post, camp, and station quartermasters were the operating force of the Corps in the field for carrying out its mission of supply and services.

Depots were important not only because of the role they played in the supply of Quartermaster items but because a number of other activities were located at these installations. For instance, a factory at the Philadelphia Quartermaster Depot manufactured Army uniforms. Such laboratories as existed at this time were to be found at the depots, as, for example, the Subsistence Research Laboratory at the Chicago Quartermaster Depot. Quartermaster schools were also located at depots. Quartermaster personnel were trained at the Quartermaster School at the Philadelphia Depot and at the Motor Transport School located at the Holabird Quartermaster Depot.[82]

The Quartermaster field organization expanded rapidly during the emergency and war periods. New depots were built and old ones were expanded. In addition, new staff functions were assigned to The Quartermaster General in relation to ASF depots. Such administrative changes as occurred after 1939 were in the direction of increased control and co-ordination of the field installations. Field offices for the centralized purchase of nonperishable subsistence emerged. Even more significant was the substitution of centralized procurement of perishable foods for the decentralized purchase of such foods which had been permitted at posts, camps, and stations in peacetime. As the Army expanded during the emergency, this could no longer be tolerated, and one of the most important innovations was the creation of new field installations called market centers.

Market Center Program

The need to co-ordinate food procurement for military agencies during the period of emergency gave rise to the market center program.

---

[81] For a discussion of their activities see Ch. X of The Quartermaster Corps: Organization, Supply, and Services, Vol. II, in preparation for this series.

[82] (1) For the work of the laboratories see Chs. III and V below. (2) For training at the Quartermaster School see Ch. VIII of volume cited above in n. 81.

The intent was to establish a centralized procurement organization which could utilize speedy commercial methods of purchasing large quantities by negotiation and would give posts, camps, and stations access to all the nation's markets. The program promoted more economical and more efficient Army procurement of perishable subsistence.[83] The original provision for the establishment of market centers was made in March 1941[84] and the program was under way in May. By 7 December some twenty-five to thirty market centers were either planned or in operation on a small scale. Approximately a year later over forty were in operation, additional facilities having been set up from time to time to serve new marketing and distribution areas or to give more adequate service to the original areas. This expansion was necessary not only to take care of the increase in personnel of the Army but to provide facilities, beginning with the spring of 1942, for the procurement of most of the perishable supplies for the Navy and the Marine Corps.

The market centers were under the direct control of The Quartermaster General. Because control could best be handled in a central geographical location, the Chicago Market Center, which was described as the "Central Office for administrative purposes," developed into the national supervisory headquarters of the program. By a slow and sometimes painful process, clear-cut lines of authority and responsibility were worked out eventually between the market centers, the Chicago central office, and the OQMG. In the summer of 1941 the Chicago central office was established as Field Headquarters, Perishable Subsistence Section, OQMG.[85] Its activities, which were purely administrative and supervisory, were differentiated from those of the Chicago Quartermaster Market Center, an operating agency. The Perishable Section of the Subsistence Branch in Washington became a liaison office for maintaining contact with the Army and government agencies and for inter-preting and co-ordinating OQMG policies and those of governmental food administrative agencies with Field Headquarters and the market centers.[86]

Food Service Program

Another important aspect of subsistence administration was the initiation of the Food Service Program. Food conservation had always been considered a normal concomitant of Army feeding, and numerous rules and regulations were aimed at enforcing moderation in the purchase and preparation of food. In the summer of 1941 the QMC contained in undeveloped form the essential elements which went into the future Food Service Program. One of these was the Bakery Section of the Subsistence Branch, OQMG, which co-ordinated the training in the bakers' and cooks' schools, produced quality bread in posts, camps, and stations, and prepared a balanced field ration menu. The central headquarters of the market center system and the Subsistence Research Laboratory comprised other components. The conservation branch of the laboratory was later described as having the same mission as the Food Service Section of the OQMG, except that its work was done before the food got to the soldier. Finally, these elements included bakers' and cooks' schools (one to each service command at that time) which were to multiply 700 percent within three years but were even then carrying out their appointed task of training men for service in the Army messes and garrison bakeries.

The difficulty was that these agencies were completely unco-ordinated and insufficiently

[83] For a detailed account of this program see H. R. Rifkind, *Fresh Foods for the Armed Forces: The Quartermaster Market Center System* (QMC Historical Studies 20, August 1951).

[84] OQMG Cir Ltr 42, 19 Mar 41, sub: Purch of Fresh Fruits and Vegetables.

[85] OQMG Cir Ltr 117, 23 Jun 41, no sub.

[86] Memo, Capt L. Morrill for Brig Gen C. A. Hardigg, OQMG, 10 Feb 43, sub: Opns of Perishable Sec.

staffed to accomplish their work to the best purpose. In the opinion of The Quartermaster General the remedy lay in establishing "a system of supervision by trained personnel." [87] This anticipated in many respects the later Food Service Program. The problem was to emphasize at the posts the need for following proper messing procedure, to provide the type of mess supervision that would guarantee the enforcement of such procedure, and to create and organize a nationwide conservation program which could be administered by a central office. The War Department early in 1943 sought to bring home to service commanders an increased sense of their responsibility for saving and properly dispensing food by re-emphasizing food preparation and consumption as command functions. About the same time provision was made for the appointment of mess officers at all posts, camps, and stations.[88] Thus the groundwork was laid for the Food Service Program which was initiated in the fall of 1943.

From the beginning of 1943, as civilian shortages increased, there developed a mounting public pressure for food conservation that led General Somervell to direct The Quartermaster General to establish an organization which would assume adequate and proper mess supervision. The OQMG promptly drafted a plan whereby it became the staff agency at ASF headquarters level for mess management, thus completing the chain of supervision for this function throughout the ASF from the mess supervisors and commanding officers of posts, camps, and stations through the food service director at the staff level of the service command.[89] The plan replaced the old Bakery Section within the Subsistence Branch with a Food Service Section having the power to supervise the preparation and service of food, to eliminate waste, and to insure adequately trained mess supervisors, mess sergeants, and bakers and cooks by developing proper material for training courses and by inspecting the effectiveness

of operation of bakers' and cooks' schools.[90] The Food Service Program was not intended to minimize the responsibility of the commanding generals of the service commands but rather to implement their authority and to co-ordinate all food activities throughout the service commands. It became the business of the field agencies to see that the measures, instructions, data, and recommendations drawn up in Washington were given significance.

Service Commands

The service commands were the nine geographical units into which the War Department divided the continental United States for administrative purposes. Known as corps areas before 1942, they were assigned to the SOS in March when the Army was reorganized, and acquired their new name in July as a result of a survey conducted by the Control Division, SOS.[91] The geographical boundaries of the old corps areas were not changed, and the major function of the service commands continued to be the operation of fixed Army installations. They were the principal field agencies for the SOS and performed its basic functions, except those technical ones relating to procurement, new construction, depot operations, and port and certain transportation activities.

The relationship of the service commands to the supply services, however, was radically

[87] Memo, Gen Gregory for CofS G-3, 24 Feb 42, sub: Tng and Supervision of Mess Pers.

[88] (1) WD Cir 16, 11 Jan 43, sub: Revised Procedure for Distr of and Accounting for Fld Rations. (2) SOS Memo S-30-3-43, 15 Jan 43, sub: Supervision of Messes and Elimination of Waste.

[89] (1) Memo, Gen Somervell for TQMG, 1 Jun 43, sub: Mess Supervision. (2) Memo, Gen Gregory for CG ASF, 26 Jun 43, sub: QM Food Sv. (3) After approval, the plan was published as ASF Cir 45, 3 Jul 43, sub: Food Sv Program.

[90] OQMG OO 25-24A, 2 Aug 43, sub: Orgn of Food Sv Sec.

[91] (1) WD GO 35, 22 Jul 42, no sub. (2) AR 170-10, 10 Aug 42, sub: SvCs and Depots.

changed. Under the former corps area setup, the supply services exercised direct jurisdiction over their representatives on the headquarters staff of the corps area commander. Under the new arrangements, the service commander had complete jurisdiction and any instructions from the supply services had to go through his office. The QMC had a dual function to perform under this system. It was charged with the performance of certain technical activities which it carried out through field installations of its own located in service commands, such as market centers, Quartermaster depots, and remount areas. In addition to these direct operating responsibilities, the QMC had a staff responsibility to the Commanding General, SOS.[92] In this relationship The Quartermaster General was in the same position as the director of a staff division of Headquarters, SOS. He advised the commanding general, issued plans, procedures, and directives to the service commanders, assisted them, and followed up performance within their jurisdictions.

When a function that was the sole responsibility of the Corps was involved, the staff relationship between The Quartermaster General and the service commander was clear cut. For example, laundry service was a function peculiar to the Corps, and the Commanding General, SOS, later ASF, looked to The Quartermaster General as his staff officer in reference to this activity. The same was true of the Food Service Program, the staff arrangement of which was characterized as "the best working staff arrangement in the whole ASF." [93] On the other hand, where a function common to the technical services was concerned and ASF had a staff division to supervise it, the relationship between the chief of the technical service and the service commander was "pretty hazy." The Quartermaster General had staff responsibility, for example, for preparing and recommending procedues for the use of the service commands with respect to the storage, issue, maintenance, and salvage of Quartermaster supplies and equipment. Within Headquarters, ASF, a Maintenance Division was established because General Somervell believed it necessary to have some one agency co-ordinate maintenance among the seven technical services. Confusion developed as to whether the Maintenance Division or The Quartermaster General worked with the service commander, an issue that in the fall of 1944 led one high-ranking officer to remark, "We have never quite clearly settled that one." [94]

Even though staff responsibilities were not always clearly defined, The Quartermaster General was responsible for formulating and publishing training doctrine and manuals for Quartermaster personnel being trained in the service commands. He was also authorized to supervise the establishment of installations for repair and salvage operations and other service installations and to insure by proper inspection the operating efficiency of Quartermaster installations and of Quartermaster units under the service commands. Specific Quartermaster activities under the jurisdiction of the service commands with staff responsibility vested in The Quartermaster General included the Food Service Program, laundries and dry cleaning plants, Quartermaster repair shops, salvage depots, service schools, replacement training centers, and cemeteries.[95]

Depots

The most important field installations of the QMC were the depots, since they constituted the backbone of the system of supply and assured the flexibility of supply operations. An

---

[92] OQMG OO 185, 5 Aug 42, sub: SvC Reorgn.

[93] Address, Maj Gen C. F. Robinson, sub: Relations of Technical Services with Service Commands, QMs' Conf, 2–4 Oct 44, Camp Lee, Va.

[94] *Ibid.*

[95] (1) AR 170-10, 24 Dec 42, sub: SvCs and Depots. (2) AR 30-2135, C3, 12 Jan 43, sub: Laundries. (3) AR 30-1840, 9 Oct 44, sub: National Cemeteries.

efficient, co-ordinated depot system was essential to winning the war, but when the United States entered World War II, each supply service was procuring its supplies and distributing them irrespective of other services. The depot system consisted of general depots jointly occupied by the supply services and branch depots operated by each supply service.

At the beginning of the emergency, storage and distribution operations, like other supply functions, were loosely co-ordinated under the joint direction of the Supply Division, G–4, in the War Department General Staff and the Office of the Assistant Secretary of War, but in practice these two agencies were often played off against each other so that the supply services were almost as autonomous as they had been in 1917, when the lack of adequate co-ordination had produced unhappy consequences. This was remedied, however, in March 1942 by the establishment of the SOS, which was given supervisory responsibilities over all the operations of the supply services. For the next five months the General Depot Service (later Division), SOS, which had inherited the staff functions associated with the construction, allocation, and use of War Department storage facilities, directed the operations of the general depots. Then, in July, the General Depot Division was discontinued,[96] and SOS transferred its operating functions in reference to jointly occupied depots to The Quartermaster General, while its staff functions went to the Assistant Chief of Staff for Operations. When the SOS became the ASF in March 1943, these staff functions were performed in the Office of the Director of Operations.

General depots consisted of supply sections of the various tenant services, each of which was organized in the same way as a branch depot of the particular service to which it belonged. The supply officers, heading these sections, were responsible to the chief of the supply service they represented rather than to the depot commander.

In prewar days the supply sections were free of any supervision save that exercised by the Quartermaster General acting for the War Department. He designated a depot quartermaster who was assigned the task of managing activities of concern to all the tenant services, such as guard, fire protection, general police, utilities, and transportation activities of the installations.[97]

Because of this autonomy, supply officers in general depots worked independently of each other, with little or no pooling of labor or equipment. This independence was further promoted by the prewar fiscal system, for funds were not allotted to general depots as such but were divided among the various supply sections. The authority of the depot commander was thus confined to "housekeeping problems" and to labor and equipment of a nature common to the supply sections. However, he had no control over labor and equipment of a particular supply section even when idle men and machines in one section might have been beneficially employed in another.

This autonomy of the supply sections was first subjected to remedial study by the General Depot Service.[98] It proposed to eliminate wasteful practices and duplication of work by organizing the general depots along functional lines and by conferring on the depot commanders enlarged powers by which they could direct the consolidation and use of both facilities and labor for the benefit of the tenant services. Warehousemen, highly trained in storing and handling supplies in civilian life, and experts in personnel administration were to be the major instruments of the depot commanders in attaining these objectives. The proposals, however, met formidable opposition from the QMC and

[96] SOS GO 22, 11 Jul 42, no sub.
[97] AR 700-10, Sec. III, 1 Jul 36, sub: Supplies: Stor and Issue.
[98] Memo, Col R. E. Duff, Actg Chief of Gen Dep Div, SOS, for CGs all Gen Deps, 13 Apr 42, sub: Functions of Gen Deps to Be Performed Under CO.

other technical services and were considerably modified.[99]

When the functions pertaining to general depots were transferred to the QMC in July, the same goals were pursued but in less drastic fashion. The general depots were temporarily called jointly occupied Quartermaster depots and subsequently ASF depots.[100] In the transfer certain staff functions were imposed on the OQMG. These included the installation of modern warehousing, space conservation, pooling of common labor, and up-to-date commercial methods of materials-handling. Funds for meeting all overhead expenses at jointly occupied installations were allotted to The Quartermaster General, who was thus freed of financial dependence upon the supply sections. The Operations Division, SOS, co-ordinated the allocation of space for branch depots, but the OQMG was responsible for handling the applications of supply services for space at jointly occupied depots in accordance with SOS instructions. The Operations Division, SOS, supervised the general inspection of operations.[101]

After the transfer, the OQMG outlined the functions the commanding officer was to exercise under the jurisdiction of The Quartermaster General. Particular stress was laid on the requisitioning, pooling, distribution, and servicing of all warehouse and materials-handling equipment (except that peculiar to a particular supply service); on the application of modern storage methods; and on the co-ordination of wage and labor policies. The depot commander was to have a qualified warehousing and materials-handling representative on his staff to assist the supply officers, and a personnel branch to handle the procurement of civilian employees.[102] These changes thus followed the same trend initiated by the General Depot Service, SOS.

Although Headquarters, ASF, continued to study the organization of operations at branch and jointly occupied depots with the objective of modernizing and standardizing storage operations,[103] it was deemed inadvisable to make radical changes in depot organization, administration, and procedures which might interfere with depot operations during the intense activity of the war period. No major changes in the administration of jointly occupied depots therefore occurred between their designation as ASF depots in April 1943 and V-J Day. Co-ordination of the work of supply sections was most strikingly demonstrated in the development of labor and materials-handling-equipment pools and in a more centralized supervision of personnel affairs. In other matters, too, the depot commander assumed more authority than in prewar days, but, generally speaking, supply officers retained control of the technical aspects of their functions, though the depot commanders could intervene if they considered the operations of a supply section inefficient. The trend was unquestionably toward a more highly centralized administration of jointly occupied depots.

Co-ordination, standardization, and control of storage and distribution operations were as inadequate at Quartermaster branch depots in

---

[99] (1) Dep Opn Div to Gen Scowden, OQMG, 20 May 42, sub: Comments on Memo, Gen Dep Sv, 11 May 42. (2) Ltr, Col T. L. Holland, CO ATGD, to Col Duff, SOS, 19 Apr 42, no sub. (3) Ltr, Col Duff to CO COGD et al., 20 Jun 42, sub: Reorgn of Gen Deps.

[100] AG Memo S210-8-43, 30 Apr 43, sub: Designation of Jointly Occupied Deps.

[101] (1) Ltr, TQMG to COs, Former Gen Deps, 12 Aug 42, sub: Reorgn of Deps Jointly Occupied. (2) Memo, Col R. C. L. Graham, Dir of Plans Div, SOS, for TQMG et al., 5 Sep 42, sub: Co-ordination of Stor and Shipping Problems.

[102] (1) Per ltr, TQMG to Brig Gen W. A. Danielson, CO MEQMD, 5 Aug 42, no sub. (2) Ltr, Col J. W. G. Stephens, OQMG, to COs QM Deps, 24 Aug 42, sub: Orgn of QM S&D Div at Deps. (3) Ltr, TQMG to COs QM Deps, 21 Oct 42, sub: Orgn of Civ Pers at QM Deps.

[103] (1) Rpt, Control Div, SOS, 17 Sep 42, sub: Ultimate Plan of Dep Opns. (2) Memo, Gen Lutes, ASF, for Chiefs of Tech Svs, 21 May 43, sub: Dep Reorgn Under Rpt 67.

1939 as at jointly occupied general depots. No single agency in the OQMG was responsible for the supervision of these operations, and field installations were at a loss to know what agency in Washington to approach when problems required immediate attention. It was feasible in peacetime, when supply activities were limited in scope, to permit the several commodity branches of the Supply Division to deal with depots, for the system could work then without close supervision. Thus each depot had multiple contacts with the OQMG and, at the same time, had great autonomy in conducting its operations. This situation persisted as late as the summer of 1942 when it was observed that Quartermaster depots and Quartermaster sections of general depots "had a tendency to operate as separate autonomies rather than as a part of the depot system." Each installation was using various methods "for doing business with little regard for the existence of similar supply organizations." [104]

Some steps toward centralized supervision were taken during the emergency period, culminating in the establishment of the Depot Division in May 1941.[105] Not until the OQMG shifted to a functional organization in March 1942, however, were storage and distribution functions concentrated in a single unit called the Storage and Distribution Division. It had managerial supervision over the operation of Quartermaster depots and Quartermaster sections of general depots, with the exception of their procurement functions, which were vested in the Procurement Division. The Storage and Distribution Division was charged with the development of depot organization and procedures, the allocation of warehouse equipment, the initiation of recommendations for the construction and expansion of depot facilities, the establishment and maintenance of stock levels, and the control of stockages, including excess supplies at posts, camps, and stations.

Between World Wars I and II, depot organization followed the OQMG organizational pattern, although there were many local variations. Some of these were traditional and others the result of exceptional responsibilities imposed on installations, such as the dual procurement and manufacturing functions of the Jeffersonville and Philadelphia Quartermaster Depots. In the interest of greater standardization, the principle of functionalism was applied to Quartermaster depot organization in 1942 as it had been at higher echelons. A year later, however, nonstandard organizations and procedures still existed to a large extent in depot operations. Although a standard framework had early been recognized as "necessary to make procedural instructions equally applicable and to place operational and managerial studies on a basis of comparability," [106] it was late in 1943 before depot organization became more or less stable.

Inasmuch as the practicability and desirability of delegating important responsibilities to the field depended upon the existence of capable and dependable field units, the OQMG divisions took measures to help the depots streamline their organization [107] and build up strong technical staffs for handling various phases of operations. This simplification and strengthening of field installations was important both to headquarters controls and efficiency in the field.

Equally important was the delegation of adequate authority to field executives. One of the prime purposes of the War Department reor-

---

[104] Dep Opn Div to Ex Off, S&D Sv, OQMG, 28 Jul 42, sub: Material for Annual Rpt of SW.

[105] See above, p. 15.

[106] Ltr, Col Stephens, OQMG, to CO BQMD et al., 24 Aug 42, sub: Orgn of QM S&D Div at Deps.

[107] For example, the Procurement Division conducted studies for the improvement of expediting and inspection organization in the depots, and the Storage and Distribution Division prescribed a standard organization for the Storage and Distribution Section of each depot.

ganization in March 1942 was to effect maximum decentralization of operations while maintaining centralization for co-ordination of broad general policies and objectives.[108] Illustrative of the application of this principle to Quartermaster operations was the steady delegation of responsibility for actual procurements and procurement expediting to the depots and the decentralization of personnel routines and records to these field establishments. The major benefit in the OQMG of this decentralization policy was that it focused attention upon the consideration of important policies and controls, but it also helped prevent an undue increase of personnel at Washington headquarters. In regard to actual operations, this policy speeded up supply by eliminating red tape and unnecessary clearances with headquarters.

At the same time considerable progress was made in improving and tightening those controls essential to activities performed by the scattered field units. Among the major improvements was the standardization and simplification of instructions on policy and procedure for a wide variety of operations, such as contracting, fiscal and property accounting, reporting, distribution of supplies, personnel actions, and salvage operations. There were also improvements in the quality of statistical and other information of operations reported by the field and summarized at OQMG for control purposes and for use by higher authority. Another improvement was the establishment of more adequate and direct contacts with the field in connection with phases of operations in which determinations in the OQMG had to reflect realistically field experience; for example, research and developmental work and the determination of requirements.

Relations with Other Agencies

In the course of fulfilling its mission the QMC found it necessary to work closely with many other agencies of the government. These ranged from the older, well-established departments of government to the newly created wartime agencies. Thus in normal times the Corps relied for laboratory testing of materials upon the National Bureau of Standards of the Department of Commerce, the official government testing agency. The bureau continued to handle a large part of this work in wartime and also undertook tests of completed experimental items in cases where close scientific observation of performance was necessary.[109] In its research and developmental work the OQMG also utilized the laboratory and reference facilities of the Department of Agriculture and the Department of Interior. The Office of Scientific Research and Development was established by an executive order in 1941 to assure adequate provision for research on scientific and medical problems relating to the national defense. This office was of increasing assistance to the OQMG in its developmental work, for through its National Defense Research Committee the facilities of governmental, university, and industrial laboratories all over the country were made available for the solution of scientific problems.[110] Fundamental research problems were ordinarily presented to it through the War Department liaison staff which had been set up for such clearance in Headquarters, ASF.

One of the most important wartime agencies was the War Production Board (WPB), established on 16 January 1942 to assure "the most effective prosecution of war procurement and production." In view of mounting military requirements and decreasing supplies of critical materials, priorities and allocations of materials

[108] Memo, Gen Somervell to Dirs of all Staff Divs, et al., 27 Mar 42, sub: Control.

[109] See, for example, Rpt, National Bureau of Standards to OQMG, 23 Aug 43, sub: Tropical Helmets.

[110] For a more detailed account see Erna Risch and Thomas M. Pitkin, *Clothing the Soldier of World War II* (QMC Historical Studies 16, September 1946), pp. 12–14.

were necessary to balance resources between the military and civilian sections of the economy. The OQMG found it necessary to co-ordinate activities with the WPB in connection with many specific problems, such as over-all program requirements of materials and allotments for them, production schedules, priorities, expediting production, allocations of materials to QMC contractors, and specifications.[111] The OQMG maintained contact with the WPB either directly or through the Army-Navy Munitions Board (ANMB) and ASF staff divisions.

The need for control of prices to check profiteering and other disruptive practices resulting from abnormal market conditions led to the enactment of the Price Control Act of 1942. At the same time, however, there was danger that the Quartermaster supply mission would be adversely affected. Consequently the OQMG established procedures and organizational units to obtain such relief from OPA price control activities as was necessary in the interest of expeditious war procurement.[112] The breadth and scope of Quartermaster purchases and the large number of civilian-type commodities inevitably brought delay and confusion in the application of OPA price controls. The OQMG, therefore, had to obtain numerous rulings on the exemptions from OPA price regulations. Quartermaster policy, however, called for the fullest co-operation with the OPA in checking inflation through price control, and the OQMG maintained active liaison with that agency. Where matters of general policy or those of concern to other technical services were involved, Headquarters, ASF, dealt directly with the OPA in solving over-all price control problems.

No one product was more essential to the winning of the war than petroleum. To assure the prosecution of the war the Petroleum Administration for War (PAW) was established with authority to formulate basic policies, plans, and programs for the conservation and most effective development and utilization of petroleum in the United States, its territories, and possessions. It issued necessary directives to the petroleum industry and as far as practicable served as the channel of communication between the units of the petroleum industry and the several departments and agencies of the federal government on matters directly involving the functions and duties of the administrator. On petroleum matters the Fuels and Lubricants Division, OQMG, worked through the Army-Navy Petroleum Board, since that agency maintained close liaison with PAW and effected close co-operation between the War and Navy Departments on all matters pertaining to petroleum and petroleum products. At the same time, specific branches of the Fuels and Lubricants Division found it essential to maintain direct relations with various divisions of PAW, as, for example, in reference to requirements, production capacity of the various refineries throughout the United States, and allocation of petroleum products.[113]

Solid fuels, like petroleum products, were also administered by a central agency, Solid Fuels Administration for War (SFAW), with the result that as the supply of coal became more critical the Solid Fuels Branch of the OQMG requested its allocations from the SFAW and then advised a depot to execute a contract with a designated contractor for so much coal to be delivered to a given post, camp, or station.

Finally, manpower problems established the need for other relationships. Early in the emergency the Labor Division of the Office of Production Management (OPM) was made respon-

---

[111] OQMG OO 25-51, 11 Sep 43, sub: Coordination of Activities with WPB.

[112] (1) OQMG OO 25-54, 24 Sep 43, sub: Orgn of Procurement Div. (2) OQMG OO 25-54A, 29 Sep 43, same sub. (3) OQMG OO 25-54D, 17 Jan 44, same sub.

[113] A fuller treatment is found in Risch, *Fuels for Global Conflict*, pp. 10–12.

sible for providing an adequate and continuous supply of trained manpower for the defense program. Later the WPB absorbed the OPM and assumed its labor supply responsibilities for several months. By 18 April 1942 these were transferred to the War Manpower Commission. Like the OPM, the commission made use of the United States Employment Service as the central exchange for labor market information and for the recruitment, placement, and control of the nation's manpower.

Quartermaster industries were particularly plagued by labor turnover which often seriously impeded vital production. This situation was a reflection of existing wage differentials which provided an effective basis for pirating on the part of rival suppliers in the same or other defense industries. The QMC was therefore much interested in manpower controls that would aid in the recruitment and retention of essential labor forces. Liaison with the above-mentioned agencies was originally maintained within the War Department by the Office of the Under Secretary of War. This activity was absorbed in March 1942 by Headquarters, SOS. Within the OQMG a Labor Section was established which developed the necessary procedures for reporting and follow-up of labor supply problems. It channeled labor problems through the Office of the Under Secretary of War to the OPM Labor Supply Branch and later through Headquarters, ASF, to the War Manpower Commission. The impact of controls imposed by the commission, the OPA, and the WPB are revealed more fully in Quartermaster operations.[114]

---

[114] See below, Ch. VII.

PART TWO

SUPPLY

CHAPTER II

Factors Shaping Research Activities

Total war requires the use of all national resources and the exploitation of all scientific knowledge and technological skills. In World War II the United States was engaged in global war which posed a supply problem of tremendous proportions. The supply responsibility of the Quartermaster Corps included the procurement, storage, distribution, and salvage of such supplies as clothing, food, petroleum products, individual and organizational equipment, and numerous "housekeeping" items. The QMC, under the provisions of the National Defense Act of 1920, was the most nearly universal supply agency of the Army. An essential part of its supply activity was research and developmental work to improve existing items and provide new equipment as the need became apparent.

To assure victory in the war it was necessary for the American soldier to be so equipped that he would be superior to his opponents in the field. As a result of the mechanization of warfare and the extension of battle fronts to all kinds of terrain in all types of climate, an enormous demand was created for a wide range of equipment of the highest attainable quality. From the standpoint of Quartermaster responsibility, this equipment included water-repellent fabrics, arctic and jungle clothing, shoepacs, ski boots, shrinkproof socks, and waterproof matches, as well as nutritious rations, mobile laundry and bath units, clothing and textile repair units, and portable field bakeries. So great

was the emphasis on research and developmental work in World War II that the war's end found such activities established as a permanent feature of military planning.

When the war began, however, the status of research and developmental activities left much to be desired. Such activities had been carried on since 1918, but there were two schools of thought as to the significance of the achievements of these twenty years. One group viewed the work done in that interval as the foundation for much that was accomplished in World War II. The second group deemed negligible the research activities of those years. The latter view was well expressed by the wartime director of the Military Planning Division.

It has been said too often that the Army started this war with the equipment with which it had ended World War I. Actually, the situation was much worse. Many items which had been developed as the result of field experience in the mud and rain of northern France in 1917 and 1918 were "modified" in peacetime to be more suitable for the garrison life at Ft. Benning, Georgia, or Ft. Sam Houston, Texas. Even after the outbreak of the war, the importance of immediately improving existing equipment was not recognized by many. . . . Furthermore, many of the items which are procured by the Quartermaster Corps are of commercial types. In peacetime research had to be carried out on Ordnance material because there were no commercial items available. On the other hand, it was felt by many that the Quartermaster Corps could and would accept standard commercial designs and items without difficulty. No single point of view has perhaps done the Army more harm than this one. There are extremely few commercial items which are suitable for military use. The demands which the Army places upon equipment are such that the use of commercial items results in lower efficiency, higher casualties, and incidentally, higher costs. The inadequacies of existing equipment and the dangers implicit in its use were brought out at once in the snow and mud of supposedly subtropical North Africa and in the early campaigns in the Aleutians.[1]

Influence of World War I Surplus Property

Research and developmental activities of any period are conditioned chiefly by economic factors which determine their character and scope. In the years immediately following World War I surplus property was such a determining factor. When World War I ended, the existence of great stocks of nearly all the items of clothing and equipment which were then standard hindered the development of new items. It was approved War Department policy to issue such stocks until they were exhausted. The War Department recognized the danger of complacency resulting from the possession of such a tremendous mass of war gear. It kept in mind, too, the fact that much of this equipment was already obsolescent at the time of its production. Accordingly, in 1922 the War Department inaugurated a policy of modernization.

The policy of the War Department is to develop and complete the best types of equipment and armament in time of peace, irrespective of the amount on hand as a result of the World War. Wherever the amount of a particular article of equipment or armament on hand precludes the possibility of production of a newer type, nevertheless the new type will be adopted, and complete specifications drawn up and approved, to the end that, in the event of an emergency, production could be begun of the latest type. It was found, during the World War, that in some instances necessity forced the quantity production of old types of equipment because improved types had never been developed, and new types of equipment

were produced without an adequate service test. . . . The War Department policy which requires the use of equipment and armament now on hand, until exhausted, should not interfere with the development of new types to be authorized for adoption for future use.[2]

To put this policy into effect the War Department directed the chiefs of branches of the Army to make an annual survey of adopted types of equipment and armament with which their troops were provided in order to determine if such types were up to date and satisfactory for an emergency. On or before 31 December of each year the chiefs of branches were to submit a report of this survey to G–4 (the Supply Division) of the General Staff. Whenever it was found that new or improved types were desirable, steps were to be taken looking toward their development in accordance with instructions which had already been issued.

These instructions of the Secretary of War, issued on 5 January 1922, directed the chiefs of the supply branches to systematize procedures for determining acceptable types of equipment, for conducting research and developmental activities in connection with the standardization of equipment, and for preparing and standardizing specifications.[3] Subsequently these instructions were formalized in Army Regulations [4] first published 15 December 1924 and revised from time to time thereafter as necessitated by the growth and reorganization of the Army. In general, both the instructions and the later reg-

[1] Brig Gen G. F. Doriot, "The Program of the Quartermaster Corps for Future Research," Proceedings of the Conference on Quartermaster Textile Research, 1945, pp. 55–56.

[2] Ltr, TAG to TQMG, 15 Sep 22, sub: Annual Survey of Adopted Types of Equip, AG 400.114 (9–14–22) (Misc) D.

[3] Ltr, TAG to Chiefs of WD Sup Brs, et al., 5 Jan 22, sub: Instructions Relative to Type, Specs, and Standardization of Specs for Articles Used by U. S. Army, AG 400.114 (12–21–21) (Misc Div) CCW/LWW/154.4.

[4] AR 850–25, 15 Dec 24, sub: Misc Types of Equip Used by USA.

ulations provided for determination of policy and general supervision in the development of equipment by the General Staff. The latter was to indicate the types of equipment which it deemed necessary and the general characteristics which they should possess. The several chiefs of the supply branches might also initiate the development of new items or changes in existing ones. The respective supply branches, with the co-operation of the using branches, were to conduct the research and developmental work in connection with those items for the procurement of which they were responsible. Each supply branch was to maintain a technical committee, on which all the supply and combat branches as well as the General Staff were to be represented. The technical committees were to pass upon proposed new or revised designs and to make recommendations for the approval of specifications and the standardization of items. Types were to be submitted to The Adjutant General for approval. Items were to be cleared for procurement through the Assistant Secretary of War to assure that, insofar as possible, they were of such design as to be readily produced in quantity in time of emergency. The General Staff, as the co-ordinating agency, was to be kept advised of the progress of research and developmental work in the various branches and of the lines along which it was being conducted.

Throughout the period between the two wars the annual surveys of equipment and reports of deficiencies based on them were continued. They constituted the principal stimulus to the improvement of designs. The War Department in 1923 called attention to the importance of these surveys and the action which it was hoped would result from them, particularly in connection with mobilization plans.

The established type of each article of equipment and supply must not only be determined in time of peace, but specifications drawn up so that in a great emergency the procurement plans can be carried out without the delay incident to seeking a suitable type. . . . It is necessary and essential for war plans that there be a standard type adopted, and the principal purpose of the annual survey of equipment is to determine this fact and to determine also the deficiencies which exist and the remedy which must be applied at the earliest practicable date.[5]

Those portions of the annual survey reports from the using services which pointed out inadequacies in items of Quartermaster issue were forwarded to The Quartermaster General for action in accordance with the provision of Army Regulations 850-25. Each year The Quartermaster General in turn submitted to the War Department a report indicating the progress which had been made in correcting deficiencies in equipment, either through the improvement of existing designs or the development of new ones.

In the first of these annual survey reports the Infantry, Cavalry, Field Artillery, and other using branches reported seventy items of Quartermaster equipment as being deficient in one or more respects. The number declined somewhat in later years, but a considerable group of items continued to be reported on each year all during the period between the two wars. Many of the complaints, especially in the earlier years, had to do with the quality of clothing and other items purchased during World War I. Because it was approved policy to issue stocks on hand until they were exhausted and large quantities of these items were available, little could be done to meet these deficiencies as far as immediate issue was concerned. Though the statement of policy laid down in 1922 warned against the tendency, it was inevitable that the existence of surpluses should tend to postpone action looking toward improvement. Nevertheless, there was a gradual development of im-

---

[5] Ltr, TAG to TQMG, *et al.*, 15 Jan 23, sub: Survey of Types of Equip and Sup, AG 400.114 (1–6–23) Misc M–D.

proved specifications so that better types would be ready to go into production when their issue became feasible. In 1927, for instance, the OQMG was able to report that, except for two items, "with reference to the Annual Survey of Equipment, it is believed that satisfactory progress is being made on all items reported thereunder by the War Department branches." [6]

Lack of Integrated Research Program

In the interval between World Wars I and II, however, the QMC established no integrated program of research. Except for motor transport planning, the Corps did little to promote a program in which the relationships of items of equipment to each other were developed. Precise objectives to be attained within any given group were not worked out. For the most part, items of clothing and equipment were taken up for improvement individually and only as deficiencies were reported in them. To be sure some efforts were made to co-ordinate Quartermaster research, both within the Corps and with other supply services. Thus, within the OQMG a Standardization Branch [7] was established in the summer of 1921, specifically charged with the responsibility of preparing specifications for approved types and co-ordinating Quartermaster research and developmental work. Never very large or active until 1935, the Standardization Branch in practice acted mainly as a clearinghouse, transmitting correspondence to the commodity branches of the Supply Division, which in turn worked through the manufacturing depots. The several Quartermaster depots, or industries co-operating with them, accomplished whatever research was done during this period. In response to instructions from the Secretary of War, The Quartermaster General established on 24 January 1922 a Quartermaster Corps Technical Committee (QMCTC) as an advisory board on equipment problems. During the process of developing types of equipment

for which the QMC had responsibility, this committee was charged with effecting a complete co-ordination among all interested branches of the Army. [8] Because the executive officer of the committee was also the chief of the Standardization Branch these two units during the next twenty years functioned almost as one in co-ordinating and promoting Quartermaster research and development.

While the early QMCTC served to bring to bear on Quartermaster research and developmental activities the several points of view of the using arms and services, neither the committee nor the Standardization Branch promoted an aggressive, integrated program of research within the QMC. Their mission was to co-ordinate and not to control or direct developmental activities. As a consequence, each of the operating branches of the Supply Division and each of the manufacturing depots was left free to develop its own research and developmental program, in the light of the annual equipment reports from the using arms. The results of these individual programs were made known, however, to the other services by the QMCTC.

Had the committee and the Standardization Branch attempted to guide an integrated research program, their efforts would have been foredoomed to failure in the period of the twenties and the thirties. Manufacturing depots, such as the Philadelphia Quartermaster Depot, would have opposed such a program. Developmental work had for many years been decentralized in the several Quartermaster depots and was for them a traditional prerogative that was jealously insisted upon long after an integrated research program was initiated in 1942.

---

[6] Ltr, TQMG to TAG, 31 Mar 27, sub: Annual Survey of Equip, 400.1141.

[7] OQMG O Memo 119, 30 Aug 21, sub: Orgn of OQMG.

[8] OQMG OO 10, 24 Jan 22, sub: Experimental, Development and Spec Procedure. Since the extant minutes of the committee date from 10 October 1921 it had been in existence before this date.

Furthermore, it was War Department policy to leave research and developmental work to the efforts of industry as much as possible. The financial limitations imposed during this period, particularly in the depression years, further restricted the possibilities of developing an integrated research program.

Financial Restrictions

The lack of adequate funds for research and developmental work was another factor—in many respects the controlling factor—limiting these activities in the years following World War I. In those years the fiscal estimates proposed by The Quartermaster General for research purposes were modest. Even so, the lack of a long-range planned program of Quartermaster research hampered a strong defense of these estimates. As a consequence the estimates were generally sharply reduced by the Budget Advisory Committee of the War Department when representatives of the OQMG appeared at its hearings to defend them. They were further lowered by the Bureau of the Budget. For the most part, the cuts made usually affected funds designed for the development of motor vehicles. In the thirties reductions were also made in the estimates for developmental work in the field of clothing and equipment. The sharpest decline in funds for research purposes took place after the depression began. Such funds, along with all others for the Army, were consistently reduced during the thirties. The trend persisted until the fiscal year 1940 and was completely reversed only in the following fiscal year. This situation was analyzed by the chief of the Fiscal Division in the following terms:

It will be noted that the policy of approving, without substantial cuts, the stated estimates for research and development has been apparent only since the "emergency" has been in full swing. In the six years prior to that time, . . . the situation was quite the opposite, and very little consideration

was given by either the Budget Advisory Committee or the Bureau of the Budget to the requirements as presented to them. During the six-year period, the Budget Advisory Committee, for example, heard estimates which included requirements of $524,650 for research and development and made deletions amounting to $290,250 or 55%. The Bureau of the Budget in their action on the estimates made cuts of 80% of the amounts presented or 36% of the requirements as originally stated. It is interesting to note that Congress made no changes in the estimates and thus appropriated funds for research and development amounting to only 9% of the money originally requested.[9]

Although there were reductions of funds, a comparable curtailment of research and developmental activities did not necessarily follow. Because of lump sum appropriation, it was possible to utilize a portion of the funds allocated for procurement or other Quartermaster operations to complete a given research project.[10] There is no way of calculating the extent to which this practice alleviated the scarcity of funds appropriated for research and developmental activities. Without it, even the modest programs of the period would have been hopelessly crippled.

Despite financial restrictions and the lack of a co-ordinated research program, there was a steady, if slow, modernization of standard equipment for which the QMC was responsible during the twenty-year interval between the wars. Particularly in the thirties much of value was accomplished. A few important new pieces of equipment, such as the gasoline-burning field range, were developed. In the textile field the basic uniform fabrics used throughout World War II were developed before 1941. These included the 18-ounce serge used in making en-

[9] (1) Ltr, Col E. B. McKinley, OQMG, to Lt Col E. S. Hoag, ACofS G-4, 22 Jan 42, sub: R&D Funds. (2) See also Mark S. Watson, *Chief of Staff: Prewar Plans and Preparations,* in the series UNITED STATES ARMY IN WORLD WAR II (Washington, D. C., 1950), pp. 42, 47–49.

[10] Interv, OQMG historian with Clay V. Davis, Chief Clk, Fiscal Div, OQMG, 18 Mar 44.

listed men's uniforms, 32-ounce melton for overcoats, elastique for officers' uniforms, and herringbone twill for work clothes. Although these textiles were modified from time to time during World War II, the basic developmental work had been accomplished prior to the outbreak of the war. Much was also done in the motor transport field, notably in the development of the jeep and other multiple-wheel-drive vehicles.

Influence of Procurement Planning

Aside from developmental work aimed at modernizing Army equipment, the OQMG was engaged in a type of research that evolved from the procurement planning undertaken during the years 1920–40. This had involved the preparation of plans to secure adequate and satisfactory raw materials for Army items in the event of a major crisis. Materials in which shortages might be expected to develop were divided into "strategic" and "critical" categories. Strategic materials were essential wartime commodities which were wholly or in large part obtained from foreign sources. Critical materials were those ordinarily produced at home but which might be difficult to procure in an emergency.

Continuous studies of the procurement of commodities were initiated as early as 1921 by the Office of the Assistant Secretary of War. At first intended to cover the whole field of Army procurement, these studies were soon confined to the strategic and critical groups of materials. In 1924 there were formed "War Department Commodity Committees" for the clearance of plans for the procurement of specified raw materials within these categories. The preparation of these plans was assigned to the several supply services on the basis of major interest in the individual commodity involved. The QMC was

thus to prepare plans for the emergency procurement of coffee, cork, flaxseed, hides, jute, manila fiber, quebracho, rubber, sisal, tin, and wool. This list was later considerably extended. The plans were revised from time to time in the following years under the supervision of the committees, and new items were added for study. Occasionally, because of the development of sufficient domestic production, a commodity was removed from the list. Plans for a given commodity embraced a full description of it, an estimate of wartime military and civilian requirements, its sources, a comparison of requirements and estimated available supply, substitutes, prices, possible conservation, recommendation of emergency control and distribution measures, and other pertinent data. The Navy finally came to participate in the program and joint "Army and Navy Munitions Board Commodity Committees" were formed for the study of materials in which the Navy had a procurement interest. Quartermaster Corps officers, drawn from the procurement planning organization in the OQMG, were active as chairmen or members of a considerable number of these committees, which continued to function into the period of the national emergency.[11]

Corollary to the preparation of plans for the emergency procurement of strategic and critical materials was research in substitutes. The necessity for such a program early became apparent to both the Office of the Assistant Secretary of War and the OQMG. The only alternative was to build huge reserves of strategic materials as Germany and Japan were doing, a course of action that the War Department, in view of the strong pacifist feeling of the time, could not pursue lest it be accused of fostering war.

In 1927 the Assistant Secretary of War requested The Quartermaster General to supple-

---

[11] Thomas M. Pitkin and Herbert R. Rifkind, *Procurement Planning in the Quartermaster Corps, 1920–40* (QMC Historical Studies 1, March 1943), pp. 31–34, 79–84.

ment his estimates for funds with additional data which would establish the value and necessity of such research, thus making defense of the request for funds easier.[12] Unfortunately, this line of action was ineffectual and the lack of funds continued to be a hampering factor. In fact, for each of the five fiscal years 1934 through 1938 — the all-important years preceding the national emergency — The Quartermaster General was forced to report to the Assistant Secretary of War that no funds had been available "for the development of substitutes for strategic and critical raw materials and, as a consequence, no work in this connection was accomplished during the year."[13]

Despite the lack of funds considerable progress was made by the QMC in developing substitute materials. Research was undertaken to develop substitutes for mercury and shellac heretofore used in manufacturing the service hat; for leather, utilized in the production of harness and items of equipage; and for silk, used in Army cravats, hat cords, and waists for Army nurses. The Corps also established close co-operation with industries engaged in developing synthetic rubber, tinless cans, and substitutes to replace shellac used in lacquering food containers. These examples are illustrative of the earnest efforts made by the Corps to develop substitutes for critical raw materials. Even after funds for such research were cut off in 1934 efforts along these lines continued. When the country entered the emergency period, frantic efforts were necessary to recover lost ground.

Once Pearl Harbor was attacked, financial stringency was eliminated as a factor. Estimates of research and developmental funds submitted by the OQMG continued to be reviewed and in some instances were cut by the War Department Budget Advisory Committee or the Bureau of the Budget. Since The Quartermaster General was authorized to transfer funds between fiscal projects, however, developmental work did not suffer.

Impact of Global War

The impact of global war greatly stimulated research and developmental activities. This fact was nowhere more apparent than in the OQMG. Prior to 1940, military planning had been based on a defensive concept which visualized operations as taking place mainly near or within the borders of the continental United States, or in similar climatic areas. As a result, comparatively little attention had been given to the possibility of waging campaigns in steaming jungles, in extensive desert areas, in arctic regions, or in extremely mountainous terrain. Operational planning by the General Staff, which envisioned no movement of large forces to extreme climatic environments, set the tone for equipment planning within the supply services of the Army.

In the interval between the wars the QMC had gradually modernized standard items of clothing and equipment for which it was responsible, but it had developed no program looking toward the preparation of specialized gear for use in areas of climatic extremes. With the rapid expansion of the Army beginning in 1940, the declaration of the unlimited national emergency a year later, and especially with the participation of the United States in the new world conflict, problems of this nature presented themselves for solution in rapid succession. The growing Japanese menace to Alaska called for an increased garrison for that territory, in much of which arctic conditions prevailed. The occupation of bases in the North Atlantic which followed soon after brought additional pressure for the design and procurement of suit-

---

[12] (1) Memo, OASW for Chiefs of Sup Brs, 23 Dec 27, sub: Research in Raw Materials Substitutes. (2) Memo, Col M. R. Hilgard, OQMG, for ASW, 15 Feb 28, same sub. Both in 400.12.

[13] Ltr, Maj M. V. Brunson, OQMG, to ASW, 26 Aug 38, sub: Development of Substitutes for Strategic and Critical Raw Materials, 400.12.

able clothing and equipment for arctic operations. The rapid and spectacular development of the technique of mechanized desert warfare in North Africa, or winter and mountain operations in northern Europe, and of airborne tactics on the continent and in Crete forced the creation of new types of military organizations and, concurrently, of new equipment. The swift Japanese conquests in the Southwest Pacific, involving operations in supposedly impassable jungles and with the use of improved amphibious tactics, called imperatively for the rapid development of countertechniques and new types of clothing and equipment. The impact of the war also brought marked changes in the field of subsistence. These developments will be discussed at length in succeeding chapters.

Effect of Materials Shortages on Design

The war also increased the need for conservation, probably the most important single factor in shaping wartime Quartermaster research and developmental work. Enemy conquests of producing areas led to shortages of many raw materials, forcing the use of substitutes. Wartime limitations in trade and the enormous increase in domestic consumption due to the defense program itself had the same effect. In many instances the use of substitute materials involved a more or less complete redesign of the item. At the same time, industrial advance in the field of plastics, in textile fabrication, and elsewhere permitted many shifts from traditional to new materials.

Some of these changes were difficult to make, and in many cases the QMC was forced to resort to inferior products, sometimes unnecessarily. The Corps regarded most of these changes as temporary expedients. However, occasionally a new material proved so satisfactory that the Corps contemplated no return to the original when it should become available.

In a number of instances, a succession of shortages forced the substitution of one material for another which was itself a substitution for something else. This situation could have been alleviated to some extent if, at the time the priority system was established, a higher relative importance had been accorded to Quartermaster items involved in the over-all supply program. This would have saved considerable time, effort, and expense.

Although some progress had been made in the development of substitute materials in the interval between the wars, the lack of funds for that purpose had handicapped such research. With the outbreak of war in 1939 and especially with the sharpening of the crisis in the following year, problems of materials shortages, actual or potential, began to make their appearance on the national horizon. From all indications these shortages would become more acute as the procurement program expanded.

The problem of the assignment of strategic and critical materials to manufacturers and defense agencies became the subject of a series of administrative measures. The Army and Navy Munitions Board (ANMB) on 17 June 1940 set up a Priorities Committee to assign priorities, as between the two services, in the materials which were becoming critical. The President some months later appointed an "Administrator of Priorities," and in January 1941 established the Office of Production Management (OPM) to direct the whole complex of defense production.[14] All matters of priorities, preference ratings, conservation studies, and the like were under its jurisdiction until it, in turn, was succeeded by the War Production Board a year later. The policies of these agencies, insofar as they affected the QMC and the other supply services of the Army, were effectuated through the Office of the Under Secretary of War until

---

[14] (1) EO, 21 Oct 40, *Federal Register*, V, 4199. (2) EO, 7 Jan 41, *Federal Register*, VI, 191–92.

the reorganization of the Army in March 1942. After that time Headquarters, SOS (later ASF), was the point of mutual contact.

By early 1941 the procurement program of the QMC had begun to be affected by scarcities in such metals as aluminum, copper, nickel, brass, and stainless steel. The shortage of basic and semifinished materials and the low priority status accorded Quartermaster equipment necessitated a comprehensive conservation program. In this the OQMG sought to substitute less critical or noncritical materials wherever possible, thereby insuring successful procurement and at the same time making critical materials available for indispensable purposes. This policy was initiated in the OQMG on 24 February 1941. Expecting the shortages to become more and more drastic as the procurement program went on, the OQMG recommended to the Under Secretary of War the following week that steps be initiated "to co-ordinate all engineering and designing branches with the procurement branches for the purpose of establishing the flexibility required to meet the necessities of substitutions of metals as such necessities arise." [15]

Conservation measures affecting the design of equipment had thus already been projected by the Corps when the Office of the Under Secretary of War took up the problem of conservation of materials by the Army through a series of directives to the supply services. These memoranda, issued at intervals during the spring, called attention to the need for the conservation of various metals. On 11 June 1941 the Under Secretary of War stressed the need for strict enforcement of a comprehensive conservation policy. He directed the supply services to conduct "a continuous study" of all specifications in order to reduce or eliminate requirements for strategic or critical materials which had been placed under allocation or priority control unless such action seriously impaired military efficiency of the equipment.[16] On the

first of each month, each supply service was to report to the Office of the Under Secretary the progress it had made in such revision of specifications.

The Quartermaster General immediately turned to the task of announcing the policy to the Corps [17] and setting up the necessary organization. A policy was outlined with reference to materials on the "Priorities Critical List." These were to be specified only when no substitution could be made without seriously impairing military efficiency. None of the materials listed as critical were to be used "except on such items or projects for which there is no known substitute that will not result in the loss of essential efficiency." Suitable substitutes should not be construed as meaning "equal" or "equivalent," but should be interpreted as meaning "those that will serve the same essential purpose even though they may be less durable and involve some increased initial or ultimate cost." This policy was to be applied immediately to new materials subsequently placed under mandatory control by the OPM.

Some months later more detailed instructions to the Corps emphasized that "conservation should not be considered of secondary importance but should be made the first order of business of all personnel concerned with specifications and procurement." In considering the suitability of substitutes, the military characteristics and efficiency of the items were of fundamental importance but the procurability, durability, and cost of substitutes were also to be duly weighed. When an item possessed definite military characteristics, that is, when it had

---

[15] (1) Memo, Lt Col Hugh B. Hester, OQMG, for USW, 3 Mar 41, sub: Substitutions. (2) Same to chiefs of all branches, OQMG, 24 Feb 41, sub: Substitution in Specs.

[16] Memo, Robert P. Patterson for TQMG, 11 Jun 41, sub: Conserv of Certain Basic and Semifinished Materials.

[17] OQMG Cir Ltr 113, 16 Jun 41, sub: Conserv of Critical Materials.

certain essential qualities which it must possess in order to fulfill a definite military purpose, the effect on these characteristics of the use of a substitute was to be carefully considered. When no definite military characteristics were in-involved, the essential efficiency of the item was to be given first consideration. The com-mercial procurability of a substitute within a reasonable time was to be weighed against the time involved in obtaining the material orig-inally specified with applicable preference ratings. Durability of a substitute was to receive due consideration, and items which could be readily repaired or replaced might be designed of materials having a shorter probable life than the original. Increase in original and mainte-nance cost was to be weighed against durability, efficiency, and procurability, but in general, where the other prerequisites were met, "cost should not be the determining factor in deciding whether or not the substitution should be made." [18]

The administrative details of the conservation program were handled initially by a Conserva-tion Steering Committee, established in July by The Quartermaster General in the Planning and Control Division. It effected co-ordination and general supervision of the conservation work of the Corps.[19] Responsibility for changes in specifications, however, remained with the division chiefs. The committee also consoli-dated and reviewed the monthly reports pre-pared by the various divisions for the conserva-tion report to the Under Secretary of War as required by his instructions on 11 June. A requirements section prepared studies on raw materials requirements for Quartermaster items. Subsequently, in a reorganization at the end of 1941, the functions of preparing estimates of raw materials requirements and of carrying out the conservation policy were grouped together in a Production Branch of the Planning and Control Division. [20] When the major reorgan-izations of the OQMG occurred in 1942, these

functions, administered by a Materials and Conservation Section, ultimately were lodged in the Research and Development Branch of the Military Planning Division.

Under the policy set forth, Quartermaster specifications were subjected to close study with a view to conserving scarce materials. Every effort was made to find suitable substitutes that could be used either wholly or in part and that possessed the same performance abilities and military characteristics as those then in use. The basic work was accomplished at Quartermaster depots, laboratories, and shops. Exceptions to OPM and later WPB conservation orders were requested only after continued research and experimentation failed to produce satisfactory substitute materials. An analysis of the specific critical materials affecting the Quartermaster procurement program reveals the scope of the Quartermaster conservation program and its impact on the design and development of items for which the Corps had responsibility.

Under the strain of the defense program, shortages in a number of metals, such as alumi-num, copper, zinc, nickel, tin, and stainless steel, were first to appear. Aluminum, which had been produced in this country by only a single firm and largely from imported bauxite, quickly came to present a very acute problem because of the extensive use of this metal in the manufacture of airplanes. The initial effort of the QMC in conserving aluminum was made in the field of garrison equipment, the purchase of which was forbidden if it required the use of aluminum.[21] But a number of Quartermaster field items also made extensive use of this metal. The necessity of maintaining satisfactory

---

[18] OQMG Cir Ltr 255, 30 Sep 41, sub: Conserv Instructions.

[19] OQMG OO 168, 24 Jul 41, no sub.

[20] OQMG OO 25–A, 31 Dec 41, no sub.

[21] (1) OQMG Cir Ltr 71, 22 Apr 41, sub: Substi-tutes for Aluminum. (2) OQMG Cir Ltr 104, 7 Jun 41, sub: Conserv of Aluminum.

military characteristics for field items precluded such blanket prohibition of the use of aluminum as could safely be applied to garrison equipment. Nevertheless, specifications for mess gear and other field items utilizing aluminum were revised to incorporate satisfactory substitute materials.

The Army field mess gear, consisting of meat can, canteen cup, canteen, knife, fork, and spoon, had for many years been made largely of aluminum. Mess gear made of this metal was easy to clean, would stand fire, did not easily corrode, and was extremely light. It had served the Army well through one war and there was great reluctance on the part of the QMC and the using arms to undertake the use of substitutes. It was easy to design a plastic handle to the knife, which effected some saving of aluminum. Redesign of the meat can, canteen cup, and canteen was another matter. Under pressure of a dwindling supply of aluminum, however, experimentation continued, and in 1943 large orders of stainless steel meat cans and canteen cups were procured. These items, though much more costly than the aluminum types, proved satisfactory and were finally standardized. Satisfactory canteens of both plastic and stainless steel were eventually produced and received classification as substitute standard items.[22]

Among other field items of Quartermaster issue making extensive use of aluminum, the most important was the field range, M–1937. Until well into the war period the QMC was harassed by serious delinquency in the delivery of spare parts and accessories for this item. Delinquencies were due in varying degrees to delays in receipt of raw materials and equipment by the manufacturer and to engineering changes made necessary by the elimination of critical materials, as well as to a lack of production capacity in the case of some contractors. To help break the bottleneck created by the materials situation the QMC resorted both to higher priority ratings and to revision of specifications.

In their efforts to eliminate strategic materials, engineers at the Jeffersonville Depot, the procuring depot for most Quartermaster mechanical equipment, soon produced a revised design for the field range. Blued steel sheets and galvanized steel replaced aluminum and stainless steel, leaving a small amount of copper, essential for the fuel lines, as the only critical metal in this important mobile cooking unit. In use this new design, which was later somewhat modified, proved entirely satisfactory as far as its basic materials were concerned. The weight was only moderately increased and the efficiency perhaps somewhat improved.[23]

Shortages of certain types of steel and of the alloy metals for making them began to be felt before the defense program had gone far. The whole group of ferro-alloy metals, such as nickel, chromium, manganese, tungsten, and the like, were on the list of materials specified as critical in June 1941.[24] Most of the world's nickel came from Canada and ample supplies of it were available in the United States until it began to be used in fantastic quantities for the tough nickel steel needed in armor plate and projectiles. Expansion of production was a slow process, involving the construction of new mills and smelters as well as the mining of more ore. Chromium, the master alloy metal in stainless steels, had a variety of other industrial uses. It was produced mainly in South Africa, Turkey, and the distant Pacific islands. The acute shipping situation contributed to the shortage of this important material. Tungsten, essential in

---

[22] (1) R&D Br to Procurement Div, OQMG, 19 Apr 43, sub: Type 430 Stainless Steel for Meat Cans and Canteen Cups. (2) R&D Br, Status Rpt, 30 Apr–31 Oct 43. (3) *Ibid.*, 31 Jul 42–31 Dec 43.

[23] (1) Ltr, Lt Col O. E. Cound, OQMG, to OUSW, 17 Jan 42, sub: Conservation. (2) Interv, OQMG historian with Eugene D. Halleck, Mechanical Sec, R&D Br, OQMG, 9 Jun 44.

[24] OQMG Cir Ltr 113, 16 Jun 41, sub: Conserv of Critical Materials.

the manufacture of tool steel, had been produced chiefly in China. Though deposits in the United States and in South America were being opened up, the growing difficulty of communication with China and the vast increase in tool making incidental to the defense program produced a temporary scarcity. Manganese, a desulphurizing and deoxidizing agent in the basic steel making process as well as an important alloy metal, was largely imported from abroad. A large stockpile of it had been built up in the United States, however, and it was considered somewhat less critical than some of the other alloy metals.[25]

A large part of the alloy steel used by the QMC in 1941 went into automotive equipment, which was then still a Quartermaster responsibility. Specification changes in the motor transport program, however, had to be viewed with caution. The elimination of some critical materials would have had unfortunate effects upon the ruggedness and performance of the vehicles involved. Substitutions also would have required complete redesigning and retooling of particular parts and of the vehicle as a whole, which would have consumed considerable time and resulted in complete production stoppage. In addition, substitutions in certain types of automotive parts would have required fuel and lubricants differing appreciably from those in use for military vehicles. Despite these handicaps the Corps liberalized specifications and substituted less essential materials for aluminum, alloy steel, rubber, and other critical materials as rapidly as suitable substitutes could be found to provide the performance considered essential for military vehicles.[26]

As shortages of ferro-alloy metals became more acute, specifications of Quartermaster items were repeatedly reviewed to conserve these critical materials. Some thirty-eight minor items, chiefly accessories in harnessware, were found in which substitutes of less critical materials could be made for nickel. At the same time

a procurement of 6,600,000 stainless steel identification tags—an item previously manufactured of monel metal which contains 60 percent nickel—was made, thus conserving approximately 50,000 pounds of nickel.[27]

Chromium was conserved largely through the substitution of other materials for stainless steel. Much of the tableware and many miscellaneous kitchen utensils of the Army had been made of stainless steel. These were now, for the most part, redesigned in tinned or enameled steel. Large quantities of corrosion-resisting steel were freed by the use of galvanized iron in laundry equipment Stainless steel was also replaced by cast iron in all mixers for bakers. In the shipbuilding program, still under Quartermaster direction in 1941, stainless steel was therefore used in the construction of vessels and equipment only where excess corrosion resulted if mild steel or other ferrous materials were employed.[28]

The sheer bulk of the requirements of the defense program and of the expanding civilian economy accompanying it, which was imposed on an industrial system that had been static for many years, soon brought about shortages in most types of steel. Pig iron and steel were placed under priority control by the OPM at the end of the summer of 1941. The QMC was instructed to make "every effort to conserve the use of iron and steel products where they are now specified and substitute wood and other

---

[25] (1) "The Crisis in Materials," *Fortune*, August 1941, p. 69. (2) Memo, Dir of Info, OEM, for editors of newspapers, Oct 41, sub: Materials for Defense.

[26] Memo, Gen Gregory, TQMG, for USW, 18 Jul 41, sub: Rpt of Conserv of Strategic and Critical Materials.

[27] (1) Standardization Br to Plng & Control Div, QQMG, 14 Mar 42, sub: Conserv of Nickel. (2) Production Br to Asst Chief of Plng & Control Div, OQMG, 19 Feb 42, sub: Nickel. (3) Standardization Br to Production Br, OQMG, 13 Mar 42, sub: Nickel. All in 410.2.

[28] Memo, TQMG for USW, 2 Jul 41, sub: Conserv of Stainless Steel, 410.2.

materials wherever possible." [29] Accordingly on numerous construction projects, which at this time were still a Quartermaster responsibility, efforts were made to conserve steel through structural designs involving greater use of wood and concrete. Wood sheathing replaced corrugated steel for siding and roofing. Construction quartermasters stopped using galvanized fencing, specifying wood in place of steel for fence posts.

A survey had revealed that the QMC purchased approximately 150 items requiring large amounts of steel. Excluding the large quantities that went into the automotive program, construction, and shipbuilding, a few important items, including field ranges, tent stoves, cots, and lockers, utilized the remainder of the Corps' steel requirements. It was a simple matter to substitute wood for steel in the procurement of office furniture and filing equipment. Little could be done, however, about eliminating steel entirely from such items as field ranges and stoves, although redesign of the range practically eliminated the more critical types of the metal. On the other hand, wood replaced steel in the standard Army cot and the folding chair while the locker box and field safe were redesigned so as to save much of the weight of steel and to effect other improvements. [30]

A considerable amount of copper, in the form of brass and bronze, has traditionally been used in the clothing and personal equipment of the soldier. Brass is considered good for ornamental purposes because it takes on a high polish and resembles gold. Copper alloys are also favored for utilitarian uses, since they are hard and strong while at the same time much more resistant to corrosion than iron or steel. Buttons for the uniform coat as well as distinctive military insignia have for generations been made of brass. Brass or bronze has been used extensively in the form of buckles and, since the introduction of webbing, in eyelets, snaps, rings, and end clips on personal gear such as cartridge belts and packs. Eyelets for shoes and canvas leggings also make use of one or another copper alloy. In organizational equipment of Quartermaster types, copper alloys are used for tent grommets, musical instruments, kitchen utensils, and incidentally in caparison equipage and various mechanical items. Although QMC consumption of copper in all forms was relatively slight when compared with the use of this metal by the Ordnance Department in such items as small arms ammunition and shell casings, its conservation was considered important in view of the scarcity of copper which developed with the defense program.

While the national copper supply had seemed ample only a short time before, direct military uses in the rearmament program beginning in 1940, with the infinitely varied uses of the metal in the expanding industrial economy, soon produced a shortage. A record production in the United States of 842,000 tons in 1937 had seemed sufficient for any possible need, but in 1941, even with the importation of 500,000 tons from South America, there was an acute shortage. Requirements for 1942 were at that time estimated at 2,500,000 tons. [31]

As the supply of copper became inadequate to meet vital military needs, requests for allocation for personal hardware—buckles, clips, grommets, and the like—were disapproved regardless of how essential they appeared to the QMC. This caused a serious delay in the procurement program. Whereas manufacturers had been working three shifts to supply the Corps, many were forced to cut down to one-shift operation and some shut down completely for

[29] OQMG Cir Ltr 221, 2 Sep 41, sub: Conserv of Iron and Steel Products.

[30] (1) OQMG Ltr 399, 22 Dec 41, sub: Purch of Steel Furniture and Office Equip. (2) Resources Div, OQMG, Rpt of Development Projects in Progress, 1 Jun 42. (3) R&D Br, Status Rpt, 31 Aug 42–31 Dec 43.

[31] "The Crisis in Materials," *Fortune*, August 1941, p. 68.

lack of materials. In addition, the shortage of skilled molders made it difficult to obtain adequate supplies of molded types of hardware and created a major chokepoint in the production of several types of buckles and clips.

Production engineers and expediters from the OQMG conferred with the Jeffersonville Quartermaster Depot and leading suppliers of hardware components. As a result of their study they recommended a comprehensive survey of the entire line of Quartermaster hardware with a view to standardizing designs and material specifications, eliminating unnecessary types and sizes, and substituting stamped for molded hardware wherever practicable. These recommendations were adopted.

At the same time the QMC endeavored to substitute for copper wherever possible. Among the substitutes considered for small hardware items of bronze and brass, such as grommets, buckles, clips, loops, and hinges, were enamel-coated iron or steel, and zinc.[32] Zinc sheet was used to replace brass in tent grommets, conserving an estimated 2,000,000 pounds of brass during a period of six to eight months, and a number of other effective substitutions were soon made in the small hardware field, largely eliminating brass from Quartermaster items of equipage.[33]

A more difficult problem was posed in the replacement of the metal used in the attachments and findings of the soldier's personal equipment. The QMC finally issued an appeal to industry to offer suggestions.[34] Zinc substitutes, tried out for the eyelets in such heavy webbing items as cartridge and pistol belts, proved too soft for use. However, plastic eyelets which met with approval after tests by the Quartermaster Board were finally developed.[35] They were not used because in the manufacturing process they were found difficult to apply. Snap fasteners, used for the pockets of cartridge belts and in a number of other items, presented a peculiar problem. They called for hard metal while their

use involved friction which would scrape off any coating applied to an iron or steel substitute, exposing it to rust. The director of the Military Planning Division was convinced that brass was essential for snap fasteners, but nevertheless under pressure the QMC allowed the use of steel snap fasteners on a few items.[36] Plastic substitutes were used in making end clips, which bound the tips of webbing belts and straps. Olive drab plastic buttons replaced the bronze buttons heretofore used to brighten the uniform.[37] Plastic proved to be one of the most effective substitutes for brass in many Quartermaster items.

Tin was used in great quantity by the QMC in the form of tin plate in cans for food packaging. In 1940, after the beginning of the limited national emergency, the Corps, in collaboration

[32] (1) Ltr, Col F. H. Pope, OQMG, to Hon. Henry Cabot Lodge, Jr., 18 Dec 41, no sub. (2) OQMG Cir Ltr 39, 19 Jan 42, sub: Conservation—Use of Zinc-Base Die Castings as Substitutes for Brass in Small Hardware Items.

[33] (1) OQMG Weekly Progress Rpt, 29 Jun 42. (2) Memo, TQMG for USW, 18 Jul 41, sub: Rpt of Conserv of Strategic and Critical Materials. (3) While coated iron and steel substitutes for brass were reasonably satisfactory in most items of equipment under normal climatic conditions, they proved entirely unsuitable for jungle use. As a result the depots were instructed that, with minor exceptions, brass should be used in the specifications for all hardware for jungle items. Ltr, Maj S. J. Kennedy, OQMG, to CO PQMD and CG JQMD, 2 Sep 42, sub: Jungle Equip.

[34] Ltr, R. R. Walton, OQMG, to Dr. M. G. Millikin, Hercules Powder Co., et al., 20 Aug 42, no sub, 095.

[35] Materials & Conserv Sec to Plastics Sec, OQMG, 25 Aug 42, sub: Plastic Eyelets on Belts.

[36] (1) Memo, Col Doriot, OQMG, for Dir of Production Div, SOS, 29 Sep 42, sub: Conserv of Brass in Snap Fasteners, 410.2. (2) Dir of Mil Plng Div to Insp Div, OQMG, 13 Oct 42, no sub. (3) Henry Rau, Jr., OQMG, to Chief of Conserv Sec, Copper Br, WPB, 18 Apr 43, sub: Construction of Snap Fasteners, 400.112.

[37] (1) R&D Br to TQMG, 24 Aug 42, sub: Plastic Buttons for Wool Serge Coat. (2) Plastics Sec to Dir of Procurement Div, OQMG, 26 Nov 42, sub: Plastic Uniform Buttons. (3) R&D Br to S&D Div, OQMG, 26 Dec 42, sub: Plastic Cap Buttons.

with the National Canners' Association and the several large can manufacturers of the country, began a series of tests of tin plate of lighter grade than that normally used for food packaging. These tests established the feasibility of reducing the tin content in food cans. After the United States entered the war the tests became the basis of a WPB order directing that no tin plate should be manufactured heavier than the light grade which had been established as satisfactory. As Japanese conquests extended through the tin-producing regions of southeast Asia, effectively cutting off the bulk of the normal supply of the metal, the QMC also directed its attention actively toward the development of substitute food-packaging materials, such as black plate, glass, and fiber containers.[38]

In addition, the procurement divisions of the OQMG were directed to survey the items for which they were responsible and report those making use of tin and tin-bearing materials, with a view to effecting substitutions wherever possible.[39] Conservation of aluminum and stainless steel in kitchenware had turned attention to the possibilities of enamel steel as a substitute. Efforts were now made to redesign, in enamel steel, cooking equipment and various containers which had been manufactured of tin-coated steel, sometimes as a substitute for aluminum.

Although zinc was a metal which had never been on the critical list, as early as February 1941 the Office of the Under Secretary of War informed the supply services that steps would have to be taken to reduce the quantities of zinc being specified in order to guard against an acute shortage. Zinc, as a component of brass, entered into the construction of a great many Quartermaster items. It was also used as a galvanizing agent in such items as buckets and G. I. cans, and as part of a compound in the manufacture of rubber goods. A few pieces of equipment used the metal in the pure state.[40]

One of the basic measures taken toward zinc conservation consisted of eliminating the "hot-dip" galvanizing process in the manufacture of items calling for a zinc coating. Instead, the less wasteful electroplating or sherardizing processes were to be used for applying zinc coatings to steel.[41] Galvanizing was eliminated entirely in many metal construction items, painting being ordinarily substituted.

Late in 1943 the increased production of zinc, together with the reduction of the small arms ammunition program, brought about a definite surplus of the metal. The supply services were then encouraged to make all possible use of zinc inasmuch as the War Department desired to keep marginal mines in operation so that their production would be available for brass in the event that the ammunition program should be expanded again.[42]

In general, by the end of 1943 scarcities in most metals had disappeared. Aluminum had become so plentiful that the supply services were encouraged to find new uses for certain types of the metal. Brass and bronze once more became available for design purposes. By that time, too, the situation in regard to chromium and stainless steel had eased so much that these metals were available for a number of important Quartermaster uses, such as identification tags, canteens, mess trays, and certain parts of the field range. Most grades and alloys of steel had become available in ample quantity and were reintroduced into various pieces of equip-

---

[38] The efforts of the subsistence and packaging staff of the OQMG and the Subsistence Laboratory at the Chicago Depot to devise effective substitutes for tin in the packaging of food are described in detail in Harold W. Thatcher, *The Packaging and Packing of Subsistence for the Army* (QMC Historical Studies 10, April 1945), pp. 27–41.

[39] Plng & Control Div to MT and Sup Divs, OQMG, 18 Mar 42, sub: Conserv of Tin.

[40] Chief of Standardization Br to Chief of Sup Div, OQMG, 2 May 41, sub: Conserv of Zinc.

[41] OQMG Cir Ltr 136, 7 Jul 41, sub: Elimination of Hot-Dip Galvanizing Process.

[42] Henry Rau, Jr., Chief of Material Sec, to Col Doriot, OQMG, 18 Nov 43, sub: Meeting on Availability of Copper and Zinc.

ment from which they had been eliminated during the period of scarcity.[43] The story of metal conservation was one of famine followed by feast.

Of all the nonmetallic raw materials in which shortages developed during the war, rubber was by far the most vital. Rubber had come to occupy a unique place in the national economy, its applications constantly broadening as the knowledge of its chemistry developed. It was always an exotic, a product of the tropics. Native to Brazil though it was, its cultivation had been developed in British Malaya and the Dutch East Indies until more than 90 percent of our imports came from these regions and nearby areas which were equally in danger of conquest by Japan, in case of war involving Japan with the white colonial powers in the Pacific.

In the period of procurement planning, the wartime supply of rubber had been the subject of a progressive commodity study by the QMC. When there was an obvious abundance of rubber and when the legend of "invincible Singapore" was still part of the accepted popular mythology, little was done to insure an adequate emergency supply. By 1940, however, the government was taking belated steps to stockpile rubber. Not until some time after Pearl Harbor, however, did rubber figure largely in the Army conservation program. Prior to that time Donald M. Nelson, then Director of Purchases, OPM, had suggested the retreading of automobile tires as a conservation measure.[44] By August 1941 rubber was listed among the materials considered most critical and The Quartermaster General had instructed the Corps to eliminate and reduce its use as much as possible.

It was the middle of January 1942, when Japanese conquest of the whole of southeastern Asia was imminent, that the Under Secretary issued his first special directive to The Quartermaster General and to the other supply chiefs on the subject of rubber conservation. "The

matter of a supply of crude rubber has reached a critical stage. Notwithstanding the drastic curtailment of civilian uses of rubber, it is evident that the armed services must also materially conserve and curtail the use of rubber by all practicable means." [45]

Rubber needed for automotive equipment, including tires, tubes, and mechanical parts, consumed 73 percent of Quartermaster rubber requirements. The rest was used in the manufacture of service shoes, overshoes, raincoats, rubber boots, and a variety of other items.[46] In the active rubber conservation program which now took place, the greatest emphasis was naturally placed on automotive items, which remained a Quartermaster responsibility for several months longer. Numerous items of clothing and equipage, however, were also affected by the program. Specifications were revised to cut down sharply the weight of rubber in the raincoat, to reduce the rubber content in rubber boots and overshoes, and to substitute plastic for rubber in all combs. The purchase of all types of rubber matting had been stopped and all outstanding contracts were canceled. At the same time The Quartermaster General set forth the policy henceforth to be observed by the Corps in conserving rubber. All specifications were to be reviewed either to reduce the quantity of rubber prescribed or to substitute synthetic or reclaimed rubber where this could be done without impairing military characteristics of the items involved.[47]

[43] (1) ASF Cir 3, Sec. IX, 3 Jan 44, sub: Conservation. (2) Memo, Chief of Minerals Sec for Chief of Steel Sec, Materials Br, Production Div, ASF, 27 Oct 43, sub: Stainless Steel for Army Flat Ware.
[44] Ltr, Donald M. Nelson to Robert P. Patterson, USW, 28 Jul 41, sub: Tire Retreading.
[45] Memo, Robert P. Patterson, USW, for TQMG, 12 Jan 42, no sub, 423.
[46] A. Daignault to Col Guy I. Rowe, OQMG, 25 Nov 41, sub: Rubber Rqmts of QMC, 423.
[47] (1) Memo, TQMG for USW, 20 Jan 42, sub: Rubber Conserv, 423. (2) OQMG Cir Ltr 32, Supplement 2, 23 Jan 42, sub: Conserv of Rubber. (3) OQMG Cir Ltr 70, 17 Feb 42, same sub.

As the Japanese conquests continued and it became apparent that very little new crude rubber would be available for years to come, the pressure on the supply services to reduce their consumption of this material increased. The elimination of all rubber from supply procurements soon came to be the objective of the QMC. This ideal was never attained, though surprising progress was made toward it. A review of rubber conservation projects prepared by the OQMG in August 1942 indicated that thirty-seven different items and groups of related items containing rubber had been under study with a view to eliminating this material. Great progress had been made in reducing the rubber content in the service shoe. All crude rubber had been eliminated from the heel, and the use of reclaimed rubber had been minimized by the adoption of a heel with a wood core. Crude rubber had been completely replaced by reclaimed rubber in shoe taps. The rubber content of the overshoe had been successively reduced by lowering the compound specifications and by the adoption of a cloth instead of a rubber top. The rubber content of hip and knee boots had been considerably reduced by changes in the specifications for the compounds involved. Oil-treated fabrics and synthetic resins were specified in the raincoat, completely eliminating rubber. The former were quickly found to be unsatisfactory, particularly in extreme climatic conditions. The synthetic resin coats, on the other hand, were developed to the point where they were equal or even superior to those using natural rubber. Waxes and other finishing materials had been found suitable to replace the chlorinated rubber formerly used in the water-repellent and fire-resistant treatment of tentage duck. Completed or under way were projects for the elimination or reduction of the rubber content in such miscellaneous items as firemen's coats, wire cutters, shoepacs, ski boots, latex-dipped gloves, gaskets for food and water containers, canvas field bags, and the elastic webbing in the suspension of the helmet liner.[48]

In the summer of 1942 a new series of items, constituting the specialized clothing and personal equipment for jungle operations, became a QMC responsibility. Jungle equipment was soon in production on a large scale, in preparation for major American offensive operations in the Southwest Pacific. Some of the items involved the extensive use of rubber and in the urgent need for this equipment first procurements had been made without question of the amount of rubber involved. Specifications for jungle items, such as the jungle boot, essentially a high-top sneaker made with a full rubber sole and heel, and the jungle food bag, used for carrying dried foods, were soon revised, however, to conserve rubber.[49]

In the course of the conservation program, every item of Quartermaster issue involving the use of rubber was carefully scrutinized. In most cases, satisfactory substitutes from the plastic field or elsewhere were eventually found for rubber items, or the crude rubber content was at least materially reduced through the use of reclaimed or synthetic material. The urgency of rubber conservation continued for a long time. Since changes in the design of Quartermaster equipment containing rubber had been pushed as far and as rapidly as possible in the direction of conservation, there remained for the time being only tightened control measures covering the use of rubber items and the suggested delay of procurement as means for further reducing rubber consumption. As the production of synthetic rubber began to take on significant proportions, however, the supply services were

---

[48] Ltr, Col Doriot, OQMG, to S. P. Thacher, Chief of Rubber Sec, ANMB, 10 Aug 42, sub: Rpt on Rubber Conserv.

[49] Ltr, Doriot to Thacher, 8 Oct 42, sub: Rpt on Rubber Conserv. (2) For a summary of the development and hurried first procurement of the jungle equipment see Thomas M. Pitkin, *Quartermaster Equipment for Special Forces* (QMC Historical Studies 5, February 1944), pp. 198–207.

urged to emphasize conversion of remaining rubber items from the natural to the synthetic product.[50] Rubber conservation measures in the QMC from the fall of 1943 on, insofar as they involved the design of equipment, centered in the application of one or another of the synthetics, as these became available, to uses formerly calling for crude rubber.

Cordage fibers, such as hemp, sisal, and jute, constituted a group of largely imported raw materials extensively used by the Corps. Jute, a product of India, was used chiefly for burlap bagging. Noting the increased shipping rates on burlap from India, the hazardous nature of such shipping, and the heavy stocks of cotton accumulated within the United States because of the loss of export markets, The Quartermaster General in 1941 directed that cotton cloth and cotton bagging be procured in the place of jute burlap whenever possible.[51]

Shortly afterward all stocks of first-class Manila fiber, produced in the Philippines and generally used for the better grades of rope, were ordered "frozen" by the OPM. Since this Manila fiber was essential to the expanding Navy, the QMC was requested to review its cordage specifications with a view to utilizing sisal and cotton rope or Grade C Manila, as far as possible, to meet its requirements. Tentage rope was the most important single classification of Quartermaster cordage. Sisal replaced the use of Manila fiber. The best sisal is obtained from Java and East Africa; somewhat lower grades are grown in Mexico. With the supply of the best grades soon cut off or reduced by the progress of the war, Quartermaster specifications made use of the less desirable Mexican variety. Also, a considerable amount of cotton rope had already been procured for a number of uses. Cotton rope has a tensile strength about half that of Manila of the same diameter. It has a high rate of water absorption and lacks resistance to mildew. The material was cheap and abundant, however, and further develop-

ment of cotton rope, with a view to its more extended use, as well as experiments with rope made of jute, of which a considerable quantity was now found available, were carried on by the Jeffersonville Quartermaster Depot and the Bureau of Standards. Ropes of jute and of both braided and twisted cotton, satisfactory for most purposes, were developed and specifications drafted.[52]

Among the items needed for the new mountain troops was a climbing rope. Such rope had to have a great tensile strength and unusual resistance to sudden shock. Climbing ropes had traditionally been made of first-class Manila. While it was believed by mountaineers that no other material would serve, under the pressure of critical shortage lower grade Manila was used. At the same time reports of experiments by manufacturers with nylon rope were followed up and actively encouraged by the OQMG. Ultimately mountain climbing rope made of nylon, actually superior to the best Manila, was produced. However, nylon itself was a critical material, and there was some difficulty at first in getting it allocated for this purpose. Limited quantities were finally made available to meet the most urgent needs for climbing rope.[53]

Developmental work in the textile and clothing program was conditioned by the need for the conservation of various fabrics. Wool was used by the QMC in great quantity for winter clothing and blankets. It had been a scarce commodity during World War I. As a consequence, during the period of procurement planning, the OQMG had studied the means of assuring a

[50] ASF Cir 70, Sec. II, 3 Sep 43, sub: Conversion from Crude to Synthetic Rubber.
[51] (1) OQMG Cir Ltr 82, 1 May 41, sub: Use of Substitutes for Jute Burlap. (2) *Ibid.*, 130, 3 Jul 41, same sub.
[52] (1) Ltr, Col Doriot, OQMG, to CG JQMD, 24 Sep 42, sub: Sisal Rope. (2) R&D Br, Status Rpt, 31 Oct 42–31 Oct 43.
[53] (1) R&D Br to S&D Div, OQMG, 23 Mar 43, sub: Climbing Ropes. (2) Pitkin, *Quartermaster Equipment for Special Forces*, pp. 97–98.

supply of it in another emergency as well as the possibilities of effecting substitutions for it. For the most part, domestic production was sufficient for ordinary needs during the early part of World War II. The prospect of a considerable mobilization of manpower, however, foreshadowed an eventual shortage and caused the OQMG in the spring of 1940 to urge that measures be taken toward building up a stockpile of Australian wool.[54] This action eventually resulted in the accumulation of a supply sufficient to meet all essential military needs.

Before this program had become effective, however, and when for a time military events threatened to cut off the larger part of wool imports, prospective shortages had considerable effect on the design of items using wool. In the summer of 1941 the OQMG reviewed its wool uses and began active consideration of substitute materials. The increased rate of mobilization resulting from our entry into the war in December and the possibility that wool supplies from abroad might be cut off or seriously reduced forced the OPM to take measures controlling civilian consumption and brought a renewed study of Army specifications.

A movement began among conservation officials to persuade the QMC to lighten the weight of the winter uniform and effect other savings in wool. The wool conservation program urged upon the Corps by the WPB centered upon four principal items and materials—blankets, 32-ounce overcoating, 18-ounce serge, and flannel shirting—which accounted for over 80 percent of Army wool purchases.[55] These recommendations, prepared in the light of civilian experience, were discussed at a conference in the OQMG between representatives of the WPB, the QMC, and civilian textile specialists. Some of the dangers involved in effecting substitutions for wool in basic field items were clarified. While 16-ounce woolen cloth, for instance, might be considered ample for ordinary civilian use, it was hardly suitable for troops

who might be ordered to extremely cold climates. The 18-ounce serge, used for much of the Army's winter clothing, was lighter than the material used in any previous war and lighter than the fabric used by other armies.

The Corps had already substituted cotton comforters for wool blankets for use in barracks. Substitutions for the field blanket, however, had to be viewed with caution. Preliminary tests had shown that a mixture of reworked wool or cotton immediately resulted in reduced warmth. The peculiar virtue of wool was that it absorbed large quantities of moisture without becoming saturated. Blankets with an admixture of cotton would be less efficient in this respect and less wind resistant. Nor would it be efficient to increase the weight of the blanket to offset the reduction in wool content, since the soldier would have to carry the added burden on his back.

Quartermaster representatives revealed that 35 percent of reworked wool was already being used in the material for overcoating and that flannel shirting was 20 percent cotton. Thus it appeared that wool requirements could not be materially reduced through lowering the weight and quality of basic Quartermaster items. Nevertheless, the OQMG undertook to cut wool consumption wherever possible and a committee was formed to study the subject of wool conservation. This committee held meetings at intervals throughout the next few months at the OQMG and at the Philadelphia Quartermaster Depot, the procuring depot for clothing.

As a result of the committee's deliberations a number of additional measures were taken.

---

[54] Memo, Brig Gen C. L. Corbin, OQMG, for ASW, 21 May 40, sub: Shortage of Raw Wool to Meet Mobilization Rqmts, 423.

[55] (1) Memo, Deputy Dir of Procurement & Distr, SOS, for Gen Corbin, OQMG, 30 Mar 42, no sub. (2) Memo for file, F. S. Blanchard, Textile Consultant, Bureau of Industrial Conserv, 4 Apr 42, sub: Wool Supply and Mil Rqmts—Mtg at OQMG, 2 Apr 42.

The "bi-swing back," designed to allow greater freedom of movement, was taken out of the service coat, effecting a 12 percent saving in the yardage of serge used on each garment. Since the introduction of the field jacket, this coat was no longer considered a combat garment nor did the return to the snug-fitting back lessen its utility for ordinary wear. The proportion of re-worked wool in overcoating material was in-increased further by 15 percent. A trench coat of water-repellent, wind-resistant poplin, with a re-movable wool lining, was proposed as a possible replacement for the woolen overcoat and the raincoat in the European theater. Blankets with a low percentage of wool content were proposed for barrack use, making all-wool blankets in use in barracks available for reissue in the field and eventually cutting down the procurement of the all-wool type. In line with the committee's recommendations, trench coats and experimen-tal blankets of various mixtures were procured for thorough testing, while investigations of possible substitute wool and rayon mixtures to take the place of the basic 18-ounce uniform serge cloth were undertaken.[56]

Tests conducted by the Quartermaster Board indicated that blankets made with as much as 35 percent of reworked wool were as warm as those made entirely of virgin wool, while any considerable admixture of rayon was inadvis-able as it increased the tendency to absorb mois-ture and lessened the fire resistence of the blanket. Trench coats were approved for use by officers, and extensive tests by service boards of similar coats for enlisted men were undertaken. The project was dropped, however, in August 1943 when the M–1943 combat ensemble was adopted. By that time, in fact, there was little need of further experimentation along the line of wool substitutions. The size of the Army was becoming stabilized and initial clothing issues were expected to decline rapidly. The military situation had so improved that there was little likelihood of interruption of the lines of com-munication with Australia and other wool-producing countries. It was anticipated that the QMC would not consume even the domestic wool clip for 1943 or 1944. The stockpile of wool in the country was large and could even be reduced with safety. While it might be de-sirable to maintain a modest reserve, The Quar-termaster General advised the WPB that "the same reasons do not prevail today, as did prevail a year and one-half ago, for carrying a reserve of the present size."[57]

Silk had always been one of the strategic ma-terials under the classification maintained during the procurement planning period. Imported largely from Japan, this material would be prac-tically unobtainable in case of a war with that power. Silk, on which the Air Corps had first claim for use in parachutes, became subject to strict conservation measures in the summer of 1941. The Supply Division of the OQMG was directed to prepare a report indicating the uses of this material in Quartermaster items and the measures that could be taken to conserve it.[58]

Silk was used extensively by the Corps in banners and ribbons for decorations and medals, in nurses' white waists and enlisted men's black ties, in hat cords, as lining or seam material in numerous items of clothing, and as thread. For most uses substitutions were readily effected. Mercerized cotton thread replaced silk thread; mercerized cotton and rayon replaced silk lin-ing; the issue of silk neckties and nurses' waists was discontinued; rayon replaced silk in hat cords and in some other items.[59] For banners and decoration ribbons, replacement was a little

---

[56] (1) Maj Kennedy to Col Doriot, OQMG, 23 May 42, sub: Committee to Review QM Wool Specs. (2) Preliminary Rpt of QM Wool Conserv Com, 8 Jun 42. (3) QM Wool Conserv Com Rpt, 11 Sep 42.

[57] Ltr, Gen Gregory to Donald M. Nelson, 10 Aug 43, no sub, 423.

[58] Plng & Control Div to Chief of Sup Div, OQMG, 29 Jul 41, no sub.

[59] Memo, Gen Gregory for USW, 1 Sep 41, sub: Conserv of Strategic and Critical Materials.

more difficult and was not at first recommended. The special weathering and draping qualities of silk, together with its high degree of strength, made it the most desirable material for such items, intimately associated as they were with individual and organizational morale. The Philadelphia Depot had, however, for a number of years been investigating all types of synthetic fibers for use as substitutes for banner silk. By June 1942 it had developed a specification for rayon banner cloth which was approved as satisfactory for procurement.[60]

It had long been known in the QMC that the facilities available for the production of cotton duck, used for tentage, tarpaulins, and many items of clothing and personal equipment, would be insufficient to meet all needs in case of a great emergency involving the mobilization of a large army. This situation had made the study of duck procurement one of the most important aspects of Quartermaster procurement planning.

Even the limited expansion of the Army which took place in 1940 forced almost immediate departures from the specifications of tentage duck. By November procurement officers in the OQMG were admittedly "securing practically every fabric that can be be considered as a possible substitute for the regular 15.5 oz. plied yarn duck."[61] Tentage made from substitute material, it was directed, was to be marked so that it could be readily identified in the field. The shortage of duck was so serious by the following year that a study of clothing items was made with a view to eliminating this material. One of the savings effected was replacement of the 10.2-ounce waterproofed duck used as the outer fabric of the mackinaw by a lighter cotton fabric that was in greater production and could be readily waterproofed.

With the increased rate of mobilization following Pearl Harbor, the Army's duck requirements approximately doubled. Every effort was made to extend the production of this material.

Carpet, plush, tapestry, and upholstery industries were converted to its production despite a substantial increase in cost to the government. The QMC was assigned the task of buying all duck for the Army. Efforts already under way were stepped up to develop a substitute material for the type of duck used in shelter tents. In the face of enormous demands, specifications for numbered and flat duck had to be revised to include the more abundant double- and single-filled flat duck, heavy twill, and other substitute materials. Because of the difficulties in procuring the heavy duck required for pyramidal and other large tents, the Army had to gear its specifications more realistically to potential supply and accept a wide variety of nonstandard tentage. Concessions were made with respect to color, weight, and width in order to eliminate the difference between commercial and Army production where possible.[62] In addition, a study was made of all items of duck and webbing equipment, primarily to reduce the weight carried by the soldier but also in an effort to make greater use of lighter and more available materials. The WPB issued an order forbidding, in general, the use of duck for civilian purposes, "unless such cotton duck has been rejected as unfit for use by both the Army and the Navy of the United States."[63]

With many new manufacturers brought into the field and with substitutions and changes in the finishing technique, the production of duck

---

[60] (1) Ltr, Col Vere Painter, PQMD, to TQMG, 2 Jun 42, sub: Banner Silk Substitute. (2) 1st ind, Maj Kennedy, OQMG, to CG PQMD, 15 Jun 42, same sub. (3) 2d ind, Col Painter to TQMG, 19 Jun 42, same sub. (4) Ltr, Lt Paul E. Walz, PQMD, to TQMG, 1 Oct 42, sub: QMC Tentative Spec for Rayon Banner Cloth. All in 400.1141.

[61] Ltr, Capt James E. Baker, OQMG, to John M. Reeves, Reeves Bros, Inc., 20 Nov 40, no sub.

[62] (1) Ltr, Col W. A. McCain, PQMD, to TQMG, 2 Oct 40, sub: Utilization of Carpet Mills for Duck. (2) Rpt, Col Robert T. Stevens and Ralph A. Butland, n. d., sub: The QMC Duck and Webbing Pool.

[63] WPB, General Preference Order M–91 to Conserve Sup and Direct Distr of Cotton Duck, 28 Feb 42.

was gradually stepped up to meet the needs of the armed forces, and procurements of substitute fabrics were made less frequently. The duck problem, however, was and continued to be one of the most serious production difficulties which the QMC was called upon to face and, for a time, a large proportion of the items into which the material entered was affected by the shortage.

Fur had been extensively used in the special list of clothing for the small peacetime Alaskan garrison. With the expansion of the Army and the establishment of large garrisons in Alaska and other far northern areas, any large dependence upon furs for cold-climate clothing became impracticable. For a time the Corps made wide use of "shearling," or yearling lambskin, in its cold-climate clothing. But there were practical objections to this material, and its use by the Air Corps was so great that by the end of 1941 it tended to become a critical material. For some years explorers and mountaineers had been tending to minimize the use of furs in their clothing, substituting loosely woven woolen protected by outer shells of closely woven, wind-resistant cotton. Textile men had also been experimenting with the use of plush or "pile" of alpaca and mohair for cold weather garments. The QMC, after conducting cold-chamber laboratory experiments with soldiers wearing different types of garments, found that pile clothing with wind-breaker shells was efficient. The clothing designers of the Corps turned more and more to pile material to meet cold-climate clothing needs. By 1943 the Army clothing list for cold areas included very few items involving the use of fur.[64]

The expansion of the northern garrison also brought to light another serious material shortage. Sleeping bags are essential equipment for troops in cold climates. Down, which consists of the soft, fluffy under feathers of ducks, geese, and other aquatic birds, is considered the most efficient filler for sleeping bags. Early in the emergency a shortage of down became apparent. Kapok, a fluffy vegetable fiber, was an obvious substitute, and this material was used for some procurements for the Alaskan garrison. It proved, however, to lack sufficient warmth to meet the rigors of the arctic winter, and Maj. Gen. S. B. Buckner, commanding in Alaska, protested vigorously against its use.[65]

Down had been largely imported from China and Europe. Most of the foreign sources were soon shut off. The WPB in February 1942 issued an order restricting the use of goose and duck feathers and down to fulfilling defense contracts, but the limited domestic supply, even when so channeled, proved insufficient to meet the needs of the Army. The QMC explored every avenue in the search for a really efficient substitute for down. Extensive experimentation was carried on with milkweed fiber, curled chicken feathers, kinked acetate fiber, and other natural and synthetic materials. Nothing as effective as the mixture of 40 percent down and 60 percent waterfowl feathers was discovered, however, though the shorter feathers of turkeys and chickens made a reasonably satisfactory material when used in a mixture not exceeding 25 percent with down and waterfowl feathers. Sleeping bags were purchased chiefly with the 40–60 percent mixture of down and feathers, although in 1944 dilution with 25 percent of chicken feathers was authorized.[66]

---

[64] Pitkin, *Quartermaster Equipment for Special Forces,* pp. 23–29.

[65] (1) Memo, Maj Gen S. B. Buckner for CG Fourth Army, 30 Sep 41, no sub. (2) Ltr, Col Robert M. Littlejohn, OQMG, to Gen Buckner, CG Alaska Defense Command, 17 Jan 42, no sub. (3) Ltr, Gen Buckner to CG Western Denfense Command, 22 Jun 42, no sub.

[66] (1) Memo for file, Materials & Conserv Sec, OQMG, 19 Dec 42, sub: Down, Feather, and Kapok Situation. (2) Ltr, Col Doriot, OQMG, to Dr. E. G. Auchter, Research Administrator, Dept of Agriculture, 11 Mar 43, no sub. (3) Special Forces Sec to Materials Sec, OQMG, 6 Mar 43, sub: Filler for Sleeping Bags.

Quartermaster items also made use of large quantities of leather of various types, much of which was normally imported. Most of the leathers used in the manufacture of equipment became critical materials sooner or later. The first serious shortage to appear was in horsehide, used for heavy leather gloves. A cowhide tannage was developed which was intended to give cowhide the same characteristics as horsehide, and this material was used as a substitute. Another substitute specification for horsehide gloves was worked out in goatskin. As cowhide itself became a critical material, a new glove design, in which leather was used only in the palm, was developed in 1942. This cut-and-sewn glove replaced the wool knit glove previously supplied as the general issue item of handwear.[67]

Within a few months after Pearl Harbor, hides, skins, and most types of leather were placed under close control by the WPB, primarily to make these materials available for military needs. The Army supply services, however, were not brought under such heavy pressure to eliminate leather as in the case of rubber and certain of the metals. Footwear consumed by far the largest part of the leather used in Quartermaster items. The most effective measure taken by the Corps to conserve leather was the initiation of a shoe-rebuilding program both in this country and in the theaters.[68] In addition, the QMC took advantage of every opportunity to reduce its consumption by effecting substitutions or eliminating leather from a number of other items, such as scabbards for rifles, carbines, and submachine guns. Specifications were relaxed to permit the use of lower grade and thinner leathers.

The most important new development in the design of the service shoe, affecting the quantity of leather used, consisted in the change from a leather to a composition sole. This step was taken primarily because of the superior wearing qualities of the composition material, but the growing shortage of sole leather was a consideration. Its effect was to reduce greatly the leather requirements for this basic Quartermaster item.[69] A further conservation measure consisted in the replacement of the leather bottom filler by a cork filler. Since the rubber situation became very tight after the United States entered the war, conservation in the footwear program from this time on was centered more in efforts to reduce the amount of crude rubber consumed than in the saving of leather. In fact, at one time it was expected that it would be necessary to return to the use of leather soles. Nevertheless, leather remained a critical commodity and the QMC continued to watch for opportunities to save this material.

A notable feature of the whole conservation program was the extensive use of synthetic plastic materials as substitutes for natural raw materials. Plastics constituted a relatively new field of industrial development. Progress in this field was immensely stimulated during the war by the needs of the QMC and the other supply services. For Quartermaster items alone plastics were considered, tested, and to some extent used as substitutes for metals, rubber, and other materials. This new group of substances also occasionally permitted the development of a new item for which no natural material was quite suitable. In a number of instances, plastic substitutes for orthodox materials were so superior to the original that no return to the latter was contemplated when it should again become abundant.

---

[67] (1) Standardization Br, Rpt of Test and Development Work in Progress, 1 Mar–1 May 42. (2) R&D Br, Status Rpts, 30 Jun–31 Jul 42, 31 Aug–30 Nov 42.

[68] See section on shoe-rebuilding program in Ch. II of The Quartermaster Corps: Organization, Supply, and Services, Vol. II, a volume now in preparation for this subseries.

[69] (1) Memo, Harold M. Florsheim, OPM, for Col Littlejohn, OQMG, 23 May 41, no sub. (2) Memo, Gen Corbin for ACofS G–4, 6 Jun 41, sub: Composition Soles for Sv Shoes, 421. (3) Ltr, Gen Littlejohn to Maj Gen W. C. Baker, 14 Feb 42, sub: Sv Shoes.

Plastic buttons not only replaced the brass buttons of the uniform, but also took the place of vegetable ivory and bone buttons of other garments. Plastic replaced brass in whistles, water bag faucets, bugles, and razors; it took the place of aluminum in knife handles and, in a limited procurement, in canteens; it replaced rubber in raincoats and other waterproof fabrics. Certain new and important Quartermaster items, such as the helmet liner and the methyl bromide delousing set, were made of plastic substances from the beginning. Rifle and other weapon covers of expendable plastic material were developed for the use of the amphibious forces. Plastic insoles for the jungle boot added to the health and comfort of troops campaigning in the steaming tropical forests of the Southwest Pacific.[70] The applications of plastics, largely but not entirely as substitutes, eventually became so extensive that shortages of these synthetic substances frequently appeared, sometimes forcing the substitution of one plastic for another.

Nylon was a new plastic material which came to have varied and useful applications in Quartermaster equipment. Best known before the war as a silk substitute from which sheer stockings were made, nylon showed protean possibilities under the stimulus of war. Mountain climbing rope, superior to the best Manila, was developed from it. Shoe laces made of filament nylon showed such excellent wearing qualities that they came to be used with all jungle footwear. Rainsuits and light-weight ponchos for tropical wear were designed in nylon. Toothbrush and shaving brush bristles were made of it, and the material was considered for a whole range of jungle fabric items. Nylon was also deemed the best material for mountain tents.[71]

Unfortunately for the Corps, nylon was the only satisfactory substitute available to the Air Forces for the Japanese silk formerly used in parachutes. It was used not only for the fabric but also for the shroud lines of the parachutes. Nylon fabric was therefore largely allocated to the Air Forces, and the supply services for some time had to do without it or to accept such quantities of rejected parachute material as became available. Production of nylon increased but so too did Air Forces' requirements. While substantial allocations were eventually made to the QMC in 1944, the organization was for a long time unable to make as free use of this amazingly versatile product as it would otherwise have done.[72]

---

[70] (1) Ltr, Col C. A. Schwarzwaelder, OQMG, to Office Chief of CWS, 21 Sep 42, sub: Scientific Info. (2) Pitkin, *Quartermaster Equipment for Special Forces,* 266, 273–75.

[71] (1) Footwear & Leather Sec to Materials Sec, OQMG, 7 Aug 43, sub: Nylon for QMC Uses. (2) Materials Sec to Textile Sec, *et al.*, OQMG, 6 Aug 43, sub: Nylon for QMC Uses.

[72] Materials & Conserv Sec to Col Doriot, OQMG, 25 Aug 42, sub: August Nylon Allocation Meeting, Hq SOS.

CHAPTER III

The Development of Army Clothing

In any discussion of wartime scientific achievement it is inevitably the spectacular—jet propulsion, new explosives, radar—which obtains the most publicity. This may obscure but by no means diminishes the importance of the research done by the Quartermaster Corps in co-operation with industrial and university laboratories in developing those items of clothing which contributed to the physical and mental well-being of the soldier in World War II.

Organization for Product Development

Quartermaster research activities were centered in the Supply Division at the beginning of the national emergency in 1939. Two units of that division—the Standardization Branch and the Clothing and Equipage Branch—were active in the development of new items of Quartermaster clothing and equipment and in the revision of specifications.[1] The Standardization Branch, the heart of which was the Specifications Section, was responsible for supervising the development, preparation, and standardization of specifications for all articles provided by the Quartermaster Corps. This supervision meant checking and clearance rather than the direction of an active program of co-ordination. The branch also handled administrative details for the Quartermaster Corps Technical Committee (QMTC), which effected co-ordination among all interested branches of the Army during the development and standardization of types of clothing and equipment for which the Corps had responsibility, and the preparation and co-ordination of specifications. Lt. Col. Letcher O. Grice was chief of the Standardization Branch and executive officer of the committee. The Clothing and Equipage Branch was under the direction of Col. Robert M. Littlejohn, later to become Chief Quartermaster of the European Theater of Operations (ETO). Although primarily concerned with procurement, this branch had been accustomed to take a dominant part in the design of items within its province and continued to be active in developmental work.

In the emergency period Quartermaster research was confined, as heretofore, largely to correcting deficiencies in items as pointed out in the annual surveys of equipment made by the chiefs of branches of the Army. Occasionally upon request new items were developed. Quartermaster research did not become an activity in its own right, however, until the end of 1941. This development resulted from the mounting international crisis, which by 1940 had forced the United States into a vast defense program, including the dispatch of a greatly enlarged garrison to Alaska.

The Alaskan clothing list, revised to some

---

[1] (1) OQMG OO 4, 7 Jan 37, sub: Office Orgn. (2) OQMG OO 24, 7 Sep 38, same sub. (3) OQMG OO 25F, 15 May 41, no sub.

extent in 1928, had remained almost unchanged until 1940. Both the Clothing and Equipage and the Standardization Branches were engaged in 1940 in revising this list and in developing and procuring suitable cold-climate clothing and equipment. A series of meetings on the problem emphasized the need for an organization, unhampered by problems of procurement, storage, and distribution, to study cold-climate equipment. As a result, Brig. Gen. Clifford L. Corbin, chief of the Supply Division, authorized the establishment of a new Cold Climate Unit in the Standardization Branch late in 1941.[2] Quartermaster wartime research and developmental activities stem from these beginnings.

Lines of responsibility for the details of the development of items of clothing and equipment necessarily remained somewhat flexible. Both the Clothing and Equipage Branch and the Standardization Branch were acquiring industrial specialists and expanding rapidly to meet their responsibilities.[3] There was a certain amount of duplication of organization and functions which was of minor consequence as long as the two branches remained in close touch within the same division under chiefs who were in harmonious relationship. The prime objective was to get the work done, and consequently specific problems were handled by personnel of either branch as the qualifications of individuals dictated.

The reorganization of the OQMG along functional lines in March 1942 altered this situation. The Supply Division was broken up. The Standardization Branch, absorbed by the new Production Service, became the Product Development Branch within the Resources Division, and was headed by Lt. Col. Georges F. Doriot. At the same time the Resources Division also absorbed the Production Branch of the Planning and Control Division, thus merging in one organization the problems of production, materials conservation, and design. This con-

solidation gave recognition to the fact that product development and production problems were closely associated. The Clothing and Equipage Branch, which kept its own research organization intact in the transfer, became a branch in the new Storage and Distribution Service.

Two distinct organizations in the OQMG, rather widely separated from a control standpoint, were now performing essentially the same functions because this divided responsibility was not clarified during the process of reorganization. The conflict was presently resolved by the adoption of a recommendation made in the Platt Report to the effect that "all design and development work at headquarters, OQMG, should be centralized in Product Development Branch; such work being carried on now in Storage and Distribution Service should be transferred to Product Development."[4] The Production Service had made good its claim to jurisdiction in this field.

Responsibility for product development was further clarified in the second reorganization of the OQMG at the end of July 1942. The Military Planning Division absorbed the Production Service, taking over its organizational units intact. Its mission was declared to be, in part, to "develop Quartermaster items to meet changing needs and conditions."[5] The Resources Division, with Colonel Doriot continuing as its

---

[2] For a fuller treatment of these developments see Pitkin, *Quartermaster Equipment for Special Forces*, pp. 8–71.

[3] (1) Col L. O. Grice, "The Standardization Branch," *QMR*, XXI (March–April 1942), 23–24, 103. (2) Gen Robert M. Littlejohn, "Clothing and Equipage," *QMR*, XXI (March–April 1942), 20–21.

[4] (1) Chief of OP&C Div to Dirs of Divs, OQMG, 10 Sep 42, with attachments prepared by survey teams, subs: Memo of Recommendations on OQMG Procurement and Memo on Basic QMC Procurement Functions. (2) For a fuller discussion of the Platt Report see Ch. I, above.

[5] OQMG OO 184, 31 Jul 42, sub: Reasgmt of QMC Functions.

chief, became the Research and Development Branch of the new Military Planning Division. Quartermaster research with some exceptions was now centralized in the Research and Development Branch, which continued to be the chief organization for product development in the OQMG during the remainder of the war.

A broad assignment of responsibility was made to the Research and Development Branch. It initiated action to insure continued practical development of Quartermaster equipment; approved all specifications for Quartermaster items; ascertained problems of production and materials, recommending solutions; and supervised conservation work as well as activities in the Corps concerned with the operations of the Controlled Materials Plan. In collaboration with other divisions of the OQMG, the Research and Development Branch prepared the Master Production Schedule and translated schedules for end items into requirements for raw materials. It co-ordinated the testing activities of the Corps, represented the OQMG on the technical committees of other arms and services, and served as the executive office of the QMCTC. The products sections of the branch had the primary responsibility for the development of specific items assigned to them. Although a number of organizational adjustments were later made within the Research and Development Branch, the organization for the development of Quartermaster items of clothing and equipment had, by the end of 1942, taken on a more or less fixed form for the duration of the war.[6]

While in theory all research activity of the QMC was centralized in the Research and Development Branch when the OQMG was reorganized along functional lines after March 1942, in practice this centralization took place slowly and was not completely accomplished during the war. For many months there was friction between the Subsistence Branch of the Storage and Distribution Division and the Research and Development Branch of the Military Planning Division over responsibility for research in subsistence and in the packaging of subsistence. It was the end of 1942 before this difficulty had been settled to the satisfaction of both divisions. Responsibility for research in packing was never vested in the Military Planning Division but remained with the Storage and Distribution Division throughout the war. Similarly, when petroleum procurement for the Army was centralized in an integrated commodity organization in the OQMG called the Fuels and Lubricants Division, that division was also given responsibility for the development of containers and petroleum equipment despite the contention of the director of the Military Planning Division that all research concerning Quartermaster items should be concentrated in the Research and Development Branch.[7]

The Research and Development Branch co-ordinated the research activities of all QMC agencies in the field. Notable among these were four of the Quartermaster procuring depots—Boston, Philadelphia, Jeffersonville, and Chicago. Boston specialized in footwear; Philadelphia in clothing and textiles; Jeffersonville in mechanical items, webbing, tentage, and tentage textiles; and Chicago in subsistence. In the years before the national emergency, the larger part of such research work as was done by the QMC was actually conducted at these depots, or by private manufacturers co-operating under their direction. Problems of equipment design, presented to the Corps from the using forces, were ordinarily cleared through the OQMG and referred to the appropriate depots for recommended solution. The Philadelphia and

---

[6] See Chart 5.

[7] (1) OQMG OO 24-37B, 25 Aug 43, sub: Responsibility for Spec, Design, R&D of Containers for Petrl Products. (2) OQMG OO 25-70, 25 Mar 44, sub: Asgmt of Responsibility for Equip Especially Designed for Handling of Petrl Products. (3) Dir of Mil Plng Div to the Deputy QMG, 4 Aug 43, no sub.

CHART 5 — RESEARCH AND DEVELOPMENT BRANCH, OQMG: 16 JUNE 1944

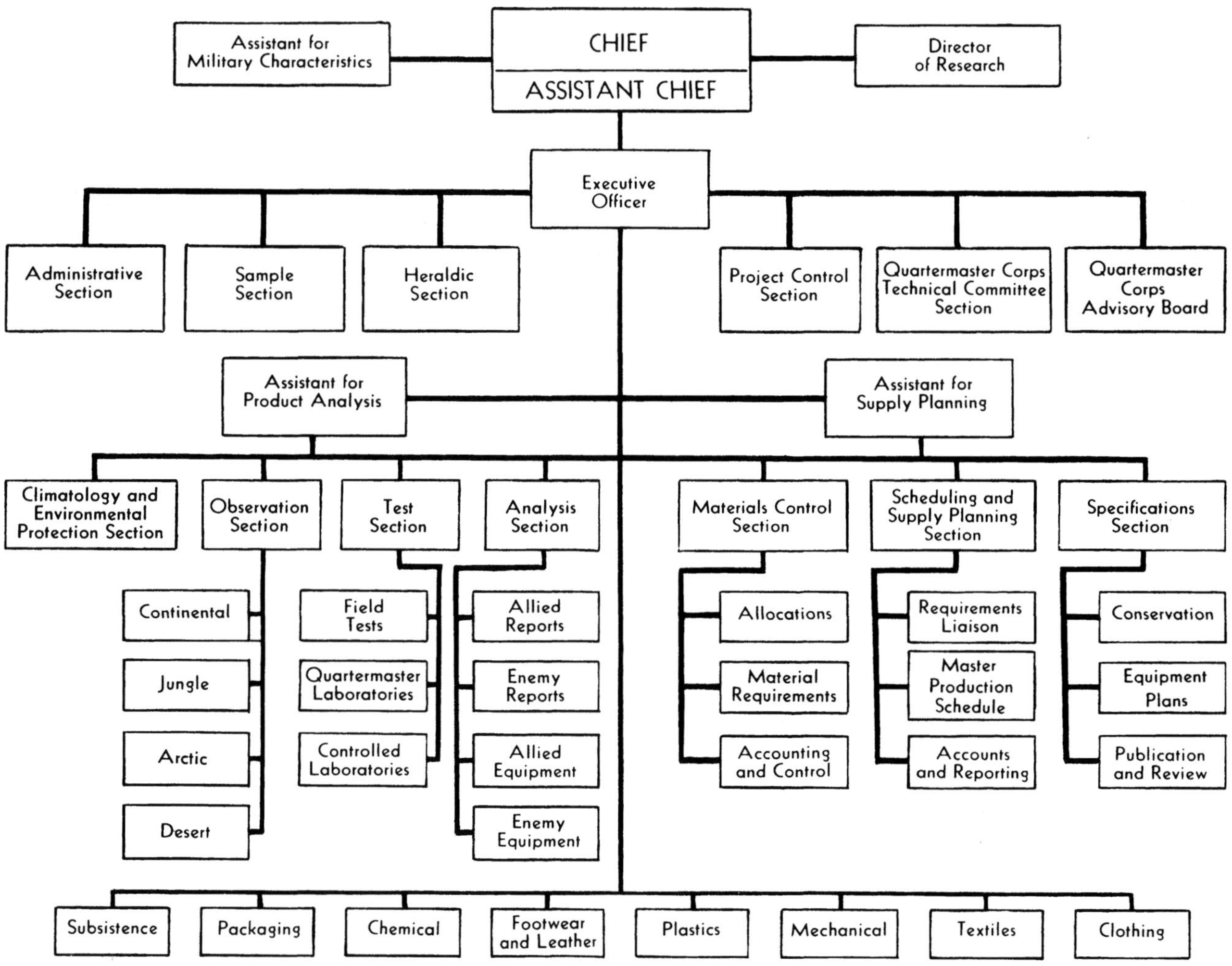

CHIEF
ASSISTANT CHIEF

Director of Research

Assistant for Military Characteristics

Executive Officer

Quartermaster Corps Advisory Board

Quartermaster Corps Technical Committee Section

Project Control Section

Administrative Section

Sample Section

Heraldic Section

Assistant for Product Analysis

Assistant for Supply Planning

Climatology and Environmental Protection Section

Observation Section

Continental

Jungle

Arctic

Desert

Test Section

Field Tests

Quartermaster Laboratories

Controlled Laboratories

Analysis Section

Allied Reports

Enemy Reports

Allied Equipment

Enemy Equipment

Materials Control Section

Allocations

Material Requirements

Accounting and Control

Scheduling and Supply Planning Section

Requirements Liaison

Master Production Schedule

Accounts and Reporting

Specifications Section

Conservation

Equipment Plans

Publication and Review

Subsistence

Packaging

Chemical

Footwear and Leather

Plastics

Mechanical

Textiles

Clothing

Jeffersonville depots maintained manufacturing plants, producing many of the items within their respective fields. These two depots contained quality-control laboratories which tested for specification purposes samples of items under procurement taken from the production line. In these laboratories, too, a certain amount of experimental work was carried on to improve existing items and develop new ones.[8]

All the varied activities of the depots were, of course, greatly expanded with the national emergency. The facilities of the Philadelphia and Jeffersonville laboratories were enlarged and modernized. In the vast developmental program incident to the preparation of suitable clothing and equipment for the wartime Army, they became a leading reliance of the QMC. Even before the great expansion of the Army, the Philadelphia Depot was engaged in a considerable variety of research and developmental projects in clothing and textiles. By August 1942 it was conducting studies and tests ranging from the water absorption of resin-coated fabrics to the reconditioning of World War I buttons. At the same time the Jeffersonville Depot was working on a number of projects looking toward the substitution of more available materials for strategic metals in Quartermaster items, the improvement of tentage duck, the study of rot- and mildew-resistant compounds, and the improvement or initial development of a number of duck and mechanical items. In September 1942 the Boston Depot reported activity on a number of projects for the improvement of the design of the service shoe as well as studies for the conservation of rubber in the arctic overshoe and the jungle boot. Such projects are illustrative of the research activities pursued by the depots — the prime agencies of the Corps in meeting its basic responsibility of supplying the Army.

If the Research and Development Branch of the Military Planning Division had difficulty in securing recognition in the OQMG of its responsibility for research, it also encountered opposition from the depots. Like other long-established field agencies in any widespread organization, they tended to generate their own *esprit de corps*, their own local loyalties, and their own jealously guarded prerogatives. In connection with developmental work they had over a period of years built up a tradition of semi-independence, which was little disturbed during the first years of the emergency. When the research and development organization within the OQMG began to take on final form, however, it started to assert control over the research activities of the depots.

Full co-ordination was not secured without some pressure. In May 1942 the depots were first required to submit to the OQMG regular monthly reports showing the status of all their projects.[9] A few months later information in the OQMG on the research activities of one of the depots was still very meager. It was necessary for The Quartermaster General to reiterate that responsibility for "supervising and coordinating all research, development and engineering of Quartermaster supplies and equipment" was vested in the Production Service. To secure better co-ordination he soon directed that all depot research and developmental projects be submitted to the OQMG for approval before work was started on them.[10]

---

[8] (1) The growth and activities of the textile laboratory of the Philadelphia Quartermaster Depot are described at considerable length in a report by James A. Barnes, The Laboratory: Philadelphia Quartermaster Depot, July 1943. (2) Two reports by David Spence Hill, The Engineering Division, June 1943, and The Manufacturing Division, September 1943, cover the work of the laboratory and manufacturing plant at the Jeffersonville Quartermaster Depot. These are all typescript reports prepared under the direction of, and filed with, the Historical Section, OQMG.

[9] Ltr, TQMG to CG PQMD *et al.*, 13 May 42, sub: R&D Projects.

[10] (1) Ltr, Col Doriot, OQMG, to Brig Gen Allen R. Kimball, JQMD, 18 Jul 42, no sub. (2) Ltr, Gen Gregory to CG JQMD, 4 Aug 42, no sub. (3) Ltr, Gen Gregory to CG JQMD, 8 Aug 42, sub: R&D Projects. All in 400.112.

The depots had traditionally written many of the specifications for the items which they procured and had a tendency to take over this function more or less completely. The responsibility of the Research and Development Branch in this respect was now underscored. It was emphasized that this office would "furnish recommendations where necessary on specifications to be written by the depots since this office is in closer contact with the varying needs of different sections of the Army and with the changing availability of materials and facilities." [11] Even emergency specifications were to be submitted to the central office for concurrence.

A policy of making frequent visits to the depots to discuss problems, the submission of regular depot reports, and the approval of research projects and emergency specifications by the OQMG brought a closer integration of the research activities of the depots with the Quartermaster program as a whole and made the organization into a more effective working team. The control of the Research and Development Branch over depot research was further strengthened in the autumn of 1943 by an order which specifically made the assignment of projects to, and the direction of technical activities in, all Quartermaster research laboratories "the direct responsibility of the Military Planning Division." [12]

The official QMC field testing agency was the Quartermaster Board, which conducted tests at the request of the Research and Development Branch. Created by direction of the Chief of Staff, U.S. Army, in 1934 at the Quartermaster School in Philadelphia, this board was re-established in 1942 at Camp Lee, Va., the chief training center for the QMC during World War II. [13] Its president was directly responsible to The Quartermaster General in all technical matters. While the Quartermaster Board had been established under a broad charter, its chief activity became that of field testing clothing and equipment. Under Col. Max R. Wainer, director of

the board, testing of various new items began shortly after the board moved to Camp Lee and increased rapidly thereafter.

Field testing, as done by the board, was not intended to be a substitute for laboratory testing but rather its complement. Field testing was divided into two main groups, normal and expedited testing. In normal testing items were used by personnel in the performance of regular daily activities. In expedited testing the life span of an article was compressed into a fraction of its normal expected life. Expedited testing was used when time was a major consideration, while normal testing permitted a finer degree of accuracy. [14]

Both special and fixed installations were used for testing items. To test various types of mechanical devices, where a high degree of operating skill might be required and the utmost control be essential, special installations which could be dismantled at the end of the test were set up for individual tests. On the other hand, fixed installations, such as the shoe test track and the combat course, [15] were set up at the Quartermaster Board for many of the tests on footgear and clothing. By the use of these proving grounds definite patterns of wear could be established. Still another method was to test under controlled conditions. Thus, a principal test method involved the use of many samples of clothing and equipment items by troops engaged in controlled activities in the field. In this type of testing actual tactical problems were devised and were executed by trained units of men under conditions designed to duplicate realistically field conditions to which the items under

---

[11] Mil Plng Div to Insp Div, OQMG, 5 Oct 42, sub: Insp Rpt at JQMD.
[12] OQMG OO 25–56, 25 Oct 43, sub: Mil Plng–QM R&D Activities.
[13] (1) AR 30-10, 8 Jun 34, sub: QM Bd. (2) OQMG OO 18, 19 Jan 42, sub: QM Bd.
[14] Rpt, Col Wainer to OQMG, Fld Testing Procedures, QM Bd, Camp Lee, Va. [circa 1943].
[15] See Charts 6 and 7.

consideration might be subjected. Another method, invariably supplemented by other approaches, employed considerable numbers of samples, and personnel engaged in their normal duties. Personnel of the regular training regiments at Camp Lee were equipped with the materials undergoing test, and observers and recorders were attached to such units during the test period.

Another important QMC testing agency for clothing and equipment, established after the war began, was the Climatic Research Laboratory, at Lawrence, Mass. This laboratory was first projected by Dr. Paul A. Siple, authority on the Antarctic, when he was temporarily employed by the Corps as an analyst of cold-climate clothing in the summer and autumn of 1941. He believed that the Corps, with its vast and increasing responsibility for clothing and equipping troops for service in varied climates, should have under its own control a fully equipped laboratory where extreme conditions of both cold and heat could be produced. There the techniques of the physiologist, the physicist, the textile expert, and the climatologist could be applied and the results synthesized to place the selection of clothing for any given environment on a really scientific basis.[16] Dr. Siple believed such a laboratory was particularly essential inasmuch as physiological laboratories had not taken into consideration the effects of clothing in their studies of climatic stress. He was given carte blanche to organize the laboratory, although by agreement with the chief of the Research and Development Branch he was not obliged to operate the laboratory. Instead he was permitted to set up a companion climatology unit in the branch in which to work out more of his ideas.

While considerable time elapsed before the laboratory was eventually established, by March 1943 it had begun the testing of cold-climate clothing and equipment. Lt. Col. John H. Talbott of the Medical Corps, who had long been

associated with the work of the Harvard Fatigue Laboratory, was appointed to take charge of the laboratory. Its work expanded rapidly. Later the Climatic Research Laboratory constructed a hot chamber where desert and jungle conditions could be simulated. The laboratory became the principal facility of the Research and Development Branch in the performance of such tests on clothing and equipment for climatic extremes as could be performed in a laboratory, though much testing of this nature continued to be done also in co-operating private laboratories.[17]

Testing of new items of Quartermaster issue by the Army service boards had long been part of the regular procedure leading to standardization. These boards were organizations set up by the chief of each technical service to test items that were developed, and such testing continued during the war. In addition, the Research and Development Branch was responsible for securing the collaboration of a considerable number of governmental and private agencies in this work. Governmental agencies which carried on laboratory work for the Corps included the National Bureau of Standards, the official government testing agency, which in normal times

---

[16] (1) Ltr, Dr. Siple to Col Grice, OQMG, 28 Oct 41, no sub. (2) Pitkin, *Quartermaster Equipment for Special Forces*, pp. 279–81.

[17] (1) Authority for the establishment of the laboratory was formally received from the Commanding General, SOS, 7 January 1943, and its activation was officially confirmed 4 February 1943. AGO Memo S 30–5–43, 4 Feb 43, sub: Establishment of QM CRL, SPX 322.29 (1–20–43) OB-I-SPQ-MP-FH. (2) Construction of the laboratory was achieved by using maximum construction funds allowable to The Quartermaster General without special approval of the SOS. Manpower as test subjects, however, had to be approved and so for the first time the SOS became aware of the laboratory. SOS approval of the laboratory was reluctant and was given only because it already existed. Ltr, Dr. Siple to Maj Gen Orlando Ward, Chief of Military History, 10 Nov 50, with incl, no sub. (3) For a fuller discussion of these developments see Pitkin, *Quartermaster Equipment for Special Forces*, pp. 282–92.

CHART 6—QUARTERMASTER BOARD SHOE TEST TRACK

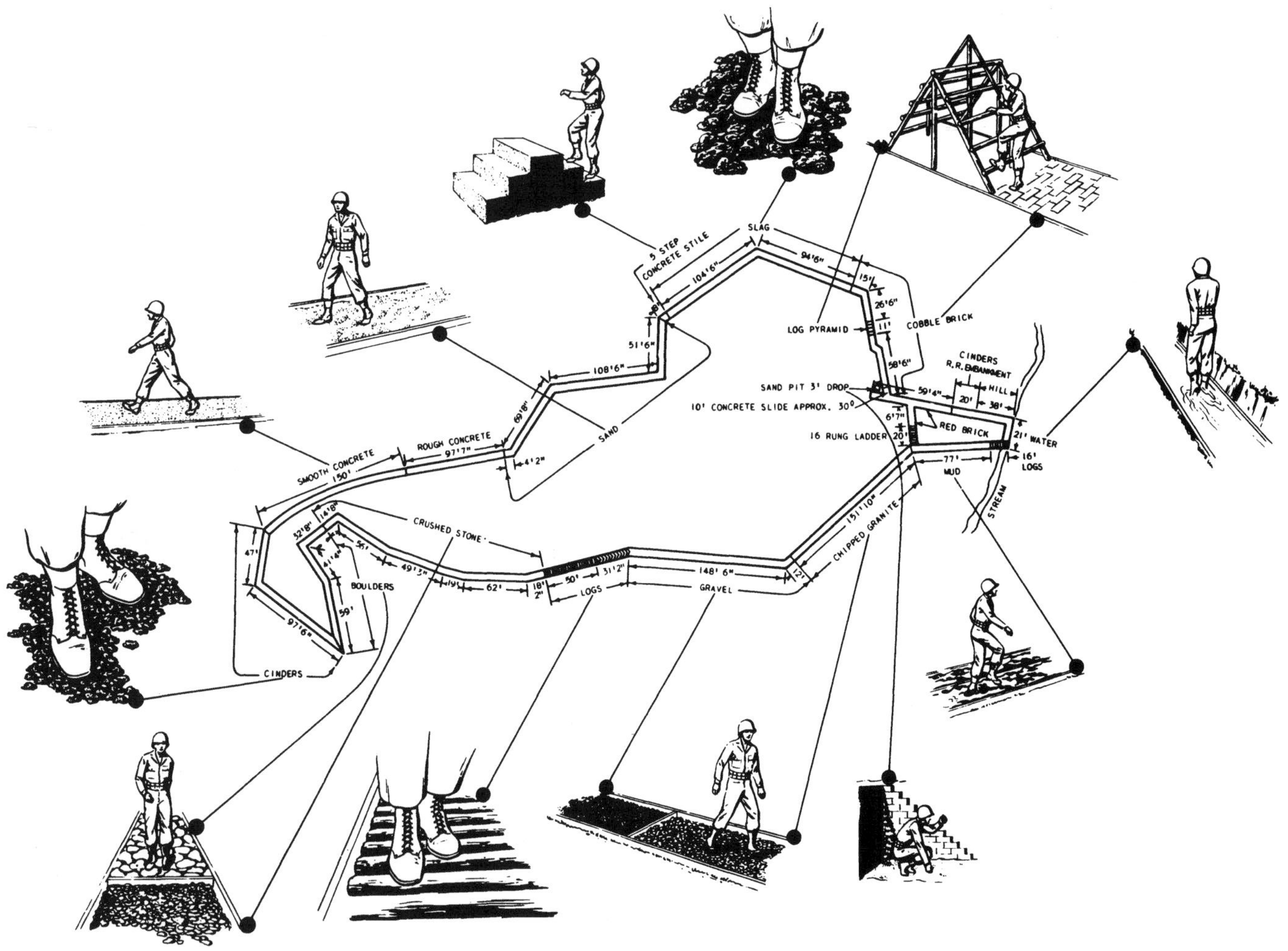

CHART 7—QUARTERMASTER BOARD COMBAT COURSE (1,700 FEET)

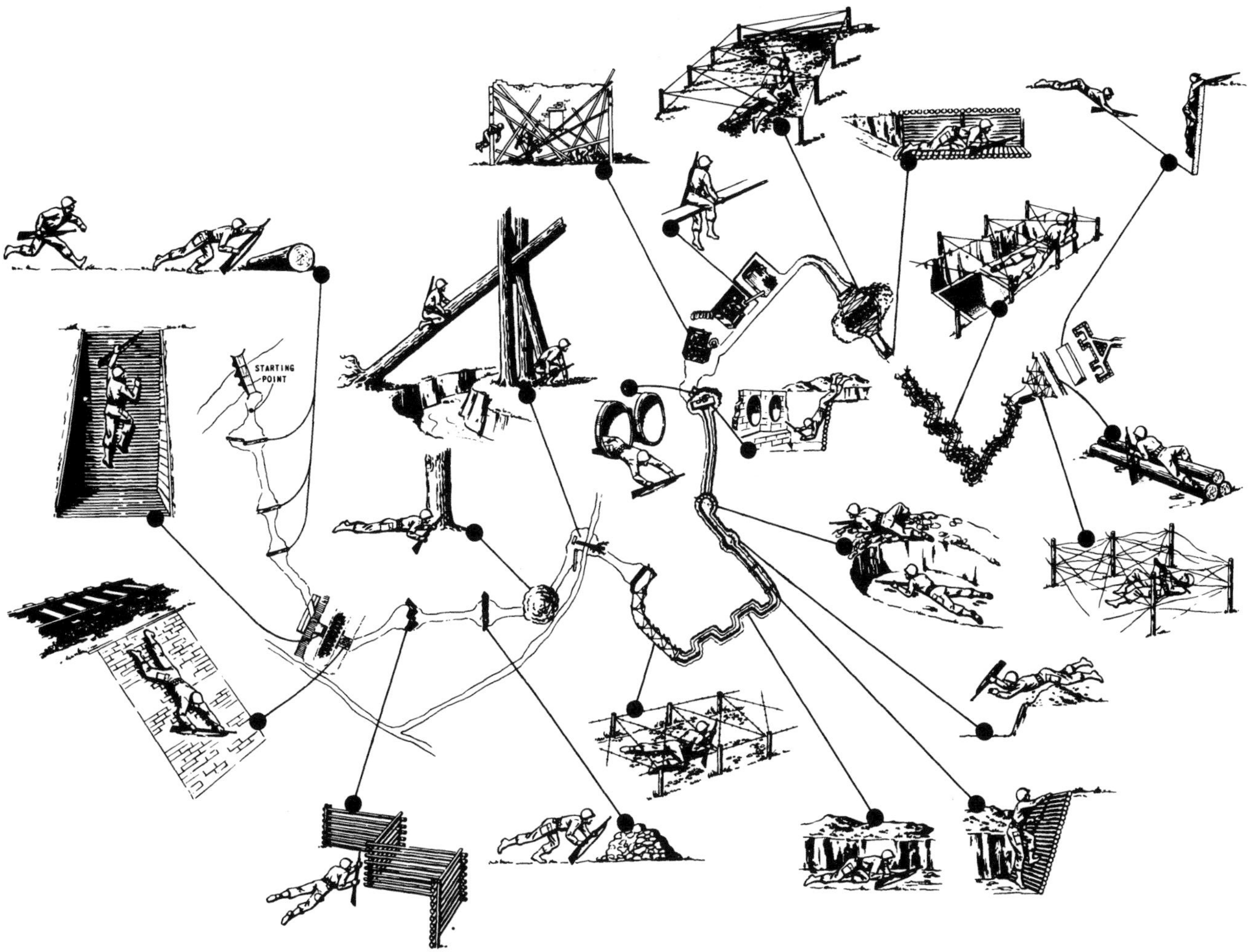

STARTING POINT

was the principal reliance of the Corps for laboratory testing of materials, and the Textile Foundation, another agency in the Department of Commerce. The laboratory and reference facilities of the Department of Agriculture and the Department of the Interior also gave considerable assistance in the work of the Research and Development Branch.

The Office of Scientific Research and Development (OSRD), established by executive order in 1941 for the purpose of assuring adequate provision for research on scientific and medical problems relating to national defense, was of great and steadily increasing assistance to the OQMG in its developmental work. Fundamental research problems were ordinarily presented to the OSRD through the War Department liaison staff which had been set up for such clearance in Headquarters, ASF. Through its National Defense Research Committee the OSRD made available the facilities of governmental, university, and industrial laboratories all over the country for the solution of scientific problems. Assisted by this committee, the Military Planning Division placed contracts with the laboratories considered most able to perform the desired research. In placing contracts the division also dealt directly with representatives of a particular industry or a university laboratory.

In addition, the Research and Development Branch had its own Advisory Board, composed of executives in various fields of research as well as outstanding scientists and explorers who were able either to contribute directly to the solution of specific problems or who headed organizations with scientific personnel whose services could be made available. This board was organized in the spring of 1942, when the product development organization of the OQMG was taking on permanent form under the direction of Colonel Doriot.

A number of university laboratories, specializing in various fields, were called upon for

assistance in the development of equipment. By posing questions and problems and by analyzing reports, the Research and Development Branch guided its co-operating laboratories in the work to be accomplished. Among the university laboratories contributing to the results achieved, the Fatigue Laboratory of Harvard University was especially notable. When the war began this laboratory was under the directorship of Dr. David B. Dill,[18] who was succeeded in 1941 by Dr. William Forbes as acting director. The laboratory had undertaken a broad program of physiological research, involving studies in all phases of the physiology of fatigue, including effects of heat, cold, and altitude on human efficiency. During the war it was engaged entirely on war research projects, nearly all of which concerned the OQMG. These included basic research on clothing principles, in particular the efficiency of Army clothing, as well as nutritional studies. Its program was integrated with that of the Climatic Research Laboratory at Lawrence and the Subsistence Research Laboratory at Chicago.[19] As the new Climatic Research Laboratory came into action, work was divided between it and the Fatigue Laboratory. In general, practical tests of completed items were made by the Lawrence Laboratory, while research into the principles of design for clothing suitable to climatic extremes remained the function of the Harvard organization.

Valuable work in the physiological testing of Quartermaster clothing for climatic extremes was also performed by Dr. Lovic P. Herrington and his staff of the John B. Pierce Laboratory of Hygiene at New Haven, Conn. The Department of Physiology at Indiana University under

---

[18] Dr. Dill, after becoming a lieutenant colonel, was transferred in the spring of 1943 from the Air Corps to the QMC to become Assistant for Product Analysis in the Research and Development Branch.

[19] For the work of the Subsistence Research Laboratory see Ch. V, below.

the direction of Dr. Sid Robinson also conducted laboratory testing of uniforms for hot climates. Assistance was given to the Research and Development Branch in the study of problems of fiber, yarn, and fabric properties by the Textile Laboratories of the Massachusetts Institute of Technology, under the direction of Professor Edward R. Schwartz. Leather problems were analyzed by the research laboratory of the Tanners' Council located at the University of Cincinnati.

In wartime, as in peace, the Corps depended on private industry for a great part of its research and developmental work. In November 1940, shortly after the first considerable enlargement of the Army had taken place, there were some nineteen firms co-operating in eleven projects of the Supply Division. In January 1942 more than 200 business firms were reported as engaged in co-operative development of seventy-five different items, aside from motor transport, for the QMC. These firms included leaders in the fields of chemicals, rubber, textiles, clothing, leather goods, light metal products, chinaware, and others.[20]

Industry generally was eager, under the stimulus of war, to contribute its inventive genius, laboratory facilities, and technical skill to the solution of Quartermaster equipment problems. Many new products were regularly brought to the attention of the OQMG as offering possibilities in the way of meeting Army needs. As early as February 1941 the flood of such offerings had become so great that there was established a special Quartermaster Equipment Board within the Supply Division for the purpose of passing upon new articles and proposed changes in design submitted by manufacturers and others. The OQMG also, through its varied technical staff, attempted to keep in touch with all pertinent technical advances in industry, and frequently inquired for samples of new materials or finished items which might have Quartermaster application.

When a new item was needed, or field reports indicated the necessity of an improvement in design, whole industrial groups were often called upon to offer their suggestions or to take up the necessary development with their own facilities. Thus, when a new stove, small and light enough to be carried in the rucksack, was needed for mountain troops, a meeting of the design engineers of nine of the leading stove manufacturers of the country was called at the Chicago Quartermaster Depot, and the problem was presented to them. When the QMC took over from the Ordnance Department the development of the liner for the new steel helmet, half a dozen manufacturers of plastics and other firms interested in the problem were brought into conference and asked to pool their resources in order to hasten the development and mass production of this badly needed item. When trouble with the burner of the M–1937 field range persisted in the field, the Coleman Lamp and Stove Company and the American Gas Machine Company, two of the leading firms in the development of gasoline-burning equipment, with the Ethyl Corporation, research authority on leaded gasoline, were asked to co-operate and produce a better burner.[21]

The Research and Development Branch dealt with industrial firms, as far as practicable, through committees and associations set up by the various industries for their common benefit. Many such associations were established during the war to handle the highly specialized problems growing out of the needs of the armed

---

[20] (1) Sup Div to Admin Div, OQMG, 29 Nov 40, sub: Commercial Cooperation in R&D, 400.312. (2) Ltr, TAG to TQMG, 18 Oct 41, same sub. AG 400.114 (10–17–41) MB–D. (3) 1st ind, Col F. H. Pope, OQMG, to TAG, 1 Jan 42, on same.

[21] (1) Dir of Production, Resources Div, to Dir of Procurement, OQMG, 21 May 42, sub: Ski Stoves. (2) Memo, unsigned, 4 Jun 42, sub: Production Program for Cold Climate Stove. (3) Conference on Helmet Liners, 14 Jan 42. (4) Ltr, Col Doriot, OQMG, to American Gas Machine Co, 17 Sep 42, no sub. (5) Ltr, Col Doriot to Ethyl Corp, 19 Sep 42, no sub.

forces. Conferences with such associations, at the call of the OQMG, were part of the regular routine of the office. Sometimes such an organization, with its member firms working on contracts for the same item, would take the initiative and call a conference to discuss and present to the QMC problems of production and suggestions for the improvement of designs.

The contributions of American industry to the development of Quartermaster clothing and equipment eventually became almost infinite in number and variety. They ranged from minor suggestions as to the design of a relatively simple piece of wearing apparel to the development, sometimes by a single firm, of a complicated mechanical item. Hundreds of industrial organizations in many fields of production aided, with consultant service, individual or co-operative design, or laboratory testing of the finished product, in the solution of the developmental problems of the OQMG.

Development and Standardization Procedure

The general procedure to be followed in the work of research, development, and classification of items of equipment for the Army was prescribed by AR 850–25. This regulation, as revised in 1943, stated in substance that research and development were functions of the technical services under the general direction of the Commanding General, ASF, or in case of Air Force items, of the Commanding General, AAF. Under established procedure a developmental project was initiated whenever a using arm decided that a given development was desirable. The using arm also formulated the statement of the military characteristics which the projected item was to possess. The development was then co-ordinated through the technical committee of the service charged with the procurement of that class of equipment. The procurement of experimental types was approved by the Commanding General, ASF, after which

the necessary developmental program was prepared by the chief of the technical service concerned. Development was pursued in close liaison with the using arm. When experimental types had been developed and procured, they underwent engineering tests, conducted by the technical service, to determine their engineering soundness, and service tests, conducted by the using arms and services, to determine their suitability for service use. The developing service co-ordinated all tests to insure that they were comprehensive, without incurring delay or duplication of effort. Classification of the item after testing was recommended by the using arm or service, co-ordinated through the appropriate technical committee. This committee submitted recommendation for classification to the Commanding General, ASF, for approval. The classification of an item as standard or substitute standard permitted determination of the basis of issue and procurement planning for production. Specifications were prepared by the technical service and submitted to the Commanding General, ASF, for approval.[22]

Within this general framework, a considerable variety of detailed procedures was possible. The actual inspiration for a new item of Quartermaster equipment might come from any one of a number of sources—the presentation of a new device by a manufacturer or inventor, the idea of a technician in the Research and Development Branch or in one of the manufacturing depots, a report from an observer or a unit on maneuvers or in a theater of operations calling attention to a deficiency or a need, the examination of a piece of captured enemy equipment, the need for conserving a critical material, or the alteration of a related item. If the project originated in or first came to the attention of the Research and Development Branch and was approved there, normal procedure called for a request to be submitted to Headquarters, ASF,

---

[22] AR 850-25, 30 Jun 43, sub: Development, Classification of, and Specs for Types of Equip.

for permission to develop the item experimentally. If the project first cleared through Headquarters, ASF, and was approved there, the Research and Development Branch would learn of the proposed item by way of a directive to carry on such experimental development. In either case, research to determine the military characteristics of the desired new item was the next step. Technicians of the branch usually secured the collaboration of personnel of the using arms in this work, which involved the study of the functions to be performed by the item, the prospective military and geographic conditions of its use, the review of similar existing equipment, and the functional relationship of the proposed item to other pieces of equipment. Preparation of the design followed, most often with the assistance of one of the Quartermaster manufacturing depots, an industrial firm, or a whole industrial group. An experimental order would then be placed with a manufacturer, or the necessary test samples might be made in a manufacturing depot.

When samples sufficient for testing had been procured, laboratory tests would be undertaken under the direction of the Test Section. These tests might be conducted in the Corps' own facilities—the manufacturing and testing depots or the Climatic Research Laboratory, for example. They might be made by a co-operating agency, such as a government, university, or industrial laboratory. Field tests followed, coordinated but not directed by the Test Section. These were usually conducted by a number of appropriate service boards, normally including the Quartermaster Board.

On the completion of the test program, the item was presented to the QMCTC for adoption. In this committee, which usually operated through subcommittees, the arms and service which were interested in the item were able through their representatives to make known their views. If the item was approved by the committee, it was forwarded to Headquarters,

ASF, for final adoption. A new item might be adopted as "standard," representing the highest qualifications for the purpose intended and therefore preferred for procurement. Or it might be classified as "substitute standard," representing something less than the most desirable qualifications but the best immediately available because of material shortage or for some other reason. It could therefore be procured as a substitute for a standard article. With the development of a new item to replace another, the latter might be reclassified as "limited standard," representing an article which did not have as satisfactory military characteristics as a standard article, but which could be used as a substitute since it was either in use or available for issue to meet supply demands. Upon the adoption of the item, a basis of issue for it was prepared, specifications were written, and a plan for its procurement was drawn up.[23]

The organizational background was identical for product development in both clothing and equipment [24] and consequently has been here presented as a unit, preliminary to discussion of the developmental work in these two fields. Since similar methods of testing were applied to items of clothing and equipment and the same general procedure was utilized to achieve their standardization, these aspects have also been treated at this point as a unit. Against this background the specific achievements in the development of clothing and equipment during the war years, as well as the trends and problems involved in research in the clothing field, are analyzed in the following sections.

The range of Quartermaster product development was wide. Hundreds of new items were developed during the war and many previously

[23] A considerable number of "case histories" of individual items have been drawn upon in the preparation of this brief account of the procedure followed in Quartermaster product development.

[24] The exceptions in the field of subsistence research are discussed below in Ch. V.

adopted items were modified in the light of criticism from the field. Projects were initiated ranging in variety and complexity from the development of asbestos mittens to the design of command tents. Since only a selective account of this work is possible, primary emphasis has been placed on the development of items of combat clothing and equipment. In combat the enlisted man and the officer wore the same combat clothing whether it was herringbone twill in the Pacific or olive drab woolens in the ETO. New items, commonly used, have been emphasized, although examples have been drawn from among the more specialized items to illustrate the impact of global war upon Quartermaster research.

Winter Combat Clothing

The American soldier went into World War II clad in a uniform evolved from that of World War I. In the wave of economy that swept Congress after 1918 it was deemed unnecessary for the Army to have a dress uniform. As a consequence, the combat uniform of World War I underwent gradual modifications in the interval of peace until it approached as nearly a dress uniform as it could. The basic uniform of World War I consisted of olive drab woolen service breeches and coat. The latter was designed as a single-breasted sack coat with a standing collar. Beginning in 1926 the "choker" collar of the coat gave way to a collar-and-lapel design, necessitating the use of a tie. A black silk four-in-hand cravat was selected. Gradually during the thirties trousers replaced breeches as a standard part of the uniform, but it was not until 1 February 1939 that they were authorized for all arms and services.[25]

At the beginning of the emergency this service coat and the trousers comprised the basic uniform. It was not really a dress uniform, and, as was promptly disclosed in World War II, neither was it a good combat uniform, although a bi-swing back had been adopted for the coat late in 1939 as a means of providing a more functional garment. To meet its shortcomings a field jacket was designed and developed in the same year to be used in lieu of the service coat in the field.[26] Under the pressure of material shortages the silk tie gave way to a black wool worsted tie in 1940 and then to an olive drab mohair tie by the end of 1941. In 1939 canvas leggings had replaced the spiral leggings of the World War I infantryman.[27]

Global war caught the Army short of clothing specialized for extreme climatic environments, and of necessity much of the early work on clothing was devoted to filling this need. In the development of cold-climate clothing, which was pushed first because of the urgent program of defense measures involving the sending of an enlarged garrison to Alaska, the OQMG utilized the principle of "layering." More and more, experienced cold-climate men had abandoned the use of furs, using instead loosely woven woolens, covered by windproof garments of light but finely woven cotton, to protect the enclosed air from wind erosion. This layering principle had become widely accepted before the outbreak of World War II, and the OQMG, after utilizing it in the development of arctic combat clothing, also applied it in the development of the standard winter combat uniform of the American soldier.

---

[25] (1) AR 600-35, 31 Dec 26, sub: Prescribed Uniform. (2) AR 600-40, 31 Dec 26, sub: Wearing of Uniform. (3) WD Cir 71, Sec. I, 23 Nov 38, sub: Sv Uniform.

[26] (1) Ltr, Brig Gen A. B. Warfield, OQMG, to ASW, 6 Feb 40, sub: Procurement Clearance on US Spec 8-31D, EM's Sv Coat. (2) 1st ind, ASW to TQMG, 7 Feb 40, on same, 400.1141. (3) Ltr, Gen Corbin, to ACofS G-4, 21 Sep 40, sub: Windbreakers.

[27] (1) Ltr, Gen Corbin, OQMG, to TAG, 7 Dec 40, sub: Neckties, and 2d ind, AG to TQMG, 2 Jan 41. (2) Ltr, Gen Corbin, to ACofS G-4, 4 Feb 42, same sub, and 2d ind, AG to TQMG, 24 Feb 42. (3) Min of QMCTC, 13 Jan 39.

SERVICE UNIFORMS OF 1918 AND 1941

In line with this development was the adoption of a plush-type or "pile" material for inner garments. The idea of shifting away from the use of furs as a major reliance in the design of cold-climate clothing was particularly stimulated in 1941 by the upholstery industry, which was in search of new business since the automobile industry, under government compulsion, was cutting down on its production of pleasure cars. Once tests had demonstrated early in 1942 that satisfactory clothing for arctic use could be made of pile, more and more cold-weather garments, such as caps and liners for field jackets and parka overcoats, were made of this material.[28]

The Army's initial emphasis on special troop organizations resulted in concentration on the development of specialized clothing to meet the needs of such units. Thus, special cold-climate clothing was designed for the new mountain troops. The Armored Force asked for and received a different winter uniform, snug fitting and with a minimum of protrusions, for wear in tanks. Another special uniform and special jumping boots were developed for parachute troops. For a time it seemed that there was to be no end to the specialty uniforms, each bringing its own new production problems. Their bewildering variety placed a heavy burden upon the system of distribution, and it was inevitable that a reaction should set in. After the first year of the war Quartermaster efforts were centered on the development of combat clothing adaptable to general issue.

Developmental work on the winter combat uniform was initiated early in the fall of 1942 when Col. David H. Cowles, then chief of the Military Planning Division, requested the early development of a combat jacket and trousers. It was proposed to use 9-ounce sateen or a fabric having similar wind- and tear-resistant characteristics for the new battle trousers and jacket in order to provide a satisfactory wind-resistant outer shell. The theory was that these garments,

when worn alone, would provide a battle dress for mild weather; when combined with pile fabric liners, they would offer adequate protection for severe weather. It was thought that the combination of wind-resistant, water-repellent, cotton outer shell and pile liner would permit the elimination of the overcoat, the mackinaw, and the olive drab field jacket.[29]

An experimental combat outfit was soon under test, but developmental work progressed slowly, since differences of opinion arose between the ETO and the OQMG as to what constituted the most desirable combat outfit. The Research and Development Branch supported the use of the layering principle. The new winter combat uniform[30] it developed consisted basically of a cotton outer shell with layers of insulation added inside as warmth was needed. The cotton outer shell consisted of olive drab field trousers and a field jacket, M-1943, both made of 9-ounce sateen, for which 9-ounce oxford cloth was later substituted in 1945 as an improved wind-resistant fabric.

In the process of standardizing a basic combat uniform, the object of the Research and Development Branch was to simplify the clothing issued to the enlisted man by eliminating many special types. Thus, the assembly of wool trousers and cotton outer shell which was standardized by the summer of 1943[31] replaced five other types heretofore issued to the soldiers. Kersey-lined trousers, winter-combat trousers, mountain trousers, wool ski trousers, and parachute-jumper trousers were all declared limited standard. Similarly, five different types of

---

[28] Pitkin, *Quartermaster Equipment for Special Forces,* pp. 26–27.

[29] Ltr, Brig Gen J. L. Frink, OQMG, to QM Bd, 21 Dec 42, sub: Battle Clo, Test QMB T–166.

[30] For a full discussion of the development of this uniform see Risch and Pitkin, *Clothing the Soldier of World War II,* pp. 47ff.

[31] QMCTC, min of mtg No. 15, 13 Jul 43.

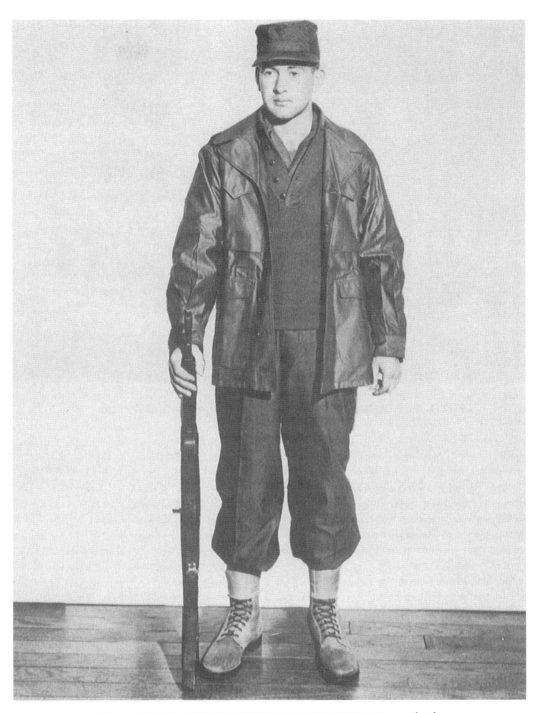

UTILIZATION OF THE LAYERING PRINCIPLE. *Note combat boots.*

FIELD JACKET M-1943. *Note buttoned collar (left) and adjustable tie cord (right).*

jackets[32] previously issued were replaced by the field jacket, M-1943, which was standardized on 12 August 1943.[33] This new jacket, developed along windbreaker lines, provided many new functional characteristics lacking in the previous field jacket. Its greatly improved closures at throat, cuff, and waist gave added protection against wind. Its four large cargo pockets provided substantial carrying capacity. Its full-bloused effect afforded freedom of movement, and its design was such that the jacket could be worn satisfactorily by itself or over successive layers of wool underwear, wool shirt, high-neck sweater, and pile jacket. This new combat uniform was tested not only in this country but also at Anzio by the 3d Division. Subsequently, when publicity on the new uniform was released, it was reported that the new battle dress

had "terrific effect on the morale of the men" who wore it on the Fifth Army beachhead in Italy.[34] As a result of the 3d Division's favorable report, the combat uniform was approved and requisitioned by the North African Theater (NATO).[35]

While the Research and Development Branch sponsored the layering principle in the new

[32] The arctic, winter combat, mountain, and parachute-jumper jackets were declared limited standard at the same time. Subsequently, the old style, olive drab field jacket was also made a limited standard article of issue.

[33] (1) QMCTC, min of mtg No. 15, 13 Jul 43. (2) Ltr, OQMG to Hq ASF, 29 Jul 43, no sub, and 2d ind, Hq ASF to TQMG, 12 Aug 43.

[34] *The New York Times,* May 6, 1944.

[35] Memo, Col Doriot, OQMG, for Lt Col James Stack, Opns Div, WDGS, 9 Oct 44, sub: New Combat Uniform.

COMBAT UNIFORM WITH HOOD

combat uniform it was developing, Headquarters, ETO, advocated a uniform similar to the British battle dress. They indorsed a short wool jacket as the outer garment of the combat uniform. As early as 1942 the idea of what later evolved into the wool field jacket was conceived by Maj. Gen. Robert M. Littlejohn, Chief Quartermaster, ETO, under whose direction the design and development of the ETO jacket were perfected by Lt. Col. Robert L. Cohen. A considerable number of such jackets was locally procured, and, after extensive tests had been conducted among the field forces in England during the summer of 1943, specific recommendations were made to the War Department.[36] In the fall of 1943 further impetus was given to this project by a letter from General Eisenhower to General Marshall, which in turn was passed on to The Quartermaster General, suggesting that a wool jacket, along the lines of the British battle jacket but with a distinctive style, be considered.

The OQMG had been working on its combat uniform to replace the multiplicity of uniforms then plaguing distribution, and it did not view favorably the development of still another uniform. From the beginning therefore it sought to place the wool field jacket in the layering pattern that it had adopted. It was aware of developments in the ETO, and upon the basis of analysis of the British battle dress, it developed a series of model jackets which, beginning in September 1943, the office sent to the Chief Quartermaster of the ETO. These were eventually modified to produce one model that incorporated all desirable features. A model of the wool field jacket developed by the Research and Development Branch was shown to the Chief Quartermaster, ETO, and his staff on 16 February 1944. They regarded the jacket as inferior to the ETO-style jacket developed in England. Furthermore, they stated that it could not be produced in quantity in the ETO. Since issues had already been made of the ETO-style jacket,

the American type, it was argued, would only complicate matters by offering two contrasting styles of the same garment.

The OQMG and the ETO were moving toward agreement on design, but there were deep differences of opinion on the place of the wool jacket in the uniform system. The OQMG, guided by a physiological-climatological approach to the problem, embraced the application of the layering principle. It was convinced that the wool jacket, which could be worn for both combat and dress, should replace the coats of the enlisted man and the officer, at least in theaters of operations.[37] From the standpoint of warmth, the garment was regarded as adequate for wear in the temperate zone when combined with the field jacket, M–1943, wool shirt, and wool undergarments. On the other hand, it felt that the proposed ETO uniform without the M–1943 jacket was "sadly lacking in water repellent items" and would not be adequate for the wet-cold weather conditions that prevailed in France.[38]

The OQMG attempted to keep the theater informed on the new items being developed, but this could only be accomplished by letter, since the office had at first no success in obtaining approval for observers to visit the theater. Early in February 1944, however, Capt. William F. Pounder was sent to the ETO as a field observer to exhibit the new combat uniform de-

[36] (1) Ltr, Gen Littlejohn to Gen Somervell, CG ASF, 3 Mar 45, no sub, and incls, of which see Sec. V, sub: Jacket, Fld, Wool, Personal Papers of Gen Littlejohn. (2) Ltr, Maj Gen John C. H. Lee, CG SOS ETO, to CG ETOUSA, 14 Sep 43, no sub, enclosing pamphlet, ETO Jacket, Fld, Wool, OD. USFET AG 421 Uniforms. (3) For details of the ETO development, see I. G. Cheslaw and W. C. Chaikin, Quartermaster Operations in the War Against Germany, in preparation for this series.
[37] (1) Memo, Gen Gregory for Gen Somervell, 28 Jan 44, no sub. (2) Memo, Brig Gen H. Feldman, OQMG, for Hq ASF, 23 Mar 44, sub: Wool Fld Jacket. Both in 421.1.
[38] Ltr, Capt W. F. Pounder, Fld Observer, to Col Doriot, OQMG, 30 Jun 44, no sub.

veloped by the Research and Development Branch, but the theater was reluctant to have him demonstrate the items to supply officers. The Chief Quartermaster had at first been much interested in the field jacket, M–1943, and its use with the wool field jacket fitted into ETO plans, but only if it could be obtained in sufficient quantities to dress units uniformly. The small amount of depot stocks then available and the low production figures were disappointing.[39] Time and availability were the problems.

General Littlejohn made a personal visit to the United States in the spring of 1944 in an effort to expedite the approval of the final design and the initiation of production of the wool field jacket. On 18 April samples of the latest jackets were reviewed by representatives of the Chief Quartermaster, ETO, the ASF, and the Military Planning Division, OQMG. Insofar as developmental questions were concerned, a basic design was agreed upon with certain modifications in detail of design recommended for further investigation. On the other hand, decisions at this conference on availability and the supply of jackets apparently were not definitive and clear and became the crux of the later controversy on winter clothing.[40] Jackets embodying the conference modifications were submitted for final approval to Headquarters, ASF, and to the Quartermaster, ETO. The following month Headquarters, ASF, directed that the wool field jacket be presented to QMCTC for classification as to type, but such action was deferred in order to give the using arms and services time to consider their requirements for the garment. Not until 2 November 1944 was the wool field jacket classified as the standard item of issue and the wool serge coat reclassified as limited standard.[41]

This wool field jacket had been designed primarily as a field garment which could also be used for dress purposes. It was a component part of the combat uniform, but in extremely cold climates the pile liner was substituted for it. The wool field jacket was supposed to be so fitted that it could be worn over the wool undershirt, flannel shirt, and high-neck sweater, and under the field jacket, M–1943. The application of the layering principle, however, broke down in practice because men would not wear the wool field jacket in combat, preferring to save it for dress wear when they were returned to rest areas.

The existing lack of knowledge of the War Department uniform as a complete unit and the limited use made of the M–1943 assembly during the war prevented a thorough combat test of the assembly. It was not used in the ETO, where the wool field jacket was not issued in quantity during hostilities, although experimental quantities were issued to troops in the field. Only in Italy during the winter of 1944–45 was the M–1943 assembly used as planned. Even when the assembly was issued as a unit, troops tended to regard the wool field jacket as a dress item and they did not wear it in combat. The sweater and the field jacket, M–1943, alone were not sufficient to keep the men warm in severe weather. Information obtained at Camp Lee from men returning from the Mediterranean Theater revealed that they obtained the additional warmth made necessary by their refusal to wear the short wool jacket for both combat and dress either by wearing two sweaters or by cutting a blanket to fit and sewing it inside the jacket, M–1943.[42]

---

[39] Ltr, Pounder to Doriot, 29 Mar 44, no sub.

[40] For the supply aspects of this controversy, see Cheslaw and Chaikin, Quartermaster Operations in the War Against Germany.

[41] (1) Memo, Dir of Reqmts Div, ASF, for TQMG, 10 May 44, sub: Wool Fld Jacket, and 1st ind, Col Doriot to CG ASF, 31 May 44. (2) Min subcom mtg, QMCTC, 16 May 44, same sub. (3) Memo, Col Doriot, OQMG, for CG ASF, 5 Oct 44, same sub, and 2d ind, Col M. M. Irvine, Actg Dir of R&D Div, ASF, to TQMG, 2 Nov 44.

[42] (1) Asst for Product Analysis to Clothing Sec, R&D Br, OQMG, 22 May 45, sub: Observation Rpt Abstract. (2) Rpt of Investigating Committee, 16 May 45, sub: Investigation Supply of Clothing in ETO. At

These facts were confirmed by the findings of a representative of the Clothing Section of the Research and Development Branch, who visited the ETO in the summer of 1945. He, too, found that soldiers had a tendency to have the jacket fitted too small for combat use because they thought of it in terms of a dress item. The difficulties in fitting the jacket had developed because it was not understood to be a component part of the field uniform. Conditions were corrected by instructing personnel responsible for the issue of the jacket on its purpose, how it should be worn, and how it should be fitted in conjunction with the various layers of the combat unit to obtain the maximum flexibility and functional benefit from the item.[43]

Fundamentally the new combat uniform of 1944 was the same uniform that the OQMG, in conjunction with a board of officers from the AGF, had recommended in March of 1943. In lieu of the pile jacket liner the short wool jacket was substituted, although for extremely cold areas the pile liner was still utilized. As a result of repeated requests from field observers, one new item was added to the outfit in 1944, namely, a hood for the field jacket, M–1943. With the new combat uniform the American soldier wore a newly designed, olive drab, cotton field cap and new combat boots, designed with a wide cuff at the top and made of leather with the flesh side turned out. In cold, wet weather he wore the shoepac.

The final design of the combat uniform was accomplished only after prolonged developmental work by the Research and Development Branch on the individual garments comprising the outfit. Only after the difficult problem of the short wool jacket had been satisfactorily solved, both as to design and its place in the combination of garments composing the combat uniform, did Headquarters, ETO, indorse the latter.

The difference of opinion between the ETO and the OQMG regarding the combat uniform had serious effects on the supply of clothing in the ETO in the winter of 1944–45. The theater had planned to supply clothing and equipment in accordance with Table of Equipment 21, the new comprehensive table for clothing and individual equipment. As changes were made in this table theater plans were changed accordingly. Of the new clothing items scheduled to become available for general issue from production during 1944, the theater included in its plans the wool jacket and the high-neck sweater but not the field jacket, M-1943. The War Department and the OQMG in accordance with the layering principle had recommended that the latter be worn over a combination of other garments to replace the overcoat in the ETO. However, the theater decision, approved by SHAEF, rejected the field jacket, M-1943, in favor of the overcoat for general issue. It was reluctant to accept the field jacket, M-1943, on the supposition that acceptance of it would preclude the adoption of the short wool jacket.

The theater intended the wool field jacket to be the basic garment for all troops. Unfortunately, although a schedule of delivery that would meet its needs was promised, it proved impossible to develop the required production in time. Production was limited by the lack of pocket-creasing machines and by the style of tailoring which required manufacture by the men's clothing industry. Every effort was made to accelerate production, but shipments lagged appreciably behind the promised schedules.

---

the direction of the Commanding General, ASF, the Assistant Director of Matériel, Brig. Gen. Albert J. Browning, appointed this investigating committee, whose report indicated that "as of 28 February no issues had been made in ETO and theater stocks were 2,100,000" of wool field jackets. (3) The report contained no explanation of why these jackets had not been issued during the period covered by the report. Memo, Maj Gen C. F. Robinson, Dir of Control Div, ASF, for CG ASF, 21 Jun 45, sub: Investigation Supply of Clothing in ETO.

[43] T. F. White to Gen Doriot, OQMG, 4 Jul 45, sub: Rpt of Insp in ETO.

Until the wool field jacket became available the theater was promised continued shipments of the earlier olive drab field jacket which was limited standard but an authorized substitute for the field jacket, M-1943. This old style jacket, however, was out of production, and supply could only be made from remaining zone of interior stocks which were exhausted before the wool field jacket became available. As a consequence, the ETO then submitted requisitions for the field jacket, M-1943. Because of the theater's earlier decision not to requisition this jacket, a cut back had been made in the originally planned production which resulted in a short stock position in the zone of interior and an inability to meet requirements when the ETO submitted its requisitions in the fall of 1944. As a result, some soldiers had the wool field jacket without the field jacket, M-1943; others had the later jacket but not the wool field jacket to wear with it. In such cases the men were not properly dressed, and it was necessary to issue the overcoat for combat wear in Europe during the winter of 1944–45, although the overcoat had come to be regarded as a dress rather than a combat item. The differences in point of view and the results stemming from them account in part for the difficulties encountered by the ETO in supplying clothing in the winter of 1944–45.[44]

Summer Combat Clothing

While winter combat clothing was used during the greater part of the year in the ETO, herringbone twill suits, though originally developed as fatigue clothing,[45] became the accepted year-round combat clothing in the tropical Pacific areas. The development of herringbone twill clothing involved a multiplicity of problems, ranging from the use of camouflage patterns and the reversibility of garments through the addition to such clothing of protective features against gas; design and construction details; manufacturing difficulties; and the relative place of the one- and two-piece suits in the clothing program.

These problems culminated in a general review of the entire subject of the battle dress in the fall of 1942. As in the case of winter combat clothing, the initial tendency of the QMC had been toward the development of a wide variety of specialized types of one- and two-piece herringbone twill suits, such as working suits, protective suits, desert suits, and jungle suits. By September 1942, however, it was felt that, except for special forces operating in climatic extremes, it would be desirable to move in the direction of a single design.[46]

At the suggestion of the Philadelphia Depot the first step in the process of simplification was taken by eliminating special protective clothing to be used in the event of a gas attack. Instead, existing herringbone twill clothing was modified by the addition of protective flaps, such as flies and gussets at the sleeve and front openings of the one- and two-piece suits, which would assist in gas protection. These protective flaps, imposed by the Chemical Warfare Service, were disliked intensely by men serving in the jungles, but they were used on all herringbone twill clothing throughout the war.[47]

[44] (1) Rpt, Investigation: Sup of Clo to ETO, 16 May 45, unsigned. Personal Papers of General Littlejohn. This report is the result of an investigation of winter clothing supply in the ETO which General Somervell instructed General Browning to make, after receipt of a letter from General Littlejohn on 2 March 1945.

[45] For an account of the development of fatigue clothing see Risch and Pitkin, *Clothing the Soldier of World War II*, pp. 64–67.

[46] (1) QMCTC min of mtg No. 9, 15 Sep 42. (2) Insp Rpt, Lt N. J. Block to TQMG, 16 Sep 42, no sub.

[47] (1) Ltr, Col Vere Painter, PQMD, to TQMG, 21 May 42, sub: One-Piece Working Suits, and 1st ind, Maj Kennedy, OQMG, to CG PQMD, 17 June 42. (2) Characteristic of the comment from the field is the following extract: "As far as the cut is concerned these things are a waste of time and cloth; the buttoning of sleeves, around ankles, flap on front of

In the fall of 1942 the desirability of using camouflage patterns for all summer combat garments was another problem under consideration. The development of camouflage patterns and all problems relating to color were responsibilities of the Corps of Engineers, which advocated no less than three color combinations. Samples of clothing utilizing different camouflage patterns were shown to the QMCTC in the summer of 1942. It was suggested that clothing could be regular herringbone twill one- and two-piece suits of standard appearance on the exterior but with camouflage patterns printed on the inside. The possibility of reversing the garments would make them useful under varying conditions.

The use of camouflage in different colors and patterns would require several different suits, multiplying the problems of issue and handling. The Corps of Engineers insisted that its studies showed that camouflage clothing should be available to all military personnel abroad. The AGF, however, opposed this view although they agreed to the necessity for outfitting snipers in camouflage suits. These conflicting opinions were resolved by the end of 1942 when a directive from Headquarters, SOS, was received by the OQMG instructing that no further consideration be given to camouflaging regular issue garments. This directive followed action by the Corps of Engineers in October to approve the use of an olive drab No. 7 green shade as the best available all-purpose camouflage color for combat clothing.[48]

However, a camouflage pattern, in a green combination on one side and tan on the other, was applied to the jungle suit but not with notable success. Reports received from the Southwest Pacific Theater criticized this camouflage jungle suit as too visible when men were in motion. A camouflage pattern was considered satisfactory for snipers, but it was felt that moving troops did not require a special suit. Subsequently, Headquarters, AGF, reported that the special jungle uniform was considered unsuited for use in jungle areas, a fact verified by officers of the United States Marine Corps who had had battle experience in jungles. "The consensus of opinion is that the dark green No. 7 shade is desired because it provides the best blending color for jungle areas."[49] The War Department General Staff directed that, after stocks of camouflage cloth on hand had been utilized, the herringbone twill camouflage jungle suits were to be reclassified as limited standard. This was accomplished by 30 March 1944, and the recommendation of the QMCTC that no further shipments of these items be made to theaters of operations was approved.[50]

A problem in relation to herringbone twill clothing demanding immediate attention in the fall of 1942 was the necessity of simplifying design in order to obtain sufficient production of the garments. Such action would enable manufacturers of work clothing to handle the large quantities of one- and two-piece herringbone twill suits. It would bring into production of military items a class of industry then contributing little. At the same time it would re-

---

trousers, and the gusset front of blouse or coat. I presume these things are imposed by the Medicos, if so, all I can say is that the fellow who dreamed it was a brother to those who say Infantry will use hammocks, and mosquito nets, and cotton gloves in combat. If he's fool enough to believe such stuff he will wake up with a bayonet in him. The first thing the soldier does is to cut all those things out of which I've written and curse those who put them in." From rpt by Capt Harold Haney, Hq, 162d Infantry, 7 Oct 44, in memo, Asst for Product Analysis to Clo Sec, R&D Br, OQMG, 3 Nov 44, sub: Jungle Uniform.

[48] QMCTC, min of mtgs No. 6, 8 Jul 42; No. 13, 27 Oct 42; No. 18, 29 Dec 42.

[49] (1) 3d ind, Maj R. J. Delacroix, Hq AGF, to CG ASF, 22 Jan 44 on Ltr, Col Doriot to same, 4 Dec 43, sub: Jungle Uniform. (2) Rpt, 1st Lt Robert L. Woodbury, QM Observer in SWP Theater, 1 Feb–15 May 43.

[50] (1) 4th ind, Dir of Reqmts Div, ASF, to TQMG, 28 Jan 44, on Ltr, Col Doriot to CG ASF, 4 Dec 43, sub: Jungle Uniform. (2) 9th ind, same to TQMG, 30 Mar 44, on same ltr. (3) QMCTC, min of mtg No. 3, 29 Feb 44.

lease other producers for the manufacture of jungle suits and winter combat outfits.

Such simplification of design was initially accomplished, for example, through the elimination of a decorative pleat in the jacket pocket of the two-piece suit and the substitution of a simple hemmed style for the shirt-type cuff of the sleeve. In February 1943, in view of the heavy procurement of herringbone twill clothing planned for the months ahead, a conference was held at Philadelphia between depot and OQMG representatives to discuss changes in manufacturing operations which would facilitate procurement. The design of herringbone twill clothing was thereupon further simplified, as, for example, by the substitution of a plain, one-piece back for the bi-swing back heretofore used in making the one-piece suit. By simplifying manufacturing operations as well as offering optional specifications, the OQMG hoped to increase production of herringbone twill garments.[51]

A problem of design that persisted throughout the war years and seemingly defied solution was the incorporation of a drop seat in the design of the one-piece herringbone twill suit. Originally requested by the Desert Warfare Board in the summer of 1942 and subsequently discarded as efforts to produce special clothing for desert troops were abandoned, the request was renewed by the AGF in May 1943.[52] At first these requests were in conflict with the efforts being made to promote greater production of herringbone twill clothing by simplifying manufacturing operations. It was the general opinion that a one-piece suit with a drop seat would cause insurmountable difficulties from a procurement standpoint. When renewed efforts at redesigning the garment were made between 1943 and 1945, it was found impossible to develop a satisfactory type of drop seat that would meet the requirements of protection against chemical warfare. Finally in the spring of 1945 the AGF decided to eliminate this requirement

from the military characteristics demanded in the design of a one-piece working suit.[53]

Jungle Combat Clothing

While the general trend in the OQMG was toward the development of one uniform suitable for summer combat wear by all troops, an exception was made for troops operating in the jungle. Although the OQMG had received no official request from any source, it had been at work for some time on the development of jungle equipment when suddenly, toward the end of July 1942, General MacArthur urgently requested 150,000 sets of special jungle equipment including a jungle uniform.[54] The AGF formally sanctioned the development of a jungle uniform having certain military characteristics on 28 July 1942. It was to be a one-piece herringbone twill suit with tight-fitting cuffs at wrist and internal adjustable suspenders to take the weight of clothing and equipment from the shoulders and collar of the garment, thus improving ventilation and preventing insect bites through clothing. The suit was to have two large cargo pockets on the sides at the hips and two medium-sized cargo pockets on the waist. The fabric was to be insect-proof and made up in camouflage pattern. The OQMG took swift action. Samples were prepared by the Philadelphia Depot and a specification was drafted.

[51] (1) See Spec PQMD 42A, 30 Oct 42, sub: Cotton HBT Trousers, and 45B, 2 Nov 42, sub: HBT Jackets. (2) Ltr, Col Doriot, OQMG, to CO PQMD, 27 Feb 43, sub: Simplification of Special One-Piece, HBT Suits and Jackets. (3) Ltr, Lt Col F. M. Steadman, PQMD, to TQMG, 1 Mar 43, same sub. All in 400.1141.

[52] (1) Ltr, Capt R. J. Delacroix, AGF, to CG ASF, 2 May 43, sub: Redesign of One-Piece Work Suit, and 1st ind, Hq ASF, to TQMG, 4 May 43. (2) See Risch and Pitkin, Clothing the Soldier of World War II, pp. 70ff.

[53] Ltr, Lt Col R. A. Meredith, AGF, to CG ASF, 23 Mar 45, sub: One-Piece Working Suits with Drop Seat, and 1st ind, Col P. R. Faymonville, Dir of R&D Div, ASF, to TQMG, 9 Apr 45.

[54] For a full discussion of the early development of jungle equipment see Pitkin, Quartermaster Equipment for Special Forces, pp. 198ff.

Within a month the jungle suit had been stand-ardized.[55]

Even as the one-piece jungle suit was being developed and procured, a second school of thought stressed the advantages of a two-piece jungle suit. Although the one-piece suit had been useful in Panama where it was first tested, in the jungles of New Guinea it proved a fail-ure. Here the "frog-skin" suit was reported as "too heavy, too hot, and too uncomfortable."[56] When wet, herringbone twill increased in weight substantially, adding to the load carried by an individual soldier under humid, tropical conditions. The most serious criticism was the lack of a drop seat in the suit. The fact that men had practically to disrobe to perform normal functions, thereby exposing themselves to the bites of any and all insects, defeated the purpose for which the uniform had been designed, namely, to give the maximum protection against the forays of insects carrying such dis-eases as malaria, dengue fever, and scrub typhus. On the basis of the arguments advanced, the advocates of the two-piece uniform were suc-cessful in substituting that outfit for the one-piece jungle suit in the spring of 1943.[57]

The two-piece jungle suits proved more pop-ular than the one-piece suits, but the OQMG felt that there was room for improvement. Crit-icism of the issue of herringbone twill garments for jungle use continued. Inasmuch as little clothing or textile design of a radical nature had been evolved to provide the necessary pro-tection against insects, terrain, and other en-vironmental hazards encountered in jungle war-fare, the Military Planning Division initiated a comprehensive project in requirements for jun-gle clothing in August 1943. This included field study at the Everglades in Florida, tests for physiological reactions in hot, humid atmos-phere conducted at Indiana University and wear tests at Camp Lee.

The Textile Section sought to perfect a jun-gle cloth which would be thin, dense, and of the lowest possible water-holding capacity. Poplin and Byrd cloth were found to be cooler, to weigh less when dry, to absorb less weight of water, and therefore to dry more quickly than any of the other fabrics tested. As tightly woven fabrics, they also gave better protection against mosquito bites. The Committee on Jungle Clothing recommended the adoption of pop-lin.[58]

At the same time the Clothing Section of the Research and Development Branch worked to perfect the most desirable design for a jungle uniform. Many modified styles of the basic two-piece suit were developed in experimental models. Jungle combat uniforms made in the new design and from the new fabrics were tested during the period from 1 July to 1 No-vember 1944 at Bougainville, and by the 41st Infantry Division during September and Octo-ber 1944 on Biak Island. In addition, they were tested in the Central Pacific Area and the China-Burma-India Theater. During the sum-mer of 1944 the Quartermaster Board also un-dertook a comprehensive field test of tropical clothing, equipment, and rations at Camp Indian Bay, Fla.[59]

A lightweight tropical combat uniform had been desired by all the theaters in which it was tried experimentally. The War Department General Staff had also expressed a desire for this

[55] [4th ind], Col W. A. Wood, Jr., Dir of Reqmts Div, SOS, to TQMG, 31 Aug 42. (An indorsement cited in brackets refers to a basic document which can-not be located.)

[56] Rpt, Lt Woodbury, QM Observer, SWP Theater, 1 Feb–15 May 43.

[57] (1) Ltr, Subcom, QMCTC, to QMCTC, 30 Apr 43, sub: Two-Piece Jungle Suit. (2) QMCTC, min of mtg No. 9, 4 May 43. (3) [2d ind], Hq ASF, to TQMG, 8 Jun 43.

[58] (1) Action min of 1st mtg on Jungle Clo, 5 Aug 43. (2) R&D Br, Status Rpt, 31 Aug 43, p. 21. (3) Com on Jungle Clo, min of mtg, 13 Oct 43.

[59] For comment on Camp Indian Bay tests see (1) Dir of QM Bd to TQMG, Rpt on QM Bd, Camp Lee, Va., 1 Feb 42 to 30 Jun 44, pp. 80ff; (2) *Ibid.*, 1 Jul 44–30 Jun 45, pp. 43ff.

uniform. Action to initiate its manufacture, however, was delayed because of the shortage of fabrics at that time. Not until June 1945 did the OQMG near its production goals. Only then was it possible to divert 5-ounce poplin to the manufacture of jungle uniforms. So great had been the demand for lightweight, wind-resistant fabrics that a choice had had to be made between the manufacture of winter combat uniforms to protect men from the cold and rain and lightweight jungle uniforms to ease the burden of the heat. On 11 July 1945 standardization of the new jungle uniform was approved by Headquarters, ASF, [60] but the war ended before the new uniform could be issued to troops in the field.

Combat Headgear

One of the important contributions to the comfort and safety of the soldier was the development of the helmet assembly.[61] In World War I the American doughboy had worn the M–1917 helmet which was neither comfortable nor an adequate protection from shrapnel flung upward from the ground. The steel helmet and liner of World War II was a radical departure from the "tin hat" of the first war. Consisting of an outer, pot-shaped, steel body and a snugly inserted plastic shell which contained a suspension to fit the whole assembly comfortably to the wearer's head, the helmet and liner were always worn in combat, except in the jungle where the liner alone was sometimes used for combat fighting.

In the forward areas of all theaters the liner was commonly worn in place of the garrison cap. It was suitable for wear both in the tropics and, with the addition of a specially designed knit cap, in the Arctic. Since the steel helmet itself was without head harness, it could be used as a wash basin or bucket and in many other ways. Made in one size to fit the conformity of the steel helmet, the liner carried an adjustable headband inside the suspension which, with a neckband (issued in three sizes), made possible a close fit to the head. Together, helmet and liner weighed approximately 3 pounds, and the liner alone weighed about 10 ounces.

While the Ordnance Department was responsible for the development of the combat helmet, the liner for it was developed as a joint product of private industry, the Ordnance Department, and the QMC. The helmet and liner idea had been originally suggested as early as 1932. The first tangible version, however, was derived in large part from a plastic football helmet and suspension invented and patented by John T. Riddell, a Chicago manufacturer of football supplies. The Infantry Board in early 1941 was the first to consider the design of the Riddell football helmet likely for adaptation in developing a substitute for the cumbersome and unsafe steel helmet of World War I. The Ordnance Department then took a hand in the development of sample liners, utilizing the football helmet suspension, but before the year was over the QMC had contributed a great deal of experimentation, and the liner, originally developed as a fiber hat worn under a steel shell, had been made a Quartermaster item.

Almost from the first, however, the fiber liner was considered unsatisfactory. From the summer of 1941 the Standardization Branch of the OQMG conducted experiments on liners, using various plastics, and enlisting the co-operation of several industrial firms. In 1942 a plastic shell was substituted for the original fiber liner, and proved to be a stronger, longer-wearing item.

---

[60] (1) [1st ind], Col M. M. Irvine, Actg Dir of R&D Div, ASF, to TQMG, 11 Jul 45, no sub. (2) For a fuller discussion of the development of the jungle uniform see Risch and Pitkin, *Clothing the Soldier of World War II*, pp. 72–77.

[61] This account is based on the more detailed study prepared by the depot historian at the Chicago Quartermaster Depot: Marion Massen, The History of the Helmet Liner (CQMD Historical Studies 5, 1944).

The first plastic liners were unsatisfactory in many ways, and the Research and Development Branch, successor to the Standardization Branch, sought to improve them. The helmet liner was anything but static in design after the first experimental stages had passed. Industry and the Research and Development Branch in co-operation with the Chicago Quartermaster Depot, the procuring agency for the item, worked long and hard to examine and perfect any suggested changes that would make the liner a more comfortable headpiece. The adjustable headband, which eliminated burdensome tariff sizes, was worked out; hardware was redesigned so as to be as comfortable as possible and eliminate many pressure points on the wearer's head; a chin strap which could be removed for the delousing operation was developed; and a textured paint coating, less inclined to chip and less reflective, was also developed.

The proposed use of the helmet assembly had led the OQMG in 1941 to undertake a comprehensive survey of all headgear for purposes of simplification. When the helmet assembly was adopted, it was necessary to develop a woolen liner to provide warmth in winter. The Chief of Infantry advocated the use of a skullcap, but the QMC, because of manufacturing difficulties limiting production, favored a knitted cap, which was adopted as a standard item of issue on 26 February 1942.[62]

The Chief of Infantry remained unfavorably disposed toward the use of the knitted cap, and in October 1942 a project was initiated to develop an all-purpose field cap. Using a ski cap as the point of departure, the OQMG continued developmental work until there was devised early in 1943 a windproof, water-repellent poplin cap with a stiffened sun visor, which gave protection to the eyes without protruding beyond the helmet liner. This field cap, M–1943, was designed to be worn with the field jacket, M–1943. It could also be worn under the hood of that jacket and with the steel helmet and

liner. At the same time a pile cap of improved military characteristics was designed for wear in extreme cold. The Research and Development Branch decided that these two items of headgear met all the requirements for temperate, cold, and arctic climates, and they were subsequently classified as standard, thereby eliminating a multiplicity of field caps previously used.[63]

Combat Footgear

Adequate footwear is essential in war, for it may determine in no small measure the outcome of a battle. The fact that World War II was fought in many climates and terrains complicated the QMC's problem of supplying adequate footwear. That problem was also made more difficult as a result of the fortunes of war which cut off many sources of raw materials.

The trend of development in both world wars was similar. The Army was caught unprepared for the emergency in both instances. In World War I the first issue of footwear was the peacetime shoe recommended for adoption by the Munson Board in 1912. A sturdier marching shoe appeared by May 1917, but it was not until the spring of 1918 that a heavier shoe with more waterproof construction was developed to suit the demands of trench warfare. The so-called "Pershing" boot, made of leather with flesh side out and a hobnailed sole, was admirably designed to meet the demands of combat service for that period.[64]

As in the case of the World War I combat uniform, so the combat shoe underwent modification after the war to emerge as a more suit-

---

[62] (1) QMCTC, min of mtg No. 7, 16 Jun 41. (2) Memo, Gen Corbin, OQMG, to ACofS G–4, 11 Feb 42, sub: Headgear for Wear Under Helmet Liner. (3) 2d ind, TAG to TQMG, 26 Feb 42, on same. Last two in 400.112.

[63] QMCTC, min of mtg No. 15, 13 Jul 43.

[64] Helen R. Brooks, Development of the Modern Service Shoe (BQMD Historical Monograph 1, July 1945), pp. 10–11.

able garrison shoe. It was developed for a small peacetime army with a regard for appearance and comfort. Made with grain side out, polished upper leather, full leather outsoles and whole leather heels, this Type I service shoe was obviously a product of an economy of surplus. Some official studies of combat-type footgear were conducted during the twenty years following World War I, but the specification for service shoes remained substantially unchanged at the beginning of the period of emergency in 1939. Until September 1941 all service shoes procured were Type I.

Instead of profiting by the lessons of World War I, the QMC entered World War II pursuing the same course of action with regard to shoes that it had taken in 1917. Starting with a peacetime shoe, it developed one of greater durability until finally a shoe of the type of the Pershing boot was again specified. Apparently no thought was given to making use of this specification to begin with, although it had proved very satisfactory during the closing months of World War I.

As the emergency period began, although the need for a sturdy combat shoe was obvious, Quartermaster personnel showed a lack of imagination in anticipating requirements. Thinking was still in terms of a peacetime army. The major question of discussion during 1939 was the possible replacement of the high-top garrison shoe with a low quarter shoe in the interest of appearance, comfort, economy, and morale.[65] With the federalization of the National Guard and the establishment of the Selective Service System in the fall of 1940, the military program began to assume wartime proportions. The year before our entry into the war was marked by considerable developmental work.

During the small-scale maneuvers characteristic of the early training period, the light service shoe, Type I, issued to the soldiers worked out satisfactorily, but complaints were

numerous that the outsole wore through in the short period of two to three weeks. Government technicians, in an effort to develop more durable soles, turned their attention to the use of composition soles. Experiments resulted in a revised service shoe, Type II, which utilized a rubber tap and heel.[66] But just as the Army succeeded in producing a sole that would wear, it was forced, because of the serious rubber shortage, to keep reducing the new rubber content of these taps until the point was reached when no new rubber was used and taps were made entirely of reclaimed rubber.

As materials shortages increased, the motivating factor behind all initial wartime developmental activities in the field of footgear became conservation of resources. During 1942 there was a considerable amount of experimental work toward such conservation, although the Boston Depot insisted that standards of current specifications ought to be maintained. Lighter insoles, strip gemming, cork filler material, reclaimed rubber taps, wood-core heels, and zinc-coated steel reinforcing nails were introduced into the manufacture of service shoes to conserve leather, duck, rubber, and brass. The service shoe was actually being weakened when the sturdiest possible footgear was needed.

About mid-1942 the Research and Development Branch, OQMG, became interested in a boot which would supplant the shoe and legging combination in use since the beginning of the war but thoroughly disliked by the troops. Laces broke, leggings wore out quickly and were difficult to put on and take off. Observers' reports subsequently indicated that rather than go

[65] (1) Ltr, Col C. A. Hunt, 5th Infantry, to CG 1st CA, 2 Feb 39, sub: Garrison Shoes. (2) Ltr, Subcom, QMCTC, to QMCTC, 20 Sep 39, sub: Low Quarter Shoes. Both in 421.5.

[66] (1) Ltr, Col Littlejohn, OQMG, to CO BQMD, 16 May 41, sub: Sv Shoes. (2) Ltr, Gen Corbin, OQMG, to TAG, 12 Apr 41, sub: Composition Soles for Sv Shoes, and 1st ind, TAG to TQMG, 16 Apr 41. Both in 421.5. (3) QMC Spec 9–6F, 19 Nov 41, sub: Sv Shoes, Type I and II.

through the tedious procedure of removing their shoes, soldiers occasionally went for long periods without taking them off, thus opening the way to foot ailments.[67]

Since the combat boot eventually produced was a product of complicated developments, it is difficult to trace any particular shoe as its predecessor. Initially the Desert Training Center had stimulated interest in a combat boot by its request for a special boot suitable for desert troops. The scope of the project was widened to develop a combat boot suitable for all troops. A thorough examination of all the service shoes in use at the time revealed that the type of construction sought was most closely approximated in the Canadian combat boot, a heavy-duty shoe with a cuff and strap at the top. The OQMG requested the Boston Depot to produce samples of boots of this type.

Development of the combat boot was stimulated by the findings of the Chief of Staff, General Marshall, after his return early in 1943 from an inspection tour of the combat zone in North Africa. He reported in conference on 1 February 1943 that the service shoes were unfit for field use and that he would request the development of a "suitable shoe along the lines of the field shoe issued in France during the last war." The shoe in use in the combat zone was "too light, and too much on the order of the garrison shoe for field service." [68]

Samples of improved shoes had been developed earlier by the OQMG, and these were submitted to the Chief of Staff on 5 February. A decision was reached to change production as soon as possible from the Type II service shoe to a new Type III shoe. The latter was to be made with flesh-out upper leather and a full rubber sole and heel, which, with the scarcity of rubber, was later changed to reclaimed and then to synthetic rubber. The use of flesh-out Army retan had been decided upon because it was more durable, it absorbed dubbing more readily, thereby increasing the qualities of flexi-

bility and waterproofing, and it was more comfortable in the breaking-in stage than grain-out leather.

At the same time it was also decided to produce a new combat boot in limited quantities for test purposes. The boot was the same as the shoe, plus a cuff and buckle top which gave it a 10-inch height as compared to the 6 inches for the Type III shoe. The boot was intended to eliminate the shoe and legging combination worn by infantrymen and the special boot worn by parachute troops.

Deliveries of the Type III shoe began April 1943. By July, experimentation on the combat boot as a replacement for Type III shoes was fairly well advanced. Field test reports were favorable and on 16 November 1943 the QMCTC approved a committee report calling for standardization of the combat boot. A few days later this recommendation was concurred in by the ASF.[69] By January 1944 the shoe industry began production of the combat boot for regular issue.

Although the combat boot was well received in most theaters, there was some complaint about it in the ETO in the winter of 1944–45. In the fall of 1944 combat troops in that theater were confronted with mud, slush, and cold—elements against which the new service shoes offered only relative protection—and trench foot appeared.

Trench foot had first showed itself as a serious problem in the summer of 1943 during the attack on Attu, in the Aleutians. Of the total 2,900 casualties during the Attu operation, 1,200 were due to exposure, resulting chiefly in

[67] Rpt, Capt Pounder, QM Observer, Rpt of QM Opns in NATO, 5 Mar–2 Jun 43.
[68] Memo, Gen Corbin, OQMG, for CG SOS, 18 Feb 43, sub: Unsuitability of Present Issue.Shoe in T/O, 421.3.
[69] (1) QMCTC, min of mtg No. 25, 16 Nov 43. (2) 3d ind, Hq ASF, to OQMG, 22 Nov 43, on ltr, QMCTC to TQMG, 19 Nov 43, sub: Combat Sv Boot, Composition Sole, 400.1141.

FOOTWEAR DEVELOPED BY THE QUARTERMASTER CORPS. *Type I service shoe (above) and field combat boot (below).*

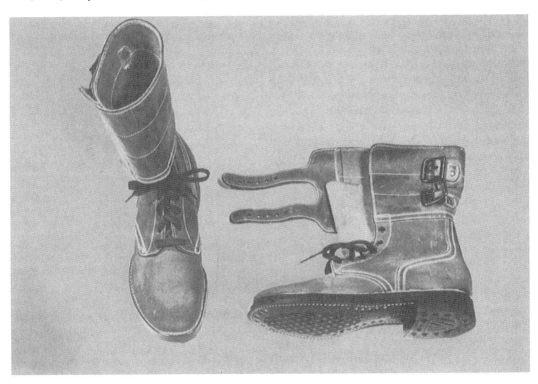

trench foot. About 40 percent of the total casualties, therefore, were not directly attributable to enemy action. In November of the same year trench foot reappeared during the first winter campaign in Italy, accounting for 20 percent of the casualties at its peak incidence. The Quartermaster of the Fifth Army took steps to prevent a recurrence of such an outbreak the following winter by issuing shoepacs and wool ski socks to combat troops and by instituting an educational campaign in foot care. At the same time the OQMG, through its observers in the field, closely followed the action taken and made efforts to explain the fit and use of shoepacs and other new items of winter clothing. As a result the incidence of trench foot declined sharply in Italy, only to rise to epidemic proportions in the ETO during the winter of 1944–45.[70]

The OQMG had long recognized the need of providing specialized footgear for operations in cold, wet climates. The shoepac, which was a well-known commercial item with a moccasin-type rubber foot and a leather top, was considered best for such conditions. When the Attu task force was getting ready to depart, in May 1943, Quartermaster cold-climate specialists had recommended shoepacs to the commanding general. Instead of the shoepac he had chosen a 12-inch leather Blucher boot, which was perhaps a more comfortable item but not so well insulated nor so efficient as the rubber-footed shoepac would have been in the slush of Attu. The director of the Military Planning Division later attributed the foot casualties suffered on this expedition largely to the failure to adopt the recommendation of his representatives.[71]

Similarly, in reviewing the proposed ETO winter combat outfit, which included the use of combat boots or service shoes and overshoes, Captain Pounder recommended the use of shoepacs. The chief of the Supply Division in the Office of the Chief Quartermaster, ETO, agreed that shoepacs were more waterproof than shoes

or boots, but he felt that the soft rubber sole wore out quickly and did not provide proper support or protection for the soldier's feet.[72] Hence he rejected the recommendation. Experience with the wet, muddy conditions in France soon forecast the need for shoepacs and the ETO submitted its first requisition for 446,000 on 15 August 1944.[73]

It was understood perfectly in the OQMG that the Type III service shoe and combat boot were not, by themselves, sufficient for foot protection in conditions like those encountered in Europe during the last winter of the war. Since leather is a permeable material, no leather boot is waterproof, no matter how carefully designed. The major leaking occurred at the seams and could not be eliminated by the use of dubbing, which furthermore inhibited rapid drying. Quartermaster specialists recommended either the addition of rubber overshoes, or the substitution of shoepacs in wet-cold conditions. With waterproof footgear, frequent changes of socks, and proper training and discipline, trench foot can be kept to a minimum, though its elimination in a winter campaign is probably impossible. Perhaps the most important reason for the prevalence of trench foot in the ETO during the winter of 1944–45 was the prolonged

---

[70] (1) 1st Lt Robert D. Orr, QM Observer, Rpt on Attu Opns, 11 May–16 Jun 43. (2) SGO to ASF, Monthly Rpt, 30 Jun 44, Sec. 7, sub: Health, p. 9. During January and February 1944 there were 2,800 hospital admissions for trench foot in the Fifth Army in comparison to 12,900 admissions for battle wounds. (3) Ltr, Maj Robert H. Bates, QM Observer with Fifth Army, to Gen Doriot, 24 May 45, sub: Observers' Bulletins, 319.25. (4) Memo, Maj Gen Norman T. Kirk, SG, for CofS, 9 Dec 44, sub: Trench Foot in ETO.

[71] Ltr, Col Doriot, OQMG, to CG, ASF, 24 Jul 44, sub: Footwear for Cool and Cold Wet Climates.

[72] (1) Memo, Col A. M. Brumbaugh, for Chief QM ETO, 2 Jul 44, sub: Comments on Capt Pounder's Rpt, 30 Jun 44. (2) See also Ltr, Capt Pounder to Col Doriot, OQMG, 13 Mar 44, no sub.

[73] Rad, Hq Com Zone to AGWAR for Somervell, 15 Aug 44, sub: Winter Clo for Special Conditions.

SHOEPACS AND WOOL SKI SOCKS *are tried on by a foot soldier of the 4th Infantry Division in the ETO, 25 January 1945.*

period of front-line service required of combat divisions. Peak efficiency, including foot care, cannot be maintained under such conditions. Lateness of supply, aggravated by a limited amount of shipping and the low priority allotted clothing and footwear items, was also a factor. By midwinter a sufficient distribution of overshoes was made to give a fairly adequate supply to combat troops, though a full distribution of large sizes was not effected until the middle of March. Shoepacs were issued to the Seventh Army early enough to be used effectively during the winter, but the First, Ninth, and Third Armies did not receive an initial issue of shoepacs until the latter part of January.

The arctic overshoe used over the combat boot or the Type III shoe was offered as a combination that would keep the feet dry. But the weight of such a combination proved a hindrance to fast movement and often caused the soldier to discard the overshoes in combat. Moreover, the overshoes first issued in quantity had been made during the worst of the rubber shortage and were provided with cloth tops which leaked badly and tore easily. This type was discontinued in favor of the all-rubber overshoe as soon as sufficient rubber was made available.

Lightness and increased insulation made the shoepac a more satisfactory item for winter wear than the boot and overshoe combination. While the shoepac had formed a part of the Alaska clothing list before the war, little attention had been paid to it as a basic military item until 1941. At that time cold-climate men in the OQMG undertook its improvement and a number of changes were made in the specification. One of its weaknesses was a tendency to pull apart at the point where the rubber foot was stitched to the leather upper. Improved shoepacs were procured only when the U. S. Rubber Co. made available to other firms its patented construction method which provided a more effective type of junction.[74]

During the next two years the shoepac underwent many modifications designed to improve its military characteristics and to meet the criticisms of the men who wore it. Early procurements had been made with a variety of commercial lasts. In 1943, the Boston Depot designed a uniform last which, in turn, necessitated other changes in the pattern. An improved heel, which gave better support to the instep, was also provided. When final details were worked out, production was converted to the new model in August 1944.[75] The shoepac was not standardized, however, until 1945.

Although a greatly improved shoepac had been developed, it could not be produced in large enough quantities to meet the increased requisitions made by the ETO in December 1944. The M-1944 shoepac, incorporating an arch support and raised heel, and made in three widths, was the most adequate item of wet- and cold-weather footgear available, but most of the shoepacs issued even in the last winter of the war did not contain these improvements. Complaints which were justified only against the earlier models were registered about shoepacs in general. Shoepacs, in any case, required time for the soldier to become accustomed to them.[76] In the winter of 1944–45 there was not always time.

If fighting in cold, wet areas posed problems in the development of adequate footgear to the technicians of the Research and Development

---

[74] Ltr, Brig Gen James R. Alfonte, OQMG, to CO BQMD, 1 Jul 42, sub: Shoepac, 400.1141.

[75] (1) Lt Col D. B. Dill, Special Forces Sec, to Col Doriot, Mil Plng Div, OQMG, 12 Jul 43, sub: Shoepacs. (2) QMC Spec BQD 570, 19 Jul 44, sub: Shoepac, 12-inch, M-1944. (3) Ltr, Col C. P. Bellican, OQMG, to CG ASF, 13 Nov 45, sub: Shoepac, 12-inch, M-1944 and 1st ind, Hq ASF to TQMG, 30 Nov 45. All in 421.3.

[76] Rpt, Maj Paul A. Siple, QMC Tech Observer, G-4, 12 Apr 45, sub: Rpt on Observations and Conclusions Concerning the Adequacy of Winter Clothing in ETO Winter 1944–45, incl in Ltr, Maj Gen T. B. Larkin, DCofS, ETO, to CofS, USA, 19 May 45. Personal papers of Gen Littlejohn.

Branch, OQMG, and of the Boston Depot, combat in jungle areas presented other difficulties. Shortly after Pearl Harbor four jungle platoons were activated and equipped for the purpose of patrolling jungle areas for considerable distances on each side of the Canal Zone. In the early days of experimental development of jungle gear in Panama under the direction of Capt. Cresson H. Kearny, it had been revealed that leather service shoes deteriorated very rapidly under conditions of heat, moisture, and parasitic growth existing in the jungle. The jungle forces had been experimenting with a boot, developed by the U. S. Rubber Co., which gave four to five times the wear obtained from leather service shoes.

The OQMG took up the development of the jungle boot and under pressure of a request from General MacArthur in July 1942 quickly completed the project. The jungle boot was standardized on 31 August 1942. The Boston Depot prepared a specification, and arrangements were immediately made for the procurement of 200,000 pairs. This procurement at once ran into difficulties. Production of the jungle boot involved the rehabilitation of the canvas footwear industry, which had been virtually shut down for several months by a WPB order forbidding the use of either crude or reclaimed rubber for canvas footwear. The trained operators of this industry had scattered to other fields. These had to be relocated or new operators trained.[77]

Production difficulties and other delays prevented extensive use of the jungle boot as well as other new items of jungle equipment in the Guadalcanal fighting and in the New Guinea campaign which began outside Port Moresby in October and closed at Buna in February 1943. These operations were carried on largely with the older standard equipment supplemented by items improvised locally. The new jungle equipment was arriving toward the close of this phase of the fighting and was being issued to troops.

The items, including the boot, attracted the favorable attention of quartermasters on the ground, and it was expected that they would have an effect on later operations.

The jungle boot was a sneaker-type shoe made with a corrugated rubber sole, to give better footing on slippery and grassy slopes, and a permeable duck top, some eleven and a half inches in height, which allowed air to reach the feet and legs, permitting ventilation and cooling and preventing tropical rashes. Thus the legging could be discarded. The boot had a removable fabric insole[78] to keep the foot from contact with the rubber sole and insulate it against ground heat. It had the advantage of being porous, light, and easily cleaned and dried.

Its disadvantages made the jungle boot unsuccessful in the field. It afforded too little support, resulting in many cases of "aching arches" and gave too little protection to the foot. Men complained that the canvas top chafed the lower leg and in the operations on Leyte "it was not an uncommon sight to see the tops folded down about half way to the sole and hanging loose." Sometimes the tops were cut off above the ankles.[79] Since the jungle boot was made over the manufacturers' own lasts and not over

---

[77] Insp rpt, A. T. Daignault to TQMG, 3 Aug 42, no sub.

[78] Since fabric insoles proved unsatisfactory, the OQMG experimented with other materials. A new plastic substance called "Saran" was finally used by Lt. Robert L. Woodbury and Earl P. Hanson to produce an insole that solved the problem. Saran insoles were a significant development, and after World War II they were put to civilian uses. It appears likely that they will be used in arctic footwear also. (1) E. P. Hanson to Col B. Robinson, OQMG, 14 Oct 42, sub: Patents on Shoe Ventilation. (2) Special Forces Sec to Patent Sec, Legal Div, OQMG, 7 Nov 42, sub: Insoles.

[79] (1) Ltr, Lt Col Glenn J. Jacoby to CG USAFPOA, 14 Dec 44, sub: QM Observer's Rpt 319.25 to PAC. (2) See also Brig Gen George E. Hartman, Hq USAFCPA, to Col Doriot, 4 Dec 44, no sub. General Hartman encloses the report of an observer who was attached to the XXIV Corps during the Leyte operations.

the Army Munson last, there was also considerable complaint about the fit.

A number of specification changes were made without producing a thoroughly adequate or satisfactory jungle boot, and developmental work was resumed. The OQMG instructed the Boston Depot to produce models incorporating various ideas with reference to materials and patterns. The object was still to develop a lightweight boot which would dry out quickly, even when soaked through by heavy tropical rains, and which would afford adequate traction in the sole. At the same time it was to be made of materials which had been subjected to some form of special treatment for preventing mildew.

In the course of experimentation and testing of models, spun nylon was selected as the most satisfactory fabric for use in the new boot. The most difficult problem involved development of a mold for the Bramani rubber sole with lugs placed in such a position as to permit stitching of the sole to the welt.[80] By February 1945 a satisfactory boot had been designed and was ready for large-scale procurement. The new tropical combat boot specification called for a 10½-inch boot of welt construction, made in a plain-toe blucher pattern without a toe cap. The top was made of spun nylon duck fastened by two straps and buckles. The boot had a leather mid sole, a full-length, cleated, rubber outer sole, and a molded, cleated rubber heel. A ventilating-type insole was to be worn with the boot.

When, after testing, favorable reports on the efficiency of the tropical combat boot had been received from the AGF, the QMCTC initiated standardization in November 1944. It was planned to substitute the tropical combat boot for the jungle boot, although the latter was to be issued until the supply was exhausted. Because of the uncertainty of requirements, since the war in the Pacific was moving northward out of the jungles, production of the tropical combat boot was not started until the summer of 1945. The end of the war brought the termination of all contracts.

Clothing for Women in the Army

The Corps' concern with the problems involved in developing and issuing clothing to women in the armed service dates from the spring of 1942, when a bill to establish a Women's Army Auxiliary Corps (WAAC)[81] was under consideration by Congress. Some uniforms had been furnished to members of the Army Nurse Corps (ANC) in the period between World War I and World War II, but Quartermaster personnel thus far had been confronted with no special problems in providing clothing for women in the Army. They had little or no past experience upon which to draw. No body of information existed in reference to design, pattern, sizing, specifications, or procurement of women's clothing such as that which had been built up over the years for men's clothing by the OQMG and the Philadelphia Depot. The OQMG was now embarking on a new venture, made more difficult by the haste with which the wardrobe for the WAAC had to be designed and procured.[82]

Between 1942 and 1945 the development of WAAC clothing at the OQMG was the responsibility of only two men. Colonel Grice, chief of the Standardization Branch, piloted the program through the preliminary stages of planning during the period February to August 1942, when the basic details of the uniform were determined. In August Maj. Stephen J. Kennedy, chief of the Textile Section in the Re-

---

[80] Ltr, Gregory J. Tobin, BQMD, to James P. Giblin, OQMG, 20 Sep 44, no sub.

[81] When the organization was incorporated as part of the Army under legislation enacted on 1 July 1943, it became known as the Women's Army Corps (WAC).

[82] For a detailed account of this activity see Erna Risch, *A Wardrobe for the Women of the Army* (QMC Historical Studies 12, October 1945).

search and Development Branch, became the officer in charge of the WAAC clothing program. To him fell the task of making the modifications in WAAC clothing necessitated by practical experience, as well as of developing new items subsequently needed by the WAC. Closely associated with the developmental work at the Philadelphia Depot throughout this period were two officers, Maj. Frank M. Steadman and Capt. William L. Johnson. None of these officers were specialists in the field of women's clothing nor were their staffs experienced. Late in 1942 this situation was modified by the addition of some officers who knew the field of women's clothing, and both the OQMG and the depot added women consultants to their staffs, primarily to present the woman's point of view. It is difficult, however, to evaluate the influence of these women consultants. Their more active participation in the program came only after the initial planning had been completed.

Both the OQMG and the Philadelphia Depot sought assistance from outside sources to acquire as rapidly as possible the necessary "know-how." They consulted manufacturers, stylists, designers, technical experts, and department store buyers of women's garments, both in conference and by means of correspondence. While such consultation was most helpful, the failure to utilize personnel trained in the women's clothing field from the beginning of the program resulted in the modifications which followed close upon the first issue of WAAC clothing at Fort Des Moines in July 1942.

It was unfortunate, too, that not until early in 1945 was a Women's Clothing Section established as a unit within the Research and Development Branch. Until that time responsibility for women's clothing, both at the OQMG and at the Philadelphia Depot, was delegated to organizations responsible for men's clothing. This could not fail to affect the course of the development of women's clothing. A particularly

noteworthy example is to be found in the case of specifications written by the depot which called for the use of haircloth and heavy canvas in women's jackets, as in men's.[83] As the result, a hard, stiff jacket was produced in place of one with the soft lines considered desirable in women's clothing.

Subject to the approval of Mrs. Oveta Culp Hobby, who participated in the preliminary planning as Director Designate of the WAAC prior to the passage of legislation establishing the organization, a design for a WAAC service uniform was developed in three months of furious activity in the OQMG between February and May 1942. The uniform evolved painfully; it was the design of no one person but the result of group work. As originally developed the uniform consisted of a six-gore skirt and a semi-fitted, single-breasted jacket, using four buttons down the front and a detachable belt of self-material with cloth-covered plastic buckle. There were two upper breast pockets with flaps and two lower, diagonal, slash pockets.[84] All subsequent modifications were improvements of this basic design.

No sooner was the first issue of the summer uniform made at Fort Des Moines in July 1942 than a barrage of criticism was let loose which resulted in further study of the appearance, fit, pattern, and functional suitability of the uniform.[85] From the fall of 1942 through 1944 modifications were made in the uniform beginning with the elimination of the jacket belt and working through improvement of patterns.

[83] (1) Interv, OQMG historian with Miss Maxine Spengler, PQMD consultant, 23 Apr 45. (2) The Philadelphia Depot justified its action by insisting that the jacket was a uniform, not a civilian outfit, and that a more substantial construction was necessary in order to eliminate the need for frequent pressings. Interv, OQMG historian with Maj Wm. L. Johnson, PQMD, 20 Apr 45.

[84] Memo, Gen Gregory for ACofS G–1, 16 May 42, sub: Uniform for WAAC.

[85] Risch, *A Wardrobe for the Women of the Army*, pp. 37ff.

THE ORIGINAL WAAC UNIFORM. *From left to right, officers' winter uniform, officers' summer uniform, and enlisted women's winter uniform.*

Much of the difficulty came from pattern defects which were eliminated only when commercial pattern makers were called in. In the hasty procurement of the first uniforms, the manufacturers rather than the OQMG or the Philadelphia Depot had made the original patterns. Since there had been no test made of their correctness prior to procurement, whatever was wrong with the basic patterns was reproduced in both the summer and winter uniforms initially procured. Later when the Philadelphia Depot incorporated many improvements in the patterns, the desired results were not achieved because the depot had to utilize the facilities of the men's garment industry. Accustomed to tailoring men's uniforms, they retained in their production of women's uniforms the characteristics of men's clothing. The manufacturers of women's clothing were not able to handle the production of uniforms at prices the depot was willing to pay, particularly when the WAAC program was greatly expanded in November 1942. Further difficulties stemmed from the fact that the quality work of a designer of high-priced clothing could not be duplicated in the mass production of the jacket. Gradually these difficulties were adjusted and a satisfactory uniform was eventually achieved.

Basic to the trend of the development of the uniform was the fact that the director of the WAAC and her associates wanted to look as much like the Army as possible. Although this policy was questioned by the OQMG, it was never changed by WAAC Headquarters. The WAAC selected Army colors for the uniform and adopted a shirtwaist and the Army regulation khaki tie. These were included in the items submitted for general staff approval by The Quartermaster General on 16 May 1942, along with an overcoat, a raincoat, an in-between utility coat, and the WAAC cap, adopted after prolonged discussion and the fashioning of innumerable samples. By 1945 this cap had been dropped in favor of a garrison cap.

Unlike the WAAC, the ANC could trace its history back to the Civil War, but only after it was established as a part of the United States Army in 1901 was the provision of adequate uniforms a possible problem. Even then the need was not recognized, and a uniform was not adopted until World War I. In the next twenty years little consideration was given to the adequacy of the nurse's wardrobe. Not until war loomed in 1940, and it was apparent that the ANC would have to expand, was any effort made to improve the outdoor uniform in design and color. At the suggestion of the Office of the Surgeon General new blue uniforms were adopted, but various complications prevented the nurses from being fully equipped with the new uniform even at the beginning of 1942. Belatedly it was discovered that the nurses' wool uniforms and overcoats were cut on masculine lines not adapted to the female figure and bore no relation in sizing to the standard forms used commercially.[86]

Early in 1941 the Philadelphia Depot began to cope with the problem of sizes and patterns. At the same time the OQMG was becoming immersed in the problem of providing clothing

for the WAAC, but not until the fall of 1942 was any effort made to correlate the development of clothing for the two organizations. Then a program of co-ordination was gradually developed, leading to the adoption of the same service uniform for both the WAAC and the ANC. Other items of the outfit, such as waist, necktie, stockings, gloves, and coats were identical for Army nurses and Waacs. The only distinctive items of the nurses' uniform were the cap, bag, and insignia. The impact of all the modifications in the WAAC uniform was felt in the nurses' outfit.

No adequate consideration was given to the development of functional clothing suitable to the various occupations performed by the women of the Army. This was particularly true of the nurses. The one set of outdoor clothing and six ward uniforms supplied nurses sent overseas could scarcely be described as sufficient for active service. An OQMG observer in the NATO wrote as follows:

There is one Service in the American Army that has been sadly neglected in the way of providing clothing for combat areas. This Service is the Army Nurses' Corps. Formerly, peace-loving Americans could only picture the nurse in a tidy established hospital well back in the rear areas; however, such is definitely not the case. Army nurses now accompany task forces on landing operations. They go through exactly the same rigors of warfare as do the soldiers, with the exception that they do not participate in actual combat. The nurse's duties are to follow as closely as is necessary the progress of the fighting troops. Thus in landing operations they disembark shortly after the invasion troops have forced a beach head and immediately upon landing begin their duties of serving the wounded. During land battles, they proceed as close to the fighting front as is reasonably safe in order to carry out their medical work. It can now be seen that the nurse travels the same route as the soldier. Consequently, she must have clothing that is as rugged and as well-designed as the combat

---

[86] *Ibid.*, p. 101.

ARMY NURSE CORPS UNIFORMS. *Old winter uniform (left) and new winter uniform (right).*

soldier's. Nurses lacked this type clothing during the Tunisian campaign. It was impossible for them to wear the usual nurse's dresses, caps, chic underwear, Cuban heel shoes, etc. In order to keep adequately warm and be able to hit foxholes when necessary, the American nurses were forced to wear regular men's G. I. underwear, shoes, HBT suits, helmet with helmet liner, etc. Needless to say, women's sizes differ from men's. Consequently, nurses were wearing shoes several sizes too large, HBT uniforms that could be wrapped around them twice, underwear that was not designed for feminine forms, and overcoats that draped around them like a tent. The only items that were satisfactory were the helmet and the helmet liner. It can be easily seen that the nurse was not as pretty a sight as she might well have been. In many cases, their

sloppy dress caused considerable laughter. It is imperative that the nurses have a uniform that will allow them freedom of movement and afford sufficient warmth and sufficient durability for wear in combat areas.[87]

When a thorough review of nurses' clothing was initiated in September 1942, hospital uniforms were studied and redesigned to satisfy functional needs as well as to improve their appearance. A new fabric, a 4-ounce brown- and white-striped seersucker, was selected for the hospital uniform to be worn in oversea areas.

[87] Rpt, Capt Pounder, QM Observer, Rpt of QM Opns in NATO, 5 Mar–Jun 43.

Later in the summer of 1944 this same uniform was also authorized to be worn in the United States. The traditional white uniform was thus discarded during the war years in favor of the seersucker dress which provided a simple, short-sleeved, wrap-around uniform with a tie belt. The design was chosen to allow ease in fitting, and in laundering under difficult conditions. A matching seersucker jacket was developed to be worn with the uniform, thereby providing the nurses with a serviceable street outfit for warm weather. As designed, the jacket was made in a semifitted, collarless, one-button, cardigan style which was approved and standardized on 14 December 1942.[88] A new seersucker cap was also designed for wear with the hospital uniform.

In the summer of 1943 it became necessary to develop other items as part of the hospital uniform of the nurses. The Office of the Surgeon General indicated that nurses needed a uniform with trousers for wear on hospital ships and trains where it was frequently necessary to climb ladders to attend patients in upper bunks. It was also needed by all nurses in oversea areas, where normal duty required from time to time that they serve in hospitals using litters instead of beds. The OQMG requested the Philadelphia Depot to develop seersucker slacks and shirts. These were standardized on 28 August 1943.[89]

Insofar as suitable work clothing was concerned, Waacs fared no better than nurses in the beginning. In the initial development of clothing neither WAAC Headquarters nor the OQMG gave much attention to work clothing,

[88] (1) Ltr, Col Doriot, OQMG, to Chief of Development Br, Reqmts Div, SOS, 30 Nov 42, sub: Standardization of Seersucker Jacket, and 2d ind, Gen Wood, SOS, to OQMG, 14 Dec 42. (2) Insp rpt, Miss Emily Alexander to TQMG, 23 Jan 43.

[89] (1) Ltr, Col R. W. Bliss to TQMG, 6 Jul 43, sub: Nurses Uniforms. (2) Ltr, Capt W. P. Barrett, OQMG, to CO PQMD, 1 Jul 43, sub: Women's Seersucker Trousers and Shirts. (3) [4th ind], Gen Wood, ASF, to TQMG, 28 Aug 43.

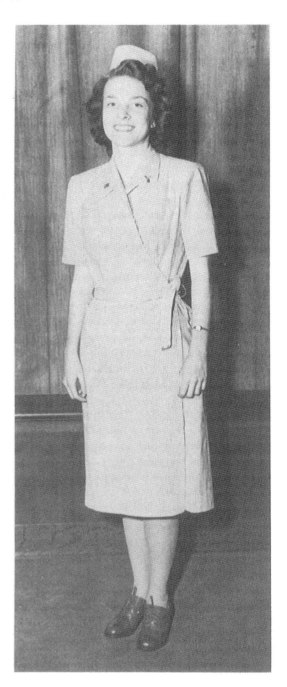

NURSE'S SEERSUCKER UNIFORM

primarily because the duties which the Waacs were to perform were not clearly defined until long after the program was under way. Originally a one-piece herringbone twill suit and later a two-piece suit provided satisfactory summer work clothing. The major portion of WAAC activity, however, was thought of in terms of clerical and administrative work for which the service uniform was regarded as adequate. It proved, however, to be wholly inadequate as winter apparel for personnel engaged in outdoor occupations, such as motor transport service, or for personnel performing many duties at unheated hangars or other buildings where warm clothing was required. In the winter of 1942–43 and part of 1943–44, WAAC personnel engaged in outdoor activities were issued whatever warm clothing was available at the discretion of the commander of the local post. This included enlisted men's items, such as overcoats, wool socks, long wool drawers and shirts, combat jackets and trousers, as well as CCC mackinaws.

At the same time that WAAC Headquarters in the fall of 1942 was requesting suitable winter clothing for motor transport units, the Office of the Surgeon General requested The Quartermaster General to standardize arctic equipment for nurses.[90] In its developmental work the OQMG used the same basic principle of layering which had been applied in fashioning men's clothing. Items developed for the men were now adapted for the use of women, and nurses and Wacs were provided with outer cover trousers and wool liners; with the field jacket, M–1943, liner, and hood; and with a battle jacket. Although in arctic clothing men continued to use pile liners, in women's arctic clothing wool liners replaced them.

Where soldiers were sent, nurses and Wacs soon followed; hence suitable tropical clothing was as essential for them as cold-climate clothing. Both the WAC and the ANC were critical of herringbone twill garments. Requests for

khaki slacks and shirts came from the NATO for WAC drivers as well as from the SWPA for nurses. Malaria control officers in the latter area would not permit nurses to wear either herringbone twill or seersucker slacks and shirts because they offered insufficient protection against mosquitoes. After considerable developmental work khaki shirts and slacks were classified as standard items of issue to women personnel.[91]

In providing appropriate women's footwear, the QMC duplicated the course of development for men's shoes. Nurses were sent overseas early in the war in service shoes wholly inadequate to the demands of field wear. Quartermaster technicians were not unfamiliar with the problem of furnishing shoes for women, but commercial lasts had always been used in shoes procured for the ANC. There was a tendency to leave the details of specifications to the discretion of the contractors, and thus the Army was unable to maintain rigid control of the quality or fit of the shoes it bought. The WAAC service shoe, originally selected and approved by WAAC Headquarters, was also made over a commercial last. Criticism from the field promptly revealed the unsuitability of this shoe.

In the fall of 1942 a trend developed for uniformity of footgear for all women in the Army. A systematic consideration of the shoe problem was begun, resulting in the development by the Boston Depot, in co-operation with industry, of satisfactory models for service and field shoes manufactured over government-owned lasts.

---

[90] (1) Ltr, Brig Gen L. B. McAfee, SGO, to CG SOS, 5 Sep 42, sub: Arctic Clo and Equip for Nurses, and 1st ind, Col Wood, Dir of Reqmts Div, SOS, to TQMG, 7 Sep 42. (2) Ltr, Gen Lutes, ACofS for Opns SOS, to TQMG, 27 Nov 42, sub: Clo for WAAC Pers.

[91] (1) Ltr, Col H. W. Roberts, Hq NATO, to TAG, 25 May 44, sub: WAC Summer MT Uniform, and 1st ind, Dir of R&D Div ASF, to TQMG, 14 Jun 44. (2) Ltr, Maj Gen George F. Lull, SGO, to CG ASF, 3 Jul 44, sub: Tropical Fld Uniform for Army Nurses. (3) QMCTC, min of mtg No. 21, 10 Oct 44. (4) 2d ind, Actg Dir of R&D Div ASF, to TQMG, on same.

Subsequently, at the request of The Surgeon General, a combat boot, identical in design to that issued the men, was developed for nurses, except that it was made over the same last as the women's field shoe.[92] Thus the gamut was run from oxfords to combat boots for field wear.

Textile and Leather Problems

The design of functionally appropriate uniforms for Army personnel was only one phase of the problem of developing Army clothing. The development of suitable military textiles also was fundamental. This field of activity had long received the attention of technicians at the Philadelphia Depot. In the interval between World Wars I and II, the laboratory of the depot had engaged in routine testing of fabrics and some experimental work directed toward the development of better military fabrics. Most of the standard fabrics used for Army uniforms, such as 18-ounce wool serge, 8.2-ounce cotton khaki, and herringbone twill, had been developed prior to 1939.

When the Military Planning Division, OQMG, initiated an integrated program of research in 1942, much was learned about both military clothing and fabrics. As the war progressed, it was realized that improvements could be made. In regard to military textiles already accepted and in use, the Textile Section of the Research and Development Branch was concerned with obtaining such improvements by raising the level of specification performance, by adopting a better fabric construction, or by using a new finishing treatment. The shrink-proofing of woolens and the development of improved water-resistant fabrics were illustrative of this trend.

One of the major fields of Quartermaster research during the war was the improvement of water-resistant fabrics. The use of cotton cloth with this characteristic had been introduced in the Army as a result of an order directing Maj.

Gen. J. K. Parsons, commanding general of the Third Corps Area, to develop a lightweight field jacket to replace the service coat for field duty in 1939. Heretofore, like most other armed forces of the world, the American Army had always fought in wool clothing. Abandonment of the use of wool in the outer garments of the Army was one of the important changes in military textiles during the war. It stemmed from the adoption of the layering principle applied to winter combat clothing. Wind-resistant, water-repellent cotton fabrics afforded the soldier better protection against wind and rain than wool. They were stronger, more resistant to tearing, and dried more quickly.

At first a wind-resistant poplin and later, about the end of 1942, a 9-ounce sateen were developed and adopted for use in such garments as field jackets and outer cover trousers. In 1943 the OQMG learned of a series of fabrics developed at the Textile Institute in Manchester, England, which produced fabrics having better water-resistant properties than any known in this country. Basically, the principle of construction involved utilizing the swelling properties of cotton when wet in such a manner as to close up the fabric, preventing the penetration of water. Full data on the construction was obtained from the Textile Institute by the OQMG and applied by the textile industry in developing improved water-resistant fabrics.[93] In 1945 a 9-ounce, wind-resistant oxford cloth became the standard fabric for winter combat clothing. It had been found in 1944 that dense fabrics were also satisfactory for a new purpose, namely, to give protection against mosquitoes. Hence they were used in the development of the tropical combat uniform.

---

[92] (1) Ltr, Gen Bliss, SGO, to TQMG, 29 Jun 44, sub: Footwear for Army Nurses Assigned to SWP and SP Theaters. (2) Risch, *A Wardrobe for the Women of the Army,* pp. 76–81.

[93] Col Kennedy, Chief of Textile Sec, "Problems for Future Quartermaster Textile Research," *Textile Research Journal,* November 1945, pp. 414–15.

The problem of keeping the soldier dry in the field was susceptible of a second line of attack. His outer garments could also be made more protective by giving them a water-repellent treatment. Although some technologists believed that improved water repellents would solve the problem largely by themselves, the most satisfactory results were obtained by applying the best available water repellent to specially designed water-resistant fabrics.

Both before and during the war the QMC carried on research to develop improved water-repellent finishes. Though such developmental work was concentrated at the Philadelphia Depot before the war, the depot's activities had been largely limited to liaison work with industry. Chemical manufacturers had for many years pursued intensive research on a competitive basis in this field, since water-repellent finishes were used on hunting and ski clothes and on tentage. They continued such research during the war years, when developmental work was undertaken by the Chemical Section of the Research and Development Branch. The Philadelphia Depot co-operated in this work.

At the beginning of the emergency the QMC was using a so-called durable type of water-repellent finish on cotton fabrics used for outer garments.[94] In the course of time deterioration of this finish resulted from either dry cleaning or laundering. As a consequence, either a more durable finish had to be developed, or such garments had to be treated again in the field to insure water repellency for the lifetime of the garment. To restore water repellency to the garment after laundering, the QMC, at the beginning of the war, was using an emulsion of waxes and aluminum salts. Not only did the Corps wish to improve this type but it was also desirous of developing an adequate solvent type of water repellent for use after dry cleaning.

Developmental work in reference to such nondurable or re-treating types of water repellents was taken up with various chemical companies in 1942. The Philadelphia Depot co-operated in this experimental work, and a contract was signed with the National Association of Dyers and Cleaners, making its facilities available for testing purposes. As a result, the existing specification was revised to provide increased water repellency and stability. Field conditions of mobile warfare, however, would never permit constant re-treating of garments. If water repellency had any military advantage at all, it was argued, it would have to be in the garment prior to issue. This raised anew the question of durability.

QMC personnel were divided between the advocates of durable and nondurable water-repellent treatments. Lack of knowledge concerning the true performance of water-repellent finishes dictated a systematic review of the whole field of such finishes. As the year 1942 closed, a program to evaluate all commercial water-repellent products was inaugurated. Under a contract with the National Defense Research Committe, the Textile Foundation and the QMC conducted a study to determine better methods of evaluating water-repellent compounds.[95] As a result of this work, four finishes were deemed sufficiently durable to meet the minimum military requirements and were approved for Army use. Out of this developmental work emerged two new tests which proved effective in correlating laboratory test methods and actual wear performance to the extent that laboratory tests alone, thereafter, proved sufficient to evaluate additional finishes for flat cotton fabrics.[96] The QMC specification, "Test Methods for Textiles," was thereupon revised to

---

[94] (1) Interv, OQMG historian with Dr. J. E. Simpson, Chemical Sec, Nov 1945. (2) Dr. J. E. Simpson, "The Army's Water Repellent Clothing," *American Dyestuff Reporter*, XXV (1946), pp. 243–52, 272, 288–90.

[95] (1) R&D Br, Status Rpts, 31 Dec 42, 31 Jan 43. (2) For the details of this work see Risch and Pitkin, *Clothing the Soldier of World War II*, pp. 95–96.

[96] R&D Br, Status Rpt, 31 Aug 44.

provide for evaluation of new water-repellent finishes, not by fixed composition limitations, but by performance tests known to measure desired characteristics without reference to tradename products. What was accomplished in reference to water repellency was applicable, however, only to cotton fabrics. Research in the use of water-repellent finishes for woolen fabrics was only beginning as the war ended.

Although woolens constituted the major portion of Army clothing, little consideration had been given before the war to the role that shrinkage played in reducing the wearability of woolens. Industry had developed the sanforizing process for cottons but had done little to produce washable woolens. By 1943 the problem of shrinkage was being forcibly brought to the attention of the OQMG not only by the comments of observers in the field but also by salvage studies which revealed that shrinkage caused the great number of failures in all woolen garments.

It was the high rate of shrinkage on socks which was the immediate cause for the initiation of a study of antishrink processes by the Research and Development Branch.[97] The branch believed that faster progress could be made by concentrating on one item. It selected the cushion-sole sock because field experience had shown that this sock was the most comfortable to wear and afforded the most foot protection. Its useful life, however, was very limited because shrinkage was so great after three to six field launderings that the sock became unwearable.[98]

Of the several commercial processes available for pretreatment of socks to prevent shrinkage, one, using a chlorination treatment called the Hypol process, was found to be most satisfactory. To obtain the benefits of washability at the earliest possible time this process was applied to at least a part of the cushion-sole socks then under production. In the meantime further research was carried on in the hosiery industry.

Through the National Research Council a project was set up for studying various shrinkproofing processes, which led to the conclusion by the late summer of 1944 that satisfactory results could be obtained with a very simple chlorination on the alkaline side. The process was simple enough for application in any mill with even the most meager equipment. Immediate attention, thereupon, was given to renegotiating contracts to provide for the application of this treatment to all cushion-sole socks, with the result that the cushion-sole sock industry was converted to the production of shrinkproof socks by the end of 1944.[99] Subsequently the same treatment also was applied to heavy wool socks and wool ski socks.

With the conversion of the hosiery industry under way it was possible for the OQMG to give consideration to shrinkage in other wool items. The information and experience gained in shrinkproofing one knitted item could be applied to another, as, for example, woolen underwear, which is usually knitted and made from the same type of merino yarn as socks. Work on the development of shrink-resistant treatments for woven fabrics was resumed simultaneously. Considerable progress was made but none of these developments reached the production stage before the war ended.

Quartermaster research was also interested in the development of any construction or finish that would make fabrics wear longer, thereby reducing the cost of Army clothing and textile equipage. One line of investigation was concerned with the development of abrasion-resistant finishes to be applied to textiles. Tests at the Philadelphia Depot revealed that greater claims for commercial treatments were made than could be verified. A second approach to the

---

[97] *Ibid.,* 31 Jul 43.

[98] Capt Harry F. Clapham, "Washable Woolens for the Army," *Proceedings of the Conference on Quartermaster Textile Research,* p. 17.

[99] See R&D Br, Status Rpts, 31 Aug, 30 Sep, 31 Oct, 30 Nov, 31 Dec 44.

problem was made through the redesign of textile fabrics. Increased durability was the goal sought by the OQMG, but although considerable experimentation was undertaken, results were not immediately applicable to textiles utilized in World War II.[100]

The QMC was interested, too, in developing clothing which would afford some protection against flash burns. The Armored Force needed flameproof clothing for tank crews under combat conditions. The problem was turned over to the Philadelphia Depot early in 1943 with instructions to "carry on the necessary investigations to develop the best fire-resistant treatment for herringbone-twill to be used by tank troops."[101] In the meantime the OQMG approached various manufacturers and co-ordinated the work with the Chemical Warfare Service. Developmental work continued into 1945. By the end of the war a process for obtaining an excellent, durable, flame-resistant treatment on clothing had been developed and was just getting into production.

The application of various treatments to textiles has been here limited to a discussion of soldiers' clothing, but it had a wider potential use. Military textiles were also utilized in the form of tents and tarpaulins to provide shelter for both soldiers and matériel, and were used in many items of personal equipage. Developments in fabric construction and finishes were as applicable to these items as to clothing. Jungle operations opened another large field of research, necessitating treatments to prevent mildew. The chief of the Textile Section in the Research and Development Branch believed that the progress made by the Army in the study of tropical deterioration of textile products would rank as a major scientific achievement in the field of biochemistry.[102]

If the Corps was concerned with improving textiles by changes in the construction of fabrics and by the application of various finishes, it was equally concerned with improving the quality

of leather used in Army footwear. Considerable developmental work in tannages was conducted at the laboratory facilities of the University of Cincinnati. Improving the water resistance of leather was a fundamental research problem which was attacked in various ways. One method was to improve the quality of dubbing, a mixture of oil and tallow used to preserve leather and increase its resistance to water.[103] Testing the relative merits of having the flesh side out or the grain side out was another approach to the same problem, although tests revealed no appreciable difference in water resistance. The ultimate solution of this problem was dependent on considerably more research which was projected for the postwar period.

Still another problem was mold and rot prevention in leather. Not only shoes but also various items of jungle equipment, such as machete sheaths, deteriorated rapidly because of the growth of molds under continual humid conditions. Mold preventive agents had been successfully applied to canvas, and some had been used commercially on leather. Information, however, was meager as to the effectiveness of such agents. The question of toxicity and resulting skin irritations had also to be considered since many of the leather items came into close contact with the soldier's skin. Under the National Defense Research Committee, a contract was negotiated with the University of Cincinnati to develop a mold-proofing treatment for leather. The scope of this project was subsequently widened to include studies of leather preservatives, shoe sterilization and disinfection,

---

[100] See R&D Br, Status Rpts, 29 Feb 44–30 Apr 45, sub: Wear Resistance of Apparel Textiles.

[101] Ltr, Col Kennedy, OQMG, to CO PQMD, 16 Jan 43, sub: Flameproofing.

[102] (1) Col Kennedy, *Textile Research Journal,* November 1945, p. 419. (2) See also William H. Weston, "Tropical Deterioration of Textile Products," *Proceedings of the Conference on Quartermaster Textile Research,* pp. 29ff.

[103] See R&D Br, Status Rpts, 1943 and 1944, sub: Dubbing.

thread preservation, and the effects of perspiration on leather.[104]

In the course of experimentation and testing at the University of Cincinnati and the National Bureau of Standards, it was established that the use of paranitrophenol was effective and safe. Its use was approved by the Office of the Surgeon General provided that the skin did not come into contact with the leather. Specifications accordingly were prepared in the spring of 1945 for the protection of upper, midsole, and insole leathers used in military footwear for tropical areas, but the war ended and shoe contracts were canceled before mold preventives were applied to footgear.[105] Experiments to improve the water resistance of leather and to prevent the growth of molds are illustrative of the trends in fundamental research in leather problems, though they by no means cover all research undertaken by the Corps in this field.

Summary

Since World War I there has been a growing awareness in the War Department of the need for continuous research in those branches which would contribute effectively to the military efficiency of the country. Unfortunately, the funds made available by Congress for this purpose in the period between World Wars I and II proved wholly inadequate. While some developmental work was accomplished by the QMC during these twenty years, no integrated program of fundamental research was initiated before 1942.

As a result of the World War II program, much pertinent data has been accumulated in reference to military clothing and the role it may play in maintaining or reducing the physical resistance of the soldier. Clothing which affords inadequate protection against moisture, for example, necessitates the expenditure of body energy to evaporate the moisture in wet clothes. If the soldier is at rest, lying in a foxhole or sleeping, he may not generate enough body heat to do this, with the result that body temperature is lowered, efficiency lost, and health endangered. Weight, too, is a drain on the soldier's reserves of resistance. The difference between a 5-pound pair of combat boots and a 3-pound pair of jungle boots is equivalent in terms of heat stress to four times that difference, or 8 pounds additional weight to be carried by the soldier. Additional weight means increased sweat production, pulse rate, and skin and internal temperature. The nearer to heat exhaustion the soldier approaches, the lower his efficiency becomes. By bitter experience the jungle fighter learned the price of weight; he discarded all but the minimum essentials. Such factors of environmental protection and weight had to be taken into consideration by Quartermaster designers of clothing. Bulk and volume had also to be weighed in terms of thermal protection as opposed to maneuverability. Finally, the designer had to assess the values of military appearance as these affected discipline and morale.

The emphasis placed on the development of suitable garrison clothing and footgear in the interlude of peace resulted in the failure to have in readiness adequate combat clothing when the emergency began in 1939. Increasingly, in the late thirties stress was placed on the development of functional clothing for general field use and there was a growing differentiation between barrack and field clothing. This interest of Quartermaster clothing designers in functionalism was further stimulated by the impact of global war and the establishment of new types of military organizations. With the advent of war numerous new types of clothing and equipment were designed for parachutists, armored

---

[104] (1) R&D Br, Status Rpt, 31 Aug 42. See monthly Status Rpts thereafter for 1943 and 1944 under heading, Leather Mold and Rot Prevention.
[105] *Ibid.*, 31 Aug 45.

and mechanized forces, ski troops, and special-type forces serving in cold climates.

In the beginning it was the tendency of the QMC to develop special garments for each new type of military organization. Procurement, storage, and issue of basic clothing by the Corps were rendered considerably more difficult by the need for processing different articles having similar functional use. The Philadelphia Quartermaster Depot early protested against this trend.

With all due respect to the desires of higher authority for perfect protection and absolute suitability for specialized personnel, the multiplicity of new items of clothing and variations in design being adopted without service tests will render the task of the Quartermaster Corps increasingly difficult if not impossible of fulfillment unless a halt is called on all but essential changes.[106]

Even before the first phase of developing specialized items of clothing had ended, the OQMG began making the specialized parts interchangeable with the component parts of the basic uniform. It was felt that while differences in climate and terrain in the various theaters of war were complicating factors, they had to be subordinated to the development of standard basic clothing for use by all arms and services. By the fall of 1942, therefore, the OQMG was moving toward the development of an all-purpose combat uniform, in the design of which the layering principle was adopted, and for the first time in Army clothing the use of wool in outer garments was abandoned. The trend in military clothing for men and women alike was from specialized types to a standardized field uniform.

By consolidating garments having the same functional utility into single types the Military Planning Division promoted the simplification of the over-all Army Supply Program. In developmental work special consideration was given to designing all-purpose items which could be substituted for one or more standard items.

Thus one field jacket replaced numerous coats and jackets and two caps were made to serve the purpose of a multiplicity of headgear for winter and arctic wear. This trend toward simplification was still predominant in the developmental work under way when World War II ended.

Using scientific methods the QMC sought improvements in both the construction of military fabrics and the finishes applied to them. Warmth without bulk, strength without weight, water impermeability without loss of air and water-vapor permeability, and elimination of shrinkage of wool without affecting its other qualities were the objectives. The scientific method necessitated careful analysis and prolonged testing, and consequently, as hostilities ended, many of the items to which its findings had been applied were just getting into production. Much of the scientific work in progress remained to be completed in the postwar period.

These considerations are equally applicable to developments in the field of design. It was futile, for example, to improve water-repellent finishes if designers used horizontal seams which permitted rain to wick through, thereby nullifying the advantages gained. As science was applied to the fundamental problems involved in the development of military textiles, it became apparent that the design of garments would have to be revised in the light of the findings. Much basic work remained to be accomplished in the postwar period before all the anticipated advantages could be reflected in military clothing and textiles. Under the stimulus of war, scientific methods have been applied to Quartermaster problems and much has been achieved. In order to maintain superior standards in Army clothing and footgear, it is obviously necessary to support a continuous program of research in peace as well as in war.

---

[106] Ltr, Col W. A. McCain, PQMD, to TQMG, 4 Nov 40, sub: Complication of Clo Sup by Adoption of New Items.

CHAPTER IV

The Development of Personal and Organizational Equipment

Among the Army supply services, the Quartermaster Corps has by far the broadest range of responsibilities in the field of equipment, which, in military terminology, includes everything needed to outfit an individual or an organization. Generally speaking, everything that is not a weapon nor so technically specialized as to fall naturally into the province of one of the other services is a Quartermaster item. In the following discussion equipment is limited to items of personal equipment, such as field packs, sleeping bags, and intrenching shovels, carried by the combat soldier, and to organizational equipment, such as field ranges, mobile shoe and clothing repair units, textile repair units, and mobile sterilizer and bath outfits, issued to units in the field.

To trace the development of each of the numerous items of personal and organizational equipment procured and issued by the Corps is neither feasible nor necessary to an understanding of the problems involved. Representative items within major groups, therefore, have been selected for detailed treatment to illustrate the difficulties encountered and the trends that developmental activity took in solving them.

Personal Equipment

Much of the personal equipment issued to the American soldier in World War II was the same kind that his father carried in 1917. The uniform of World War I had been modified in the interval of peace to provide an improved garrison outfit, but little or no change had been made in personal equipment, primarily because large quantities of such supplies were on hand from World War I. Some refinements had been introduced, particularly in the thirties, but these were minor in character. Not until World War II was well under way were any significant modifications made to improve items of equipment.

Field Packs, Bags, and Carriers

The basic equipment of the soldier in the field has always included some sort of knapsack, or pack, to carry spare clothing, miscellaneous small equipment, blankets, personal articles, and sometimes rations. Since the U. S. Army pack was made of duck and webbing and since brass was used in the form of buckles, rings, grommets, and other small hardware to join, open, close, or suspend its various parts, wartime shortages in these materials affected the pack's design. All developmental work in textile finishes, such as that with regard to abrasion resistance and water resistance, was applicable to textiles used for packs and other equipage, just as it was to those converted into clothing. Mildew-resistant treatments were also applied to all textile equipage items during the war.

Virtually no change had taken place since 1918 in the infantry pack used in the field. Some refinements had been made in it, but when World War II began the Army retained the haversack with a detachable pack carrier as one of the two basic items for carrying personal equipment in the field. Known collectively as the field pack, M–1928, it was difficult to separate when a light field pack was needed. Actually, the haversack was a canvas wrapper in which equipment was rolled. It was complicated to assemble, and the completed pack was long and narrow, with a high silhouette. The other basic item was a relatively small canvas field bag, M–1936, based upon the design of the French musette bag. It had a number of compartments in which a few personal effects as well as maps and papers could be carried. Originally intended for the use of officers, in World War II it was also issued to motorized units and various other types of troops.

As in the design of clothing, attention in 1941 was first concentrated on the development of equipment for specialized troops. Neither the haversack nor the canvas field bag was adequate for arctic or jungle use. For example, a more suitable carrier had to be developed for troops sent to the defense of Alaska. The standard Army pack was too small to carry the personal equipment necessary to a soldier operating in extremely cold weather. The load shifted around too much for safe skiing, and the pack restricted free movement of the arms essential in skiing and climbing. Brig. Gen. Simon B. Buckner, Commanding General, Alaska Defense Command, recommended the use of the "Norse Pac," a form of rucksack carried by Norwegian and other European ski troops.[1]

The OQMG and the Jeffersonville Quartermaster Depot, following this recommendation, co-operated with industry in developing a special type of carrier for arctic and mountain troops called the rucksack, based on the design of the Norse Pac. This was a large-capacity canvas sack, closed at the top by a drawstring, with a covering flap and pockets at the back and sides. It had web shoulder straps and a web belly strap which encircled the body and prevented the sack from swinging while the soldier was in motion. The sack was mounted on a light, tubular, steel frame so constructed that the weight of the whole pack was distributed low around the hips. Two of the frames, when detached from their sacks, could be attached to skis to form an emergency sled. A white cover for camouflage use in snowy country was issued with the rucksack.[2]

During the Attu operations, soldiers complained that the rucksack was too large and was extremely uncomfortable because it rested so heavily on the hips. The Quartermaster observer thought that the discomfort was caused by the frame and the improper packing of the rucksack. Even when heavier items were put on the top, however, the pack was "none too comfortable."[3] While there were no subsequent changes in the basic design, a number of modifications to increase the efficiency of the rucksack were made during the war years.

Jungle troops also needed a specialized type of carrier. The haversack, M–1928, was unsatisfactory for use in tropical swamps, where there was no dry or level ground on which to lay out a roll of cloth and insert personal effects according to a prearranged system. The jungle pack evolved from the experimental work conducted by Capt. Cresson H. Kearny in Panama. It consisted of a rainproof bag attached to the webbing of the standard issue pack. Pairs of enclosing straps ran horizontally and vertically,

---

[1] Ltr, Brig Gen S. B. Buckner to CG Ninth CA, 3 Mar 41, sub: Reduction in Number of Items of Alaskan C&E and Modification of Specs.

[2] (1) QMC Spec JQD 88, 14 Mar 42, sub: Rucksack, 400.1141. (2) Pitkin, *Quartermaster Equipment for Special Forces*, pp. 101–02.

[3] 1st Lt Robert D. Orr, QM Observer, Rpt on Attu Opns, 11 May–16 Jun 43.

permitting adjustment of the pack to any desired size. The bag was large enough to carry a considerable load. It closed at the top with a cord and was covered by a rainproof flap. On top of this flap was a small zippered pouch for canteen, medical kit, and other small articles. Separate waterproof bags in the main pack kept the hammock, spare clothing, and rations dry and gave added buoyancy to the pack when it was necessary to swim with it.[4]

On the whole the jungle pack was satisfactory in its first large-scale use in the Southwest Pacific. It had definite advantages over the haversack, M-1928. There was, however, some complaint because the arrangement for fastening on the bayonet was so far back that a man wearing the pack could not reach it. The web strap proved uncomfortable, and the canvas surface which rested on a man's back caused sweating and produced prickly heat. Critics from New Guinea complained that the bag was not waterproof, but the Quartermaster observer noted that this criticism arose from a misunderstanding of the use of the waterproof clothing bag. Intended as a liner to the jungle pack, the waterproof clothing bag, he found, was used as a field equivalent of the barracks bag. Renaming it a "pack liner," he felt, would clarify its real purpose.[5]

When the QMC had completed its developmental work on the jungle pack in the summer of 1942, it continued to study possible modifications of the item, including enlargement to carry a heavier load, which would make it adaptable for general Army use. The pressure of other priority projects, however, prevented any progress from being made until the beginning of 1943 when experimental models embodying these modifications were developed.

By the spring of 1943 contracts for haversacks and pack carriers were expiring and new procurements were required. Headquarters, AGF, favored the replacement of haversacks, pack carriers, and canvas field bags by the jungle pack,

JUNGLE PACK

except where the canvas field bag was issued to officers and enlisted men in cavalry and mountain units.[6] Tests of the enlarged jungle pack were under way at the Quartermaster Board when a subcommittee of the Quartermaster Corps Technical Committee recommended standardization of the jungle pack, renamed the field pack, M-1943. The committee, however, sponsored only limited procurement of the

---

[4] (1) QMC Spec JQD 190, 10 Aug 43, sub: Jungle Pack, 400.1141. (2) Pitkin, *Quartermaster Equipment for Special Forces,* pp. 200ff.

[5] Rpt, 1st Lt Robert L. Woodbury, QM Observer, SWP Theater, 1 Feb–15 May 43.

[6] (1) Ltr, Col D. H. Cowles, OQMG, to Hq ASF, 12 Apr 43, sub: Substitution of Jungle Pack for Haversacks, Pack Carriers, and Canvas Fld Bags. (2) 1st ind, Capt R. J. Delacroix, AGF, to CG ASF, 27 Apr 43, on same. (3) 4th ind, Col R. R. Robins, ASF, to TQMG, 18 May 43, on same. All in 428.

item. Standardization was held in abeyance pending further test before final adoption.[7] In the field this enlarged pack was not well received because of its bulk and the difficulty of packing and adjusting it. At the same time officers returning from the Pacific commented favorably upon the versatility of the Marine Corps pack.[8]

Personnel in the AGF were experimenting with a pack embodying the best ideas of the Marine pack, the canvas field bag, and the jungle pack. The salient characteristic of this experimental pack was its construction in two separable sections, which permitted the soldier to drop a part of it, retaining a small lightweight pack for combat. Salvage crews gathered the dropped portion. This pack was the prototype of the cargo-and-combat field pack ultimately developed. In the spring of 1944 the AGF proposed that this field pack be standardized without tests. The OQMG opposed adoption of any untested item, but it was willing to supply the pack if requested by the AGF, provided the latter realized that production could not be halted immediately after adoption to make improvements or modifications. Meanwhile, the Infantry Board expressed an adverse opinion of the item. This field pack was not standardized but the QMCTC recommended development of a new pack along the general lines requested by Headquarters, AGF. On the basis of a directive issued by Headquarters, ASF, the QMC, in co-operation with the AGF, began work to develop a divisible type of pack.[9]

As developed, the field pack, M-1944, consisted of two parts. The upper part, called the combat pack, was about the size of the former canvas field bag. The lower part, known as the cargo pack, was similar to an overnight bag but somewhat larger. A small canvas handle was attached so that it could be used as a traveling bag in garrison. It was standardized as the cargo-and-combat field pack, M-1944, on 20 July 1944. Many modifications recommended

by the Infantry Board were approved in the standardization action.[10]

Under test by the Infantry Board, the quick-release buckles used on the pack were found unsatisfactory. They did not provide a connection tight enough to prevent the pack from swaying. Straps running under the cargo bag and attached to three-bar buckles on the combat pack were therefore substituted. This change was the chief difference between the modified pack and the original M-1944 model. The AGF recommended the incorporation of this modification into current procurement at the earliest possible moment.[11]

Standardization of the improved M-1945 cargo-and-combat field pack, however, was held up for some time pending a decision to eliminate the canvas field bag in favor of the new field pack in the Table of Equipment (T/E) 21. The AGF felt that improved items of equipment should be issued to combat troops as soon as available. The OQMG, on the other hand, preferred to issue haversacks, pack carriers, and canvas field bags until the supply was exhausted. It indicated that there would be difficulty in manufacturing sufficient cargo-and-combat field packs because the supply of duck and webbing

---

[7] (1) Rpt, Subcom, QMCTC, to QMCTC, 27 May 43, sub: Fld Pack. (2) QMCTC, min of mtg No. 12, 8 Jun 43. Both in 428.

[8] Maj D. L. McCaskey, *The Role of Army Ground Forces in the Development of Equipment* (AGF Studies 34, 1946), p. 84.

[9] (1) QMCTC, min of mtg No. 5, 28 Mar 44. (2) *Ibid.*, No. 6, 4 Apr 44. (3) Maj W. H. McLean, Ex Off QMCTC, to TQMG, 6 Apr 44, sub: Fld Pack, and 3d ind, Hq ASF to TQMG, 15 Apr 44, on same. All in 428.

[10] (1) Rpt, Subcom, QMCTC, to QMCTC, 23 Jun 44, sub: Cargo-and-Combat Pack. (2) QMCTC, min of mtg No. 12, 27 Jun 44. (3) Ltr, Col Doriot, OQMG, to CG ASF, 5 Jul 44, sub: Cargo-and-Combat Pack, and 2d ind, Hq ASF to TQMG, 20 Jul 44, on same. All in 428.

[11] Ltr, Dir of Inf Bd to Chief of Ground Reqmts Sec, ASF, 24 Oct 44, sub: Cargo-and-Combat Fld Pack, and 1st ind, Hq ASF to CG ASF, 1 Nov 44, on same, 428.

was very critical. Despite the supply difficulties the cargo-and-combat field pack, M–1945, was standardized on 9 April 1945, at which time the M–1944 pack was reclassified as limited standard.[12]

The design of new tools and new weapons for the soldier forced Quartermaster development of new carriers, sheaths, and scabbards to enable him to carry such equipment, or of new ways for attaching them to his webbing gear. Thus the creation of a new intrenching shovel required a new carrier so that the soldier might attach it to his pack. When the Ordnance Department procured and began to issue a new carbine, .30-caliber M1, the QMC in the fall of 1942 was called upon to develop a canvas scabbard for carrying it that could be strapped to the leg. In field use this item proved impractical and was subsequently declared obsolete. Development of an 18-inch machete for jungle troops necessitated the design of a suitable canvas sheath.

Similarly, new types of ammunition required the development of new ammunition carriers, such as the general-purpose ammunition bag, standardized in the spring of 1943 and capable of carrying nineteen different types of ammunition, and a rocket-carrying bag, completed about the same time, to carry ammunition for the 2.36-inch rocket launcher (bazooka). A new but unsuccessful approach to this problem was the utilization of cargo pockets as ammunition carriers. These pockets were used in the jungle suit, in herringbone twill trousers, and in experimental models of cotton trousers. Although the OQMG enthusiastically endorsed them, the soldier in the field was just as vigorously opposed to their use. An adverse report from NATO noted that cargo pockets on combat trousers "bulged like the chaps of a Hollywood cowboy." It was found preferable to carry grenades in an empty canteen cover. From the Pacific came word that troops regarded cargo pockets as a "nuisance."[13] Actually, cargo pockets were never used extensively as ammunition carriers and in fact had disappeared entirely from combat uniforms by 1944.

The new duffel bag, developed to replace the denim barracks bag, contributed much to the comfort and convenience of the soldier. The blue denim barracks bag had been issued in World War I and, after modification and standardization in 1929, was being procured when World War II began. Late in 1941 the Standardization Branch proposed redesigning this bag, making it longer and narrower in shape, and substituting the more durable olive drab duck for denim. The impact of war requirements on the duck industry, however, was so great that duck was not available. Denim therefore was retained as the fabric but its color was changed to an olive drab. This barracks bag, made with a round bottom, was 32 inches high and 14½ inches in diameter. It used a drawstring closing.[14]

The QMC knew at the time that a denim bag would not compare favorably with one made of duck, and field reports soon made the fact painfully apparent. The barracks bag was criticized because of its poor shape. When packed, it bulged at the sides and took the form of a ball, awkward to stow or to carry. Each soldier required two barracks bags to contain his clothing, making the handling extremely difficult. The usual method was to tie the strings together and put the loop over the shoulder, carrying one bag in front and the other in back.

[12] (1) 2d ind, Gen Doriot, OQMG, to Hq ASF, 21 Feb 45, on ltr, Hq AGF to CG ASF, 7 Feb 45, sub: Basis of Issue for Cargo-and-Combat Fld Pack. (2) Rpt, Subcom, QMCTC, to QMCTC, 27 Feb 45, sub: Cargo-and-Combat Fld Pack. (3) Ltr, Gen Doriot, OQMG, to CG ASF, 12 Mar 45, same sub, and 2d ind, Hq ASF to TQMG, 9 Apr 45, on same. All in 428.
[13] (1) Capt W. F. Pounder, Jr., QM Observer, Rpt of QM Opns in NATO, 5 Mar–2 Jun 43. (2) Rpt, Lt Col W. J. Preston, Jr., to CG AGF, 1 May 45, sub: Observations During Recent Opns of XXIV Corps in POA.
[14] Standardization Br, Rpts of Test and Development Work in Progress, 2 Jan–1 Apr 42.

BARRACKS BAG *with drawstring closing.*

DUFFEL BAG *with improved closure.*

This soon proved tiresome, whereupon the soldier resorted to dragging both along the ground behind him. The bags quickly wore through and their contents were lost. The barracks bag proved thoroughly unsatisfactory when the soldier was shipped overseas. At debarkation it frequently burst. One of the bags was stored in the hold of the ship, and when the soldier went ashore and moved away from the port area it frequently happened that it never caught up with him. A more substantial bag similar to that of the Marine Corps was generally indorsed.[15]

In the light of this field experience, the QMC began to develop experimental duffel bags large enough to carry the soldier's entire issue of clothing and equipment. In conjunction with representatives of the New York Port of Embarkation, the OQMG worked out dimensions which would accommodate the soldier's full allowance of clothing and equipment and take cognizance of space requirements on board ship. It was soon apparent that a better means of carrying the bag was needed than that offered by the Marine model. A double-purpose handle was therefore devised which permitted the bag to be carried at the side, like a suitcase, or slung over the shoulder, like a golf-bag. An improved closure was also contrived. The mouth was fitted with a long metal staple on one side. The eyelets on the three remaining sides could be slipped over this staple and held in place by a snap link attached to the end of the shoulder strap. The bag could be locked if desired. Despite the fact that it was still in short supply, duck was used in the improved duffel bag which was standardized in April 1943. It was approximately 12½ inches square and 37 inches in length. Because of fabric shortages and limitations of production, priority of issue was given to troops already overseas or embarking for theaters of operations.[16] During the critical shortage of duck and webbing in 1944–45 it was necessary to utilize substitute materials, but despite such occasional compromises in quality the duffel bag was stronger and more portable than the barracks bag.

Shelter Half

An important item of personal equipment carried by each soldier was a piece of canvas called a shelter half. Two soldiers, by matching shelter halves and the poles and pins they carried, were able to erect a field shelter for themselves, the familiar "pup tent." Each shelter half consisted of a rectangular piece of canvas with a triangular piece sewed to one end. When the two pieces were buttoned together and assembled, they formed a tent closed at the rear and open at the front. In an effort to keep dry, soldiers hung their raincoats over the front of the pup tent when it rained, but the shelter afforded little protection from the elements. Though the item was generally execrated by the troops who used it in 1918, nothing was done for the next twenty years to improve it. At the beginning of the emergency period all shelter halves on hand and in use had been bought during World War I.

In the course of maneuvers during the emergency, suggestions for providing additional protection were offered. A subcommittee of the QMCTC dismissed them as unsatisfactory but recommended that the Standardization Branch study the possibilities of improving the shelter half.[17] Shelter halves with triangular pieces sewn on both ends, to form completely enclosed tents, were tested by various service boards. The tests indicated that such shelter

---

[15] (1) Capt Pounder, QM Observer, Rpt of QM Opns in NATO, 5 Mar–2 Jun 43. (2) Maj C. M. Burnhome, Rpt 8 to Chief of Mil Plng Div, 29 Mar 43.
[16] (1) Rpt, Subcom, QMCTC, to QMCTC, 19 Mar 43, sub: Overseas Bag. (2) 4th ind, Dir of Reqmts Div, ASF, to TQMG, n. d., on same, 428.
[17] Rpt, Subcom, QMCTC, to QMCTC, 14 Aug 40, sub: Redesign of Tent, Shelter Half, 400.112.

halves would provide more protection and tent space. As a result this new shelter half was standardized in October 1941, and the old type was reclassified as substitute standard.[18] At the same time the subcommittee of the QMCTC recommended that stocks of the old type shelter half still on hand be modified by the addition of a second triangular piece.

While the OQMG concurred in the recommendations it noted that a duck shortage existed and recommended that no modification of the old style shelter halves be made for about a year, or until an adequate supply of duck became available.[19] Not until the fall of 1943 were sufficient quantities of duck on hand for the production of the new shelter half, which required slightly more duck than the old. The old type shelter half was then reclassified from substitute to limited standard. By the end of 1943 all contracts for this type had been completed.[20]

Shelter-half tents were rarely pitched in operations near the enemy, since they made obvious targets. When not pitched as a tent, the shelter half could be used as a ground cloth. It was not waterproof, however, and troops in the field continued to be critical of the item. The greater versatility of the German shelter tent was called to the attention of The Quartermaster General.[21] It weighed one pound less than the American type, it could be made up into tents of varying size, and it could also be used as a poncho.

Early in the war the Special Forces Section of the OQMG had investigated the desirability of equipping desert troops with a poncho in lieu of a shelter half and a raincoat. In October 1942 the Research and Development Branch initiated a project to develop a sectional poncho tent, but this was dropped in mid-1943 upon directive from Headquarters, ASF. In the meantime synthetic-resin-coated ponchos were developed and procured. When the possibility of using coated nylon arose, Headquarters, ASF, requested the OQMG to develop as soon as possible a lightweight poncho for use in the Southwest Pacific area. By 1944 a lightweight nylon poncho was standardized.[22] Versatility was its chief characteristic, since it could be used as a raincoat, an individual shelter, a sleeping bag, or, if several were combined, a tent.

The shelter half, unlike the German model, could not be utilized as a poncho. With slight modification, however, it could be assembled into tents of varying size. In September 1944 the Research and Development Branch began to investigate the possibility of combining six shelter halves to form a six-man tent. This combination was accomplished by the use of ten buttonholes placed along the lower edge of the shelter half. On the strength of a report by the Field Artillery Board, the AGF requested that all future shelter halves be fabricated with this modification and that existing stocks also be modified. The Textile Section, OQMG, advised that contractors were working at capacity and estimated that the addition of ten more buttonholes to each shelter half would reduce production by 30 percent. The QMCTC therefore recommended that the change be accomplished "in future production as soon as possible consistent with maintenance of necessary production."

---

[18] (1) Ltr, Brig Gen C. L. Corbin, OQMG, to TAG, 22 Aug 40, sub: Shelter Tents. (2) Memo, Actg Chief of Test Sec for Dir of Inf Bd, 1 Aug 41, no sub. (3) 6th ind, TAG to TQMG, 20 Oct 41, on rpt, Subcom, QMCTC, to QMCTC, 1 Oct 40, sub: Redesign of Tent, Shelter Half.

[19] 4th ind, Gen Corbin, OQMG, to ACofS G–4, 11 Oct 41, on rpt cited in n. 18.

[20] (1) Rpt, Subcom, QMCTC, to QMCTC, 23 Nov 43, sub: Tent, Shelter Half (Old Style). (2) 3d ind, Hq ASF to TQMG, 15 Dec 43, on memo, Ex Off QMCTC, for TQMG, 30 Nov 43, same sub. (3) 4th ind, Col Doriot, OQMG, to CG ASF, 4 Jan 44, on same.

[21] Ltr, Maj Gen C. H. Gerhardt, Hq 29th Inf Div, to TQMG, 4 Oct 44, sub: German Shelter Tent, 424.1.

[22] (1) Rpt, Subcom, QMCTC, to QMCTC, 22 Feb 44, sub: Lightweight Poncho. (2) QMCTC, min of mtg No. 3, 29 Feb 44. (3) [3d ind], Hq ASF to TQMG, 19 Mar 44, 422.3.

This action was approved by Headquarters, ASF, early in 1945.[23]

Sleeping Bags

The necessity for providing better shelter for the soldier in the field turned Quartermaster attention to the problem of improved sleeping gear. Traditionally, blankets had been issued as a part of the personal equipment of the soldier. They were so provided in World War II. While the GI blanket was durable, it was not very warm for its weight and afforded inadequate protection no matter how artfully a bed was contrived.

Protection was especially needed by troops stationed in extremely cold areas. Because of enlarged garrisons in Alaska, the OQMG placed primary emphasis on the development of specialized sleeping gear for arctic and mountain troops. The arctic and the mountain sleeping bags, developed by the Corps early in the war, used down and feathers which were considered the best fillers available for sleeping bags.

The problem in developing sleeping bags was to secure maximum insulation with a minimum of bulk and weight. The outer shell had to be water resistant but sufficiently permeable to enable body vapors to escape and thus prevent condensation within the bag. In addition to these basic characteristics the sleeping bag had to be easy to get out of, durable, portable, and washable.

Early in the war Quartermaster consultants, in the interest of adding to the comfort of troops and increasing their efficiency, suggested the desirability of issuing sleeping bags to all troops in lieu of all or part of the blankets furnished them. Because practically all materials used in the production of sleeping bags were on the critical list, the wool-conservation committee did not recommend adoption of a sleeping bag for the enlisted man as proposed in May 1942.

Developmental work, however, continued and in the fall of 1942 the first specification for the wool sleeping bag was published.[24] Unlike the arctic and mountain sleeping bags, the wool bag was not filled with down or feathers and was made of knitted wool cloth. It was mummy-shaped and provided with a 30-inch heavy slide fastener. Because of the extreme shrinkage, which occurred when the knitted wool cloth bag was laundered, the OQMG substituted a woven, 21½-ounce napped wool cloth in the summer of 1943. Thereafter wool sleeping bags were made of wool blanket material equivalent in weight and durability to that of standard Army blankets. The design was somewhat altered so that the bag could also be used inside the mountain sleeping bag. During the summer the Philadelphia Depot further amended the specification, and altered the pattern to conserve cloth and reduce cost.[25]

Consistent reports from the British Isles and other places with raw, cold climates emphasized the inadequacy of two blankets as sleeping gear. Headquarters, AGF, therefore requested standardization of the wool sleeping bag in the fall of 1943 and its issue on a basis of one for each man except in the tropics, the arctic, and in cold mountain operations.[26] Early in 1944 the item was standardized. Because sufficient sleeping bags could not be manufactured immediately, the proposed basis of issue was modified to provide one for each individual in the-

---

[23] (1) Textile Sec to QMCTC Sec, OQMG, 10 Jan 45, sub: Tent, Shelter Half, Modified. (2) Rpt, Subcom, QMCTC, to QMCTC, 9 Jan 45, same sub. (3) QMCTC, min of mtg No. 2, 16 Jan 45. (4) 1st ind, Hq ASF to TQMG, 25 Jan 45, on ltr, Col Doriot to CG ASF, 22 Jan 45, same sub. All in 424.1.

[24] QMC Spec PQD 273, 29 Sep 42, sub: Wool Sleeping Bag, 400.1141.

[25] (1) QMC Spec PQD 273B, 21 Jun 43, and 273C, 30 Aug 43, sub: Wool Sleeping Bag. (2) Ltr, Maj Francis Boyle, OQMG, to CO PQMD, 4 Mar 43, same sub. Both in 400.1141.

[26] Ltr, Hq AGF to CG ASF, 22 Nov 43, sub: Wool Sleeping Bag, 427.

aters of operations in temperate climates when approved by the commanding general of the theater. This issue was in lieu of the mandatory allowance of two wool blankets.[27] After the wool sleeping bag became an item of issue for combat troops, further changes were made to conserve materials. At the same time a simpler method of construction speeded production of the bags, which were also increased in length and girth.

During the winter of 1944–45 wool sleeping bags were issued in quantity to troops in Italy and northern Europe. Many modifications were suggested as a result of this first large-scale use of the item. There was general agreement that a longer zipper was needed to facilitate rapid egress from the bag. One observer reported:

The bag, sleeping, wool is the best item of equipment that has ever been issued for the purpose of allowing men in the front areas to sleep. It is suitable for use by everyone except those actually in the very forward foxholes, i. e. by anyone who can reasonably expect 30 seconds warning before he must personally fight.[28]

Not all reports, however, agreed with this view. Some held that the wool sleeping bag was not practical for front-line soldiers, who had to respond rapidly to an alarm, and indicated a preference for blankets.[29] The mummy-shaped bag was an issue bitterly fought over throughout the war. One of the problems was that soldiers had to learn new sleeping habits because of the restricting confines of the bag. Large individuals particularly had difficulties, and an oversized bag finally proved essential.

An integral part of the sleeping-bag problem throughout the war was the development and use of a sleeping pad to minimize heat loss to the ground or snow under the pressure of the body. Although no acceptable solution was found, an experimental half-length air mattress which weighed only half a pound showed promise.

In the closing weeks of the war the wool sleeping bag underwent further modifications to meet the criticisms made. The slide fastener was lengthened to provide a closure at least seventy inches long, and a simplified construction was provided in the new pattern which eliminated waste portions of cloth at the end and center of the pattern lay. The wool sleeping bag, M-1945, was standardized as the war ended.[30]

Intrenching Tools

An indispensable item of individual equipment for combat use in World War II was the intrenching shovel. As a Quartermaster observer in Tunisia commented:

This is one of the few items that the fighting soldier will not discard, but will actually carry right into battle with him. It is probably the most useful utensil that he has in his possession. In every new position that he takes, either advancing or retreating, it is absolutely necessary that a foxhole be dug. When foxholes are needed, they are usually needed IN A HURRY—and DEEP![31]

In contrast to the trench warfare of 1917–18, World War II emphasized the importance of individual shelters and foxholes. Each soldier had therefore to be provided with such tools as he would need under varying conditions of isolation and in varying types of soil.

[27] (1) Rpt, Subcom, QMCTC, to QMCTC, 26 Nov 43, sub: Wool Sleeping Bag. (2) 3d ind, Hq ASF to TQMG, 18 Jan 44, on ltr, Ex Off QMCTC to TQMG, 7 Dec 43, same sub. Both in 427.
[28] Ltr, Col Albert H. Dickerson, WD Observers Bd, Hq ETO, to CG AGF, 12 Feb 45, sub: AGF Rpt 638: Wool Sleeping Bag, 427.
[29] (1) AGF Bd, MTOUSA, 8 Apr 45, sub: Rpt 370. (2) Ltr, Hq 10th Mountain Div to CG MTOUSA, 30 Mar 45, sub: Comment on Wool and Mountain Sleeping Bags. Both in 427.
[30] (1) Rpt, Subcom, QMCTC, to QMCTC, 19 Jun 45, sub: Sleeping Bags and Cases for Same. (2) Ltr, Hq AGF to CG ASF, 25 Jun 45, sub: Wool Sleeping Bag and Others. (3) 3d ind, Dir of R&D Div, ASF, to TQMG, 30 Jul 45, on same. All in 427.
[31] Capt Pounder, QM Observer, Rpt of QM Opns in NATO, 5 Mar–2 Jun 43.

When the United States entered the war in 1941, the American soldier was equipped with a number of intrenching tools adopted before World War I. These included an ax, a pick mattock, and a shovel standardized in 1910. The shovel was 22 inches long and weighed 29¾ ounces. In the spring of 1942 several minor changes were introduced. In particular, the cutting edge of the shovel was to be sharpened during manufacture so as to be ready for service when issued to the soldier.[32]

Shortly thereafter, upon oral directive of the Deputy The Quartermaster General, the Special Forces Section initiated a new project to improve the intrenching shovel. The T-shaped grip of the M-1910 shovel had a tendency to catch in barbed wire. It could not be used as a pick and its handle was not long enough. The object was to increase the effectiveness of the shovel without increasing its weight. Samples of Japanese and German Army shovels were studied with a view to incorporating their best features in the new design. The Special Forces Section sought to develop a combination tool to replace the shovel and pick mattock. Samples were developed of an experimental intrenching shovel which had one side of the blade sharpened and the other serrated for cutting through roots and low undergrowth. This shovel had a detachable handle designed for use as a pick.[33] By the end of 1942 small quantities of these shovels had been procured and distributed for test purposes to various service boards. A Quartermaster observer in the Southwest Pacific Theater carried a sample with him to New Guinea where it was well liked. "It was the consensus that this type of shovel was worth the extra weight, although it was thought that the weight could well be reduced. In coming over the Owen Stanley Mountains, a man with a shovel could never find a companion with a pick or vice versa; hence the enthusiasm for this new design."[34] ·

During the winter of 1942–43 the OQMG awaited the results of the tests being made. In March the Quartermaster Board reported that, with slight modifications, the intrenching shovel with a pike handle was for most purposes a satisfactory replacement for the M-1910 intrenching shovel, the pick mattock, and the ax. Two months later, however, the Research and Development Branch closed this project on intrenching tools until formal authority for its continuance could be obtained from Headquarters, ASF.[35]

In July 1943 the AGF urged the adoption of an intrenching tool similar to the German shovel.[36] The chief distinguishing characteristic of the German item was its folding blade. When extended it was used as a shovel; when folded at right angles to the handle and locked, it served as a pick. For carrying, it could be folded completely against the handle. Exact duplication of the German shovel was neither desirable nor possible. At the request of the Mechanical Section, the Ames Baldwin Wyoming Co. developed a shovel similar to the German type but adapted to American mass-production methods. High-carbon steel was substituted for the high-chrome-alloy steel, which was not available in this country. The construction of the shovel was strengthened, and it was made slightly longer and heavier than the German model. Despite the lack of service tests the QMCTC approved its adoption as a standard item of issue. The M-1910 in-

[32] QMC Spec JQD 104, 15 Apr 42, sub: Intrenching Shovel, M-1910, 400.1141.

[33] (1) Special Forces Sec to Product Test & Review Sec, OQMG, 23 Dec 42, sub: Japanese Intrenching Shovel. (2) Ltr, Capt John W. Mockabee to National Inventors Council, Dept of Commerce, 14 Nov 42, no sub.

[34] Rpt, Lt Woodbury, QM Observer, SWP Theater, 1 Feb–15 May 43.

[35] (1) R&D Br, Status Rpt, 31 Mar 43. (2) QMB Rpt, Project T-125, Rpt of Test of Intrenching Shovel, with Pike Handle, 16 Mar 43. (3) R&D Br, Status Rpt, 31 May 43.

[36] Ltr, Hq AGF to CG ASF, 14 Jul 43, sub: Individual Intrenching Tools.

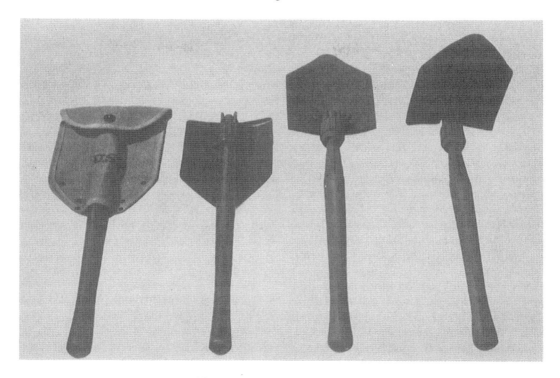

INTRENCHING SHOVEL M-1943

trenching shovel was reclassified as limited standard.[37]

This M-1943 intrenching shovel, which had been hurriedly standardized and put into production at the insistence of the AGF, was "an adequate shovel, a good hoe, only a fair pick and an indifferent axe." [38] At the time of standardization the OQMG had requested the QMCTC to recommend further developmental work on intrenching tools in order that a better all-purpose tool might be devised. The fact that the various arms and services insisted that the pick mattock and ax were essential in addition to the M-1943 intrenching shovel was evidence that such research was justifiable. This recommendation, however, was rejected by Headquarters, ASF, on the ground that reports from NATO indicated that the intrenching shovel

was satisfactory for the purpose intended.[39]

Although QMC activity was not continued at this time, the Infantry Board was developing and testing combination intrenching tools. It reported on a design which, it claimed, would, "when refined as to design for production," be a satisfactory and desirable combination intrenching tool, suitable for standardization and

[37] (1) Rpt, Subcom, QMCTC to QMCTC, 12 Jul 43, sub: Intrenching Shovel M-1943. (2) QMCTC, min of mtg No. 16, 20 Jul 43. (3) [4th ind], Hq ASF to TQMG, 28 Jul 43.

[38] (1) Insp Rpt, Eugene D. Hallock, Mechanical Sec, to TQMG, 13 Feb 45, no sub, 400.112. (2) Rpt, Subcom, QMCTC, to QMCTC, 12 Jul 43, sub: Intrenching Shovel, M-1943. (3) QMCTC, min of mtg No. 16, 20 Jul 43.

[39] (1) Ltr, Col Doriot, OQMG, to Hq ASF, 30 Jun 44, sub: Intrenching Tool, M-1944. (2) 1st ind, Hq ASF to TQMG, 12 Jul 44, on same. Both in 400.112.

issue in lieu of the intrenching shovel, M–1943.[40]

The OQMG agreed that there was a need for a combination intrenching tool which the shovel did not fill, but it did not concur in the conclusions drawn by the Infantry Board on the basis of its test. From a supply viewpoint, the OQMG objected because the manufacturing cost of the proposed design was prohibitive. In addition, it was a heavier tool than the intrenching shovel, adding weight to the soldier's load. Action by the QMCTC was deferred, and the OQMG initiated a project, utilizing the experience gained in the Infantry Board test, to produce test samples of improved combination intrenching tools, incorporating design features that would lend themselves to low cost and to mass-production facilities readily available.[41]

With the assistance of the Ames Baldwin Wyoming Co. several designs were worked out and were then submitted to tests by the several service boards. The Infantry Board and the Quartermaster Board agreed that the design which combined the shovel with a separate pick hinged on the same pin as the blade was most satisfactory. On the basis of the findings of the Infantry Board, Headquarters, AGF, recommended that this type of intrenching tool be standardized on the basis of one for each individual.[42]

A subcommittee of the QMCTC recommended that the combination intrenching tool be declared standard without further service tests. It further recommended that the new tool be issued immediately to combat and combat support units as replacement for the M–1943 shovel, the pick mattock, and the ax, regardless of the condition of the intrenching tools in the possession of these units. The M–1943 shovel, pick mattock, and ax were reclassified as limited standard and were to be issued to units other than the combat and combat support units until exhausted. The new combination intrenching tool was standardized on 21 September 1945.[43] Because the war had ended before this action

was completed no procurement was made.

In design the new tool was similar to the M–1943 shovel, but it was made of heavy steel and was of more rugged construction. The folding pick was attached to the same hinge as the blade and could be locked in any one of three positions by the nut that locked the blade in position. These positions were (1) along the back of the handle, to be out of the way when the tool was used as a shovel; (2) at right angles from the handle for use as a pick; and (3) extended to 180 degrees from the folded position for use as a probe. When completely folded for carrying, the tool was 20½ inches long. In extended position it was about 28 inches long and weighed slightly less than 50 ounces.

18-Inch Machete

The basic tool essential for combat troops in jungle operations was the machete, useful for disposing of sentries and in ambush attacks at night, as well as for clearing a path through tangled vegetation. A commercial machete with a 22-inch blade and a leather sheath had been standardized in 1937 for issue to certain troops

---

[40] (1) IB Rpt 1549B, Intrenching Tools, 19 Oct 44. (2) 2d ind, Capt Holman Hamilton, AGF, to CG ASF, 29 Nov 44, on Hq AGF to Pres, Inf Bd, 27 May 44, sub: Combination Intrenching Tool.

[41] (1) Mechanical Sec to Col Doriot, OQMG, 28 Dec 44, sub: Rpt of IB 1594B, Intrenching Tools. (2) 4th ind, Col Doriot, OQMG, to Hq ASF, 24 Jan 45, on Hq AGF to Pres of Inf Bd, 27 May 44, sub: Combination Intrenching Tool. Both in 400.112.

[42] (1) Ltr, Lt Col R. A. Meredith, AGF, to CG ASF, 30 Jun 45, sub: Combination Intrenching Tool. (2) 1st ind, Hq ASF to TQMG, 4 Jul 45, on same. Both in 413.17.

[43] (1) Rpt, Subcom, QMCTC, to QMCTC, 7 Aug 45, sub: Combination Intrenching Tool. (2) QMCTC, min of mtg No. 18, 14 Aug 45. (3) Ltr, Gen Doriot, OQMG, to CG ASF, 5 Sep 45, sub: Combination Intrenching Tool. (4) 1st ind, Hq ASF to TQMG, 21 Sep 45, on same. All in 413.17.

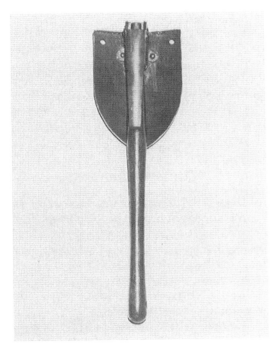 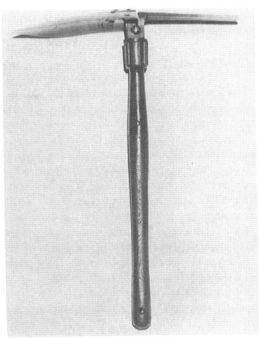

COMBINATION INTRENCHING TOOL, *folded (left) and open (right).*

in Panama.[44] Not until World War II, however, did the machete become an important item of personal equipment.

When Capt. Cresson H. Kearny organized an experimental jungle platoon in Panama during the emergency period, he developed, among other items of jungle equipment, a machete with an 18-inch blade. This was a straight-back modification of the Collins commercial-type machete, proved by extensive use in the tropics. Machetes had been manufactured commercially in the United States for 150 years, but no manufacturer had ever bothered to find out how they were actually used. As a consequence, the handle, with a sharp corner at the rear of the butt, was designed to be gripped tightly like a hatchet. The machete, however, depended on velocity rather than weight for its cutting action, being allowed to pivot in the hand during the stroke while held only with the thumb and the index and middle fingers. In this loose, free-swinging grip the sharp corner on the butt caused blisters. South American Indians had plenty of time to grind this corner down, but Army equipment had to be ready for use when issued. In the redesign of the commercial machete this corner was rounded off. A hole was also drilled in the handle for a wrist cord, which kept the machete from being dropped or lost.

In commercial practice it had also been customary to grind only a token edge on the blade, leaving the edge to be completed in the field. The Quartermaster specification remedied this omission by requiring the factory to do all the

[44] Ltr, Lt Col C. A. Hardigg, OQMG, to ASW, 27 Sep 40, sub: Procurement Clearance, 400.1141.

grinding. To avoid the action of tropical rot and mold upon leather, the OQMG replaced the leather sheath with one made of heavy, water-repellent duck.[45]

When General MacArthur requested delivery of jungle equipment in the summer of 1942, the AGF recommended that immediate steps be taken to adopt an 18-inch machete and sheath. The military characteristics of these items conformed to those which had been evolved by Captain Kearny and the OQMG. Standardization was quickly accomplished.[46] The first specification for the 18-inch machete had already been issued by the Jeffersonville Quartermaster Depot. This original specification was revised many times to incorporate modifications which improved the machete, such as the substitution of a Bakelite pistol-grip handle for the wooden one which often caused blisters. Both styles of handles, however, continued to be specified and procured.[47]

At the same time consideration was given to the problem of camouflage. Jungle troops recommended that the 18-inch machete be furnished with an unpolished blade. Instead of going through the final processes of manufacture, the blades were taken immediately after forging, when they were still dark in color and scaled from oxidation. After being subjected to a tumbling process to remove the excess scales, the blades were left with a rough, dark finish. Tests in Panama indicated that not only did the "carbon-colored," unpolished finish of the blade reduce rusting but it also decreased the risk of the blade's reflecting the sun's rays and thus revealing positions to the enemy. Furthermore, the use of unpolished blades cut down the cost of manufacture and speeded production by eliminating bottlenecks in grinding machinery. Consequently, in November 1942, the OQMG directed the Jeffersonville Depot to change the existing contracts on the balance of the machetes being procured to incorporate this finish.[48]

The 18-inch machete proved an unqualified success. It was used, as intended, by jungle troops for cutting trails, and for a great variety of other purposes by natives who obtained possession of it. "The natives in New Guinea . . . use our machetes for everything imaginable, for building quarters, for constructing storage huts, for clearing air strips, for hacking out roads and trails and even, among the wilder natives, for taking Jap heads." [49]

Organizational Equipment

Organizational equipment underwent few modifications in the decade following World War I. Limited Congressional appropriations during that period, as well as quantities of surplus equipment left from World War I, largely accounted for this lack of progress. By the mid-thirties, however, developmental activity was resumed in a leisurely manner.

Modern warfare was increasingly characterized by mechanization, with emphasis on automotive and motorized items. Aside from developments in the field of automotive design, Quartermaster effort was predominantly devoted to motorizing various types of organiza-

[45] (1) Rpt, Capt C. H. Kearny, 4 Sep 42, sub: Description and Use of New Indiv Jungle Equip. (2) Lt Woodbury to Hist Sec, OQMG, 11 Sep 43, sub: History of Development of Jungle Equip. (3) Ltr, Maj Bestor Robinson, OQMG, to The Collins Co., 25 Jul 43, no sub.

[46] (1) Ltr, Hq AGF to TQMG, 28 Jul 42: Standardization of 18-Inch Machete. (2) Memo, Hq SOS for TQMG, 31 Jul 42, sub: Jungle C&E. (3) 4th ind, same to same, 31 Aug 42, on same. All in 422.3.

[47] (1) QMC Spec JQD 188B, 19 Nov 42, sub: 18-Inch Machete and Sheath. (2) Ltr, 2d Lt R. M. Toucey, OQMG, to CG JQMD, 20 Oct 42, sub: Tentative Spec JQD 188, 6 Aug 42 for Machete. Both in 400.1141.

[48] (1) Ltr, Lt Col H. E. Rounds, OQMG, to CG JQMD, 30 Nov 42, sub: 18-Inch Machete, M–1942, enclosing extracts from Rpt on Tests of Jungle Equip, 17 Nov 42, by Capt Kearny, 474.7. (2) QMC Spec JQD 188E, 18 Feb 43, sub: 18-Inch Machete, M–1942, 400.1141.

[49] Rpt, Lt Woodbury, QM Observer, SWP Theater, 1 Feb–15 May 43.

tional equipment in order to keep pace with the rapid advances made by mobile armies. When modern armies moved, practically all the services of a municipality had to move with them. Quartermaster mobile supply columns became "Main Street on wheels." [50] The QMC had to develop and perfect portable and mobile kitchens, bakeries, laundries, baths, and shoe, clothing, and textile repair units.

The tempo of development was greatly accelerated after 1939. Much of the preliminary developmental activity was accomplished in the emergency period so that when the United States entered the war in December 1941, the QMC was prepared to take the field with units equipped for mobile warfare. The use of such organizational equipment in Army maneuvers and particularly in the campaigns in NATO revealed shortcomings in portable and mobile equipment which were corrected by subsequent modifications.

Two Quartermaster installations co-operated in this developmental work. Until August 1942 the Holabird Quartermaster Motor Base, center of motor transport activities, and, throughout the war, the Jeffersonville Quartermaster Depot, were active in developing mobile organizational equipment. Within the OQMG the initial developmental work was accomplished through the co-operative efforts of the Motor Transport Division and various branches within the Supply Division responsible for particular phases of Quartermaster activity, such as the Laundry Branch, and the Subsistence Branch of the Storage and Distribution Division. Although responsibility for automotive equipment was transferred to the Ordnance Department in the summer of 1942, responsibility for the different kinds of mobile organizational equipment remained in the QMC and was centralized by the following summer in the Research and Development Branch of the Military Planning Division, which thereafter undertook such modifications as field experience dictated.

The one exception to this development was that responsibility for petroleum-handling equipment, despite the objections registered by the Director of the Military Planning Division, was vested in the newly created Fuels and Lubricants Division.

Automotive Equipment

Under Army regulations[51] the responsibility of the QMC in regard to the development of motor vehicles was limited to the general-purpose vehicles which were used for hauling cargo, ammunition, personnel, or equipment. Combat vehicles, such as tanks and armored cars, came under the jurisdiction of the Ordnance Department.[52] Quartermaster vehicles were further divided into two general classes. Administrative vehicles, closely paralleling normal commercial products, were used for housekeeping purposes in the zone of interior. Tactical vehicles, distinguished from the administrative type by always having the all-wheel drive—the most notable difference between military and commercial trucks—filled the requirements of the field forces for transporting supplies, personnel, and equipment under maneuver or combat conditions.

Among the contributions of the QMC to the war effort, the development of the jeep [53] was

[50] Address, Lt Col E. S. Van Deusen, MT Div OQMG, before Metropolitan Chapter, SAE, New York City, 19 Feb 42.

[51] AR 850–15, 29 Sep 39, sub: Mil Mtr Vehs.

[52] The QMC Motor Transport Service of 1918 became a separate Motor Transport Corps in the same year and was returned to the QMC in 1920. Here it remained until 1 August 1942 when all functions relating to both types of vehicles were consolidated under one organization by the transfer of the entire QMC Motor Transport Service to the Ordnance Department. WD Cir 245, Sec. IV, 25 Jul 42, sub: Transfer of Certain MT Activities.

[53] For a detailed account see Herbert R. Rifkind, The Jeep—Its Development and Procurement Under the Quartermaster Corps, 1940–42 (typescript copy on file, Hist Sec, OQMG).

probably the most spectacular single accomplishment. Officially known as the ¼-ton 4x4 truck,[54] it was developed primarily as a tactical vehicle, although its remarkable versatility made it useful for a host of administrative purposes. The project originated in the thirties, when a program for the replacement of obsolete equipment and the complete motorization of the Army was begun. The QMC and other services and arms, particularly the Infantry, were aware of the need for a lightweight vehicle to replace the motorcycle for cross-country reconnaissance and messenger purposes. At the same time the Army was also aware of its need for a light weapons carrier to give quick and close support to attacking infantry. The Motor Transport Division, OQMG, carried on considerable experimentation with extra light models of the regular 1 ½-ton 4x4 cargo truck and later a ½-ton 4x4 was adopted as a standard model.[55] The latter, however, did not fill the Infantry's requirement for a light car for reconnaissance purposes.

In the summer of 1940 the Chief of Infantry emphasized the need for a vehicle that would have a maximum height of 36 inches and a weight of 750 to 1,000 pounds. This vehicle, possessing a low silhouette and four-wheel drive, was to have a cross-country and grade ability equal to that of standard cargo vehicles, an integral or detachable .30-caliber machine gun mount, and a capacity of at least two men, one machine gun including accessories, and 3,000 rounds of ammunition. If feasible, and if the production of test vehicles would not be unduly delayed, the frame and body were to be designed with amphibious characteristics.[56] Thus the concept of an amphibious complement to the light reconnaissance car was born simultaneously with the land model idea.

The Adjutant General forwarded this proposal for comment and recommendation to both The Quartermaster General and the Chief of Ordnance. The Quartermaster General suggested that the Holabird Quartermaster Depot, center of motor transport activities, be authorized to investigate the light passenger car of the American Bantam Co. as a possible solution of the problem, a suggestion that was passed along to the Chief of Ordnance.[57] On 19 June 1940 a special subcommittee, appointed by the Chief of Ordnance, met with officials and engineers of the American Bantam Co. at their plant at Butler, Pa. It drew up and recommended for adoption a set of military characteristics for the vehicle. These limited the weight to a maximum of 1,200 pounds, the wheel base to approximately 75 inches, and the maximum height to 36 inches. It was also recommended that 70 of these cars be procured for service testing. Since the vehicle was a commercial wheeled type without armor and fell within the general purpose classification, the subcommittee also recommended that the QMC be charged with its development and procurement.[58] The Secretary of War approved the subcommittee's recommendation and authorized the expenditure of not more than $175,000 of Quartermaster funds for the project.[59]

The Infantry and Cavalry were interested in a four-wheel-steer type of jeep, and eight of the seventy trucks procured for testing were provided with this feature. These two arms wanted the four-wheel-steer feature because of the greater mobility and maneuverability that it gave to the jeep, but it was never standardized.

---

[54] Official designation of Army trucks indicates the number of wheels and driving wheels. Thus a "4x4" means four wheels, all of which are driving wheels.

[55] QMCTC, min of mtg, 18 Nov 38.

[56] Ltr, CofInf to TAG, 6 Jun 40, sub: Light Veh Dev, 400.112.

[57] (1) 2d ind, AGO to TQMG and CofOrd, 14 Jun 40, on ltr cited in n. 56. (2) 3d ind, TQMG to CO Holabird QMD, 14 Jun 40, on same. (3) Ltr, TAG to CofOrd, 15 Jun 40, sub: Light Veh Dev. All in 400.112.

[58] Rpt, Subcom on Automotive Equip to Ord Committee, Tech Staff, 22 Jun 40, sub: Dev of Light Inf and Cav Vehs, 400.112.

[59] 4th ind, TAG to CofOrd and TQMG, 5 Jul 40, on rpt cited in n. 58.

Viewing the problem from the standpoint of production and standardization, the Motor Transport Division opposed its adoption because it would have used four instead of two of the critical bottleneck items so essential to the all-wheel drive and its standardization would have meant one more maintenance problem.[60]

On the basis of competitive bidding the QMC awarded the order for the first seventy jeeps to the American Bantam Co. on 25 July 1940.[61] Earlier in the month a tentative specification had been drafted at the Holabird Depot. Engineers of the company and the depot co-operated in ironing out engineering difficulties. During the construction of the first pilot model it became evident that it would be necessary to increase the weight of the truck, and substantial changes were made before the model passed the severe Holabird test. After testing under supervision of the test boards of the using arms, the QMCTC co-ordinated their findings and recommended standardization of the jeep on 22 January 1941.[62]

The success of the jeep was instantaneous and sensational. So versatile did it prove that its uses multiplied in a fashion never even dreamed of by its creators. When news reports began to come in from theaters of operations all over the world, it was realized that the ¼-ton 4x4 truck had attained for itself and the QMC a reputation equal in its way, perhaps, to that of the famous Flying Fortress of the Air Forces, or the General Sherman tank, the pride of the Ordnance Department. Ernie Pyle, famous war correspondent, who characterized the jeep as "a divine instrument of wartime locomotion," eulogized it as follows:

Good Lord, I don't think we could continue the war without the jeep. It does everything. It goes everywhere. It's as faithful as a dog, as strong as a mule, and as agile as a goat. It constantly carries twice what it was designed for, and still keeps on going. It doesn't even ride so badly after you get used to it.[63]

However spectacular the success of the jeep, it represented but one of many developmental projects undertaken by the QMC in the automotive field before August 1942. Other trucks developed included the amphibious jeep, nicknamed the "waterbug," and the 2½-ton 6x6 truck, the basic cargo truck of the United States Army, which became known as "the workhorse of the Army" and enjoyed a success equal to that of the jeep.[64]

The development of motor vehicles for military purposes in World War II required a meeting of minds between the QMC, which set forth the specification for a given item, and the automobile industry, which translated it into an acceptable motor vehicle. Technically, the Army's functions in the development of any new vehicle ended with the preparation of military characteristics by the using arms and the writing of specifications by the QMC. The automotive engineers of private industry carried on from that point, designing, engineering, and building the pilot model in accordance with the stated specification. Collaboration and consultation, however, on all aspects of each automotive development, including design and engineering, had to take place between the QMC and industry if the undertaking was to be successful.

The drafting of specifications was significant in relation to the development of a standard-

---

[60] For a discussion of the experimentation with the four-wheel-steer jeep see Rifkind, The Jeep, pp. 159–70.

[61] (1) Current Procurement Br, OQMG, to ASW, 10 Jul 40, sub: Procurement of Trucks, Light Recon and Comd Cars, ¼-ton, 4x4. (2) 1st ind, ASW to TQMG, 11 Jul 40, on same. (3) Ltr, Holabird QMD to TQMG, 24 Jul 40, sub: Invitation for Bids 398–41–9. (4) 1st ind, OQMG to CO Holabird QMD, 25 Jul 40, on same. All in 451.

[62] QMCTC, min of mtg No. 1, 22 Jan 41.

[63] Ernie Pyle, The Washington Daily News, June 4, 1943.

[64] The design and development of the 2½-ton 6x6 by the Motor Transport Division, OQMG, was essentially complete when it was taken over by the Ordnance Department in August and standardized by it on 23 October 1942. OCM, item 19107, 23 Oct 42.

ized fleet of motor vehicles, consisting of a minimum number of types and sizes, which was the objective of the Corps throughout the period of its responsibility for motor transport. A specification, however, was no better than the procurement policy on which it was based, and Quartermaster specifications for motor vehicles were written to dovetail with the productive ability of the manufacturers. Under established procurement policy,[65] making mandatory the use of competitive bidding methods, the QMC had to draft motor vehicle specifications in such general terms as to enable several makers to meet them with vehicles of their own design. This procedure differed entirely from that governing the detailed specifications provided for other Quartermaster items of supply. A specification for a service uniform, for example, could be prepared to a single design, which all clothing manufacturers could produce without the necessity of making drastic changes in their operations or facilities.

In general, it was not feasible for automotive concerns in peacetime to make identical vehicles, or for one plant to manufacture a truck in accordance with the design of another maker. The cost of the extensive retooling that would be required, considered in relation to the small amount of the normal peacetime contract, precluded this. As a consequence, there was no peacetime alternative to the use of general specifications for motor vehicles, which meant that they could be met by the standard commercial chassis of any manufacture making a truck in the desired class. All of this was basically incompatible with the whole concept of standardization which held that, in order to escape in future conflicts the rather disastrous maintenance experience of World War I, motor vehicles would have to be standardized into a few basic sizes and types, thus holding the spare parts supply system down to a minimum number of spare parts and assemblies.

Between World Wars I and II the QMC made strenuous efforts to achieve standardization, even to the extent of venturing into the manufacture of trucks of its own design at the Holabird Depot, a procedure forbidden by War Department directive after the fall of 1933.[66] Thereafter all vehicles purchased were commercial models with such modifications as would make them suitable for military use. A multiplicity of makes and models of trucks were purchased in the following years, creating, in the event of war, an impossible maintenance problem.

By 1939 military requirements in the general-purpose tactical category were limited to five chassis types,[67] which were expanded to nine during the war years.[68] Within the limits of existing War Department policies, procurement, law, and the decisions of the Comptroller General, however, standardization could not be achieved. Only when Congress enacted legislation in 1940 [69] permitting exceptions to the mandatory use of competitive bidding methods could any real progress be made by the QMC in standardizing the motor fleet. It was then possible for the Corps to negotiate contracts

[65] The basic policy provided that the procurement of motor vehicles, other than combat vehicles, was to be limited to models produced commercially by two or more companies, "with the minimum deviation from standard commercial chassis necessary to conform to approved military characteristics." AR 850–15, par. 3b, 29 Sep 39, sub: Mil Mtr Vehs.

[66] WD GO 9, Sec. I, 11 Sep 33, sub: Policies Pertaining to Mtr Vehs.

[67] These were the ½-ton, 1½-ton, 2½-ton, 4-ton, and 7½-ton types. (1) See ltr, Brig Gen R. H. Jordan, OQMG, to TAG, 15 Jun 39, sub: Standardization of Mtr Vehs. (2) Ltr, TAG to TQMG, 12 Aug 39, same sub.

[68] The ¼-ton was introduced in 1940. The ¾-ton replaced the ½-ton while the 4–5-ton, 5–6-ton, and 6-ton chassis were added to fill the gap between the 4- and 7½-ton groups.

[69] (1) On 2 July Congress authorized war contracting "with or without advertising." PL 703, Sec. 1 (a). (2) The Secretary of War immediately issued a directive permitting awards to be made without formal competitive bidding whenever such methods "will serve to expedite the accomplishment of the defense program." Ltr, SW to Chiefs of Sup Arms and Svs, 2 Jul 40, sub: Procurement Without Advertising.

which achieved a greater degree of standardization by restricting purchase of truck models to those of the one commercial manufacturer in each weight classification whose product most closely approached military requirements, or by requiring vehicles to be assembled by the automobile industry from the standard commercial units and assemblies that came closest to meeting military needs. Thus, in the heavier field, it was planned to have the 6-ton prime mover made of standard major units by the White, Federal, and Autocar companies. For the medium types, Chevrolet and Yellow Truck and Coach, both divisions of General Motors, were first selected to make exclusively their 1½-ton and 2½-ton trucks, respectively. In the lighter field, the outstanding example of identical construction was the jeep, which ultimately was to be made by both Ford and Willys from the designs and blueprints of the Willys model. When the exigencies of World War II compelled procurement by negotiation, a greater degree of standardization resulted.

Petroleum Products

Equally important in World War II was the standardization and simplification of the different kinds of petroleum products used in maintaining and operating automotive equipment. The many kinds of fuels and lubricants required by Army vehicles created an acute problem of supply for the QMC. Under combat conditions, however, only a minimum number of grades of fuel could be supplied by tank cars, tank trucks, portable pipelines, and cans. In industrial life a special lubricant could be designed to give the best possible performance in each given type of bearing. What the Army needed, however, were fuels and lubricants which would be as universal as possible in application.

At the beginning of 1941 a number of official and quasi-official organizations, such as the supply services of the Army, the Navy Department, the Federal Specifications Board, and service advisory committees from industry, were all concerned in setting specifications for fuels and lubricants. Both the QMC and the Ordnance Department recommended the creation of a committee which would supervise the preparation of specifications for the whole field.[70] As a result, on 24 April 1941 the War Department Committee on Liquid Fuels and Lubricants was established[71] and emerged as the co-ordinating and expediting committee on specifications during World War II.

At the same time that The Quartermaster General was recommending co-ordinated action on specifications, he was also urging the standardization of specifications, reducing the number of grades to one for gasoline and one for diesel fuel. The Chief of Ordnance was in entire agreement with these proposals, and the Ordnance Department took an active part in the initial standardization of Army specifications.[72]

When this standardization program began, three types of gasoline were used for combat and motor transport vehicles. The Ordnance Department, assisted by the Coordinating Research Council and test data obtained from theaters of operations, Army installations, and industrial organizations, developed a specification for an all-purpose gasoline designed to meet the year-round combat requirements of all vehicles of the ground forces from ¼-ton trucks to tanks. This new specification for 80-octane gasoline, issued 3 November 1943, eliminated the necessity of differentiating between summer and winter grades by providing an all-purpose gasoline which assured maximum operating

---

[70] (1) Ltr, CofOrd to USW, 14 Feb 41, sub: Formation of Committees on Liquid F&L. (2) Ltr, TQMG to TAG, 25 Feb 41, sub: Liquid Fuels. Both in 463.

[71] For a fuller discussion of the work of this committee see Erna Risch, *Fuels for Global Conflict* QMC Historical Studies 9, rev ed (Washington, 1952), pp. 77–78.

[72] (1) Ltr, TQMG to TAG, 25 Feb 41, sub: Liquid Fuels. (2) Memo, CofOrd for ACofS G–4, 28 Mar 41, same sub. Both in 463.

efficiency regardless of temperatures, except in extreme arctic conditions where a special arctic grade was used. With the centralization of petroleum procurement and distribution in the Fuels and Lubricants Division, OQMG, 1 June 1943,[73] that division accomplished the final work of co-ordination on the 80-octane gasoline specification by insuring its use by all the services, by arranging for the Petroleum Administration for War to assure its supply, and by promoting co-ordination with the British.

In a similar manner the two types and seven grades of gear lubricants utilized before the war were reduced to one type and three grades. In line with the trend in gasoline it seemed advisable to have an all-purpose diesel fuel, an objective that was accomplished largely under the direction of the Fuels and Lubricants Division, OQMG.[74]

Petroleum-Handling Equipment

Since complete responsibility for the development of equipment especially designed for handling petroleum products was not centralized in the Fuels and Lubricants Division until the spring of 1944, the original developmental work on many such items was accomplished in other supply services, such as the Ordnance Department, the Transportation Corps, and the Corps of Engineers. For example, the 100-gallon-per-minute portable gasoline dispenser was approved and standardized on 23 December 1943 by action of the Ordnance Technical Committee.[75] On the other hand, developmental work on "Mareng" cells, or collapsible containers made of canvas impregnated with synthetic rubber, was initiated in 1942 by the Transportation Corps. Subsequently responsibility for development was vested in the Corps of Engineers. It carried development of four types to the point of standardization before responsibility was transferred to the QMC.[76] As a result of conferences, it was later decided that the Corps

of Engineers should continue developmental work and testing in this field upon specific directive from the Fuels and Lubricants Division.[77]

After responsibility for the development of petroleum-handling equipment had been centralized in the Fuels and Lubricants Division, a number of refinements in such equipment were undertaken. The division also developed new items, such as the portable can cleaner, and the 2,500-gallon tank truck and 2,500-gallon trailer, which increased the facility of handling petroleum products in the field.

One item, the popular 5-gallon "blitz" can, was developed by the QMC long before centralization of responsibility for petroleum-handling equipment had been achieved. Made of 20-gauge steel, the blitz can was equipped with carrying handles. It was·designed primarily as an item of issue for fuel-consuming vehicles and gasoline companies. However, it had a wider use than this implies. Not only was the blitz can used as a distribution medium for motor fuel between railhead or fuel dump and the combat zone, but it was also the primary basis of initial and continued supply to beachheads until port facilities permitted the use of tankers and pipelines.

The blitz can was an adaptation to American usage of the 5-gallon German can, or "Jerry Can," a sample of which was brought to the OQMG in the summer of 1940. The Motor

[73] (1) ASF Cir 33, 26 May 43, sub: Procurement, Storage and Distr of Petrl Products, Fuels (Liquid and Solid) and Lubricants. (2) OQMG OO 25–37, 29 May 43, sub: Establishment of F&L Div.

[74] Risch, *Fuels for Global Conflict*, p 81.

[75] Memo, OCO for CG, 23 Dec 43, sub: Pump, Gasoline, Dispensing, 100 GPM—Standardization Recommended.

[76] AGO Memo W 850–15–43, 10 Apr 43, sub: Asgmt of Responsibility for Handling Liquid Fuel Equip.

[77] Ltr, Brig Gen W. E. R. Covell to CG ASF, 23 Aug 43, sub: Responsibility for Development and Procurement of Collapsible Liquid Fuel Units.

FILLING BLITZ CANS FROM RAILROAD TANK CAR *by use of portable gasoline pump.*

Transport Division instructed the Holabird Quartermaster Motor Base to prepare specifications for a 5-gallon galvanized can following generally the pattern of those captured from the Germans in Europe.[78] In order to use the assembly-line technique and mass production, the QMC constructed the blitz can in three pieces instead of the two used by the Germans, who welded the parts together and assembled them by hand. Other changes were made including the use of an American type of closure, which would take a flexible nozzle essential to servicing vehicles, and automatic venting, which permitted complete discharge of contents in a minimum of time.[79] Procurement was initiated in the fall of 1940. Although a number of refinements were later developed by the Fuels and Lubricants Division, the blitz can used during World War II was essentially the same as the model developed by the Motor Transport Division in 1940.

Field Range

A portable, gasoline-burning field range was one of the more important items of development among those used in the storage, handling, and preparation of food. Wood-burning field ranges No. 1 and No. 2, as well as so-called rolling kitchens consisting of horse-drawn ranges and accessories, were developed and used in the field during World War I. These ranges were limited as to the variety and desirability of the food prepared on them, and the smoke they emitted enabled the enemy to determine the location of Army units.[80] This equipment continued to be used in the years following, and, in fact, field ranges No. 1 and No. 2 were procured even in the early period of World War II but only because equipment recognized as superior could not be supplied in quantities sufficient to fill the demand at that time.

The need for a portable, gasoline-burning field range was recognized, and the Jefferson-

ville Quartermaster Depot began developmental work in 1932. By 1937 it submitted a specification to the Standardization Branch, OQMG. In its original form the M–1937 field range consisted of one or more self-contained cabinets, constructed of aluminum and stainless steel, each of which contained a roast or bake pan with griddle cover and a steel cradle for supporting a large boiler and a fire unit. It was designed to be transportable on a 2½-ton truck and could be operated while in transit. The newly designed range underwent extensive field tests which resulted in numerous alterations in the original design.[81] In May 1939 it was classified as a standard item of issue,[82] not because these tests had demonstrated that it worked with maximum efficiency but to permit immediate procurement. Many problems, from the use of leaded gasoline to the design of proper utensils for an efficient field range, remained to be solved.

Since the M–1937 range was developed in peacetime, it was designed of materials—chiefly aluminum and stainless steel—judged best for the purpose rather than of those most readily obtainable in a period of scarcity. As war became imminent, the necessity to conserve raw materials forced the redesign of the field range and the use of substitute materials.[83] Inasmuch as these changes increased its weight from 138 to 178 pounds and numerous minor breakdowns of parts were reported, it was with considerable

[78] Rpt, Lt Heller to Lt Col H. B. Hester and Col Doriot, OQMG, 27 Oct 41, sub: History of the Gas and Water Can Procurement Program.

[79] Risch, *Fuels for Global Conflict*, pp. 90–91.

[80] Maj O. E. Cound, "The Army's New Field Range," *QMR*, XIX (September–October 1939), 10.

[81] (1) Memo draft, Brig Gen A. B. Warfield, OQMG, to CofInf, 23 Feb 39, sub: Tests for Improvement of QM Portable Fld Range. (2) Capt Cound to TQMG, 20 Mar 39, sub: Outline of Changes to be Made in 17 Units of QM Portable Gasoline Fld Range, M–1937.

[82] 2d ind, TAG to TQMG, 16 May 39, on ltr, Col Hardigg, OQMG, to TAG, 10 May 39, no sub.

[83] See above, Ch. II.

FIELD RANGE M–1937, *set up in the box of a two and one-half ton truck near Haller, Luxembourg, January 1945.*

relief that the Mechanical Section of the Research and Development Branch returned to the use of aluminum and stainless steel when the metal situation improved in the late summer of 1944.

The fire unit of the field range provided the most troublesome problem in design, and underwent considerable modification during the war. As a gasoline-burning unit, it used either white or leaded gasoline. Its design was simple, but maintenance proved extremely difficult, as a direct result of the type of gasoline used. While the use of white gasoline created no particular problems, the gasoline most readily available in

the field was motor fuel, a high-test leaded gasoline. The use of this fuel posed two problems. The toxicity of burner fumes created a hazard to health. The lead in the gasoline, deposited in tubes, valves, and burner slots, clogged the burner parts, creating maintenance difficulties.

In order to remove the lead the original fire unit used an asbestos disc about three inches in diameter and one eighth of an inch thick. It was located in a special case at the mid point of the generator tube and all vaporized gasoline had to pass through this filter. It removed about 60 to 70 percent of the lead in the gasoline, but

GASOLINE COOKING STOVES *M-1941 (left) and M-1942 (right)*.

this type of filter had to be replaced after two to six hours of operation. In actual practice filter changing appears to have been required after the preparation of almost every meal. One report from the field stated that, even after the leaded gasoline had been filtered through five or six gas mask canisters, "it was still necessary to tear the range down at least three times per day in order to have it work at all." [84] Frequently the lead not stopped by the filter clogged other parts of the fire unit.

Before the North African campaign, experience with the fire unit had been limited to maneuvers in which operating personnel had usually obtained white gasoline by one means or another. In North Africa, when only leaded gasoline was available, no one was prepared to meet the maintenance problem because of inexperience as well as lack of parts for the range.

The fire units therefore failed to give adequate service.

Even before the North African campaign demonstrated the acute need for improving the maintenance characteristics of the fire unit, the Research and Development Branch instituted a program to solve the problem of lead removal and to simplify and redesign the burner. It asked the Ethyl Corporation, the American Gas Machine Co., and the Coleman Lamp & Stove Co. to pool their engineering knowledge for this purpose.[85]

The net result was the adoption of a tube

---

[84] Capt Pounder, Rpt of QM Opns in NATO, 5 Mar–2 Jun 43.

[85] (1) Ltr, Col Doriot, OQMG, to Ethyl Corp, 19 Sep 42, no sub. (2) Ltr, Doriot to CG JQMD, 30 Sep 42, sub: Research Work on Fire Unit. (3) See R&D Br, Status Rpts, 31 Aug 42–31 Mar 43, under heading: Deleading of Gasoline for Fld Range.

packed with steel wool as a filter generator. The new generator could be operated for 200 to 300 hours before requiring renewal, and it increased the amount of lead removed up to 95 percent or more, thereby reducing maintenance considerably.[86] The design of the fire unit was modified to incorporate the changes necessitated by the use of the new filter. At the same time the design of the flame valve was altered to make it self-cleaning. This improvement, together with the more satisfactory filter, reduced flame valve cleaning from once in 4 to 8 hours to once in 50 to 100 hours. These improvements were immediately made applicable to new procurements of the field range. A conversion kit was designed and procured to convert equipment, especially that already in use in the field, where the problem was most acute. The new generator, an adequate supply of spare parts, and the cumulative effects of an educational program on repair caused the field range and fire unit thereafter to be considered entirely acceptable.

Small Stoves

Centralized messing facilities were not always available to soldiers in World War II. Circumstances frequently called for wide dispersal of units. The possibility of operations in cold-climate areas first raised the problem of providing cooking and heating facilities for the individual soldier or for small groups. In the summer of 1941 the QMC attacked the problem in behalf of mountain and ski troops. The Primus stove, a light, compact stove burning liquid fuel, had been used by arctic explorers and mountaineers for many years, but a one-burner gasoline stove that would satisfy military requirements was not available on the commercial market. Stoves used by campers were too heavy and operated only on white gasoline. At the request of the QMC the Coleman Lamp and Stove Co. in the summer of 1941

designed a functionally satisfactory stove which was known as the cold-climate stove.[87] Essentially it was the same stove subsequently called the M–1941, a one-burner gasoline stove. This stove, compact in size and rugged in construction, weighed thirty-seven ounces and would burn over two hours on either white or leaded gasoline. The burner was designed to light instantaneously without priming, even at low temperature. Pending the outcome of tests, the stove was classified as a limited procurement type.[88]

In the meantime desire for an even more compact and a lighter stove led the QMC to call a conference of eight of the leading gasoline stove manufacturers at Chicago on 9 February 1942. They were invited to produce a new single-burner unit for use in mountain operations and also to incorporate two of the burners in a larger stove to serve vehicle crews. The ensuing developmental work resulted in the design of a new stove called the M–1942 model. By test in the Bureau of Standards the M–1941 and M–1942 stoves were considered practically identical on the basis of heating, fuel consumption, and general efficiency. The M–1942 gasoline stove, however, weighed less than half the earlier one (17 ounces as against 37 ounces), was more compact, and required only half as much material in its manufacture. It was also believed to have better igniting characteristics at low temperatures. The stove had tripod folding legs and tripod folding brackets on top of the burner. When folded the whole stove could be carried within a straight-sided pot seven

[86] (1) Rpt, Carl H. Rasmussen, Mechanical Sec, R&D Br, Unit Fire, Range Fld, M–1937, 15 Nov 45. (2) 3d ind, Col Doriot to Hq SOS, 5 Dec 42, on ltr, Hq 72d Fld Artillery Brigade to CG AGF, 16 Nov 42, sub: Rpt on Use of Fld Ranges.
[87] (1) Ltr, Col Robinson to JQMD, 5 Jun 41, no sub. (2) Ltr, same to Lt Col H. M. Schofield, WDGS, 14 Jun 41, no sub. (3) QMC Spec JQD 33, 10 Oct 42, sub: Cold-Climate Stove.
[88] QMCTC, min of mtg No. 6, 8 Jul 42.

inches in diameter and four inches deep.[89] In the fall of 1942 the new model was standardized while the M–1941 stove was reclassified as substitute standard.[90]

Where weight and bulk were primary factors to be considered as in the case of equipment used by ski troops, mountain forces, and special task forces, the M–1942, one-burner gasoline stove was considered the best small stove. In all other cases, particularly when the stove would be used by mechanized forces, the M–1941 model could be utilized to good advantage. Although the later model, which was subsequently somewhat modified, had been intended to replace the M–1941 stove, production difficulties made it necessary to procure both till the end of the war.

The one-burner gasoline stove proved to be one of the most popular items of equipment developed by the QMC. Ernie Pyle wrote:

One of the most practical pieces of equipment our Army has got around to is the little Coleman stove for cooking. . . .

Almost every group of front-line soldiers has one now. They heat their C-rations in it, make coffee several times a day, heat water for shaving, and if they're in an enclosed place such as a dugout they even use it for warmth.

You have no idea what a big thing some practical little device like a successful stove is in the life of a man at the front.[91]

The 1942 stove as combined with a mountain cookset and issued as a one-burner cooking outfit would serve about five men. The mountain cookset consisted of two aluminum pots, nesting into each other, with a stainless steel cover which also served as a frying pan. When not in use the stove fitted within the pots, and a steel wire handle on the cover folded out of the way and locked all units together securely.[92]

Other cooking outfits for small groups of men operating away from organizational mess facilities were developed by the QMC. Among these was the 20-man cooking outfit, initially "developed under the auspices of Major

Clements of the Storage and Distribution Division" [93] and later taken over and modified by the Special Forces Section of the Research and Development Branch. Designed to be used particularly by antiaircraft and searchlight detachments, it was recommended for standardization by the QMCTC on 15 September 1942. The outfit consisted of two gasoline stoves of the two-burner type; two metal cases, one for each stove, which could be used as a cooking vessel and a frying pan; a set of nested cooking vessels including two coffee pots; and miscellaneous utensils, such as can openers, paring knives, and a ladle. The complete outfit weighed about fifty pounds and was packed in a canvas carrying bag.

This 20-man cooking outfit was criticized in test reports because food, unless closely watched by the cook, burned easily. An intensely hot, localized flame was furnished by the burners, which were the same as those used in the M–1941 one-burner stoves. In addition, the frequent clogging of generators posed a maintenance problem. Within a year a considerable number of modifications had been made to overcome these difficulties as well as to redesign the components of the outfit.[94]

Because of the inadequacy of the 20-man cooking outfit, a project had been initiated

[89] Special Forces Sec, Mil Plng Div, to Mil Intel Div, OQMG, 10 Oct 42, sub: One-Burner Gasoline Stove, M–1942, 414.2.

[90] (1) QMCTC, min of mtg No. 9, 15 Sep 42. (2) By an oversight the reclassification of the M–1941 stove was not accomplished until the summer of 1943. Ltr, Col Cowles, OQMG, to CG ASF, 11 Jun 43, sub: One-Burner Gasoline Stove, M–1941, and One-Burner Cooking Outfit, and 2d ind, Hq ASF to TQMG, 21 Jun 43, on same, 414.2.

[91] Ernie Pyle, "Krauts and Tedeschi," *The Washington Daily News*, May 1, 1944.

[92] R&D Project Register, Case Record on the Mountain Cookset, 10 June–26 Oct 42.

[93] (1) Col Robinson to Capt McLean, Mil Plng Div, OQMG, 18 Dec 42, no sub. (2) QMCTC, min of mtg No. 9, 15 Sep 42.

[94] (1) [2d ind], AAABd to CG AACmd, 28 May 43. (2) Ltr, Col Doriot, OQMG, to CG AGF, 25 Sep 43, sub: 20-Man Cooking Outfit. Both in 414.2.

about March 1943 to develop a more satisfactory item. In the months following a considerable amount of research was accomplished, resulting in the development of the small detachment cooking outfit to provide hot meals for 20 to 30 men. Standardized at first on a basis of limited procurement, the new outfit proved superior in tests to the 20-man cooking unit. As a consequence in the summer of 1944 the QMCTC recommended its standardization and the reclassification of the 20-man cooking outfit as substitute standard.[95]

This small detachment cooking outfit weighed 80 pounds but was so constructed that it could be packed in two equal parts, which could be carried on pack boards by two men. When set up for cooking, the stove was a rectangular box measuring 18 by 24 by 12 inches in size, with a sectional stovepipe about 6 feet long. This stove was operated by a flow of liquid fuel from a 5-gallon gasoline can. Components of the outfit included aluminum cookpots of assorted sizes, stainless steel frying pans, a sterilizing pan for mess gear, and various other small accessories. For packing purposes, the cooking utensils fitted together in the upper half of the stove, while the stovepipe—telescoped into one short length—and the burner were packed in the lower half.

Field Bakeries

When World War II began the Army was using the same kind of field bakery equipment utilized without change for twenty-three years. The regular item of issue to bakery companies was the Army field baking oven No. 1, which required that all mixing, moulding, and dividing of dough be done by hand. It was a portable, knock-down piece of equipment, designed to be assembled in the field. Since its gross weight was 3,714 pounds when assembled, and since it included eighteen separate pieces when packed for shipment, the field baking oven was

obviously not well designed for use under difficult field conditions.

The QMC was aware of the need for improving field bakery equipment. As early as 1931 the Motor Transport Board at Holabird was instructed to study the problem of mobility in connection with such equipment.[96] For the next ten years this problem was studied in a leisurely fashion by the Corps. Not until 1940, however, when the need had become urgent, was the Jeffersonville Depot instructed to develop a field bake oven and a mixer designed to use gasoline as fuel.[97]

By June 1941 the depot had developed equipment which was ready for preliminary inspection. Informal tests revealed that further developmental work was required, and it was suggested that qualified engineers from the best manufacturing companies of bakery equipment be consulted. With the co-operation of industry, working models were constructed. Among the various models tested at Fort Meade, Md., early in 1942, the oven constructed by the Century Machine Co. of Cincinnati was deemed best by the Subsistence Branch, OQMG, which opposed further experimentation as fruitless. In consequence it directed the Jeffersonville Depot to make "no purchases of Field Bake Ovens other than that developed by the Century Machine Company" until further notice.[98] In the summer of 1942 the field bake oven, M-1942, was standardized and used by the services as

[95] (1) Rpt, Subcom, QMCTC, to QMCTC, 26 Oct 43, sub: Small Detachment Cooking Outfit. (2) Rpt, Same to same, 17 Aug 44, same sub. (3) QMCTC, min of mtg No. 16, 22 Aug 44. (4) This action was approved by Hq ASF, 8 Sept 44. 2d ind, Hq ASF to TQMG, 8 Sep 44, on ltr, Col Doriot to CG ASF, 28 Aug 44, same sub, 414.2.

[96] Ltr, Lt Col B. Taylor, OQMG, to CO Holabird QMD, 1 Apr 31, sub: Mobile Bakeries, 414.2.

[97] Ltr, Gen Corbin, OQMG, to CO JQMD, 3 Aug 40, sub: Development of Fld Bakery.

[98] Ltr, Gen Hardigg, Chief of Subs Br, OQMG, to CG, JQMD, 14 Apr 42, sub: Portable Fld Bakery Units.

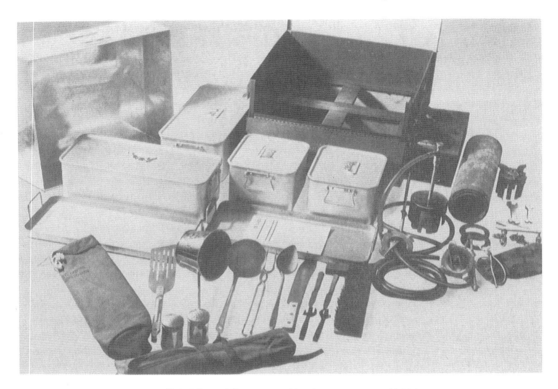

SMALL DETACHMENT COOKING OUTFIT

standard field equipment throughout World War II.[99]

Although the field bake oven, M–1942, was developed by the Subsistence Branch, OQMG, and the Jeffersonville Depot in co-operation with industry, responsibility for subsequent modifications of it and the development of a mobile bakery was vested in the Research and Development Branch by the end of 1942. Despite the reluctance of the Subsistence Branch to admit the need for additional research, the Mechanical Section of the Research and Development Branch began further developmental work on ovens and made a number of modifications to improve the operations of the M–1942 model.[100]

The M–1942 oven was definitely an improve-

ment over the old equipment. It was a two-section oven. Each section weighed about 550 pounds and was equipped with bars so that it could be lifted and carried by four men. The upper section consisted of two separate baking decks, while the lower contained the burners and a built-in proofing chamber. Later pot-type gasoline burners were substituted for the two

---

[99] (1) Ltr, Col Doriot, OQMG, to Chief of Dev Br, Reqmts Div, SOS, 5 Aug 42, sub: Fld Baking Outfit. (2) 2d ind, Hq SOS to TQMG, 26 Aug 42, on same. Both in 414.2.

[100] (1) Rpt, Mil Plng Div, Summary of Rpt on New Fld Bake Ovens, 4 Jan 43. (2) Chief of Subs Br to Dir of S&D Div, OQMG, 28 Jan 43, sub: Comments on Rpt of Development of Fld Bake Oven, M–1942. (3) Insp Div to TQMG, 1 Feb 43, sub: Insp–JQMD & Cincinnati, Ohio, 6–10 Dec 42.

20-MAN COOKING OUTFIT

M-1937 fire units originally used. Hand mixing of dough was eliminated by the use of a dough-mixing machine powered by a gasoline engine. While the M-1942 oven was portable in comparison with the Army field baking oven No. 1, it was in no sense mobile, and it operated mechanically only in respect to the mixer. Manual handling of the dough—which was not conducive to cleanliness—was still necessary to prepare, divide, weigh, mould, and set the dough in pans.

When the M-1942 baking outfit began to operate in the field, defects in the equipment became apparent and criticisms were directed to the OQMG from theaters of operations. The routine of assembling the equipment manually to begin baking bread and dismantling it to evacuate a location was time consuming. When marching orders were received a Quartermaster truck company had to furnish forty-five trucks to move the equipment of an American baking company.[101] The M-1942 field bakery lacked the mobility demanded by modern war. In addition, the equipment itself was criticized. The proofing chamber was not used because it was too hot in summer and too cold in winter; instead, in the field, proofing racks were improvised by Quartermaster bakers. The gasoline engine for the mixer failed to operate satisfactorily over an extended period, since it was apparently too small for the mixer. Maintenance

---

[101] A Quartermaster bakery company was equipped with 32 ovens, 16 dough mixers, 64 insulated fermentation cans, and complementary equipment.

ARMY FIELD BAKE OVEN No. 1 *in operation at New Caledonia, April 1942.*

was difficult and replacement parts were not readily available.[102]

Generally, "so called mobile equipment" was considered by one Quartermaster observer to be "too large and too complicated." "Movable" rather than "mobile" was the term applicable to it. In particular, he found British bakeries more efficient than American. "The British bakery can be moved in much shorter time than ours can. It takes fewer personnel to operate it and it produces the same amount of bread." [103] All reports from the ETO supported this view. Many American bakery units in the ETO made use of the British mobile bakery, all of the major items of which were mounted on two-wheel, high-platform trailers.

Through the ingenuity of the American soldier fresh bread was being delivered to the troops, but the cost in time, morale of using troops, efficiency, transportation, maintenance, and spare-parts supply problems made it apparent that major improvements would have to be effected. Early in 1944 the Research and Development Branch requested permission of Headquarters, ASF, to develop a field bakery unit with mobility "equal to that of a 2½-ton truck."[104] This mobile equipment was to have adequate productive capacity for supplying large concentrations of personnel. The M–1942 portable bakery equipment would continue to be issued to supply small bodies of troops primarily in the Pacific areas where such groups were isolated and the use of mobile equipment, capable of producing for large numbers, was not justified.

The M–1942 equipment was to be modified, however, to meet the criticisms that had been made. Leading industrial firms co-operated with the Jeffersonville Depot and the Mechanical Section, OQMG, to improve the oven, mixer, and gasoline engine. Mixers having larger bowl capacity were designed, and a new engine, capable of standing constant hard use for longer periods, was substituted for the original model.

Work on an improved oven, lighter in weight than the M–1942 model but rugged in construction, continued for many months. It remained uncompleted when the war ended.[105]

In the meantime developmental work on a truly mobile bakery unit had been started in 1944.[106] The design of the mobile bakery was undertaken only after a thorough study of field bakery operations and of the deficiencies and advantages of both the British mobile bakery and the M–1942 bakery. The Research and Development Branch consulted the best engineering talent of the country, and over fifteen companies participated in the development of the mobile bakery unit.

Components of the bakery unit consisted of one machinery trailer carrying mixing and make-up machinery, two oven trailers, and two generator trailers. Auxiliary equipment, such as dough troughs, racks, conveyors, scales, and tentage, was also included. This equipment was factory tested at the respective manufacturing plants and then assembled in complete units at the Jeffersonville Quartermaster Depot, where necessary engineering changes were effected as a result of further preliminary tests. Early in the summer of 1945 extensive baking tests were undertaken at Fort Knox, Ky.

World War II ended before the mobile bakery unit could be put into combat service, but the tests had demonstrated its superiority to the

---

[102] (1) Abstract, 1st Lt Owen N. Tucker, Rpt of Investigation of Am Fld Bakery Equip in NATO, 30 Aug 43. (2) Rpt, Maj Burnhome, European-North African-Persian Areas, Nov 1943. (3) Asst for Product Analysis to Mechanical Sec, R&D Br, OQMG, 26 Aug 43, sub: Fld Bake Oven.

[103] Rpt, Maj Burnhome, European-North African-Persian Areas, Nov 1943.

[104] Ltr, Col Doriot to Hq ASF, 28 Jan 44, sub: Mobile Fld Bakery.

[105] (1) R&D Br, Status Rpts, 31 Aug 44–31 Aug 45, under heading Portable Fld Bakery, M–1944. (2) R&D Br to General Supplies Br, S&D Div, OQMG, 23 Mar 45, sub: Fld Bakery Equip.

[106] See R&D Br, Status Rpts, 31 Jan 44–31 Aug 45, under heading, Bakery, Fld, Mobile.

old equipment in conservation of manpower, in productive capacity, and in mobility. Limited procurement was requested by the QMC and initiated as the war was ending in order to provide equipment for training and to obtain field experience on production models. The new mobile bakery unit was intended for use wherever requirements had to be met for 5,500 or more pounds of bread per day. Where less than that amount was required, the M–1942 bakery was to be used. The mobile bakery unit, M–1945, was standardized in the fall of 1945.[107]

Responsibility for Refrigeration Equipment

The development of mechanical equipment to handle the storage of perishable food was an essential part of the task of feeding the Army. Unfortunately, uncertainty over the question of responsibility for developmental work on refrigeration equipment prevailed throughout the war, inevitably hindering work in this field. Prior to World War II responsibility for the development of all military refrigeration had been vested in the QMC. When Congress by legislative action on 1 December 1941 transferred construction, real estate activities, and repairs and utilities from the QMC to the Corps of Engineers, responsibility for refrigeration equipment was included. War Department implementation of the law, however, left unclarified for three months whether a complete transfer or a division of responsibilities had been directed insofar as the development of refrigeration equipment was concerned. By March 1942 the Chief of Engineers had been directed to assume responsibility for such developmental work. An exception to this transfer was the developmental work on refrigerated semitrailers, the responsibility for which remained in the Motor Transport Division, OQMG.[108]

In the summer of 1943, however, at the request of the Chief of Engineers the problem was taken up by the Procurement Assignment Board, ASF, which reassigned to the Corps the responsibility for preparing specifications and procuring mechanical and ice-cooled refrigerators, including frozen-food storage units to be used in new facilities or in portable or mobile equipment.[109] Refrigerators for marine and rail use and for aircraft were excluded. In the OQMG the function of developing refrigeration equipment was centralized in the Military Planning Division.[110]

The division of responsibilities, however, between the Engineer Corps and the OQMG for each major type of refrigeration equipment had not been entirely and satisfactorily clarified. Repeated conferences between the two services solved these difficulties, and in April 1944 a new War Department circular spelled out in detail the assignment of responsibilities. In general, the Corps of Engineers was responsible for larger refrigeration equipment for fixed installations, such as permanent ice-making plants, while the QMC was responsible for small

---

[107] (1) Ltr, Gen Doriot, OQMG, to CG ASF, 6 Aug 45, sub: Procurement of US Mobile Bakeries. (2) Rpt, Subcom, QMCTC, to QMCTC, 21 Aug 45, sub: Mobile Bakery Unit, M–1945. (3) QMCTC, min of mtg No. 19, 11 Sep 45. (4) Ltr, Gen Doriot to CG ASF, 17 Sep 45, same sub, and 1st ind, Hq ASF to TQMG, 8 Nov 45. All in 414.2.

[108] (1) WD Cir 248, 4 Dec 41, sub: Transfer of Constr and Real Estate Activities from QMC to CE. (2) WD Cir 69, 7 Mar 42, sub: Definition of Responsibility. (3) For a period of five months responsibility for refrigerated semitrailers was vested in the Ordnance Department: from 1 August 1942, when the Motor Transport Division was transferred to Ordnance, to 24 December 1942, when research, design, and developmental responsibility for special purpose vehicles pertaining to the QMC were returned to its jurisdiction. WD Cir 245, 25 Jul 42, Sec. IV, sub: Transfer of Certain MT Activities, and WD Cir 418, 24 Dec 42, sub: MT Responsibilities.

[109] AGO Memo S5–103–43, 8 Jun 43, sub: Asmgts of PAB.

[110] (1) OQMG OO 25–46, 10 Aug 43, sub: Asgmt of Functions Transferred from CE. (2) About the same time responsibility for the development of the refrigerated semitrailer was also transferred to the division. OQMG OO 25–48, 14 Aug 43, sub: Transfer of Functions.

equipment for fixed installations and for practically all portable and mobile refrigeration equipment.[111]

Refrigerated Semitrailers

One of the earliest items developed for handling perishable subsistence was the refrigerated semitrailer. The purpose of the developmental work, begun in the spring of 1941, was to provide a semitrailer of the van type with a refrigerator body capable of handling at least one day's meat and vegetable supply for one division. Various industries co-operated with the OQMG and the Holabird Quartermaster Depot in the early developmental work.

The first specification drafted by Holabird was made broad enough to cover several commercial models, which were purchased for experimental purposes.[112] The semitrailer was made principally of steel and insulated with corkboard and fiberglass. The refrigerating system was an integral part of the semitrailer, capable of maintaining temperatures of 10° F. for frozen foods and 35° F. for fresh foods. As a result of tests made by the Quartermaster Board and field use by a quartermaster refrigerator company during maneuvers in the fall of the year, several modifications, such as increased cork insulation in the floor, sides, and ceiling, were incorporated in a new specification.[113] In June of 1942, the 10-ton, two-wheel, refrigerated semitrailer, utilizing a 4–5 ton 4x4 tractor, was standardized.[114]

Shortly thereafter motor transport activities, including the development of the refrigerated semitrailer, were transferred to the Ordnance Department. By the end of the year, however, responsibility for the design and development of special-purpose motor vehicles pertaining to the QMC had once more been restored to the Corps. In the following summer the Research and Development Branch reviewed the entire problem of providing fresh meat and vegetables

to troops in forward areas. Tests were conducted both in the laboratory and in the field to determine the mobility and usefulness of the refrigerated semitrailer in accomplishing its mission.

As a result the Quartermaster Board reported that the refrigerated semitrailer was satisfactory for operation in rear echelons only, inasmuch as greater mobility was required in forward areas. The size and the weight of the semitrailer were such that it could not leave a road quickly to seek shelter from an air attack. Moreover its size, weight, and slowness would definitely impede traffic on important supply roads. On the other hand, the semitrailer had capacity to supply a greater number of troops than it had mobility to reach. The Quartermaster Board recommended that "consideration be given to the development of portable equipment to be mounted on 2½-ton 6x6, cargo trucks and 1-ton cargo trailers to replace the van-type, two-wheel, semitrailers and 4–5 ton, 4x4 tractors."[115] Reports from theaters of operations amply supported the findings of the board.

Although refrigerated semitrailers of the heavy type were still being delivered as late as May 1945 to fill the requirements of the Service Installations Division, the Mechanical Section had, in July 1944, initiated a project to decrease the weight of this item to permit greater maneuverability and to increase the payload. A

[111] (1) Memo, Brig Gen H. Feldman, OQMG, for CG ASF, 9 Feb 44, sub: Asgmt of Responsibility for Refrigeration Equip. (2) WD Cir 156, Sec. V, 20 Apr 44, sub: Refrigeration. (3) These provisions were slightly modified in the fall. WD Cir 446, Sec. VI, 23 Nov 44, same sub.

[112] Ltr, Col Van Deusen, OQMG, to CO Holabird QMD, 17 May 41, sub: Development of Semitrailer, Refrigerated Body Type, 400.112.

[113] Ltr, Capt E. H. Holtzkemper, OQMG, to CO Holabird QMD, 31 Dec 41, sub: Mobile Refrigerator Unit, 400.1141.

[114] (1) Memo, Col Van Deusen, OQMG, for CG SOS, 12 Jun 42, sub: Standardization of Semitrailer, 10-ton, 2-wheel (2dt), Refrigerator. (2) 3d ind, Hq SOS to TQMG, 30 Jun 42, on same. Both in 451.3.

[115] QMB Rpt, 10 Sep 43, sub: Project S–63, Rpt of Test of Mobile Refrigeration Unit, pp. 8–9.

plug-in type of refrigerating system was to be used because, as a separate and self-contained unit, it could easily be removed and replaced.[116] The heavy model of the refrigerated semitrailer weighed 14,700 pounds. An experimental model, weighing about half the amount, or 7,500 pounds, was ordered by the Mechanical Section. This weight reduction was accomplished by the use of aluminum and featherweight insulation. It was expected that a payload of 15,000 pounds could be carried as compared with 10,000 pounds carried in the heavy model.

The pilot model of the aluminum semitrailer was completed in September and driven cross country from Spokane, Wash., to Camp Lee, Va. This road test revealed minor defects but aside from a few changes the Quartermaster Board considered that unit satisfactory. The first production model of the aluminum trailer body was completed and inspected in May 1945 and found to be "highly satisfactory." [117] The project was thereupon closed, since the developmental work was considered completed.

The development of the lightweight semitrailer was accomplished without too much difficulty but developing a satisfactory separate refrigerating unit raised many problems. The chief one was the inadequacy of the small gasoline engine to provide power for the refrigerating unit. In a test it broke down completely after 107 hours of operation, and the Quartermaster Board was therefore unable to test the refrigerating unit according to plan.[118] The problem had not been satisfactorily solved when the war ended and all contracts were canceled. The OQMG was convinced, however, of the need for a long-range developmental program for small gasoline engines, which was accordingly planned.

Although a small number of lightweight semitrailers were produced in the summer of 1945 they were not placed in service in the field. Any claims to superiority of the new design over the earlier heavy model must rest on the

conclusions drawn from tests made during the developmental program. The question of its usefulness in delivering perishable food to troops in forward areas remained speculative.

150-Cubic-Foot Portable Refrigerator

The need for a refrigerator unit more portable than the 10,000-pound semitrailer resulted in the initiation in August 1943 of a project for the development of a 150- (at one time planned as a 125-) cubic-foot portable cabinet that could withstand rough handling in forward areas. Comparative tests of the serviceability and mobility of the 10-ton semitrailer and various sized portable units were made at Camp Lee, Va.[119]

This project was barely begun when a requisition for several hundred 150-cubic-foot refrigerators, operated by gasoline engines, was received from the South Pacific area under the mistaken belief that the units already in use there were Army items. Actually they were issued by the Navy. Theater requests for the Navy-type, 150-cubic-foot refrigerator led to the development of the Army unit, since the Navy refrigerator was found to be too heavy for easy transportation.[120]

The Mechanical Section continued developmental work on a 150-cubic-foot refrigerator in co-operation with various manufacturers who produced experimental models for testing at Camp Lee. By the beginning of 1944 a preliminary report covering refrigeration and structural performance had been received from the Quar-

---

[116] (1) R&D Project Record, 189–44, sub: Semitrailer, Two-Wheel, 10-ton gross, Refrigerator Body, Improved. (2) See also R&D Br, Status Rpts, 31 Jul 44–31 May 45, under same title.

[117] *Ibid.*, 31 May 45.

[118] QMB Rpt, 23 Mar 45, Project S–132, Preliminary Rpt of Study of Semitrailer, Two-Wheel, 10-ton, Refrigerator Body, Lightweight (Refrigerating System), T–1579.

[119] R&D Br, Status Rpts, 31 Aug–30 Sep 43.

[120] Asst Chief of R&D Br to QMCTC Sec, OQMG, 31 Jan 45, sub: Walk-In Portable Refrigerator, 414.1.

termaster Board. It was sufficiently complete so that prior to the drafting of a specification and drawings the Research and Development Branch could recommend purchase by the Procurement Division of the best model tested.[121] By the end of February the drawings and specification had been completed.

This portable refrigerator unit, weighing about 3,900 pounds, utilized steel in its construction and corkboard for insulation. It had a twofold purpose. It was designed for the transportation and storage of frozen food up to approximately 4,200 pounds of boneless beef, for which purpose its temperature could be automatically held at about 10° F. When used for the transportation and storage of unfrozen perishable produce, the temperature could be automatically held at about 35° F. Designed for rough usage, this "all-purpose, all-temperature refrigerator" could be operated while being transported over good roads on a 2½-ton truck or over rough terrain on a 4-ton truck.[122]

Although deficiencies in the unit were recognized, this model was produced to fill immediate requirements in the field but it was never standardized. Simultaneously, the Mechanical Section began developmental work on an improved model. The ratio of the weight of the refrigerator to its payload, which was about 1:1, was not considered uneconomical but it was felt that it could be improved. A lighter weight model was also desired. At a meeting attended by representatives of the OQMG, the Jeffersonville Quartermaster Depot, and industry, the details and component parts to be incorporated in an approved pilot model were settled. In developing the experimental featherweight models, manufacturers used aluminum alloys in their construction while the mechanical units were of the plug-in type.[123] Early in 1945 the Bureau of Standards made tests of the thermal characteristics of the lightweight refrigerators. In the meantime an electric-driven, as well as a gasoline-engine drive, plug-in, refrigerating system was developed by the OQMG and tested by the bureau.

This new lightweight model of the 150-cubic-foot refrigerator was standardized on 16 June 1945 although it had not been service tested.[124] In contrast to the earlier model the lightweight refrigerator with an electric-motor-driven refrigerating unit weighed about 1,900 pounds but had the same payload. When a gasoline-engine-driven unit was plugged in, the refrigerator weighed 2,200 pounds. Made of aluminum sheet and insulated with rubber board in the floor and semi-rigid glass wool in the walls and ceiling, the refrigerator was also provided with lifting rings at the top corners for convenient handling. Runners were provided for dragging the refrigerator during loading and unloading operations.

The lightweight refrigerator had other advantages over the earlier heavy model. Unlike the latter, the lightweight refrigerator and refrigerating unit were independent components, which simplified the problems of procurement and maintenance. In the event of a major breakdown the plug-in unit could easily be replaced. Where power was available, the electric-motor-driven refrigerating unit was satisfactory for use in a stationary field refrigerator. As in the case of the heavy model, a gasoline-engine-driven generator was used to operate the lightweight refrigerator while in transit on a truck. The inadequacy of the small gasoline engine, however, handicapped development in the refrigeration field as it did in reference to many other Quar-

---

[121] R&D Br, Status Rpt, 31 Jan 44, p. 23.

[122] Capt Wetherbee to Chief of Mechanical Sec, OQMG, 26 Jun 44, sub: Comparison of 26½, 50, 125 cu. ft. Refrigerator Units.

[123] R&D Br, Status Rpts, 31 Mar–30 Jun 44, under heading Refrigerator, ·Portable, 125 cu. ft.

[124] (1) Rpt, Subcom, QMCTC, to QMCTC, 16 May 45, sub: Portable Refrigerator, Walk-In, Plug-In Type, 150 cu. ft. (2) QMCTC, min of mtg. No. 10, 22 May 45. (3) Ltr, Gen Doriot, OQMG, to CG ASF, 29 May 45, same sub, and 1st ind, Hq ASF to TQMG, 16 Jun 45. All in 414.1.

termaster items which it powered. Since the war ended before the lightweight portable refrigerator was put into field use, its advantage over the heavy model in field operation cannot be evaluated.

Mobile Salvage Equipment

When the modernization and expansion of the Army began in 1940, all QMC tactical organizations were restudied. This led to the organization of new mobile units, such as laundry companies, sterilization and bath companies, and shoe and textile repair companies. These so-called comfort organizations rendered important service to troops in the field, for high morale is partly attributable to comfortable shoes, clean clothes, and baths. At the same time the requirements of the expanding Army for clothing and equipage were enormous, emphasizing the need to conserve these items by salvage operations since the supply of wool, duck, leather, and other materials was not limitless.

With the authorization of such mobile units by the War Department, the QMC began action to purchase the necessary equipment for them. For example, in the spring of 1941 the OQMG requested and received permission to purchase two semitrailers with equipment mounted in them for the repair of barracks bags, blankets, coats, shirts, trousers, and shelter-half tents. This equipment was to be used for experimental and training purposes at Camp Lee with a view to standardization.[125] By August semitrailers with commercial equipment appropriate for each of the new mobile units were standardized.[126]

This equipment—in the case of the mobile clothing repair shop it included a sewing machine, together with a tack button, darning, and button-sewing machine—was operated by an electric generator powered by a gasoline engine. It was mounted on one or more two-wheel, van-type semitrailers which measured 22 by 8

feet, with a height of 6½ feet, and which weighed approximately 20,000 pounds each when fully equipped. The prime movers were in all cases 4–5 ton 4x4 tractors. These, like the semitrailers, had been standardized by earlier action of the Motor Committee of the QMCTC.

A considerable number of these mobile units were sent overseas. By the following summer of 1943 reports from the North African Theater began to come in. The shoe repair and the clothing and textile repair units were doing a good job, but it was observed that they were set up as semipermanent installations, chiefly in the salvage depot at Casablanca. Mobile laundry units operating in NATO were for the most part attached directly to hospitals. They handled hospital laundry exclusively, and early in the campaign they remained with the larger base hospitals in rear areas. The mobile sterilization and bath units "performed a fine job for front line troops in the Tunisian campaign." Because of their size, however, they could not proceed too close to the forward lines. The vans were set up just out of artillery range of the enemy, and division quartermasters arranged schedules for the fighting troops to come back to the mobile units during their period of relief from combat duty. On the other hand, men within artillery range relied on the combat engineers to erect shower facilities by means of portable shower pipes. According to one observer, twice the number of mobile laundry and sterilization and bath units could have been used to good advantage in NATO. The limited number of such units available was due to the fact that their size precluded getting shipping priority

---

[125] Ltr, Gen Corbin, OQMG, to ACofS G–4, 25 Mar 41, sub: Mobile C&E Repair Units, and 1st ind, TAG to TQMG, 1 Apr 41, 413.8.

[126] (1) Memo, TQMG for ACofS G–4, 29 Jul 41, sub: Mobile Clo Repair Shop. (2) Memo, same to same, 30 Jul 41, sub: Mobile Shoe Repair Shop. (3) Memo, same to same, 29 Jul 41, sub: Mobile Laundry. (4) 2d ind, AGO to TQMG, 2 Aug 41, on each memo. All in 413.8.

for them. A great amount of deck space and special handling was required to transport the mobile semitrailers. The use of a more compact unit was recommended. It was obvious, too, that these units were not sufficiently mobile or maneuverable to be used in tactical situations as had been intended.[127]

By this time the experiences of the Army provided a basis for appraisal of the field operations of the mobile units hurriedly organized in 1941. It was now possible to institute desirable improvements, and, as a preliminary step, the OQMG directed the Quartermaster Board to conduct a series of studies on mobile units for the purpose of accumulating data on their mobility, operating efficiency, tactical employment, maintenance requirements, and on the adequacy of tables of organization and equipment.[128]

The findings of the Quartermaster Board supported the criticisms made in the field about mobile equipment. Mobile semitrailers lacked mobility and maneuverability for operations in forward areas. "Not only were they found to be easy targets for attacking aircraft and vulnerable to attack and capture by ground action, but it was disclosed that their low speed and maneuverability constitute a definite danger if employed on important supply roads on which other military traffic demands are heavy."[129]

At the same time responsibility for the research, design, and development of special vehicles peculiar to the QMC was transferred from the Mobile Equipment Branch of the Service Installations Division to the Military Planning Division.[130] The Research and Development Branch thus became responsible for designing more suitable mobile equipment.

In January 1944 the Mechanical Section initiated a project to design, in co-operation with industry and the Jeffersonville Quartermaster Depot, more portable and mobile salvage repair units.[131] A new approach was taken. The cumbersome two-wheel, van-type semitrailers

were eliminated and replaced by one-ton, two-wheel cargo trailers which weighed about 3,900 pounds equipped, and measured 5 feet 7 inches in width by 9 feet in length by 5 feet 6 inches in height. These trailers were towed by 2½-ton 6x6 trucks in place of the 4–5 ton 4x4 tractors. The new equipment used in the shoe, clothing, and textile repair units was basically similar in general operating characteristics to that used in the earlier units. Unlike the early mobile units, which mounted the equipment in a semitrailer for both movement and operation, the new design provided for boxing the machinery and arranging it compactly in special compartments in each trailer for transit. In operation this equipment was dismounted from the trailer and installed on the ground in tentage or buildings.

In addition to mobility, maneuverability, compactness, and lightness, the QMC by the summer of 1944 was considering the desirability of adding another military characteristic to mobile and portable units, namely, capability of being transported by air.[132] The success of airborne supply in theaters of operations suggested the possibility of greater use of this method, particularly in the Asiatic and Pacific theaters. It was proposed to bring the matter before the QMCTC for decision and, if favorably acted upon, to obtain from the Air Forces information as to the types of planes or gliders in which each

[127] (1) Capt Pounder, Rpt of QM Opns in NATO, 5 Mar–2 Jun 43. (2) Compare, Lt Morison, Rpt of Observation, Desert Tng Center, Sep–Oct 1943. (3) Product Analysis Sec to Mechanical Sec, OQMG, 8 Jul 44, sub: Semi-Mobile Units, giving extracts from rpt, Capt Orr, SWP base, 9 Jun 44.

[128] Dir of QM Bd to TQMG, Rpt on QM Bd, Camp Lee, Va., 1 Feb 42–30 Jun 44, p. 102.

[129] *Ibid.*, pp. 103–04.

[130] OQMG OO 25–48, 14 Aug 43, sub: Transfer of Functions.

[131] (1) R&D Project Record, R–103–44, 29 Jan 44, sub: Salv Repair Unit. (2) See also R&D, Status Rpts, 31 Mar–30 Nov 44, under heading Salv Repair Units.

[132] Lt Col David B. Dill to Maj McLean, OQMG, 6 Jun 44, sub: Air Transport of QM Mobile and Portable Units.

PORTABLE REPAIR UNITS. *Clothing repair unit set up for operation (above) and trailer type shoe repair unit (below).*

class of items would be transported. The new military characteristic was approved and the completed mobile trailer units were made so that they could either be towed by 2½-ton 6x6 trucks or carried in C–47 airplanes or CG–4A gliders.

Tests of the new salvage repair mobile units by the Quartermaster Board proved satisfactory. The Jeffersonville Depot prepared specifications by November. In the following month the QMCTC recommended standardization of the new mobile units and reclassification of the earlier models as limited standard.[133] As the war ended these new salvage repair units were just beginning to come from the factories.

Laundry Equipment

The laundry equipment standardized in the summer of 1941 was a vast improvement over that used in World War I but suffered from the same defects as other mobile equipment utilizing van-type semitrailers.[134] Early in 1944 the Mechanical Section initiated a project to develop a more mobile laundry unit. Jeffersonville Depot technicians contributed to each phase of the development. It was proposed to design a new laundry unit mounted on two small-sized two-wheel trailers. The tires and the wheels of the latter were made interchangeable with those of a 2½-ton 6x6 truck. One trailer was equipped with a washer, extractor, drain bin, electric auxiliary pump, and an automatic water heater which operated on either automotive or aviation-type gasoline. This trailer with its equipment weighed 4,720 pounds. The second trailer carried a drying tumbler with a gasoline-fired air heater, an electric generator providing power for equipment on both trailers and lighting for night operations, and a hose reel for storing all water hose. This trailer weighed 4,420 pounds. Fuel tanks, spare parts, and exhaust hose were carried on each trailer. These

trailers could be towed by 2½-ton trucks which carried personnel as well as equipment and supplies. When the wheels were removed from the trailer bed, the units could also be transported by C–47 airplanes. The unit was capable of processing 1,000 pounds of clothing per 8-hour shift. On the basis of 5 pounds a week for each man, one laundry company could serve 48,000 troops.[135]

The two-trailer type mobile laundry was first tested at Camp Indian Bay, Fla., by the Quartermaster Board during the summer of 1944. While it was satisfactory in most respects, a number of deficiencies were revealed affecting the capacity of the unit. On the assurance of the manufacturer that the burner defects could be corrected, the mobile laundry was standardized on 5 January 1945 because of the urgent need for this type of equipment in the field.[136]

Because of production difficulties a tumbler made by the Huebsch Co. was substituted for the Hoffman Co. model used in the developmental work. As a consequence it was necessary to engage in more experimental work to adapt the Huebsch standard tumbler to the new-type gasoline air heater. Tests of this model completed by the Quartermaster Board during the first week in July revealed that the operation of the tumbler prevented the laundry from reaching its rated output capacity. In addition, repeated attempts failed to make the original

---

[133] (1) Rpt, Subcom, QMCTC, to QMCTC, 28 Nov 44, sub: Two-Wheel, Tractor, Shoe Repair *et al.* (2) QMCTC, min of mtg No. 25, 5 Dec 44. (3) Ltr, Col Doriot to CG ASF, 11 Dec 44, same sub, and 2d ind, Hq ASF to TQMG, 5 Jan 45. All in 412.

[134] For a fuller treatment of the development of laundry equipment see Louis Filler, *Laundry and Related Activities of the The Quartermaster General* (QMC Historical Studies 13, March 1946).

[135] R&D Project Record, R–102–44, Feb 44.

[136] (1) Rpt, Subcom, QMCTC, to QMCTC, 28 Nov 44, sub: Two-Trailer Type Mobile Laundry. (2) QMCTC, min of mtg No. 25, 5 Dec 44. (3) Ltr, Col Doriot to CG ASF, 11 Dec 44, same sub, and 2d ind, Hq ASF to TQMG, 5 Jan 45, 412.

burners operate satisfactorily.[137] A conference with the manufacturers was held immediately to effect modifications. After the war ended, developmental work to perfect an improved tumbler was continued as a postwar project.

Mobile Bath Units

Like other mobile equipment developed during 1940–41, the sterilization and bath unit proved unsuitable for use in forward areas. There were about four such units in the North African Theater during the Tunisian Campaign. These, however, were left behind in Africa during the Sicilian Campaign. The first unit to reach Italy was moved into the rear area of the Fifth Army in late November 1943. Few infantry troops in Italy used the massive sterilization and bath unit for it was not "considered practical to place it within their reach." [138]

The sterilization and bath equipment consisted of four tents and a trailer. The four tents were set up near the trailer and used for undressing, physical examination, salvaging soiled clothes, and providing new clothes and dressing space. The trailer was equipped with a steam chamber in which the soldier's clothes were steamed under pressure at 252° for fifteen minutes. Outside the chamber were twelve shower heads for baths. The trailer was also equipped with a boiler. No field complaint was made of the serviceability of the shower facilities, but it was found that the sterilization equipment was not used to any great extent for clothing. It was used primarily to sterilize blankets and mattresses. While hospitals needed sterilization equipment a Quartermaster observer suggested that the only fumigation equipment needed by the soldier was the individual methyl-bromide bag.[139]

The QMC employed two types of delousing—steam and methyl bromide. The latter was intended eventually to replace the steam units but both methods continued to be used throughout

the war. Early in 1942 as a result of conferences between the Sanitation Division of The Surgeon General's Office and the Laundry Branch, OQMG, the conclusion was reached that steam sterilization was not necessary to kill disease germs and that fumigation would suffice. Fumigation chambers used less critical material in their construction and were lighter in weight than the older steam sterilizing chambers. As a consequence they could be moved closer to combat areas.

The Department of Agriculture for many years had been interested in the use of methyl bromide as a fumigant. At the request of The Surgeon General, the Bureau of Entomology and Plant Quarantine of the Department of Agriculture designed a mobile methyl-bromide chamber.[140] Tested at Camp Lee, this chamber was found to be too small and not properly constructed for use with a mobile sterilization company. From this preliminary design, however, the QMC evolved a satisfactory 330-cubic-foot chamber made of plywood panels which was capable of holding 60 barracks bags. The sterilization and bath unit was reclassified as limited standard and the new mobile fumigation and bath unit was standardized in March 1943.[141]

In the following months a considerable amount of developmental work was carried on

---

[137] Memo, Gen Doriot for TQMG, 3 Aug 45, sub: Two-Trailer Type Mobile Laundry.

[138] (1) Col Dill to Dir of Mil Plng Div, OQMG, n. d., sub: Rpt of Travel to NATO, 26 Oct–13 Dec 43. (2) Capt Pounder, Rpt of QM Opns in NATO, 5 Mar–2 Jun 43.

[139] Col Dill to Dir of Mil Plng Div, OQMG, n. d., sub: Rpt of Travel to NATO, 26 Oct–13 Dec 43.

[140] (1) Louis Filler, *Laundry and Related Activities of The Quartermaster General*, pp. 154ff. (2) Ltr, OSG to Hq SOS, 20 Jun 42, sub: Delousing of C&E, 727.4. (3) 2d ind, Lt Col T. M. Duff, OQMG, to CG SOS, 11 Jul 42, on same.

[141] (1) Rpt, Subcom, QMCTC, to QMCTC, 21 Jan 43, sub: Mobile Fumigation and Bath Unit. (2) 1st ind, QMCTC to OQMG, 26 Jan 43, on same. (3) 4th ind, SOS to TQMG, 16 Mar 43. All in 414.4.

to improve the construction of the fumigation chamber. After 14 August 1943 this was accomplished by the Mechanical Section, following the transfer of responsibility for research and developmental work on fumigation chambers from the Service Installations Division. About two months earlier the QMC had been given the responsibility for the procurement of all portable and mobile delousing equipment, including the writing of specifications.[142]

The fumigating chamber was not used to any great extent in the field, largely because there was no more need for it than there had been for the sterilization unit. Infestation among combat troops was uncommon, and when it occurred other methods, particularly the use of DDT, were effective. Less than 100 cases of infestation occurred in the Fifth Army during the entire month of January 1944.[143] On the basis of these findings The Surgeon General's Office was queried on the desirability of continuing procurement of the methyl-bromide chamber. In the spring of 1944 he recommended discontinuance as soon as possible.[144]

While the successful use of DDT diminished the need for fumigation chambers and raised the question of the reorganization of the fumigation and bath company, the OQMG found there was a real need for highly mobile field bathing facilities. Until the very end of the war responsibility for field bathing equipment was divided between the QMC and the Corps of Engineers. The pioneer work in the development of shower facilities for soldiers in the field was carried out by the Corps of Engineers. Its activities in this undertaking dated from the period immediately following the termination of World War I. The use of improvised types of field showers during that war had demonstrated that troop morale and health could be improved by adequate bathing facilities. Quartermaster interest also dated from the period after World War I and was further stimulated by the organization of the sterilization

and bath companies just before the United States entered World War II.

When the QMC initiated development of a new fumigation and bath unit and dropped procurement of the sterilization unit after January 1943, it was most interested in providing a more mobile outfit. For a new bathing unit the Military Planning Division turned to a mobile eight-head shower unit developed by the Corps of Engineers and favorably tested in 1941. It had been rejected for standardization by the Assistant Chief of Engineers because he felt that rubber tires and manufacturing facilities should not be wasted in "providing luxuries and excessive convenience as implied by trailer mounting." Procurement had been limited to sixty sets which were turned over to the QMC and subsequently standardized.[145] The OQMG revised the design to provide for units with twelve instead of eight shower heads for use in the new mobile fumigation and bath unit. Subsequently a twenty-four-head shower unit replaced the twelve-head unit, and the fumigation chamber and shower unit were standardized separately, thereby facilitating the practice of setting up bath units independently of sterilization and fumigation activities.[146] Unfortunately for purposes of operation by the trained personnel of the fumigation and bath companies, the fumigation and bath units were not separated. Because fumigation facilities were not required in the various theaters to any

[142] (1) OQMG OO 25–48, 14 Aug 43, sub: Transfer of Functions. (2) ASF Memo S5–103–43, 8 Jun 43, sub: Asgmts of PAB.

[143] Col Dill to Dir of Mil Plng Div, n. d., sub: Rpt on Travel to NATO, 26 Oct–13 Dec 43.

[144] (1) Ltr, Col Doriot, OQMG, to OSG, 18 Mar 44, sub: Methyl Bromide Fumigation Chambers. (2) 2d ind, OSG to TQMG, 1 Apr 44, on same. Both in 414.4.

[145] 4th ind, Hq SOS to TQMG, 16 Mar 43, on rpt, Subcom, QMCTC, to QMCTC, 21 Jan 43, sub: Mobile Fumigator and Bath Unit, 414.4.

[146] 4th ind, Hq ASF to TQMG, 30 Nov 43, on rpt, Subcom, QMCTC, to QMCTC, 19 Oct 43, sub: Equip for Fumigation and Bath Co.

considerable extent, the complementary mobile shower units were not provided to the fullest extent possible.[147] As a consequence, by the middle of 1944 many complaints were being received from the theaters concerning the inadequacy of the bath facilities provided for the troops. To remedy this situation the Military Planning Division in October proposed the use on maneuvers of small mobile shower detachments operated by six men and equipped with one bath unit and one 2½-ton truck. Such a test would provide the basis for a decision on the advisability of providing this equipment as part of the organizational set-up for a division and for corps and army troops.[148] Later the ASF provided for essentially the same bath unit in a revised Table of Organization and Equipment 10–500, published 10 January 1945.[149] There is no indication, however, that any of these units were ever activated.

The Jeffersonville Depot published a specification for the separate bath unit which provided for an oil-fired water heater mounted on a steel channel frame. The fuel pump, water pump, and air blower were operated by a single-cylinder, four-cycle, air-cooled gasoline engine mounted on the trailer. Piping, shower heads, and hose were designed to be mounted on brackets on the side of the unit when the trailer was being towed. The complete unit weighed about 3,800 pounds, and the trailer was so designed that the front wheel could be folded under for transport by a C–47 or C–54 plane.[150]

Shower facilities were tremendously effective morale builders. They were extremely popular, particularly when set up in connection with a clothing exchange unit which enabled the soldier to don an entirely clean outfit after bathing. A number of deficiencies in the bath units were revealed in use, however, and on the basis of theater criticism the Military Planning Division initiated a project in April 1945 to eliminate the defects, reduce the over-all weight,

and improve performance. The developmental work on this lightweight model was continued after the war ended.

In April the AAF requested the development of a portable eight-head shower unit which would be an improvement over the shower unit developed by the Corps of Engineers. Headquarters, ASF, called upon the Chief of Engineers for comment, and the latter took the opportunity of recommending that the development of shower equipment for field use be assigned to his office to avoid competitive development between the QMC and the Corps of Engineers. Headquarters, ASF, concurred.[151] The OQMG, however, protested promptly and vigorously, outlining its case so effectively that Headquarters, ASF, on 27 July 1945 rescinded its earlier order and concentrated in the QMC the responsibility for the development of all mobile and portable bath equipment to accompany troops in the field.[152]

Tentage

In the developmental work initiated to provide the Army with suitable tents, the OQMG and the Jeffersonville Quartermaster Depot analyzed and investigated problems of design, fabric construction, and finishes which increased the resistance of cotton duck to water, fire, and mildew. At first the QMC was most concerned with the performance of tentage. The desire for a superior finish and color for tentage duck had

[147] Memo, Col Doriot, OQMG, to CG AGF, 18 Oct 44, sub: Use of 24-Showerhead Mobile Fld Bath Unit, 412.2.

[148] *Ibid.*

[149] 3d ind, Hq ASF to TQMG, 8 Dec 44, see memo cited in n. 147.

[150] JQD 1035, 21 Nov 44, sub: 24-Showerhead Mobile Bath Unit.

[151] 5th ind, Hq ASF to CE, 4 May 45, on ltr, AAF to ASF, 15 Feb 45, sub: 8-Head Portable Shower Unit.

[152] Memo, Brig Gen H. A. Barnes, OQMG, for CG ASF, 21 May 45, sub: Fld Shower Equip, and 1st ind, Hq ASF to TQMG, 27 Jul 45, 412.2.

crystallized throughout the Army during 1940 and 1941. In anticipation of decisions to be taken, the Air Corps had conducted exhaustive visibility tests in 1935, and subsequently the Corps of Engineers, responsible for camouflage, made studies to develop the most suitable color for Army matériel.

Ever since World War I Army tentage had been made of 15.5-ounce duck, colored to a khaki shade with mineral colors and then treated with aluminum acetate, soap, and wax to gain water repellency. The weight of this finish added only slightly to the weight of the goods. On the eve of World War II, to promote uniformity, the QMC adopted the standard olive drab shade No. 3 for all personal and organizational equipment using duck and webbing. Later, to conceal military equipment and matériel more effectively, the dark green olive drab shade No. 7 was adopted because this color was less visible from the air than the No. 3 shade.[153]

As a protection against incendiaries, the QMC also decided to treat Army canvas with a fire-resistant finish. This "746" finish had been developed during the thirties through the cooperative efforts of private industry, the Department of Agriculture, and the QMC.[154] The application of the finish[155] to 15.5-ounce duck increased its weight by nearly 50 percent, but in view of the advantages to be gained through its use the factor of increased weight had to be disregarded. To compensate for the additional weight, however, the QMC substituted a 12.29-ounce duck for the 15.5-ounce duck, thereby lightening the weight of the treated duck by about 5 ounces per square yard.[156] The 746 finish had the advantage of giving fire and water resistance and of providing longer life and good color for camouflage to the heavy tentage canvas used in making large tents.

The national emergency soon directed attention to the finish applied to tentage fabric, since chlorinated rubber was used as a fireproofing and waterproofing agent. Both crude rubber and chlorine were on the list of strategic and critical materials. A study was therefore undertaken to find suitable substitutes. This project was completed by the spring of 1942 when waxes and other materials were substituted for crude rubber.[157] Efforts to develop an improved finish continued for many months at the Jeffersonville Depot, resulting in the replacement of the 1939 performance specification by a new one clearly stating which materials were mandatory in the preparation of the finish and which were prohibited.[158]

A comparatively new requirement for Army tentage was mildew resistance. Prior to World War II mildew-proofing had not been a major military problem. Warfare in humid, tropical jungles, however, created a demand for preservative treatments of textile items of both equipment and clothing to prevent loss of service through the action of mold-rot and mildew. In the summer of 1942 the Jeffersonville Depot began a study of mildew and mildew-resistant compounds. Certain fungicides were on the market and under commercial development, but it was necessary to evaluate their claims of effectiveness, durability, and safety as well as to set up test methods for acceptance purposes. Through the work of the Department of Agriculture, long engaged in study of the preven-

[153] (1) QMCTC, min of mtg No. 2, 26 Jan 43. (2) Ltr, Col Kennedy, OQMG, to Hq SOS, 30 Dec 42, sub: Color for C&E. (3) 1st ind, Hq SOS to ACofS G-4, 1 Jan 43, on same. (4) Memo, ACofS G-4, for CG ASF, 30 Mar 43, same sub. All in 400.1141.

[154] Memo for file, James R. Redmond, Chief of Fire-Resistant Duck Sec, JQMD, 19 Apr 43, no sub.

[155] Fed Spec CCC-D-746, 17 Feb 39, sub: Cotton Duck, Fire, Water, and Weather Resistant.

[156] Rpt, Col Robert T. Stevens, Deputy Dir for Purchases, OQMG, and Ralph A. Butland, Textile Technologist, 1 Feb 44, sub: QMC Duck and Webbing Pool.

[157] Ltr, Col Doriot to S. P. Thacher, Chief of Rubber Conservation, ANMB, 10 Aug 42, sub: Rpt on Rubber Conserv.

[158] QMC Spec JQD 242, 2 Dec 42, sub: Cotton Duck, Fire, Water, and Weather Resistant.

tion of the growth of microorganisms on fabrics, and the Jeffersonville and Philadelphia Depots, several fungicides and treatments proved reasonably satisfactory for the purpose intended and were accepted on procurements of military items.[159] Since it was believed that the fundamental principles of mildew-proofing should be clarified and established and that treatments could be improved, research continued in this field throughout the war years.[160]

The progress made in solving the problems of water, fire, and mildew resistance was applicable to textile items of clothing and of equipment. Similarly, what was learned about fabric construction in the development of water-resistant fabrics for use in combat clothing could also be applied to tentage fabrics. From the beginning of 1944 the high-sley oxford principle of construction was carried into heavier weight fabrics. Since a critical shortage of cotton duck developed during that year, this experimentation proved helpful in solving the problem. Tests conducted by the Textile Foundation showed that flat ducks made in a jo-cloth[161] type were superior in water repellency to numbered ducks of equal weight. This was extremely significant since it made possible the use of single yarn material in place of plied yarn during the duck shortage then facing the QMC. The importance of restudying fabrics used for tentage was evident to the Textile Section, and developmental work in this field was continued through the war period.[162]

Squad Tent

Development of newly designed tents began in 1942. Improved construction techniques were not then factors for consideration. The QMC was concerned primarily with the production of special types of tents for a particular use. When the war started the Corps was procuring and utilizing the pyramidal eight-man squad tent of

World War I, which was commonly used for housing personnel. In addition, the Army used various other tents—command post, storage, hospital ward, surgical operating, and assembly—as well as a large wall tent, which served for general utility, and a smaller one for officers' quarters.

Reviewing this situation, the OQMG initiated the development of a twelve-man experimental tent to effect simplification of the tent procurement program and conservation of cotton duck.[163] Since the Army had adopted the twelve-man squad as a tactical unit, this new tent was called the squad tent and was designed to house the entire squad in training or overseas. It was twice as large as the pyramidal tent which it was intended to replace, but it conserved duck by using somewhat less material than two pyramidal tents.[164]

Simplification of issue through reduction in the number of types of tents was to be promoted by the substitution of the squad tent for the storage, hospital ward, and large wall tents as well as for the pyramidal tent. These by action of the QMCTC, were reclassified as limited standard items to be issued until the supply was exhausted. The squad tent, which retained the basic conceptions of the pyramidal tent, was

[159] Ltr, Col Doriot to Dr. E. C. Auchter, Dept of Agriculture, 12 Feb 43, no sub.

[160] See R&D Br, Status Rpts for 1944 and 1945 under headings: Finish, Mildew, Pretreatment, for Military Fabrics; and Finish, Textile, Resistant to Degradation of Microorganism and Tropical Exposure.

[161] This was the Quartermaster name applied to fabrics using the principle of construction derived from the Textile Institute of Manchester, England. Officially the specifications read high-sley oxford.

[162] R&D Br, Status Rpts, 31 Oct 44, pp. 56–57; 31 Dec 44, p. 56; 30 Apr 45, p. 57; 31 Jul 45, pp. 47–48.

[163] (1) Standardization Br, Rpt of Test and Development Work in Progress, 2 Jan 42. (2) QMCTC, min of mtg No. 10, 6 Oct 42.

[164] (1) Lt Earl M. Savitt to Chief of R&D Sec, OQMG, 15 Feb 42, sub: Squad Tent, Model 1942 (Experimental). (2) Memo, Gen Corbin, OQMG, for ACofS G–4, 5 Mar 42, same sub. Both in 400.112.

standardized on 16 December 1942.[165]

The Jeffersonville Depot objected to the proposed substitution of the squad tent for the other four tents because it would disrupt the procurement program and result in a serious loss of production. "The present program *will meet the needs of our troops*, and why make changes when the change will not materially affect any factor in winning the War?"[166] It was suggested that procurement be limited to an experimental quantity of 10,000 squad tents so that the difficulties of production could be determined before a complete change-over was made. These views, supported by the Procurement Division, OQMG, were not concurred in by the Military Planning Division, which advocated the substitution.[167]

The views of Quartermaster procurement personnel prevailed because of the necessity for continuing large-scale production of the old-style tents after the United States entered the war, inasmuch as no new design was immediately available. Even after a new design had been developed, many months would elapse before volume production could be attained. By the time the new squad tent had been standardized in 1942, more than a million of the four old-type tents had been manufactured, a quantity sufficient to meet immediate Army requirements. Only 19,000 squad tents were delivered in 1943.[168] Although production of this item increased many times to meet the large requirements of 1944 and 1945, the squad tent did not replace the storage, hospital ward, large wall, and pyramidal tents during World War II, and thus the simplification objective of the Research and Development Branch was not attained.

No radical changes in construction were embodied in the design of the squad tent. The construction of tents was still viewed chiefly as a matter of providing a desired amount of covered floor space by using certain conventional elements of construction, such as walls and sloping decks, and by utilizing fabrics of such strength that their structural design presented no particular problem when they were used, as heretofore, over relatively short periods of time.

In 1944, however, when the production of the squad tent was to be greatly increased to meet the large quantities requisitioned from the field, the structural soundness of the tent and the principles of its construction were questioned. When reports of excessive tent failures began to come in from the Pacific early in the war, the explanation at first was in terms of inadequate protection against fungus attack. Later it became evident that basic structural weaknesses existed in the tents used by the Army. Contrary to the principles employed in other types of housing, the entire support of the tent was provided by the roof fabric itself. Concentrated stress at various points led to excessive elongation of the fabric, resulting in leakage at the seams and rupture of the fabric.

Through the National Research Council, the Military Planning Division entered into a contractual arrangement with the Institute of Industrial Research at the University of Louisville to study the problem of stresses and strains placed on tentage fabrics when used in tents. The study of tent design and construction was later broadened to include other phases, such as the problem of heating and ventilating tents.[169]

Based on the findings of the Institute of Industrial Research, certain constructional modifi-

---

[165] (1) [2d ind], Hq SOS to TQMG, 16 Dec 42. (2) QMCTC, min of mtg No. 12, 20 Oct 42. (3) The hospital ward tent remained in use for field hospitals having more than 500 beds.

[166] Ltr, Brig Ben Allen R. Kimball, CG JQMD, to TQMG, 2 Nov 42, sub: Squad Tents, 424.1.

[167] (1) Mil Plng Div to Procurement Div, OQMG, 11 Nov 42, sub: Squad Tent. (2) Procurement Div to Mil Plng Div, OQMG, 21 Nov 42, same sub. Both in 424.1.

[168] *Statistical Yearbook of the QMC, 1945*, p. 53.

[169] (1) Institute of Industrial Research, University of Louisville, Tent Design and Construction, Textile Series, Rpt 15, Tent Research Rpt, 1, n.d. (2) R&D Br, Status Rpts, Feb–Aug 45, under headings: Tent, Construction and Material; Tent, Design and Material.

cations of the squad tent design were proposed early in 1945. To eliminate the strain placed upon canvas used in the tent roof, it was planned to suspend the roof canvas on a webbing frame which would carry the load.[170] At the same time consideration was also given to raising the height of the side walls of the squad tent from the approved 4½ feet to 6 feet. Information from Pacific theaters had indicated that tents were being erected over built-up frames to raise the tent higher from the ground, thereby providing better ventilation and more efficient use of interior floor space.[171]

Unfortunately the proposed modifications required the use of more duck for the side walls and more cotton yarn to produce the required webbing. The limitations of production again prevented the procurement of a new design. The findings of research were therefore not applied to the production of tents during the war.[172]

Portable Squad Shelter

One development in design that evolved out of the critical shortage of duck in 1944 grew out of the effort to find substitutes for tentage duck. At the request of Headquarters, ASF,[173] a project was initiated to develop a lightweight portable shelter which would use less duck yet be comparable in size and shape to the squad tent. The shelter was also to provide more storage space than the storage tent and to be transportable in a 2½-ton 6x6 truck.[174] Developmental contracts were given to a number of engineering concerns, and experimental models employing aluminum, steel, or plywood roofs, and cotton duck sides and ends, were designed.

On the basis of these models the OQMG drafted a specification embodying the best features of each. Models constructed along the specified lines were tested during the summer of 1945. In the meantime, to meet immediate

needs, The Quartermaster General requested authority to procure 30,000 of the portable shelters as direct substitutes for the squad tent.[175] To permit this procurement, the QMCTC recommended, and Headquarters, ASF, approved classification of the item as a limited procurement type.[176] The war ended before results could be obtained, but developmental work continued.

Maintenance Shelter Tent

The development of one other type of tent merits attention since it involved a basic change in design, namely, the use of a rigid frame in lieu of poles and pins. The mechanization of the Army gave rise to a need for portable shelters in which to repair vehicles under blackout conditions. This need was particularly stressed by Armored Force observers returning from

[170] By this type of construction "the entire strain of the tent is carried from the ridge line through a piece of heavy webbing to a D-ring at the eave-line to which the tent rope is attached through a movable bar." The roof canvas was simply laid on the webbing and stitched to it but carried no strain other than its own weight. Textile Sec to QMCTC Sec, OQMG, 3 May 45, sub: New Type Tent Construction, 424.1.

[171] (1) Col Dill, Rpt on Observations in SWPA and POA, Oct–Dec 1944. (2) Ltr, Gen Doriot, OQMG, to Hq ASF, 21 Mar 45, sub: Modified Squad Tent, 424.1.

[172] (1) 7th ind, Hq ASF to TQMG, 19 May 45, on ltr, Gen Doriot to Hq ASF, 21 Mar 45, sub: Modified Squad Tent. (2) QMCTC, min of mtg No. 9, 8 May 45. Both in 424.1.

[173] (1) Memo, Hq ASF for TQMG, 11 Nov 44, sub: Substitute for Duck. (2) Ltr, Hq ASF to TQMG, 5 Dec 44, sub: Substitutes for Tents.

[174] (1) R&D Br, Project Record SD 4–45, Jan 45, sub: Substitute for Tents. (2) R&D Br, Status Rpts, 31 Jan–31 Jul 45, heading, Substitute for Tents.

[175] Ltr, OQMG to Hq ASF, 10 Mar 45, sub: Substitute for Tents, 400.112.

[176] (1) Rpt, Subcom, QMCTC, to QMCTC, 30 Jun 45, sub: Portable Squad Shelter. (2) QMCTC, min of mtg. No. 14, 2 Jul 45. (3) 1st ind, Hq ASF to TQMG, 16 Jul 45, on ltr, OQMG to ASF, 11 Jul 45, sub: Portable Squad Shelter.

Libya, and in the summer of 1942 Headquarters, Armored Force, Fort Knox, Ky., requested standardization of a blackout maintenance shelter at an early date.[177] It was recommended that the tent be made large enough to accommodate a medium M3 tank or a 2½-ton truck without interference from uprights or ridge pole.

Headquarters, SOS, directed The Quartermaster General to initiate a project for developing such a tent.[178] The Jeffersonville Depot manufactured a tent according to the proposed military characteristics. The tent was suspended over a steel frame to eliminate interior poles that might interfere with maintenance work. A 9-by-10-foot opening was provided in the tent roof to enable cranes located outside the tent to raise or lower heavy parts of equipment. In order that the tent might be used for other purposes than motor repair, this opening was equipped with heavy-duty slide fasteners. A number of the maintenance shelter tents were tested and found satisfactory by the Armored Force Board. The tent was standardized on 24 July 1943.[179]

Sectional Hospital Tent

One other feature introduced in tent construction during World War II was the use of a liner. The value of a layer of dead air as an insulator had long been well known, but prior to 1943 no attempt had been made to use a lightweight liner[180] to trap an insulating body of air beneath the roof of a tent. Troops operating in hot climates had discovered the merits of this principle and some had improvised their own insulating liners from salvaged parachute cloth. A liner was particularly needed in hospital tents, and when a developmental project was initiated in 1944 to modify the existing hospital ward tent, a white liner made of 4-ounce cotton sheeting to cover the entire inside of the tent was incorporated in the newly designed sectional hospital tent, standardized on 7 July of that year.[181]

The sectional hospital tent unit was rectangular in shape. Supported by a web frame, the tent was constructed so that a complete end section, including roof, side walls, and blackout doors, could be detached from the main body. Additional center sections could be added to extend the tent to any desired length. At the time of standardization it was the intent of the QMCTC to utilize the sectional tent to replace all miscellaneous tentage. Any of the special purpose tents, including the squad tent, could be constructed by adding or removing sections. Because of the stringency of the duck supply in the summer of 1944, however, it was inadvisable to make this change. The goal of standardization in tentage, therefore, could not be achieved and remained a postwar objective.

These selected items of tentage by no means included all developmental projects on tents. The QMC devoted considerable attention to the development of such tents as the command post tent and the surgical operating tent for the Medical Department. Discussion has been limited, however, to only such developmental projects as contributed to basic changes in the

---

[177] Ltr, Hq Armored Force to CG ASF, 11 Aug 42, sub: Proposed Mil Characteristics and Request for Standardization of Blackout Maint Shelter, 424.1.

[178] 2d ind, Hq SOS to TQMG, 25 Sep 42, on above ltr, 424.1.

[179] (1) Rpt, Subcom, QMCTC, to QMCTC, 18 Jun 43, sub: Maint Shelter Tent with Frame. (2) 4th ind, Hq ASF, 24 Jul 43, on ltr, Hq AAF to TQMG, 24 Jun 43, same sub. Both in 424.1.

[180] A washable liner of tent twill, coated white, had been used in the heavy operating surgical tent, but was intended chiefly for sanitation purposes and to reflect and diffuse light within the operating chamber.

[181] (1) Ltr, Brig Gen R. W. Bliss, SGO, to TQMG, 2 Mar 44, sub: Hospital Ward Tent. (2) Memo, Col Doriot for QMCTC, 1 Jun 44, sub: Tents. (3) QMCTC, min of mtg No. 10, 6 Jun 44. (4) Ltr, Col Doriot, OQMG, to CG ASF, 10 Jun 44, sub: Sectional Tent, and 3d ind, Hq ASF to TQMG, 7 Jul 44, on same. All in 424.1.

design of tents or to the trend toward standardization.

Summary

In the years between World Wars I and II, War Department appropriations permitted scant allowance for continued research in the field of personal and organizational equipment. At the same time the existence of large stocks left on hand from World War I tended to stifle initiative toward new designs, particularly in the relatively simple items of personal equipment. The American soldier went to war in 1941 equipped, for the most part, with items familiar to the doughboy in 1918. The larger part of the funds made available to the QMC for developmental work in these years was channeled into the field of automotive equipment, enabling the Army to enter World War II equipped with the 2½-ton 6x6 truck and the jeep, two of the major contributions of the Corps to the winning of the war.

The nature of the war placed initial emphasis on the development of special items of personal equipment as well as specialized clothing. Immediate attention therefore was given to the development of a jungle pack and other items for the use of jungle troops, and such gear as rucksacks and arctic sleeping bags for troops operating in Alaska. The ultimate trend in this field, however, as in the development of clothing, was toward the use of standard items of equipment by all troops, with specialized gear developed only for use by troops operating under extremes of climatic conditions.

While the demands of war required the development of many new items, such as carriers for new types of ammunition and tools, the QMC emphasized a program of simplification which would make one item serve the purpose of several, thereby simplifying the problem of supply. Thus the M–1943 shovel, pick-mattock, and ax were intended to be replaced by the new combination intrenching tool developed late in the war. In the field of organizational equipment, the sectional tent was designed to replace all miscellaneous tentage.

Unfortunately, the program of simplification was often nullified by other factors. The stringency of the duck supply in the case of tents, for example, prohibited changes in procurement to effect the standardization desired by the QMC. Similarly, the immediate war needs in 1942 resulted in the initiation of procurement of old-style items of equipment which continued to be used throughout World War II.

The QMC came to place primary emphasis upon reduction in the weight of equipment which it designed. The Germans had been particularly successful in this field because of the large supply of aluminum available to them. The QMC, handicapped by a lack of that lightweight metal, was forced to work with substitutes. As a consequence, the objectives of weight reduction and conservation of critical raw materials were frequently in conflict. The use of substitute metals resulted in an increase in the weight of the field range, for example, which could be lessened only when improvement in the metal situation in the late summer of 1944 permitted the Corps to return to the use of aluminum and stainless steel. This factor of weight was particularly important in mobile equipment of various types. The original models had all proved too heavy and slow for use in modern warfare. These handicaps were overcome by the use of aluminum, as in the new refrigerated semitrailer, or by substituting for the van-type semitrailer with repair machinery installed in it, a one-ton two-wheel cargo trailer in which the machinery was boxed and compactly arranged for transit but set up in tents or buildings for operation. Factors of weight and compactness became increasingly important during the war as the use of supply by air increased. The capacity of being transported by air came to be accepted as a necessary military characteristic of Quartermaster organizational equipment during World War II.

Standardization, simplification, and weight reduction were the major trends in the development of equipment. These, however, had to be achieved within the limits of the prevailing program of conservation of critical materials and of adjustments necessary to achieve and maintain the maximum production needed for winning the war. As a consequence, immediate procurement could not always be initiated for an item of equipment developed by the QMC. Critical reports from the field led to efforts to improve existing items of equipment. More often than not the final improvement came too late to see service in the field during World War II.

CHAPTER V

The Development of Subsistence

Food supplied by the Quartermaster Corps to the Army is called subsistence. It has always been among the most important items of military supply. Food must be adequate in quantity, varied enough to provide all the ingredients of a properly balanced diet, and acceptable to the soldier. To furnish energy his diet must contain fats and carbohydrates; to build and repair his body it must provide proteins and minerals. At the same time his food must have sufficient vitamins and bulk to foster health. The regular serving of palatable food is the greatest single factor in building and maintaining high spirit and morale.

In time of peace supplying the United States Army with food was a relatively simple task. In the years between the two world wars, the strength of the Army was less than 200,000 men. Small groups of soldiers were located at scattered, permanent stations, and it was convenient for each post, camp, or station to purchase its own food. Perishables were obtained from local sources, while nonperishable foods were bought by the depots for direct delivery in regular quantities. The Army prescribed the use of a garrison ration in peacetime for all persons entitled to it, the ration being "the allowance of food for subsistence of one person for one day." [1] It consisted of thirty-nine components, the quality of which was prescribed by federal specifications. These components included not only the meat, vegetables, fruit, dairy products, and beverages served at mealtimes but also the

ingredients used in their preparation. This ration, however, was not issued in kind but was a money credit based on the cost of a definite quantity and quality of specified subsistence items, both perishable and nonperishable. Using this credit, organization commanders might purchase a wide variety of subsistence items to provide a balanced diet. The ration permitted what was called a ration savings privilege, permitting any savings from the money credit of a certain month or period to be carried over for subsequent use. It could be used by the officer in charge of an organization mess to provide supplemental food and beverages on special occasions. Under this system the commissary of a post, camp, or station was organized to provide daily a wide variety of subsistence items in accordance with the individual wishes of organization commanders. Such supply offered no problems of research for the QMC.

In time of national emergency and war, however, the garrison ration system was not used. Instead, the Army prescribed the items of food to be issued for consumption on a certain day or during a prescribed period of time, both as to variety and quantity. Each messing organization drew its share of the prescribed food items and prepared menus accordingly. The components of the field ration had to be diversified to meet existing conditions of supply, availability of transportation, storage space, and messing

---

[1] AR 30–2210, Sec. I, par. 1, 15 Mar 40, sub: Rat.

facilities available to the consuming organizations.

Only four of the field rations of World War II existed in 1939, but considerable confusion over ration nomenclature had developed by that time. To clarify the situation a subcommittee of the Quartermaster Corps Technical Committee in the fall of that year proposed the substitution of the single term "field ration" for all old names, and the use of letters to distinguish among them. Consequently, the field ration was classified into four types—A, B, the then new C, and D.[2] Each was intended for issue in a given military situation. This nomenclature was used throughout World War II but was greatly expanded during the war years by the addition of a number of other rations, such as the jungle, mountain, five-in-one, ten-in-one, and K rations. Additional special rations were developed for the Air Corps.

Although it was once customary for armies to subsist at least partly "on the country," supplementing basic supplies by foraging, most modern armies, including that of the United States, found it necessary to use field rations for feeding their troops in combat zones. Regardless of the military situation, American troops had to be fed. The fact, also, that during World War II they were widely distributed in many areas of varying climatic conditions, thousands of miles and many days away from the home source of supply, introduced other elements which had to be considered in subsistence research. The development of adequate rations posed problems ranging from the maintenance of their nutritional adequacy to their acceptability, utility, and stability, despite prolonged shipment and storage under a variety of adverse conditions.

In addition, Quartermaster subsistence personnel were concerned with problems of packaging and packing and the conservation of shipping. The limited amount of shipping space dictated the use of such techniques of food

processing as dehydration, while the need to reduce the weight carried by soldiers, particularly members of special task forces, necessitated processing food so that it would occupy the smallest amount of space and yet provide the required nutritional values. An emergency food supply might be compressed into special chocolate bars. Military requirements imposed by war could not be satisfied by the extremely short shelf life and simplicity of packaging characteristic of commercial products. Hence foods of long shelf life which maintained their nutritional value, vitamin content, and palatability had to be developed. Moreover, foods had to be packaged to afford protection from the elements, rough handling, gas contamination, and insect infestation. The solution of these problems formed a vital phase of subsistence supply.

Administrative Background

Administrative responsibility for research and developmental activity in subsistence and in its packaging and packing was subjected to a number of changes in the opening years of World War II. When the war began, all responsibilities for subsistence, including research in this field, were centralized in a Subsistence Branch within the Supply Division. A Subsistence Research Laboratory,[3] established in Chicago in the sum-

---

[2] (1) Rpt, Subcom, QMCTC, to QMCTC, 15 Sep 39, sub: Fld Rat. (2) 2d ind, TAG to TQMG, 1 Nov 39, on memo, Brig Gen A. B. Warfield, OQMG, for TAG, 5 Oct 39, no sub. (3) See Harold W. Thatcher, *The Development of Special Rations for the Army* (QMC Historical Studies 6, September 1944), pp. 7–8. Hereafter cited as Thatcher, *Special Rations.*

[3] The laboratory will be referred to by this name although after its reorganization in February 1944 it was renamed the Subsistence Research and Development Laboratory. In the postwar period, after 1 March 1946, it became known as the Quartermaster Food and Container Institute for the Armed Forces. (2) For an extended account see Walter Porges, *The Subsistence Research Laboratory* (CQMD Historical Studies 1, 1 May 1943).

mer of 1936, gave the Subsistence Branch technical advice, carried on research and development for rations and subsistence items, and prepared specifications governing their procurement. Responsibility for subsistence had for many years been vested in an independent Subsistence Department, which was absorbed by the QMC in 1912 and was thereafter organized on an integrated commodity basis, first as the Subsistence Branch and then as a division. Thus a tradition of autonomy was fostered, which conditioned many of the organization's administrative relationships during the war.[4] By December 1942, in line with the functional reorganization of the OQMG, responsibility for research and developmental activity in subsistence had been transferred to the Research and Development Branch of the Military Planning Division.[5] By reason of its membership in the Subsistence Research Project Board, however, the Subsistence Branch continued to maintain an active interest in research.

The Subsistence Research Laboratory remained administratively a division of the Chicago Quartermaster Depot, but after December a Subsistence Section in the Research and Development Branch of the Military Planning Division became responsible for assigning projects to, and directing the technical activities of, the laboratory. From the fall of 1944 the director of the laboratory also acted as chief of the Subsistence Section.[6]

Insofar as research in the packaging and packing of subsistence was concerned, responsibility in 1939 was distributed among several offices within the QMC. The distinction between packaging and packing was not always clearly drawn, but, officially, packaging contained the product itself and frequently was designed along with the product. Packaging was usually accomplished at the production point. Packing referred to the exterior or shipping container.[7] Initially research in subsistence packaging was carried out by the Subsistence Branch, OQMG,

and the Subsistence Research Laboratory at Chicago. As in the case of subsistence research, by December 1942 responsibility for it was vested in the Research and Development Branch of the Military Planning Division. Responsibility for packing, on the other hand, was transferred from the Standardization Branch to the Depot Division early in 1942 and in July of that year was vested in the Storage and Distribution Division where it remained during the war years.[8]

Because the facilities of the Subsistence Research Laboratory for research on, and testing of, packaging and packing were limited, the Military Planning Division early in 1943 made arrangements to set up a physical testing laboratory, called the Washington Package Research and Development Laboratory, at the Washington Quartermaster Depot in Cameron, Va., for conducting research on the packaging and packing of all Quartermaster supplies. The testing of materials and the interpretation of the results were the joint responsibility of the Military Planning Division and the Storage and Distribution Division.[9] Functions were divided between this laboratory and the Subsistence Re-

---

[4] See above, Ch. I, section on Evolution of Functional-Commodity Type Organization.

[5] OQMG OO 25–24, 14 Dec 42, sub: Subs R&D Activities.

[6] (1) Activities Report of the QM Food and Container Institute for the Armed Forces, Vol. I, No. 3 (August, 1948), 298–99. (2) CQMD Activity Rpt, 1–15 Oct 44.

[7] ASF Cir 29, 13 May 43, sub: Staff Responsibility for Packaging and Packing.

[8] (1) OQMG OO 48, 20 Feb 42, sub: Asgmt of Responsibilities to Depot Div. (2) OQMG OO 184, 31 Jul 42, sub: Reasgmt of QMC Functions. Under this order the Depot Division became the Depot Operations Branch of the Storage and Distribution Division. (3) It was subsequently renamed the Storage Branch, OQMG OO 25–38, 31 May 43, sub: Establishment of Storage Br, S&D Div.

[9] Ltr, Col G. F. Doriot, OQMG, to Reqmts Div, SOS, 12 Mar 43, sub: Packaging Program, and 2d ind, Brig Gen W. A. Wood, Jr., Hq SOS, to TQMG, 1 Apr 43, on same.

search Laboratory to eliminate any duplication of research activities in this field.[10]

Efforts to develop food products for military use were centered at the Subsistence Research Laboratory. Starting as a small, ill-equipped, understaffed organization in 1941, the laboratory added more people and equipment as its activities increased during the war. In the early part of the war the laboratory's facilities were adequate for rather rough storage, utilization, and acceptability testing and for chemical, bacteriological, and vitamin evaluations. Subsequently additional equipment enabled it to perform more refined testing of all these as well as to undertake other developmental work.

For lack of time the results of a true research program could neither be established nor utilized during the war. Although a considerable body of technological and production knowledge and skill existed in industry, it had not been related to military requirements for food products, which, in any case, were being determined as the war progressed. During the first two years of the war, the laboratory was occupied with learning the latest production methods and applying these to the manufacture of products which would meet military needs. In the last two years of the war, the laboratory, with more people, increased facilities, and added knowledge and experience, was able to concentrate to a large extent on the development of new and more satisfactory products and more suitable rations. Its achievements were always attained with the wholehearted co-operation of industry, whose contributions to the development of Army subsistence are too numerous for detailed discussion.

In carrying out its mission the laboratory acted "as the hitherto missing military link between research groups and production groups." [11] University laboratories, as well as the facilities of industry, were called upon to assist in the solution of technical problems involved in developing food for Army use. Such assistance was early sought by the Subsistence Branch, OQMG, and was continued under contractual arrangements by the Subsistence Section of the Research and Development Branch, OQMG, after December 1942. Many universities and colleges contributed to subsistence research either through direct contact with the QMC concerning special problems referred to them, or as a result of experimentation undertaken in conjunction with various bureaus of the Department of Agriculture, its experimental stations, and its regional research laboratories.

In addition to dealing with food and food packaging concerns and with university groups, the QMC also had connections with other service laboratories interested in similar problems, such as the Medical Nutrition Laboratory of the Office of The Surgeon General and the Aero Medical Research Laboratory at Wright Field. To these must be added the informal and formal relationships with a number of other government agencies, among them the Department of Agriculture and the Fish and Wildlife Service of the Department of Interior. The achievements made in subsistence research during the war therefore represented the cumulative knowledge and co-operative efforts of all these organizations, both public and private.

The Development of Special Rations

The Subsistence Research Laboratory was concerned chiefly with the development of rations designed for use under operational conditions. Packaged operational rations were required not only for troops in actual contact with the enemy but for those cut off from their

---

[10] (1) Ltr, B. E. Proctor, Chief of Subs Sec OQMG, to Dr. J. H. White, Actg Dir SRL, 14 Apr 44, sub: Asgmt of Responsibilities and Functions. (2) Harold W. Thatcher, *Packaging and Packing of Subsistence for the Army* (QMC Historical Studies 10, April 1945), p. 16. Hereafter cited as Thatcher, *Packaging and Packing.*
[11] Activities Report of the Quartermaster Food and Container Institute, Vol. I, No. 3 (August 1948), 298.

normal source of supply or advancing so rapidly that their field kitchens could not keep pace with them. The problem of feeding soldiers in such situations was not new, but modern warfare, with its emphasis on mobile units, parachute-troop action, commando raids, and rapid armored advances, broadened this subsistence problem.

Even during the relatively immobile warfare of World War I, several special rations were used, such as the reserve ration, the trench ration developed in 1918, and the emergency ration, popularly known as the "Armour ration" or "iron ration." [12] In the years following this war the QMC made efforts to improve the reserve ration, but ration planning during this period was for the most part an academic exercise. The history of subsistence research parallels that of other Quartermaster items of supply in that lack of funds and personnel during the interlude of peace narrowly limited developmental activity. After the mid-thirties interest in preparation for national defense began to revive, and by the outbreak of war new field rations C and D had been developed to replace the obsolete reserve and emergency rations then officially in use. As a result of the lack of interest in ration planning between the two world wars, however, the Corps was compelled to solve the ration problem hurriedly and under pressure during World War II, a procedure that emphasized the necessity for a program of continuous research.

In the development of packaged rations the Subsistence Research Laboratory had to take into account factors which were often in conflict. Whatever the military or individual requirements were, they could be satisfied only within the limitations of the availability of the nation's food supply. Out of experience the laboratory eventually formulated four requisites for a satisfactory ration: acceptability, nutritional adequacy, stability, and military utility. [13]

The particular kind of ration needed depended on the military operation in which it was to be used, but in general any ration had to be "economical of space and weight in transportation and storage, of facilities and labor in unloading, carrying, issue, preparation, and consumption." [14] Eleven special rations [15] were standardized to meet specific tactical situations during World War II. These included types of rations designed for survival, combat, and group feeding, from which the following illustrative examples have been drawn for analysis.

D Ration—Survival Type

One of the subsistence problems confronting the QMC was that of issuing food for the individual survivor who could not get or expect outside help. In World War I this problem had been met by the use of the Armour ration, issued as an individual emergency ration. This was replaced in World War II by the D ration, which had been developed before the outbreak of the war.

Field ration D was strictly an emergency ration. As a result of an OQMG directive, work on it was begun in 1935 by Capt. Paul P. Logan, then head of the Subsistence School in Chicago.[16] This work was completed by 1937.

_____

[12] Porges, *The Subsistence Research Laboratory*, pp. 33–38.

[13] SR&DL, A Report of Wartime Problems in Subsistence Research and Development (13 vols projected by Quartermaster Food and Container Institute for the Armed Forces), Vol. XII, *Ration Development*, prepared by Capt John P. Samuels *et al.*, June 1947, pp. 4–5. Hereafter cited as SR&DL, *Ration Development*.

[14] *Ibid.*, p. 5.

[15] These were as follows: field rations D, C, K, and ten-in-one; the life raft, parachute emergency, and lifeboat rations, which were of emergency character; and the hospital supplement, aid station beverage pack, kitchen spice pack, and aircrew lunch, which were considered supplemental in nature.

[16] (1) Ltr, Lt Col Paul P. Logan, OQMG, to Col Gillespie, Fort Lewis, Wash., 1 May 41, no sub, 430.2. (2) Porges, *The Subsistence Research Laboratory*, Appendix IV, ltr to Col R. A. Isker, OIC SRL, 26 Apr 43, no sub.

The D ration was the result of hundreds of experiments in combining chocolate, the basic ingredient, with different cereals. In the beginning developmental work was based on the theory that an emergency ration should not be palatable lest it be consumed before an emergency arose. Subsequently, at the instigation of G–4 of the general staff, palatability was made a requisite in order that the D ration might also be used to supplement other food, such as reserve and regular field rations, in the theaters of operations.[17]

In the end a palatable 4-ounce bar, containing 600 calories, was developed. The chief ingredients were chocolate, sugar, oat flour, cocoa fat, skim milk powder, and artificial flavoring. The chocolate was unique in that it was stabilized to a high melting point; it could withstand temperatures up to 120° F. Except for minor changes in ingredients and in fortification of the chocolate with vitamin B_1,[18] no changes were made in the formula for the D ration during World War II. A ration consisted of three of these bars with a total weight of 12 ounces and a total caloric content of 1,800.[19] This new ration was always regarded as one to be used strictly as a last resort, and then for only a brief period covering very few meals. The caloric content was therefore deemed adequate for such a stop-gap use.

In the summer of 1937 the new ration was tested on a reasonably large scale in the field and provision was also made for storage testing. The results of both proved favorable. Having passed its early tests successfully, the "Logan bar," as it was popularly called, was recommended for standardization in the fall of 1938.[20]

In addition to being used as a separate meal in emergencies, the D ration was used as a component of other Army rations. A two-ounce D bar was included as a part of one of the meals of the new K ration. It remained a component of the supper unit of this ration. It was also included in the "bail-out ration" of the Army

Air Corps and in one of the menus of the ten-in-one ration when the latter was standardized in the late spring of 1943.

The D ration fulfilled the most rigid Army requirements for minimum space and weight. From the standpoint of energy yield it was an especially good food source. Experience indicated, however, that the D bar was not completely satisfactory even when used as a means of survival. While many soldiers found it useful as a concentrated, tasty, and quick means of acquiring energy, it produced nausea in some cases and it made men thirsty. This disadvantage alone made use of it inadvisable if drinking water was limited in supply.[21]

Although it had been developed as a strictly survival food item, the D bar was used extensively to supplement C and K rations. Men ate it as candy or used it for making hot chocolate. Kitchens utilized it in baking pies and cakes and in making puddings and cocoa.[22] Similarly, in the Southwest Pacific Area, the D ration was "rarely issued, except as a supplement to 'C' Ration."[23]

In this area, certain defects were particularly noticed. D bars stored in hot, dry places were subject to crumbling, a process that was preceded by the appearance of a white "bloom" on

[17] *Ibid.*
[18] (1) Ltr, Maj J. J. Powers, OQMG, to CO CQMD, 24 Jul 40, sub: Addition of Thiamin Chloride to Type D Rat, 400.112. (2) For a fuller account of the development of the D ration as well as other special rations see Thatcher, *Special Rations,* pp. 4–15.
[19] Col Rohland A. Isker, "Army Foods—Army Menus," *QMR,* XXXII (July–August 1942), 90.
[20] (1) Rpt, Subcom, QMCTC, to QMCTC, 9 Nov 38, sub: Further Consideration of Emergency Rat. (2) QMCTC, min of mtg 6, 18 Nov 38. Both in 400.112.
[21] SR&DL, *Ration Development,* p. 62.
[22] (1) Asst for Product Analysis to Sub Sec, OQMG, 24 Apr 45, sub: Rpt 18—Hq ComZ, ETO, OofCQM, 5 Mar, signed Littlejohn. (2) Same to same, 8 Feb 45, sub: Rations, extract from QM Fld Obsn Rpt 5, Maj Gen R. L. Littlejohn.
[23] Memo, Maj Carl R. Fellers for CO QM Subs Depot, USASOS, 3 Sep 43, sub: US Army Rat D, RAC ORB AFWESPAC QM Sec 430.2 Rat.

the surface of the bar. This bloom was a crystallization of the fat mixed with oat flour and powdered milk in the bar itself. It did not impair the food value of the ration, and, even when crumbled, the D bar was still acceptable for use in cocoa.

The D ration, developed before World War II began, was available for immediate issue. During the war other types of survival rations were developed, particularly for the Army Air Forces. The Subsistence Research Laboratory, working in co-operation with the Aero Medical Laboratory, developed several different food units, such as the life raft ration and the parachute ration, for inclusion in Air Forces kits.

C Ration—Combat Type

While the D ration was the first modern emergency ration, it was not designed to fill the need for a nutritionally balanced combat ration, which could be readily carried by the soldier, and which would provide three satisfying meals a day, independent of outside sources of supply and of central messing facilities.

When the Subsistence Research Laboratory began in 1937 to study the problem of the combat-reserve ration, it was interested primarily in revising the existing reserve ration. Not until March 1938 did this study take a new turn. Then the director of the laboratory became convinced that "some system of individual carrying of rations must be devised immediately." [24] By June the main features of a new combat ration had been worked out, and the director enthusiastically described this revolutionary development to the OQMG. Packed in three cans, the ration, having a weight of 36 ounces and providing 4,200 calories, had "all the vitamins, fuel and regulating foods, and is far better in edibility and palatability than any meal that can be cooked in a peacetime Army mess, let alone a rolling kitchen in gas and shell attack." [25]

Two forms of the ration were proposed: one

for general use on a campaign and the other, a more Spartan diet, to be consumed under actual combat conditions. The latter consisted of two cans containing the meat and vegetable components, one 12-ounce can containing 8 ounces of bran cereal, a 3-ounce chocolate jam bar, and 1 ounce of soluble coffee. In September the ration was shown to members of the General Staff and representatives of the Navy and Marine Corps. All were keenly interested. The OQMG, however, felt that the caloric value of the ration ought to be checked and increased and directed the laboratory to undertake further study along these lines. [26]

The laboratory soon discovered that the total of 4,200 calories claimed for the ration was based on a miscalculation of the nutritional value of the chocolate jam bars. The actual caloric content of the three cans was only slightly more than 2,000. Since it was not feasible to increase this content to the required amount, the only alternative was to include more cans in the ration. The laboratory therefore recommended that the ration be composed of six 12-ounce cans. Three of them would contain meat and vegetable components. These were later designated as the M unit. The other three, subsequently called the B unit, would contain bread, coffee, and sugar components. The total would have a caloric content of 3,348. By the addition of 8 ounces of the chocolate emergency ration, called the D bar, this content could be raised to approximately 4,500 calories. [27]

In the fall of 1938 the QMCTC approved a subcommittee recommendation that this ration

---

[24] (1) Ltr, Maj W. R. McReynolds, SRL, to Capt Logan, OQMG, 24 Mar 38, no sub, SRL File 430.02 Combat Rat. (2) For a full account of the early development of the C ration see Porges, *The Subsistence Research Laboratory*, pp. 53ff.

[25] Ltr, Maj McReynolds, SRL, to Capt Logan, OQMG, 3 Jun 38, no sub, SRL File 430.02 Combat Rat.

[26] Ltr, Capt O. E. Cound, OQMG, to CO CQMD, 18 Sep 38, sub: Combat Rat, 400.112.

[27] SRL, Research Rpt 95, 15 Oct 38, 400.112.

be considered as a replacement for the reserve ration, and that it be developed until completely perfected.[28] In the meantime the Subsistence Research Laboratory had been investigating existing commercial products for possible use in the M unit, but these were rejected because of their poor quality. By the summer of 1939 the laboratory was ready to report its findings to the OQMG. It listed ten varieties of the M unit it had developed as well as three types of biscuit for the B unit, all differing from each other in flavor and texture. The ration weighed 5 pounds, 10 ounces, and contained 4,437 calories. At the same time the laboratory adopted the standard cylindrical sanitary can, holding about 16 fluid ounces, for packaging the ration in lieu of the 12-ounce rectangular can which was no longer produced commercially in sufficient quantities to make large-scale procurement feasible.[29]

Developmental work had now reached the stage where the new reserve ration could be considered for adoption by the Army. In the fall of 1939 a subcommittee of the QMCTC, reviewing the whole field of ration nomenclature, recommended standardization of the new reserve or combat ration as field ration, type C. The ten varieties of the M unit, suggested in the June report of the Subsistence Research Laboratory, were reduced to three: beef stew, pork and beans, and meat hash. The B unit was confined to a single type, which included all three varieties of crackers developed by the laboratory. Subsequently, to simplify production line operation, a kind of biscuit known as the "C square biscuit" was substituted for these three types. Formal announcement of the adoption and standardization of the C ration was made by The Adjutant General on 1 November 1939.[30]

Standardization of the C ration was accomplished before a field test was arranged. The first large-scale tests were conducted during the 1940 maneuvers. The C ration was not unqualifiedly popular with the troops. The awkwardness and bulk of the containers made it almost impossible for the soldiers to carry a full day's rations. They wanted a flat, rectangular type of can, and recurrently expressed this preference during the war.[31] The men complained that there was an excessive quantity of food, that it lacked variety, and that in some instances it caused nausea.[32] As a result, the size of the can was reduced in December 1940 to 12 ounces, and the amount of biscuits and coffee was also decreased.[33] At the same time there was added to the B unit a 1-ounce chocolate bar. This was a type of fudge and not to be confused with the 1- or 2-ounce D bar previously suggested for inclusion. Later hard candy was substituted for the chocolate bar because it was felt that soldiers would and should carry hard candy to eat between meals.

The Subsistence Research Laboratory engaged in extensive developmental work on the com-

[28] QMCTC, min of mtg 6, 18 Nov 38.

[29] SRL, Research Rpt 111, 21 Jun 39.

[30] (1) Rpt, Subcom, QMCTC, to QMCTC, 15 Sep 39, sub: Fld Rat. (2) QMCTC, min of mtg 6, 28 Sep 39. (3) 2d ind, TAG to TQMG, 1 Nov 39, on memo, Gen Warfield, Actg TQMG, for TAG, 5 Oct 39, no sub.

[31] As late as the summer of 1945 an observer in the ETO reported: "Preference for the K ration over the C still continues, in spite of the fact that on several occasions new menus have been available to troops. This preference, it seems, is due to the bulkiness of the C ration and the difficulty encountered in carrying it. For example, during the two recent river crossings made in this area, those across the Rhine and the Roer, generally one ration was carried by the individual and this ration was predominately the K ration. . . . If the C ration were manufactured in a flat can approximately the size of a K ration package, it would no doubt be more popular, especially as new menus become more plentiful." Hq ETO, OofCQM, Rpt 20, sub: Comments and Recommendations on QM Equip, ETO, n. d. (circa May 1945), 319.1 Sullivan Papers.

[32] (1) Memo, Maj McReynolds, QM Sec Third Army Depot, Alexandria, La., for TQMG, 22 May 40, no sub, 430.2. (2) Lt Col F. V. Hemenway, Hq Third Div, Ft Lewis, Wash., to CG Ninth Corps Area, 6 Jun 40, sub: Test of Fld Rat, 400.112.

[33] 2d ind, Col Logan, OQMG, to TAG, 16 Dec 40, on memo, Maj P. B. Mayson, Hq Fourth Corps Area, for TAG, 2 Dec 40, no sub.

ponents of the C ration. It found most commercial canned meat products unsuitable for military use. The more satisfactory of them, such as pork luncheon meat, corned beef, and roast beef, were being used in the B ration. In formulating recipes for canned meat products and developing processing methods, the laboratory at first emphasized nutritional adequacy and balance. As it became apparent, however, that all nutritive factors could not be combined in a single product, palatability became the primary goal.[34] When satisfactory formulas had been evolved they were submitted to the OQMG.

As previously stated, the ten different kinds of M unit suggested by the laboratory were reduced to three at the time of standardization. The C ration had not been designed for continuous consumption over long periods of time. It was not to be issued for more than 72 hours and, within this limit, its three meat components were satisfactory. In actual theater operations, however, the ration was frequently used for long periods. Instances were reported of soldiers being fed the C ration for as long as 90 days. Such prolonged wartime use had not been anticipated. In the summer of 1940 the Subsistence Branch had indicated that the ration was intended for use in emergencies in the forward areas of the combat zone, where it was impracticable to use cooking or heating facilities. "The use of this ration will, therefore," it prophesied, "be very infrequent and consequently a large variety is not essential."[35]

The Subsistence Research Laboratory recognized that a greater variety of meat components was desirable, but variety had to be subordinated to other considerations. When the first large-scale procurement of the C ration was instituted in August 1941, it had to be confined largely to items available in great volume and from as many sources of supply as possible. Throughout the war there was a constant struggle in the canned-meats program between quantity and quality. The Subsistence Research Laboratory and the Subsistence Section of the Research and Development Branch, OQMG, were intent on widening the variety of canned meats for ration components, improving existing commodities, developing new types, and attempting to get the more desirable into production. The buyer of canned meats at the Chicago Depot and the procurement agencies of the QMC generally were responsible, despite shortages of materials and labor, for filling procurement demands with nutritionally adequate products which could be obtained most simply, uniformly, and in the largest amounts. The buyer was interested in quality but he tended to favor the products he was sure to get in sufficient amounts at the time desired.[36]

Even the limited variety of meats specified for the C ration, however, was greater than that sometimes received by the soldier in the field. The ration was supposed to be assembled with equal quantities of each meat component, but assemblers who had exhausted their stock of one meat unit would substitute one or two of the others. The result was that packed cases sometimes contained quantities of one or two meat units but none of the third.[37]

The monotony of the C ration, the first of the special rations perfected that contained meat, was heightened by the fact that its meat components, stew or hash, also appeared in the B ration. Such duplication was opposed in principle by the laboratory but this agency was not responsible for filling supply requirements. The factor of monotony was of minor importance to

[34] SR&DL, A Report of Wartime Problems in Subsistence Research and Development (13 vols projected by Quartermaster Food & Container Institute for the Armed Forces), Vol. XI, Meat Products, prepared by Capt Joseph Czarnecki et al., July 1948, p. 61. Hereafter cited as SR&DL, Meat Products.

[35] Subs Br to Chief of Sup Div, OQMG, 28 May 40, no sub, 430.2.

[36] Marion Massen, Canned Meats Procurement for the Armed Forces During World War II (CQMD Historical Studies, Rpt 7, March 1946), p. 295.

[37] SR&DL, Meat Products, p. 63.

procurement personnel who were confronted with the many problems involved in providing canned meats in large quantities. As a consequence, the low degree of acceptability of such foods as canned hash and luncheon meat was repeatedly reported during World War II.

The C ration retained its original form for several years of the war. Its three meat components underwent only minor revisions. In response to the changing supply situation, the grades, cuts, and proportions of the meat ingredients were changed.[38] An attempt was made to meet the criticism that the meat particles were ground too small by increasing their size from one half to three fourths of an inch. It was well into 1944, however, before automatic packing of larger chunks of meat was at all successful.

By the spring of 1944 the need for an improved combat ration had become imperative. There had been an interminable use of stew and hash as staple B and C ration components. As a result of this overuse, complaints that the rations were unpalatable mounted steadily. In an effort to relieve the monotony the laboratory had developed in 1942 four additional meat units, but nothing came of them at the time.[39] In December 1943, however, one new unit consisting of ground meat and spaghetti was added.

Major changes in the C ration were made in the summer of 1944 when a new specification[40] was issued providing for ten different kinds of meat units, including such items as chicken and vegetables; ham, egg, and potato; frankfurters and beans; and ham and lima beans. The M unit of meat and vegetable hash was dropped from the ration at this time. In April 1945 the meat and vegetable stew also was replaced by a new type of beef stew. In an effort to insure that the variety provided by the new meat components would actually be made available to the men in the field, the new specification listed six specific menus along with packing schedules. These menus were rotated so that no

one meat would appear more than four times in the same packing case. The ten components were to be procured in equal quantities. Unfortunately, assemblers were again permitted by the Procurement Division to make substitutions when they ran out of certain components, and thus the procurement history of the old C ration was repeated in the new type.[41]

Although the most conspicuous of the changes in the C ration was the increased variety of the meat components, the B unit of the ration was also modified. To increase variety and acceptability the Subsistence Research Laboratory provided six B units. The bread component was changed by the use of three types of biscuits or crackers rather than the standard C biscuit. Although crackers were still used, pending the outcome of studies on canned bread, the inclusion of jam components in the new C ration made them more palatable. In addition, several new confections were included to relieve the former emphasis on hard candy.

The original beverage of the C ration was soluble coffee, which was included in each of the three B unit cans. By the summer of 1942 a greater variety had been achieved in beverage components. It was decided that one of the B unit cans should contain soluble coffee, one cocoa beverage powder, and one the lemon powder which had also been used in the K ration.[42] The lemon juice powder, as well as other beverage crystals introduced later, carried ascorbic acid (Vitamin C). In theory three beverages were thus provided for the soldier, but the men in the field refused to use lemon powder, whether in C or K rations. There was

[38] Thatcher, *Special Rations*, pp. 26–27.

[39] *Ibid.*, p. 28. These units consisted of ham, eggs, and potatoes; beef and noodles; ham and eggs; and meat and spaghetti.

[40] CQD 183, 28 June 44, sub: Rat, Type C, Assembly, Packaging, and Packing, 400.1141.

[41] SR&DL, *Meat Products*, pp. 69–70.

[42] Ltr, Col Logan, OQMG, to CG CQMD, 30 Jun 42, sub: Changes in the B Units of the Type C Rat, 430.2.

not always enough sugar to sweeten it, and whether it was sweet or sour, few men eating in the cold wanted a cold beverage. There were reports of its use as a cleaning agent for stoves or even as a hair rinse! A quartermaster of the 2d Infantry Division noted:

We used K ration lemon powder dissolved in buckets of water for scrubbing the floor when we were living in buildings, and it worked out exceptionally well, cutting dirt spots and more or less bleaching the wooden floors.[43]

When the new specification for the C ration was published in April 1945,[44] synthetic lemon juice powder was eliminated.

The new C ration was further improved by the addition of an accessory kit. Cigarettes and matches had been included in two of the B units since March 1943. They were now increased in quantity, and gum was also added. The usefulness of toilet paper as an accessory item had been shown in the ten-in-one ration and was therefore now added to the new C ration. All of these items, including halazone tablets for purifying water, and a small can opener, were assembled in accessory packets which were made from foil laminated to kraft paper, and were inserted between the round cans when they were packed in shipping cases.

Soldier opinion of the old C ration, as well as of all other rations, was expressed in a number of reports, most of which were received by the QMC during the last year of the war. Excerpts from some of these reports became available to the Subsistence Research Laboratory, but soldier comments were apt to be too general and too conflicting in nature to be of much use as a guide to corrective action. The laboratory was permitted to send very few technically trained observers overseas. Hence it did not know precisely what was being praised or criticized—under what specifications the item had been produced, whether or not it had deviated from specifications, how the item was issued or

served, or other details necessary for guidance in further developmental work. Instead of practical field experience the laboratory had often to rely upon its simulations of field conditions in taking corrective action on subsistence items.

Insofar as the old C ration was concerned the reports showed that the biscuits of this ration were not very acceptable. Soldier comments reflected a deep-seated dislike for hash, stew, and lemon juice powder. So powerful was the prejudice against the C ration in the Pacific theaters that it was questionable whether the new type of C ration could overcome it. The Assistant for Product Analysis in the Research and Development Branch, OQMG, suggested the desirability of changing the labeling or the packaging of the new ration to eliminate this handicap.[45] When the new C ration began to reach the field, however, it was praised very highly, leading one observer to conclude that "the simplicity of supplying and preparing C ration, the acceptability of its new components, and the filling properties of this ration as modified, all insure it a leading role in future operations." [46]

K Ration—Assault Phase

The C ration was a combat ration but the combat situation had to be sufficiently stable to permit daily resupply. When the soldier was actually fighting, as in the assault phase of combat, he required a different type of ration. For

---

[43] (1) Hq ETO, OofCQM, QM Fld Observation Rpt 14, 1–7 Jan 45, 319.1 Sullivan Papers. (2) See also Lt Col D. B. Dill to Dir of Mil Plng Div, OQMG, Rpt on Travel to NATO, 26 Oct–13 Dec 43.

[44] CQD 183B, 12 Apr 45, sub: Rat, Type C, Assembly, Packaging and Packing, 400.1141.

[45] Asst for Product Analysis to Subs Sec, OQMG, 23 Nov 44, sub: C Rat.

[46] (1) Col Dill, Rpt on Observation in SWP and POA, Oct–Dec 44. (2) USAFFE Bd Rpt 138, 29 Mar 45, sub: QM Bull #11 (Rat). (3) See also the voluminous analysis of observers' and soldiers' comments by the Assistant for Product Analysis on file in the R&D Br, OQMG.

this situation the Subsistence Research Laboratory developed the K ration.

Although the laboratory had been experimenting in 1940 and 1941 with pemmican as the chief ingredient of a ration for mobile troops, the origin of the K ration dates from June 1941 when the Chief of Infantry requested the development of a ration which could be carried in the pockets of paratroopers' uniforms. It was suggested that, in order to fit such pockets, each packaged ration should be 6 inches long by 2½ inches wide by 1 inch thick, with a weight of not more than three fourths of a pound. The recommendation proposed the inclusion of four sodium chloride tablets, to be used to replace salt lost from the body by excessive perspiration, and suggested consideration of the use of chocolate, peanuts, raisins, concentrated soups, bouillon cubes, and fruit juice powder because of their food value and compactness.[47]

Working in co-operation with Dr. Ancel Keys of the University of Minnesota, the Subsistence Research Laboratory had been experimenting with pemmican biscuits, cervelat sausage, beverage concentrates, and special confections, and it was therefore able to make counterproposals.[48] In particular the laboratory objected to the small size of the ration, proposing instead dimensions of 6½ by 3¼ by 1¼ inches. The laboratory viewed favorably the use of all the proposed ration items except sodium chloride tablets, which were already being issued by the Army, and concentrated soups, which required boiling water for preparation. Two sample rations were sent for consideration to the Provisional Parachute Group. One of these, containing 12 pemmican biscuits, a 1½-ounce cake of Type D chocolate, a meat preparation, and a lemon or orange powder soluble in cold water, may be considered the direct prototype of the K ration. Early experimentation of the laboratory had demonstrated that a ration must be appealing as well as nutritious. Emphasis was therefore placed on securing the greatest variety of palatable, stable, and nutritious foods obtainable within the imposed limits of space and weight. Maximum palatability of the K ration was sacrificed to these limitations, which exerted the primary influence in the development of this ration.

Late in the summer of 1941 development of this ration, usually referred to as the parachute ration, had reached the point where field tests were desirable. About the same time the Chief of Infantry emphasized that there was no conflict between the needs of parachute troops and other types of troops, and he recommended that "all-around suitability rather than a highly specialized use be the objective." [49]

Shortly thereafter representatives of The Quartermaster General and the Chief of Infantry agreed to designate the new item as Field Ration, Type K, thereby eliminating any limitation as to the function which the ration might fulfill.[50] Extensive tests were made of the K ration in the fall and winter of 1941–42, and it emerged with flying colors.[51]

The commanding general of the Army Ground Forces felt that the findings of some of the tests were sufficiently conclusive to warrant standardization of the K ration without waiting for completion of all the comprehensive tests. In the summer of 1942 the QMCTC recommended adoption of the K ration. Official an-

---

[47] (1) Ltr, Lt Col W. C. Lee, Hq Provisional Parachute Group, Ft Benning, Ga., to CofInf, 17 Jun 41, sub: Rat for Use by Parachutists. (2) 2d ind, OCI to TQMG, 27 Jun 41, on same. Both in 400.112.

[48] (1) 4th ind, Col Henry B. Barry, CQMD, to TQMG, 22 Jul 41, on ltr cited in n. 47. (2) Ltr, Col Isker, SRL, to Col Lee, Ft Benning, Ga., 22 Jul 41, sub: Parachute Rat. Both in 400.112.

[49] 2d ind, Col M. S. Lough, OCI, to TQMG, on memo, Col Lee, Ft Benning, Ga., to SRL, 28 Jul 41, no sub, 400.112.

[50] Ltr, Col Logan, OQMG, to Col Isker, SRL, 13 Nov 41, no sub.

[51] For an extended discussion of these tests see Thatcher, *Special Rations*, pp. 43–48.

nouncement of the standardization, however, was delayed until November.[52]

Development tended toward designing the K ration in meal packages rather than a single package for an entire day. These were labeled "breakfast unit," "dinner unit," and "supper unit." In the course of development the weight of the K ration increased to 36½ ounces net weight or 46½ ounces including the outer wrappings, but the caloric content remained about the same. The composition and the packaging of the K ration varied in many minor details during the war period. To trace these changes in detail would be tedious, and a graphic presentation (Chart 8) is sufficiently explanatory.[53]

The successive revisions of the K ration increased its palatability but it remained inferior in this respect to the improved C ration. Like the latter it included, by the end of the war, nonfoodstuff items intended to provide additional comfort for the soldier. Similarly, the trend of development moved from the use of finely ground potted meats to the use of sliced meat or chunk meat products. A number of these—chicken solid pack, ham steak, and pork steak—were developed by the Subsistence Research Laboratory and approved by the OQMG, but the war ended before these items could be procured. Field criticism had underscored the need for revision of the K ration, but priority of development at the laboratory was given to the new C ration and the ten-in-one.

The K ration was intended for use in the assault phase of combat. The first and succeeding waves of troops would go into action carrying K rations, with D rations in their pockets for use in case they were cut off. As positions were consolidated, the C ration would be issued to the troops. In actual operation in the theaters, however, both C and K rations might be utilized during this period until, with the establishment of a beachhead, groups of men could be supplied with the ten-in-one ration.

When pressed, soldiers would admit that the K ration was a necessary item, but it was soundly criticized nonetheless. Similar complaints flowed into the OQMG from all theaters. All troops disliked the biscuits—Defense, K-1, and K-2—whether on Attu, in North Africa, or on Leyte. They were decidedly opposed to the use of lemon powder and were extremely critical of the inclusion of nonpopular brands of cigarettes.

In general the men will not eat K rations after a few days. They will pick out the chocolate bar, drink the coffee, and eat the soda crackers if they are the salted type. They will usually eat the cheese for about a week, after which they get tired of it.[54]

Although from a nutritional viewpoint it was necessary for a soldier to eat all portions of the K ration in order to receive full food value, observers agreed that troops threw away disliked items, thereby upsetting the nutritional balance the laboratory had sought to achieve in this ration.[55]

The K ration represented only one of several rations developed for use during the assault phase of combat. On the basis of requirements in the Pacific theaters the Subsistence Research Laboratory in 1944 undertook the development of a ration that would satisfy troops in the first phase of an amphibious assault. As a result an assault lunch was perfected. The provision of in-flight food for air crew members opened up

[52] (1) Memo, Maj J. R. Dryden, AGF, for TQMG, 11 May 42, sub: Test of Fld Rat, Type K Emergency, 400.112. (2) QMCTC, min of mtg 4, 25 May 42. (3) 2d ind, Hq SOS to OQMG, 27 Nov 42, on memo, Col Doriot, OQMG, for Chief of Dev Br, Reqmts Div, SOS, 17 Nov 42, sub: Standardization of Rat Type K, 430.2.

[53] See Thatcher, *Special Rations*, pp. 56–58.

[54] Dir of Mil Plng Div to Dir of Subs Div, OQMG, 30 Mar 45, sub: Rat, giving extracts from a report of a captain of the Medical Corps recently returned from Leyte.

[55] See the voluminous file on soldiers' and observers' comments on the K ration from all theaters, covering the period 1943–46, extracts from which were compiled by the Assistant for Product Analysis and are now on file in the Research and Development Branch, OQMG.

CHART 8—PRINCIPAL CHANGES IN K RATION COMPONENTS

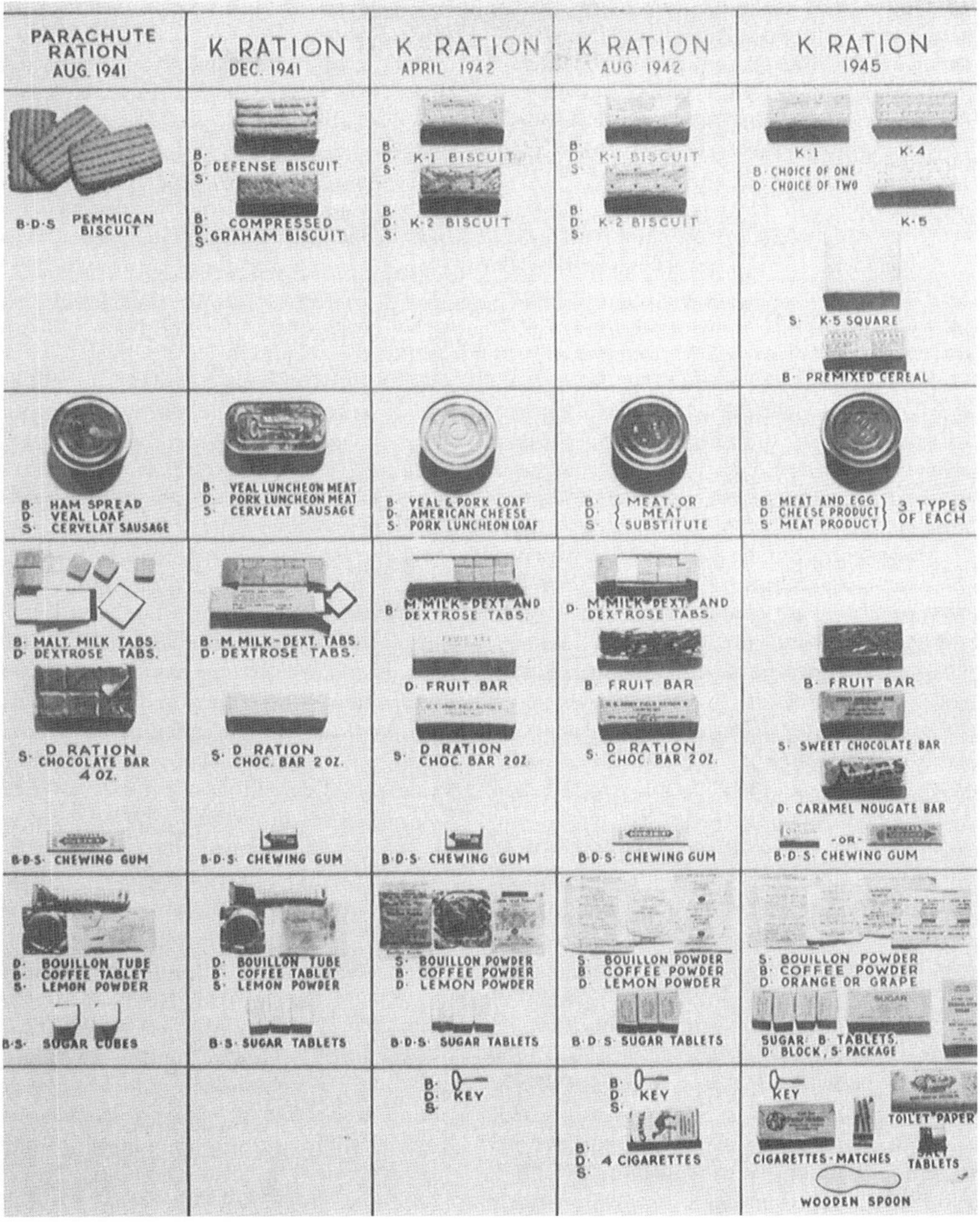

PARACHUTE RATION AUG. 1941	K RATION DEC. 1941	K RATION APRIL 1942	K RATION AUG 1942	K RATION 1945
B·D·S PEMMICAN BISCUIT	B· D· S· DEFENSE BISCUIT B· D· S· COMPRESSED GRAHAM BISCUIT	B· D· S· K·1 BISCUIT B· D· S· K·2 BISCUIT	B· D· S· K·1 BISCUIT B· D· S· K·2 BISCUIT	K·1 K·4 B· CHOICE OF ONE D· CHOICE OF TWO K·5 S· K·5 SQUARE B· PREMIXED CEREAL
B· HAM SPREAD D· VEAL LOAF S· CERVELAT SAUSAGE	B· VEAL LUNCHEON MEAT D· PORK LUNCHEON MEAT S· CERVELAT SAUSAGE	B· VEAL & PORK LOAF D· AMERICAN CHEESE S· PORK LUNCHEON LOAF	B· D· S· { MEAT, OR MEAT SUBSTITUTE }	B· MEAT AND EGG } D· CHEESE PRODUCT } 3 TYPES S· MEAT PRODUCT } OF EACH
B· MALT. MILK TABS. D· DEXTROSE TABS. S· D RATION CHOCOLATE BAR 4 OZ. B·D·S· CHEWING GUM	B· M. MILK–DEXT. TABS. D· DEXTROSE TABS. S· D RATION CHOC. BAR 2 OZ. B·D·S· CHEWING GUM	B· M. MILK–DEXT. AND DEXTROSE TABS. D· FRUIT BAR S· D RATION CHOC. BAR 2 OZ. B·D·S· CHEWING GUM	D· M. MILK–DEXT. AND DEXTROSE TABS. B· FRUIT BAR S· D RATION CHOC. BAR 2 OZ. B·D·S· CHEWING GUM	B· FRUIT BAR S· SWEET CHOCOLATE BAR D· CARAMEL NOUGATE BAR – OR – B·D·S· CHEWING GUM
D· BOUILLON TUBE B· COFFEE TABLET S· LEMON POWDER B·S· SUGAR CUBES	D· BOUILLON TUBE B· COFFEE TABLET S· LEMON POWDER B·S· SUGAR TABLETS	S· BOUILLON POWDER B· COFFEE POWDER D· LEMON POWDER B·D·S· SUGAR TABLETS	S· BOUILLON POWDER B· COFFEE POWDER D· LEMON POWDER B·D·S· SUGAR TABLETS	S· BOUILLON POWDER B· COFFEE POWDER D· ORANGE OR GRAPE SUGAR: B· TABLETS, D· BLOCK, S· PACKAGE
		B· D· S· KEY	B· D· S· KEY B· D· S· 4 CIGARETTES	KEY CIGARETTES·MATCHES TOILET PAPER TABLETS WOODEN SPOON

a large field of development posing many intricate problems. In the beginning little or no attention had been given to in-flight feeding, but by the spring of 1943 the laboratory, in co-operation with the Army Air Forces, was developing the air crew lunch.[56]

Ten-in-One Ration

Among the special rations developed by the QMC the ten-in-one was the most important packaged ration for group feeding. It was intended for use in combat situations not sufficiently stabilized to permit kitchen-prepared meals, though still allowing a minimum of food preparation. It could be used for troops isolated in small groups, such as gun crews, armored vehicle crews, and small tactical groups. However, when developmental work on rations for group feeding was first initiated, the operational conditions for which they were to be used were not clearly foreseen.

The ten-in-one ration had three predecessors—the mountain, the jungle, and the five-in-one rations.[57] The first two of these originated during 1941 and 1942 in the OQMG, where the Army's emphasis on the organization of special troops, such as parachute troops, jungle troops, mountain troops, and armored forces, was translated into Quartermaster concentration on specialized clothing, equipment, and food for such troops. The developmental work on these two rations, each intended to feed four men for one day, was chiefly accomplished by the Special Forces Section of the OQMG. However essential a special ration might be for mountain troops, considerable doubt existed as to the need for special types of food for troops operating in jungle areas. The Subsistence Research Laboratory was extremely critical of these two rations and urged that procurement be held to a minimum until field reports demonstrated their adequacy. Although these rations were not standardized considerable quantities of them

were nevertheless procured before they were finally dropped.

Concurrently the Subsistence Research Laboratory was developing a five-in-one ration, which was planned as a unit assembly of sufficient food to take care of five men for one day. This ration grew out of the need of the Armored Force to supply rations to individual tank crews and to fast-moving organizations. It was intended to provide a ration as much like the regular B ration as possible but one which would enable men to be completely self-sufficient in the field. Hence the selection of foods was suggested by the B ration but was modified to the extent that soluble coffee and pre-cooked readily prepared cereals were used. Such foodstuffs were selected as could be easily prepared by troops with limited cooking experience and more limited cooking facilities. They were commercially produced items both as to type of product and size of container. Three menus were developed by the laboratory for this ration, which included forty different food items. By August 1942 developmental work was approaching completion, and a considerable quantity of the five-in-one ration was procured, although like other group-feeding rations it was not standardized.

A special ration providing food for ten men for one day had been under consideration in this same period, but the project remained dormant until the spring of 1943. Then it was suddenly revived and rapidly pushed to a successful conclusion as a result of two factors. One was the great success of the British Composite Pack during the North African campaign in the fall of 1942. This "Compo" ration, packaged to feed fourteen men for one day and containing nine different menus, was intended to provide the only subsistence in new operations

---

[56] For elaboration of this development work see SR&DL, *Ration Development*, pp. 49–59.

[57] For an analysis of the development of these rations see Thatcher, *Special Rations*, pp. 64–90.

for as long as forty-two days. The Research and Development Branch made a complete study of this ration in the spring of 1943, and it undoubtedly had much influence on the development of the ten-in-one ration.[58]

The second factor was the movement for simplification of rations which gathered impetus in the fall of 1942. The trend toward diversification, illustrated by the mountain and jungle rations, reached its climax in the spring. A critic described the situation as follows:

Development during the last two years in an effort to furnish a suitable type of combat ration having the qualities of light weight, small bulk and adequate nutritional value has been highly successful insofar as bulk, weight, nutritional value and palatability are concerned, but has also had the undesirable result of producing a large number of different types of packaging and types of components to fit local conditions of terrain and climate, and even to fit particular types of equipment. The resulting complexity has so involved both the supply problem and the problem of the ultimate breakdown for use that an immediate simplification is considered essential.[59]

As a result of a series of conferences in the fall and winter of 1942–43, representatives of the AGF and the QMC agreed upon the development and standardization of two special rations (in addition to the type A and type B field rations) that should eventually replace all the special rations then being procured for the AGF. The two special rations included an individual combat ration and a small-group field ration. Development of the former proved unsuccessful, and consequently the C, K, and D types of field rations continued to be utilized during World War II. On the other hand, the quest for a small-group ration was successful and resulted in the standardization of the ten-in-one ration in June 1943.[60] It replaced the mountain, jungle, and five-in-one rations, which were classified as limited standard.

In March 1943 the military characteristics of the ten-in-one ration had been determined at a conference between representatives of the OQMG and the AGF. Since theater reports stressed the need for speed, the Research and Development Branch, in collaboration with the Subsistence Research Laboratory, undertook to complete development of the ration within 30 to 45 days. A weight limitation of 40 pounds had been imposed, necessitating a considerable use of dehydrated foods. During the course of development the laboratory evolved two versions of the ration, each containing three menus. The chief difference between them was that in one set all meals were arranged on a group basis, and in the other a unit of the K ration was substituted for the dinner in each menu, thus permitting individual distribution of the midday meal.[61] The use of the K ration permitted the inclusion of a greater number of items for the two group meals and resulted in a higher caloric value for the entire ration. Accordingly it was this set which was selected for adoption. It had also been decided that distribution to smaller tactical units would be materially aided by packing the ration on a double five-in-one basis. Before standardization in June some additional changes were made, including the increase of the number of menus to five and the addition of towels to the nonfood items in the ration.

Although a number of other minor changes were made, the most important modification of the ten-in-one ration was initiated in 1944. In the original development it had been assumed that tactical considerations would necessitate an

[58] R&D Br to Opns Br, Mil Plng Div, OQMG, 16 Mar 43, sub: Lessons Derived from Opns at Casablanca and Oran.
[59] Ltr, Lt Col J. S. Tanner, Asst Ground Adj Gen, to CG ASF, 28 Mar 43, sub: Simplification of Rat for Active Fld Opns.
[60] (1) Rpt, Subcom, QMCTC, to QMCTC, 7 Jun 43, sub: Ten-in-One Rat. (2) QMCTC, min of mtg 12, 8 Jun 43. (3) 4th ind, Hq ASF to TQMG, 25 Jun 43, on subcom rpt. Both in 430.2.
[61] Ltr, Col Isker, SRL, to George Burgess, R&D Br, OQMG, 13 Apr 43, no sub.

TEN-IN-ONE ARMY FIELD RATION, *September 1943.*

individual issue at noon. Use of the ration in theaters of operations, however, demonstrated that, except in the case of the most exposed infantry, it was possible to heat all three meals. Reports from overseas indicated that the five-in-one ration with a group noon meal was more acceptable than the ten-in-one ration with individual dinners. Furthermore, complaints from NATO about the similarity of the K ration and the K type lunch provided for the noon meal of the ten-in-one ration led to suggestions to modify it.[62]

The K ration noon meal had been included as the best immediate solution of the problem in the rapid development of the ten-in-one ration. Since its limitations had been recog-

nized, the Subsistence Research Laboratory started developmental work toward increasing the food value and bulk of the noon meal, improving its acceptability and getting away from the K type lunch. This had to be accomplished, however, without substantially exceeding a slightly increased weight of 45 pounds per unit and without sacrificing individual messing at the noon meal.[63] The weight factor was

[62] (1) Ltr, Brig Gen J. P. Sullivan, Hq Fifth Army, to Col W. H. Middleswart, Hq SOS NATOUSA, 19 May 44, no sub. (2) Ltr, Col Middleswart to Brig Gen H. Feldman, OQMG, 25 May 44, no sub. Both in 430.2.

[63] Ltr, Gen Feldman to Col Middleswart, Hq SOS NATOUSA, 3 Jun 44, no sub, 430.2.

deemed to be especially important for operations in the Pacific.

The laboratory was successful in developing new products permitting menus of greater variety. Such meat items as hamburger, pork tenderloin, pork and corn, pork and apple, and sausage and apple were substituted for the disliked hash-type products. At the same time the size of the meat cans was increased from 4 to 6 ounces. New confections were introduced and a can of pudding was included as a dessert in the noon meal. It was expected that the change to the new meat items and confections could be effected in six weeks, although it would take a little longer to get production established and include the puddings.[64] To the accessory kit, containing cigarettes, halazone tablets, matches, can opener, soap, paper towels, and toilet paper, were added other items, including a sponge for cleaning mess gear used in cooking. Where space permitted, the allotment of cigarettes was increased to twenty per man.

Further developmental work on the ration during 1945 was aimed at increasing the acceptability of its components, and revision of the ration was authorized accordingly in February 1945.[65] The Subsistence Research Laboratory undertook to plan a ration that would be acceptable and nutritionally adequate, would permit standardization of container sizes and interchangeability of components from menu to menu, and would, at the same time, be practical from a production and procurement viewpoint. The production requirements were particularly important in the spring of 1945 because shortages and transportation difficulties were affecting the quality of the ten-in-one ration then being procured.

In February the laboratory revised the ration by changing the noon meal from an individual to a group issue basis.[66] In this revision a fresh start was made in menu planning. Although the OQMG favored the use of three menus because of the popularity these had achieved in

the five-in-one ration, the laboratory successfully defended the use of five on the basis of their effect on acceptability. The commodity branches of the laboratory were called upon to recommend components on the basis of maximum acceptability and availability.

New menus, No. 6 through No. 10,[67] were submitted to the OQMG for approval. The greatest single advance in the new ten-in-one was undoubtedly the use of canned breads instead of the usual biscuits. Canned fruits were added to all five breakfast meals, and the beverage components were increased. The acceptability of the noon meal was greatly improved by the use of two popular chunk meats—beef and gravy and roast beef—as well as canned hamburgers and frankfurters. For the first time, too, canned tuna and salmon were included as main meal items. Chunk meats were also used for the supper meals. In addition, canned whole white potatoes and sweet potatoes were added as components separate from meat to avoid any similarity to the stews which had been found so universally monotonous. The varieties of confections were increased, and all accessories were standardized throughout the menus.

The revised ten-in-one ration met with such approval in Washington that Headquarters, AGF, recommended that the standard menus No. 1 through No. 5 be reclassified as limited standard and that future procurement be made of the new menus. It was understood that this revision had increased the weight of the unit to 58 pounds, but this was considered unimportant in view of the increased acceptability of the ration. Troops, according to Headquarters, AGF,

---

[64] (1) Ltr, Feldman to Middleswart, 26 Jun 44, no sub. (2) Memo, Capt Walter A. Maclinn for George W. Burgess, OQMG, 14 Jun 44, sub: Modifications in the Ten-in-One Rat, 430.2.

[65] For an analysis of the laboratory's work in the following months, see SR&DL, *Ration Development*, pp. 90–100.

[66] R&D Br, Status Rpt, 28 Feb 45, p. 54.

[67] For reproduction of the proposed menus, see SR&DL, *Ration Development*, pp. 95–99.

would seldom be required to carry the ration by hand for any appreciable distance, and it could easily be divided into a two-man load.[68] A trial procurement of the revised ration had been approved by the QMCTC, but the end of the war suspended the procurement of all special rations. Theater evaluation of the new ten-in-one during World War II is therefore not available.

Development of Components of A and B Rations

The development of packaged operational rations constituted a primary, but not the only, interest of the Subsistence Research Laboratory, since the QMC had to feed troops behind the combat lines in theaters of operations as well as those located in the zone of interior. Field rations, types A and B, the latter of which required considerable developmental work, had been designated for these purposes. Field ration A corresponded as nearly as practicable with the components, or substitutes therefor, of the garrison ration.[69] It was issued daily whenever circumstances permitted. Ordinarily it included such items as fresh fruits and vegetables. With a few exceptions, field ration A was first prescribed for all posts, camps, and stations within the United States for a 3-month trial period beginning 1 May 1941.[70] This directive was later extended to provide throughout the war for the use of the A ration within the zone of interior at all posts, camps, and stations of more than 2,500 strength, with some few exceptions.[71] The A ration was also used overseas where availability of local perishables and refrigerated transportation permitted.

In overseas theaters, however, the limited amount of refrigerated storage and refrigerated transportation greatly restricted the quantity of perishables which could be used. Often it was not possible or practical to use the A ration. Field ration B was normally used in operations overseas as well as during field training in the

zone of interior. It was issued behind the combat lines wherever troops were removed from the sources of fresh foodstuffs and sometimes even at the front itself. Front-line fighting troops, however, normally consumed combat or emergency rations, such as C, K, or D.

The B ration corresponded as nearly as was practicable with the components of field ration A except that nonperishable processed or canned products replaced those of a perishable nature. Thus canned meats were substituted for fresh meats; dehydrated and canned fruits and vegetables for fresh ones; evaporated or dried milk for fresh milk; hard bread or crackers and canned jelly or jam for fresh bread and butter. The B ration was a nonperishable one which did not require refrigeration facilities and could be stocked at depots and railheads. It usually required full field kitchens and ordinarily also needed field bakeries, although these might be eliminated by the use of hard bread or biscuits.

The American meal pattern, which included meats, vegetables, and dairy products, was reproduced in the Army subsistence program. The adaptation of many of the normal American food items to mass production and field use brought a variety of developmental problems.

Boneless Beef

Because of limited refrigerated storage and transportation facilities, the only fresh meats available in overseas theaters were fresh frozen meats, such as Army-style boneless beef and semiboneless pork loins. When possible these were used to supplement the B ration. The de-

---

[68] Ltr, Hq AGF to CG ASF, 14 Jul 45, sub: Ten-in-One Rat, 430.2.
[69] AR 30–2210, Sec. I, par. 4d, 15 Mar 40, sub: Rat.
[70] WD Cir 28, par. 1, 17 Feb 41, sub: Rat.
[71] (1) WD Cir 170, Sec. I, 16 Aug 41, sub: Rat. (2) WD Cir 195, 18 Sep 41, sub: Sales Commissaries, Fld Commissaries, and Rat.

velopment of boneless beef [72] was the result of many years of experimentation. The idea of using it on a large scale in the field had originated with Col. William R. Grove, Chief of Subsistence, during World War I as a means of eliminating the waste of carcass beef and of saving shipping space.[73] The method used for boning, freezing, and packaging beef in 1918 was rudimentary.[74] At the end of the war, moreover, further developmental work was suspended since no civilian or military demand existed for boneless beef. The Army returned to the use of carcass beef.

Developmental work on boneless beef was revived in 1934 at the Quartermaster Subsistence School and was continued after 1936 by the Subsistence Research Laboratory at Chicago.[75] This work was promoted by Dr. Jesse H. White, who had supervised the production of boneless beef for the Navy during World War I. His efforts, however, received little or no support until the late thirties, when the laboratory enlisted the co-operation of Armour & Co. and Swift & Co. in the development of this purely military item. It was anticipated that the savings to be effected in storage, shipping space, weight, and packaging materials would more than compensate for the additional cost of preparing boneless beef. A number of problems were involved in this developmental work. The first was the utilization of all edible meat from each carcass to avoid prohibitive costs for the product. A boning method had to be perfected that would result in the economical use of the edible meat of the carcass and, at the same time, produce cuts of meat suitable for roasting, slicing into steaks, stewing, or grinding. Furthermore, the problem of packaging had to be solved to provide for easy removal of coverings and easy separation of individual pieces of frozen meat to promote ease of use in the field with a minimum of preparation time. It was 1938 before a satisfactory boning technique was perfected and the QMC could write instructions

for the preparation of Army boneless beef. The basic characteristics of the technique thereafter remained much the same. Changes made subsequently were effected to improve the cuts of meat, the distribution of cuts, and the packaging.[76]

Late in 1939 the OQMG directed the Subsistence Research Laboratory to make a study of the feasibility of using boneless beef on maneuvers. It was proposed to test its use during the Second Army maneuvers in the spring of 1940. The laboratory recommended that the meat be packaged in three groups instead of the two used heretofore. It proposed packing 40 percent for roasting and frying, 40 percent for stewing and boiling, and 20 percent as ground meat. This division, it was urged, would result in the most satisfactory use of the whole carcass.[77] The introduction of the third class of boneless beef was a new development in the preparation of the product. The Subsistence Branch, OQMG, did not concur. It believed only two classes of meat should be provided on a 50-50 percent basis—(1) roasting and frying meat and (2) stewing, boiling, and grinding meat. Since the equipment of the field range included a hand-operated grinder, the grinding of meat before shipment was not deemed essential.[78] Later in the summer of 1941, as a result of criticisms

---

[72] For a full discussion of this development see Elliott Cassidy, *The Development of Meat, Dairy, Poultry, and Fish Products for the Army* (QMC Historical Studies 7, October 1944), pp. 4–15.

[73] Ltr, Col William R. Grove to Maj Gen E. E. Booth, 15 Sep 38, no sub.

[74] For an elaboration of this method see SR&DL, *Meat Products*, pp. 10–11.

[75] Col Paul P. Logan, "Food's Part in Defense," *QMR,* XXI (May–June 1942), 63.

[76] Cassidy, *Development of Meat, Dairy, Poultry, and Fish Products for the Army,* p. 6.

[77] SRL, Research Rpt 125–40, 6 Mar 40, sub: Army Boneless Beef, 431.

[78] (1) Subs Br to Chief of Sup Div, OQMG, 11 Mar 40, sub: Boneless Beef for Fld Rat. (2) Ltr, Lt Col Carl A. Hardigg, OQMG, to CO CQMD, 25 Mar 40, same sub. Both in 431.

made during tests on maneuvers, the specification was revised to include ground beef.

Boneless beef proved so successful during the 1940 maneuvers that various posts, camps, and stations requested it. In September 1940, for the first time since World War I, boneless beef was procured on other than a test basis. By January 1941 the OQMG was giving attention to procuring boneless beef in quantity.

World War II experience confirmed the advantages which the laboratory believed boneless beef possessed over carcass beef. Approximately 60 to 70 percent savings were made in transportation and storage space, and a saving of about 30 percent was effected in weight.[79] From 45 to 55 pounds of meat could be packed in one fiberboard box,[80] and these boxes could be easily and uniformly stored. The satisfactory storage life of boneless beef was greatly increased over that of the usual carcass beef. Since boneless beef was packed according to definite uses for which the respective cuts were adapted, its use largely eliminated the need for butchers in the field to cut meat for distribution. The time required for preparing boneless beef in the field was only a fraction of that needed for thawing, boning, and cutting carcass beef. Furthermore, the beef was 100 percent edible as compared to a yield of approximately 70 percent for the best carcass beef. By excluding inedible and unusable portions from delivery, its use also reduced to a minimum garbage disposal problems and loss. An unanticipated advantage of frozen boneless beef was that it could be used extensively in the field to chill other perishable foods while it was thawing. Boneless beef proved to be one of the most popular meat items used by the Army during World War II.

Undoubtedly the success of boneless beef spurred the initiation during the war years of developmental work applying similar techniques to other meat products. Pork was second to beef among meats used by the Army. Fresh chilled pork was used primarily by installations in the continental United States which were close to sources of supply. The successful development of partially boned pork loins was accomplished in 1942, and frozen pork accordingly was shipped overseas. Lamb represented only a small percentage of the total meat procurement, but it was desirable to provide it to vary ration menus. Boneless lamb was developed during 1942, but it was not procured because the yield of edible lamb was low in comparison with the cost of the labor involved. In 1945, however, the laboratory developed a method of breaking down and packing the carcass of lamb, called telescoping, which not only required little labor but saved about 40 percent of the shipping space. In 1945, too, the laboratory initiated developmental work on "fabricated" veal. This experimentation was brought to a successful close only after the war ended.[81]

Smoked Meats

Ham and bacon are among the most familiar meats in the American diet. The objective of the QMC was to provide the Army with smoked meat products that would remain palatable and stable without refrigeration. During the Spanish-American War ham had been developed that would stand up under field conditions without refrigeration. Dry salt bacon had been used at an even earlier date. Unfortunately the excessive dryness and saltiness of the meat made it unpalatable. The experiences of World War I had yielded similar and unsatisfactory results. With the advent of refrigeration, meat packers developed a new type of mildly cured ham and bacon for the commercial market. These products, however, were perishable, and required constant refrigeration. As a conse-

---

[79] SR&DL, *Meat Products*, pp. 15, 21.

[80] Packers were allowed to fill boxes with ground meat to a maximum of 62 pounds, net weight.

[81] For discussion of these developments see SR&DL, *Meat Products*, pp. 22–31.

quence, commercial smoked meats were of limited use to the Army in time of war.[82] They were used at installations in the United States, but they could not be shipped overseas since refrigerated space was extremely critical early in the war, and food had to be held months before consumption.

With the enactment of selective service legislation in 1940 and the resultant expansion of the Armed Forces, the OQMG and the Subsistence Laboratory became interested in developing ham and bacon that could be used in the field without refrigeration. Developmental work was begun under Dr. Jesse H. White of the laboratory, who worked in close co-operation with Mr. Harry Williams of the Research Department of Wilson & Co. of Chicago.[83] Most of the preliminary laboratory work had been accomplished by February 1941. Smoked hams were prepared according to formulas prescribed by the laboratory. By April a proposed specification provided for two types of hams.[84] Those prepared by the long-cure method were destined for overseas. "Defense" hams, essentially a short-cured product, were developed for use in this country, Puerto Rico, and Alaska, and dry salt-cured bacon for issue in the Hawaiian, Panama Canal, and Philippine Departments.

Defense hams were expected to keep from two to four weeks under field conditions, but the first reports received from the field in June 1941 indicated unsatisfactory performance.[85] Complaints of the development of slime and mold on the hams caused the laboratory to review the processing and packaging procedure. The changes made were incorporated in a new specification,[86] and resulted in better products. The defense ham was regarded as satisfactory for Army use and was procured throughout 1941.

Defense ham and bacon, however, were not designed for and hence were unsuitable for shipment overseas, as was demonstrated by their failure to withstand nonrefrigerated transporta-

tion to Hawaii in March 1942.[87] This failure resulted in intensified developmental work on smoked meat products for overseas shipment. The processing method used for such products required long curing and produced a rather salty meat that was not highly palatable. In the conversion of perishable to nonperishable products the QMC was not completely successful in achieving its goal, but the laboratory's developmental work did make smoked meat products available overseas, adding variety to the soldiers' food.

Surface mold, however, remained a wartime problem. In an effort to eliminate it, the laboratory early in 1942 investigated and experimented with various packing methods.[88] Packing hams in salt was the best method available at the time of adoption, but it had disadvantages. In particular, over a long period of storage it increased the brackish taste of the product. The laboratory experimented with packing ham in lard. This method was found to be quite successful, but the OQMG did not follow up the experiment. As a result of many complaints, the packing of overseas hams and bacon in salt was discontinued in January 1944. A few months later the use of ventilated boxes was specified to permit the circulation of air which would vaporize the moisture condensing on hams or draining from them. This new packing method

[82] Col Logan, Subs Br, to Col Hardigg, Sup Div, OQMG, 17 Feb 41, no sub.

[83] Ltr, Col Hardigg, OQMG, to Col Barry, CQMD, 21 Feb 41, sub: Travel Orders.

[84] (1) Proposed Army Spec drafted by CQMD, 16 Apr 41, sub: Smoked Hams. (2) Cassidy, *The Development of Meat, Dairy, Poultry, and Fish Products for the Army*, pp. 17–18.

[85] Ltr, Col Barry, CO CQMD, to Col Logan, OQMG, 25 Jun 41, sub: Defense Hams.

[86] U. S. Army spec drafted by CQMD, 16 Jul 41, sub: Smoked Ham.

[87] Ltr, Capt W. O. Kester, Food Insp, to Subs Off, Hawaiian QM Depot, 10 Apr 42, sub: Rpt on Condition of Defense Ham.

[88] (1) Cassidy, *The Development of Meat, Dairy, Poultry, and Fish Products for the Army*, pp. 20–21. (2) SR&DL, *Meat Products*, pp. 39–41.

was fairly successful in preventing slime and mold resulting from wet hams. As refrigeration facilities increased in the ETO, the problem diminished in importance, not because the problem of developing smoked ham capable of retaining its palatability and stability without refrigeration had been solved, but because refrigeration kept difficulties with this method of packing to a minimum. The overseas ham, however, was not suitable for shipment to the Pacific theater where refrigeration facilities were not similarly available, and an extreme shortage of hams existed there.

Canned Meats

In the early stages of an invasion, troops existed on combat rations for a period varying from a week to a month. Thereafter the B ration was utilized for a period of 60 to 90 days, or until refrigeration became available in the new theater, after which the B ration was supplemented with perishable products. Until then frozen meats could not be used, and troops were entirely dependent upon canned meats. The bulk of canned meats procured for the B ration at the beginning of the war consisted of corned beef hash, meat and vegetable stew, meat and vegetable hash, pork luncheon meat, and Vienna sausage. The products were quite similar to those sold commercially and, in fact, prior to the issuance of specifications by the Chicago Quartermaster Depot, were obtained in their commercial forms.

Although the B ration was described by one Quartermaster officer in Italy as the "best field ration the Army ever had," it was the target of considerable criticism from the North African and Pacific theaters of operations.[89] Most of the complaints centered about the distaste the troops had acquired for certain meat components, particularly the stews, hashes, Vienna sausage, and pork luncheon meat. Regardless of the source of production, the soldier disparag-

ingly called all pork luncheon meat "Spam." Through its overissue to troops, it became the butt of many jokes. A Quartermaster observer at Biak, referring to corned beef, corned beef hash, and meat and vegetable stew, inquired:

When are those items going to be eliminated? Troops in this theater have been fed those three items so often that they simply pass them up now when they appear on the table. . . . It is an old contention of mine that GI Joe has become thoroughly allergic to stews and hashes. He wants whole meat products.[90]

So deep-seated was this dislike that when the observer showed a list of new meat components, including one called beef and vegetables, to officers at Biak the general reaction, without their having even seen the new ration, was: "Look, they are giving meat and vegetables a new name."

It was the contention of the laboratory that it was not the products so much as the methods of distribution and preparation which were at fault.[91] Certainly the frequent use of the same meat components, whether indifferently or well prepared in overseas kitchens, made for monotony and promoted criticism of the items. The laboratory had pursued a program of continuous developmental work to obtain a wide variety of canned meat products which had been submitted to the OQMG. As a result of the complaints the OQMG approved a wider variety of palatable and nutritious canned meats. Before the war ended more than fifty kinds were being produced for the B ration and the various combat rations.[92] As in the case of packaged rations,

[89] See, for example, Lt Col D. B. Dill to Dir of Mil Plng Div, n. d. (circa Apr 44), sub: Rpt on Travel to NATO, 26 Oct–13 Dec 43.

[90] Memo for file, Asst for Product Analysis, R&D Br, OQMG, 24 Oct 44, giving an extract from Letter 22, Capt Robert D. Orr, 19 Sep 44.

[91] SR&DL, *Meat Products*, p. 94.

[92] See chart of canned meats procured for the Armed Forces during the war in Marion Massen, *Canned Meats Procurement for the Armed Forces During World War II*, p. 320.

the trend was toward the use of chunks of meat so that by the end of the war such items as beef and gravy, pork and gravy, and ham chunks were being procured. Canned boned chicken and turkey were also procured for the B ration.[93]

Fruit and Vegetable Products

Vegetables, which form an important part of any American meal except breakfast, are generally acceptable in the following order of preference: fresh, frozen, canned, and dehydrated. Fresh and frozen vegetables and fruits, the procurement and inspection of which were under the direction of the Chicago Quartermaster Market Center, were important in the A ration as used at installations in the United States. Their use involved no developmental problems for the QMC. The use of frozen foods resulted in savings of money, packaging materials—a highly important factor during the tin shortage—and shipping space for the Army. The lack of sufficient refrigerated storage and transportation equipment, however, limited the extent to which frozen foods could be used in World War II.

Canned fruits and vegetables had long been extensively used by the Army because they were relatively easy to handle, prepare, and store. However, they were bulky and heavy and used strategic materials, especially tin. Such canned products were used in the A ration only when fresh foods were out of season or frozen vegetables were too expensive. They formed the basis, however, of the B ration.

Commercial canning of fruits and vegetables had been so perfected by industry that the QMC had no need to initiate special developmental projects. On the other hand, special storage problems, which had not heretofore confronted industry, were posed by the global nature of World War II. This was particularly true of canned vegetables destined for the tropics. Freezing and extreme cold also affected

such products in various ways. As a consequence, the Subsistence Research Laboratory had to test these commodities to determine their suitability for extended use overseas. Illustrative of the stability problems investigated by the laboratory was the control of thermophilic spoilage. Thermophilic bacteria are present in many canned foods, but they are generally harmless unless such products are exposed to temperatures from 100° to 130° F. In storage conditions at many overseas installations such temperatures prevailed. Under these circumstances the bacteria multiply rapidly, causing spoilage of the canned products.[94]

Reports in 1943 indicated that considerable spoilage was occurring in canned peas and corn stored for any length of time in the tropics. An investigation by the National Canners Association showed that specific spots in the processing line were foci of thermophilic bacterial infection in pea- and corn-canning plants. At a meeting held at the laboratory in May 1943, attended by representatives of the National Canners Association, the American Can Co., the Continental Can Co., and the Owens-Illinois Glass Co., it was decided that a control program for nonacid canned products should be instituted. Mobile laboratories were to be placed in operation to investigate causes of spoilage.

Because the OQMG wanted the National Canners Association to participate actively in this program, it took no further action until September 1943. Then, supplied with information by the research laboratories of the association and as a result of a number of conferences, the Subsistence Research Laboratory made plans

---

[93] For specific developmental problems involved in the evolution of these items see SR&DL, *Meat Products*, pp. 94–107.

[94] For a discussion of the different types of spoilage see SR&DL, A Report of Wartime Problems in Subsistence Research and Development, Vol. IX, *Fruit and Vegetable Products*, prepared by Maj Matthew E. Highlands et al., September 1947, pp. 19–20. Hereafter cited as SR&DL, *Fruit and Vegetable Products*.

DEHYDRATED FOOD PRODUCTS

for the construction and operation of a mobile chemical and bacteriological laboratory. This mobile laboratory was completed and utilized for making two surveys of 50 pea-canning plants and 77 corn-canning plants in the summer of 1944. So successful were these surveys that the program was expanded by the construction of two additional mobile laboratories which were placed in operation in the summer of 1945. It had been estimated that, by preventing Army procurement of unsatisfactory canned peas and corn for overseas use, the first mobile laboratory in 1944 saved a total of $2,350,000.[95]

Wartime conditions compelled the use of dehydrated products, which had special advantages for meeting the restrictions imposed by World War II. Foremost among these was the

saving in weight and ship tonnage that could be made through the removal of moisture from vegetables, fruits, and other food products shipped overseas. Furthermore, the fact that nonrigid containers instead of tin cans could be used for packing many dehydrated products resulted in large savings of strategic materials. With few exceptions, too, dehydrated foods withstood extremes of temperature as well as, or better than, certain canned foods. Since precooked dehydrated foods required only the addition of water or milk to reconstitute them for use, preparation in the field was greatly simplified. Some dehydrated products required special treatment by the cook for proper rehydration,

_____
[95] *Ibid.*, p. 33.

and unless directions were followed an inferior food resulted. If improperly handled, dehydrated vegetables acquired a grasslike flavor and aroma, although their nutritive value was retained. New techniques, however, tended to minimize this loss of flavor, which had caused the doughboy of 1917 to sing:

> They feed us carrots every day
> Which taste just like alfalfa hay
> Hinky, dinkey parley voo.

While dehydrated vegetables were not a new development,[96] and had been used during World War I, the return of peace in 1918 led to an abrupt slump in the dehydration industry. Not until early in 1941 did the QMC begin to study dehydration seriously, although the Subsistence Research Laboratory had been examining and testing samples of dehydrated products submitted by industry for some time before 1941, and Quartermaster personnel had kept themselves informed of technical development in this phase of food processing. With the outbreak of war in 1939 general interest in this problem was stimulated. A special committee of the Institute of Food Technologists was appointed in 1940 to study the food needs of the Armed Forces.[97] The Department of Agriculture expanded its studies of dehydration, in which it had been interested since 1935, and the War Department conducted an extensive survey of the production facilities of the entire industry in 1941–42.

Aside from promoting expansion of the dehydration industry to meet its requirements,[98] the QMC was concerned with such problems as the improvement of processing procedures, the design and construction of equipment, and the improvement of the quality and storage life of dehydrated products. To this end the OQMG and the Subsistence Research Laboratory instituted a program for the collection and dissemination of information to dehydrators, with the laboratory acting as the focal point in this activity. Improving the quality of dehydrated vegetables involved selection of suitable varieties of raw materials for dehydration, studies of each step in the preparation of dehydrated foods, and analysis of the desirability of adopting such practices as blanching, sulfiting, and reducing moisture content to very low levels. The mobilization of all research facilities—in government, industry, and educational institutions—and the formulation of a co-ordinated research program directed and supervised by the Army and the Department of Agriculture were the most feasible approaches to solving the many perplexing problems in a relatively short time. This method made possible simultaneous engagement in a variety of different tests and experiments. After December 1942 this program of co-ordinated research was directed and supervised for the Army by the Military Planning Division.[99]

The accomplishments of this co-ordinated program resulted not only in greatly increased production but also in the development of new dehydrated products and the radical improvement of all dehydrated foods. The research on dehydrated vegetables produced many foods

---

[96] For a full account of developments in this field see Elliott Cassidy, The Development of Dehydrated Foods for the Army, June 1946, 525 pp. Typescript study on file at Hist Sec, OQMG.

[97] Ltr, S. C. Prescott to Maj Logan, OQMG, 2 Nov 40, no sub.

[98] On 8 May 1941 Capt Cecil G. Dunn, assistant professor of food technology at the Massachusetts Institute of Technology, was called to active duty in the Subsistence Division, OQMG, and assigned the task of directing the planning and co-ordinating of the dehydration program for the War Department. This work became a major assignment in April 1942.

[99] No major research project was supervised after that date by the Subsistence Division, which had research responsibility until then for subsistence items. Thereafter many research projects were undertaken by the Research and Development Branch of the Military Planning Division upon request of the Subsistence Division, such projects as sulfiting, and bacteriological examination of equipment and processes in dehydration plants. Ltr, Col Cecil G. Dunn to Dr. Harold W. Thatcher, OQMG, 7 Dec 45, no sub.

having a bright natural color and improved aroma and flavor. Nevertheless, dehydrated vegetables were never very popular with the troops.

Quartermaster interest in dehydrated fruits had been aroused anew in 1937 when a field test was requested for a number of such fruits. The Subsistence Research Laboratory also made some tests. While dubious of the usefulness of the dehydrated products, the laboratory recommended that constant contact be maintained with the manufacturers and that the Army keep itself informed of developments.[100] Before World War II the Army's attitude toward the use of dehydrated fruits was passive. During the war research in the field was emphasized after other phases of the dehydration program were well advanced. It resulted in the introduction of new processing methods. Research on blanched, dehydrated apricots, peaches, and pears was accomplished at the University of California. Members of the California Dried Fruit Association and the Subsistence Research Laboratory participated in the developmental and trial production conducted in 1944 and 1945. When the war ended, however, developmental work on blanched, dehydrated fruits satisfactory for military use was still in an experimental stage.[101]

Egg and Dairy Products

The progress made in dehydration included its application to other food products, such as milk and eggs.[102] The extensive research and developmental work conducted by the QMC in these fields can only be suggested here. The need of the Army for huge quantities of dry whole milk, intended primarily for beverage purposes, resulted in a concentration of effort on this product. It was believed that the findings in this field could be applied to nonfat dry milk solids, that is, dry skimmed milk, used mainly in baking. When World War II ended considerable developmental work had been accomplished. Improved methods of gas packaging dry milk had been put into effect, and copper contamination had been reduced. These measures helped prevent milk fats from becoming rancid through oxidation. Thereafter other off-flavors became apparent, stressing the need for further research. Work in this field continued after the war.

Dried whole eggs were improved over the prewar product by rigidly controlling the quality of the raw materials, by reducing the moisture content, and by using multistage dehydration. Partly because of poor preparation in the field, dried eggs were not very popular with the troops during the war.

The research accomplished to develop dehydrated foods was probably as extensive in scope and as varied as any experimental work performed in Army subsistence during World War II. Certainly more progress was made in improving dehydrated food products from 1942 to 1945 than in the preceding thirty years, and it was of the utmost importance in feeding the Armed Forces.

The use of butter by armies is unusual, for it is regarded as a luxury food. During World War II butter was supplied at the rate of two ounces per man per day whenever it was available in sufficient quantity and where refrigeration facilities were adequate. Since butter becomes rancid during unrefrigerated storage and melts at high temperatures, what the Army needed was a product that would remain stable without refrigeration. The Subsistence Research Laboratory and the Kraft Cheese Co. began developmental work on a modified butter prod-

---

[100] (1) Ltr, Capt Logan to Commandant, School for Bakers and Cooks, Ft Slocum, N. Y., 23 Apr 37, no sub. (2) Rpt, SRL, 28 May 37, sub: Research Rpt 39–37.

[101] For an elaboration of the research undertaken see Cassidy, The Development of Dehydrated Foods for the Army, pp. 395ff.

[102] See Cassidy, *The Development of Meat, Dairy, Poultry, and Fish Products for the Army,* pp. 37–41, 47–50.

uct late in 1941. By January of the following year the laboratory submitted to the OQMG a tentative specification for what came to be called Carter's spread, a combination of butter and hydrogenated vegetable shortening.[103] It had the advantage of a high melting point, but the hydrogenated oil component gave the spread a waxy body. It was procured and used in the North African campaign but not without eliciting considerable adverse criticism. One observer remarked that no single item had been the butt of more jibes than Carter's spread. It was described by one soldier as having a "greasy tang."[104] By 1943 its procurement had been discontinued. It was replaced by a more acceptable butter and cheese combination known as Army spread, which had been developed in the meantime by the Subsistence Research Laboratory and the Kraft Cheese Co. This was widely used in the later campaigns of World War II.

So extensive was the subsistence research program of the QMC that the discussion here has been necessarily limited to the major aspects. Only passing mention can be made of the developmental work done on a variety of other components, such as dehydrated soups, desserts, and beverage powders used in the B and special combat rations.[105] No discussion of subsistence would be complete, however, that omitted mention of the research directed toward the development of effective methods of packaging and packing the Army's food. No matter how high the quality of the food obtained for the troops, unless it was delivered in edible condition the efforts of laboratory technicians would be in vain. As a consequence a major part of subsistence research had to be devoted to this problem.

Development of Packaging and Packing

At the outset of World War II the vital need for special overseas packaging and packing of subsistence was not fully appreciated by industry or the QMC.[106] Industry's peacetime packaging efforts were based largely on eye appeal and low cost. The fact that commercial products were consumed within a few months and that handling in transit was closely controlled eliminated any need for more than a minimum amount of protective packaging.

No Army specifications covering packaging and packing for overseas shipment existed at the outbreak of the war. Federal specifications covered packs for commercial use only, and early procurements of subsistence were packaged and packed accordingly. Flexible packaging materials, such as cellophane and coated or waxed glassine, offered little moisture protection, and industry had given slight attention to sealing bags and cartons tightly. Corrugated fiber boxes were generally used as shipping cases.

These commercial techniques, suitable to domestic distribution, were inadequate in the field. Early shipments of canned goods packed in commercial containers arrived at overseas destinations with cases broken open and the cans scattered loose in the holds of ships and over docks.[107] Furthermore, packages broke and

---

[103] Rpt, ASF Food Sv Conf, 11–14 Aug 43, address by Col Logan, p. 239.
[104] Rpt, Col Dill to Dir of Mil Plng Div, OQMG, n. d. (circa Apr 44), sub: Rpt on Travel to NATO, 26 Oct–13 Dec 43.
[105] (1) For development of these items see SR&DL, Fruit and Vegetable Products, pp. 63–70. (2) SR&DL, A Report of Wartime Problems in Subsistence Research and Development, Vol. X, General Products, prepared by Capt Vernon M. White et al., November 1947.
[106] (1) For a thorough analysis of the developmental work in this field see Thatcher, Packaging and Packing. (2) SR&DL, A Report of Wartime Problems in Subsistence Research and Development, Vol. V, Subsistence Packaging and Packing, prepared by Maj Robert R. Melson et al., January 1947.
[107] For illustrations of the rigorous conditions to which subsistence packages were subjected see the comments of observers, analyzed in Thatcher, Packaging and Packing, pp. 1–13.

spilled their contents, and foods in flexible packages picked up moisture. Subsistence losses due to the failure of packaging and packing materials at the beginning of the war were substantial.

The qualities required for military packaging and packing, gradually revealed during the progress of the war, were many and varied. Such subsistence packages had to provide adequate protection for a minimum of at least a year, in all kinds of weather and under all extremes of climate. Because of the excessively rough handling of shipping cases, packing materials had to be durable and rigid enough to permit stacking without crushing the case or its contents. They also had to be resistant to the effects of both high and low humidity and of water. Some foods contained ingredients requiring special properties in packaging materials to afford protection against rancidity or against acid reaction with the package. Packaging and packing materials also had to be resistant to the destructiveness of molds, insects, and rats. At the same time wartime shortages compelled the QMC to avoid the use of scarce materials or those which were not adaptable to production with existing machinery. Finally packs had to be so designed as to conserve as much shipping space as possible. Meeting such rigid requirements challenged the ingenuity of experts in the QMC and industry.

By the end of 1942 the Army had established the necessary military characteristics for subsistence packaging and packing materials. The translation of military characteristics into precise functional requirements was a continuous process, for, as new materials were developed during the war, new requirements were formulated. By December 1942 the confusion in administrative responsibility had been clarified by vesting responsibility for packaging in the Research and Development Branch of the OQMG and the Subsistence Research Laboratory, and responsibility for packing in the Packing and Crating Section of the Storage and Distribution Division, OQMG.[108] As a consequence, specifications on many items were prepared by 1943, and industry had acquired a better understanding of the Army's needs. During the last eighteen months of the war the QMC improved and refined its packaging and packing materials and types of containers. It also developed substitutes for some of the materials which were becoming increasingly scarce, and amended specifications accordingly.

In this developmental work, basic research on the qualities of a raw material was done either by private industry, trade associations, or government laboratories. The work on packaging and on the outer shipping container was closely correlated and the finished products were tested by the Subsistence Research Laboratory and the Washington Package Research and Development Laboratory. When the specification for a new package was drafted, industry was consulted on any changes which might affect its conversion of equipment to the production of the new item, and the QMC co-operated fully in facilitating the changeover.[109]

Packaging

Most of the packaging problems arose out of the necessity for conserving tin. The packaging of subsistence would have been greatly simplified had there been no restrictions on the use of tin plate, inasmuch as hermetically sealed cans were the best means of packaging food. Unfortunately, tin was listed as a strategic material in 1940 and Japanese conquests cut off most of the supply two years later. Quartermaster efforts were therefore devoted to conservation of this metal, which was accomplished by reducing the

---

[108] See above, p. 176.
[109] Ltr, Col Doriot, OQMG, to Reqmts Div, SOS, 12 Mar 43, sub: Packaging Program, 400.162.

thickness of the coating of standard tin plate,[110] lowering the tin content of the solders, eliminating the tin coating on keys, and using bonderized plate wherever possible.[111] The success of the conservation program as well as the development of a small supply of Bolivian tin made tin plate more available for essential military uses by January 1944, permitting the elimination of some substitute types of containers. For example, the use of composite fiber cans—paperboard containers with metal ends—which had been utilized for packaging such items as hard candy, cocoa, gelatin, spices, dessert powders, and tea, was discontinued as far as possible. Their performance in the field had been unsatisfactory and a large percentage of food spoilage had been reported from the North African and Pacific theaters.[112]

While tin conservation measures were promoted, steps were also taken to protect more adequately the tin cans in use. Reports from the theaters[113] indicated that cans were rusting under the severe conditions encountered, resulting in the spoilage of large quantities of food. Paper labels, by holding moisture, accelerated rusting. In addition, the paper labels often became detached from the cans, making identification of the contents difficult. These developments, as well as the need for camouflage in combat areas, led to the decision to cover food cans with a corrosion-resistant coating and to replace the paper labels with an abbreviated statement of the contents embossed or imprinted in ink on the end or side of each can.[114]

To further the conservation program and to develop substitutes which in their own right could help to meet the great demand for packaging food products, the QMC investigated a variety of flexible packaging materials, such as cellophane, glassine, waxed papers, and foils, which were used as carton liners, wrappers, small bags, and unit packages for combat rations. There was continuous developmental

work in this field during the war years.[115] Illustrative of this work was the development of laminated (bonded) foils and films.

The most promising flexible packaging materials were aluminum foil and pliofilm. Unfortunately, the shortage of the raw materials—aluminum for foil and crude rubber used in pliofilm—precluded the use of these materials, although a small quantity of aluminum foil was made available for packaging soluble coffee in certain of the special rations. When aluminum foil became available early in 1944, a laminated foil made from sulphite paper, aluminum foil, and kraft paper was developed and specified for use with the K ration. According to the Subsistence Research Laboratory the laminated foil wrap employed in the K ration carton was the chief example of an entirely adequate flexible package developed during World War II.[116]

---

[110] By this means an estimated saving of 4,588,000 pounds was made by the summer of 1942. Ltr, Col Doriot, OQMG, to Dir of Resources Div, SOS, 8 Aug 42, sub: Rpt by the Conservation Div, WPB, 400.3.

[111] (1) Thatcher, *Packaging and Packing,* pp. 30–40. (2) Any sheet steel plate suitable for manufacture into containers was known as black plate. To prevent corrosion it had to be lacquered, and the easiest way to make the lacquer stick was to treat the black plate at the steel mill in a zinc phosphate solution, a process which was called "bonderizing." This gave the steel a matte surface and formed a film affording protection against rust. Supplementary rpt, Advisory Com on Metals and Minerals, NRC, National Academy of Sciences, n. d. (circa Jun 42), sub: Conservation of Tin in the Food-Canning Industry.

[112] (1) Transcript of proceedings, mtg of Subcom of Container Coordinating Com on Fiber Boxes, Drums, and Cans, 10 Nov 43. (2) Ltr, Gen Gregory to all purchasing depots, 7 Apr 42, sub: Packing of Subs Items for Overseas Shpmt.

[113] (1) See, for example, ltr, Brig Gen F. Gilbrath, CG SFPE, to Col D. H. Cowles, OQMG, 9 Sep 42, no sub, quoting CG SOS, New Caledonia. (2) Rpt, 1st Lt R. L. Woodbury, QM Observer in SWP, 1 Feb–15 May 43.

[114] (1) For a discussion of the procoating program see Thatcher, *Packaging and Packing,* pp. 41–45. (2) Cir Ltr 46, 9 Mar 43, sub: Permanent Identification Marking.

[115] For a discussion of this developmental work see SR&DL, *Subsistence Packaging and Packing,* pp. 37–48.

[116] *Ibid.,* p. 48.

At the beginning of the war other flexible packaging materials were available in large quantities but they were not exceptionally protective. Development of materials with high water-vapor transfer resistance was a primary problem. Since cellophane and glassine did not have moisture protective qualities adequate for Army use, industry developed and the Subsistence Research Laboratory tested laminated sheets of these materials. After considerable experimentation industry developed improved materials by laminating two coated films together with a material similar to microcrystalline wax. Such materials were widely used for packaging the smaller components of the special rations.[117] Although flexible packaging materials could not take the place of tin cans as the sole source of protection, these materials were important in providing inner packaging for overseas shipment of subsistence items.

The use of flexible packaging materials as possible substitutes for tin cans was only one line of investigation pursued by the Subsistence Research Laboratory. Other methods of solving the conservation problem were examined, among them the use of waterproof bags and wax-dipped cartons and boxes. The latter were used during the war for packaging D, K, jungle, five-in-one, and ten-in-one rations. Their successful use was the result of a continuous wartime developmental program initiated in 1941. It was concerned with methods of constructing the carton and with experimentation directed toward the development of new waxes.[118] Like other substitutes the wax-dipped carton did not offer a final solution to the problem of material shortages, but the wax-impregnated and coated folding carton was widely and satisfactorily used during World War II.

The use of waterproof bags, whose chief value was in protecting foods by providing a barrier to moisture, afforded still another approach to the problem of packaging foods satisfactorily without utilizing tin. Waterproof bags had not been widely employed as case liners before World War II, but ultimately the use of three types was specified by the Chicago Quartermaster Depot. Two of these—the Reynolds bag and the X-crepe bag—were developed and in large-scale production by mid-1942.[119] A third type, the two-ply case liner, was developed by industry and the Subsistence Research Laboratory in 1943.[120]

Packing

Failure of shipping cases used for overseas movement caused the first major repercussion of the war insofar as packing was concerned. The first intimation that commercial corrugated fiber boxes were inadequate for Army use had come during maneuvers in the summer of 1941.[121] Shipments to Iceland had further emphasized their shortcomings, but a veritable storm of criticism followed deliveries to North Africa and the Pacific. The inadequacy of commercial boxes raised the problem of whether to pack subsistence supplies originally in more durable containers or simply to overpack commercial containers before shipment overseas. It was found impractical to purchase all canned goods in wooden or solid fiber containers. Overpacking, though considered unsatisfactory, at first appeared to be the only solution. In the fall of 1941 a definite program was evolved of using wirebound boxes for overpacking paperboard commercial containers.[122]

[117] See Thatcher, *Special Rations, passim.*
[118] For the details of this technical development see SR&DL, *Subsistence Packaging and Packing,* pp. 65–78.
[119] For their development see Thatcher, *Packaging and Packing,* pp. 48–49.
[120] For its development see SR&DL, *Subsistence Packaging and Packing,* pp. 85–87.
[121] Memo, Brig Gen E. Reybold, Actg CofS, for TQMG, 11 Aug 41, sub: Containers for Canned Rat, 457.
[122] (1) Ltr, Col Logan to QM Sup Off, SF Gen Depot, 2 Dec 41, no sub. (2) Memo, Col Hardigg for TAG, 26 Dec 41, no sub.

Two days after Pearl Harbor a general specification was issued by the Office of the Under Secretary of War for packing canned goods for overseas shipment. This stop-gap measure provided for the use of corrugated and solid fiber boxes, nailed wooden boxes, and wirebound wooden boxes.[123] Since this was not in line with the policy of overpacking previously adopted, it is obvious that considerable confusion existed. During the winter of 1941–42, however, the various government agencies reached agreement on specifications for packing articles for overseas shipment that, for the most part, eliminated overpacking. The first comprehensive set of directions for the packaging and packing of subsistence items for overseas shipment in the QMC was issued in April 1942.[124] It permitted the use of either the new type of weatherproof solid fiber containers, or wirebound or nailed wooden boxes. Later instructions made clear that overpacking was to be retained only in the case of food in glass containers.

Except for the special rations, which were packed in nailed wooden boxes, it was the Quartermaster policy by the summer of 1942 to utilize weatherproof fiber containers in preference to wooden boxes. Their use saved weight, space, and cost. Field experience, however, demonstrated that the weatherproof fiber containers did not have sufficient strength when wet. More and more the trend was toward the use of wooden containers. Since the supply of wood was becoming critical, however, its use could not be viewed as a permanent solution.

In June of 1942 the QMC was investigating the possibility of developing a new, durable fiber container in which to pack the five-in-one ration.[125] In their developmental work the Subsistence Research Laboratory and industry pursued new lines of investigation, including the use of an asphalt barrier lamination in the kraft paper used to construct the fiberboard and the utilization of sisal in the construction of the

kraft paper itself.[126] The "sisal box" originated from this experimentation.

Meantime the container industry worked to meet the challenge imposed by wartime conditions, developing a superstrength, all-kraft, solid fiber box. These boxes had many advantages. They withstood rougher handling than nailed boxes, hitherto considered the best containers for overseas shipment. They took up less space than wooden boxes and their color was better for camouflage purposes. On the other hand, they lacked the rigidity of wooden boxes and hence did not stack as well. At the suggestion of the Chief, Packing and Crating Section, OQMG, the new material was dubbed "V-board." The development of V boxes represented a major triumph of wartime research. Specifications for several new types of containers made from these materials were issued on 2 December 1942. Three grades of V board were used. The first grade, V1, was made of virgin fiber. Its use was intended for boxes shipped to areas of heavy moisture. The V2 grade combined both virgin and used fibers to produce containers destined for areas of moderate rainfall. The V3 grade was the poorest, merely increasing the protective qualities of the former weatherproof solid fiber box.[127] Although the grades of fiberboard were intended to be correlated with the moisture of given

[123] U. S. Army Spec 22–273, 9 Dec 41, sub: Gen Specs for Packing Canned Goods (Subs) for Overseas Shpmt (Boxes, Strapping, and Marking).

[124] QMC Tentative Spec 12–A, 27 Apr 42, sub: Gen Specs for Packing Overseas Shpmt, Canned Fruits and Vegetables and Other Items of Subs.

[125] SRL, Rpt of R&D Projects for Month Ending 31 Aug 42, p. 2.

[126] (1) Ltr, Col Logan, OQMG, to CG CQMD, 16 Aug 42, sub: Rpt on Five-in-One Ration by Desert Warfare Bd, 400.1141. (2) Memo, Col Doriot, OQMG, for Resources Div, SOS, 15 Sep 42, sub: Conservation of Wood and Metal by Use of Fiber Containers, 457.

[127] For a full discussion of the development of the V boxes see Thatcher, *Packaging and Packing*, pp. 65–70.

areas, in actual use it was impossible to control the delivery of boxes in the field in this way. In practice an effort was made to use V1 solid fiberboard boxes for the front lines and V3 boxes for the rear. The critical shortage of kraft pulp that developed with the advent of V boxes contributed to delays in procurement, but the boxes were put into use as fast as they were produced during the spring of 1943. C, D, and K rations continued to be packed in wooden boxes but other special rations were packed in V boxes.

Burlap and osnaburg were other packing materials that became critical early in the war. It was commercial practice to pack flour, sugar, and salt in bags made from these materials. War shortages necessitated a search for substitutes. Multiwall paper bags, made of heavy virgin kraft paper, of three to five walls, intersticed with layers of asphalt to make them moisture proof, had been used commercially for packing cement and fertilizer. When the need for substitutes arose, such multiwall bags were tested in the spring of 1942 and adapted by the QMC for packing flour and granular foods.[128] They were extensively used throughout World War II.

Summary

In subsistence research as in other fields of Quartermaster developmental work, the decade following World War I was characterized by a dearth of activity, resulting in large measure from the lack of funds allotted for this purpose. The interest of Congress and of the public in national defense was at a low ebb. At the same time, military planning in subsistence was conditioned by the type of warfare conducted during World War I. The demands and problems of the "blitzkrieg" had not yet stirred the imagination of military planners. By the mid-thirties, however, interest in preparation for national defense, including rations, began to revive. The Subsistence Research Laboratory

was established and research was initiated, resulting in the development of the D and C rations prior to the outbreak of World War II.

Laboratory personnel were primarily concerned with the development of special rations, which also involved considerable work on packaging. While the supply of perishables involved problems of procurement and distribution, their use called for no research other than the application of principles of nutrition to the preparation of menus. The development of special rations involved many considerations. Neither subsistence personnel nor the food industries could be called experienced in ration design when World War II began. Out of experience obtained early in the war the laboratory formulated four requisites for a satisfactory ration: acceptability, nutritional adequacy, stability, and military utility.

At the outset of the war nutritional value was the primary requirement of special ration items. Subsistence personnel attempted to develop food components which would provide the greatest nutritive value in the smallest space and weight. Acceptability was of secondary importance. Although the Army never went to the extreme of sacrificing acceptability for nutritive value as, for example, by using soy beans for meat, nevertheless at times nutritive value was stressed at the expense of palatability. Actual experience demonstrated that troops would not eat what they did not like. No matter how perfectly balanced a diet was provided in a special ration, its value was reduced if it was not completely consumed. As the war progressed, although nutritive values continued to receive due consideration, greater stress was placed on acceptability. The development of the C ration from the old to the new type clearly illustrated this shift in objective.

It is to be observed that other factors beyond

---

[128] A detailed account of the work accomplished in developing multiwall bags for Army use is found in Thatcher, *Packaging and Packing*, pp. 89–93.

the control of the laboratory worked in opposition to the principle of acceptability. While variety of components promoted acceptability, it was subordinated in the early stages of the war to procurement consideration. Items which could be obtained in great volume and from as many sources as possible were purchased. Throughout the war a conflict existed between quantity and quality. The lack of variety promoted monotony and was responsible for the stream of criticism that flowed into the QMC from the field.

An initial insistence by Quartermaster planners in 1941–42 upon the development of special rations for special troops was an ephemeral trend that characterized subsistence research as well as the development of clothing and equipage. Illustrative were the rations developed for jungle and mountain troops. They gave way to the ten-in-one ration, suitable for group feeding in a variety of military situations.

Weight and space were limiting factors not only in the development of packaged rations but also of meat products. These considerations led to the production of boneless beef and semi-boned pork loins for overseas use. They also stimulated renewed interest in the dehydration industry, which was greatly expanded through the co-operative efforts of the QMC. Dehydrated fruit, vegetables, milk, and eggs were shipped abroad in large quantities, saving critical shipping space. Dehydration enabled the Corps to provide foods which otherwise might not have reached the field at all.

Weight and space likewise were considerations in subsistence packaging and packing. The development of packaging and packing, sufficiently protective to permit distribution of foods in satisfactory condition at the consumption point, had to be accomplished, however, despite material shortages and the necessity for conservation. This not only imposed major limitations upon the form that the development of packaging and packing took, but also led to a search for substitutes to replace such critical materials as tin, aluminum foil, wood, burlap, and osnaburg. The development of flexible packaging materials that would be moisture resistant was stimulated, as well as the production of new packs far superior to anything utilized by industry before the war. Even these packs, however, were not indestructible. This fact stressed the necessity for more intensive training to eliminate careless handling and storage of subsistence. The lack of an integrated research program between 1918 and 1941 was responsible for the hurried experimentation and production of subsistence items during World War II. Nevertheless, the United States Army was well fed, although the rations issued to the troops were not always the best possible, in view of all the factors involved in ration planning. Under the spur of criticisms from the field, subsistence personnel overcame the initial defects of their program. Unfortunately, experimentation was time consuming, and many of the best products developed by the laboratory failed to reach the field before the war ended. The concerted effort of industry and the QMC achieved gratifying results during the war, but a continuing research program in peace as well as in war would pay larger dividends.

CHAPTER VI

Forecasting War Requirements for Quartermaster Supplies

A primary step in the logistical planning of the Army was the determination of war requirements for the myriads of items that went into the supply line to provide for training and alerting units in the zone of interior and to sustain overseas combat operations during World War II. Insofar as Quartermaster supply was concerned, this included many thousands of items of clothing, equipment, subsistence, fuels and lubricants, and general supplies for which the OQMG forecast requirements from one to three years in advance of Army needs, but not items of reserve stock needs.

The problem of supply in World War II was one of great complexity. It involved the supply of a large number of men who for the first time in our history were widely distributed, fighting in all kinds of climates and in geographic areas encircling the globe. This great dispersion complicated maintenance of the supply line. The multiplicity of equipment items furnished the American soldier also increased the difficulties of supply. Moreover, the United States not only supplied its own troops but also contributed extensively to equipping those of its allies, a reversal of the situation in World War I. Under lend-lease arrangements it shipped overseas a vast variety of both military and nonmilitary supplies. Subsequently, the necessity for providing for civilians in liberated areas increased the supply responsibility of the Quartermaster Corps. All of these factors sharpened the need for forecasting requirements with the greatest degree of accuracy.

In time of peace, industry and agriculture were able to fill the relatively small Army demands without benefit of advance planning. Even during the emergency period and the early phases of the war, when military requirements were increasing sharply as mobilization progressed and industries were converting to war production, the lack of accuracy in forecasting requirements made little difference. The major problem was buying sufficient quantities to keep ahead of demand. Practically everything that could be produced could be used effectively by the armed forces. Any errors of oversupply could be and were absorbed by an army still in the process of expansion and needing to be initially equipped. Once a stockpile had been built up and the filling of initial demands gave requirements personnel time to review developments, a more careful balancing of supply and demand was necessary. As the Army approached its full strength, requiring primarily maintenance and the replacement of equipment, and as the problem of allocations of scarce materials to industry became acute, refinements in forecasting requirements occurred. Since raw materials and manpower were not inexhaustible and the maintenance of the civilian economy was essential to the prosecution of the war, accuracy in forecasting was underscored and new techniques for supply planning were adopted.

Administrative Background

The supply process from the computation of requirements through the manufacture and delivery of supplies and equipment to the troops is an integrated whole, the control of which should be directed by a single head. At the beginning of World War II, however, the War Department did not have a proper system for the control of supply. Nor did it have in use proper methods for computing requirements, or uniformity of basic records.[1] These deficiencies had to be corrected during the course of the war.

At the time of Pearl Harbor responsibility for the supervision of supply was divided between two independent offices of the War Department as provided by the National Defense Act in June 1920. The Office of the Under Secretary of War[2] was responsible for supervising the actual procurement of supplies. Purchasing policy, the determination of new production facilities, the control of the flow of raw materials, labor problems, production expediting, and inspection all came within the scope of this authority. On the other hand, G–4 of the War Department General Staff was responsible for determining supply requirements of the Army and, after delivery was made, for supervising the storage, transportation, distribution, and issue of supplies and equipment. Each of these offices dealt directly and separately with the supply services. Co-ordination between G–4 and the Office of the Under Secretary of War was inadequate. As a result of this situation, it was not uncommon for a supply service to play one office against the other.[3]

World War I had emphasized the importance of forecasting requirements. The lack of adequate plans for industrial mobilization and procurement had been a costly experience, the repetition of which, it was realized, could not be permitted. As a consequence, the National Defense Act made the Assistant Secretary of War responsible not only for current procurement of Army supplies but also for the preparation of plans for procurement and industrial mobilization to be used in the event of another major conflict.

Disagreement immediately arose as to the division of responsibility between the Assistant Secretary of War and the War Department General Staff. This problem was settled by making the General Staff responsible in procurement planning for the determination of supply requirements for the Army. In other words, under its mobilization plans the General Staff determined the gross requirements of the Army—when supplies would be needed, and what quantities would be required. The Office of the Assistant Secretary of War controlled the computation of procurement requirements. From a computation of stocks on hand it determined the amount of additional supplies which would have to be procured to meet the demands of the General Staff. It also determined how and where such supplies might be procured within the time limits of the mobilization plan. Procurement requirements were the supply requirements of the General Staff minus the stock on hand.[4]

Both the General Staff and the Assistant Secretary of War were dependent on the supply services for carrying out these functions. The

---

[1] Lecture, ICAF, Lt Gen LeRoy Lutes, 23 Sep 46, sub: The ASP, pp. 10–11. On file in Hist Sec, OQMG.

[2] Until 1941 this office was designated the Office of the Assistant Secretary of War. See WD Bull 1, Sec. I, 22 Jan 41, sub: Act of Congress—Apmt of USW.

[3] (1) John D. Millett, The Organization and Role of the Army Service Forces, a volume in preparation for the series U.S. ARMY IN WORLD WAR II, Ch. II. On file in OCMH. (2) Millett, "The Direction of Supply Activities in the War Department: An Administrative Survey, II," *The American Political Science Review*, XXVIII (June 1944), p. 494.

[4] (1) Harold W. Thatcher, *Planning for Industrial Mobilization, 1920–1940* (QMC Historical Studies 4, August 1943), pp. 6–9. (2) See also Thomas M. Pitkin and Herbert R. Rifkind, *Procurement Planning in the Quartermaster Corps, 1920–1940* (QMC Historical Studies 1, March 1943), *passim*.

services did the actual work of computing the supply requirements and also furnished the information on the amount of stock on hand and the additional sources of supply. Under the National Defense Act of 1920 supply planning for war for the first time became a recognized function of the OQMG, which computed Quartermaster war requirements to be used in various plans for mobilization drafted during the next twenty years.

Within the OQMG the responsibility for the computation of such requirements, initially vested in the Executive Office, had by 1937 come to be a function of the War Plans and Training Branch of the Administrative Division.[5] There it remained until January 1941. Quartermaster requirements computed for procurement planning purposes in the twenty-year interval of peace, however, were not used in World War II. Other estimates prepared by operating branches were used and the war plans were disregarded. Primarily this situation resulted from the fact that mobilization plans were drafted on the premise that they would be used at a specific time, whereas events developed so gradually during the emergency period that problems were resolved by personnel in the operating divisions rather than by the planners.

Throughout this same twenty-year period the estimating of current Quartermaster requirements of the Army was accomplished by the operating branches of the Supply Division. Although much had been learned during World War I,[6] in the interval between the wars the OQMG resumed its prewar system of estimating requirements by the use of the Yearly Estimate of Funds—a statement of Quartermaster expenditures for the next fiscal year based on requests from the various Corps installations. It was prepared by the operating branches—Subsistence, Clothing and Equipage, and General Supplies—of the Supply Division to obtain congressional appropriations necessary for carrying

on the normal peacetime functions of the Corps. By a system of apportionment the OQMG allotted funds to field installations in accordance with their requests.

Until 1942 no successful attempt was made to combine the estimating of current requirements with those for planning purposes so as to develop common methods and reports. When in January 1941 the war planning activities of the Administrative Division were transferred to the Planning and Control Division, the computation of requirements both for specific plans and for current estimates was included in its mission. However, responsibilities for preparing estimates for current requirements were not withdrawn from the operating branches of the Supply Division and, in fact, were reaffirmed to them in May 1941.[7] As a consequence dual responsibility for requirements continued, and the Planning and Control and the Supply Divisions each prepared a set of requirements. Actual procurement, however, was not based on either set, both of which were designed for long-range planning—in the one case, for future mobilization plans and in the other, for current estimates on the basis of which congressional appropriations were obtained. Actual procurement instead rested on short-range requirements, prepared by the commodity branches, on the basis of which action was taken to procure cloth or end items and to maintain proper stock levels and proper distribution of stock by the depots.

---

[5] (1) OQMG Office Memo 119, 30 Aug 21, sub: Orgn of OQMG. (2) OQMG OO 4, 7 Jan 37, sub: Office Orgn. (3) OQMG OO 10, 15 Jan 41, sub: OO 4, 1937 amended.

[6] For an analysis of the determination of requirements in World War I see Donald F. Bradford, *Methods of Forecasting War Requirements for Quartermaster Supplies* (QMC Historical Studies 14, May 1946), pp. 5–27. Hereafter referred to as *Methods of Forecasting*.

[7] (1) OQMG OO 10, 15 Jan 41, sub: OO 4, 1937 amended. (2) OQMG OO 25A, 31 Dec 41, sub: Orgn and Functions, Plng & Control Div. (3) OQMG OO 25F, 15 May 41, no sub.

The duality of control in the OQMG and in the higher echelons of the War Department continued until March 1942 when the Army was reorganized into three major commands. In the process certain procurement and planning functions of the Office of the Under Secretary of War and certain supply planning functions of the Office of the Assistant Chief of Staff, G–4, were combined and vested in Headquarters, Services of Supply (later Army Service Forces). This concentration of the major phases of the supply process "under one top management had a tremendous influence on the Army Supply Program."[8]

Within the OQMG these changes were reflected in the reorganization of the office along functional lines. The requirements functions of the Planning and Control Division were assigned to the Production Service, which was charged with the primary responsibility for requirements forecasting. The newly created Storage and Distribution Service, which took over the commodity branches of the Supply Division, was directed to collaborate with the Production Service in determining requirements to insure conformity to "actual experience factors." [9]

Within four months the Requirements Division of the Production Service was transferred as a branch to the Military Planning Division, where it remained during the war. In the meantime, it had initiated a program to improve requirements forecasting by securing personnel trained in economics, statistics, and business methods and by obtaining the necessary data for making more accurate estimates.

It was the primary function of the Requirements Branch to compute requirements for the Army Supply Program (ASP), designed for fiscal purposes and as a guide to the War Production Board for long-range planning of the country's wartime production program. These long-range forecasts were for Quartermaster items of clothing, equipment, general supplies

food, and, until the summer of 1943, petroleum products. Short-range requirements were computed by the commodity branches of the Storage and Distribution Division. Their actual operations were based not on the ASP but on the Master Production Schedule, changes in which were initiated by the operating branches, a system which provided for some flexibility within the over-all limits of the ASP.

In the process of computing requirements programs the Requirements Branch developed a fair degree of co-operation with the operating branches of the OQMG. The exception was the Subsistence Branch. Relations with this branch were complicated by the fact that the War Department designated its chief, Brig. Gen Carl A. Hardigg, as the official Army representative on all interagency food committees.[10] Petroleum requirements also presented special problems. As a consequence of the partial centralization of petroleum procurement for the Army in the Fuels and Lubricants Division, which was established in May 1943, responsibility for petroleum requirements was vested in that division. Included were all Army petroleum requirements except fuels and lubricants used for Army Air Forces aircraft.[11] While the responsibilities of the Requirements Branch were reduced by this action, they were expanded in another direction. Except for fuels and lubricants, the branch was given the additional responsibility of estimating requirements for Quartermaster items for the civilian populations of liberated areas. It also supplied Headquarters, ASF, with advance estimates of shipping space and tonnage needed for such supplies and, for planning purposes, prepared potential

---

[8] Lecture, ICAF, Gen Lutes, 23 Sep 46, sub: The ASP, p. 3.

[9] OQMG OO 84, 31 Mar 42, sub: Orgn of OQMG.

[10] Ltr, Maj Gen Lucius D. Clay, ACofS for Matériel, to Roy Hendrickson, Dir of Food Distribution Administration, Dept of Agriculture, 29 Jan 43, no sub.

[11] For discussion of both subsistence and petroleum requirements see sections in this chapter, below.

requirements for civilian populations in territories still held by the enemy.[12]

Theory of Forecasting Requirements

The QMC tried to achieve balance between supply and demand by anticipating the quantity of goods it would be required to deliver to the troops at given periods of time. If demand were known far enough in advance to gear production to meet it, then the Army could be supplied without dislocating the civilian economy. Requirements had to be computed for both expendable and nonexpendable items. The determination of these requirements was based on different elements and each is therefore discussed separately. Expendable items are illustrated by subsistence and petroleum products. Nonexpendable items are represented by clothing and equipment. The theory and the elements underlying the computation of requirements for nonexpendable items are analyzed first, but much of this discussion must necessarily be basic to the computation of all requirements.

Estimating requirements always had to be applied to definite periods of time, since it would be meaningless to say, for example, that the Army needed 10,000,000 pairs of shoes. The estimate would have to indicate the number of shoes required for a certain length of time. The determination of supply requirements was therefore the process of forecasting required production. Such procurement forecasting was complicated by the fact that it was based on a number of variables. Among the more important of these were troop bases, probable rate of induction and possible geographic distribution of troops, probable life of items, operational plans, possible overseas procurement, and losses due to enemy action.

The military demand for nonexpendable items which Quartermaster forecasters sought to measure was comprised of three elements:

initial issue, replacements, and distribution.[13] Added together, these components stated total demand, or gross requirements for a specified period of time. To make a final estimate of new supplies needed, however, the amount of the stock on hand had to be determined and subtracted, giving the net requirements for the same period of time. The basic formula for computing requirements for nonexpendable items therefore stated that required production, or net requirements, was equal to total demand, or gross requirements, minus stock on hand.[14] This is a highly simplified statement of the theory upon which the computation of requirements was based. A closer examination of requirements forecasting will indicate some of the difficulties inherent in it as well as the nature of the modifications made by the Requirements Branch, OQMG, in its efforts to establish a scientific basis for estimating requirements.

Elements in the Determination of Requirements

Initial Issue

The first of the elements in total demand was initial issue. Initial issues were the numbers of articles authorized by various Tables of Basic Allowances (T/BA's), Tables of Equipment (T/E's), and Tables of Allowances (T/A's) to be issued to an individual or organization for the first time. The T/BA listed the clothing and organizational equipment authorized for issue to individuals and units, to be taken with the organizations or individuals wherever located. The T/A showed items of equipment not contained in the T/BA but which were needed by

---

[12] OQMG OO 25-56A, 2 Nov 43, sub: Establishment of Civ Supply Sec, Reqmts Br.

[13] Much of this discussion of theory and methods is based on (1) Bradford, *Methods of Forecasting.* (2) Dr. Sidney Hoos, Chief, Methods & Factors Sec, OQMG, Lectures on Elements of Quartermaster Requirements, Feb 44. A mimeographed copy is in the National War College Library. Hereafter referred to as Elements of QM Reqmts.

[14] Hoos, Elements of QM Reqmts, p. 2.

the organizations in posts, camps, and stations. Such equipment—mattresses and barracks chairs for example— was not usually taken with a unit into the field or on change of station. The T/E, however, listed the items of equipment authorized to be taken with an organization on change of station and, under normal conditions, into the field.

Individual equipment was usually issued at reception centers and organizational equipment at the station at which the unit was activated. Initial issues were therefore partly determined by the rate of induction and the troop basis, which presented a detailed breakdown of the projected number of men and the number of each type of organization in the Army.[15] To compute initial-issue quantities for a given period of time, therefore, it was necessary to know the projected troop strength or troop basis and the probable authorized allowances for the period in question. The troop basis was prepared by the War Department General Staff, but it had to be combined with Tables of Organization (T/O's) and various T/BA's and T/A's to obtain initial-issue requirements for organizational equipment and for items of individual clothing and equipment for the period used.

The value of initial issues depended upon the accuracy with which the troop basis reflected the actual troop strength organization. Unfortunately, instead of one authoritative troop basis from which to compute requirements, several troop lists were prepared by different divisions of the General Staff, with resulting inconsistencies. "One troop list prepared by G–3 showed the activation of units, another prepared by the Operations Division showed the contemplated deployment, and still another planned sailing of units overseas. There was a tendency to buy on one basis and try to supply on another."[16] At the end of the war there was still more than one troop basis, but some improvement had occurred. As the troop basis provided more and

more specific information, forecasts of requirements became more accurate.

The troop basis prepared by G–3 stated the number of units of each type authorized to exist by a specified date in the future. From the T/O's forecasters obtained the number and classes of men, animals, and a few of the major items of equipment of military units. Forecasters had to know the number and grades of officers and enlisted men in order to determine the quantities needed of such items as gloves or cook's clothing. The number and kinds of animals made it possible for them to determine the quantities needed of saddles, pack equipment, and similar items. Such equipment as motor vehicles had to be specified to enable them to determine, for example, the number of gasoline drums required. These tables were revised from time to time in the light of experience in the field.

It would be inaccurate to assume that the use of these T/BA's and T/A's involved a relatively simple process of calculation in estimating initial-issue requirements. These tables were subjected to frequent revision with the result that estimates, requisitions, and issue were not always based on the use of the same table. Changes were constantly being made in the T/BA's. New items were added as they were developed, obsolete items were deleted, and authorized allowances were increased or decreased as field experience dictated. Such changes generally reached the supply sergeant in the field months after they had been inserted in the T/BA.[17] His requisitions would therefore be based on one table while issue was made on another. From time to time the tables were gen-

---

[15] *Ibid.,* p. 4.

[16] Lecture, ICAF, Gen Lutes, 23 Sep 46, sub: The ASP, p. 5.

[17] Special Studies Sub-Sec, Reqmts Br, 28 Jul 43, sub: Rpt on Analysis of Reqmts, Study 5-28. This was a study of the time-lags between the date of an ASF authorization of a change in allowances in T/BA's and the date of field change.

erally revised. During the period of the emergency each arm or service had its T/BA—fourteen in all. By the fall of 1941 the difficulties of computation for the issue of Quartermaster items had become so great that simplification of the tables was a necessity. The OQMG prepared a consolidated table which listed all Quartermaster items of clothing and individual equipment for issue to troops, regardless of arm or service. This table was issued by the War Department as T/BA 21 on 1 October 1941, covering clothing and individual equipment.

Items of organizational equipment remained in the T/BA's of the respective arms and services, but since they were fewer in number they were somewhat easier to handle. Subsequently, early in 1943, T/E's replaced the cumbersome T/BA's, excepting T/BA 21.[18] Tables of Equipment included the initial allowances for only one designated type of organization in the Army instead, as in the old T/BA's, of allowances for all types of units of an entire arm or service. Within a short time these new tables were combined with the T/O's to provide Tables of Organization and Equipment (T/O&E's), thereby simplifying the work of the supply officer in the field.[19]

Issuance of T/BA 21 marked progress toward simplification, but it was rapidly nullified by the adoption of special clothing for the many new types of organizations, such as parachute units and amphibious troops. This produced a complicated table that not only confused computation of requirements but resulted in supply difficulties in the field. Developments reached their peak about mid-1942 and again emphasized the problem of simplification. It was attacked this time by the Requirements Branch from the angle of climatic distribution of the troops, and the co-operation of the Research and Development Branch was sought in connection with its environmental protection studies. A new table was prepared and published by the War Department on 10 March

1943 as Table of Equipment 21. This table was used until the end of the war. In theory at least, it permitted determination of issue to be made at a glance since all items of issue were listed and the quantities entered under three columns—Arctic, Temperate Climate, and Tropics—according to the amount of each item authorized for the type of climatic region indicated.

Although simplification had been promoted, T/A's were not always clear-cut or simple to use. Generally allowances were related to manpower, being expressed as the quantity of each item per individual. But World War II was global in nature, and highly specialized equipment was used by the Army. Authorized allowances for each piece of equipment also had to be related to a particular unit of the Army, to a specific use, to special areas, and to particular periods of time.[20] Some articles were issued only for a particular occupation or duty assignment. For example, because of the nature of his work, each mechanic was furnished a mackinaw. The problem was further complicated by the fact that some articles were issued at the discretion of the commanding general of the theater of operations. Special considerations, such as the intensity of climate or the logistical situation, dictated such issues. Thus, where the glare of the sun was too great for ordinary vision to withstand, sun glasses were authorized for issue by the commanding general of the theater. A certain clairvoyance was needed by Quartermaster forecasters in trying to "prognosticate the Commanding Officers' thinking" in such cases.[21]

Wherever a qualification to an allowance existed, it was necessary to establish an "initial factor." Tables of Basic Allowances provided for

---

[18] (1) AR 310–60, 12 Oct 42, sub: T/O's, Tables of Distribution, T/E's, T/B's, and T/A's. (2) *Ibid.*, change 1, 8 Jan 43.
[19] WD Cir 129, 1 Jun 43, sub: T/O&E's.
[20] Bradford, *Methods of Forecasting*, p. 71.
[21] Hoos, Elements of QM Reqmts, p. 4.

the issue of two pairs of service shoes, but each inductee did not automatically receive these shoes. The issue was regulated by the type of work to which he was assigned. Instead of deriving initial issue through multiplying the allowance by the number of inductions listed in the troop schedule, a weighted average initial factor was computed from past experience. Supposing that the forecaster was concerned with the initial issue of service shoes in 1943, he would ascertain the number issued as initial issue in 1942 and then by dividing that figure by the number of inductees for that year, he would have an average initial factor that could be applied against the number of inductees contemplated in 1943.[22] The difficulties of determining an accurate initial factor increased when representative experience in issue was not available, or when the bases of issue were so complex as to render past data valueless for interpretative purposes.[23]

Replacement

The second element in calculating military demand was replacement.[24] Items of clothing and equipment initially issued to the troops wore out under the strain to which they were subjected during training as well as in combat where they were exposed to all the destructive forces of battle. In many instances they were lost, pilfered, or destroyed before they could be used. Replacement was, therefore, the estimate of the quantities of items needed to replace losses and maintain the full complement of initial issues of most items at all times. In estimating total military demand, replacement became the controlling influence when the Army reached its full strength. Except for inductions of men necessary to maintain the Army at its authorized strength, initial issues ceased. Procurement then was largely concerned with filling replacement needs. The replacement ele-

ment was not only important for forecasting consumption but also for maintaining stock levels which were computed on the basis of replacement issues rather than initial issues after the strength of the Army was stabilized.[25]

In estimating the quantities of replacements that would be needed, Quartermaster forecasters made use of replacement factors. A replacement factor was expressed as a percentage figure to indicate for each authorized allowance of initial issue the rate per month at which it disappeared in the hands of troops through wear, tear, consumption, and loss. For example, if the authorized initial allowance of cotton khaki shirts was four per man and experience showed that, on the average, they lasted two years, then the monthly replacement factor was 4.2 percent. In other words the four shirts wore out at the average rate of 4.2 percent per month, and two shirts would, on the average, have to be replaced at the end of a year.[26]

This percentage replacement factor was one of two general types of factors used in forecasting requirements. It was used for determining requirements for nonexpendable items. However, in estimating requirements for expendable items, such as soap, as well as for subsistence, a consumption factor was used. Unlike the replacement factor, the consumption factor was not a rate expressed in terms of percentage but was instead expressed in terms of the consumption of a specific number of units of an item by a specific number of men during a particular

---

[22] *Ibid.*, p. 7.
[23] For further elaboration see Bradford, *Methods of Forecasting,* pp. 73–74.
[24] Until the fall of 1943 this element was also referred to as maintenance. WD Cir 297, 13 Nov 43, Sec. II, sub: Maint—Change in Terminology.
[25] (1) Bradford, *Methods of Forecasting,* p. 75. (2) Lecture, Dr. Sidney Hoos, Deputy Chief of Reqmts Br, OQMG, 1945, sub: The Development and Revision of Repl Factors.
[26] (1) *Ibid.* (2) Bradford, *Methods of Forecasting,* p. 76.

period of time, usually per month. Thus, if the consumption factor for soap was 1,350 pounds per 1,000 men per month, then on the average each group of 1,000 men had to be supplied with 1,350 pounds of soap each month.[27]

Replacement and consumption factors were also divided into zone of interior and theater of operations categories. The former reflected replacement or consumption experience at posts, camps, and stations in this country, whereas theater factors reflected combat conditions in the theaters. During the course of the war, theater factors came to be subdivided into a different factor for each theater. By the end of the war there were a number of factors in use for each initial allowance of an item.

During the war years not only was the concept of replacement factors considerably refined, but accuracy was also increased by the expansion of data on replacement experience in the zone of interior and in the major theaters of operations. One of the major problems confronting Quartermaster requirements personnel was the determination and measurement of the elements influencing the replacement factor. This difficulty arose partly out of the definition of the term "life expectancy," which combined the incompatible ideas of wear and tear and combat loss.

The *expected life* of an item of equipment is its estimated average length of serviceable life from the time of its original issue to total loss or unserviceability. The actual life may vary from zero, in the case of an item destroyed or lost on its first day of issue, to a period greatly in excess of its expected life when the item is used under the most favorable conditions of upkeep and wear.[28]

The first efforts of the Requirements Branch, OQMG, were directed towards measuring the rate of wear and tear. Progress in improving the accuracy of factors was delayed because emphasis during the period of an expanding army was on initial issue and not on replacement. Throughout 1942 and during much of 1943

most of the armed forces were in this country. Replacements were needed only for losses sustained in training and during maneuvers. Insofar as battle losses were concerned, it was assumed that theater rates would be generally twice the zone of interior rates. This was a practice inherited from peacetime planning.[29]

Many new items for which no experience existed were developed in the early years of the war. For such an item the Requirements Branch established a replacement factor for the zone of interior as close as possible to that already approved for a comparable article. However, the accuracy of previously established factors was open to question. The only data available for verifying that accuracy were the reports of total shipments contained in the records of distributing depots. These were not always reliable and did not distinguish between issue for initial supply and issue for replacement. In other words, in 1942 no scientific method for determining realistic factors had been evolved.

The OQMG was aware of this need and attacked the problem in the summer of that year. To check the accuracy of existing records, it directed the Quartermaster Board at Camp Lee to examine stock records at that camp and derive replacement factors from them.[30] As the year ended the Requirements Branch had initiated field studies which were broader in scope. Field survey teams began in September to collect experience data on which to base replacement rates. On the basis of their findings many Quartermaster replacement factors were reduced. In this activity the Quartermaster General set the pace for the Army. The Corps was using such teams in the zone of interior before the policy was extended by Headquarters, ASF,

[27] Lecture, Hoos, 1945, sub: Development and Revision of Repl Factors.
[28] AGO Memo S 700-9-43, 20 Feb 43, sub: Determination and Use of Maint Factors and Distr.
[29] Bradford, *Methods of Forecasting*, p. 77.
[30] Ltr, Col D. H. Cowles to Pres, QM BD, 19 Aug 42, sub: Verification of Maint Factors.

in 1943 to all technical services.[31] The introduction of the Stock Control System in June of that year made provision for monthly reports which subsequently supplied data on replacement issues to troops at posts, camps, and stations, on the basis of which revisions of zone of interior factors were made thereafter periodically.

The development of accurate theater factors was equally essential. At the beginning of the war a single over-all factor was used to determine requirements for replacements in the theaters of operations. As early as the summer of 1942, however, the Requirements Branch, OQMG, regarded this as an oversimplification of the problem of determining requirements.[32] Variations in climate and terrain demanded that the theaters of operations be divided into several areas. The branch proposed six such areas, but until 1944 Headquarters, ASF, refused to permit their establishment on the theory that any variations in the rate of deterioration arising from geographic conditions would be offset by the use of an average factor.[33]

The application of an average factor to the needs of a theater of operations was also questioned by Quartermaster requirements personnel.[34] There was as much difference, it was contended, between the use of items and their life expectancy in the areas comprising a theater as among the different theaters of operations. Each theater was divided into a combat area and a supply or noncombat area. It would have been more accurate to establish a factor for each of these areas. Certainly the amount of wear and tear in some parts of a theater of operations was no greater than in the zone of interior. This argument was partially accepted by the ASF in the August 1943 ASP, when zone of interior replacement rates were applied to inactive theaters, such as the Caribbean Defense Command.[35]

It was not until the spring of 1943 that ASF interest in theater replacement factors was emphasized. As a consequence no provision had

been made for obtaining loss and expenditure rates in the North African campaign. The OQMG had been interested in acquiring such data but could send no teams overseas until officially directed to do so in June 1943.[36] By directive at that time each technical service sent specially trained officers into the theaters to collect the required data for selected items of its issue. Each theater commander was responsible for submitting complete data on replacement issues in monthly and quarterly reports to the ASF. The QMC again took the initiative. It was the first service to organize and utilize replacement data teams. Quartermaster teams made an outstanding record in compiling data on replacement and expenditure rates resulting from combat conditions.[37]

The data supplied by the theater reports covered all issues to troops except initial supply, losses due to spoilage and shrinkage, quantities repaired for stock or for reissue, and initial issues for the period covered by the report. By the fall of 1943 such reports were being

[31] (1) Reqmts Div, ASF, Manual, July 1943, sub: Determination and Use of Maint Factors and Distr, pp.11–12. (2) Hist rpt, Lt Col Simon M. Frank, The Determination of Army Supply Requirements, n. d., p. 122. This is a typescript report, accompanied by 4 volumes of documents, on file in OCMH.

[32] Lecture, Hoos, 8 Jul 42, sub: Method of Determining Reqmts.

[33] Memo, Col L. A. Denson, Dir of Reqmts Div, ASF, for TQMG et al., 22 May 44, sub: Computation of Sec. I, ASP, 1 Aug 44, 400.314.

[34] Hoos, Elements of QM Reqmts, p. 9.

[35] Memo, Brig Gen W. A. Wood, Jr., Dir of Reqmts Div, ASF, for TQMG et al., 15 Jun 43, sub: Computation of Reqmts, Sec. I, ASP, 1 Aug 43, 400.314.

[36] Memo, Actg TAG for CinC, SWPA, et al., 24 Jun 43, sub: Determination of Maint Factor and Rates of Consumption and Expenditure, AG, 400 (21 Jun 43) OB–S–SPOPP–M.

[37] (1) Frank, The Determination of Army Supply Requirements, p. 121. (2) For an elaboration of their work see Lt Sidney Karasik and Lt Robert Stott, "Quartermaster Replacements in the North African Theater," QMR, XXIV (November–December 1944), 28, 120. (3) Maj William G. Ashmore, "Supply Planning for Beachhead Operations," QMR, XXIV (January–February 1945), 18.

received in sufficient numbers to warrant their use as a basis for procurement estimates.[38] Innumerable revisions were made in replacement factors, a large percentage of which were downward. More accurate and realistic theater replacement factors were developed. As a consequence special factors were set up for the ETO, MTO, SWPA, CPA, and CBI.[39] The overall replacement factor for all theaters with which forecasters had begun their work was superseded in the supply and demand studies by a much more realistic different factor for each theater for which issue experience became available.

Distribution Requirements

The third basic element in the computation of requirements for nonexpendable items was the stock level. Variously referred to as "distribution," "pipeline," "carry-over," "working stock," and "inventory," this term meant the amount of stock which had to be on hand at any particular point in time to serve as a working inventory and as a reserve. Since the summer of 1942 the Requirements Branch had centered its attention upon this element. As in all cases it questioned the validity of each general assumption whenever it was based on "accepted procedure" rather than upon statistical analysis or the operating needs of the QMC. Thus it rejected the distribution factors inherited from the war planning agencies.

In mobilization planning, requirements for distribution had presumably been computed by percentages known as distribution factors which were derived from past experience. Such distribution requirements represented an allowance for additional stock necessary to fill the pipeline, to provide goods in transit, and to allow depots a working inventory. Where size tariffs were applicable, the factor was increased in proportion to the number of sizes listed in the tariff table. These distribution factors were then applied to the sum of initial and maintenance requirements for the period having the largest requirements, which in mobilization planning was the first month. Application of the distribution factor only to the first period was based on the theory that distribution requirements became frozen stock and that once this stock had been established for the maximum amount to be distributed in any one period, it remained available.[40] This concept was accepted and incorporated by Headquarters, SOS, in its directive for computing the 1 September 1942 ASP but was even more restrictive in that it limited application of distribution factors only to initial requirements.[41]

The computation of requirements for distribution by this factor method was rejected by the Requirements Branch, OQMG, as basically unsound. The distribution factors which had been inherited were inadequate, logically unsound, and statistically indefensible. As supply lines lengthened and stockage points increased, they were too inelastic for determining the quantities of distribution required. The Army distribution process involved the establishment of stocks as working inventories at several supply points. In the zone of interior, stocks in general moved from factory to depots and thence to posts, camps, and stations for issue to the enlisted man. If the stocks were destined for a theater of operations, they were normally shipped from factory to filler depot, to port of embarkation, to port of debarkation, to base depot, intermediate depot, and advance depot, and thence to supply dumps of the armies where eventual issue to the soldier took place. Not

---

[38] [1st ind] Col Cowles, OQMG, to Dir of Stock Control Div, ASF, 22 Sep 43, sub: Maint Factors.
[39] Ltr, TAG to CinC, SWPA, *et al.*, 11 Jul 44, sub: Determination of Repl Factors, Rates of Consumption and Expenditures, AG 400 (7 Jul 44) OB-S-C-M.
[40] Maj George H. Horkan, "The Computation of Requirements," *QMR*, XIX (March–April 1940), 58.
[41] Memo, Dir of Reqmts Div, SOS, for TQMG *et al.*, 15 Jul 42, sub: Recomputation of Sec. I, Equip, Ground Reqmts for ASP.

only were supplies needed to start and maintain a normal flow but also they had to be available at all these supply points to insure continuation of that flow. The distribution factor, however, was static and inflexible. "It was valid for all points in time only if troops in the areas, the rate of inductions, and the supply system remained constant." [42] Obviously such a combination was unlikely to occur in modern warfare.

During the summer and fall of 1942 the Requirements Branch had developed a procedure for estimating stock needs called the "carry-over method," [43] which stated supply levels in terms of days and would reflect the expansion and contraction of inventories as required by supply operations. This method of computing distribution had grown out of the need for flexibility and a more accurate knowledge of stock levels. By this method distribution requirements for nonexpendable items were computed by multiplying cumulative initial-issue requirements for any given period by the replacement factor for the given item, and then multiplying the result by a figure representing the number of months of maintenance or replacement authorized by the War Department to maintain the desired stock level. Instead of distribution referring to percentage distribution based with reference to initial issue as in the SOS directive, the OQMG proposed to make distribution refer to carryover based on established stock levels expressed in terms of months. Since supplies tied up in storage and in transit varied according to changes in the military program and could not be reduced to a predetermined distribution factor, flexibility was promoted by the carry-over method.[44]

The carry-over method would not have been completely accurate without a careful consideration of the size-tariff problem. As a consequence a size-tariff adjustment for sized items was incorporated in distribution as determined by the carry-over method. The development of the size-tariff adjustment factors, although large-ly a mathematical and statistical problem, was extremely important in determining how much stockage must be carried at various points in the pipeline.[45]

The OQMG proposed including a further refinement in the theory of distribution. This was the classification of all Quartermaster items into four groups depending upon their importance to the combat function. The more essential the item the higher the distribution level authorized. Thus service shoes would be in Group I and handkerchiefs in Group IV. However, no reduction by reason of decreased importance of the item was made in stock levels established for initial issue because the rate of induction changed so frequently that supply had to be assured for this allowance.

At a conference on 13 July 1942, attended by representatives of both the Requirements Division, SOS, and the OQMG, the latter registered their objections to the existing method of computing distribution requirements and outlined

---

[42] (1) See Chart 9. For the various supply points see Charts 10 and 11. (2) Bradford, *Methods of Forecasting*, p. 35. (3) Hoos, Elements of QM Reqmts, pp. 13ff.

[43] The practical development of this method grew out of the remarkably co-operative teamwork of the requirements group. Although Dr. Hoos, Chief, Methods and Factors Section, Requirements Branch, participated in a leading way in the development of the carry-over method, many others played helpful and significant roles in its administrative development and modification. In collaboration with Col. Henry W. Bobrink, Dr. Hoos also developed the idea that stock level needs should vary in accordance with the importance of the item to combat operations.

[44] (1) Memo, Maj Gen E. B. Gregory for CG SOS, 23 Jul 42, sub: Supplemental Computation of ASP. (2) Memo, Col Cowles, OQMG, for Reqmts Div, SOS, 21 Oct 42, sub: Proposed Method for Recomputing Sec. I, ASP, dated 9 Oct 42, 400.314.

[45] (1) Bradford, *Methods of Forecasting*, pp. 82–85. (2) Hoos, Elements of QM Reqmts, pp. 16, 27. (3) Lecture, Hoos, n. d., sub: Explanation of Size Tariff Factor Used in Deriving Depot Stock Levels. (4) Rpt, Methods & Factors Sec, Reqmts Br, OQMG, 2 Jul 45, sub: Determination of Depot Stock Levels Based on Operating Experience.

CHART 9—SUPPLY PIPELINE (QUARTERMASTER ITEMS)

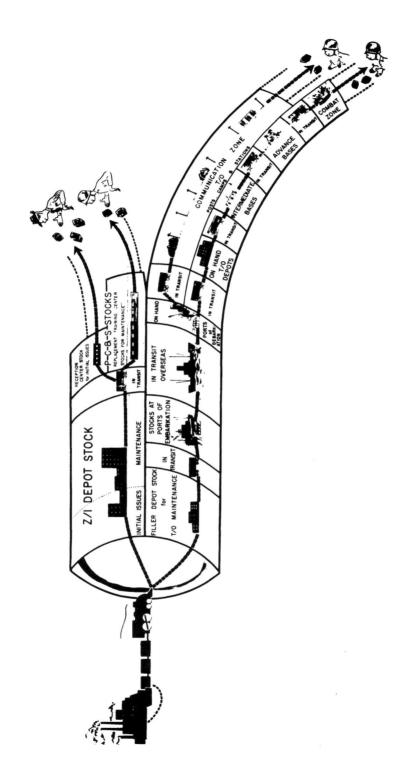

the carry-over method.[46] Although refused permission to use this method in computing Quartermaster requirements for the 1 September 1942 ASP, the OQMG prepared an alternative program in the hope that the advantages of the new method would be recognized by Headquarters, SOS. After this program was submitted on 7 September, conferences were held between representatives of the OQMG and Headquarters, SOS, which resulted in acceptance of the Quartermaster method of computing distribution requirements but not of the levels proposed nor of the idea of grouping items by their importance to the combat function. The QMC supply program prepared by the carry-over method was not published by Headquarters, SOS, because an acute shortage of certain critical raw materials led to an economy drive in the fall of 1942. It was used, however, as a planning document by the OQMG in preparing contracts and delivery schedules for end items and contributory material.[47]

It was the persistence of the Requirements Branch, OQMG, that won gradual adoption of the carry-over method by Headquarters, ASF. The directive for the February 1943 ASP did not accept this method. With Headquarters' permission, however, the OQMG calculated and used realistic distribution factors employing most of the elements used in the carry-over principle. If not officially recorded in a directive, in substance the method was accepted. In the directive for the August 1943 ASP, however, Headquarters, ASF, for the first time gave official recognition to the carry-over principle of estimating stock requirements by directing the use of this method by all technical services.[48]

Evolution of the Army Supply Program

In a narrow sense the ASP may be defined as a printed document which periodically set forth during World War II the requirements of the Army for supplies and equipment. Broadly defined, however, it was a system developed during the war for

> estimating the future needs of the Army for supplies and equipment, correlating these needs with assets already in the hands of the Army, and coordinating them with production capabilities in terms of facilities, raw materials, components, manpower; governing and scheduling purchasing and production; adjusting pricing, and controlling stockages and stock levels.[49]

The ASP evolved gradually. In 1939 War Department requirements for equipment, munitions, and supplies were determined by the use of what was called the "Rearmament and Reequipment Program." This program had been started by G–4 in the fall of 1932. It was a limited and unrefined statement of procurement needs which was designed to provide for the existing strength of the Regular Army and National Guard units.[50]

During the period of emergency, budget and equipment preparation activities of the War Department were delayed reactions to adverse events in Europe. A number of increases were made in the authorized strength of the Army necessitating recomputations of requirements. The big expansion, however, came with the collapse of France in the early summer of 1940. Then, on the recommendation of a special com-

---

[46] Min of mtg concerning reqmts for ASP, 13 Jul 42, 400.314.

[47] (1) Memo, Dir of Reqmts Div, SOS, for TQMG, 16 Oct 42, sub: Supplemental Computation of Sec. I, ASP. (2) Memo, TQMG for Dirs of S&D, Fiscal, Sv Instls, and Procurement Divs, OQMG, 17 Nov 42, sub: QMC Reqmt Program for Planning Purposes, 400.314.

[48] Memo, Actg Dir of Reqmts Div, ASF, for TQMG *et al.*, 15 Jun 43, sub: Computation of Reqmts Sec. I, ASP, 1 Aug 43, 400.314.

[49] Lecture, ICAF, Gen Lutes, 23 Sep 46, sub: The ASP, p. 1.

[50] (1) Lecture, ICAF, Maj Simon Frank, 17 Jan 45, sub: History of the Army Requirements Program, pp. 4–5. On file at Hist Sec, OQMG. (2) See also a more extended account in Frank, The Determination of Army Supply Requirements, pp. 3ff.

mittee appointed by the President, Army requirements were raised to nearly six billion dollars. This program of 30 June 1940 was the first of the munitions programs. To control the unprecedented expenditure, an "Equipment Expenditure Program" was developed by G–4 of the General Staff. It was intended to facilitate the administration of the Munitions Programs. The first of this series of Expenditure Programs was published on 12 August 1940 and the last on 30 June 1942. Thereafter the ASP became the means for authorizing procurement.[51]

In effect the Expenditure Programs were a breakdown of the monies appropriated by Congress for supplies and equipment for the Army into specific items or categories of items and quantities which the procuring services were authorized to buy after G–4 approval of the programs. They were, however, an inadequate means of governing the supply program of the Army. They were limited in scope and did not cover all necessary items nor did they indicate when the items would be needed, whether in 1941, 1942, or 1944. In other words, they were not phased in time, a fact which compelled a revision of the program when the United States entered the war. Although these programs were inadequate as a basis for production planning and scheduling and for determining the Army's needs for raw materials and industrial facilities, they were a "meager but important beginning in determining the requirements of the Army and translating these requirements into feasible production schedules."[52]

The attack on Pearl Harbor in December 1941 necessitated the establishment of time objectives for the procurement program. Awareness of this need had been growing in various quarters. In September 1941 Donald M. Nelson, then Executive Director of the Supply, Priorities, and Allocations Board (SPAB) sought a more realistic approach to the problem of setting procurement objectives. His goal was to relate over-all requirements to the supply of materials and to the productive capacity of available facilities. He requested information from the Secretary of War on the Army's schedule of requirements by quarter periods to be sent to the Office of Production Management.[53]

In the meantime the War Department General Staff was preparing a revised troop basis estimating the force required to defeat the country's potential enemies. On the basis of this troop schedule a supply program known as the "Victory Program" was completed and transmitted early in October to the OPM. After 7 December 1941 the need to set up time objectives for the procurement program became urgent. On 27 December a revised troop basis, indicating the periods in which units would be activated, was obtained. The supply program computed on the basis of this troop schedule was completed in February 1942. It was called the "War Munitions Program" but was never authorized for procurement because its requirements were too high to be met. It proved to be in the nature of a "dry run" edition of the ASP. In addition to stating production goals in terms of calendar-year periods, it had other desirable features, namely, the incorporation of Navy and lend-lease requirements.[54]

An immediate revision of this program was called for by the Office of the Under Secretary of War and G–4.[55] Such revision was dictated by production possibilities and the availability

[51] Memo, Hq SOS for TQMG et al., 22 Jul 42, sub: Equip Expenditure Program.

[52] Lecture, Gen Lutes, 23 Sep 46, sub: The ASP, p. 2.

[53] (1) Memo, Nelson for SW, 17 Sep 41, sub: Military Reqmts and Probable Production of Finished Products. (2) See Mark S. Watson, Chief of Staff: Prewar Plans and Preparations, in U. S. ARMY IN WORLD WAR II (Washington, D. C., 1950), pp. 331ff.

[54] Frank, The Determination of Army Supply Reqmts, pp. 17–20.

[55] (1) Memo, OUSW for Chiefs of Sup Arms and Svs, 5 Feb 42, sub: Equip Sec of ASP. (2) Memos, ACofS G–4, for TQMG et al., 20 Feb 42 and 2 Mar 42, same sub, 400.314.

of shipping. Thus was initiated the first comprehensive ASP which appeared in April 1942 shortly after the major phases of the supply process had been concentrated under one top management in the newly organized Headquarters, SOS.

During 1942 the problem of production possibilities was of primary concern to those responsible for supply. Within the War Department the ASP was the medium by which balance was to be attained in production and in over-all supply and demand among the several military programs and between end items and their components. The program was therefore developed and operated under two phases. In the first an initial long-range program was to be developed and immediate broad analysis and adjustment were to be made. In Phase II periodic, detailed, short-range analysis and adjustments of the long-range program were to be made.[56] Until a realistic relationship between military requirements and industrial capacity had been determined, Phase I was of great importance. Its significance waned, however, after the early stages of the war.

Phase I gave effect to such considerations as significant changes in planned troop strength, availability of raw materials, the capacity of industry, and limitations on shipping. During 1942 the ASP was adjusted radically to attain the balance sought. For example, a revision was necessary when the President authorized a new troop strength in August. By October another critical decision was made placing production emphasis on the aircraft and escort vessel programs. The WPB indicated that the production capacity of the country would not support the ground equipment program as stated in the ASP as well as provide for accelerated production of the aircraft and escort vessel programs. As a result a 20 percent cut in ground equipment had to be taken.[57] Revisions of the ASP were made because of changes in the troop basis, in allowance tables, in strategic plans, and in availability

of raw materials and facilities. The standardization of new items of equipment and the elimination of the use of programmed items were also primary causes for revision of the ASP.

The scope of the ASP extended to all types of equipment procured by the Army for the armed forces of the United States and its allies. The development and supervision of this program were responsibilities of Headquarters, SOS, but the implementation of its directives was accomplished by the technical services. The program set forth the procurement objectives of the several technical services by calendar years in terms of end items. It was divided into a number of separate sections which varied at times but included such categories as ground equipment, air equipment, expendable supplies for ground forces and for air forces, miscellaneous supplies for international aid, and construction supplies.

After July 1942 the ASP was used as the sole source of procurement authority for the QMC and the other supply services. To relate the program to availability of critical materials and industrial facilities, The Quartermaster General and the other supply service chiefs, at the direction of the Production Division, SOS, translated end items listed in the ASP into terms of raw materials. The raw material requirements were determined by compiling bills of materials obtained from contractors or by estimation. These were transmitted to the WPB and Army and Navy Munitions Board where the information on availability of supply enabled Headquarters, SOS, to adjust the ASP when necessary and secure an appropriate tentative allocation of materials. The ASP therefore served as a guide for allocation of raw materials by the WPB and the ANMB.

---

[56] Memo, Brig Gen Lucius D. Clay, Deputy CofS for Reqmts & Resources, SOS, for Chiefs of Operating Divs, SOS et al., 5 Apr 42, sub: Procedure in the Development and Execution of ASP, 400.314.

[57] Lecture, Frank, 17 Jan 45, sub: History of Army Reqmts Program, p. 12.

In this connection, controlling the flow of critical materials, such as aluminum, into essential war programs was one of the most vexatious problems early in the war. An effort to solve this difficulty through the use of a priority system failed. The Production Requirements Plan, which attempted to allocate materials on the basis of manufacturers' estimates rather than on end item programs, was equally unsuccessful. In the fall of 1942 the materials problem was solved through the development of the Controlled Materials Plan which provided for an allocation of materials to claimant agencies in accordance with scheduled programs of requirements. Since the QMC was a comparatively small user of critical metals, it did not figure as prominently in the operations of the Controlled Materials Plan as did other technical services.[58] The use of this plan required the translation of the ASP into scheduled quantities of the various controlled materials. Headquarters, ASF, supplemented the ASP with a document issued quarterly and known as the "Army Requirements for Controlled Materials" from the second quarter of 1943 to the end of the war.

In addition to being used as the sole source of procurement authority and as a guide for the allocation of raw materials, the ASP served other purposes. It was used for co-ordinating the demands of the Navy and of international aid which the Army had to procure. Finally the ASP was used as a basis for budget estimates submitted to Congress. The total amounts of equipment, expressed in dollars, were incorporated in the budget for securing funds for future appropriations. The ASP was also used as a basis for defending these estimates in Congress.[59]

Quartermaster Contributions to Improved Techniques

Between April 1942 when the first ASP was published and October 1944 when the seventh

and last edition of the ASP appeared, the program underwent many developments. Techniques of computing it were improved and principles of forecasting were refined. In this process of development the Requirements Branch, OQMG, "not only anticipated but formulated, refined, and induced the ASF to accept most of the requirements policies and procedures that were eventually adopted by that agency."[60] Foremost among these was the carry-over method of computing distribution requirements. This concept of stock levels as operating reserves that fluctuated in accordance with anticipated issues was carried over into the supply and demand and supply control systems that later superseded the ASP.

Since the carry-over method related stock level requirements directly to initial and maintenance issues, it enabled a new concept of stock on hand to be incorporated in the estimate by adjusting the number of months of maintenance used in the computation.[61] Formerly emphasis was placed on estimating total assets and total consumption, but attention could now be centered only on the increases to these assets and on consumption as reflected by issues from the depots.

The OQMG was interested in eliminating from the definition of tangible assets such vagaries as stocks in the hands of troops. At best such figures could only be "computed estimates for the large majority of Quartermaster items."[62] One of the outstanding features of the

[58] For a full discussion on controlling the flow of materials to Quartermaster contractors see Harry B. Yoshpe, *Production Control in the Quartermaster Corps, 1939–1944* (QMC Historical Studies 8, December 1944), pp. 36–41.
[59] Frank, The Determination of Army Supply Reqmts, pp. 38–39.
[60] Bradford, *Methods of Forecasting*, p. 46.
[61] Dir of Mil Plng Div to TQMG, 18 Jun 43, sub: Comparison of QM Subsections, 1 Feb 43, ASP Sec. I and 1 Aug 43, ASP.
[62] Memo, Col Cowles, OQMG, for Reqmts Div ASF, 22 Sep 43, sub: On Hand Figures for 1 Feb 44 Revision of ASP.

August 1943 ASP was the deletion of stocks in the hands of troops from the on hand figure. Data for the program were based only on actual stocks in storage. The on hand figure included stocks at posts, camps, stations, and depots, which were ready for issue, as well as reserves at ports of embarkation. It also included the stock in transit to these installations and the quantities consigned as port reserves to ports of embarkation. It did not include supplies actually in transit and consigned for shipment overseas since these were considered part of the assets of the theater of operations. The inventory was limited to stocks located in the continental United States.[63] Calculated on hand figures took the place of totaled inventories. Although the Stock Control Division, ASF, proposed inclusion of the stocks in the hands of troops in the February 1944 revision of the ASP the validity of the OQMG objections was recognized, and the QMC program included only those elements incorporated in the August 1943 program.[64]

The ASF directive for the August 1943 ASP showed acceptance of other Quartermaster concepts. The application of zone of interior replacement factors to supplies in noncombat areas physically located in theaters of operations had been advanced by the Corps. It received partial recognition by the ASF when zone of interior replacement rates were applied to inactive theaters of operations, such as the Caribbean Defense Command. A more realistic approach was further promoted by the official recognition given for the first time in this directive to overseas procurement. The total of required production for each period was to be reduced by the amount of anticipated overseas procurement as determined by the chiefs of the supply services from theater reports.[65] Reverse lend-lease was included in overseas procurement since it was supply which did not need to be manufactured in this country. The effect of overseas procurement on production schedules

had been considered in the OQMG a year earlier in the summer of 1942.[66]

Still another Quartermaster concept proposed as early as July 1942 found acceptance in the August 1944 ASP. The OQMG had urged the division of the world into a number of separate areas in order to reflect geographic peculiarities in the computation of requirements. In the directive for the August 1944 program Headquarters, ASF, took the first step in this direction by authorizing a European Area and a Pacific Area in the computation of requirements.[67]

It was Quartermaster persistence which won ASF acceptance of improved techniques developed by the OQMG. Problems of operations were naturally realized at the technical service level before they became known to the higher echelons. Solutions to these problems could be and were devised at that level but ASF approval came slowly. This had the effect of discouraging the presentation of other improvements to the technique of determining requirements. Thus the difficulty of winning acceptance of the carry-over method made the OQMG reluctant to urge acceptance in the fall of 1942 of a method for forecasting supply needs and for controlling their procurement and distribution which embodied all the essential features of the supply control system established by Headquarters, ASF, two years later in the fall of 1944.[68]

[63] AGO Memo S700–18–43, 26 Mar 43, sub: Determination of "On Hand" Figures as of 1 Jul 43, for use in ASP.

[64] (1) Memo, Stock Control Div, ASF, for TQMG et al., n. d. (circa Sep 43) sub: On Hand Figures for 1 Feb 44 Revision of ASP. (2) Memo, Col Cowles, OQMG, for Reqmts Div ASF, 22 Sep 43, same sub.

[65] 1st ind, Gen Clay to TQMG, 2 Jul 43, on memo, TQMG for CG ASF, 24 Jun 43, sub: Computation of Reqmts Sec. I ASP, 1 Aug 43.

[66] Brig Gen F. F. Scowden to TQMG, 24 Aug 42, sub: Reverse Lend-Lease.

[67] Memo, Col Denson, Reqmts Div, ASF, for TQMG et al., 22 May 44, sub: Computation of Sec. I ASP, 1 Aug 44, 400.314.

[68] Bradford, Methods of Forecasting, p. 46.

Development of Supply Control System

Supply and Demand Study

During the early phases of the war when the problem of supply was confined to provisioning an expanding Army with initial equipment and stockage, the ASP served its purpose of guiding procurement activities although forecasting was only on a long-range basis. Short-range forecasting was accomplished by the commodity branches of the Storage and Distribution Division. When the shortage of scarce materials allocated to industry became critical and when the problem of supplying the Army shifted to the maintenance of men and pipelines, the necessity of estimating requirements as accurately as possible became increasingly important. Underestimating requirements was as serious as overestimating them. The latter would produce a dislocation of industry and an unjustifiable curtailment of civilian supply. Underestimation meant the loss, probably beyond recovery, of raw materials and the capacity for production of other vital work. This was particularly significant for Quartermaster items which were in direct competition with civilian commodities.[69]

The ASP was not so much a control measure as a planning document, setting future objectives and providing the basis for appropriation requests. By the summer of 1943 it was clear that the ASP was a none too accurate "horizon setter" rather than a mechanism for achieving smooth production schedules, integration of the production processes, sufficient raw materials, and effective control of stocks.[70] The need for closer co-ordination between production and consumption required that the supply status be established on a monthly basis.

The ASP provided a statement of annual needs but no guide existed for scheduling demand within the year. In the QMC the requirements forecasts of the Requirements Branch had only a limited application as a basis for pro-

curement. Its estimates were accepted as guidance data by the operating branches but were often bypassed in actual procurement by the practice of "forward buying." This, for example, enabled the operating branch to procure some of the 1943 requirements of a given item in 1942 on the plea that all the 1942 requirements had been procured early in the year and continuous production was necessary to retain the facilities for the manufacture of Quartermaster items. This practice grew out of fear that the QMC would be caught in short supply. Such fear could be dispelled only by a statement of demand for shorter periods than those used in the ASP which provided for semiannual computations of demand and supply. To be sure there were interim changes computed for the program but these were sporadic and discretionary in nature. Not until the later days of the ASP were revised estimates processed for approval on the basis of continuing modification and revision in line with experience.

The necessity for periodic review of requirements in the light of operating needs gave rise to the development of the supply and demand study.[71] During the latter part of 1943 the Requirements Branch developed methods of computing requirements on the basis of forecasts of depot issues. Forecasts of depot issues were prepared so that adequate stocks could be maintained "to meet all legitimate requisitions by

---

[69] Address, Alvin Mayne, Reqmts Br OQMG, sub: Supply and Demand Studies and Field Information Essential to Computation of Reqmts, QM Conference, 2–4 Oct 44, Camp Lee, Va.

[70] Dir of Mil Plng Div to TQMG, 8 Feb 44, sub: Comments on Atchd Memo concerning ASP by Mr. Bruce.

[71] Like the carry-over method, the development of the supply and demand study was the product of the co-operative effort of personnel in various operating divisions of the OQMG. Within the Requirements Branch, Alvin Mayne crystallized the concept and Hyman G. Landau performed the detailed work. The resulting technique was submitted to the Deputy The Quartermaster General for Supply Planning and Operations on 20 January 1944.

regional and filler depots." [72] The planning of supplies was confined to the depot level, since the method was devised to enable The Quartermaster General to control his supply, and he lost that control when supplies left the depot.

The OQMG assumed that field experience had advanced sufficiently to be used as the basis for forecasting. The method developed was explained to representatives of the ASF at a conference in November 1943. The ASF did not approve the use of this system as a substitute for the method it prescribed for the ASP. Maj. Gen. Lucius D. Clay, Director of Matériel, opposed the use of the method because he believed it would cause Army demands to fluctuate sharply from month to month. The changes would be reflected in production schedules and the frequency of them would be detrimental to Army procurement and to industry. While the use of this method was opposed for official requirements, the ASF representatives found sufficient merit in it to suggest its use and continued development for checking and reviewing requirement estimates. Furthermore, Mr. Howard Bruce in the Office of the Director of Matériel was assigned to study and evaluate the method. [73]

His report criticized the system because it relied too much on recent, actual experience instead of upon a combination of experience and judgment as heretofore. The method was found applicable, however, to certain types of items. He suggested that one group of items be estimated in strict compliance with directives formulated by Headquarters, ASF, and a second group, by reference to inventory and issue data. The Requirements Branch objected to the assumption that it used experience without analysis and questioned the value of the proposed grouping of items. [74]

Supply Control System

When on 7 March 1944 Headquarters, ASF, published Circular 67, it acknowledged the validity of experience as a basis for determining requirements and in essence accepted the procedures already developed by the Requirements Branch, OQMG. [75] It replaced the ASP with the Supply Control System, which was made applicable to all Quartermaster items except subsistence. During December 1944, however, it was extended to these items. The Supply Control System established an integrated method of requirements forecasting, production scheduling, stock accounting, stock control, and disposal of excess supplies. Continuous short-term review was the keynote of the system, which provided data on a monthly basis, in contrast to the ASP, which was concerned with annual procurement requirements.

Procedures were set forth for attaining the objectives of the program. To facilitate control all military property was divided into two broad groups. Group "P" included all items of major importance from a military or monetary standpoint, on which centralized control was therefore desirable. It also included those items the demand for which could not be adequately estimated solely on past experience. Group "S" comprised all other matériel. [76] These groupings followed the same general division of items recommended in the Bruce memorandum.

As a method of reviewing items in both categories, the circular directed the technical services to prepare supply and demand studies in order to regulate procurement more closely and correlate it and requirements to current needs. These studies were to embody three

[72] Address, Mayne, Supply and Demand Studies and Field Information Essential to Computation of Reqmts, QM Conf, 2–4 Oct 44, Camp Lee, Va.

[73] Bradford, *Methods of Forecasting*, p. 51.

[74] Dir of Mil Plng Div to TQMG, 8 Feb 44, sub: Comments on Atchd Memo Concerning ASP by Mr. Bruce.

[75] (1) Memo, Gen Clay, for Dir of Purchases Div, ASF, *et al.*, 26 Jan 44, no sub. (2) For an analysis of Quartermaster methods see Bradford, *Methods of Forecasting*, pp. 47–51.

[76] ASF Cir 67, Sec. II, par 3, 7 Mar 44, no sub.

major phases: (1) a forecast of future issues, (2) the computation of authorized stock levels, and (3) the determination of status and adjustment of procurement schedules and stocks. Where items did not have a readily predictable rate of issue, the ASF directed the technical services to follow the ASP method in developing issue forecast. For items having a stable rate of issue the determination of future issue requirements was to be based on a critical evaluation of past issue experience and a projection of this experience into the future.

Stock levels excluded amounts already shipped overseas as well as quantities under the control of posts, camps, and stations in the United States. They were based upon anticipated depot issues to the extent authorized. For distribution in the zone of interior a 45-day level of supply was prescribed; for the theater of operations it was established at 60 days. An additional 30 days of supply, entitled "overseas contingency reserve" was authorized for those items issued overseas which did not have a strategic reserve.[77] Basing levels on anticipated issues, as calculated in the supply and demand study, changed the concept of stockage as set forth in the ASP directives as a static quantity to one which fluctuated as estimated issues varied and as the number of days authorized was changed.

The method to be used in determining the status of an item and adjusting its procurement schedules and stocks was left to the judgement of the technical service. The objective was "to bring stocks in line with the total authorized stock levels (U. S.) at the earliest practicable date, and thereafter to make procurement schedules accord with future demand."[78] This date depended on the status of production and the procurement problems involved, but unless an extension was specifically authorized by Headquarters, ASF, the necessary adjustments were to be accomplished within six months.

Insofar as it related to Quartermaster requirements, the history of supply control during 1944 was one of conferences and reports concerning the extent of the presentation of supply control data.[79] The OQMG recommended adequate but minimum accounting; the ASF requested detailed information. The Supply Control Form developed as the reporting document for the principal items was divided into seven major areas of functions: (1) identification of the item, (2) past supply status, (3) present supply status, (4) future supply status, (5) stock status, (6) disposal, and (7) annual data comparisons.[80] These forms were prepared for each item reported. Collected and published monthly they were called the Monthly Progress Report, Section 20. This replaced the ASP as the official statement of required production and the authority for procurement.

The Supply Control System required the closest co-ordination between all requirements, procurement, and stock control agencies. Within the QMC the administration of the system was worked out without establishing a central authority for requirements forecasting, production scheduling, and the other closely related functions.[81] A greater degree of co-ordination was effected but the determination of requirements remained a joint responsibility in the OQMG because the Military Planning Division still had to obtain concurrence in its forecast

[77] WD Cir 85, Sec. III, 25 Feb 44, sub: Stock Level within Z/I.
[78] ASF Cir 67, Sec. II, par 5 e (3), 7 Mar 44, no sub.
[79] (1) Chief of Reqmts Br to Chief of Mil Plng Div, OQMG, 20 Mar 44, sub: Tentative Form of Sup and Demand Rpt. (2) Same to OP&C Div, OQMG, 9 Aug 44, sub: Conf on Sup Control Rpts. (3) Memo, Col Doriot, OQMG, for CG ASF, 3 Nov 44, sub: Proposed Revision of Sup Control Rpt. (4) Memo, Doriot for same, 13 Nov 44, sub: Comments on Proposed Sup Control Form.
[80] For an analysis of this form see Bradford, *Methods of Forecasting*, pp. 60–70.
[81] (1) OQMG OO 25–72, 31 Mar 44, sub: Asgmt of Responsibilities. (2) OQMG OO 25–72A, 11 Jul 44, same sub.

studies from other interested divisions.

The Supply Control Report was an improvement over its predecessor, the ASP, to the extent that administratively it tended to force the requirements and procurement groups to work together more closely than heretofore. Embodying a close supervision over supply planning and operations, it represented the final instrument adopted by the War Department during World War II as a solution to the whole control problem. It had one vital deficiency for it was basically weak in the forecasting of issues. The validity of the entire report depended on forecast of issues to the Army but the report had no check as to the accuracy of that one element. While the report contained data on the most recent issues and cumulative issues for each item from the beginning of the year, these data were insufficient to permit the reviewing group more than a cursory review of the issue forecast. There was no explanation of the interpretations given to authorized allowances, nor was it indicated what portion of the issues were in anticipation of consumption by troops or how many articles were to be shipped as additions to the stocks required overseas.[82]

Computation of Task Force Requirements

In addition to calculating requirements for supply programs which involved long-range planning, the Requirements Branch was also responsible for computing immediate initial and replacement requirements for task forces. The most essential element here was time. Task forces generally moved on short orders, and personnel of the Overseas Requirements Section of the branch had to compute requirements for them quickly, based on War Department movement orders. Beginning inconspicuously with the computation of supply requirements for forces assigned to garrison bases obtained from Britain in trade for a number of over-age destroyers, this activity "grew to staggering proportions with the mounting of the North African and Normandy operations."[83] During the war the section prepared approximately 4,000 requirements reports for task forces and for various other special operations.

International Business Machine (IBM) tabulation was vital in computing such data. Before the outbreak of hostilities every computation—every addition, subtraction, multiplication, and division—was performed manually by a clerk with the aid of an adding machine or calculator. One computation, for example, prepared shortly before Pearl Harbor for a relatively small task force required approximately six weeks. Such laborious procedures were unsuited to the tempo of modern war, which demanded the use of machine methods and the conversion of all basic data needed for requirements computation to electrical accounting machine punch cards. Within a short time after the outbreak of war, the section, with the co-operation of the Machine Tabulating Branch, had developed an efficient and flexible system for the accurate preparation of all the various types of requirements reports.[84]

Computing task force requirements involved not only the initial issue and replacement quantity of each item of food, clothing, equipage, regular supplies, and fuels needed by a particular force, but also the total weight and cubic displacement of this shipment. Such data served

---

[82] (1) Bradford, *Methods of Forecasting*, p. 70. (2) According to Dr. Hoos, if requirements and procurement personnel could have been brought to work together more closely under the latest ASP procedures, the "net result would have been even better because ASP forecasting record, analyses would show, was the more accurate largely because it was less mechanistic and not hindered with random non-controllable variations." Ltr, Dr. Hoos to Chief of Military History, 21 Dec 50, no sub.

[83] Rpt, Overseas Reqmts Sec, Reqmts Br, Mil Plng Div, OQMG, Oct 45, sub: History and Record of Accomplishment, p. 12.007. Copy on file at Hist Sec, OQMG.

[84] For elaboration of the problems involved see *ibid.*, pp. 12.010ff.

as the basis for requisitions directing shipment from depots, as the basis for planning rail and water shipping requirements, and as a check list for conducting showdown inspections of troops and equipment at staging areas and ports of embarkation. They were the key instrument for the shipment of supplies for forces moving into theaters of operations.

Overseas Requirements Tables

Obviously if forecasts of requirements estimated in the War Department and requisitions for supplies prepared in overseas commands were based on common assumptions, the statements of requirements would be more accurate. Perhaps the chief deficiency in the method of determining requirements during World War II was the lack of co-ordination between the assumption underlying the estimates of the Requirements Branch, OQMG, and the basis of requisitions from the theaters of operations. The desirability of such co-ordination had always been recognized, but its necessity was sharply emphasized when supply planning shifted from long-range planning under the ASP to short-term operations under the Supply Control System. A more precise correlation between forecasts and requisitions was demanded by the short-term estimates of that system. The OQMG sought to achieve co-ordination through the development of overseas requirements tables.

Personnel at ports of embarkation and theater commanders were both in need of lists of consumption and replacement factors. Although the Requirements Branch recognized this need, it was in no position to provide realistic factors for each theater in 1942. In the meantime, while it collected and analyzed data, the Storage and Distribution Division, as an operating division in closer touch with problems in the field, sought to fill this need by drafting a pamphlet

to serve similar ends. This "Guide for Use in Preparing and Editing Requisitions for Quartermaster Supplies in the Theater of Operations" was sent to all ports and theaters on 1 March 1943.[85] The shortcomings of this pamphlet were recognized, and therefore its use was recommended only as a guide for future needs in the absence of accurate consumption data in any theater.[86]

In the meantime data obtained by overseas teams were being screened and converted by the Requirements Branch into tentative replacement factors by theaters. In response to a request of the Central Pacific Base Command, the Requirements Branch in December 1943 prepared an Overseas Requirements Report. At about the same time a preliminary computation was made covering the United Kingdom. This became the first Overseas Requirements Table, and it was submitted to the New York Port of Embarkation for review. Various recommendations made by the port were accepted. The Requirements Branch suggested that the replacement factors derived from theater issue experience supplant the over-all replacement percentage approved by the War Department.[87]

Overseas requirements tables were thereupon prepared during the next few months for the six theaters of operations showing the total authorized initial allowances, stock level, reserve requirements, the monthly replacement factor, and the replacement quantities for 1,000 individuals for 30 days in each of the theaters

---

[85] The Guide was subsequently revised and published as a War Department supply bulletin, SB 10–12, 11 Feb 44, sub: Guide for Use in Preparation of Requisitions in Overseas Commands and Editing Thereof by Ports of Embarkation. It was succeeded by SB 10–98, 21 Jul 44, and was rescinded on 21 March 45. Both bulletins advised use of the overseas requirements tables, if available, because of their more direct applicability.

[86] For further analysis of the pamphlet see Bradford, *Methods of Forecasting*, p. 86.

[87] Travel Rpt, Capt H. A. Naisbitt to TQMG, 21 Jan 44, sub: Rpt of Inspection of QM Activities at NYPE.

of operations. These tables were not applicable to all items. They covered clothing and equipment, expendable supplies, spare parts for selected items, certain groups of sales items, and salvage repair supplies. They did not apply to such Class I supplies as rations, or to fuels and lubricants, or certain Class IV supplies requiring special justification, as tentage for housing and storage.[88]

After the tables had been used for several months and their contribution to efficiency demonstrated, Headquarters, ASF, directed the preparation of similar tables by the other technical services.[89] The overseas requirements tables attained almost universal acceptance and contributed markedly to promoting co-ordination between the theater commands, the ports of embarkation, and the War Department in the estimating of requirements. Although the tables were widely used at ports of embarkation and overseas commands, they were not consistently and regularly used by the analysts of the Requirements Branch itself. For several reasons their use was more limited in preparing estimates for supply control. The most important reason was the lapse of time between receipt of data requiring a change in the estimate of requirements and the incorporation of that data in the quarterly revision of the Overseas Requirements Table. Since this information was available to the analyst, there was no point in his waiting for the table's publication before taking corrective action. To achieve greater co-ordination in this area a Factor Control Committee was established in the Requirements Branch in November 1944 to bring about as complete agreement as possible between the factors and allowances used in the supply program computations and those computed for the Overseas Requirements Tables. Although some success was thereby achieved, complete co-ordination between the supply programs and the tables was not effected before the war ended.

Subsistence Requirements

Administrative Background

In the forecasting of subsistence requirements close working relations were necessary between the Requirements Branch, Military Planning Division, and the Subsistence Branch (later Division). Harmonious relationships, however, were not easily achieved, in part because of the tradition of independence long enjoyed by the subsistence organization. As a commodity unit, it had been accustomed to computing its own requirements. The Subsistence Branch viewed long-range requirements estimated by the Requirements Branch as too theoretical in nature and too dissociated from its day-to-day operating problems to have much practical application.

Headquarters of SOS and later of ASF did not actively engage in detailed supervision of food requirements during most of World War II as it did for other matériel. Nor did it represent the War Department in matters of subsistence production and procurement.[90] Instead, on 29 January 1943 the Chief of Staff for Matériel, SOS, advised the Department of Agriculture that the "War Department has centered its responsibility with respect to the food requirements of the Army" under the specific supervision of Brig. Gen. Carl A. Hardigg, Chief of the Subsistence Branch, OQMG.[91] Since this branch was also procuring food, influencing production, and making the actual operating decisions, it followed that agencies of the Department of Agriculture tended to confine their relations with the War Department to the Subsistence Branch, OQMG. The Requirements

[88] Bradford, *Methods of Forecasting*, p. 88.

[89] Memo, Gen Somervell for Chiefs of Tech Svs, 8 Jul 44, sub: Computation of Allowances for Overseas Bases.

[90] Memo, Deputy Dir of Resources & Production Div, SOS, for TQMG, 2 Feb 43, sub: Transfer of Food Functions, 430.

[91] Ltr, Gen Clay to Roy Hendrickson, Dir of Food Distribution Administration, 29 Jan 43, no sub.

Branch, as a means of keeping in touch with current development and probable future trends for long-range planning in subsistence, tried in vain to secure representation on the Inter-Agency Food Allocations Committee established by the Department of Agriculture. Not until 4 August 1945 was the Military Planning Division definitely assigned to represent the QMC on the commodities sub-committees of the Food Requirements and Allocation Committee—successor to the Inter-Agency Food Allocations Committee—for the purpose of presenting and justifying Army food requirements. The Subsistence Division continued to represent the War Department in all matters of food procurement.[92]

Despite the irritations that grew out of these relationships, the personnel of the Subsistence Branch and of the Requirements Branch collaborated in preparing requirements for subsistence and post exchange items. In time a working arrangement was evolved. Before beginning a computation, personnel from the two branches discussed the method and assumptions to be used. The decisions made included agreement as to consumption factors, strength data, shipping time, stock levels overseas and in the zone of interior, loss allowances, and other data. During the computation frequent checks were made by the Subsistence Division to catch errors before the work was completed. Subsequently, when the Supply Control Reports replaced the ASP, the work of preparing them was done jointly by these two agencies. The actual forms were computed by personnel of the Requirements Branch from requirements previously concurred in by the Subsistence Division. The reports were then reviewed and approved by personnel of the Subsistence Division. Both agencies were represented at review meetings conducted by Headquarters, ASF.[93]

Requirements had to be estimated for perishable and nonperishable foods and for special rations as well as for post exchange items and ration accessory packets. Field ration A, consisting of fresh foods supplemented by some canned foods, was issued to troops in the zone of interior except when they were on maneuvers. Front-line combat troops received special rations, such as C, K, or ten-in-one. Other theater troops were issued field ration B, which included a large number of nonperishable foods.

Basic Formula

In computing the net ASP requirements[94] for these foods, the personnel of the Requirements Branch used a basic formula that remained unchanged during the war, although elements composing it underwent many refinements to effect greater accuracy of the forecasts made. In anticipation of further analysis, this formula may be stated simply. Net Army requirements equaled the quantities of food consumed by the troops, plus necessary closing stock inventories in the zone of interior and theaters of operations, minus the actual opening inventories. The net purchases of subsistence made in the United States by the QMC included not only these net requirements, minus anticipated local procurement overseas, but also the quantities purchased for and transferred to other agencies, such as the Navy and the Red Cross, as well as the subsistence provided for civilians in occupied areas. The necessary closing inventories consisted of post, camp, and station stock levels for zone of interior personnel and theater levels for overseas personnel authorized by the War Department on the basis of a certain number of days of supply for the personnel being sub-

---

[92] OQMG OO 30–74, 4 Aug 45, sub: Representation on Inter-Agency Food Subcommittees of Requirements and Allocation Committee.

[93] Rpt, Reqmts Br, OQMG, Oct 1945, sub: Army Subs and PX Reqmts, Jul 42–Aug 45, Pt. I, p. 10.

[94] The following discussion of methodology is largely based on a report prepared by the operating personnel of theRequirements Branch. Rpt, Reqmts Br, OQMG, Oct 45, sub: Army Subs and PX Reqmts, Jul 42–Aug 45, Pt. III, pp. 14–32, 40–56.

sisted at the end of the month. These inventories also comprised stock levels required at filler depots, including normal operating levels and production reserves. Opening inventories consisted of the stocks on hand at posts, camps, and stations, and at filler depots in the zone of interior and at base depots in the theaters of operations.

To compute the quantities of food consumed by the troops the forecaster multiplied the number of rations by consumption factors in order to arrive at the issue demand. The first step in the process was to determine the "multiplier" to be used for the area for which the computation was being made. It was obtained by multiplying the average number of personnel in each feeding category, such as prisoners of war, liberated allies, allied military personnel, and Army personnel fed in organized messes, who were being fed each month, by the number of days in the month. Beginning with the ASP of 1 February 1944 an average month of 30.5 days was used instead. The list of all multipliers was known as the ration schedule, and for convenience in computation a ration schedule was set up for each area for which requirements were computed. Separate computations were made for the zone of interior and overseas. In the theater computation, allowance was also made for loss by pilferage, spoilage, and ship sinkings.

Elements in Subsistence Forecasting

Strength Data

In computing subsistence requirements a number of elements were important. Obviously, accurate strength data were as essential to computing requirements for expendable items as they were to nonexpendable items. In both cases the Troop Basis and later the War Department Troop Deployment were used to obtain cumulative strengths for the zone of interior

and overseas. Both computations suffered from the fact that such data could not be obtained from the General Staff sufficiently far in advance to allow for the proper computation of requirements and the implementation of procurement programs. "It just seemed impossible to get the Staff to understand the importance of lead time in production." [95] Furthermore, since strength figures were given on a quarterly or semiannual basis, it was necessary to assume uniform monthly changes in order to compute monthly subsistence schedules.

For subsistence requirements one of the main inadequacies in these figures was the fact that they contained no information on non-Army personnel being fed by the Army. Such data had to be obtained from whatever sources could be secured at the time ration schedules were prepared, and had to be adjusted to reflect correctly the strength actually being subsisted by the Army. In general, such personnel were grouped by type of menus in order to reduce the number of categories involved in the computation of issue demand requirements. Thus in the Mediterranean Theater of Operations (MTO) native cooks, waiters, and mess attendants were grouped with prisoner of war strength because of the similarity in menus supplied rather than as an indication of military status. By the February 1945 program the lack of data had become serious because the various groups of non-Army personnel represented a substantial portion of the total strength. As a result of continued agitation by the Requirements Branch, G–4 finally included a "Subsistence Rations" section in the Supply Supplement to the War Department Troop Deployment. Beginning with the March 1945 issue official strength figures became available on an area basis for non-Army personnel.[96]

---

[95] Lecture, Gen Lutes, 23 Sep 46, sub: The ASP, p. 5.

[96] Rpt, Reqmts Br, OQMG, Oct 45, sub: Army Subs and PX Reqmts, Jul 42–Aug 45, Pt. III, pp. 27, 50–51.

Consumption Factors

Strength figures were necessary for the preparation of ration schedules, but before total quantities of subsistence could be estimated consumption factors also had to be established. Unlike the forecast for nonexpendable items, the basic equation used in estimating subsistence requirements did not use the element of initial issue nor replacement factors. Instead, consumption factors were utilized which expressed the rate at which pounds of a particular subsistence item were consumed by a specified strength during a specified period of time.[97]

Since consumption rates derived from actual issue experience were not available, consumption factors in practice were based in 1942 upon authorized menu rates. These menus were prepared by the Subsistence Branch. The master menu, known as the domestic menu, was intended as a guide for the company mess in the zone of interior. Composed of perishables and nonperishables collectively known as ration A, the master menu contained a menu for three meals a day, for each day of the month, each menu differing from the others. It was published each month, three months in advance. The overseas menu, planned for use in the theater, consisted of two separate menus—No. 1 for use in tropic and temperate zones and No. 2 for frigid zones. It included only nonperishable foods collectively known as ration B.[98]

The use of such data, although in many cases the best available, was not entirely satisfactory. Because menu rates for subsistence items were authorized it did not necessarily follow that actual usage in either the theaters or the zone of interior was in accordance with such prescribed rates of issue. The European Theater of Operations (ETO), for example, operated during the war on its own menu. Even under the best conditions the menu could not be followed exactly because a certain amount of latitude was given commanding officers to make permissible

substitutions of the food included in the menu. Local conditions of supply also caused a certain number of substitutions to be made.[99]

Personnel of the Subsistence Division and of the Requirements Branch were not in agreement on the use of consumption factors. The latter viewed consumption factors derived from menu rates as appropriate for the immediate future only because conditions likely to prevail at a more remote date were not adequately considered. The Subsistence Division insisted on relating factors rather closely to the present availability of supplies, and difficulties were encountered in obtaining its concurrence to factors not established on that basis. Subsistence personnel thought it desirable to use whatever factors were appropriate for the next few months regardless of how adequately or inadequately they might reflect conditions at a later date. As a consequence the issue demands computed actually represented quantities required, based on the assumption that the current demand situation would continue to the end of the period for which the computations were being made.[100]

To overcome the difficulties stemming from reliance on menu rates, the Requirements Branch sought to develop consumption factors for the zone of interior based on actual issue experience. In the February 1943 ASP the Requirements Branch no longer relied wholly on the master menu in computing zone of interior requirements. Instead menus were obtained from a cross section of forty camps, and rates of consumption were computed from these. By

---

[97] Hoos, Elements of QM Reqmts, p. 28.

[98] Ltr (tentative draft), Maj C. L. Campbell, Subs Br, to Spencer Platt and Edward J. Bennett, Bureau of the Budget, 1 Dec 42, sub: Food Reqmts of US Army, 430.

[99] (1) *Ibid.* (2) Lecture, Dr. R. M. Macy, Reqmts Br, OQMG, 16 Jan 43, sub: Talk Given on Rqmts before Group of Officers from Camp Lee, Va. (3) Messing in the ETO.

[100] Rpt, Reqmts Br, OQMG, Oct 45, sub: Army Subs and PX Reqmts, Jul 42–Aug 45, Pt. III, p. 52.

this period of the war the need for greater accuracy in forecasting subsistence requirements was emphasized by the necessity to conserve food. To achieve this end the War Department in 1943 attempted a more rigid control of rations for Army messes and ordered a reduction in the authorized allowances for field rations. This action was based on extensive studies of Army food consumption and wastage initiated at the Quartermaster Board shortly after Pearl Harbor upon directive of The Quartermaster General.[101] In order to accumulate the necessary subsistence data on issue experience the Requirements Branch sent field survey teams to visit representative posts, camps, and stations in the United States. While this study[102] was originally projected to cover all Quartermaster items, in the spring of 1943 it was reorganized to exclude all but subsistence items. As a result of this study detailed consumption rates in the zone of interior were derived from actual issue experience for each subsistence item. It was possible for the first time to reflect in the 1 February 1944 ASP the reduction in subsistence issues in the zone of interior due to "absenteeism" from messes. The effect was to produce "a $117,000,000 savings in 1944 requirements as stated in the current ASP." [103]

For theaters of operations the Requirements Branch based its consumption factors on the authorized menu rates of overseas menus No. 1 and No. 2. Wherever feasible it also used shipping rates. Shipping rates to the South Pacific Area (SPA) and such bases as Alaska and Iceland were considered suitable for determining subsistence requirements. The use of shipping rates, however, had certain disadvantages. It was difficult to determine what the experience rates actually were. Furthermore, shipping rates did not take into account a change in the use of subsistence sent to a theater. Thus quantities of subsistence which accumulated in excess of the needs of a given theater could be transferred to allied military personnel, used for civilian sup-

ply, or left to deteriorate because troops moved to a different island, for example, and it was not feasible to ship their supplies with them. This would not be reflected in shipping records.[104]

Insofar as perishable items were concerned, overseas requirements could not be related entirely to either menu rates or shipping rates. Forecasted issue demands had to be related to the quantities that could be shipped based upon availability of "reefer" (refrigerator) ships. Requirements personnel had to take into consideration the effect on consumption factors of the use of substitute nonperishable foods. A substantial change in the number of reefer ships available for shipping fresh butter, meat, and other perishable foods to a given area, for example, meant that the use of canned butter and meats and other substitute items would be altered correspondingly.[105]

Similarly, determination of requirements for special rations could not be based upon total strengths and average consumption factors because of the emergency nature of the issue of such items. During the first two and a half years of the war, requirements for special rations were computed as a percentage of the total quantity of menus No. 1 and No. 2 B rations

[101] (1) WD Cir 16, 11 Jan 43, sub: Revised Procedure for Distr of and Accounting for Fld Rations. (2) WD Cir 179, 7 Aug 43, Sec. II, sub: Authorized Allowances for Fld Rations. (3) Dir of QM Bd to TQMG, n. d., sub: Rpt on the QM Bd, Camp Lee, Va., 1 Feb 42–30 Jun 44, pp. 89–95.
[102] (1) Standard Fld Procedure for Reqmts Study 18, revised 21 Apr 43. (2) Carroll Belknap to Chief of Reqmts Br, OQMG, 15 Apr 43, sub: Reqmts Study 18. (3) Chief of Subs Subsec to Chief of Reqmts Br, OQMG, 17 Nov 43, sub: Necessity for Continuation of Reqmts Study 18 for Subs.
[103] (1) Memo, Col Doriot, OQMG, for Dir of Reqmts Div, ASF, 17 May 44, sub: First Rpt of Reqmts Study 18, 430. (2) See section on Food Service Program in Ch. XII of Quartermaster Corps: Organization, Supply, and Services, Vol. II, in preparation for this series.
[104] Rpt, Reqmts Br, OQMG, Oct 45, sub: Army Subs and PX Reqmts, Jul 42–Aug 45, Pt. III, p. 22.
[105] Ibid.

required for use in overseas areas. In the September 1942 ASP and the one of February 1943, for example, 25 percent of the total B rations for overseas consumption was used in computing special rations requirements. These percentages were fixed by Headquarters, SOS, but the apportionment of the requirements among the C, K, and D rations was determined by the Subsistence Branch.

By August 1944 sufficient information had been obtained from requisitions, cables, and theater reports to permit special rations requirements for some areas to be computed for the first time on an individual area basis. Before the war ended the method of computing requirements for special rations had been greatly refined. The procedures, however, were complex, for an attempt was made to arrive at the number of troops who would be using special rations in each theater and the extent to which such rations would be used each month. In the process, personnel of the Requirements Branch gave an increasing amount of attention to the influence of anticipated military operations upon special rations requirements in the several theaters. Thus in the computation of the program for April 1945, it was assumed that the European war would end that summer. Procurement requirements for special rations would therefore drop sharply, but when operations against Japan increased, they would probably rise again. An attempt was therefore made to determine the extent of these needs in the Pacific, in order that the complex process of producing and assembling the components of the special rations might not be interrupted by cutbacks to the point where it would be impossible for production to rise in time to meet these needs.[106]

Reserves and Inventory Data

Essential to computing net subsistence requirements of the Army were the necessary closing stock inventories and the actual opening inventories in the zone of interior and in theaters of operations. Except for inventories at regional and filler depots, which were adequately reflected in ASP computations, actual stock on hand was not used as a beginning credit in computing subsistence requirements. Forecasters simply assumed that stocks at posts, camps, and stations in the zone of interior and at overseas bases were authorized levels.

In the February 1943 ASP an effort was made to use actual inventories insofar as these were available. Thus stock figures covering quantities on hand in depots, ports, and commercial or contractors' warehouses were used. Actual data on post, camp, and station inventories were used for the first time in computing the April 1943 ASP, but the figures were limited to only certain items.[107] In most programs, forecasters continued to assume that stocks were at authorized levels for posts, camps, and stations, and for overseas bases.

Actual overseas stocks were not included in any of the calculations during the war because adequate information was not available. Had such information been available it might have been applied to reduce requirements in theaters of operations. A study made by the Subsistence Section of the Requirements Branch for the period January to July 1945 revealed that subsistence stocks overseas were on the average 55 percent above the authorized levels. The excess stocks were greater for perishable items than for nonperishables. One third of the items were in excess of 100 percent or more. Of the items above authorized levels the average excess was about 80 percent; of items below authorized levels, the average deficit amounted to about 30 percent.[108]

---

[106] Rpt, Reqmts Br, OQMG, Jan 46, sub: Army Forecasted Reqmts and Procurement of Special Rations During the Period, Jul 42–Aug 45, *passim.*

[107] Rpt, Reqmts Br, OQMG, Oct 45, sub: Army Subs and PX Reqmts, Jul 42–Aug 45, Pt. II, pp. 10, 16.

[108] *Ibid.,* Pt. III, p. 41.

Each post, camp, and station in the zone of interior and each overseas theater was permitted to carry supplies equivalent to a certain number of days of supply for the personnel being subsisted at the end of the month. These authorized operating levels were changed periodically by the War Department. As supply conditions changed, authorized levels in the various theaters were revised from time to time. Although revisions were also made in zone of interior depot levels, these tended to remain at about 45 days projected issue for the zone of interior and 60 days for filler depots backing up overseas shipments. In addition to these operating reserves production reserves were established for certain subsistence items requiring additional stocks because of importing hazards, manufacturing obstacles, such as setting up assembly lines for canned butter, and seasonal availability, particularly in the case of processed fruits and vegetables. Such seasonal reserves were forecasted in terms of months of supply— for example, of canned peas—necessary to be on hand at the end of the calendar year to meet requirements until the new supply became available. Procurement of canned peas took place during a certain season of the year but since consumption occurred generally during the whole year, the advanced procurement carried in stock became seasonal reserves.[109] Operating and production reserves insured a continuous flow of subsistence through the supply pipeline to feed our troops at home and overseas.

Overseas Procurement

In estimating issue demand for overseas areas, allowance had to be made not only for pilferage and spoilage, as in the case of nonexpendable items, but also for local procurement. During the war considerable quantities of subsistence items, particularly perishables, were obtained by local procurement overseas. Data on the quantities of subsistence so obtained

were fragmentary and unsatisfactory. This information was used, however, to adjust gross overseas issue demands by deducting the amounts estimated as procurable in any given theater. Using the gross overseas issue demand rather than net requirements permitted a larger margin of safety.[110]

The February 1943 ASP was the first program in which an adjustment was made for estimated local procurement in the overseas theaters. By agreement with General Hardigg this adjustment was made applicable only to the 1943 requirements and not to those of 1944. In the beginning such adjustments were made for the United Kingdom (UK), SPA, and the Southwest Pacific Area (SWPA). Thus with the exception of coffee, canned fruits and vegetables, multivitamin and salt tablets, all requirements for troops in the SWPA, computed on menu No. 1 factors, were eliminated. This was made possible by very extensive local procurement in Australia. In subsequent programs consideration was given to local procurement in other theaters.[111]

Because of the limited usefulness of local procurement information, allowances were made only in the case of principal items. It was realized that local procurement of other items occurred, but such quantities were considered supplemental supplies. A preliminary study of local procurement for subsistence items was begun in June 1945 but not completed. On an area basis it showed that the bulk of the local procurement was concentrated in the SWPA, averaging about 60 percent of the total. For the rest, 25 percent was procured in the ETO, 10 percent in the SPA, and only 5 percent in all the other areas. These percentage distributions, however, tend to indicate a more precise set of

[109] *Ibid.*, Pt. III, pp. 28, 29.

[110] *Ibid.*, Pt. III, p. 29.

[111] Memo, Col Cowles, OQMG, for Reqmts Div, ASF, 29 May 43, sub: Data on Foreign Procurement of Subs for ASP, and 1st ind, Hq ASF to TQMG, 11 Jun 43, 430.

information than actually existed.[112]

As in the case of forecasting requirements for nonexpendable items, each of the elements entering into estimating subsistence requirements was scrutinized by personnel of the Requirements Branch to promote greater accuracy of the final results. While the scientific approach used in forecasting requirements frequently fell short of the goals of accuracy and co-ordination deemed desirable by the Requirements Branch, many modifications toward those ends were effected. Subsistence forecasts in 1945 rested on a sounder basis than in 1941.

Petroleum Requirements

Administrative Developments

Petroleum products are among the most important items of supply for a modern mechanized army. The enormous demands for these products during World War II led to the gradual evolution of an organization which exercised centralized control over petroleum supply to the Army.[113] In the process, responsibility for the computation of long-term petroleum requirements was rapidly shifted from one unit to another in the OQMG.[114] In the spring of 1942 when the OQMG was reorganized along functional lines, responsibility for determining Quartermaster petroleum requirements for the ASP was vested in the Requirements Branch of the Military Planning Division. By the end of the year, however, this responsibility had been transferred to the newly created Petroleum Branch in the Procurement Division. The Military Planning Division was to collaborate with the Petroleum Branch in the compilation of long-term petroleum requirements but in actuality the Petroleum Branch became responsible for them. The Military Planning Division thereafter merely acted as an agency through which requirements were submitted to Headquarters, SOS, in order that a more uniform presentation of the Quartermaster program

might be made. Six months later on 1 June 1943 the Petroleum Branch was replaced by the Fuels and Lubricants Division. For the remainder of the war this division computed petroleum requirements and was responsible for all petroleum functions assigned to the QMC. The Military Planning Division remained the channel through which supply programs were transmitted to Headquarters, ASF.[115]

Prior to the war and until the summer of 1942 each supply service computed its own petroleum requirements. These were assembled in a more or less haphazard manner and were usually greatly out of line with actual requirements. By mid-1942, in view of the prospect of nationwide gasoline and fuel oil rationing, it was essential that Army petroleum requirements be accurate in order that shortages might be forecast and supply programs planned accordingly. Though Army requirements were small in comparison with those of the Navy or the Air Forces, it was advisable to anticipate them well in advance of actual need.

The first step toward bringing requirements into line was taken on 19 August 1942 when Headquarters, SOS, directed the Requirements Branch, OQMG, to make a study of the problem. In particular it was to draw up the petroleum requirements of the Army for the balance of 1942 and all of 1943 and 1944 for incorporation into the September 1942 ASP. To accomplish this it was necessary for the Requirements Branch to obtain estimated requirements from each of the various supply services and ascertain the basis for calculating such requirements

---

[112] Rpt, Reqmts Br, OQMG, Oct 45, Army Subs and PX Reqmts, Jul 42–Aug 45, Pt. III, p. 47.

[113] See above, Ch. I, pp. 34–35.

[114] For a full analysis of the development of the petroleum organization and the computation of petroleum requirements see Erna Risch, *Fuels for Global Conflict* QMC Historical Studies 9, rev ed (Washington, 1952) pp. 1–17.

[115] (1) OQMG OO 25-22, 3 Dec 42, sub: Reasgmt of QM Functions Relating to Petrl. (2) OQMG OO 25-37, 29 May 43, sub: Establishment of F&L Div.

in each instance.

In the course of preparing this program it became apparent that standard methods of requesting requirements, presenting and submitting them, and setting up reserve stocks would have to be established. In the interest of accuracy and as a means of co-ordinating the requirements of all services, the Requirements Branch proposed that one individual be appointed in each supply service and the Army Ground Forces with the responsibility for collecting, compiling, and submitting petroleum requirements. This proposal was acted upon favorably and such "custodians" were appointed. A referee, named by the director of the Requirements Division, SOS, acted as the clearing agent for that organization. Where discrepancies in the estimates submitted were observed by the Requirements Branch, OQMG, and the matter could not be resolved informally with the service concerned, the question was laid before the referee of the Requirements Division, SOS, for decision. In no event, however, "would the Requirements Branch of OQMG go directly to the Services involved in an attempt to iron out discrepancies in requirements." [116] It was hoped that this procedure would insure complete coverage for all services, prevent duplication of requirements, and establish standard methods in computing them. The computation of accurate petroleum requirements was needed not only for purposes of the ASP but by Brig. Gen. Walter B. Pyron, Chief for Operations, Fuel Section, Resources Division, SOS, who at this time was responsible for co-ordinating the total petroleum requirements of the Army—exclusive of the AAF—with the Office of the Petroleum Coordinator, the Army-Navy Petroleum Board, and with other governmental agencies.

The procedure of channeling requirements through the OQMG continued when the Petroleum Branch was established in December 1942. The branch computed requirements for gasoline, oil, and lubricants for all armored motor and track-laying vehicles. It secured from the other supply services and from the AAF in relation to its ground equipment all other petroleum requirements, which were then assembled into the ASP and submitted to the Resources Division, ASF.[117] Staff responsibilities were lodged with the Fuels Branch of this division, which screened [118] and adjusted requirements in the light of long-range production possibilities and transmitted them to the Requirements Division, ASF, for inclusion in the ASP, and to the Army-Navy Petroleum Board. The chief of the Fuels Branch continued to act as the War Department liaison officer for petroleum.

When the Fuels and Lubricants Division was established, it retained all the operating responsibility formerly exercised by the Petroleum Branch and in addition was made responsible for the performance of all staff functions necessary to the discharge of these operating responsibilities, with the exception of certain ones specifically assigned to Headquarters, ASF.[119] Thus, insofar as requirements were concerned the Planning Division, ASF, was to screen requirements and requisitions received from theaters of operations. Within two weeks, however,

---

[116] (1) Dr. Macy to Dr. Baker, Reqmts Br, OQMG, 23 Sep 42, sub: Conf with Brig Gen W. B. Pyron on Petrl Reqmts. (2) Memo, Maj John L. King, Chief of Fuels Sec, Resources Div, for Gen Pyron, Chief for Opns, Resources Div, SOS, 1 Oct 42, sub: Army Petrl Reqmts—Exclusive of Aircraft of AAF. (3) Memo, Dir of Resources Div, SOS, for Dir of Reqmts Div, SOS, 3 Oct 42, sub: Reqmts for Petrl. (4) 2d ind, Col Cowles, OQMG, to Hq SOS, 17 Oct 42, on same. All in 463.

[117] (1) WD Cir 317, Sec. III, 17 Sep 42, sub: Responsibility for Gasoline, Lubricants and Misc Items. (2) ASF Adm Memo S–20, 20 Mar 43, sub: Procedure, Storage and Distr of Petrl Products.

[118] Screening was a process of evaluating estimates against all the known factors and included the elimination of duplications which might otherwise have been overlooked.

[119] ASF Cir 33, 26 May 43, sub: Procurement, Storage, and Distr of Petrl Products.

this responsibility had been delegated to the Fuels and Lubricants Division.[120] In effect, the Requirements Branch of that division inherited the responsibilities formerly exercised by the Fuels Branch of the Resources and Production Division, ASF.

In the performance of its staff functions pertaining to requirements of petroleum products, excluding those for AAF aircraft, the Fuels and Lubricants Division formulated policies governing the technical services in their computation of requirements, it supervised and standardized methods, and it screened and adjusted such requirements in accordance with consumption factors and records of consumption collected and maintained by the OQMG.

From the summer of 1943 to the end of the war the Fuels and Lubricants Division was responsible for estimating petroleum requirements for the entire United States Army throughout the world, except petroleum used in aircraft. It was solely responsible for estimating the gasoline, lubricating oil, grease, and other products to be used in all general purpose vehicles, in motorcycles, passenger cars, trucks, and tanks, regardless of the service or branch of the Army using the vehicle or product, either in the zone of interior or overseas. In addition, it was responsible for estimating the quantity of petroleum used in many types of special equipment. Of course, the individual technical services developed basic estimating data incidental to petroleum requirements for their special purpose vehicles and equipment, such as crash-trucks in the Air Corps, barges, ferries, and locomotives for Transportation, fog oil and gasoline for bombs for Chemical Warfare Service, petrolatum for the Medical Department, gasoline and diesel fuel for the operation of power units by the Signal Corps, and asphalt for roads and fuel oil for utilities for the Engineers.

Once the division had assembled, screened, and adjusted these requirements they were submitted for review and approval to the Require-

ments Division, ASF. This review was, in fact, an acceptance of the program. In addition, the Fuels and Lubricants Division assembled and submitted to the International Division, ASF, the petroleum requirements for civilians in occupied territories. These requirements were then submitted to the Combined Civil Affairs Committee for final review, approval, and incorporation into the ASP. All requirements were then forwarded to the Army-Navy Petroleum Board. It is significant that the director of the Fuels and Lubricants Division acted as deputy to the Commanding General, ASF, in his capacity as a member of this board. The board reviewed and combined Army requirements with those of the AAF aircraft and the Navy and transmitted them along with lend-lease requirements to the Petroleum Administration for War. There the requirements were reviewed and screened by the Requirements Committee, of which the director of the Fuels and Lubricants Division was a member and his chief of the Requirements Branch was an alternate. Thereafter allocation of material was made by the WPB. Subsequently the Fuels and Lubricants Division notified the technical services of the approval, or, if reductions occurred, it made allocations between the technical services and the AAF and notified them accordingly.[121]

Elements in Forecasting Petroleum Requirements

The collection and analysis of factors of experience and service were fundamental to improvement in estimating petroleum requirements. When the Requirements Branch of the Military Planning Division was called upon to compute petroleum requirements for the September 1942 ASP, it found itself then and later

---

[120] Memo, Dir of Opns ASF, for TQMG, 10 Jun 43, sub: Screening Reqmts and Reqns, 463.

[121] Address, Chief of Reqmts Br to officers of branch, Dec 43, sub: Staff Responsibilities of Reqmts Br.

suffering from a lack of basic data. The branch had barely begun to use the improved methods it was developing for computing requirements for other Quartermaster items when changes in organization transferred these problems first to the Petroleum Branch and then to the Fuels and Lubricants Division. Each of these organizations built upon the work of its predecessor, collecting data on factors and improving the techniques used in the computation of petroleum requirements.

Three factors—consumption, service, and usage—had to be considered in computing petroleum requirements.[122] Petroleum products were expendable items, and the consumption factor was, therefore, the amount of fuel or lubricants that a given piece of equipment consumed in a given period of time. Consumption of gasoline by a vehicle varied in periods of actual combat, during inactive periods, when operating in cold, moderate, or temperate climates, or according to topography, that is, in the desert, mountains, plains, or jungle. While the various types of terrain and climate had a considerable effect on the requirements for petroleum products, insufficient information was available for quantitative determination of these effects.

The service factor was the time period of operation. Consideration had to be given to the length of time that a certain piece of fixed equipment was operated; for example, the number of hours per day that a company used its cooking stove, the number of hours per day that generating equipment for a radio station operated, or the number of hours per day necessary to provide heating in a base or field hospital. Some equipment was both mobile and stationary, using petroleum on both counts. Thus, a truck-mounted air compressor consumed fuel while moving under its own power and when operating as a piece of stationary equipment. The usage factor was obtained by multiplying the consumption factor by the service factor.

The first step in computing petroleum requirements was to determine the consumption factors in gallons of fuel per day or per mile as might be appropriate for each individual type of equipment, ranging from a kerosene lantern to a searchlight, and from a motorcycle to a tank, operating under normal conditions. When the requirements for each kind of product for all equipment in a military unit using such products were added together, consumption factors could be estimated for the unit. The total unit consumption factors for all the units in the Army equaled the total requirements of the Army, but only for normal conditions. It was necessary to adjust the normal unit consumption factors for variations in climate, terrain, and other special conditions of the season or region in which the vehicles would operate by multiplying the consumption factor by an operation factor. The latter was the ratio of gasoline consumed under special or irregular conditions of operation to that consumed under normal conditions. This result multiplied by the estimated average miles per day which the vehicles were expected to travel—thereby giving the vehicle consumption factor in gallons per day—times the number of days in the period equaled the total requirements for petroleum products.

Consumption factors for stationary equipment were listed in gallons per day. Since most of this equipment was used intermittently, these factors were based on an average use of the equipment for a certain number of hours per day. The average number of hours of operation per day for some of the equipment was fairly constant under all conditions, as for example, field ranges, stoves, water heaters, and radios. The hours of operation per day of other equip-

---

[122] The following discussion of factors is largely based on a report prepared by a firm of statistical enginers for the Fuels and Lubricants Division. Rpt, Skidmore, Owings & Merrill and W. Earle Andrews for F&L Div, OQMG, 30 Nov 43, sub: Rpt of Fuels and Lubricants Survey. See particularly the section, Factors for Estimating Petrl Reqmts.

ment might vary widely according to the conditions of use, as in the case of a fog generator, a surgical power unit, or a water purification unit.

One important approach to the problem of accuracy in computing petroleum requirements was the formulation and establishment of adequate records on consumption and inventory both in the zone of interior and the theaters of operations. Headquarters, ASF, required The Quartermaster General to "collect and maintain records of petroleum consumption factors." [123] To this end the Petroleum Branch initiated a recurring report, further refined by the Fuels and Lubricants Division, which started an experience record for the zone of interior. [124] By the end of 1943 the problem of securing an accurate determination of stocks, issues, and requirements of the Army (except AAF aircraft) in the zone of interior was well in hand.

Basic information from the theaters of operations, however, was inadequate. The petroleum analyst had no one standardized report from the theaters. Instead he was dependent for information on the automatic supply report prepared by ports of embarkation, the "stat report" of the area petroleum officer in the theater, and a number of miscellaneous reports. None of these produced any real information of value in obtaining either consumption or future requirements of the Army. To replace this variety of inadequate reports the Requirements Branch of the Fuels and Lubricants Division designed a monthly report called "The Fuels and Petroleum Report" to be submitted from all overseas commands showing stocks and receipts by sources, issues to claimant agencies, and requirements of the United States Army for thirty-one classifications of petroleum products as well as for 5- and 55-gallon drums. This report became the basis for the successful control of petroleum allocation by the Army-Navy Petroleum Board, for accurately estimating requirements for theaters of operations, and for providing an accounting system for lend-lease in reference to various types of petroleum products. [125]

By mid-1944 great strides had been made in the collection of data and the improvement of techniques upon which to base the computation of accurate petroleum requirements. As conditions changed, the basis of estimating requirements changed; hence the problem remained one of continuous study for the Fuels and Lubricants Division. While the computation of petroleum products has been selected for illustrative purposes here, it should be noted that this division was also responsible for computing the requirements of the Army for solid fuels and for containers for petroleum products.

Summary

Whether requirements were being computed for clothing, equipment, subsistence, or petroleum products, the basic needs at the beginning of World War II were accurate data and records on which forecasters might base their estimates. A dearth of such information existed in 1941, but until material shortages appeared this had no untoward effect. During 1942 the problem of procurement planning and requirements forecasting became more difficult. Then the need for logically sound concepts and ideas concerning requirements, for scientific statistical methods, and for the development of basic records was evident. Trained personnel were brought into the OQMG for this purpose, and methods were modified in the light of their findings. Refinements of methods continued till the end of the war. By that time, too, the fundamental procurement authority was no longer based upon the ASP but upon the Supply Control Report, which embodied a close supervision of supply planning and operations.

---

[123] ASF Adm Memo S–20, 20 Mar 43, sub: Procurement, Storage, and Distr of Petrl Products.

[124] For elaboration of these reports see Risch, *Fuels for Global Conflict*, pp. 26–27, 33–34.

[125] This report was put into effect by WD Letter, 29 Mar 44, file AG 463.7 (21 Mar 44) OB–S–D–SPDDL–M.

CHAPTER VII

Procurement Policies and Procedures

Military procurement is a complex, fluid, and integrated process in which the various phases of supply—from research and development of items to their purchase, distribution, maintenance, and salvage—are closely interdependent. In this discussion, however, procurement is more narrowly defined to include the policies, procedures, and administrative arrangements under which Quartermaster contracts were placed and production on them was controlled to insure delivery in the quantity, quality, and time required.

The huge volume and complexity of war procurement placed unprecedented demands on the Quartermaster Corps and its suppliers. The procurement mission of the Corps involved much more than contracting for the production and delivery of the approximately 70,000 different items assigned to it for purchase. Not only did the OQMG have to streamline its procurement organization and procedures to insure efficiency and economy of operations but Quartermaster personnel had to perform many tasks inextricably interwoven with the job of purchasing. These included servicing contracts at every stage to insure delivery of needed supplies; relentlessly following up contract performance and rendering engineering assistance to eliminate chokepoints in production; developing and implementing techniques to guarantee a steady flow of materials and component parts to Quartermaster suppliers; and inspecting

goods efficiently and promptly to permit their rapid movement to the points where they were needed.

The Quartermaster Supply System in 1939

The essential character of the war supply system of the Corps had been fairly well developed in peacetime. During World War I and in the interlude of peace following the war years, centralized purchase of the basic items of supply became the core of Quartermaster operations.[1] The OQMG was the procurement control agency for the centralized purchase operations conducted by a few key depots. It formulated and supervised the execution of policy, issued procurement directives, maintained liaison with higher authority, and helped to eliminate procurement bottlenecks. The key depots, to which were allocated certain classes of items for purchase either for depot stock or for distribution to other depots or points of consumption, fed the regional distributing areas into which the country was divided. The basic feature of the

---

[1] H. B. Yoshpe and M. U. Massen, *Procurement Policies and Procedures in the Quartermaster Corps During World War II* (QMC Historical Studies 17, June 1947), pp. 7–12. Hereafter cited as *Procurement Policies and Procedures*. The following discussion of procurement is largely indebted to this study and to Yoshpe, *Production Control in the Quartermaster Corps, 1939–44* (QMC Historical Studies 8, December 1944). Hereafter cited as *Production Control in QMC*.

field purchasing system was this centralized purchase of specialty items. Thus, all footwear was contracted for by the Boston Quartermaster Depot, clothing by the Philadelphia Depot, motor transport items by the Holabird Depot, and tentage and manufactured canvas articles by the Jeffersonville Depot. These depots drew upon the entire country for their requirements, soliciting formal sealed bids from all interested suppliers, awarding contracts to the lowest responsible bidders, and servicing these contracts through every stage to completion.

A substantial amount of regional and local buying of various articles of a general nature supplemented this centralized procurement system. Quartermaster installations in the distributing areas procured not only all Quartermaster supplies of a general nature but also any item which a central procurement depot or another supply service requested them to purchase. The posts, camps, and stations were the final link in the procurement chain. They were responsible for the local purchase of subsistence, forage, maintenance items, and such emergency items as were ordered by corps area or district quartermasters.

Centralization of procurement control in the OQMG and concentration of purchase responsibility for certain classes of items at designated key depots thus characterized the procurement organization of the QMC in 1939. Contracts, however, might be placed in any section of the country. By the beginning of World War II the QMC had developed the utmost confidence in the effectiveness of its supply system for meeting both normal and expanded Army needs.

To meet the requirements of its peacetime supply system, the Corps purchased directly from industry and from government agencies, or under contracts executed by them. It also participated in the interbranch procurement system.[2] This system was a product of World War I experience and had the effect of making the QMC "the most important of the War Depart-

ment purchasing agencies."[3] In an effort to avoid the consequences of harmful interagency competition, the President had consolidated Army purchasing through the establishment of an interbureau procurement system on the authority granted by the Overman Act of May 1918. It permitted one supply service to purchase goods for another. This wartime emergency idea was carried over into the National Defense Act of 1920. The Corps' part in the program was especially large because under this act The Quartermaster General was charged with "the purchase and procurement for the Army of all supplies of standard manufacture and all supplies common to two or more branches."[4] Other supply services were required to participate in indefinite-quantity contracts executed by The Quartermaster General or any agency under his control, except when the needs of the requiring service did not permit the delay incident to such purchase. Before World War II, however, this program of centralizing the purchasing function for items common to the needs of various supply services developed very slowly.[5]

The elimination of interagency competition was also promoted by the system of interdepartmental procurement.[6] Dictated by laws or other instructions, this system consolidated requirements of various agencies and centralized sup-

---

[2] Interbranch procurement is the procurement of supplies by one supply arm, service, or bureau for another such arm, service, or bureau. AR 5–300, 10 Dec 36, sub: ASW: Procurement of Supplies.

[3] Annual *Report of The Quartermaster General, 1919* (Washington, 1920), p. 19.

[4] 41 *U. S. Statutes* 766.

[5] For steps taken in the decade of the thirties see Yoshpe and Massen, *Procurement Policies and Procedures,* pp. 21–22.

[6] As distinguished from interbranch procurement, interdepartmental procurement is the procurement of supplies by one executive department or independent agency of the government from another such department or agency, or under a contract executed by the latter. AR 5–300, 10 Oct 36, sub: ASW: Procurement of Supplies.

ply responsibility. It was particularly effective in peacetime, when the need for supplies could be estimated in advance and the necessary arrangements made for satisfactory delivery. Under the system, the supplying agencies—for example, the Treasury Department—issued schedules containing detailed information as to the items, procedures to be followed, and the departments that were required to participate in this manner of purchase. The QMC merely drew a purchase order on the contractor of the supplying agency at the prices designated in the contract, and goods were made available direct to posts and stations.

Many Quartermaster items were acquired through participation in contracts negotiated by other federal departments. The most important of these purchases were made under the General Schedule of Supplies of the Treasury Department. Among the basic items covered by such indefinite-quantity contracts were: tires, tubes, and other motor vehicle accessories and parts; gasoline, fuel oil, and diesel engine oil delivered in tank cars, tank wagons, and drums; machine tools, small machinery, and accessories and parts; electrical supplies; and office furniture and equipment. It was mandatory for the QMC to obtain these supplies from such Treasury Procurement Schedules. Even before the establishment of the Procurement Division in the Treasury Department in 1933, the Corps participated in lubricating oil contracts entered into annually by the Navy Department. After 1933 the Navy Department continued to be designated as the procuring agency for lubricating oils and for gasoline, fuel oil, and diesel engine oil for marine deliveries.[7] Unless the "Contract Bulletin" of the Navy Department stated otherwise, or unless exemption was specifically obtained, the QMC purchased these supplies on contracts executed by the Navy Department.

It was also compulsory for the Corps to purchase such goods as met its requirements from federal prison industries and from the Committee on Purchases of Blind-Made Products.[8] These purchases included such items as brooms, pillowcases, and cotton felt mattresses. The Corps acquired various supplies from still other federal agencies, such as plain and printed envelopes from the Post Office Department, and inks, glues, and other supplies carried in stock by the Government Printing Office.

The requirements of the Corps' peacetime supply system also were filled through the manufacturing operations of certain of its depots. Such depot factories had been in existence since the early days of the nation's military history.[9] A large plant at the Philadelphia Depot manufactured and renovated a great variety of clothing and textile and canvas products. In the decade before World War II this factory produced all the outer clothing for the enlisted personnel of the Regular Army and was an important source of supply for the National Guard. Various shops at the Jeffersonville Depot manufactured and repaired leather products, such as harness items and saddles. They also produced tents and other canvas articles as well as metal, woodworking, tin, and sheetmetal products. A third center of manufacturing operations was located at the Holabird Depot, where motor transport activities were centralized. With the great automotive industry professing its readiness to furnish the QMC anything it required, it was contrary to War Department policy to make trucks. Fire-fighting vehicles, however, were assembled at Holabird, and maintenance

---

[7] (1) See OQMG Cir 1–4, 1 Mar 39, sub: Procurement and Distr of Supplies. (2) Erna Risch, *Fuels for Global Conflict*, QMC Historical Studies 9, rev ed (Washington, 1952), p. 43.

[8] (1) 46 *U. S. Statutes* 392, Act of 27 May 30. (2) 52 *U. S. Statutes* 1196, Act of 25 Jun 38.

[9] For a detailed account of one such plant see Paul R. Doolin, The Factory at the Philadelphia Quartermaster Depot (PQMD hist rpt, Jul 46). On file at Hist Sec, OQMG.

units were engaged in the general repair and re-building of all types of motor vehicle equipment from 1918, when the work was first begun at the depot, until the summer of 1942, when this responsibility was transferred to the Ordnance Department.

The National Defense Act of 1920 authorized the Assistant Secretary of War to have manufactured at the government arsenals or government-owned factories all supplies needed by the War Department which they could produce on an economical basis. Notwithstanding this legislative mandate, repeated efforts were made by business interests and their congressional spokesmen to curtail or abolish these manufacturing operations, on the ground that they constituted unfair competition with commercial enterprise. Such charges were made particularly in depression periods. In the years following the panic of 1929 persistent pressure resulted in a substantial reduction of some Quartermaster manufacturing operations, a reduction which continued until the outbreak of World War II.[10]

Factors other than their ability to meet supply requirements justified the continued existence of depot factory operations. Depot experience in production provided yardsticks for establishing minimum costs which became governing factors in setting prices to be paid contractors, thereby reducing profiteering. The depot factory also served as a manufacturing laboratory for testing new manufacturing methods, for manufacturing pilot samples of new items, and for experimenting with substitutions of materials and equipment. Furthermore, when the need arose, the depots were in a position to furnish expert guidance to industry in the interpretation of Army specifications. The continuous operation of the depot factories also served as a cushion in meeting the initial demands of mobilization and offsetting the inevitable delays incident to putting unusual requirements into production.

The policies, laws, and regulations governing

Quartermaster procurement remained generally static in the two decades preceding the declaration of the emergency. The Corps purchased supplies on the basis of competitive bidding, and, except under special conditions, it adhered to the formal advertising procedure by means of circular proposal rather than newspaper advertising. Articles or services could be procured by open-market purchase, but the use of this method was limited to emergencies when the public exigency required immediate delivery or performance, to purchases of relatively low cost—a maximum of $500 was placed on any such purchase—and to those instances where advertising was impracticable. In addition, the Corps used indefinite-quantity contracts for services and supplies, such as perishable subsistence, the demand for which was so variable that it could not with safety obligate itself to purchase definite amounts.[11]

War Procurement Plans

During the years when the operating personnel of the QMC were developing a centralized procurement system, the planners were formulating their war procurement plans based on a radically different concept. The need to plan for war production and procurement in advance of an emergency resulted directly from the unhappy supply experience of World War I. The purpose of such planning was to eliminate the disastrous interagency competition of World War I; to minimize production delays; to direct the national resources into essential channels; and to avoid industrial congestion, transportation difficulties, skyrocketing prices, undue cur-

[10] Yoshpe and Massen, *Procurement Policies and Procedures*, pp. 16–18.

[11] (1) See *ibid.*, pp. 22–24 for elaboration of these peacetime contracting practices. (2) Regulations governing contracting procedures are to be found in the 5-series of Army Regulations and in OQMD Circular 1–3.

tailment of civilian needs, and unnecessary post-war dislocations.[12]

In contrast to the peacetime central procurement system, the war procurement plans of the Corps revolved around the idea of decentralization to procurement districts that were more or less coterminous with the corps areas into which the country was divided for military purposes. These districts were to draw upon the production facilities within their own regions for the food, clothing, shelter, and equipment needed by the troops to be mobilized in the corps areas. The procurement planners furthered the objective of regional self-sufficiency in wartime by surveying the industrial facilities of these districts, allocating them to the needs of the Corps, and executing schedules of production with plants earmarked for the use of the Corps. Furthermore, on M Day and during the subsequent war the procurement plans provided for abandonment of the formal advertising method and the negotiation of contracts with the allocated facilities in accordance with these detailed, periodically revised plans. All these plans were to go into effect on M Day, when procurement planning activities were to be absorbed by current procurement.

As it turned out the transition from a state of limited emergency proclaimed by the President in 1939 to war was so gradual that no M Day was recognized. Despite the expanding purchasing program, the QMC procurement organization and techniques underwent no radical changes following the declaration of limited emergency. No authority was granted for allocating orders as proposed in the Industrial Mobilization Plan. Not until the spring of 1942 did the Corps abandon formal advertising. As the emergency progressed, it gradually extended contract negotiation, but the principle of competition remained the basis of Quartermaster procurement. No immediate merger of procurement planning with current procurement occurred. For ten months after Pearl Harbor

procurement planning in the Corps went on as a separate activity side by side with current procurement. During this period the planners aided the depots in advising manufacturers on Quartermaster requirements and procurement policies, investigating contract delinquencies, and performing other useful services. The official existence of procurement planning was ended on 3 October 1942[13] when the OQMG discontinued its offices and made its personnel and equipment available to the commanding officers of the depots.[14]

Developments in Procurement Organization

As a result of World War I experience, Congress provided in the National Defense Act that responsibility for supervision of the procurement of all military supplies should be vested in the Assistant Secretary of War. By congressional action in 1940 his title was changed to Under Secretary of War. His procurement supervisory duties expanded as the procurement activities of the supply arms and services grew. Until March 1942 the line of authority on procurement matters extended directly from the Office of the Under Secretary of War to The Quartermaster General and the chiefs of the

---

[12] (1) For an exhaustive analysis of the evolution of plans for the over-all administrative and industrial controls required in war consult Harold W. Thatcher, *Planning for Industrial Mobilization, 1920–40* (QMC Historical Studies 4, August 1943). (2) For a comprehensive account of the development of Quartermaster procurement plans developed in accordance with the requirements set forth in the Industrial Mobilization Plan, see Thomas M. Pitkin and Herbert R. Rifkind, *Procurement Planning in the Quartermaster Corps, 1920–40* (QMC Historical Studies 1, March 1943).

[13] Ltr, Gen Corbin, Procurement Div, OQMG, to CO BQMD, 3 Oct 42, sub: Discontinuance of War Procurement Plng. Other depots were notified by an identical letter.

[14] For an analysis of the contributions made by the procurement planners during the period 1939 to 1942 see Yoshpe and Massen, *Procurement Policies and Procedures*, pp. 30–38.

other supply services. At that time the creation of the Services of Supply interposed another office between The Quartermaster General and the Under Secretary of War.

Outside the War Department the national defense program established other governmental agencies which had a direct and very definite influence on procurement operations within the QMC. The principal agency in this respect at first was the National Defense Advisory Committee, which was originally designed to encourage the expansion of industrial production and to assist and advise all national defense agencies procuring supplies in the co-ordination of their efforts where these were in conflict. It was followed by the Office of Production Management, which in turn was replaced by the War Production Board, the most important single agency directing economic mobilization during the war.

Within the OQMG, procurement responsibility in 1939 was vested in a supply Division.[15] This commodity-type organization, which had evolved many years before the emergency, continued to function until early in 1942. Five branches of the Supply Division—Clothing and Equipage, General Supplies, Remount (animals), Subsistence, and Fuel and Construction Materials—were responsible for procuring the various Quartermaster commodities.

As the procurement program of the Corps expanded, however, the OQMG in 1940 established a Procurement Control Branch within the Administrative Division[16] in an effort to assure compliance with all acts of Congress and all policies, instructions, and regulations of superior defense agencies. Generally this branch performed staff functions. It was charged with controlling and co-ordinating all matters relating to procurement policy and procedure. It furnished legal advice on all procurement questions, such as those relating to preference ratings, assignment of contracts, making advance payments, the issue of tax amortization

certificates, and the execution of emergency plant facilities contracts and Defense Plant Corporation leases. The branch maintained liaison on all matters of procurement policy and procedure with other divisions of the OQMG, with higher echelons, and with other agencies.

Early in January 1941 this branch, together with others concerned with the determination of requirements, procurement plans, and the expediting of production, was transferred to a Planning and Control Division, newly created to strengthen staff supervision in the OQMG.[17] This division became responsible for continuing the review and co-ordination of procurement policies and procedures. Shortly after Pearl Harbor the Procurement Control Branch was replaced by the Purchase and Contract Branch in the same division. By that time its functions had been widened so that it was also charged with authorizing the negotiation of contracts, reviewing proposed financing of Quartermaster contractors, co-ordinating and supervising the distribution of defense orders, and reporting on labor difficulties to the Office of the Under Secretary of War.[18] A Contract Examination Branch in the same division reviewed contracts and handled change orders.

Running throughout the procurement process in this period were the policies and procedures established and supervised by the Planning and Control Division. It administered all matters pertaining to priorities, conservation, contract distribution, labor, general procurement policies of higher authority, and all pertinent legal problems. This did not mean that the division scrutinized all steps in a

---

[15] The Motor Transport and the Water Transport Branches of the Transportation Division procured motor vehicles and water transport supplies. OQMG OO 4, 7 Jan 37, sub: Office Orgn.

[16] OQMG OO 32, 22 Jun 40, no sub.

[17] (1) OQMG OO 10, 15 Jan 41, no sub. (2) OQMG OO 25A, 24 Mar 41, no sub.

[18] OQMG OO 25A, 31 Dec 41, sub: Orgn and Functions, Plng & Control Div.

procurement process, nor that papers had to be routed to and cleared by it. Its functions might be "properly likened to the general background of the entire process rather than specific operations in connection with each individual procurement." [19]

Although staff supervision had been strengthened, a commodity-type organization continued to function in the OQMG until March 1942, when the establishment of the SOS led to a move to realign the technical services and their field organizations in a similar functional pattern. In the OQMG a Procurement Service (later Division), headed during the war years by Brig. Gen. (later Maj. Gen.) Clifford L. Corbin, acquired the procurement control functions of the former Planning and Control Division and the procurement directing functions of the old Supply Division. [20]

The concept of placing all procurement activity under the control of one division organized along functional lines, however, was not realized. Clothing, textiles, general supplies, and equipment were purchased by the Procurement Division, but the handling of petroleum products and subsistence items raised problems which could not be solved by a division of purchasing and distribution activities among the functional divisions. As a consequence, these items were purchased throughout the war by branches or divisions organized on a commodity basis. [21] With these exceptions procurement remained organized along functional lines during World War II.

In the fall of 1942 the OQMG turned its attention to improving the procurement organizations of its depots. In accordance with a directive from Headquarters, SOS, early in the following year, it initiated a program for the purpose of installing a standard procurement organization in all Quartermaster procuring depots. [22] This provided for seven branches: buying and production, cost and price analysis, legal, government-furnished materials, inspec-

tion, contract termination, and procurement services. It was anticipated that the reorganization would define executive responsibility, reduce paperwork, improve the planning and scheduling of procurement activity, and clarify the relations of depot legal and fiscal divisions to the new procurement set-up. [23]

These organizational developments, the expansion of Quartermaster procurement, and the changes in procedures emphasized the need for a new kind of personnel in buying operations. The QMC had a nucleus of Regular Army and Reserve officers trained for wartime procurement duties. With the advent of the emergency, outstanding experts in the industrial field were commissioned from civil life to assist in the supervision and direction of the Quartermaster war procurement program. Numerous civilian specialists were added to the staffs of the OQMG and its central procuring depots as procurement specialists, market specialists, and expert consultants. Accustomed to a faster tempo than that found in government organization prior to the war, these new Army buyers contributed to the stepping up of operations in the Corps.

Expansion of Centralized Procurement

Preceding and accompanying efforts to organize the OQMG and the field procuring depots along functional lines were the steps taken by the QMC to strengthen and expand its centralized procurement system to meet emergency

---

[19] Chief of Purch & Contract Br to Chief of Plng & Control Div, OQMG, 5 Jan 42, sub: Steps in Procurement Opns.

[20] OQMG OO 84, 31 Mar 42, sub: Reasgmt of QMC Functions.

[21] See Ch. I, above.

[22] Ltr, Col H. A. Barnes, OQMG, to all QM Fld Installations, 6 Mar 43, sub: Elimination of Organizational Duplications, Overlappings, and Conflicts, 321.5.

[23] Yoshpe and Massen, *Procurement Policies and Procedures,* pp. 53–57.

and war needs. Such developments were especially apparent in the purchase of subsistence and of fuels and lubricants. Confronted by the needs of a rapidly expanding Army in 1940, the OQMG found its decentralized and localized system of purchasing perishables inadequate. In its place was substituted a market center system in the spring of 1941, which combined coordinated and centralized control at Field Headquarters, Chicago, with field operations centralized in a number of market centers.[24]

Similarly, to overcome the interdepot competition and unwholesome effects upon the civilian market of the prewar system of regional-depot procurement of nonperishables from wholesale grocers and distributors, the OQMG centralized procurement and made purchases directly from producers before and during the producing season. Three depots—Chicago, New York (later Jersey City), and San Francisco (later designated California)—were made responsible for the centralized purchase in large lots of most of the nonperishable foods, including dried, dehydrated, and canned foods. Distribution was effected either directly to the posts or through the various distributing depots. The Chicago Depot became the chief procurement agency of the war for nonperishables, procuring approximately 70 subsistence items by the end of 1942. The Jersey City Depot procured about 44 items and the California Depot 23.[25]

The need for centralizing the purchase of petroleum products was apparent early and became acute in the face of growing shortages and the necessity to ration supplies. Under the uncontrolled and un-co-ordinated decentralized procurement system which had prevailed in the Army ever since World War I, all of the supply services, commanding generals of armies on maneuvers, and, after December 1941, practically all of the ports of embarkation were individually directing the purchase of petroleum products in which they were interested. Centralization of purchase evolved slowly. It

was not until June 1943 that procurement control of petroleum products for the Army, excluding those for aircraft, was centralized in the Fuels and Lubricants Division, OQMG, with field operations centralized in a number of specified depots.[26]

Some measure of co-ordination had been achieved in prewar days through interdepartmental procurement of petroleum products by the Treasury and Navy Departments. The bulk of the Army's petroleum requirements for the zone of interior continued to be supplied under Treasury Department contracts during World War II, but control was centralized by channeling such requirements through the Fuels and Lubricants Division. The latter was able to obtain exemption from such contracts for lubricating oils, but was only partially successful in reference to greases and gear lubricants. Direct purchase of these items was made by key procuring depots acting upon the division's instructions. Purchases of petroleum products for maneuvers and overseas shipment were exempt from Treasury Procurement Schedules. The Jersey City Depot handled the bulk of gasoline requirements for the east coast while the Washington Depot procured most of the lubricants and greases required for offshore shipment. On the Pacific coast the bulk of petroleum requirements was handled by the California and Seattle Depots. The purchase of containers and petroleum equipment was accomplished centrally by the Jeffersonville Depot at the direction of the Fuels and Lubricants Division.[27]

A corollary of this policy of extending centralized procurement was the trend toward reducing local purchasing by posts, camps, and stations. The purpose was not only to avoid

---

[24] See Ch. I, above.

[25] OQMG Cir Ltr 399, 30 Oct 42, sub: Procurement, S&D of Nonperishable Subs Supplies.

[26] See Ch. I, above.

[27] For a more detailed discussion see Risch, *Fuels for Global Conflict*, pp. 43–60.

duplication of Army demand in the market but also to control the buying of scarce articles so as to disturb the civilian economy as little as possible. While local purchase of some nonperishable subsistence continued throughout the war, the operation of the market center program virtually eliminated local purchases of fresh foods within the zone of interior. Soon after Pearl Harbor the OQMG also found that general supplies could not be procured satisfactorily on a local basis. By the end of 1942 centralization of procurement of various general supplies had been effected. Thus the purchase of paper and paper products became the responsibility of the Jersey City Depot while requirements for rope and noncotton type cordage were assigned for purchase to the Jeffersonville Depot.[28]

Although the policy of reducing local purchases was followed by the QMC, neither the results achieved by it nor those attained by the other technical services were deemed satisfactory by Headquarters, ASF, which urged a material reduction in the "excessive" number of small orders being placed. The Quartermaster General took steps to centralize procurement of other supplies and gave the regional depots much closer control over local purchases by posts, camps, and stations.[29] By May 1944 the bulk of QMC purchases was being procured by central procuring depots and by the market centers.

In the assignment of items to central procurement depots consideration had to be given to the proximity of depots to sources of supply and the desirability of centralizing the purchase of closely related items within a particular depot. Before the emergency, however, these objectives had not been fully realized. Subsequently, with a view to preventing the overloading of any one depot, the OQMG made some changes in the assignment of items for centralized procurement. For example, since the Chicago Quartermaster Depot already bought

beds and cots, it was logical to transfer mattresses and mattress covers to it, thereby relieving Philadelphia of the burden. Similar action was taken in regard to other items to spread the purchase load.

With the greatly extended purchasing activities of the Corps during the emergency and war periods, the OQMG made changes in the designation of supply points and activated numerous additional depots. Where 8 principal purchasing depots had existed in 1939, after expansion the procurement organization included 17 depots—11 major and 6 minor depots—apart from the network of market centers and field buying offices for perishable subsistence.[30]

Experimentation with Decentralized Procurement Operations

Although centralized procurement was the heart of the QMC supply organization, persistent pressures in the summer of 1942 from higher authority, Congress, and business groups led to an experiment to decentralize procurement operations from the central procuring depots to other sections of the country. Decentralized purchasing would permit a wider distribution of orders, an objective stimulated by the passage of the Small Business Act in June. It was anticipated that a geographic distribution of procurement

---

[28] (1) Ltr, Col F. C. Harding, OQMG, to CO's of all depots, 5 Nov 42, sub: Local Purch of Gen Supplies Items, 400.13. (2) Ltr, Capt D. L. Lawton, OQMG, to CG JQMD, 3 Dec 42, sub: Designation of JQMD for Procurement of Rope and Cordage. (3) Ltr, Col Roy C. Moore, OQMG, to Hq SOS, 7 Dec 42, sub: Centralization of Paper and Paper Products.

[29] (1) Memo, TAG for Chiefs of Tech Svs, 22 Aug 43, sub: Procurement Procedures and Small Orders, 400.12. (2) OQMG Cir Ltr 129, 26 Aug 43, sub: Restricted Purch and Distr. (3) Memo, Gen Corbin, OQMG, for Purchases Div, ASF, 28 Sep 43, sub: Corrective Action in Connection with Small Purchases, 400.13.

[30] (1) See OQMG Cir 1–4, 1 Mar 39, sub: Procurement and Distr of Supplies. (2) WD SB 38–3–QM, 19 Oct 44.

would promote speed and economy in the servicing of contracts by bringing about closer contact with manufacturing sources and WPB field offices, by avoiding long hauls and unnecessary expense in distributing items from plants to storage depots, by facilitating the work of surveying plants, inspecting goods, investigating contract delinquency, and by assisting in the elimination of production bottlenecks.[31]

By way of experiment a portion of Quartermaster requirements for clothing items was allocated to the Seattle and California Depots for their procurement from manufacturers on the Pacific coast. Since in some instances similar items were procured both centrally and regionally, the spheres of operation of the central and regional depots were clearly defined to eliminate any confusion in the soliciting of bids.[32] A branch procurement office representing a number of the central procuring depots was established in New York City to enable the Corps to award more contracts in that distressed area.[33] This trend toward decentralization culminated in the fall of 1942 in the establishment of fifteen procurement districts, the boundaries of each of which corresponded to the distributing area of its depot. Each district was to act as an agent in the negotiation and servicing of contracts. Unlike other supply services which had completely decentralized their purchasing to procurement districts, this effort was a "combination set up," designed to permit centralized buying by commodity, yet at the same time establish a nationwide organization permitting closer contact with the local manufacturing situation throughout the country.[34]

This decentralization of procurement responsibilities was viewed with hostility by the major central procuring depots that felt their traditional contractual prerogatives threatened. The plan did not work smoothly and was not invoked to any appreciable extent despite the belief of the OQMG that its advantages outweighed its disadvantages. The depots remained unco-operative. The problem of contract administration was settled by the creation of a zone inspection system late in 1943,[35] but responsibility for letting of contracts remained largely with the central procuring depots. The opponents of decentralization were favored by the complexities of war procurement. The impact of tight market conditions, material allocations, and labor shortages required a centralized control. As a consequence, the experiment with decentralization ended after about a year in a renewed emphasis upon centralized procurement.

Streamlining Procurement Methods

When World War II began in Europe, the peacetime procurement machinery of the QMC was simply expanded and adjusted to meet the increased load imposed by the events of the emergency period. The basic War Department policies and procedures in procurement, however, were materially though slowly altered during the war. Procurement procedures in the Corps, as in all supply services, were based on the legislation enacted to promote national defense, directives of the superdefense agencies, such as the Advisory Commission to the Council of National Defense and particularly the OPM and its successor, the WPB, and on

---

[31] (1) Ltr, Gen Corbin, OQMG, to Brig Gen W. A. McCain, PQMD, 9 Jun 42, no sub. (2) Ltr, Corbin to CG JQMD, 12 Aug 42, sub: Procurement Policy.

[32] (1) Ltr, Corbin to CG PQMD, 29 May 42, sub: Allocation of Procurements to Seattle General Depot. (2) Ltr, Corbin to CO Seattle General Depot, 29 May 42, sub: Allocation of Certain Items of Clothing. Both in 421.

[33] (1) Ltr, Corbin to CO PQMD, 21 Jul 42, sub: Branch Office in NYC. (2) 1st ind, Col T. W. Jones, PQMD, to TQMG, 29 Jul 42, on same.

[34] (1) OQMG Cir Ltr 409, 14 Nov 42, sub: QM Procurement Districts, and Supplement 1, 3 Dec 42. (2) Memo, Col Barnes, OQMG, for CG SOS, 8 Feb 43, sub: Rpt of Survey on Red Tape in Army Procurement.

[35] See below, Ch. VIII.

the various regulations—procurement circulars, Army Regulations, and Procurement Regulations—issued by the War Department to implement these directives. Specific provisions of the Procurement Regulations, which by the summer of 1942 had superseded all earlier War Department instructions in this field, were interpreted or extended by the OQMG in a "Supplement" intended for use of personnel procuring Quartermaster supplies.

Abandonment of Formal Advertising Method

Although by December 1941 Congress had enacted a variety of laws designed to remove obstacles to the speedy placement and execution of contracts and had in particular freed Army procurement in July 1940 by authorizing the Secretary of War to enter into contracts "with or without advertising," [36] Quartermaster contracting officers, in common with all other contracting officers of the War Department, continued to follow the long-familiar method of soliciting formal bids in the purchase of supplies until after the attack on Pearl Harbor. Then speed in placing contracts and obtaining deliveries became of prime importance, and the chiefs of the supply services were urged to put Army procurement "into the highest gear at once." [37]

During the emergency period, however, there was, in practice, little deviation from the principle of awarding contracts on the basis of formal and informal advertising. Even when Quartermaster contracting officers negotiated a contract, the principle of competition was deemed essential to the government's interest. They were required to solicit quotations from responsible suppliers of the articles in question, and awards were made to the lowest bidder meeting the terms of the invitation. The fact that it was the general practice to invite bids of all known interested manufacturers gave the

procedure close resemblance to formal advertising, the only substantial difference being that informal bids were not opened publicly.[38] Thus, even when contracts were negotiated, the methods used were much the same and consumed the same amount of time as the old formal advertising method. Severe limitations imposed on The Quartermaster General by higher authority and the several superagencies resulted in a natural reluctance to delegate much purchase responsibility to the field. Many interoffice restrictions were imposed to prevent abuse of the novel process of negotiating contracts.[39] In particular the Procurement Control Branch closely supervised the operating divisions and procuring depots to maintain safeguards against any charges of favoritism, collusion, or improper awards in the procurement of items by negotiation.

Nevertheless, even before Pearl Harbor, a widened use of negotiated contracts was stimulated by the efforts to aid small business concerns by a wide dispersion of defense orders. Unlike the period of formal competitive bidding when the small businessman saw slight prospect of competing successfully with large firms, the authorization of procurement without advertising permitted the procurement officer to exercise discretion in the award of contracts and enabled him to place contracts with small plants in order to increase production capacity. More than any other supply service the QMC, because of the commercial character of many of its items, felt the impact of the pressure to spread contracts among small plants and

---

[36] (1) 54 *U. S. Statutes* 712, 2 Jul 40. (2) Memo, Dir of Current Procurement, OASW, for TQMG *et al.,* 2 Jul 40, sub: Procurement Without Advertising, 400.13.

[37] Memo, Robert P. Patterson, USW, for Chiefs of Sup Arms and Svs, 8 Dec 41, no sub.

[38] Col Guy I. Rowe, Chief of Plng & Control Div, to TQMG, 27 May 41, sub: Negotiating Contracts with Best Qualified Manufacturers, 161.

[39] For elaboration of these controls see Yoshpe and Massen, *Procurement Policies and Procedures,* pp. 60–66.

in labor-surplus areas throughout the country.[40] Interest in negotiation was further stimulated by the needs of an expanding Army and lend-lease requirements which increasingly taxed production facilities.

The real stimulus, however, for a more streamlined purchasing system came soon after Pearl Harbor. Under authority of the First War Powers Act, approved 18 December 1941, and the Executive Order of 27 December, vesting broad procurement powers in the Secretary of War, substantially all legal restrictions on Army buying were suspended except those provided in certain labor laws and limitations on profits.[41] The War Department was permitted to negotiate contracts in much the same way that ordinary commercial transactions were handled.

The Under Secretary of War in the meantime advised the chiefs of the supply arms and services that awards of defense contracts entered into without advertising required his approval only when they amounted to $5,000,000 or more. Contract awards and changes required clearance by the OPM when they amounted to $1,000,000 or more. To expedite the war effort the actual work of procurement was to be deputized to the field as far as consistent with efficiency and the public interest.[42]

The WPB promptly swept away the formal advertising method when it replaced the OPM on 16 January 1942. All supply contracts relating to war procurement were to be placed by negotiation, but, "when consistent with the required speed of war procurement," notification of the proposed purchase was to be given to "qualified possible contractors and quotations secured from them." Special factors were to be considered in negotiating contracts. Contracts were to be placed so that difficult production problems were handled by those facilities whose resources were best suited to the task, while items of simple production were to be placed with smaller concerns. Contracts also

were to be negotiated with firms "needing to acquire the least amounts of additional machinery and equipment for performance of the contracts." [43] The use of formal advertising was to be permitted only upon specific authorization of the Director of Purchases, WPB, or such persons as he might designate.

In accordance with the directive of the Under Secretary of War, The Quartermaster General took steps to put the program into effect. He advised field purchasing officers that they could negotiate contracts up to $50,000 by soliciting as many bids as was practicable and making awards to the lowest bidders without reference to higher authority. Unless otherwise directed, the procuring depots could negotiate purchases without regard to the amount by securing bids on the "QMC Form of Request for Informal Bids (Negotiated Contracts)" from all known prospective bidders. No individual award or change in contract amounting to $1,000,000 or more was to be made without submitting the proposal to the OQMG for the approval of higher authority.[44]

When the WPB directive was sent to the field, negotiation of all contracts became a "must." Awards were made after negotiation on the basis of quotations solicited and received from a number of responsible and qualified suppliers by telephone, telegraph, or letter, or in response to request for informal bids. Such factors of sound procedure as speed in procurement, price, plant facilities, compliance with

---

[40] For a detailed discussion of the early contract distribution program, see Harry B. Yoshpe, *The Small Business Man and Quartermaster Contracts, 1940–42* (QMC Historical Studies 2, April 1943), *passim*.

[41] (1) 55 *U. S. Statutes* 838. (2) 9001, 6 *Federal Register* 6787.

[42] (1) OUSW P&C General Directive 81, 17 Dec 41, sub: Decentralization of Procurement. (2) *Ibid.*, 87, 17 Dec 41, sub: Procurement Without Advertising.

[43] WPB Directive 2, 3 Mar 42, no sub.

[44] (1) TQMG to Chief of Sup Div, OQMG, 19 Dec 41, sub: Decentralization of Procurement, 400.13. (2) OQMG Cir Ltr 336, 19 Dec 41, sub: Procurement Without Advertising.

specifications, financial responsibility, and dependability of management continued to be considered by contracting officers.[45] Since clearance of contract awards by the Director of Purchases, WPB, was no longer required, no matter what the amount, the full power of The Quartermaster General to make awards or changes in contracts without regard to higher authority (i. e., up to $5,000,000) was delegated to field procurement offices.

Six months after the United States had entered the war, the responsibility of the Procurement Division and other purchasing divisions in the OQMG had become primarily directive and supervisory. They directed the central depot procurement officers to purchase, and advised on delivery schedules. Essentially their task was to see that the depot procurement officers took timely and suitable action, although there might be instances in which they selected a specific plant and directed a particular award.

Delegation of Broader Responsibility

During the emergency period controls exercised by higher authority and the superdefense agencies had the effect of throttling what little initiative contracting officers might have enjoyed. Desirable as their objectives might have been, these controls seriously delayed the execution of contracts. The Office of the Assistant Secretary of War had to approve all contracts of $500,000 or more and all deviations, however insignificant, from standard contract forms and clauses. Not until after Pearl Harbor were these checks loosened or eliminated. Then broader responsibility was delegated to field installations, such as the right to negotiate contracts of increasing value—eventually up to $5,000,000— without the necessity of obtaining clearance from the OQMG in the case of the Corps. To facilitate procurement the War Department extended the authority of contracting officers in

various ways. Thus, two weeks after Pearl Harbor, the Under Secretary of War authorized the chiefs of the supply arms and services to make "minor deviations" from the language of standard and approved contract forms and clauses. Any "material change" in contract provisions or policies, however, still had to be approved by his office. The chiefs of the supply arms and services were authorized to delegate this power to their contracting officers.[46]

Distinguishing between minor and material changes, however, posed difficulties. Situations were constantly arising in the QMC necessitating deviations from standard contract forms and the drafting of substitute clauses to reflect more precisely the rights and liabilities of the contracting parties. Among the major deviations from standard contract provisions which the OQMG was being called upon to make were escalator clauses providing for price adjustment on the basis of changes in ceiling prices set up by the OPA; a clause protecting the contractor with respect to wage increases "resulting from an increase in zone standard wage rates"; a clause protecting a contractor "in regard to increased labor or material costs due to the forced migration of Japanese labor"; and a contract designating a private corporation as an agent of the United States "for the performance of war work in a foreign country."[47] It was suggested that the government's interest would be better served by permitting deviations "in exceptional cases" subject to the approval of The Quartermaster General.[48]

To meet these and other contingencies arising out of the expanding and increasingly complex

---

[45] (1) OQMG Cir Ltr 114, 17 Mar 42, sub: Procurement Without Advertising. (2) OQMG Cir Ltr 175, 27 Apr 42, sub: Negotiated Purchases.

[46] OUSW, P&C Gen Directive 93, 23 Dec 41, sub: Deviations from Approved Contract Forms or Clauses, 161.

[47] Memo, TQMG for Deputy Dir of Procurement & Distr Div, SOS, 7 Apr 42, no sub, 310.

[48] Memo, TQMG for CG SOS, 9 Mar 42, no sub.

procurement program, Headquarters, SOS, approved for general use by all the supply services many new contract forms and clauses. In addition, it approved the general use by a particular supply service of contract forms devised by it to meet the needs of "a recurrent situation of a special type," provided these complied with the appropriate contract provisions. The supply services were authorized to make such contracts without further approval by higher authority. They could also make other contracts without approval if these embodied applicable contract clauses and contained no provision or policy matter, such as important or doubtful legal issues or decisions involving uniformity among the supply services, which, in the opinion of the supply service, should be passed upon by higher authority.[49]

Effecting amendment of contracts through change orders and supplemental agreements[50] with the least possible delay also contributed to expediting the procurement program. Early in the emergency, however, Quartermaster contracting officers could make changes without prior approval of The Quartermaster General only if they involved $500 or less. Regulations provided for modification of a contract by supplemental agreement only when it was "for the benefit of the United States" or "when a new valuable consideration" passed to the government. Any effort to correct mutual mistakes in contracts by supplemental agreement was dependent upon the presentation to the General Accounting Office of "the most convincing evidence" as to the intent of the contracting parties.[51]

As the procurement program expanded, such restrictions imposed by higher authority had to be relaxed. In the fall of 1941 the Secretary of War designated The Quartermaster General and certain officers of the OQMG as his representatives for the purpose of approving changes in standard supply contracts which did not exceed $100,000. After Pearl Harbor this sum was increased to $5,000,000, and The Quartermaster General was authorized to delegate this authority under such safeguards as he saw fit to impose.[52]

Since The Quartermaster General could not approve personally the large number of change orders and supplemental agreements that it was anticipated would flood his office, he took steps to deputize this responsibility. He authorized certain division chiefs—Supply, Motor Transport, Transportation, Memorial, and Planning and Control—to give approval in cases involving an increase in contract price of no more than $1,000,000. Branch chiefs of these divisions could act on amounts up to $100,000. Subject to instructions from the OQMG, commanding officers of Quartermaster depots and quartermaster supply officers of general depots also were authorized to handle cases involving the same amount of money. Instructions limited the authority to approve change orders and supplemental agreements involving not more than $100,000 to the five main procuring depots, while all other purchasing depots were granted this authority up to $50,000. By April 1942, in line with the policy to decentralize procurement responsibility as much as possible, the full authority of The Quartermaster General to award contracts or execute changes had been

---

[49] WD PR 3 (9–5–42), par. 304.3, and (11–12–42), pars. 306.1 and 306.2.

[50] Change orders and supplemental agreements were instruments by which original contracts could be altered to fit conditions arising after they had been signed. Change orders required only the signature of the contracting officer because the right to make the change was reserved to the government in the original contract. Supplemental agreements were not so authorized and therefore, like an original contract, required acceptance and consent of the contractor.

[51] AR 5–200, pars. 19a, 20d (4), 2 Jan 40, sub: ASW: Procurement of Supplies; Contracts, Formal and Informal.

[52] (1) OUSW P&C Gen Directive 18, 17 Dec 41, sub: Decentralization of Procurement. (2) WD Procurement Cir 91, 29 Dec 41, no sub. (3) OQMG OO 6, 6 Jan 42, sub: Designation of Representatives to Approve Changes in Sup Contracts for SW.

delegated to all the field agencies under his control.[53]

In recognition of the need for speed in the correction of errors which were unavoidable under the extensive wartime procurement program, procurement regulations later granted authority to the chiefs of supply services, under certain circumstances, to correct mistakes by supplemental agreement. The Quartermaster General delegated this authority to the Director, Procurement Division, OQMG.[54]

Removal of Restrictive Controls and Regulations

Various federal and state laws also hampered the freedom of the Corps to purchase items. Chief among the federal laws were those relating to the purchase of foreign-manufactured goods, the mandatory procurement of certain items from the Federal Prison Industries, Inc., and the Committee on Purchases of Blind-Made Products, and the purchase of other items through the Treasury Department. At both the federal and state level various tax and price-fixing laws interfered with effective procurement. Although these legislative controls were not completely removed during the war, certain relaxations did take place.

Under the "Buy American" Act of 1933, the Corps was required to purchase supplies of domestic production only, unless the Secretary of War determined that it was inconsistent with the public interest, or considered the cost unreasonable.[55] The defense program soon caused the Under Secretary of War to issue certificates of determination making the provisions of the act inapplicable during the emergency for the purchase of items from foreign suppliers and essential materials that could not be produced in the United States.[56]

In the interest of hemispheric solidarity special consideration came to be given to articles produced in the western hemisphere. Such purchases, of course, had to be limited to hides, wool, nitrates, manganese, tin, and other items listed in the Under Secretary of War's certificates of determination. When, for example, a Chilean shoe manufacturer wanted an opportunity to bid on Army shoe requirements, the OQMG advised him that it would be contrary to the Buy American Act. Similarly, when an effort was made to allow Argentine corned beef hash to compete with domestic products, the Subsistence Branch was advised that no authority existed for purchasing this item in Argentina or any other foreign country. If the price difference was great enough to justify a request for purchase authority, the essential facts and recommendations were to be furnished to the Under Secretary of War.[57]

After Pearl Harbor, on the recommendation of the Joint War Production Committee of Canada and the United States, such restrictions were eliminated insofar as Canada was concerned. In line with the new policy announced by the Office of the Under Secretary of War, The Quartermaster General advised his procurement officers that purchases of Canadian products were to be on "an equal basis" with

[53] (1) Chief of Plng & Control Div, OQMG, to TQMG, 31 Jan 42, sub: Delegation of Authority to Approve Change Orders and Supplemental Agreements, 161. (2) OQMG OO 29, 3 Feb 42, same sub. (3) OQMG Cir Ltr 175, 27 Apr 42, sub: Negotiated Purchases.

[54] (1) OQMG OO 30–16, 13 Mar 43, sub: Delegation of Authority to Correct Mistakes in Contracts. (2) WD PR 3 (3–26–43), par. 308–B.

[55] 47 *U. S. Statutes* 1520. The law did not apply to items used outside the United States or to articles or the materials for their manufacture which could not be supplied in the United States "in sufficient and reasonably available commercial quantities and of a satisfactory quality."

[56] OUSW Memos, 18 Apr and 24 Jul 41, sub: Determination Under Buy American Act.

[57] (1) Ltr, Lt Col H. B. Hester, Chief of Production Control Br, OQMG, to G. Klammer, Latin American Commercial Office, 19 Mar 41, no sub. (2) Lt Col O. E. Cound, Production Control Br, to Subs Br, Sup Div, OQMG, 3 Nov 41, sub: Purch of Corned Beef Hash.

and subject to the same restrictions as purchases of articles of domestic origin.[58] The Quartermaster General urged, however, that action be taken to permit the purchase of materials produced in the western hemisphere "without regard to the country of origin." By March 1942 the Under Secretary of War issued a certificate of determination freeing war purchases of all supplies, except food and clothing not heretofore specifically exempted, from the restrictions imposed by the Buy American Act.[59]

The necessity of obtaining special clearances—frequently in each individual case—from the Federal Prison Industries, Inc., and the Committee on Purchases of Blind-Made Products before certain of their items could be purchased from commercial sources hampered expeditious procurement. Even when clearances were issued the administrative procedures were time consuming. Each clearance had to be published in a circular letter, and all posts, camps, and stations had to keep their files up-to-date and cite a clearance on every purchase order placed outside the schedules.[60]

While the OQMG held that Executive Order 9001, 27 December 1941, afforded ample legal authority to enter into contracts without regard for limiting legislation, Headquarters, SOS, thought it more expedient to evolve a workable plan that would not cut off these agencies from furnishing such items of their manufacture as the War Department used.[61] Except for the automatic clearance granted for purchases requiring delivery within two weeks, no new arrangements seem to have been worked out with the Committee on Purchases of Blind-Made Products. The Federal Prison Industries, Inc., continued to grant periodic clearances, but blanket clearances were granted for commercial procurement of any articles in cases where cost-plus-a-fixed-fee construction or supply contracts were used; when certain government-furnished materials were used in the execution of lump-sum contracts; when the public

exigency required immediate delivery or performance; or when second-hand or used articles could be procured.[62]

Throughout the war the QMC continued to purchase many items under the General Schedule of Supplies of the Treasury Department. Where limitations on quantities, for example, might compel a contracting officer to procure outside the schedule, each such action had to be justified to insure payment. Obtaining the necessary clearance was too time consuming during an emergency or war period. Under the accelerated purchasing program many instances arose of purchases inadvertently made outside the schedule. A major bottleneck was removed when the Procurement Division of the Treasury Department approved an amendment to the War Department Procurement Regulations authorizing the chief of the supply service concerned to ratify such purchases when it appeared that the oversight represented "an isolated instance and not a continued course of neglect."[63] This ratification greatly expedited payments for

[58] (1) OUSW P&C Gen Directive 94, 27 Dec 41, sub: War Production Policy for Canada and US. (2) OQMG Cir Ltr 127, Supplement 1, 7 Aug 42, sub: Buy American Act.

[59] (1) Memo, TQMG for CG SOS, 9 Mar 42, no sub. (2) Hq SOS Gen Directive 30, 16 Mar 42, sub: Buy American Act. (3) WD PR 5 (9–5–42), par. 503.2.

[60] (1) Memo, Col Cound, OQMG, for Col H. Feldman, SOS, 11 Mar 42, sub: Reqmts of Higher Authority Hindering Procurement, 310. (2) Memo, Col Cound for Gen Corbin, OQMG, 24 Mar 42, sub: Ltr to CG SOS, 9 Mar 42.

[61] (1) Col Cound, Production Control Br, to Chief of Sup Div, OQMG, 22 Jan 42, sub: Clearance from Federal Prison Industries, Inc. (2) Memo, Hq SOS, 14 Apr 42, sub: Expediting the Administration of Procurement.

[62] OQMG Cir Ltr 280, 10 Jul 42, sub: Clearance for Items Manufactured by Federal Prison Industries, Inc. (2) OQMG Cir Ltr 9, 14 Jan 43, sub: Purchases from Federal Prison Industries, Inc.

[63] (1) AGO Memo S5–31–43, 8 Feb 43, sub: Inadvertent Purchases Outside the Gen Schedule of Supplies. (2) WD PR 6 (2–19–43), par. 606.5. (3) OQMG 30–15, 6 Mar 43, sub: Ratification by Dir of Purchases.

such purchases since it eliminated the need for handling them as claims.

Tax laws, both federal and state, as well as a variety of state regulations, hampered effective procurement. The policy of the War Department with respect to federal excise taxes changed materially during the war. Prior to the war it was accepted War Department policy to purchase free of tax. The contractor had the right under the tax law to receive from the contracting activity a certificate of exemption, approved by the Treasury Department, exempting the transaction from the federal tax.[64] This policy was based on the idea of budgetary savings which would result from cutting down the amount the military services would expend from their own appropriations. If the contractor paid the tax he would pass it along to the services in an increased contract price.

The use of tax exemption certificates was continued during the opening years of World War II.[65] It was a cumbersome procedure, however, necessitating records from both contractors and contracting officers. As the volume of war procurement mounted, the desirability of eliminating exemptions was underscored. This elimination would cost the government nothing but would save a considerable amount of paper work and manpower expended in issuing tax exemption certificates. Early in 1943 the War and Navy Departments adopted a new policy on the payment of, and the exemption from, federal excise taxes. The Under Secretary of War and the Under Secretary of the Navy issued a memorandum making this policy effective on 1 March 1943.[66] The policy was limited in that it provided for the elimination of exemptions only with respect to various subsidiary articles or components used in the performance of a prime contract but continued the use of exemptions for final finished products. On 25 February 1944 Congress passed the Revenue Act of 1943 over a presidential veto. It abolished the former exemption on sales to the federal gov-

ernment for everything except radio and radio products and on the purchase of a certain limited number of items which in the opinion of the Secretary of the Treasury could be handled most economically on a tax-exemption basis. Thereafter all purchases were made on a tax-inclusive basis.[67] The passage of this act largely eliminated the work load connected with the administration of the tax clause used in Army contracting.

State and local tax laws were not uniform in their application but as a general rule government purchases were exempt from such taxes. There were, however, various other state regulations which hampered Quartermaster procurement. These included labor laws, particularly those which limited hours of work and regulated female employment; transportation regulations pertaining to maximum truck loads and licensing of trucks; and egg and milk marketing laws, designed to protect trade.[68] Most of these difficulties were resolved by securing waivers through appeal to state boards and by administrative orders.

Milk control legislation fixing prices under a state authority posed a problem not so readily resolved. Some nineteen states had such legislation which, by subjecting the Army to an artificially controlled market, was disadvantageous to its procurement program. The fact that the state laws varied widely and prices were subject to change at any time made impossible the formulation of a central administrative policy on fluid-milk purchases. The Office of the Judge Advocate General, the legal officers of the Na-

---

[64] See, for example, AR 5-100, par. 7, 20 Jul 37, sub: ASW: Procurement of Supplies.

[65] 7 *Federal Register* 579, Treasury Decision 5114, 27 Jan 42.

[66] For this memorandum see PR 8 (2-19-43) par. 809-A.1.

[67] See PR 8 (5-18-44), Appendix, par. 890ff.

[68] Ltrs, Col Cound, Chief of Purch & Contract Br, OQMG, to Stanley F. Teele, Special Asst to Deputy Dir of Procurement & Distr, SOS, 22, 23, 27 Apr 42, sub: State Laws Hampering War Production.

tional Defense Advisory Commission, the Department of Justice, and the OQMG were
agreed that the application of state milk marketing laws to purchases made by the Army was
an unconstitutional interference with the operations of the Army.[69]

Various means short of court action were
used to secure price concessions early in the
war. Nevertheless the problem remained troublesome. It was not until March 1943 that the
Supreme Court, hearing appeals on cases involving the state laws of California and Pennsylvania, rendered its decision. If the land on
which the consuming Army camp was located
belonged to the state, the price regulation was
applicable; otherwise it was not. Congress
might, of course, override these state milk laws
if the national interest required such action.[70]

Developments in Contractual Procedures

During World War I many undesirable situations had developed as a result of the great dis-
similarity in the contractual relations between
the various producers and the government.
These caused delay and created confusion in the
letting and settlement of contracts. In order to
avoid a repetition of that experience, procurement planners sought to evolve standardized
contract forms which would be adaptable to wartime use. Their work resulted in the approval,
shortly after the outbreak of World War II,
of six war contract forms. These were intended
for use in an emergency, but although the country was already in a "limited" emergency and
gradually drifted into a vigorous defense program, no authority for the use of these forms
was granted by the War Department.

The peacetime standard contract forms continued to be used. As experience developed and
purchasing shifted to a negotiated basis, special
contract provisions and new forms were promulgated as additional standard forms. Where
conditions demanded, contracting officers were

also authorized to draw contracts in a form to
meet special circumstances. Such contracts were
to include clauses from approved or standard
forms or clauses that might have been specially
approved by the Under Secretary of War for use
when special circumstances required them. All
such contracts had to be approved by the Under
Secretary of War. Although decentralization of
authority to place contracts was vigorously pursued by the War Department, the Under Secretary of War was reluctant to decentralize authority to the various arms and services to promul-
gate new contract forms or to deviate from
standard contract clauses on their own responsibility.[71]

The first of the standard contract forms perfected for defense supply purchases—War Department Supply Contract Form 1—was adopted
in September 1941.[72] Thereafter during the war
years many other standard forms and clauses
were adopted and amended. By the end of the
war some 22 standard contract forms approved
for general use by the War Department and
some 74 additional contract forms approved for
use by particular technical services and the Air
Forces were listed in the Procurement Regulations.[73]

Special Quartermaster standard contract forms
grew out of practical experience. Some were intended for the purchase of coal and petroleum
and oil supplies. One form was devised for storage contracts and another for a uniform burial
contract. Some contracts were developed in a

---

[69] See, for example, ltr, Col Rowe, Chief of Plng &
Control Div, OQMG, to JAG, 25 Feb 41, sub: State
Milk Marketing Laws, and 1st ind, Col E. C. McNeil,
Actg JAG, to TAG, 28 Mar 41, on same.

[70] (1) *Penn Dairies, Inc., et al., vs. Milk Control Commission of Pennsylvania*, 318 *U.S. Reports* 261. (2)
*Pacific Coast Inc., vs. Department of Agriculture of Cali-
fornia et al., ibid.*, 285.

[71] Rpt, History of Purchases Division, ASF, n. d., p.
312. Mimeographed copy on file at Hist Sec, OQMG.

[72] OQMG Cir Ltr 283, 22 Oct 41, sub: WD & Sup
Contract Form 1.

[73] PR 3 (8-23-45), par. 304.1, and PR 13 (8-23-
45).

short form to expedite procurement by eliminating the tremendous amount of paper work and time involved in the use of existing forms. For example, the procurement of subsistence supplies in the open market emphasized the need for a simple, concise contract. To expediate on-the-spot subsistence procurement the OQMG prepared an informal "Offer and Acceptance," which, with slight amendments, was approved by the Under Secretary of War. Its use was authorized in the procurement of all supplies and services, except coal, whenever the issue of written invitations for bids or quotations was considered impracticable.[74]

The most popular short form of contract was QMC Form 308, a unilateral purchase order that had been used by the Corps before the war. Its provisions on the amount of the transaction and delivery time were liberalized. The form was commonly employed not only by the QMC but also by the Transportation Corps and the Chemical Warfare Service. Initially purchases were restricted to transactions of $5,000 or less, but the limit was increased to $500,000 by May 1943. This form was used provided delivery or performance time did not exceed 180 days. By the fall of the year, because procurement was leveling off, the flexibility needed in the early phases of the war procurement program could give way to standardization, and this form was replaced by a standard purchase order form—War Department Contract Form 18.[75]

Various shortcuts in contracting were also devised to expedite purchases in the expanding procurement program and to speed up production. These included letters of intent or "letter contracts" and letter purchase orders. There was a slight difference between a letter of intent and a letter contract, although both conveyed the "intention" of the government to purchase. The letter of intent was a preliminary agreement which authorized a contractor to undertake preparatory measures and start production for intended purchase at once, with the assurance

of indemnity for costs in the event a formal contract was never consummated. Letter contracts were preliminary contractual agreements customarily used in situations wherein the items, quantities, prices, and delivery dates were known but where the principal contract provisions required additional time consuming negotiations.[76]

Some contractors to whom letters of intent had been issued refused to proceed promptly to production, insisting instead on more attractive unit prices or escalator clauses. To overcome this difficulty a new form, "Letter Purchase Order," was approved by the Under Secretary of War on 10 January 1942. It could be used for the placing of orders in those instances where the need for the supplies was so urgent as to render impractical prior negotiations regarding prices, schedules of deliveries, or other terms, or where such negotiations had failed to result in an agreement.[77]

The OQMG initiated the use of letters of intent in the summer of 1940. On 1 July clothing and equipage stocks were entirely inadequate to meet the requirements of the expanding Army. The Quartermaster General had obligated under contract all available funds for the purpose, and the Munitions Bill had not yet passed Congress. Additional bids had been issued and opened, and he proposed to send out letters of intent to successful bidders informing them that when and if funds became available under the Munitions Bill, the contracting officer would enter into a contract with them at the bid price. Thus production could be started in anticipation of

[74] Memo, Col Cound, OQMG, for USW, 2 Feb 42, sub: Proposed Form of Informal Negotiated Contract, and 1st ind, OUSW to TQMG, 11 Feb 42, on same, 161.
[75] History of Purchases Div, ASF, pp. 320–322.
[76] (1) TICAF, Glossary of Terms in Use at The Industrial College of the Armed Forces, 1946, pp. 18–19. (2) Report of The Secretary of War, 1941 (Washington, 1941), p. 30.
[77] OUSW P&C Gen Directive 5, 13 Jan 42, sub: Form for Ltr Purch Order, 400.138.

the contract, a procedure approved by the Assistant Secretary of War. Since it took approximately nine months to "convert dollars into appreciable quantities of clothing and equipage," troops were supplied during the first nine months of the fiscal year 1941 by initiating procurements on letters of intent prior to the availability of funds.[78] During the emergency period, letters of intent were also used to secure immediate production of certain bottleneck items, such as axles, joints, and transfer cases, "in anticipation of the award of contracts for motor vehicles." [79]

As the character of the war procurement changed, letters of intent ceased to be used. Letter purchase orders continued to be employed for some time, but only when it was essential to give the contractor a binding commitment to permit of preparatory work without delay, or where it was impossible to negotiate a definitive contract because of the experimental nature of the work involved. The Corps used this form particularly in contracts for dehydrated vegetables and for the purchase of frozen foods.[80] By 1944 the use of these instruments of procurement had been discontinued except as authorized by the Director of Procurement in specific exceptional cases.[81]

Elimination of Duplication in Purchase Responsibility

In the course of streamlining procedures, the War Department attacked the problem of coordinating and consolidating procurements of the supply arms and services more vigorously. Interbranch procurement to eliminate interagency competition for similar items had been established in 1918, but the program had made slow progress during the ensuing years of peace. In 1940 and 1941 the impact of the expanding defense program upon the supply of raw materials and the production of finished items emphasized anew the wisdom of consolidating and

co-ordinating the procurement of supplies. This objective was promoted by the work of the Procurement Assignment Board in the Office of the Under Secretary of War (later in the Purchases Division, SOS), which reviewed items and assigned purchase responsibility to the appropriate supply service.

In the summer of 1941 the board was directed to make a comprehensive study of the allocation and procurement of supply items for the entire Army. At the request of the board, the QMC furnished a report suggesting the assignment to it of eighteen items of clothing, textiles, equipment, and general supplies.[82] The OQMG itself undertook a study of the conflicts existing between the Corps and other supply arms, services, and defense agencies. The Quartermaster General was convinced that centralized purchase was imperative for those items for which productive capacity was inadequate. In the face of growing shortages of critical materials and keen competition for them, co-ordination and orderliness of procurement was "almost nonexistent." The consolidation of procurements wherever possible and the co-ordination of procurements in all other cases would, he urged, "result in a steady flow of these essential materials in an amount sufficient to fill our

---

[78] (1) Memo, TQMG for ASW, 29 Aug 40, sub: Ltrs of Intent, and 1st ind, OASW to TQMG, 30 Aug 40, on same, 161. (2) Ltr, TQMG to Julius H. Amberg, Special Asst to SW, 25 Jun 41, sub: Senate Investigation—Progress of Program to Date, 333.9.

[79] Ltr, TQMG to OASW, 31 Oct 40, sub: Weekly Progress Rpt, 319.1.

[80] (1) Lt Col Paul P. Logan, OQMG, to CG CQMD, 18 Feb 42, sub: Contract for Dehydrated Onions. (2) Col Logan to same, 9 Apr 42, sub: Contract for Dehydrated Carrots, 161. (3) Ltr, Lt Col E. H. Foley, Jr., OQMG, to Legal Br, Purchases Div, ASF, 27 May 43, sub: Ltrs of Intent, Ltr Orders, and Termination, 164.

[81] OQMG OO 30–49, 25 Sep 44, sub: Discontinuance of Ltrs of Intent and Ltr Orders.

[82] (1) Memo, Chairman of PAB for TQMG, 8 Aug 41, sub: Asgmt of Items of Sup and Equip. (2) Ltr, TQMG to USW, 26 Aug 41, same sub. Both in 400.12.

needs." [83] Shoes, cotton duck, webbing, textiles, rope, paper (other than technical), hand tools, hardware fittings and findings for equipage, and kitchen appliances were among the items The Quartermaster General recommended for centralized procurement by one agency on requisitions from all using agencies.

Consolidation of procurement progressed slowly. It was in late December 1941 that the Procurement Assignment Board directed that the purchase of all canvas, duck, and webbing for the entire War Department be accomplished by the QMC. [84] In January procurement of paper and paper products was centralized in the Corps. The board recommended co-ordination rather than consolidation for the other items proposed for centralized procurement. By mid-1942 the trend toward consolidation, while not remarkable, was well defined. When the war ended, the number of items for which the Corps had central procurement responsibility for the War Department agencies totaled several thousand. [85]

Of all the items assigned to the QMC, the centralized procurement and distribution of cotton duck and webbing, as carried out by the QMC Duck and Webbing Pool, offered a wartime experiment that was unique in its conception, operation, and control. There had been a duck shortage in every major war in which the United States had been engaged. Recalling the experience of World War I when demand had far outstripped the ability of industry to produce, the QMC had collaborated closely in 1939 and 1940 with various carpet and plush manufacturers who could convert their facilities to duck production. In the light of that experience, too, procurement planners in the Office of the Assistant Secretary of War had long before the declaration of the emergency proposed to assign to the QMC the war procurement of duck and webbing for all supply arms and services of the Army. [86]

While no such action was initiated before the attack on Pearl Harbor, a very heavy load was placed on the duck and webbing industries by the increased Army requirements of the defense program, to which were added those of the British and other foreign purchasing commissions. Until 1942 the various services purchased their articles in a finished state, leaving to their contractors the task of obtaining the necessary duck and webbing. In this competition, Quartermaster contractors experienced considerable difficulty in procuring these materials in sufficient quantities to meet their needs. Moreover, a lack of co-ordination existed not only among the services but also among the operating units in the OQMG.

The pyramiding of priorities for duck and heavyweight webbing in limited supply industries caused all military agencies to experience difficulties in procuring these materials in the fall of 1941. The Quartermaster General, certain that centralized procurement was the only solution, requested the Under Secretary of War to designate the Corps as the central purchasing agency for all canvas used by the War Department. [87] In anticipation of the assignment of this responsibility, he took action to centralize the procurement of duck within the Corps itself and to furnish it to contractors. Conferences were held in the OQMG to develop a workable plan for the centralized purchase of duck and webbing for all arms and services, the responsibility for which was assigned to the Corps two weeks after the attack on Pearl Harbor. [88]

---

[83] Ltr, TQMG to USW, 25 Oct 41, same sub.

[84] Memo, Dir of Purchases & Contracts, OUSW, for TQMG *et al.*, 22 Dec 41, no sub.

[85] See PR 6, Appendix I (6–21–45).

[86] (1) Ltr, Col H. K. Rutherford, Dir of Plng Br, OASW, to TQMG, 21 Jun 39, sub: War Procurement of Duck and Webbing. (2) 1st ind, Maj M. V. Bronson, OQMG, to ASW, 30 Jun 39, on same.

[87] Memo, TQMG for USW, 1 Oct 41, sub: Centralized Purch of Canvas.

[88] Memo, Dir of Purchases & Contracts, OUSW, for TQMG *et al.*, 22 Dec 41, no sub.

A new unit was established as a special group in the Equipage Section of the Supply Division to work on duck, webbing, tentage and equipment items only. Headed by Colonel Robert T. Stevens, who until this time had been an active civilian advisor on textile matters to the OQMG, this unit operated the duck and webbing pool during the war years. It consisted of a compact group of officers and civilians with extensive textile experience who were permitted a far wider area of judgment and discretion in handling the program than was customary in Quartermaster procurement.[89]

As soon as the new responsibility had been assigned to the Corps, it requested the various services to submit estimates of their requirements for duck and webbing. The pool was created from emergency experience, and in the beginning there was confusion concerning the responsibility for the execution of contracts for these items, the allocation of facilities, the transfer of funds, the control of the materials purchased, and the handling of shipments. Careful study, however, evolved procedures that were satisfactory to all concerned.[90]

Duck requirements for all arms and services were consolidated to simplify procurement operations. The pool procured by personal negotiation, which proved to be more effective in securing a favorable price than the invitation to bid system. The pool tapped all known sources of production, with the Jeffersonville Quartermaster Depot controlling contract operations and the dyeing and finishing of duck. Since the pool bought duck chiefly in the grey state, it acted as a converter for most of the known production of grey duck in the country. Yardages of any one type or width were given various colors and finishes, dependent upon the characteristics wanted by the several arms and services. Huge savings to the government resulted, for the pool tied duck production into all of the known duck finishing capacity of the type desired, operating with efficient use of storage and a minimum of backhaul. Originally the pool was intended to provide for Army needs only, but it always maintained close relations with the Navy and the Marine Corps. It often furnished duck to fill their requirements, and in addition its activities were soon expanded to provide for the needs of the War Shipping Board, the Maritime Commission, and war aid requirements.

Competition and shortages of critical materials also emphasized the need for Army-Navy co-ordination. Wartime developments in joint procurement occurred sometimes as the result of practical needs and sometimes through the co-operative inclinations of purchasing officers in the two services. Procurement of subsistence for the War and Navy Departments, for example, was not formally assigned to a central agency, but beginning in mid-1942 the QMC bought many subsistence items, both perishable and nonperishable, for the Navy. The trend toward joint procurement crystallized during 1945 in two formal actions affecting Quartermaster procurement. These developments were stimulated in part by a joint Army-Navy study initiated in the fall of 1944 upon directive of the Under Secretary of War and the Secretary of the Navy to determine to what extent and by what methods procurement in the War and Navy Departments could be further co-ordinated.[91]

[89] Rpt, Col R. T. Stevens and R. A. Butland, 1 Feb 44, sub: The QMC Duck and Webbing Pool, p. 2.

[90] For a comprehensive discussion of the evolution and operation of the duck and webbing pool, see (1) *ibid.* (2) Rpt, Stevens and Butland, 20 Aug 45, sub: Supplement to QMC Duck and Webbing Pool Rpt of 1 Feb 44.

[91] Rpt, Col William H. Draper, Jr., GSC, and Capt Lewis L. Strauss, USNR, Feb 45, sub: Coordination of Procurement between the War and Navy Depts, 3 vols. Hereafter referred to as the Strauss-Draper Rpt. The general conclusion of the report was that a definite need existed for further co-ordination of procurement policies in connection with a large number of functions and of actual procurement activities in connection with large classes of similar matériel procured by various services and bureaus.

Although these developments did not bring about an actual consolidation of procurement for the two military services, they put co-ordination on a definite basis and may be considered as the fruits of the wartime experience of working together.

The establishment of the Quartermaster Purchasing Office in New York City represented an attempt to further co-ordination with the Navy in reference to textiles.[92] During most of the war the QMC centralized procurement of textiles in the Philadelphia Depot, while the Navy negotiated its textile contracts in Washington. The two military departments in March 1945 engaged space for adjoining offices in New York City. When collaborative procurement of clothing and textiles was approved in the summer of 1945, the Navy immediately transferred its procurement activities to New York. The advent of V-J Day delayed the transfer of clothing and textile contracts from Philadelphia until December 1945. Thus the war ended before actual joint activity took place at the Joint Purchasing Office, but some progress had been achieved in the direction of co-ordination and collaboration.

A similar development took place in reference to the procurement of fuels and lubricants. A centrally located Joint Army and Navy Petroleum Purchase Agency was approved by the War and Navy Departments on 11 January 1945.[93] It was June before the petroleum-purchasing units of the QMC, the AAF, and the Navy came to occupy joint office space in Washington. The units, however, continued to report to their respective commands. The recommendation of the Joint Procurement Committee for a unified command charged with staff responsibility for the control of requirements, specifications, purchase, inspection, storage, and distribution of petroleum, petroleum products, and containers for the Army and Navy was not accomplished. It remained a problem for postwar study.[94]

Contract Placement Policies and Problems

In peacetime procurement, price was the determining factor in awarding contracts. Many other considerations, however, had to be taken into account by contracting officers in the placement of contracts during World War II. The burden of military demands on industry compelled the use of every means of production, and a wide dispersion of contracts became a factor of increasing importance. It was the part of wisdom, too, to contract with small manufacturers for the simpler, civilian-type items that were required, reserving the more complicated production problems for plants geared to handle them. The avoidance of areas of congestion and labor shortage had also to be considered in the placement of contracts. Price continued to be a factor but a much more complicated one in its application. Prices had to be controlled to prevent dissipation of government funds, excessive profits to contractors, and inefficient production that would be wasteful of critical facilities, materials, and manpower. Moreover, price control would forestall public criticism. The variety of factors used in selecting contractors fluctuated in importance as the war progressed, but performance on time, in the amount and quality required, always remained the primary consideration of contracting officers.

Smaller War Plants Program

Contracting officers were harassed by seemingly contradictory pressure at every stage of the emergency. On the one hand, they were

---

[92] *Ibid.,* I, 13; III, 36–41.
[93] (1) *Ibid.,* I, 15; III, 42–55. (2) Memo, Sec of Navy and USW for CG ASF *et al.,* 11 Jan 45, sub: Joint Procurement of Fuels and Lubricants, and 1st ind, Lt Gen W. D. Styer, ASF, to TQMG, 12 Jan 45.
[94] For elaboration of joint Army-Navy procurement of petroleum see Erna Risch, *Fuels for Global Conflict,* pp. 12–15.

urged to obtain speedy delivery of high-quality goods, and, on the other, they were confronted with public and congressional pressures for the consideration of such matters as dispersion of orders, relief of industrial distress, and subsidization of marginal producers. The urgency of the demand for supplies, particularly after Pearl Harbor, caused contracting officers to dismiss as sheer politics all such considerations except the ability to perform at the lowest cost to the government. In time, however, it became evident that concentration on a small number of low-cost suppliers might not only prove detrimental to the small business structure of the nation but might impair war production itself. Broadening the production base became imperative if the heavy demands on industry were to be met.

The QMC, more than any other supply service, felt the impact of the pressures to spread contracts among small plants and in labor-surplus areas throughout the country. The commercial nature of the great majority of its items permitted the Corps to make maximum use of existing capacity, to reduce to a minimum requirements for additional facilities and equipment, and to relieve the distress of firms and communities hard hit by material shortages and the curtailment of production for civilian consumption. In anticipation, and later on receipt of directives from higher authority, the QMC sought to achieve a wider dispersion of the load on facilities making its items. For this purpose it split large orders; it invited bids on an f. o. b. factory basis, disregarding the cost of transportation to government destination; and it participated in fairs, exhibitions, industrial conventions, and "Defense Special Trains" in order to uncover useful sources of supply. It encouraged subcontracting wherever feasible, and distributed contracts to firms in "distressed areas" and to small plants and production pools throughout the country under prescribed contract distribution policies and procedures.[95]

During the emergency period the Corps built up an impressive record in aiding distressed plants and communities, but after the attack on Pearl Harbor contracting officers temporarily relegated the program to the background and concentrated a disproportionate share of orders with large firms. Even as the contract distribution machinery was being discarded in the spring of 1942, it became apparent that in an all-out war effort all existing production resources, small as well as large, would have to be utilized to the fullest extent.

The failure of the War Department to check the trend toward concentration of defense business spurred Congress to action and a Smaller War Plant Corporation (SWPC) was created, with a capitalization of $150,000,000. It had extensive powers, including the authority to enter into contracts with any government agency and to arrange for the performance of these contracts by subletting. It was also authorized to lend money, build facilities, purchase equipment, or set up such facilities or equipment as it might deem necessary to provide small plants with production facilities for war or essential civilian purposes.[96]

The passage of the act went more or less unheralded in the QMC and the War Department generally, but by the fall of 1942 Congress had impressed upon General Somervell its determination to see both the spirit and letter of the act carried out.[97] Headquarters, SOS, sought to achieve the desired contract distribution and formally implemented the Small Busi-

---

[95] For elaboration of these developments see Yoshpe, *The Small Business Man and Quartermaster Contracts, 1940–1942*, pp. 2–4, 22–33, 74–82.

[96] 56 *U. S. Statutes* 351.

[97] (1) Address, Maj W. S. Holmes, OQMG, 18 Jun 43, sub: Insp Problems in Connection with Small War Plants, Verbatim Rpt of Insp Conf, 16 Jun 43, PQMD, and 17–19 Jun 43, NYQMPO, pp. 182–84. (2) Testimony of Gen Somervell, 15 Oct 42, Hearings before Special Committee to Study and Survey Problems of American Small Business Enterprises, U. S. Senate, 77th Cong., 1st Sess, Pt. X, pp. 1171ff.

ness Act in October 1942 by issuing policy statements and directives bearing upon relationships with the SWPC. In the course of time these relationships and operational procedures were considerably simplified and decentralized to the field as a result of recommendations made by the OQMG.[98]

The QMC also pursued a number of specific policies which fostered increased participation of small firms in the war effort. It entered into an agreement whereby WPB representatives conferred with the OQMG, previewing procurement plans at the time they were first initiated. This agreement permitted the Small War Plants Division to take the necessary steps which would facilitate the participation of small plants in appropriate Quartermaster procurements. Quartermaster inspectors aided and advised small contractors on management and production problems. Loans were made available to them by the SWPC, and price premiums up to 15 percent were given if necessary to bring their production up to desired levels of efficiency. The OQMG also pursued a policy of the utmost leniency in assessing damages for delays in performance under such contracts. Complicated items, like the field range, on which small manufacturers were unable to bid directly, were broken down and procured as single components and subassemblies. These and numerous other policies of aid were pursued to facilitate Quartermaster contract placement with small plants.

In carrying out the smaller war plants program, the commercial nature of the bulk of QMC procurements, the teamwork, and the zeal of all personnel concerned enabled the Corps to place twice as many awards with small manufacturers as all the rest of the technical services combined. In 1943, 1944, and 1945, 71, 65, and 67 percent, respectively, of all Quartermaster contracts, representing approximately 50 percent of the total value of procurements, went to smaller war plants.[99] The objectives of the

Small Business Act were realized while at the same time the Corps conserved special abilities, kept needed concerns intact, and enabled some of the larger plants that had been consistently efficient and co-operative to continue in operation.

Avoidance of Congested Labor Areas

As the war progressed, the question of the availability of labor became increasingly important in the placement of contracts. The heavy war production loads placed on industry by the QMC and other supply services soon brought congestion and critical labor shortages in many localities. Quartermaster suppliers were seriously handicapped in their efforts to recruit and maintain an adequate labor supply, primarily as a result of the lower wages paid their workers. The greater opportunities offered by shipbuilding, ordnance, and aircraft plants and their more apparent relation to the war effort were responsible for the loss of workers in industries supplying the QMC. While the full impact of these factors was not felt early in the defense period, labor difficulties grew after Pearl Harbor, contributing in an increasing degree to the problem of contract delinquency. Since plant capacity for Quartermaster items was generally abundant and widely dispersed, it was imperative that contracts be sharply curtailed in tight labor market areas as a means of helping to offset this situation.

The withholding of contracts in labor shortage areas would not only assure adequate manpower for performance on these contracts when they were placed elsewhere but also on those remaining in such an area. Contracts could be placed in localities where small war plants were

---

[98] (1) Memo, CG SOS for Chiefs of Sup Svs, 30 Oct 42, sub: Procedure on Relationship with Small War Plants Division, WPB. (2) Yoshpe and Massen, *Procurement Policies and Procedures,* pp. 132–37.

[99] *Ibid.,* p. 141.

badly in need of work and manpower pools were still untapped. Competition for manpower in critical areas would thereby be avoided, and procurement goals would be achieved.

Little attention had been given to these objectives during the emergency, or defense period, despite the suggestions offered by the Office of the Assistant Secretary of War and the Advisory Commission to the Council of National Defense. In the spring of 1942 Headquarters, SOS, took the lead in cautioning the supply services to avoid congested labor markets in the allocation of new contracts. It felt that where other considerations were equal, the relative supply of manpower should "weigh heavily" in the decision as to where contracts should be placed.[100]

The Labor Section in the OQMG urged procurement personnel to place contracts in labor surplus areas, for it found many delinquent contractors located in areas of labor shortages. Procurement personnel, however, saw little cause for alarm at the time, and it was late in the summer before the Director of Procurement called the attention of the depot commanders to the SOS memorandum.[101]

In the meantime, SOS investigation of Quartermaster awards in Seattle clearly indicated the folly of undue concentration of contracts in critical labor areas. Since 1 May Quartermaster depots had placed clothing, equipage, and general supplies contracts of over $4,000,000 with Seattle manufacturers, in the face of serious labor shortages experienced by many war plants with higher wage scales in the area. Delinquency was inevitable. At the same time the Army was under criticism for failure to place more business in the New York area where some 400,000 workers were unemployed. The Quartermaster General was requested to "explore the possibility" of transferring as many current contracts as possible out of the Seattle area to localities where the labor supply situation was less critical.[102] As a consequence,

action was taken to prohibit further awards for the manufacture of Quartermaster supplies in the Seattle area and to provide for the transfer of delinquent contracts.

The policy of avoiding congested labor areas was given official standing in the fall of 1942 by the WPB and the War Manpower Commission. In outlining the various considerations which were to govern the negotiation of war contracts, WPB gave high priority to the avoidance of labor-shortage areas, and the War Manpower Commission was to certify to the war procurement agencies the necessary labor market information for putting this policy into effect.[103] Representatives of all the supply services collaborated in working out procedures whereby due consideration would be given to labor surplus and shortage areas in contract placement. On the Pacific coast and in a number of other areas where unusually critical labor shortages developed, Production Urgency and Manpower Priorities Committees were established, with appropriate Army representation, and particularly stringent contract placement policies were applied.[104]

The OQMG sought to give maximum effectiveness to these policies. It circularized lists of labor-market areas prepared by the War Manpower Commission and provided guidance to field installations on all details of policy. It was not, however, always possible to avoid tight

[100] SOS Memo, 25 Apr 42, sub: Consideration of Labor Sup in Awarding Contracts.

[101] (1) Maj W. E. Downs to Col Cound, OQMG, 22 May 42, sub: Labor Shortages as a Cause of Contract Delinquency. (2) M. C. Bishop to Dir of Procurement, 12 Aug 42, sub: Withdrawal of Contracts from Labor-Shortage Areas. (3) Ltr, Dir of Procurement, OQMG, to CG JQMD, 15 Aug 42, sub: Consideration of Labor Sup in Awarding Contracts.

[102] Memo, Hq SOS for TQMG, 22 Aug 42, sub: Contracts Awarded by QMC in Seattle.

[103] WPB Directive 2, amended, 10 Oct 42, sub: Placing War Contracts by Negotiation, 7 *Federal Register* 8179.

[104] Yoshpe, *Labor Problems in Quartermaster Procurement*, pp. 55–57.

labor areas. Circumstances sometimes justified such awards, as for example, the inability of other manufacturers to meet required delivery schedules or the failure of manufacturers in other areas to bid on requirements after due solicitation. However, the fact that staff jurisdiction in connection with the policing of the labor-area problem was shared by a number of components of the War Department organization made adequate control impossible. Until the end of the war avoidance of labor-shortage areas continued to be an important factor in contract placement, and Quartermaster field installations were cautioned to obtain proper clearance in all cases and exercise great care in the placement of contracts in tight labor areas in accordance with established policies and procedures.[105]

Cost Analysis and Forward Pricing Program

The growth of price policies was a development concomitant with the departure of Quartermaster purchasing policies from the traditional practice of awarding contracts on advertised procurements to the lowest bidder.[106] In the years of peace before 1939 no thorough planning of pricing methods had been undertaken; in fact, such matters had been subordinated in the public mind to the problem of profit control. The QMC, like other procurement agencies, entered World War II poorly equipped for contract cost analysis and negotiation of contracts.

During the period following Pearl Harbor, emphasis in military buying was, of necessity, on production and plant conversion rather than on price. Although early awareness of the price problem existed,[107] not until production became stabilized and cost experience had begun to be accumulated did improved purchasing and pricing methods become practicable. Effective price supervision was dependent on careful cost studies, skillful contract negotiation, and appro-

priate contract provisions. These were basic devices to the achievement of certain Quartermaster objectives, common to all War Department procurement agencies, namely, the maintenance of incentives for efficient low cost and maximum production, the control of inflation, the securing of fair prices on contracts, and the prevention of the dissipation of government funds as well as the accumulation of excessive profits.

The QMC, even more than the other technical services, had to deal with suppliers who could find civilian business attractive and exempt from the regulation of profit margins. With civilian demand greater than industry could satisfy, with profits often very high on civilian sales, and with the necessity of competing in procurement against civilian bidders, the Corps had to steer a careful course in price supervision and contract renegotiation to avoid jeopardizing the critical job of Army purchasing.

Under normal conditions procurements obtained as a result either of competitive bidding or negotiated contracts gave the government a price that was fairly reasonable. During the defense and war periods, however, the market became a seller's market. Under the impact of an expanding procurement program, free competitive market conditions were impaired or became inoperative. Even when formal competitive bidding still prevailed, the OQMG had noted a tendency for prices to "step-ladder" on successive invitations, the highest of several bids receiving an award on one invitation becoming the lowest bid on the next. The need for regular auditing of prices, manufacturing costs, and profits became obvious as the basis for negotiating contracts. To stabilize prices and protect the

---

[105] For elaboration see *ibid.*, pp. 53–58.

[106] For a fuller discussion of price policies see Yoshpe, *Production Control in the Quartermaster Corps*, pp. 60–78.

[107] See, for example, Donald B. Smiley to Col Hester *et al.*, OQMG, 25 Oct 41, sub: Expediting Procurement of Certain Defense Reqmts.

government's interest the Corps at first resorted to the use of a "ceiling price," above which no awards could be made. This price was determined by averaging the high and low bids submitted on earlier procurements of the same article, taking into consideration fluctuations in material and labor costs since the previous awards.[108]

It soon became apparent that where wide variations in cost existed and where all facilities of industry were needed, the use of a ceiling price in buying was an unfeasible method. The fairest approach was to negotiate with contractors on the basis of their individual costs and offer prices which would yield a profit comparable to that which they would realize from commercial operations on a normal basis. Such procedure required the establishment of cost analysis and auditing facilities. In establishing these facilities in the spring of 1942, The Quartermaster General directed the Corps to seek the "voluntary co-operation" of manufacturers in this program, which was to be presented as not only necessary but mutually beneficial.[109]

Cost studies made possible a policy of closer pricing which resulted in fairer prices being paid by the War Department for its purchases. Where careful purchasing and contracting kept prices close to cost, the producer had to exercise careful management and ingenuity to increase production and decrease costs in order to earn a reasonable profit. To achieve this the producer had to eliminate inefficiency and conserve both materials and labor. Forward pricing—the method of utilizing cost analysis studies to establish close prices at the time of making an award or during the life of a contract—promoted efficiency and contributed enormously to producing and expediting the flow of war materials.[110] Unlike the process of renegotiation, which by repricing after the completion of a contract recaptured profits after they had been earned, forward pricing prevented the creation of excessive profits.

In the summer of 1942 such cost studies were undertaken on the production of various Quartermaster items. By the spring of the following year the procuring depots were advised that more accurate pricing could be achieved by using "actual cost figures," and they were directed to obtain a cost "breakdown," explaining and accompanying his bid, from each bidder on each major procurement except subsistence.[111] The Cost Analysis Branch, OQMG, prepared studies establishing "yardstick costs" which were made available to Quartermaster procurement officers.

Within a short time complaints developed that the gathering of cost data irritated contractors, that the new procedure "created obstacles, increased the work, led to confusion and generally was unworkable or would lead to poorer rather than improved results."[112] The shift from the ceiling method of pricing to the use of cost data was so radical a change that Quartermaster procurement and renegotiation officers had to be given considerable instruction in the correct use of the procedure.

In bringing about this change a price administrator was established in the summer of 1943 in the Procurement Division, and under his guidance the organization for cost analysis was expanded and procedures were further developed and improved. Cost and price analysis work was installed in all major procuring depots. All phases of cost analysis, forward pricing on new contracts, liaison with the Office of Price Administration, adjustment of contract prices, statutory renegotiation, and settlements

---

[108] Ltrs, Gen Gregory to Sen Kenneth McKellar, 21 Apr, 5 and 8 May 42, no sub.

[109] TQMG to Gen Corbin, Chief of Procurement Div, OQMG, 12 May 42, no sub.

[110] Rpt, Cost & Price Analysis Br, OQMG, n. d., sub: Pricing Opns in QMC, *passim*.

[111] Ltr, Gen Corbin, OQMG, to CO PQMD, 10 Mar 43, sub: Negotiating Contracts with Each Contractor on Estimated or Known Costs.

[112] Memo, Gen Corbin for CG ASF, 18 Jan 44, sub: Status of Pricing Activities, 161.

on terminated contracts were co-ordinated in the Procurement Division under a deputy director for contract adjustment.[113] Contracting officers and price analysts were given appropriate training, and certain industries, particularly textile suppliers, were made aware of their responsibility in the war effort.[114]

These steps had the effect of strengthening and making more effective the cost analysis work of the Corps. By insuring reasonable prices for Quartermaster requirements, cost analysis and forward-pricing work stimulated economical and efficient management, reduced the need for statutory renegotiation of contracts, and brought substantial savings through voluntary reductions of contract prices.[115]

Improvement of Contract Negotiation Techniques

In the development of purchasing and pricing procedures, the War Department adopted policies and methods which would promote closer pricing and better original negotiation of contracts. At the same time, the policy of closer pricing carried with it the necessity of introducing new contract provisions to minimize the risks contractors incurred from unpredictable contingencies. Among the major types of contracts employed, War Department policy permitted the use of the cost-plus-a-fixed-fee contract only when absolutely necessary. In the QMC, after the transfer of construction work to the Corps of Engineers late in 1941, the use of this type of contract was practically eliminated from procurement operations.[116] Whenever conditions permitted, fixed price contracts were employed to provide financial incentives for economy and efficiency in production.

Lump-sum contracts, however, were not always practicable in their ordinary form. The war created certain types of risks which the contractor could not foresee and against which he could not protect himself. He was deterred from

bidding on long-term contracts because of his inability to estimate with reasonable accuracy the costs which would actually exist during the production under these contracts. In the case of new items, the lack of cost experience prevented the setting of a fair price at the time the contract was negotiated. And even when the item was familiar to the contractor and cost experience did exist, the impact of material shortages and priority and allocation policies, labor turnover, wage increases, changes in price regulations, increased freight rates, changes in the quantities and rates of delivery, the need for overtime and multiple-shift operations, the execution of the War Department policy of more intensified subcontracting, and many other situations might seriously affect costs during performance of the contract. As a consequence there was an increasing demand from prospective suppliers for price adjustment provisions in lump-sum contracts to cover changes in operating expenses.

War Department policy was to reduce or

[113] (1) *Ibid.* (2) OQMG OO 25–44, 31 Jul 43, sub: Asgmt of Responsibilities for Collecting and Using Cost and Price Information. (3) OQMG OO 25–54, 24 Sep 43, sub: Orgn of Procurement Div.

[114] Textile suppliers co-operated with the Corps but were not in the beginning receptive to a close pricing procedure. The number of contractors involved in numerous procurements—in one case the contracting officer had to deal with 400 bids—made application difficult. Habit undoubtedly had much to do with the attitude of the contractors who had long been accustomed to the use of the "ceiling method" of pricing by the Philadelphia Depot in the procurement of textile items.

[115] For example, the Jersey City Depot, on a procurement from one contractor involving 3,400,000 bottles of water purification tablets, accomplished a reduction in price from 7 cents to 6 cents per bottle, effecting a total saving of $34,000. Similarly on six contracts on razor blades the Procurement Division estimated that a saving was achieved of $2,858,327 for the six-month period, July to December 1943. Memo, Gen Corbin, OQMG, for CG ASF, 18 Jan 44, sub: Status of Pricing Activities, 161.

[116] Yoshpe and Massen, *Procurement Policies and Procedures*, pp. 89–90.

eliminate these risks as far as possible and to assume certain of them which were unpredictable and not subject to the control of the contractor.[117] This policy was carried out by the introduction of a number of novel contract provisions, such as escalator clauses, which were designed to protect the contractor against increased costs of production arising out of conditions beyond his control, redetermination or renegotiation articles, which permitted a tentative price to be fixed and later adjusted on the basis of production experience after part performance, and termination articles, which protected the supplier when his contract was reduced or terminated because of changes in the Army Supply Program or the cessation of hostilities.[118]

This policy was also furthered by granting adjustments in price without contract provisions in appropriate cases under the extraordinary powers conferred by the First War Powers Act, which permitted modification of contracts "without consideration" [119] in order to facilitate the prosecution of the war. Although War Department policy in the relief of hardship cases was as liberal as safety would permit, requests had to be based on conviction in the QMC that an upward adjustment in contract prices was essential to the prosecution of the war effort.

The Corps tried to keep the use of this authority to an absolute minimum but instances inevitably arose where relief by this method was necessary to prevent serious hardship and preserve contractors' facilities for war production. Tentage production was illustrative of this problem. The enormous increase in the demands for tentage after Pearl Harbor caused many new sources to be brought into production at unduly low prices. Some suppliers had taken on contracts during the off-peak season, expecting a fair return on the year's business from the profits they would make on the later sale of awnings to civilian buyers.[120] They soon found they could not continue at the existing price level and some were threatened with ruin.

Expediters of the Jeffersonville Depot and the OQMG urged the need for increasing prices and relieving those who had taken contracts at a price that was too close to the actual cost of manufacture. In order to reduce the number of cases requiring relief under authority of the First War Powers Act, the contracts of some tent manufacturers were modified to accelerate production with a corresponding adjustment of the price to a point fair and sufficient to enable them to meet their costs. In other cases, the matter was taken up with Headquarters, SOS, and the OPA, and after due consideration of profit and loss statements, balance sheets, and other pertinent data, a just and mutually satisfactory solution was effected.[121] The fact that such relief would be granted encouraged manufacturers to submit close estimates without excessive allowances in the price to guard against unforeseen risks.

Impact of OPA

The maximum efficiency in war production was dependent on the judicious manipulation of the profit motive. In the supervision of prices

---

[117] Min of Orgn Mtg of Purch Policy Advisory Committee, 11–12 Feb 43, remarks of Col A. J. Browning, pp. 9–12.

[118] Yoshpe, *Production Control in the Quartermaster Corps*, pp. 64–66.

[119] By "consideration" was meant some benefit, such as expedited delivery, accruing to the government in return for a change in the terms of a contract that would be in the interest of a contractor.

[120] Price Adjustment Sec to Textile & Equipage Sec, Procurement Div, OQMG, 29 Aug 42, sub: Adjustment Upward of Tent Contracts.

[121] (1) Dir of Production to Dir of Procurement and Dir of S&D, OQMG, 29 May 42, sub: Expediting Deliveries of Critical Items. (2) Insp Rpt, Lt J. M. Ballentine to TQMG, 3 June 42, sub: Insp of QM Activities at JQMD and Plants Located in Toledo, Ohio. (3) For correspondence and other pertinent documents on some of the firms involved, see files in Mail & Records Br, OQMG, on Foster Mfg. Co., Inc., M. Sloane Co., Inc., and Norfolk Tent & Awning Co.

to limit profits, the government had to choose a method that would prevent excessive profits but at the same time stimulate output. Close initial pricing of contracts upon the basis of cost-estimate analysis was used as one means of preventing excessive profits while providing incentives for efficient production. Profit control through the imposition of price ceilings was another approach to this problem.

The power of the QMC and other War Department procuring agencies to negotiate prices with their prime contractors "remained virtually untouched by the early price schedules" established by the Office of Price Administration and Civilian Supply and its successor, the OPA, created during the emergency period.[122] Upon the assumption that price stabilization was best transmitted from early to late stages of the production-distribution process, a policy of piecemeal control of prices of basic raw materials had been initiated. Since the early price schedules were primarily concerned with raw materials, it was not until the OPA decided on the "big freeze," the General Maximum Price Regulation affecting prices at retail, wholesale, and manufacturing levels, that the Corps became more actively concerned with the supply aspects of price control.

Shortly after Pearl Harbor, Congress enacted the Emergency Price Control Act of 1942 [123] as a means of checking profiteering and other disruptive practices resulting from abnormal market conditions. The law validated all existing price schedules, gave the price administrator express powers to issue maximum price regulations, and rendered purchases made above prescribed levels illegal. General price increases were becoming a grave threat to the efficient production of war materials and to the stability of the national economy. As a consequence on 28 April 1942 the OPA issued a General Maximum Price Regulation as "the cornerstone for a comprehensive program to eliminate the danger of inflation." [124]

This regulation placed a price ceiling on practically all commodities and services sold or rendered by manufacturers, wholesalers, and retailers, if not covered by special individual price ceilings or specifically exempted from price control. Maximum prices prescribed by the regulations were the highest prices charged by each individual seller for each commodity or service during the month of March 1942. In those cases where the seller did not deal in the same or a similar commodity or service during March 1942, the maximum price was to be the highest price charged during that month by the most closely competitive seller of the same class.

The OPA had conferred with Army and Navy representatives in advance of the promulgation of this regulation. It had explained the purposes of the regulation and its intention to exempt most specialized military items but to include Quartermaster and other standard commercial items. Within two weeks, on 13 May 1942, the OPA issued Supplementary Regulation No. 4,[125] which exempted many finished assemblies of combat items, the parts and subassemblies for them regardless of who bought them, and a long list of other items. It did not exempt finished articles purchased by the armed forces which were the same as, or similar to, articles commonly entering into private civilian use. These included finished articles such as standard commercial foods, clothing, and many other Quartermaster items. The philosophy behind this action was that exemptions of commercial or civilian-type items, whether directly or indirectly purchased by the war agencies, would make it difficult to maintain price stabilization of such items in their civilian uses. Such exemptions would tend to cause price competition between military and civilian buy-

---

[122] History of Purchases Div, ASF, p. 196.
[123] 56 *U. S. Statutes* 23, approved 30 Jan 42.
[124] OPA Bull 1, 28 Apr 42, sub: GMPR.
[125] 7 *Federal Register* 3724.

ers and perhaps undue diversion of goods to the military.[126]

The Quartermaster General, as the largest buyer affected by the General Maximum Price Regulation, immediately protested vigorously.[127] He charged that its application would seriously hamper Quartermaster procurement activities. The regulation's definition of "similar commodities or services" was broad enough to include changes in design and specification that did not substantially affect serviceability or the price line in which the commodities would usually have been sold. Necessary price increases would thereby have been precluded from changes ordinarily made in Quartermaster items because of altered military requirements, the demands of the conservation program, or other factors. Operational problems of the Corps under this regulation also arose from the failure to make any provision for price adjustments to cover increased costs of overtime or multiple shift operation frequently needed to expedite deliveries, and the lack of provision for covering many Quartermaster suppliers who had delivered goods in March 1942 at prices negotiated months earlier when costs were lower and who could not be expected to continue to use March delivery prices. It was anticipated too that difficulties would arise in reference to contractors producing new items introduced since the base period, items which could not be priced by reference to base-period prices. Finally, the urgency of war demands did not permit resort to the appeal procedures prescribed by the OPA.

The Quartermaster procurement program quickly felt the effect of the General Maximum Price Regulation. Its impact was somewhat eased by the postponement until 1 July 1942 of the effective date of the regulation with respect to contracts of the War and Navy Departments. Such aid was limited, however, because most deliveries on proposed Quartermaster contracts were to be made after 1 July and many contrac-

tors were unwilling to sell at March prices. The Quartermaster General complained of the paralysis of Quartermaster procurement and of his inability to fulfill his mission because of this regulation.[128]

The bottleneck was broken during this interval by a number of concessions obtained from the OPA. One of the most important was won on 3 June 1942, when the OPA promulgated Maximum Price Regulation No. 157. Effective 1 July, it covered the fabrication and sale of yarns, textiles, and apparel, including in addition to articles made of cloth, leather shoes, other leather goods, fur products, rubber fabrics, and rubber apparel when made to military specifications. It allowed for certain increased labor and material costs not reflected in the prices set by the General Maximum Price Regulation and for certain costs resulting from changed specifications. Changes in delivery requirements necessitating delivery rates different from those at which the same goods were delivered prior to 1 April 1942 were later deemed "a change in specification" within the meaning of this new regulation.[129]

For reasons of military expediency or out of consideration for special circumstances surrounding production on Quartermaster requirements, the OPA made a number of other concessions. Within one week after the promulgation of Maximum Price Regulation No. 157, a number of essential military items procured by the Corps—all of which "were urgently needed to equip task forces" then moving overseas—were completely exempted from the provisions

---

[126] Thomas B. Worsley, *Wartime Economic Stabilization and the Efficiency of Government Procurement* (Washington, 1949), p. 138.

[127] (1) Memo, Col Cound, Deputy Dir of Procurement Sv, OQMG, for CG SOS, 2 May 42, sub: GMPR. (2) Memo, TQMG for Deputy Dir of Procurement & Distr, SOS, 13 May 42, sub: Price Reg.

[128] Memo, TQMG for CG SOS, 23 May 42, sub: Unsatisfactory Current Status of Procurement.

[129] Ltr, David Cobb, Asst General Counsel, OPA, to Gen Corbin, OQMG, 8 Jul 42, no sub.

of the General Maximum Price Regulation.[130] The exemptions were to last throughout 1942, but from time to time at Quartermaster request some were extended for stated periods (90 days), or if production and cost experience warranted they were "lopped off" the exempted list. At about this time the OPA also exempted from the General Maximum Price Regulation many motor transport items, field jackets, and emergency field rations and other subsistence items. At the request of the Director of Procurement the OPA removed the $1,000 limitation from emergency purchases and also exempted sales and deliveries through Army sales stores, commissaries, canteens, and post exchanges from all price regulations.[131]

The legal responsibilities of Quartermaster procurement personnel with respect to OPA price controls were also clarified. Because price regulations and the Emergency Price Control Act contained prohibitions against buying or receiving goods or services above prescribed ceilings, questions arose as to the liability of government contracting and disbursing officers. To expedite procurement the OPA in the summer of 1942 relieved contracting and disbursing officers from liability and from the criminal and civil penalties for paying more than ceiling prices.[132]

By the time OPA price regulations became effective for Army procurement after 1 July 1942, the QMC had won important concessions and gained greater latitude for its procurement officers. Still the bulk of its purchases came under these regulations. If the attitude of the Corps had originally been "belligerent" toward price control as an OPA survey charged,[133] by this date it was co-operating to the fullest extent with the OPA in checking inflation through price control. To obtain rulings on questions of application and administration of regulations and to avoid delays and confusion, the QMC maintained active liaison with the OPA to prevent any delay in contract perform-

ance. Matters of general policy or of concern to other services were handled by Headquarters, ASF, which dealt directly with the OPA in expediting the solution of over-all price control problems.

Statutory Renegotiation of Quartermaster Contracts

Attempts to control excessive profits through price ceilings, negotiation based on cost-estimate analysis, and redetermination of contract prices after cost experience, failed to eliminate them entirely. Consequently, the government also resorted to the use of other devices—excess profits taxes and statutory renegotiation—to recover such profits.

The profiteering scandals in World War I lent force to the determination to eliminate excessive profits in war contracts in World War II. During the early stages of the war, when speed in procurement was emphasized, time could not be taken for extensive negotiations as to terms and prices of contracts. It was more important to get production started. Since many companies were asked to produce items the special construction of which was peculiar to military use and on which experience and data on the costs of production were lacking, cost estimates were necessarily unreliable and proved much too high when production got into full swing.

Insofar as the QMC was concerned, this element of novelty and lack of experience in pro-

---

[130] (1) Ltr, Gen Corbin, OQMG, to Leon Henderson, OPA, 29 May 42, sub: GMPR. (2) Amendment 2 to Supplementary Reg 4 to GMPR, 9 Jun 42. The items exempted included, among others, ski troop equipment, field ranges and spare parts, canteens, canteen cups, meat cans, helmet liners, and field rations C, D, and K.

[131] Yoshpe, *Production Control in QMC*, p. 69.

[132] OPA Supplementary Order 7, effective 11 Jul 42, sub: Removal of Liability.

[133] Worsley, *Wartime Economic Stabilization and the Efficiency of Government Procurement*, p. 146.

duction and purchasing was not so significant. Most of the articles purchased by the Corps had a commercial counterpart commonly produced by the same contractor. Quartermaster procurement had at least the guidance of comparable commercial price levels and prior commercial experience in the awarding of its contracts. According to the chief of the Price Adjustment Section, prices were "in nearly all cases below the level of comparable commercial items." When excessive profits did accrue under Quartermaster contracts, they resulted chiefly from the unprecedented expansion in volume of both the government and civilian business of the contractor. This increase in sales was the "most potent contributing factor to excessive profits in the field of Quartermaster procurement." [134]

Shortly after Pearl Harbor, congressional investigation into the operations of defense brokers and war contractors disclosed exorbitant profits and made restrictive legislation imperative. The result was the passage of Section 403 to the Sixth Supplemental National Defense Act, approved 28 April 1942, and known as the Renegotiation Act. Under this act, as amended in October, the War, Navy, and Treasury Departments and the Maritime Commission were given authority to renegotiate contracts, determine fair profits, refix prices, and recapture excessive profits realized on government war business with these departments. The act was later extended in the spring and summer of 1943 to include the War Shipping Administration and the Reconstruction Finance Corporation. War contracts and subcontracts were to include a provision requiring renegotiation of price at a period when, "in the judgment of the Secretary, profits could be determined with reasonable certainty." [135]

Even before Congress had taken legislative action the War Department had created a Price Adjustment Board in the SOS for the purpose of controlling profits and adjusting prices on contracts. With the passage of the Renegotia-

tion Act, this board was redesignated the War Department Price Adjustment Board and acted as the co-ordinating agency of the War Department in renegotiating contract prices. It laid down the policies to be followed by the chiefs of the supply services who were directed to establish price adjustment and cost analysis sections.[136]

The board determined that renegotiation and pricing should be carried out in a manner to encourage and reward the production of war materials.[137] The War Department recognized that it would be difficult to maintain any incentive for contractors to reduce costs in order to increase their profits if all these additional profits were taken from them by renegotiation. A basic principle of renegotiation was the contractor's right to a reasonable profit.

In deciding on a reasonable profit margin for a contractor, price adjustment officers were expected to give consideration to certain variable factors. Among these were a comparison of the prices charged the government and those charged by the contractor's competitors; the amount of capital he employed and the portion supplied by the government; the extent of the risk he assumed, as evidenced by pricing policy, the difficulty of conversion to war work, and the loss of the contractor's civilian markets; his inventive contribution and technical improvements, particularly in the development of new materials, production methods, and labor and material saving devices and substitutions; and

[134] Memo, Col Moore, OQMG, for WD Price Adjustment Bd, 25 Oct 43, sub: Price Reductions on Future Deliveries, 161.

[135] (1) For a more detailed discussion of the background of this legislation see Yoshpe, *Production Control in QMC*, pp. 71–73. (2) See also Joint Statement by the War, Navy, and Treasury Depts and Maritime Commission, 31 Mar 43, sub: Purpose, Principles, Policies, and Interpretations of the Act.

[136] Yoshpe, *Production Control in QMC*, pp. 73–74.

[137] See Min of Orgn Mtg of Purch Policy Advisory Committee, 11–12 Feb 43, remarks of Col Browning and Maurice Karker, Chairman of WD Price Adjustment Bd, pp. 9–12, 38–44.

his co-operation with competitors. Still another factor to be considered was the contractor's efficiency in reducing costs, maintaining quality of production, and economizing in the use of manpower and materials. It was recognized that the low-cost, efficient producer was entitled to a higher margin of profit both as recognition of his efforts and as an incentive for further and even more satisfactory endeavor. The general policy was to renegotiate with a contractor or subcontractor on an over-all basis, arriving at decisions through a study of profits realized or likely to be realized from his war contracts taken as a whole. When suppliers were engaged in both civilian business and war contracts, as most Quartermaster suppliers were, the Renegotiation Act applied only to the war contract portion of their business.

The War Department desired to effect forward pricing as a part of over-all renegotiation. The OQMG recognized the importance of revising prices downward so as to preclude the future accrual of excessive profits. In view of the closer pricing practiced by the Corps and the impossibility of predicting what a given contractor's volume of business would be, the OQMG found it was impossible in most Quartermaster contracts to provide for future price reductions in renegotiation agreements. It was Quartermaster practice to include a general provision for periodic re-estimates of cost when specific price reductions on individual contracts were not agreed upon. It supplemented the financial data accumulated and the findings determined through renegotiation by unit cost studies. Contracts were then awarded on the basis of a comparison of unit cost figures submitted by the contractor with his bid and yardstick costs, the cost of other contractors, and financial data obtained through renegotiation.[138]

In the summer of 1942, when the planning and conduct of procurement operations were reaching their peak of intensity, the QMC had to establish an organization for the elimination of excessive profits. Over-all control of renegotiation activities in the Corps was vested in a Price Adjustment Section (later Renegotiation Branch) in the Procurement Division.[139] Progress, however, was slow. By July 1943 the work accomplished in all War Department renegotiation units was for the most part preliminary and in the nature of advance planning. Securing qualified personnel and developing procedures made for delay. In conformity with a directive of the Under Secretary of War early in 1943 to speed renegotiation, the QMC expanded its staffs engaged in cost analysis and renegotiation work, and established five district renegotiation offices in New York City, Boston, Chicago, San Francisco, and Greenville, S. C.[140] The OQMG continued to review all settlements before approval and handled the more difficult cases in which efforts in the field had reached an impasse.

Quartermaster renegotiation posed special problems. For one thing, the number of contractors assigned to the Corps for renegotiation proved particularly large. The job of renegotiation was especially difficult because the Corps had to deal with many comparatively small contractors, who were often marginal producers, had no cost accounting units, and lacked reliable figures on production costs. Unlike contractors of other services, Quartermaster suppliers generally took war orders while continuing civilian business in substantial volume. Renegotiation in the Corps therefore had to be prosecuted with caution, lest contractors aban-

[138] (1) Memo, Col Moore, OQMG, for WD Price Adjustment Bd, 25 Oct 43, sub: Price Reductions on Future Deliveries. (2) Memo, Dir of Renegotiation Div, ASF, for QM Price Adjustment Sec, 3 Nov 43, no sub. Both in 161.

[139] Procurement Div, OQMG, OO 24, 12 Aug 42, sub: Reasgmt of Functions of Procurement Div.

[140] (1) Ltr, USW to TQMG, 9 Feb 43, sub: Pers and Volume of Renegotiations. (2) Ltr, TQMG to USW, 1 Mar 43, same sub. (3) OQMG OO 25-30, 6 Mar 43, sub: Establishment of Br Offices. (4) OQMG OO 25-30C, 20 Aug 43, same sub.

don their work in favor of their civilian contracts, which provided a less restricted and more lucrative field. Despite these difficulties the Quartermaster renegotiation program showed progress, the refunds at the end of the calendar year 1943 amounting to more than $75,000,000.[141]

This renegotiation had been accomplished with a staff smaller in proportion to the work load of assignments than that in any other major renegotiating agency of the War Department. It was also achieved in the face of considerable agitation for the revision of the Renegotiation Act. During the summer and fall of 1943 Congress was considering various amendments which threatened to emasculate the Renegotiation Act. As a consequence, contractors were reluctant to furnish data or make agreements, either oral or written, since they hoped that changes in the law would enhance their rights or possibly would exempt them altogether.[142]

Most of the proposed amendments met with strong opposition from the QMC and other renegotiating agencies.[143] As a result, some of the most objectionable proposals were omitted from the Revenue Act of 1943, which extended the renegotiation provisions to 31 December 1944 and permitted an additional six months' extension by the President. Congress later extended these provisions to 31 December 1945.[144] The substantial changes that were made in the renegotiation statute resulted in a great unsettling of its basic procedures and imposed many new burdens on the QMC.

One of the most troublesome problems created by the amended act involved the application of a retroactive provision with regard to inventory profits. It exempted from renegotiation the profits in certain industries which could be attributed to the appreciation in value of that part of the inventory in excess of the requirements for fulfilling existing contracts. Since the majority of the companies affected by

this provision—primarily cotton textile mills—were assigned for renegotiation to the QMC, this provision of the law fell with particular severity on Quartermaster renegotiation personnel. Because the provision was retroactive and contractors could file a claim within ninety days of the enactment of the Revenue Act of 1943, many cases had to be reopened for the calculation and refunding of these inventory profits.[145]

Similarly, the inclusion in the act of a provision for "agricultural exemption" burdened Quartermaster renegotiations since most of the food processing companies were assigned to the Corps. A number of other statutory and administrative provisions further complicated Quartermaster renegotiation efforts and served to prolong the renegotiation process. These difficulties more than offset the benefit gained by the decrease in the work load which resulted from exempting from renegotiation those contractors whose volume of government sales in a fiscal year amounted to less than $500,000 in lieu of the previous limit of $100,000.

One of the most interesting of the problems faced by Quartermaster renegotiation personnel involved the application of the act to textile selling agents. Over the past fifty years, selling agents had acquired increasing importance in the textile industry. Their functions had

[141] Memo, Col Moore, OQMG, for Dir of Renegotiation Div, ASF, 5 Jan 44, sub: Recoveries on Renegotiation and Through Forward Pricing to 31 Dec 43 inclusive, 161.

[142] (1) Memo, Col Moore for WD Price Adjustment Bd, 14 Oct 43, sub: Effect of Pending Legislation on Current Renegotiation, 161.

[143] (1) Memo, Col Moore for WD Price Adjustment Board, 30 Nov 43, sub: Exemption Proposed for Canners. (2) Memo, Hq ASF for Price Adjustment Sec, OQMG, 7 Dec 43, sub: Hearings—Senate Finance Committee on Renegotiations, inclosing statement of Chairman of WD Price Adjustment Bd, 161.

[144] (1) 58 *U. S. Statutes* 21ff., approved 25 Feb 44. (2) 59 *U. S. Statutes* 294–95, approved 30 Jun 45.

[145] Rpt, Statutory Renegotiation in QMC, incl in ltr, Lt Col R. G. Haines, Sup Div, OQMG, to Chairman of War Contracts Price Adjustment Bd, OASA, 10 Jun 49, sub: Completion of Renegotiation, p. 11.

expanded from that of merchandising cottons and woolens to the point where the largest of the agents exercised fairly complete supervision and financial control of many of the mills they represented. Although many of their peacetime functions were unnecessary during the war years, some of these agents aided government officials in developing new fabrics, worked closely with procurement officers on specifications, and were particularly useful in accepting large contracts and distributing production to affiliated mills best able to manufacture the required item. This pooling of production to meet a large government need spared procurement officers the difficult task of having to make arrangements with numerous mills at a critical time.

Textile selling agents were paid commissions which had to be subjected to renegotiation, but the normal technique of renegotiation was not applicable to them. It was not excessive profits that had to be renegotiated but excessive commissions received above rates agreed upon by representatives of the QMC and the Association of Cotton Textile Merchants of New York. The Corps in consultation with the War Contracts Price Adjustment Board and the War Department Price Adjustment Board evolved the "gross commission basis" of renegotiation. This meant that renegotiation was conducted on the basis of the gross commissions received from the mills which the selling agents represented.[146]

Despite the complications of the amended Renegotiation Act, the Corps made considerable progress in the cases it handled during the 1944 fiscal year. As the year ended, it was evident that a sound pricing program had been developed in the Corps, and it was believed that "when the back stop of renegotiation has been removed by law," Quartermaster contracts would be let at a price that would "preclude the accumulation of undue profits."[147]

Between 28 April 1942, when the Renegotia-

tion Act was approved, and 31 December 1945, when the provisions of the law expired, some 75,000 cases were assigned to the Army for renegotiation. The QMC's share in this renegotiation was impressive, since it handled 18,000 cases and fulfilled its mission with fewer personnel compared with total assignments than any other service. Its gross recoveries totaled approximately $390,000,000, equivalent to $112,000,000 net after tax credit. This was accomplished at a cost of about three cents per net dollar recovered.[148]

Special Procurement Responsibilities

Lend-Lease

During World War II the QMC was also assigned two special procurement responsibilities—the purchase of certain Quartermaster items for lend-lease use and for supplying civilians in occupied areas. When the Lend-Lease Act was approved on 11 March 1941, the Corps became responsible for administering the lend-lease aid of Quartermaster items. The QMC furnished beneficiary nations with thousands of types of items, but the main class of goods supplied during the war consisted of clothing and textiles. Before the transfer of motor transport activities to the Ordnance Department, however, trucks and other motor transport equipment constituted the chief items which the Corps purchased and distributed under lend-lease arrangements.

Approval of the Lend-Lease Act made it necessary for each supply service in the War Department to provide administrative means

---

[146] *Ibid.*, pp. 13–17.

[147] Memo, Chief of Procurement Div, OQMG, for CG ASF, 16 May 44, sub: Progress Rpt on Status of Pricing Activities, OQMG, 161.

[148] Rpt, Statutory Renegotiation in QMC, incl in ltr, Col Haines, Sup Div, OQMG, to Chairman of War Contracts Price Adjustment Bd, OASA, 10 Jun 49, sub: Completion of Renegotiation, p. 20.

for handling this new activity. During most of 1941 Quartermaster organization for this purpose was in a developmental stage. Before Pearl Harbor, however, the branch, originally established in the Planning and Control Division to maintain liaison with other government agencies and foreign governments and to administer lend-lease operations in the Corps, had become a division—the Defense Aid (later International) Division—a status it retained during the war years.[149]

In the complicated, formal process of channeling and screening requisitions for aid, the Defense Aid Division, OQMG, played a relatively small part. On an informal basis, however, it was important in facilitating the handling of requistions. It was the practice of the OQMG to gain information through informal meetings with representatives of the foreign nations desiring aid. They were permitted direct contact with the division or branch charged with an item's procurement in order to clarify any questions in reference to the item. Such meetings not only afforded opportunity to thrash out questions of specifications, availability, use of substitutes, and effect on the supply program but also provided the initial opportunity to evaluate and screen foreign requests for aid. As a consequence, when requisitions were actually filed, many potential obstacles to their approval had been cleared away.[150]

Quartermaster personnel participating in these informal discussions came to be regarded as a subcommittee of the Defense Aid Supply Committee established in the War Department, to which the OQMG sent a representative. This concept of the subcommittee was formalized in October 1942 when subcommittees in each of the supply services were directed to screen requests on behalf of the International Division, SOS. The Quartermaster subcommittee consulted the operating units of the OQMG in each instance for advice on the desirability of approving specific requisitions, which were

passed on to higher authority by the defense aid unit.[151]

No procurement procedures peculiar to lend-lease operations were evolved; instead, regular Army facilities and procurement procedures were used. In order to simplify procurement, it was War Department practice from the beginning to confine requests for matériel, wherever possible, to common rather than noncommon items.[152] In the QMC, however, noncommon items, such as bulk leather, Russian shoes, and overcoating for Russia, and suiting, cotton textiles, and battle dress uniforms for the United Kingdom, frequently comprised the larger part of international aid.[153] Even during the first year of lend-lease the War Department also took steps to co-ordinate specifications of foreign governments with those of the Regular Army so that transfers might be made by diverting Regular Army contracts in lieu of placing special orders.

Ordnance matériel naturally comprised the bulk of lend-lease aid. Quartermaster items, however, ranked second in importance among the supplies. In the four and a half years of lend-lease operations the Corps shipped 867 million dollars' worth of supplies to foreign governments. This figure does not include

---

[149] (1) OQMG OO 74, 11 Apr 41, no sub. (2) OQMG OO 245, 30 Oct 41, no sub.

[150] Memo, Col Hester, Chief of Procurement Control Br, OQMG, for Col H. S. Aurand, Defense Aid Director, 10 Oct 41, sub: Defense Aid Sup Committee, 334.8.

[151] For examples see (1) [1st ind] Maj Nathan Thumin, OQMG, to Defense Aid Div, OUSW, 16 Oct 41, sub: Truck Contract with Amtorg Trading Corp. (2) Ltr, Col E. Santschi, Jr., Dir of Defense Aid Div, OQMG, to Dir of Defense Aid Supply Committee, 8 Nov 41, sub: Motor Transportation Reqmts of Great Britain. Both in 451.

[152] A common item was an item required and used by the Army of the United States and by one or more of the other United Nations. A noncommon item was any other item authorized for shipment to one of the United Nations.

[153] Rpts, Statistics Br, OP&C Div, OQMG, n. d., sub: Statistical Rpts to TQMG, 1945, p. 177.

Quartermaster supplies transferred within the theaters. Clothing and textiles constituted 73 percent, equipage 15 percent, and other items 12 percent of these supplies. Russia received 49 percent of all shipments of Quartermaster items while the British Empire received 34 percent.[154]

Reverse lend-lease, a method of reciprocal aid under which American armed forces received goods and services from allied nations, was inaugurated early in 1942. It consisted largely of subsistence, and fuels and lubricants, although clothing and textiles and various equipment items as well as services and labor were furnished. Such reverse lend-lease meant an equivalent reduction of Quartermaster procurement from production in the United States.

Civilian Supply

The Joint Chiefs of Staff formalized an accepted principle of international law on 19 April 1943 when they declared that "civilian supply is a military problem during the period of military occupation." To handle the problem the Secretary of War established a Civil Affairs Division in the Special Staff. During the early years of the war, however, considerable uncertainty existed as to whether the military or a civilian agency should furnish this relief aid during the period of military occupation.[155] It was November 1943 before responsibility for supplying relief to liberated areas was officially thrown upon the War Department.[156]

Because of the nature of the commodities involved—food, sanitary supplies, clothing, and fuels and lubricants—the QMC inherited the main burden of this supply responsibility. Each of the technical services, however, prepared and recommended civilian supply requirements for each area in which operations were contemplated. These were based upon studies of the national economies involved and upon the operational assumptions furnished by higher authority. The latter established the policies and most of the procedures for supplying civilians in occupied areas as it did in the case of lend-lease procurement.[157] The technical services submitted their recommended requirements for approval to the International Division, ASF. When these applied to a theater of combined civilian supply responsibility, the division discussed the requirements with the British Army Staff, as well as with the theater, prior to their formal approval by the Combined Civil Affairs Committee. As apportioned by combined boards to the United States for supply action and as allocated by United States supply authorities to the Army, these requirements were set up as approved programs against which the theater commander could submit requisitions.

To carry out his additional supply mission, The Quartermaster General established a Civilian Supply Section in the Requirements Branch of the Military Planning Division.[158] Except for fuels and lubricants, this section not only originally computed for planning purposes the potential requirements of civilian populations and supplied advance estimates of required shipping space and tonnage but, as operations developed, it reviewed and analyzed requirements submitted by theater commanders. Fur-

---

[154] *Ibid.,* p. 182. Figures corrected in accord with data compiled by Program Review and Analysis Div, Office Comptroller of the Army, for inclusion in forthcoming statistical volumes for this series.

[155] Civilian supply in North Africa was originally charged to the State Department, which carried out its assignment through the Office of Foreign Relief and Rehabilitation Operations, established on 21 November 1942. Experience demonstrated that civilian agencies were powerless to act without military support.

[156] Ltr, Pres Franklin D. Roosevelt to SW, 10 Nov 43, no sub, incl C, p. 17, International Div, ASF, Civ Supplies Opn Handbook, n. d.

[157] See hist rpt, International Div, ASF, n. d., sub: Civ Sup: A History of the Civ Sup Br, International Div, ASF, on file in OCMH.

[158] (1) OQMG OO 25–56A, 2 Nov 43, sub: Establishment of Civ Sup Sec. (2) OQMG OO 25–56B, 20 Dec 43, same sub.

thermore, when the various freed governments made plans to supplement military aid after liberation was accomplished, it also analyzed such plans and examined their effect on requirements.

Other branches and divisions of the OQMG shared in carrying out the civilian supply responsibility of the Corps. The various divisions having procurement responsibility—Fuels and Lubricants, Subsistence, Procurement—purchased their respective items. The Fuels and Lubricants Division also computed and recommended requirements for its items, while the Subsistence Division, besides planning and preparing the basic rations for civilian feeding, processed requests to allocating agencies to meet the food requirements. The Storage and Distribution Division carried out its usual functions and, among other duties, arranged for reconditioning of existing stocks for filling civilian supply requisitions, provided for utilization of excess stocks, and established stock piles. Except on technical matters and where such responsibility was delegated to other divisions and branches, the Operations Branch of the Military Planning Division co-ordinated all civilian supply activities within the OQMG and maintained liaison with the International Division, ASF, and other government agencies.[159]

The first Army Supply Program for purely civilian supply requirements was prepared in July 1943 at the request of the ASF. From July 1943 to the end of the war the United States shipped about 6,310,000 long tons to the European and Mediterranean theaters, where it had combined responsibility with the United Kingdom and Canada for civilian supply, and to the Pacific, where, prior to August 1945, the Army had unilateral civilian supply responsibility for the Philippines and a small part of the Netherlands East Indies.[160] These supplies were valued at about $878,000,000. Foodstuffs and coal procured by the QMC made up 65 percent

and 33 percent, respectively, of the total tonnage shipped. In dollar value these two items accounted for 88 percent and 3 percent, respectively. Figures for petroleum products are not available because these items were shipped as military supplies and issued to civilians from pooled United States-United Kingdom stocks in the theaters.

Food shipments consisted chiefly of canned meats, wheat flour and grain, dehydrated soups, dried and evaporated milk, and dried beans and peas. The Corps shipped a wide variety of clothing items and shoes in the closing years of the war. These goods were supplemented with cotton piece goods, canvas and paulins, wool knitting yarn, and baled cotton. Initially these items were procured and shipped by the Foreign Economic Administration. By the spring of 1944, however, the Corps had assumed responsibility for storage and issue and by July 1945 was also procuring clothing, textiles, and shoes.[161] The principal classes of general supplies furnished by the QMC were soap, insecticides, paper products and ink, agricultural supplies and equipment, and light construction materials.

Most of the civilian supplies were shipped by the Corps, with shipments reaching their peak in the second quarter of 1945. After V-J Day a rapid decline occurred in this activity because Army responsibility in liberated areas was turned over to liberated governments which continued to obtain needed supplies through civilian agencies. Military responsibility for civilian supply in the theaters, of course, continued long after V-J Day.

[159] OQMG OO 25–103, 5 Dec 44, sub: Civ Supplies—Asgmt of Responsibilities and Functions.

[160] See Statistical Analysis of Quartermaster Supply in C. L. Kieffer and Erna Risch, Quartermaster Corps: Organization, Supply, and Services, Vol. II.

[161] (1) OQMG OO 25–79, 16 May 44, sub: Sup Matters—Civ Sup. (2) Memo, Gen Doriot, OQMG, for CG ASF, 31 May 45, sub: Procurement Responsibility for Clo, Shoes, etc.

CHAPTER VIII

Production Control

The need for prompt delivery of defense supplies was recognized from the very beginning of the emergency. To speed the purchase of Army supplies, procurement procedures were streamlined by various means. But greater facility in placing contracts had also to be preceded and accompanied by measures designed to expedite production.[1] By the spring of 1941 speeding up the production program was deemed "vital to our national existence." All agencies of the War Department were called upon to intensify the control and expedition of production, to strengthen their organization for this purpose, and to make every effort to equip American troops and those of the foreign democracies "at the earliest date which is humanly possible." [2]

The accumulation of complete up-to-date information on the status of contracts, particularly on the plants and items of procurement which were delinquent, was a procedure immediately useful in expediting production. It permitted remedial measures to be taken for shortening the period of delinquency and insuring satisfactory performance on subsequent orders.[3] While contract delinquency was no new problem in Quartermaster procurement operations, its elimination became of paramount importance in the emergency period.

Organization for Production Control

Under the National Defense Act of 1920 responsibility for the supervision of the procurement of all military supplies rested with the Assistant Secretary of War. A vital factor in this obligation was the supervision of production control, responsibility for which was charged to a Production Branch. Its activities were concerned primarily with insuring proper co-ordination and compliance with the laws pertaining to procurement and with expediting production when this was not accomplished by the lower echelons.[4] The actual letting of contracts and the day-to-day follow-up of production, however, was the primary responsibility of the supply arms and services.

In this production control program, the Office of Production Management also played an important role, for it formulated and executed measures to accelerate production, developed new or expanded facilities, sources, and methods, and insured effective co-ordination of the activities of the various governmental agencies. Close co-operation was maintained with the OPM, but this did not relieve the War Depart-

---

[1] The following discussion is largely based on the more detailed study prepared by H. B. Yoshpe, *Production Control in the Quartermaster Corps, 1939–1944* (QMC Historical Studies 8, December 1944). Hereafter cited as *Production Control in QMC.*

[2] Memo, USW for Chiefs of Sup Arms and Svs, 25 Apr 41, sub: Expediting Production.

[3] F. X. Reynolds, Chief of Production Expediting Sec, to Lt Col H. B. Hester, Chief of Procurement Control Br, Plng & Control Div, OQMG, 14 Jul 41, sub: Orgn of Production Expediting Sec.

[4] For a detailed discussion of the overhead organization for production control see H. B. Yoshpe, *Organization for Production Control in World War II* (AIC Research Project 28, February 1946), pp. 9ff.

ment of its "primary responsibility" for control and follow-up of production for which it had contracted.[5]

Within the OQMG the various operating divisions had long been responsible for following up and expediting the production of items called for under procurement directives issued by them. The actual burden of production control, however, fell on the procuring depots, which reported to the OQMG items that were not meeting schedules, and all labor difficulties. Where manufacturers were having trouble securing either raw materials or fabricated parts, the depots or the Procurement Control Branch, OQMG, granted preference ratings or sought remedial action at the Army and Navy Munitions Board or the Priorities Division of the OPM.[6]

Although the Corps always recognized the importance of production follow-up, the quality of production organizations in the depots varied. While not alarming, the increase in contract delinquency during the emergency period emphasized the necessity for expanding and strengthening the production control organizations in the field. A directive from the Under Secretary of War in the spring of 1941 served to focus attention on this problem with the result that the OQMG established a Production Expediting Section in the Procurement Control Branch.[7] It served as a clearing house for production problems affecting Quartermaster requirements and rendered production engineering assistance when necessary to maintain production balance. A number of industrial specialists were brought into the section to serve as expert technical advisers on production and management problems. It was their job to collaborate with headquarters and the field units in studying production problems in order to eliminate obstacles to production; to maintain contacts with contractors and their suppliers to determine reasons for delays; and to make continuous surveys of manufacturing plants and production methods in order to improve plant layout and equipment, to increase industrial capacity, and to solve problems of labor and raw materials supply.

From the summer of 1941 until the spring of the following year the Production Expediting Section pursued a program that resulted in reducing delinquency in production among Quartermaster suppliers and insuring smooth procurement. Thereafter it became little more than a record-keeping agency and ultimately lost its identity by absorption in a new section.[8] The initiation and execution of measures designed to promote production control, however, were not confined exclusively to the Production Expediting Section. Because of the variety of the corrective measures taken by the OQMG, this responsibility was diffused through many of its organizational units. A separate Labor Section, for example, directed and executed labor policies affecting the Quartermaster procurement program. A Priorities Section administered priorities policies, instructed and supervised field personnel in all priorities matters, audited preference ratings issued by procuring depots to insure compliance with rules and regulations, and dealt with higher authority in clarifying policy intentions and breaking priorities bottlenecks. The vitality of these and other administrative units grew increasingly as the war progressed.

The gradual disintegration of the Production Expediting Section, however, began in March

---

[5] Memo, USW for Chiefs of Sup Arms and Svs, 25 Apr 41, sub: Expediting Production.

[6] Plng & Control Div to TQMG, 24 May 41, sub: Expediting Production.

[7] (1) Memo, Robert P. Patterson, USW, to Chiefs of Sup Arms and Svs, 25 Apr 41, sub: Expediting Production. (2) Col G. I. Rowe, Plng & Control Div, OQMG, to TQMG, 24 May 41, same sub. (3) TQMG to Chief of Plng & Control Div, 4 Jun 41, same sub. (4) OQMG OO 25A, 15 Oct 41, sub: Orgn and Functions, Plng & Control Div.

[8] For elaboration of its history see Yoshpe, *Production Control in QMC*, pp. 13ff.

1942 when the OQMG was reorganized along functional lines. At that time separate organizations were established for procurement and production control. Procurement administration became centered in the Procurement Service (later Division) which acquired the procurement control functions, including expediting, of the Planning and Control Division. The Production Service, on the other hand, became responsible, among other functions, for planning and scheduling production, accelerating general production scheduling, developing production programs in collaboration with the Procurement Service, and furnishing the latter advisory service on production problems.

The March order reorganizing the OQMG, drafted in haste, permitted considerable ambiguity in the responsibilities assigned to these two services, particularly in respect to expediting. Personnel of each service often carried on expediting work independently, making for utter confusion and duplication of effort, a situation that was not improved until late in the summer of 1942 when it was agreed that the Military Planning Division—which absorbed functions of the Production Service—would engage in expediting activities only at the request of the Procurement Division. By that time a reassignment of functions had abolished the Production Service and made the Procurement Division responsible for laying out production programs to meet directed procurements and for technical control and co-ordination of field purchasing and production.[9]

Causes of Contract Delinquency

The underlying causes· of contract delinquency during World War II were complex in character and scope. Among the more serious bottlenecks to the maintenance of production at a level sufficient to meet scheduled deliveries were material shortages and priority difficulties.

The Corps had ample production capacity upon which to draw but it could only meet requirements if supplied with enough raw materials, component parts, and machine tools. Under emergency and war conditions, however, demand far exceeded supply. Critical shortages developed, resulting in slow, spasmodic production.[10] The lack of a regular and known flow of materials to war contractors made it impossible for them to meet production schedules.

Labor problems were also frequently an underlying cause of contract delinquency. The QMC relied for the bulk of its requirements on low-wage industries, but the migration of textile workers, miners, and agricultural, canning, and food processing workers to higher-wage munitions, aircraft, and shipbuilding industries often resulted in material delays in essential Quartermaster production. The injudicious placement of contracts in tight labor areas, where the Corps was in hopeless competition with other arms and services for much needed labor, inevitably resulted in delinquency on the part of Quartermaster suppliers. The failure of management to sponsor training programs permitted dislocation of production with the loss of skilled workers to military service or more remunerative employment. Discrimination because of race, color, creed, or national origin, and the reluctance to employ aliens in defense industries were bad for morale and prevented the maximum utilization of available labor resources. Various federal, state, local, and union-imposed restrictions hampered the integration of available labor forces into necessary work schedules. Low morale, slowdowns, strikes, and

---

[9] OQMG OO 184, 31 Jul 42, sub: Reasgmt of QMC Functions.

[10] (1) Col Hester, Chief of Procurement Control Br, to Chief of Plng & Control Div, OQMG, 23 Oct 41, sub: Delinquent Contracts. (2) Lt A. C. Blanchard to Col Hester, 19 Dec 41, same sub. (3) Memo, Col Hester for Chief of Procurement & Distr Div, SOS, 21 Mar 42, sub: Difficulties of Production Program.

lockouts contributed their share to production delays and contract delinquency.[11]

Processing difficulties and managerial problems further served to delay production on Quartermaster contracts. Not all Quartermaster suppliers were financially sound, reasonably alert to improvements in manufacturing methods, and gifted with high standards of business ethics. Inexperienced firms repeatedly overestimated their capacity to produce and, after undertaking their contracts, found themselves seriously hampered by poor organization and the limitations of their plant facilities. Overzealous bidders undertook the manufacture of items with which they were unfamiliar and promised delivery schedules which they were unable to meet. Such factors as failure to interpret contract instructions, laxity in placing orders for materials, delay in starting work on a contract, recurring breakdowns of machinery, the necessity of replacing poor material in order to meet specifications, and the delinquency or loss of anticipated subcontracting facilities limited production. Only if suppliers' capacity, equipment, and ability were analyzed prior to the placement of orders, and only if adequately equipped, qualified, and diligent suppliers were allowed to undertake performance on contracts, could such delays be avoided. If marginal producers had to be brought into production, it was imperative to give them all possible help with their problems.[12]

The fact that Quartermaster suppliers were also at work on other defense contracts and on commercial orders was often responsible for contract delinquency.[13] Large percentages of plant capacity were devoted to nonpriority contracts as a result of the desire to accommodate regular commercial customers. In addition, the overloading of contractors and the overlapping of awards and final delivery dates often brought trouble. Contractors frequently accepted orders from various supply services and from different depots of the Corps. Since there was no depot exchange of information on the status of performance on contracts, awards were often made to contractors who were still delinquent on earlier orders.[14] Obviously, systematically planned and adequately spaced continuation orders for the same item would prevent overloading and conflicting contracts, and would make for specialization, standardization, and assembly-line techniques that were most conducive to optimum performance.

The overloaded condition of large plants was alleviated through subcontracting and the wider diffusion of prime contracts. While this practice had certain advantages, subcontracting and contract distribution often brought production difficulties. Subcontracting deprived the depots of a definite measure of control. Subcontracts were frequently assumed by small concerns, and the lack of effective follow-up and co-operation by the prime contractors in furnishing necessary materials, machines, and engineering assistance often delayed production.[15] Similarly, in the use of small plants as prime contractors, innumerable problems arose because of their unfamiliarity with Army standards, inexperience with multiple-shift opera-

---

[11] H. B. Yoshpe, *Labor Problems in Quartermaster Procurement, 1939–1944* (QMC Historical Studies 11, April 1945), *passim.*

[12] (1) Chief of Procurement Control Br to Chief of Plng & Control Div, OQMG, 23 Oct 41, sub: Delinquent Contracts. (2) F. X. Reynolds, Statement of Delinquencies on Selected Items as of 15 Nov 41. (3) Chief of Procurement Sec, Sup Div, to Chief of C&E Br OQMG, 9 Jan 42, sub: Delinquent Contracts.

[13] (1) *Ibid.* (2) Ltr, Chief of Procurement Sec, Sup Div, OQMG, to CG JQMD, 20 Apr 42, sub: Delinquent Contracts, and 1st ind, JQMD to TQMG, 24 Apr 42.

[14] Lt Chas. W. Morgan to Col O. E. Cound, Chief of Purch & Contract Br, OQMG, 20 Apr 42, sub: Overloading of Contractors and Manufacture of Different Items by Some Contractors.

[15] (1) J. Sloss, Jr., to Chief of Production Expediting Sec, OQMG, 8 Feb 42, sub: Subletting of QM Contracts. (2) Chief of Production Br to Chief of Plng & Control Div, OQMG, 5 Mar 42, sub: Subletting Contracts for Personal Equip.

tions, and lack of credit with which to replenish promptly raw material inventories. Their lack of elaborate cost-accounting systems often caused them to take contracts at prices that afforded little or no prospect of profit, with the result that they attempted to "cut corners" in an effort to reduce costs.

Finally, contract delinquency was considerably increased by specification problems, particularly by changes made in the design and manufacture of items and by rejections caused by suppliers' inability to meet specifications and produce items of approved quality. Rejections had to be kept to a minimum if critical raw materials, machinery, and labor were to be conserved. For this purpose specifications had to be revised to eliminate rigid and exacting qualifications, while still preserving the needed military characteristics, and to simplify operations, bringing them more into line with standard commercial practice. The necessity for using substitutes in the face of ever-increasing shortages of material produced innumerable specification changes, resulting in stoppages of production.[16] These changes in design and manufacture not infrequently necessitated the retooling of a plant to produce the substitute item. Delay was also occasioned by the change orders which had to be issued to authorize the substitutions. The only solution was to keep abreast of the changing materials situation and to review specifications before procurement directives were issued.[17]

Production on Quartermaster contracts was impeded by a considerable number of other factors. Many of these resulted from the shortcomings of procurement policies and techniques under which contracting officers operated well into the war period. Innumerable procurement controls and restrictions long hampered the Quartermaster production program. Delay resulted from the time required for the negotiation of contracts. Expediting production was inextricably interwoven with the streamlining

of procurement techniques in the Corps. Maximum production could also be promoted only through a co-ordinated, centralized, long-range plan of procurement for materials used by the Corps and by various other government procuring agencies. Not only did competition between Quartermaster depots have to be eliminated but also the unco-ordinated procurement of similar items, such as duck, textiles, chinaware, and cutlery, by various procurement agencies in the Army, by the Navy, Marine Corps, and Maritime Commission. By pooling requirements and centralizing purchase responsibility in the agency having the largest over-all needs, production for such items could be scheduled in an orderly fashion, industrial capacity mobilized, and maximum production obtained without delay.

Expediting Efforts of Contractors and Depots

Depot contracting officers were zealous in attempting to expedite delivery on contracts. Contractors, too, were usually co-operative in their efforts to reduce contract delinquency. They sought to correct fabricating defects and to eliminate production difficulties. They reorganized their plants and acquired additional space, new equipment, and skilled labor to increase production. They trained labor for additional shifts and sought exemptions from laws or penalty payments restricting multiple-shift operations. To expedite deliveries they sublet por-

---

[16] See Ch. II above, section on Impact of Materials Shortages on Design, for a discussion of the use of substitute materials and changes made in specifications.

[17] (1) Digest for file, F. X. Reynolds, 11 Jul 41, sub: Rpt from COs QM Depots—Recommendations. (2) Col Cound to TQMG, 11 Jul 41, sub: Rpt of Insp at JQMD. (3) Col Cound to Dir of Production Sv, 5 May 42, sub: Substitution for Critical Materials. (4) Chief of Production Expediting Sec to Col Cound, OQMG, 2 May 42, sub: Orgn of Material Unit to Review Specs.

tions of their contracts. To reduce rejections they inspected goods more thoroughly, re-worked faulty materials, and requested inspection at plants prior to shipment. These and many other steps were taken by contractors to speed production on contracts.

In order to remove production difficulties, depot contracting officers called conferences with contractors and advised them on how to improve workmanship and comply with delivery schedules. They expedited the shipment of government-furnished materials, issued preference rating certificates, and tried to get higher ratings when necessary. They often revised delivery schedules rather than cancel delinquent contracts and executed change orders extending the time for performance. They obtained the aid of the OQMG on priority and labor problems. They authorized the use of substitute materials and accepted substandard items at a discount.[18]

These ameliorative measures helped reduce the period of delinquency, but broader and more basic policies had to be initiated by higher authority if contract delinquency was to be eliminated. The OQMG met the problem of material shortages in part by providing the contractors with government-furnished materials and components. To mitigate these shortages it also pursued a comprehensive conservation program, and adjusted specifications to make them conform more closely to commercial practices. It sought to improve the Corps' position in the priorities system in order to insure a flow of needed critical materials to its contractors. The OQMG co-operated actively in the location of materials and idle machine tools required by its suppliers for successful performance, and, when necessary, it extended them financial aid. In addition, it made efforts to eliminate bottlenecks in production by devoting greater attention to production planning and scheduling. The prosecution of these policies made possible the achievement of Quartermaster procurement goals.

Flow of Materials and Equipment

Government-Furnished Material and Equipment

To overcome the serious problem created by shortages of critical materials, the QMC undertook to furnish its contractors with necessary raw materials and components. Cloth and minor findings for uniforms had been furnished to clothing contractors by the Philadelphia Depot for a number of years. Beginning in 1941 the depot established rationing of cloth, supplying contractors on a schedule of availability sixty days in advance of delivery of end items. At the request of the depot, the OQMG authorized administration of a Minor Findings Pool in April 1942, which permitted a stock of minor findings to be carried under certain stock levels at this depot.[19] This procedure on cloth and minor findings was continued throughout the war. The development of the practice into a general policy of procurement of raw materials and components for issue to contractors was much debated in the months before Pearl Harbor.[20]

While the adoption of such a program was beset by numerous problems in stocking, accounting, and supervision, its advantages could not be ignored. In too many cases production had been held up pending delivery of necessary materials. Rather than have their skilled operators pirated by other defense plants when their production lines were curtailed or shut down for lack of materials, producers of Quartermaster items would "string the contract out" until

---

[18] Yoshpe, *Production Control in QMC*, pp. 11–12.

[19] Rpt, OP&C Div, OQMG, 10 May 44, sub: Project 343: Survey of Organizational Responsibilities and Procedures with Regard to Industrial Materials.

[20] (1) Chief of Production Expediting Sec to Chief of Procurement Control Br, OQMG, 19 Aug 41, sub: Production Expediting—Shoes. (2) Chief of Procurement Control Br to TQMG, 16 Sep 41, sub: Contributory Items. (3) Chief of Clothing Sec to Chief of C&E Br, OQMG, 27 Sep 41, same sub.

the needed materials arrived. It was also argued that providing government-furnished material (GFM) to contractors would enable the Corps to use centralized procurement, thereby effecting a substantial reduction of cost of the net item to the government. Such a program would make the small manufacturer, whose facilities had to be used by the Corps, less dependent upon the limited service of the manufacturers of industrial materials, who logically favored the old and big customers.

Despite the difficulties, particularly that of accountability, inherent in such a program, the QMC gradually extended its application by furnishing duck, webbing, and hardware to manufacturers of tents and equipage; dubbing, laces, and other findings to shoe contractors; and packing materials and components of special rations to assemblers. The five major procuring depots all provided some GFM, but clothing, equipage, and subsistence accounted for its greatest use.

Because procedures for the issue of GFM were costly and laborious, the outright sale of such materials to contractors was thought to be "the most practical solution of the problem." Under authority of Executive Order 9001, Headquarters, SOS, authorized the sale of GFM when it would facilitate the performance of war contracts.[21] Subsequently, the desirability of reducing credit transactions to a minimum and of keeping records with contractors in order, as well as protecting the government against the misuse of GFM in the hands of contractors, led to a survey of procedures early in 1944. From this survey the OQMG developed the GFM plan, containing a framework of policies, principles, and procedures that were applied until the end of the war.[22]

In order to expedite the manufacture and delivery of war goods, contractors were also furnished with GFE, a term used rather loosely to cover government-owned equipment and facilities. Such equipment was either purchased directly by the government and loaned or leased to the contractor, or it was acquired by the contractor for the government and amortized over the life of government contracts.[23]

At the Philadelphia and Jersey City Depots the provision of GFE to contractors was negligible. On the other hand, the GFE program assumed large proportions at the Chicago, Jeffersonville, and Boston Depots. The Chicago Depot, for example, encouraged canners and occasionally independent producers to build and install procoating equipment under GFE arrangements. About a hundred procoating installations were so established. Procoating of Army canned goods destined for oversea shipment was undertaken to inhibit rust under long and exposed storage and to camouflage cans in open storage dumps or in discard.[24] Subsistence contracts, however, accounted for most of the GFE furnished by this depot. The larger part was special equipment, such as drying bins, sulfiting equipment, and cyntron feeding screeners, used by producers in dehydrating vegetables. Some special facilities, representing plant expansions for the production of dried yeast and parboiled rice produced for the armed forces, were also included.[25] The Boston Depot utilized a considerable amount of GFE in the form of molds, patterns, templates, and lasts. GFE at the Jeffersonville Depot included sewing machines, cloth cutters, and baling machines used

[21] (1) Ltr, Gen Corbin, OQMG, to Hq SOS, 22 Jun 42, sub: Govt Materials Available for Govt Contractors. (2) 1st ind, Hq SOS to TQMG, 15 Jul 42, on same.

[22] (1) OQMG OO 25-89, 8 Jul 44, sub: Industrial Materials and GFM Plan. (2) QMG Cir 34, 12 Jul 44, same sub.

[23] See PR 3 (9-5-42), par. 332.

[24] (1) Marion Massen, Central Procurement Operations at the Chicago Quartermaster Depot (CQMD hist rpt 8, Jun 46), p. 196. (2) H. W. Thatcher, *The Packaging and Packing of Subsistence for the Army*, pp. 41-45.

[25] Erna Risch, *Demobilization Planning and Operation in the Quartermaster Corps* (QMC Historical Studies 19, April 1948), pp. 67-68.

in the manufacture of textile items, and welders, presses, grinders, lathes, and numerous specialized items required in metal work. GFE at this depot, either leased or amortized, amounted to about $100,000,000 at the end of the war. Included were about 500 separate contractors' plants, with the major portion of the equipment furnished consisting of some 3,000 to 5,000 sewing machines.[26]

Priorities

To guide and direct the flow of critical materials into military and essential civilian channels and to attain maximum production for war, the nation's defense program relied upon a patchwork of controls developed during the emergency and war periods. The first steps were taken in the summer of 1940 when by joint action of the Army, the Navy, and the National Defense Advisory Commission a priorities system was established to insure preferential treatment of defense production. Preference ratings were issued on individual preference certificates which gave precedence to the military services in the use of industrial facilities. A scale of preference ratings from A–1 to A–10 was assigned to individual contracts for items in accordance with their strategic importance, with a rating of AA reserved for emergencies. For essential civilian needs a B series was established.[27] The contracting officer applied the appropriate rating to a contract, determining it by reference to the Priorities Critical List and the Priorities Directive. The list designated the item to which preference ratings might be assigned, and the directive stipulated the preference rating to be assigned to each of the various items in the Priorities Critical List.

Within a few months, however, it became evident that this initial rating pattern was inadequate for guiding the flow of materials into the defense program. From the beginning more and more Army and Navy projects were placed in the top priority category, inflating it to the point where in order to relieve the congestion in the A–1 band, a graduated priority status had to be established. As a consequence, on 27 November 1940 the Priorities Committee, ANMB, subdivided the A–1 classification into preference ratings of A–1–a to A–1–j inclusive for Army and Navy procurements, and reserved ratings A–2 to A–10 for essential civilian needs. These ratings could be changed only by appeal to the ANMB with respect to individual contracts.[28]

This priorities system was effective in controlling the use of production facilities, but it was not a practical method for controlling materials required in defense production. As the volume of defense contracts expanded, the demand for raw materials under various preference ratings far exceeded the available supply. Although the priorities system determined the order of preference, it controlled neither the quantity of material distributed nor the time of delivery. It was therefore unable to insure orderly and integrated procurement by all the supply services. Orders with low priority ratings could be continually deferred while successive higher rated orders were processed and shipped. A balanced production of all items needed in the Army supply program became impossible.

In this priorities system the QMC received the low rating of A–1–i for 90 percent of its procurements. Many of its items were of a commercial nature and at the outset were readily procurable with the low ratings assigned, although raw materials, particularly metals, soon became virtually unobtainable without an increased rating. In the case of items not com-

---

[26] Interv, OQMG historian with James Bayless, GFE Sec, JQMD, 7 Feb 47.

[27] Memo, ANMB, 17 Jun 40, sub: Establishment of Priorities Committee, ANMB.

[28] (1) Directive, Priorities Committee, ANMB, 27 Nov 40. (2) ANMB, Priorities Committee, Cir 1, 9 Dec 40, sub: Description of Preference Rating System.

mercially procurable, the situation was soon acute. In these fields the Corps competed directly with other supply arms and services and with bureaus of the Navy, which were authorized to assign a much higher rating for similar equipment. Not infrequently, supplies on order by the Corps were "lifted" by other services by the simple method of placing higher ratings on them.

As a consequence, the OQMG was forced to ask for more and more assistance from the ANMB. This was no solution to the problem, since the flood of requests for more favorable priority treatment resulted in a further inflation of the priorities system that threatened to unbalance the entire defense program. On the other hand, "priority conscious" industries refused to bid on Quartermaster requirements unless assured of preference ratings sufficiently high to enable them to secure the necessary materials and component parts in time to complete their contracts on required dates.[29]

Whenever the supply of materials became critical, it was usually the QMC that was asked to curtail its program. This was a reflection of the belief entertained by both Headquarters, SOS, and the WPB that offensive weapons, such as guns and tanks, were far more important to ultimate victory than the items of clothing and equipment furnished by the Corps. As a consequence, the need for a well-rounded Quartermaster supply program in order to achieve a balanced supply program for the Army as a whole tended to be overlooked.

To prevent a complete breakdown of Quartermaster procurement, the ANMB gradually placed various items under higher priority. A preference rating of A-1-b was assigned to the Corps on 1 November 1941 for use when necessary to obtain delivery of metal components and accessories of individual fabric and leather equipment. Later this rating was made applicable when necessary on metal components and accessories of all individual and organizational

equipment other than motor vehicles. The rating of the motor vehicle program was raised to A-1-c and the alloy and carbon steel requirements of the QMC 1942 Truck Program were rated A-1-a.[30]

To prevent "lifting" of materials by services enjoying more favorable priority status, the ANMB on 23 December 1941 directed that orders of higher priority were not to pre-empt material specifically produced for a previous defense order of lower priority if the material was completed at the time of acceptance of the higher rated order or was scheduled for completion within fifteen days thereafter. Because this directive could be variously interpreted, critical materials continued to be siphoned off by projects with higher ratings.[31]

The ANMB recognized that the priorities system would have to be modified, but it was not until after Pearl Harbor that steps were taken to adjust preference ratings so as to insure balanced production of all military items needed by the Army. Instead of concentrating complete production programs in one level of priority, the ANMB proposed a percentage assignment whereby at least partial top priority would be provided to all programs to permit balanced production. Under this arrangement, the prior-

---

[29] (1) Rpt, Chief of Plng & Control Div to TQMG, 23 Apr 41, sub: Recent Procurement Problems of Div. (2) Memo, TQMG for USW, 16 Aug 41, sub: Revision of Priorities System. (3) Col Doriot, Chief of Production Br, to Col Cound, OQMG, 30 Mar 42, sub: Effect of Priority Ratings on Contract Performance and Material Substitution. (4) Ltr, Lt Col J. Van Ness Ingram, OQMG, to ANMB, 13 Apr 42, sub: Lifting of Materials.

[30] (1) Ltr, ANMB to All Sup Arms and Svs et al., 1 Nov 41, sub: Change in 20 Aug 41 ANMB Priorities Directive. (2) Ltr, ANMB to same, 1 Jun 42, sub: Increased Priority Rating for 1942 Motorcycle Program. (3) Chief of Priorities Br, OQMG, to Dir of MTS, 25 Jun 42, sub: Increased Priority Rating for Motor Vehicles.

[31] (1) Ltr, Col Ingram, OQMG, to ANMB, 13 Apr 42, sub: Lifting of Materials. (2) ANMB Memo, 16 Feb 42, sub: Interpretation of Par. 944.7 (c) Priorities Reg 1, as amended.

ity assigned to each production program would be spread over three or four grades, and no individual program would receive top priority in its entirety. All supply arms and bureaus would receive a percentage of the A–1–a and other ratings in accordance with the relative military importance of their programs. The result would be delivery of items for all armed forces on "an integrated basis." [32] The OQMG felt that the plan would "greatly alleviate the present critical situation" and urged that it be placed in operation. [33]

Early in the summer of 1942, the WPB accepted this new preference rating scheme which embodied the basic idea of establishing quotas in all priority bands. Four new preference rating categories were set up—AA–1, AA–2, AA–3, and AA–4—with an emergency category of AAA to break bottlenecks in the production of specific items. These new grades were superimposed upon all existing preference ratings and were authorized for issuance on approved listings of items covering virtually the entire military production goals of the calendar year 1942. Procurement agencies could execute rerating certificates on undelivered balances of existing contracts, and the initial assignment of these ratings to new contracts could be made after 15 July 1942 for the remainder of the calendar year within the quotas fixed for each item under each rating. Items not covered by these ratings, and quantities of applicable items in excess of the prescribed quotas continued to be rated in accordance with existing regulations. [34]

This rating pattern with some modification continued in operation until the end of the war. Under this system, the importance of Quartermaster items in the supply of the Army was recognized. Various Quartermaster items were covered by the new ratings, and established quotas limited the quantities to which each of the new ratings was to be assigned. By placing new contracts in these high priority

categories and rerating existing contracts, Quartermaster contracting officers enabled many of their suppliers to obtain materials in sufficient volume to sustain production. [35]

Allocation, Conservation, and Limitation Orders

Although the priorities system had been improved, it still was inadequate as a control for guiding the distribution of critical materials. Experience in the administration of the defense effort had early indicated the need for other types of controls to supplement the priorities system. Of these the most important were allocations which would gear the entire defense program to the available supply of critical materials. Only by allocating these materials to the end use could a balanced production program be realized and competition between the services to complete their requirements be eliminated.

Early in the defense effort the OPM and later the WPB fully realized that only an allocation system would provide a regular and known flow of materials to war contractors, eliminate interagency competition, and permit efficient production scheduling. During the OPM period various allocation orders were devised to supplement the existing priorities system and insure adequate supplies for military production. These distribution control orders were

[32] Memo, ANMB for Sup Arms and Svs of Army, Bureaus and Offices of Navy Dept *et al.*, 24 Jan 42, sub: Transmittal for Study and Comment of Proposed Revision of ANMB Priorities Directive.

[33] (1) Ltr, TQMG to ANMB, 7 Feb 42, sub: Comments on Proposed Revision. (2) Ltr, TQMG to ANMB, 20 Mar 42, sub: Priorities Affecting QM Procurement.

[34] (1) Memo, ANMB to All Sup Svs *et al.*, 29 Jun 42, sub: Priorities Directive of 12 Jun 42. (2) WPB Priorities Reg 12, 26 Jun 42.

[35] For a fuller account of the priorities system see H. B. Yoshpe, *Priorities and Allocations: A Study of the Flow of Materials to War Suppliers* (ICAF Research Project 28, September 1946), pp. 3–36.

called M orders when they dealt with materials and E orders when they dealt with equipment. They were a mandatory grouping of orders which controlled and curtailed the flow of materials and equipment into industry. The earliest of these mandatory orders were applied in February 1941 to aluminum and to machine tools. Copper, nickel, tungsten, neoprene, steel, and other critical materials came under the mandatory priorities of OPM. Included in the M series were conservation orders which restricted the uses to which a given material might be put. Such restrictions stimulated the conservation program in the QMC and led to the use of substitute materials.[36]

Finally, these distribution control orders also included L orders, or limitation orders, which curtailed the production of various types of goods requiring critical materials and thereby brought pressure on the consumer durable goods industry to convert to war production. Application of L orders, for example, brought a halt to the production of passenger cars and light trucks. Fitting into this pattern of priorities and allocations was a system of inventory control designed to curb overbuying of materials and hoarding of them in anticipation of future scarcities. It was applicable to all materials for which individual mandatory control did not exist. Manufacturers, dealers, public warehouses, railroads, and public utilities were required to report their inventories of scarce materials. Those having large stocks were forbidden to deliver them and buyers were prohibited from purchasing them without specific authorization of the Director of Priorities.[37]

As in the case of preference ratings, curtailment orders provided no real control over the flow of materials. They constituted a negative approach to the problem. They either stopped or reduced the manufacture of less essential end products, or they curtailed the use of critical materials in the manufacture of such products. They were useful tools in cutting off such pro-

duction and consequently freeing materials and facilities for more important ends. They could not serve, however, as "sensitive instruments for achieving a balanced flow of materials to the multiplicity of military, export, and essential civilian production programs."[38] Furthermore, under such individual allocation systems, each operated autonomously under a particular WPB materials branch, and hence there was no correlation of the activities and policies of the different commodity groups, with the result that co-ordination in the flow of materials was completely lacking.

Production Requirements Plan

Along with such piecemeal allocations of particular materials, however, there also developed a new control that came to be known as the "Production Requirements Plan," or PRP. It stemmed from a Defense Supplies Rating Plan which the OPM instituted in May 1941 to meet the problem of manufacturers whose business required small amounts of materials which they generally supplied from inventory stock. Under this plan, such producers estimated the proportion of their business that could be classified as defense work on the basis of their sales records for the preceding quarters. This percentage they applied to their total material requirements for the next quarter as revealed by production schedules. For this proportion they were assigned a preference rating which they applied to procure stock for quarterly supplies. Thus they were aided in securing a steady flow of materials into their plants.[39] This method of allocating materials on a quarterly basis in advance of the actual placing of orders

---

[36] See above, Ch. II.

[37] CPA, *Industrial Mobilization for War* (GPO, 1947), I, 177–181.

[38] Ibid., p. 455.

[39] (1) Yoshpe, *Production Control in QMC*, pp. 37–38. (2) Yoshpe, *Priorities and Allocations*, pp. 38–41.

was a feature that was developed in the PRP and announced on 3 December 1941.

The purpose of the plan was to balance the supply and demand of critical materials each quarter, directing the available supply into the production of necessary end products in accordance with their relative essentiality. To achieve such balance the total demand for a given period had to be known in advance. Hence the PRP necessitated a close check of essential raw material requirements through quarterly estimates submitted by manufacturers. It also required a knowledge of their inventories, the scarcity of the particular materials, and the possibility of reducing the demand by substitution and conservation. Product group committees which included SOS representation reviewed these estimates and determined the need for an extent of any "cuts" to be made. The ANMB then informed the WPB as to which broad programs might be cut and by what percentages of their requirements.

The WPB adjusted requirements in line with available supply, and distributed materials among end-product groups according to the relative essentiality of the product to the prosecution of the war. Code symbols designated the end use of such items and were shown on all purchase orders so that the ultimate supplier of the raw materials would be automatically apprised as to their end use. Allocated materials were distributed among manufacturers within the end-product group with adjustments made to reduce any excessive inventories of these materials. To meet contingencies not covered by allocation, a reserve was maintained. Preference ratings applied only to the end item, component parts, and subassemblies, and not to raw materials. The ratings designated the order of shipment of materials within an end-use symbol bracket during the three-month period.

PRP was described as a "great national budget of materials, uniform accounting system, to balance supply against demand." [40] It rested

entirely on the ability of WPB to obtain the necessary information for measuring and balancing requirements against supply and to direct definite amounts of materials for specific purposes within a limited time. PRP seemed to hold out the prospect of effective controls never achieved under the old priority system.

Until June 1942 PRP was entirely voluntary. However, almost immediately after WPB's establishment that agency began to take steps to make the plan mandatory for American industry. After Pearl Harbor, the necessity for maintaining rigid control over critical materials and co-ordinating their flow emphasized the need for a master control system. The search for such a system engendered a lively debate over the relative merits of "horizontal allocation" (PRP) and "vertical allocation" (the Controlled Materials Plan, or CMP).[41]

Neither the military services nor all of the policy-making and top operational personnel of WPB fully supported PRP. While Headquarters, SOS, co-operated with the WPB, it was more favorably disposed toward a different scheme for controlling the flow of materials. Known as the Commodity Warrant Plan, it had been developed by the Ordnance Department in the fall of 1941 and called for a vertical allocation of claims to materials. Under this plan, the war agencies would compute accurate raw materials requirements for a given period. WPB would determine the quantities allocable to the ANMB, which would divide the amount

[40] "Now in Search of a Policy: Allocations," *Fortune,* June 1942, p. 101.

[41] See CPA, *Industrial Mobilization for War,* pp. 457–501. A horizontal system was one in which authorization for critical materials was passed directly from a government agency (WPB) to the contractor or subcontractor. In a vertical system, material control was established at the end-product level of manufacturing and extended from purchaser to seller. In other words, allocation would be made to each branch of the military services which would in turn distribute authorizations for material procurement to its prime contractors, and they would pass it on to their subcontractors.

between the Army and the Navy. SOS, in turn, would allot the Army amount among the various services, each of which would then have a "bank account" of a critical item against which it could issue "checks" or warrants. Each service would use its allocated quantity in the manner it deemed best for executing its procurement program.[42]

In considering the two rival control systems which had been devised to supplement the priorities method of distribution of critical materials, the OQMG opposed the Commodity Warrant Plan. Because of the complexity and diversity of the items procured by the Corps, this plan was not adaptable to its needs. On the other hand, the OQMG Allocations Planning Committee enthusiastically endorsed the PRP.[43]

While the supply services were at odds over the control system to be adopted, WPB went ahead with its plans to make PRP mandatory for all industries using more than $5,000 worth of scarce materials in any quarter. This action was to become effective on 1 July 1942 but was subsequently postponed to 1 October.[44] By that date more careful plans had been made for its application to practically all of the metal-consuming industries, and PRP had been much improved. PRP did not function smoothly, but despite the doubts about it, this system provided the basic control of the flow of materials during the third and fouth quarters of 1942 and the first quarter of 1943. In the second quarter of 1943 both PRP and CMP were in operation as the transition to CMP was effected. PRP went out of existence on 30 June 1943.[45]

Controlled Materials Plan

PRP had scarcely been launched when the WPB announced a new allocation system—CMP. Since PRP had never been supported wholeheartedly, consideration for some time had been given to developing an alternative materials-control system. By September 1942

WPB had decided to abandon PRP as soon as another system could be established. The CMP was publicly announced on 2 November. It was a vertical system of allocation, not much different from the Commodity Warrant Plan.[46] Because they were the most critical and were required for a wide variety of items, steel, copper, and aluminum were the first to come under the CMP. Although the QMC was a comparatively small user of critical metals and hence did not figure prominently in the operation of the plan, nevertheless the CMP placed the supply program of the Corps on a more even basis with those of the Navy, the Air Forces, and the other technical services.

The fundamental purpose of the plan was to assure a balance between supply and demand of controlled materials by an allocation of them on the basis of the total requirements for controlled materials presented by each claimant agency. These requirements were based on bills of material and planned production schedules. Each claimant agency had to adjust its program to the amount of controlled materials allotted to it. All other materials continued to be distributed through the priorities system. The CMP was deemed flexible enough to permit materials other than steel, aluminum, and copper to be included in its coverage, but such action was never taken.

As the CMP went into effect in the spring of 1943, its application presented many difficulties in the OQMG. The plan provided for a separation of Class A and B products. Class A items,

---

[42] Memo, Brig Gen C. Hines, Dir of Resources Div, SOS, for TQMG, 18 May 42, sub: Commodity Warrant Plan and Inclosures, 400.314.

[43] Allocations Plng Committee to TQMG, 13 May 42, sub: Allocations, 400.314.

[44] (1) WPB, Priorities Reg 11, 10 Jun 42. (2) ASF Annual Rpt FY 1943, p. 66.

[45] For the merits and shortcomings of PRP see (1) Yoshpe, *Priorities and Allocations*, p. 52. (2) CPA, *Industrial Mobilization for War*, pp. 457–74.

[46] Rpt, WPB, 14 Nov 42, sub: CMP: Gen Instructions on Bills of Materials.

end-product items such as guns and tanks built to specifications for the Army, were reported in the form of material requirements, and material allotments for them were received directly from the War Department. Class B products included civilian-type end products, industrial machinery and equipment, products requiring small amounts of materials, and components usually stocked for commercial purposes. Their requirements were reported in unit or dollar values, and producers of B items got their allotments of material from the WPB. The OQMG protested vigorously against the B list as it applied to items of Quartermaster procurement. It objected to the inclusion on the B list of any item that could be handled satisfactorily on the A list on the ground that the Corps was charged with the power to contract, schedule, and obtain delivery of these items and could not fulfill its obligation without "the power to allot and schedule the necessary material." In February 1943, Headquarters, SOS, and the WPB resolved this problem by placing in Class A many of these items essential to the war effort.[47]

The administration of the CMP in the Corps cut across the functional responsibilities of various divisions in the OQMG, involving as it did the computation of requirements, production scheduling, and the handing down of allotments to procuring depots. The division of responsibility between the Materials Controller in the Military Planning Division and the Procurement and Storage and Distribution Divisions accounted for many of the difficulties encountered in putting the plan into operation in the Corps. Later controls were more closely integrated under the Director of the Military Planning Division, facilitating the execution of the plan.[48]

Cotton Textile Controls

Among the special controls devised in 1944, those which controlled the distribution of cot-

ton broad-woven goods to claimant agencies were of particular interest to the QMC. During the defense period and the first year of the war, the supply of most cotton goods was ample to cover total civilian and military demand. A serious unbalance did develop for a small number of specialized fabrics such as, for example, cotton duck. Controls were applied to freeze cotton duck stocks and to convert selected facilities to the production and distribution of cotton textiles.[49] Such controls as existed, however, permitted unrestricted military procurement of cotton fabrics. The chief weakness of this system was the absence of quantitative control which would limit military procurement.

By the summer of 1943 serious shortages had begun to develop. Production had started to decline, primarily because of the drift of mill labor to better paying munitions industries. At the same time military requirements rose sharply as a result of replacement needs and the necessity of meeting relief and rehabilitation requirements for peoples in liberated areas. Under the impetus of expanded consumer incomes, civilian demands were also increasing. All of these factors "converged simultaneously on the shrinking cotton textile supply."[50]

A control program was established for cotton fabrics in the third quarter of 1944. The plan was to establish budgetary controls over procurement by the military and export agencies. These agencies were to maintain accountability both for fabrics procured and for the estimated

---

[47] (1) Memo, Col Doriot, OQMG, for Chief of Material Program Br, Production Div, SOS, 18 Dec 42, sub: CMP Class B List, 400.314. (2) Memo, Hq SOS for TQMG, 29 Feb 43, sub: Questions on CMP Opns.

[48] (1) OQMG OO 25–25, 31 Dec 42, sub: CMP. (2) OQMG OO 25–50, 13 Dec 43, sub: Issuance of Instructions to Contractors. (3) OQMG OO 25–61, 13 Dec 43, sub: Contacts with Higher Authority.

[49] David Novick, Melvin Anshen, and W. C. Truppner, *Wartime Production Controls* (New York, 1949), pp. 247–48.

[50] CPA, *Industrial Mobilization for War*, p. 828.

fabric content of the end items procured. Specific yardages of cotton fabrics in thirty-two categories established by the Combined Production and Resources Board were allotted by program determination to each procuring claimant. The claimants would be prohibited from placing purchase orders beyond the quantity limitations authorized by the program determination. To win the support of the military services to operate within predetermined fabric budgets, it was proposed to remove two restrictions which at that time were interfering with the fulfillment of military programs. Under Priorities Regulation 1, mills had been able to avoid taking certain rated orders. It was now proposed to strengthen the system by establishing in each fabric category a minimum for the acceptance of rated orders that would be high enough to absorb the total preference rated demand. The second restriction to be eliminated was a maximum percentage limitation placed on the rated orders that could be accepted by mills.

The existing limitation and conservation orders and budgetary control over procurement proved usable devices but did not solve the distribution problem inasmuch as full conversion of looms from nonessential to essential production was not achieved. The system worked reasonably well for the military services, and the end of the war was in sight before the effect of the full impact of shortages on the civilian economy became evident.[51]

Set-Aside Orders and Other Mandatory Measures

The War Department preferred to depend upon the voluntary co-operation of industry, but this was not always forthcoming. Mandatory measures were applied by the Corps primarily in the procurement of subsistence, particularly in 1943 and 1944 when shortages of certain commodities became more and more

frequent. The increasing activities of black market operators and the unwillingness of producers to sell their products to the Army even at the prevailing maximum prices established by the OPA caused the Corps considerable difficulty in procuring various necessary subsistence items. Normal procurement procedures proved ineffective in the face of the shortages. The Corps therefore used compulsory orders and the requisition of personal property. It also employed the set-aside order imposed and administered by the War Food Administration (WFA) for the benefit of War Department subsistence procurement.

Under the Selective Training and Service Act of 16 September 1940, the President, through the heads of the War and Navy Departments, was empowered to place a compulsory order with any producer for any item of the type he usually produced or was readily capable of manufacturing, for a fair compensation. Such orders took precedence over all other orders and contracts.[52]

This policy was not implemented until after Pearl Harbor. Authority to place or to delegate the placement of orders had been intrusted to the WPB. The Under Secretary of War requested the delegation of this authority to the War Department, but in the early days of the war the WPB was somewhat reluctant to do this. To this unwillingness the War Department attributed its omission of any general instructions on the use of mandatory powers in 1942.[53]

It was not until 1944 that the WPB decided to delegate completely its authority to approve mandatory orders. Similar action was taken by the WFA, to which agency jurisdiction over food had been transferred from the WPB in

---

[51] *Ibid.*, 828–30. (2) Novick *et al.*, *Wartime Production Controls*, pp. 242–67.

[52] Memo, OASW for TQMG *et al.*, 17 Oct 40, sub: Compulsory Orders.

[53] Rpt, History of the Purchases Div, ASF, n. d., p. 376. Mimeographed copy on file at Hist Sec, OQMG.

December 1942.[54] This authority was then re-delegated to the technical services but limited to persons in the headquarters office of each chief. The Under Secretary of War retained the authority to determine what constituted a "reasonable price" in compulsory orders.[55]

Early in the war the QMC contemplated that this measure would be used "only in extreme cases" because of the adequacy of facilities for Quartermaster items. The Clothing and Textile Branch reported late in 1942 that it had not made use of this device but was prepared to do so "in the event of necessity." [56] The Subsistence Branch, however, in the spring of 1942 anticipated difficulties in obtaining food, particularly meat and meat products, as a result of the promulgation of the General Maximum Price Regulation by the OPA. The Quartermaster General therefore requested authority to place compulsory orders when the need arose, not only for these products but for any other Quartermaster supplies.[57] On 14 May the WPB delegated to the War Department, with power to redelegate to The Quartermaster General, authority to issue mandatory orders for subsistence items but limited the duration to three months. Subsequently the WFA took similar action. This authority was extended periodically thereafter until complete delegation occurred in 1944.

Although this authority was granted, The Quartermaster General issued no orders under it in 1942.[58] In 1943 and 1944, however, the Corps issued 8 mandatory orders to food processors, 7 for the production of boneless beef and 1 for milled rice. The order for milled rice was superseded by a voluntary contract at a new ceiling price. Of the 7 orders for boneless beef, 3 were complied with; 4 were not. Six orders were served by the Corps in 1944 on producers of field jackets, 1 of which was replaced by a voluntary contract. A mandatory order which was satisfactorily completed was also served on a manufacturer of rubber heels. On the basis of subsequent information, the Purchases Division, ASF, concluded that 11 of these mandatory orders—4 for boneless beef, 1 for milled rice, and 6 for field jackets—could have been avoided by "proper consideration of the facts, or proper negotiations, or both." [59]

Requisitioning of property [60] was sanctioned by the enactment of legislation in October 1940 and 1941. Under the Act of 10 October 1940, property which was produced and intended for export but which was barred from shipment by the Export Control Act of 1940 could be requisitioned for the prosecution of the war. Under the Property Requisitioning Act of 16 October 1941, as amended, requisitioning of personal property was permitted whenever it was needed for national defense; when the need was immediate, permitting of no delay or resort to other sources of supply; and when all other means of obtaining it upon reasonable terms had been exhausted.

During the greater part of the emergency period, the Corps apparently took little or no action to requisition property remaining in the United States because exportation of it was prohibited. The Army and Navy Munitions Board circulated lists of such blocked materials which, beginning in the summer of 1941, the OQMG called to the attention of its various operating

---

[54] Exec Orders 9280, 5 Dec 42, and 9344, 19 Apr 43.

[55] PR 14 (6–7–44), pars. 1450.2, 1450.3.

[56] (1) Chief of Price Adjustment Sec to Deputy Dir of Procurement, OQMG, 27 Nov 42, sub: Memo on Statement of Purch Policies. (2) Lt Col R. T. Stevens to same, 24 Nov 42, same sub.

[57] Memo, TQMG for Dir of Procurement & Distr Div, SOS, 7 May 42, sub: Compulsory Orders.

[58] Memo, Legal Br, Purchases Div, SOS, for OUSW, 27 Nov 42, sub: Procedure in Obtaining Authority for Compulsory Orders from WPB.

[59] History of Purchases Div, ASF, p. 383.

[60] Personal property within the purview of this legislation included any military or naval equipment or munitions, or parts thereof, or critical materials, machinery, tools, or supplies needed for their manufacture, servicing, or operations.

divisions. By 1942 some requisitioning of this type had taken place.[61]

As procurement of certain subsistence items became acute in the summer of 1943, the OQMG became interested in requisitioning under authority of the 1941 act as amended. In particular, The Quartermaster General requested authority to issue requisitions for fresh or frozen carcass beef and frozen boneless beef whenever necessary to meet his requirements. Despite an earlier unfavorable decision by the Judge Advocate General, another attempt was made to delegate the requisitioning authority to the technical services. In June 1943 the Under Secretary of War determined that the OQMG, with concurrence of the WFA, could compel sale of the needed supplies.[62] All cases, however, had to relate "to food not delivered under priority rated orders and food ordered set aside for sale to the armed forces, and in violation of such set-aside order, refused [sic] to be sold." This authority was invoked by the Corps to secure fresh and frozen carcass beef and frozen boneless beef. It was also used to seize poultry needed by the Army.[63]

Title III of the Second War Powers Act of 1942 [64] contained mandatory features which could have been invoked to obtain fair prices on the production of war material. "Apparently little question arose of the necessity for the mandatory use of these powers," administered by the WPB and the WFA, "probably because these allocation powers were accepted by industry generally" and formed the basis for the entire war procurement program.[65] Although no formal statement was published of War Department policy on the use of priorities and allocation powers as mandatory methods of procurement, the QMC made broad use of two special devices—priority ratings and set-aside orders—in the procurement of subsistence.

The WPB took the initial steps to obtain food by regulatory measures with the issuance of priority ratings—the first used in World War II. Subsequently, when the control of food was lodged in the Department of Agriculture, priority ratings continued to be issued and administered by the WFA. Under War Food Order 71 of March 1943, which superseded an earlier WPB regulation, the director of the Office of Supply in the Commodity Credit Corporation [66] was authorized to assign priority ratings to any disposition of food and to the use of food in any process of production. Under this regulation ratings ranged from the lowest, FR-10, which automatically applied to every War Department procurement contract for food, to the highest, FR-1. These ratings did not apply to goods subject to rationing or set-aside orders.[67] A priority-rated order of the WFA required a producer to sell to the War Department on the terms and in the quantities specified in accordance with the priority given in such order, or else he could not sell to his civilian customers. The contractor was not required to produce for the War Department, but this, in effect, was the end achieved.

---

[61] (1) Ltr, Asst to Chief of Requisitioning Div, Office of Exports, to Lt Col L. C. Webster, OQMG, 26 Aug 42, sub: Canned Salmon. (2) Ltr, Col Webster to BEW, 24 Sep 42, sub: Canned Pineapple and Salmon Stored at Lackawanna Warehouse Co, 431.

[62] (1) Memo, USW for TQMG, 19 Jun 43, sub: Requisitioning of Food by TQMG. (2) For the details of how this delegation of authority was worked out see History of Purchases Div, ASF, pp. 365ff.

[63] (1) Lt Col E. H. Foley, Jr., to OIC, Fld Hq, Perishable Sec, Subs Br, OQMG, 14 Aug 43, sub: Reqs for Beef, 430. (2) *The New York Times,* July 22, 1943. (3) See also HR Docs 367 and 566, 78th Cong, 1st and 2d Sess, sub: Requisitioning and Disposition of Property Required for National Defense.

[64] (1) 56 *U. S. Statutes* 177. This act was approved 27 March 1942 and amended by act of 20 December 1944. (2) 58 *U. S. Statutes* 827.

[65] History of Purchases Div, ASF, p. 357.

[66] The functions of the Commodity Credit Corporation were later turned over to the Food Distribution Administration, subsequently reorganized and renamed the War Food Administration.

[67] OQMG Cir Ltr 69, 13 Apr 43, sub: Food Priorities.

The QMC was extremely cautious about invoking any high priority ratings, the highest and only one used being FR–9. In connection with it an "emergency order" could be used to compel contractors to deliver when no voluntary contract could be drawn. Though considered less forceful than mandatory orders or requisitions, the emergency order had to be accepted within five days. It was served only after diligent efforts had been made to negotiate a voluntary contract at a fair price and only when it had been determined that the proposed producer had on hand a supply of food sufficient in quantity to fill the order and could produce it without adding to his facilities.[68] By the spring of 1945 only about a dozen emergency orders had been served upon various food suppliers, generally with successful results. One such order was used by the Quartermaster market centers to obtain large purchases of shell and frozen eggs in April 1945.[69]

Set-aside orders, applicable to purchases of both the Department of Agriculture and the Army, specified in each case a percentage of total production which was to be held for purchase by government agencies. Immediately after Pearl Harbor when a "tight situation" developed in the procurement of canned fruits and vegetables, the government resorted to Conservation Order M–86, the first mandatory set-aside regulation of World War II. Issued by the WPB in March 1942, it was the joint accomplishment of civilians and officers who had been buying canned vegetables and fruits for the Army under the central procurement plan, and of members of the WPB.[70] M–86 and its companion order M–86a provided for set-aside orders on twenty-three fruits and vegetables. In general the canners accepted these orders favorably because they defined and imposed equal obligations on all.

Subsequently the WFA issued other set-aside orders. These were imposed not only on processed products but also on raw foods. On some

items the set-aside was complete, that is, 100 percent, but on many items a percentage of production of a selected base period was specified, and the duration of the order was for a temporary period of shortage. Set-aside orders included not only canned vegetables and fruits, but also dried fruits, rice, fish, peanuts, dried milk products, butter, cheese, poultry, fresh beef, pork, and other meats. Set-aside quotas were changed from time to time. QMC subsistence officers were consulted frequently in reference to the percentages to be placed on reserve and were instrumental in having the amounts raised to meet War Department needs.

Infractions of set-aside orders were numerous, resulting frequently from failure to understand them fully. The initial set-aside orders on beef were not immediately successful in making available greater quantities of beef to the armed forces. Instead they seemed to have the effect of sending more beef into black-market channels. Evasion of the set-aside orders on beef by a small percentage of the packing industry continued throughout 1944.[71] In the long run, however, the set-aside orders proved effective in

---

[68] (1) Ltr, Gen Hardigg, OQMG, to CG CQMD, 31 Sep 44, sub: Instructions on Use of Food Priorities. (2) 1st ind, Actg Dir of Purchases Div, ASF, to TQMG, 4 Sep 44, on memo, Maj W. R. Compton, OQMG, for Dir of Matériel, ASF, 27 Jul 44, sub: Use of Priority Rating FR–9 in Procurement of Subs Supplies. Both in 430.

[69] (1) Ltr, OIC Perishable Br, Fld Hq, to OQMG, 12 Jun 45, sub: Emergency Order for Shell Eggs. (2) 1st ind, Lt Col Logan Morrill, OQMG, to CG ASF, 10 Jul 45, on same. Both in 430.

[70] For a detailed discussion of the use of set-aside orders see (1) Marion Massen, *Canned Vegetables: A Case History in Central Procurement at the Chicago Quartermaster Depot During World War II* (CQMD Hist Rpt 3, October 1943), pp. 17–27. (2) Massen, *Canned Meats Procurement for the Armed Forces During World War II* (CQMD Hist Rpt 7, March 1946), pp. 125–44.

[71] For a detailed discussion of the orders as they applied to beef and other perishables see H. R. Rifkind, *Fresh Foods for the Armed Forces: the Quartermaster Market Center System, 1941–48* (QMC Historical Studies 20, 1951), pp. 70–73.

reserving needed quotas of food for the Army and other government agencies.

Production Planning and Scheduling

Closely tied to the allocation of scarce materials was the problem of planning and scheduling production to meet requirements. Production scheduling [72] in the QMC during the emergency was inadequate; in fact, as late as the fall of 1941 little thought had been given to the problem. Because procurement plans covered too short a period—usually one to three months—and were too incomplete, satisfactory scheduling of production was impossible. Such procurement plans were prepared by the operating branches of the Supply Division for the purpose of initiating the procurement of items. Each plan outlined the quantities of an item needed for one to three months, the rate of production, allocation of funds, and other information, on the basis of which the necessary procurement directives were prepared and sent to the depot. Short-range procurement did not permit contractors to make adequate plans for scheduling their production.

Production was impeded also by the fact that procurement directives were issued on a piecemeal and repetitive basis, involving numerous purchases of the same item. About twenty-five days elapsed between the issue of a procurement directive and the award of a contract, and, depending on the item, the contractor needed from thirty to ninety days to reach the rate of production necessary to meet scheduled deliveries. Each separate procurement meant the loss of two or three months before desired production and delivery rates could be attained. Quartermaster expediters recognized that long-range procurement was basic to successful production.[73] Procurements made on the basis of the entire requirements for at least a fiscal year would eliminate the time lag in the procurement program and simultaneously insure the maximum and economic utilization of the production facilities available for Quartermaster supply requirements.

Production continuity was as essential as long-range planning in securing the desired delivery of items. For most Quartermaster items productive capacity, however, far exceeded requirements. Unless the requirements were equivalent to the full productive capacity of the plants, the assignment of continuous production schedules was impractical. The Quartermaster situation was unlike that which prevailed in the purchase of Ordnance items, where procurement was scheduled up to the maximum capacity of output. Manufacturers of Quartermaster items operated in an atmosphere of uncertainty with respect to future awards. Repeatedly the lack of continuity of contracts forced them to disband their labor forces, tear down their production lines, disrupt the steady flow of materials, and transfer equipment to other jobs. To maintain full productive capacity, contractors took on commercial orders or concurrent contracts from various depots or other supply services.[74]

Quartermaster expediters recognized the necessity of using repeat orders in sufficient volume to insure production continuity at an economic level. In this they had the support of the Office of the Under Secretary of War and the WPB. To insure continuity of production at desired rates, Headquarters, SOS, authorized The Quartermaster General to place "advance

[72] Production scheduling was a procedure for controlling the flow of components and end items in order that deliveries of balanced quantities of specific requirements could be made within specified times.

[73] (1) Memo for file, F. X. Reynolds, Chief of Production Expediting Sec, OQMG, 15 Sep 41, sub: Long-Range Procurement. (2) Reynolds to Col Hester, Chief of Procurement Control Br, OQMG, 8 Jul 41, sub: Insp Rpt, Procurement Plng District, Jeffersonville, Ind. (3) Insp Rpt, Col Cound to TQMG, 11 Jul 41, sub: Activities at JQMD.

[74] Memo for file, Carl Rasmussen, OQMG, n. d. [circa Dec 41], sub: Procurement and Production.

orders for standard material" within the limits of the Army Supply Program whenever he deemed such action desirable and when necessary funds were available.[75] In general the OQMG developed the policy of arranging delivery schedules with a manufacturer in such a way that once he attained maximum desired output, deliveries would be made in approximately equal monthly amounts until the contract was completed, and additional orders would be placed to keep up production at about the same rate until the supply program was accomplished.[76]

This earmarking of orders for specific suppliers and keeping them in continuous production, however, was in direct opposition to the War Department's policy of wide dispersion of defense orders. It provoked a storm of criticism from manufacturers who had no contracts and feared they would be left out of the program for the duration of the war. The Murray Committee of the Senate, studying the problems of the small businessman, raised considerable objections, and under pressure Headquarters, SOS, ordered the discontinuance of the practice of earmarking unless "absolutely necessary." [77] In the QMC, earmarking of orders was considerably reduced, and restricted to cases where there was "urgency of delivery," where the supplier was the "only available source," or where there was need for "developmental work." [78] Production continuity, however, remained a cardinal principle of Quartermaster procurement, but it was accomplished without sacrificing the Corps' responsibilities under the small war plants program.

To accomplish procurement objectives, production planning had to be correlated with requirements. Requirements during the emergency period, however, were forecast by two groups within the OQMG—by the Requirements Branch of the Planning and Control Division and by the operating branches of the Supply Division. As the staff agency for re-

quirements in the OQMG, the Planning and Control Division furnished requirements programs to higher echelons of authority. As the operating agency responsible for initiating procurement, the Supply Division based its procurement program on the requirements estimated by its operating branches. No relationship, therefore, existed between official requirements and the procurement of items in the Corps at this time. By the fall of 1941, as shortages of materials, facilities, and labor increased the difficulties of procurement, the need of converting procurement into a planned program of production executed in accordance with scheduled requirements became obvious.[79]

Dual responsibility for requirements was finally eliminated in March 1942, and a balanced program of requirements was developed in the Army Supply Program, which became the source of procurement authority for all the supply services and the guide for the WPB in allocating materials. It permitted long-range planning and a closer relationship between official forecasts and actual procurement.[80]

It was no guide, however, for scheduling demand within a year. A breakdown of require-

---

[75] (1) OUSW memo, 29 Dec 41, sub: Broadening the Base of Defense Production. (2) Memo, Hq SOS for Chiefs of Sup Svs, 12 May 42, sub: Continuance of Going Contracts, quoting a WPB ltr of 28 Apr 42. (3) Memo, Dir of Procurement & Distr Div, SOS, for TQMG, 1 May 42, sub: Placement of Advance Orders.

[76] OQMG Cir Ltr 175, 27 Apr 42, sub: Negotiated Purchases.

[77] (1) Memo, Hq SOS for Chiefs of Sup Svs, 14 Oct 42, sub: Procurement Directives. (2) Ltr, Sen James E. Murray to TQMG, 14 Nov 42, no sub.

[78] (1) Ltr, TQMG to Senator Murray, 24 Nov 42, no sub. (2) For a fuller discussion of small war plants program see Yoshpe, *The Small Business Man and Quartermaster Contracts, 1940–42*. (3) Yoshpe and Massen, *Procurement Policies and Procedures*, pp. 128–141.

[79] F. X. Reynolds, Chief of Production Expediting Sec, to Col Hester, Chief of Production Control Br, OQMG, 24 Oct 41, sub: Production Program.

[80] See above, Ch. VI.

ments on a monthly basis was needed. But first attempts to establish monthly procurement schedules consisted solely of dividing the year's requirements by twelve, a useless method under an allocation system. Nor did it take into consideration other factors, such as allowance for lead time in production or the possibility of seasonal variations in production capacity. These problems were solved by the Military Planning Division during 1942. On the basis of these developments a Master Production Schedule was gradually evolved and applied, although it did not take its final form until the summer of 1943. It translated official requirements for each item purchased by the Corps into a monthly schedule, setting forth the rate at which required production was to take place in order to accomplish the mission of the Corps.[81] The allocation of scarce materials accelerated this development, for, in order to obtain such allocations, schedules of production had to be submitted to Headquarters, SOS, and to the WPB. With the introduction of the Controlled Materials Plan, involving quarterly allotments for specific programs, it was imperative that delivery schedules be geared to the allocation of materials.

Procurement plans and directives had to conform to the Master Production Schedule. Such adherence was not immediately obtained in the Corps, but as the need for agreement between materials allocation and production rates was pointed up conformity was attained. Since material was only made available to the extent called for in the Master Production Schedule, any changes in the Army Supply Program necessitated a review and rescheduling of all items of procurement in .the Master Production Schedule. Subsequently, in 1944, when short-term review of requirements was introduced in the Supply Control System to replace the Army Supply Program, supply and demand studies became the basis of the Master Production Schedule.[82]

At the beginning of the war the emphasis in the QMC, as in all supply services, was on getting enough of the needed goods in time. By the summer of 1943 the Corps had caught up with war needs and in response to the changing logistical situation, the objective, as procurement leveled off, became that of securing the right supplies at the right place at the right time. The scheduling of deliveries to correspond more closely with actual requirements became increasingly important. Hence a Master Production Schedule was established as an upper level on purchasing, and efforts were made by the depots to reduce buying not controlled by such schedules. Greater attention began to be paid to stock levels and to surplus and excess stocks. Close scheduling tended to prevent the building up of surpluses and to diminish termination claims. The more effectively this could be accomplished the less would be the problem of liquidating stocks on hand after the war ended.

Other Aids for Expediting Production

Location of Idle Production Equipment

To expedite production the QMC participated in a program supervised by the ANMB and later by the WPB to uncover and distribute idle and critical machine tools. The OQMG compiled lists of its suppliers who needed machine tools to complete their contracts. These were sent to the WPB in order that the names of such contractors would be placed on the "urgent list" to receive machine tools. Whenever bottlenecks developed in machine tools, Quartermaster procurement officers and inspectors consulted with regional Critical Tool Service offices established by the WPB before they

---

[81] OQMG OO 25–47, 10 Aug 43, sub: Responsibility and Procedure for Preparing MPS.

[82] OQMG OO 25–47A, 17 May 44, sub: Responsibility and Procedure for Preparing and Maintaining MPS.

endorsed preference rating certificates for new tools.[83]

When changes were made in program schedules or when production techniques were improved, machine tools were frequently rendered idle as a result. To obtain the maximum use of these tools, WPB could direct their transfer when not in use and, if necessary, could requisition them. To speed the reporting of all surplus or idle tools, all the technical services maintained liaison with a Machine Tool Section established in the Resources and Production Division, SOS.[84]

In addition to applying to higher authority for assistance in obtaining needed machine tools, the OQMG made use of its own expediters to uncover machine tools and materials that might be useful to Quartermaster contractors. In this way, for example, Singer sewing machines stored by the Work Projects Administration in Denver were made available to expedite the manufacture of critical tentage.[85] The liquidation of the WPA and the National Youth Administration released over 20,000 heavy industrial sewing machines, and Quartermaster expediters were instrumental in getting the appropriate agencies to work out procedures for selling them to government contractors.

Expansion of Plant Facilities

Expansion of plant facilities was necessary to expedite production for national defense. In the QMC no major construction, expansion, or conversion projects were undertaken, however, since so many of the items the Corps procured had their commercial counterparts. As Quartermaster requirements assumed unanticipated proportions, production capacity did have to be expanded. This was particularly true for the production of items needed in the motor transport program prior to its transfer to the Ordnance Department. Furthermore, the introduction of new items, such as helmet liners and jungle equipment, necessitated the development of adequate sources of supply.

The expansion of facilities was accomplished in a number of ways—through the use of special "Expediting Production" funds available to The Quartermaster General, by lease agreements with the Defense Plant Corporation, and through private financing with the aid of tax amortization benefits. The latter method accounted for most of the facilities expansion which was undertaken by Quartermaster contractors to meet the Corps' requirements. It was not, however, of significant proportions, since only a small percentage of such contractors applied for tax amortization benefits.[86] These benefits resulted from legislation enacted by Congress in 1940 which permitted corporations to amortize over a five-year period, for income and excess profits tax purposes, the cost of emergency facilities when these were certified as necessary to national defense.[87] The depreciation allowance was not deductable from the corporation's taxes but was only an allowable deduction in computing its taxable income.

From the beginning of the emergency, special Expediting Production funds and Defense Plant Corporation lease agreements were used to expand facilities producing items needed in the motor transport program. In January 1942, for

---

[83] (1) Ltr, ANMB to All Sup Svs et al., 22 May 42, sub: Idle Tools and Idle Machine Hrs. (2) Priorities Br to Chief of Purchases Div, OQMG, 3 Jun 42, same sub. (3) D. A. Henderson to Chiefs of all Brs, Purchases Div, OQMG, 20 May 42, sub: Machine Tools.

[84] AGO Memo S5-34-43, 10 Feb 43, sub: Direction for Machine Tool Transfers.

[85] Ltr, Capt C. W. Weikert, OQMG, to Stewart Miller, JQMD, 24 Jul 42, sub: WPA Sewing Machines.

[86] Memo, TQMG for USW, 17 Jul 41, sub: Proposed Procurement Cir—Non-Reimbursement Applications. As of that date The Quartermaster General indicated that no more than one percent of all Quartermaster Corps contracts are being performed by contractors who have applied for amortization certificates."

[87] 54 *U. S. Statutes* 998ff, 8 Oct 40.

example, the War Department apportioned $12,750,000 to The Quartermaster General in special Expediting Production funds for this purpose.[88] Such funds were also used to expand facilities for the manufacture of steel helmets, the dehydration of subsistence items, and to finance many other projects when the contractor was unable or unwilling to do so.[89] Upon QMC recommendation, the Defense Plant Corporation, a subsidiary of the Reconstruction Finance Corporation, entered into an agreement with a contractor who expanded his plant and then leased the facilities from the Defense Plant Corporation at an agreed rental. Where the rental did not fully reimburse the corporation, part of the financing was generally borne by the War Department. Such lease agreements were used not only in the motor transport program but also to expand facilities which were badly needed for the production of fork-lift trucks and industrial tractors, the manufacture of helmet liners, and the dehydration of subsistence items.[90] In contrast to other technical services, the expansion of plant facilities was not a major problem for the QMC, although steps had to be taken to assure the fulfillment of procurement goals.

Financial Aids to Quartermaster Contractors

To expedite production the QMC found it necessary to assist contractors in financing their operations under government contracts. In the rush to obtain supplies, contracts were often let without adequate investigation of a contractor's financial status. Since financially weak contractors could not always obtain bank financing, government aid was necessary if they were to deliver on their contracts. Even sound companies became overextended and required assistance. As a consequence, various measures—the assignment of claims under contracts as collateral for loans from banks, advance payments on contracts, and the extension and guarantee of loans to contractors—were taken in an effort to solve the financial problems of the contractors upon whom the Corps relied for its supplies.

Legislation enacted in 1940 enabled the Corps to come to the assistance of its contractors. Under the Assignment of Claims Act it was possible to assign to any bank, trust company, or other financial institution all claims under contracts entered into after 9 October 1940 whenever the amount involved exceeded $1,000 and such action was not expressly prohibited by the terms of the contract.[91] Such assignments became collateral for bank loans with the government agreeing to make all payments under the contract directly to the assignee. Quartermaster contracting officers were instructed in the expeditious handling of contracts involving the assignment of claims. This action relieved the government in many cases of the necessity of making advances or extending and guaranteeing loans to contractors. By increasing the working capital available for performance on Quartermaster contracts, the assignment of claims expedited the procurement program.

Under Congressional legislation direct government financing was also made available to contractors in the summer of 1940.[92] When necessary for national defense purposes, the

---

[88] Ltr, Col F. W. Browne, Office of Budget Officer, WD, to TQMG, 7 Jan 42, sub: Apportionment, 004.4.

[89] (1) Memo, Brig Gen H. A. Barnes, OQMG, for Dir of Resources & Production Div, ASF, 14 May 43, sub: Senate Investigation of Facilities Opns. (2) Production Svs Br to Management Control Br, Procurement Div, OQMG, 2 Jun 44, sub: Annual Rpt of Production Svs Br.

[90] (1) Ltr, Col Rowe, OQMG, to USW, 26 Nov 41, sub: Bendix Aviation Corp—Lease Agreement for Weiss Joints Facilities. (2) Ltr, Col Rowe to JAG, 2 Feb 42, sub: Towmotor Co. Defense Plant Corp Lease Agreement. (3) Memo, Gen Barnes, OQMG, for Dir of Resources & Production Div, ASF, 14 May 43, sub: Senate Investigation of Facilities Opns.

[91] 54 *U. S. Statutes* 1029–30, 9 Oct 40.

[92] 54 *U. S. Statutes* 731, approved 2 Jul 40, amended *ibid.*, 875, approved 9 Sep 40.

War Department could make advance payments to a contractor up to 30 percent of the contract price. In line with the cautious policy adopted by the War Department in the beginning, Quartermaster contracting officers were directed to make no recommendations for advance payments unless a "definite and clear-cut" showing could be made that such advances would result in "advantage to the government." In general the aim was to restrict advances to firms which had "sufficient ability and reliability to complete their contracts." [93]

After Pearl Harbor the policy on advance payments was liberalized. Procedures, decisions, and administration were decentralized to the supply services and their field procurement officers. The Quartermaster General and other chiefs of supply services could now approve advances on contracts under $5,000,000 without reference to the Under Secretary of War. Within limits he could delegate this authority to his contracting officers in the field. Furthermore, advances up to 50 percent of the contract price could be made without regard to higher authority, but only if required by special circumstances, or if contractors agreed to advance to subcontractors who required financing the entire amount of advance in excess of 30 percent of the contract price. [94]

Under the new policy it was no longer necessary for Quartermaster contractors to show that they could not obtain adequate financing elsewhere. Quartermaster contracting officers had to report all cases of requests for advances that were refused. Authority was delegated to them to approve the making of advance payments wherever The Quartermaster General was authorized to do so and where the aggregate amount of the advance under a contract did not exceed $100,000 (later $250,000) or 30 percent of the contract price, whichever was less. Such advance payments were made only upon the furnishing of adequate security to protect the government against loss. The extent of such

security was left to the discretion of the contracting officers and varied according to the financial strength and responsibility of the contractors. Decentralizing authority to the field expedited the handling of advance payments. In the QMC such advance payments were made on numerous contracts involving the production of trucks, trailers, and other motor transport equipment; textiles; shoes; dehydrated foods; parts for field ranges; and containers. [95] The more liberal extension of advance payments contributed to the successful accomplishment of the war production program.

Under presidential authorization the War Department was also able to make or participate in direct loans or to guarantee loans by financing institutions to contractors engaged in war work. [96] It was War Department policy to use guarantees of loans, up to 90 percent of the principal amount of the loan, in preference to making direct loans or participating in loans. The Federal Reserve banks acted as agents in carrying out these powers. A contractor applied to his local bank, directly to a Federal Reserve bank, or to a liaison officer for a loan. On the basis of information provided by contracting officers, the Federal Reserve bank determined whether a loan or guarantee should be given, and a "Statement of Necessity" was issued. Arrangements for War Department loans or guarantees not in excess of $100,000 to one borrower (including any Navy or Maritime Commission loans or guarantees) were then completed by the Federal Reserve bank on such

---

[93] (1) OQMG Cir Ltr 178, 30 Jul 41, sub: Advance Payments on Sup Contracts. (2) OQMG Cir Ltr 256, 22 Jun 42, sub: Advance Payments.

[94] (1) *Ibid.* (2) OQMG Cir Ltr 25, 15 Jan 42, sub: Advance Payments.

[95] (1) Memo, Col Cound, OQMG, for USW, 2 Oct 41, sub: Advance Payments Made to Contractors. (2) Memo, Col Cound for Hq SOS, 11 Apr 42, same sub. (3) Memo, Lt Col C. F. von dem Bussche, OQMG, for Fiscal Div, SOS, 14 Jul 42, same sub.

[96] 7 *Federal Register* 2367, Exec Order 9112, 26 Mar 42.

terms as it deemed advisable.[97] This provided an additional method of financing contracts for the war effort.

Various other steps were taken to aid the contractors in financing their defense orders. Efforts were made to overcome delays in the negotiation and execution of contracts. Banks were reluctant to loan on the strength of letters of award. To speed contract execution, the War Department authorized contracting officers to make use of one instrument combining the invitation to bid, the bid, and the acceptance by the government. The contract was fully executed when the contracting officer endorsed his acceptance on behalf of the government, and the contractor could borrow money promptly on it. Legislation and administrative action which relaxed the requirements for performance and payment bonds executed in connection with contracts to secure the fulfillment of all agreements was also of considerable assistance to contractors. In addition, Quartermaster contractors were protected from financial hardships resulting from slowdowns, curtailments, and terminations of production. Interim financing enabled them to preserve their productive capacity and continue operations or convert to other work.[98]

Assistance on Labor Problems

The fulfillment of the Quartermaster procurement program was dependent not only on the degree to which its suppliers obtained materials and facilities for production but also on their success in obtaining and utilizing manpower. To assist Quartermaster suppliers on labor-supply and labor-relations problems the QMC established a labor organization in the OQMG and in the field.[99] It made known Quartermaster needs to established manpower agencies. As manufacturers of commercial items, Quartermaster suppliers found themselves without

essential ratings under manpower control programs. Not only did they have no priority on manpower but their workers could be drawn off by essential industries without the need for releases. Quartermaster labor officers worked steadily to improve the "essentiality status" of the Corps' suppliers and advised them on the necessary procedures to be followed in submitting their labor requests.

The QMC aided contractors in obtaining reasonable relaxation of state, local, and union-imposed restrictions on all-out war production. Restrictions on the hours of employment of women particularly hampered Quartermaster production, since they prevented the operation of vital plants on a multiple-shift basis. To meet the heavy war procurement objectives and overcome labor shortages, it was necessary to relinquish a number of gains which labor had won in the past. At the same time the Corps was also concerned for the maintenance of adequate labor standards in order that high production levels might be sustained during the war. Contractors were advised not only on the need for sound working conditions but on industrial engineering problems involved in setting up production lines and on work schedules that would make the best use of manpower.

To overcome labor shortages Quartermaster labor officers urged the maximum use of all potential laborers. As a result, women, minors, physically handicapped workers, and members of racial and minority groups formerly discriminated against in employment were brought into war production in increasing numbers. The QMC increased the skilled workers available to suppliers by assisting in training programs. Where the local labor supply proved inade-

[97] OQMG Cir Ltr 242, 10 Jun 42, sub: Guarantees, Loans and Commitments Under Exec Order 9112.
[98] Yoshpe, *Production Control in QMC,* pp. 58–59.
[99] For an elaboration of this brief summary of Quartermaster activities see Yoshpe, *Labor Problems in Quartermaster Procurement, passim.*

quate, the services of immigrant labor, foreign workers, Japanese internees, convicts, and prisoners of war were obtained. Quartermaster housekeeping and shelter equipment was made available to contractors for use by seasonal workers in agriculture and food-processing plants. When inductions of skilled operators jeopardized critical production, Quartermaster labor officers supported deferment requests. In extreme emergencies they arranged for the furlough of troop units for work in agriculture and food-processing industries.

Since labor disputes curtailed production, Quartermaster labor officers sought to maintain harmonious labor-management relations. Efforts were made to iron out differences before work stoppages occurred. Labor disputes of sufficient severity brought direct action in the form of contract terminations, removal of items from strike-bound plants, and government seizure and operation of plants. Finally the Corps participated in a broad morale-stimulation program, involving rallies, speeches, exhibits, and "E" awards, in an effort to impress upon both capital and labor their contribution to the war effort and to elicit greater co-operation and more efficient production.

Inspection of Quartermaster Procurements

Improvement of the organization and techniques for inspection of Quartermaster procurements strengthened production control considerably. In order to achieve the desired ends of procurement, however, there had to be co-operation between inspection personnel, purchasing and contracting officers, and personnel engaged in drafting specifications. Specifications and any subsequent changes in them were prepared by personnel of the Research and Development Branch who naturally were primarily interested in quality, that is, in giving the Army the best equipment obtainable. On the other hand, the contracting officers were primarily interested in quantity. They were under constant pressure to

secure delivery of supplies in accordance with the requirements of the delivery schedules, which were determined by the Storage and Distribution Division according to the needs of the service. In this conflict between quality and quantity, inspection found itself squarely in the middle. Inspectors were bound by the legal aspects of the contract and consequently were obliged to insist upon deliveries conforming to specifications and other terms of the contract. Where conflicts between quality and quantity occurred, a compromise had to be evolved by co-operation among these three groups so that delivery of supplies would not be delayed. It mattered little how accurately and scientifically specifications were drawn if commodities were not kept up to the established standard by means of careful testing and inspection. At the same time, proper inspection, by insuring a smooth flow of adequate equipment from production line to training camp and battlefield, constituted a vital link in the chain of Quartermaster supply.

Clothing, Equipment, and General Supplies

For fifteen years following World War I, inspection was not an urgent problem in the QMC inasmuch as the Army could be supplied for the most part from surplus stocks. Purchases were largely confined to subsistence for a small, peacetime Army. The necessity of supplying the newly created Civilian Conservation Corps in 1933 created an inspection problem, and thereafter inspection procedures underwent many modifications.

As in the case of procurement, responsibility for prewar inspection of clothing and equipage was centralized in the procuring depots—for example, shoe inspection at the Boston Depot. No co-ordinated system of inspection had been established. The OQMG exercised little or no control of inspection until the beginning of the emergency. There existed no uniformity of inspection policies or procedures, no over-all training policies, and no standard of quality control. Each procuring depot had its own inspection system. It sent out roving inspectors who performed advisory inspection at plants, but final inspection and acceptance occurred at the procuring depot. Rejected items were shipped back to the contractor while accepted items were sent to issuing depots for distribution.[100] Depot laboratories afforded inspection and testing services. These were supplemented by the facilities of other government agencies, such as the National Bureau of Standards. It was anticipated that in event of war commercial laboratories would be called upon to assist in performing inspection and tests.

This inspection organization, which was most satisfactory for peacetime operations, although wasteful of manpower and transportation, proved inadequate to the needs of an expanding procurement program in the emergency and war periods. As the QMC came to appreciate the many problems involved in supplying an expanding Army, its inspection organization changed materially. In the beginning the depots resorted to the use of branch offices and field supervisory organizations in order to relieve the extreme burden on the home depots. The inadequacy of peacetime procedures first became apparent in the case of clothing and equipage. The Philadelphia Depot led the way in replacing its traveling inspectors by a permanent field organization. Ten branch offices were established in areas of greatest production capacity, each of which kept in touch with the contractors and inspectors in its designated area and co-ordinated its activities with the headquarters office at Philadelphia.[101]

At the same time, the OQMG was moving toward a decentralization to the various supply depots of the responsibility for final inspection and acceptance of items procured by central purchasing depots. It proposed activating such a plan in the summer of 1940.[102] This program

happened to coincide with a plan advocated by the Advisory Commission to the Council of National Defense to decentralize responsibility for the execution and administration of contracts in order to alleviate economic distress by a wide dispersion of defense orders. Both were bitterly opposed by the Philadelphia Depot.

The decentralization of purchasing was temporarily shelved, but the OQMG went ahead with plans to decentralize inspection of clothing and textile items. The final inspection and acceptance of various clothing items was to take place at designated supply depots. It was anticipated that such procedure would effect savings in freight, storage, and handling of Quartermaster procurements, but the Philadelphia Depot was certain that the expense of equipment and added personnel needed to establish a textile inspection system at depots would outweigh any such advantages. The commanding officer marshalled his arguments against the plan, which he thought would not operate satisfactorily or be economical. In the end he made recommendations for the transfer of key personnel necessary to launch the program according to the request of the OQMG. After some modification of the original plan, a definite step was taken toward decentralization.[103]

Obviously the plan could not be put into

---

[100] OQMG Cir 1–4, Sec. III, 1 Mar 39, sub: Procurement and Distr of Supplies.

[101] Verbatim Rpt of Insp Conf, 16 Jun 43 at PQMD, and 17, 18, 19 Jun 43 at NYQMPO, pp. 258–59. Hereafter cited as Insp Conf Rpt.

[102] (1) Ltr, Col Hardigg, OQMG, to CO PQMD, 6 Jun 39, sub: Coordination of Insp at Depots–C&E, 400.163. (2) Ltr, Gen Corbin, OQMG, to QMSO San Francisco Gen Depot, 18 Jul 40, sub: Policy Regarding Delivery of C&E, 400.163.

[103] See the following for the points at issue: (1) Ltr, Col Littlejohn, OQMG, to CO PQMD, 28 Sep 40, sub: Insp of Clo. (2) 1st ind, Col W. A. McCain, PQMD, to TQMG, 2 Oct 40. (3) 2d ind, Gen Corbin, OQMG, to CO PQMD, 16 Oct 40. (4) 3d ind, Col McCain to TQMG, 21 Oct 40. (5) 4th ind, Gen Corbin to CO PQMD, 26 Oct 40. (6) 5th ind, Col McCain to TQMG, 31 Oct 40.

effect at one stroke. The depot had to be given considerable discretion in the development of the program. Inspection of coats, overcoats, and mackinaws was the central issue, and until the depot had accumulated the necessary reserve for immediate anticipated needs, decentralization to the designated depots at Chicago and Atlanta was to be delayed. When this reserve had been built up by mid-February 1941, the Philadelphia Depot still opposed decentralization. It rehearsed arguments grown familiar since the first discussion of the problem in 1936. The depot, however, was waging a losing battle. The OQMG was adamant and in April 1941 issued an order directing and setting out procedures for the decentralized inspection of clothing and equipage.[104] The depot thereupon co-operated fully in the inauguration of this program and in building up adequate inspection services at the receiving installations.

Under this system centralized technical control of field inspection at the procuring depots was retained, but final inspection and acceptance was decentralized to several receiving depots. This was the first step toward decentralization of final inspection and acceptance, but the system had developed no uniformity of inspection standards and continued wasteful of manpower and transportation.

For a time these inspection organizations were able to handle satisfactorily the military supplies flowing to the depots. The mounting requirements of 1942 and 1943, however, placed a severe strain on depot inspection organizations. As late as the summer of 1942, most Quartermaster procurements of clothing and equipage items were still being sent to depots for inspection and acceptance. Under the full impact of war, however, depot inspection had to give way wherever possible to final inspection and acceptance at contractors' plants in order to keep rejections to a minimum, conserve critical materials, labor, and transportation, and to expedite delivery of supplies to

using stations. In June 1942 the Director of Procurement, OQMG, called upon the various procuring depots to adopt this principle.[105]

The Boston Depot had been following this principle for some time in the inspection of shoes, and the results had proved satisfactory. Acting upon the directive, the Jeffersonville Depot went over completely to factory inspection, and other depots began to put the same principle into effect on their contracts. At the Philadelphia Depot, however, the proposal met with vigorous opposition. It was not that the depot did not appreciate or use field inspection as a check on quality, specification compliance, and economy in the use of materials, but it regarded its plant representatives as "quality controllers" rather than inspectors. Philadelphia's contracts totaled 6,000, and proper inspection at factories, it was argued, would require a force of at least 15,000 inspectors. Depot inspection was advocated as a conserver of trained manpower. Furthermore, depot personnel agreed that the caliber of suppliers on whom the depot had to depend was such as to prevent final inspection and acceptance at factories. Decentralized inspection among the depots had proved effective despite the initial fears of the depot and, in the light of its peculiar problems, the Philadelphia Depot opposed the substitution of plant inspection for depot inspection.[106]

[104] (1) Memo, Lt Col W. H. Middleswart, Procurement Div, PQMD, to Maj B. E. McKeever, S&D Div, PQMD, 12 Nov 40, sub: Decentralization of Insp Facilities, and 1st memo ind, 14 Nov 40. (2) Ltr, Col Littlejohn, OQMG, to Lt Col T. W. Jones, PQMD, 27 Feb 41, no sub, and reply, 4 Mar 41, 400.163. (3) OQMG Cir Ltr 53, 3 Apr 41, sub: Insp of C&E.

[105] Ltr, Gen Corbin to CG CQMD, 15 Jun 42, sub: Inspection, 400.163. An identical letter was sent to the other procuring depots.

[106] (1) 1st ind, Col R. C. Brady, PQMD, to TQMG, 23 Jun 42, on ltr, Gen Corbin, OQMG, to CG PQMD, 10 Jun 42, sub: Insp. (2) For the views of the depot see addresses and comments of Col Brady, Col Jones, Lt Col H. M. Manderbach, Lt Col G. Christie, Jr., Lt Col A. E. Dennis, and others in Insp Conf Rpt, *passim*.

Though it was not proposed to establish any arbitrary rule, the trend in the Corps was toward final inspections at contractors' plants in all cases where this could be done with adequate protection of the government's interests. Insofar as the Philadelphia Depot was concerned, the OQMG suspended its instructions pending further study of the principle of plant inspection by the depot. As a result the depot did simplify and expedite inspection procedures in a number of ways. It also tried out plant inspection for officers' clothing, confining the test to several manufacturers of high-class clothing. This trial revealed the percentage of defective garments to be so high that the depot abandoned plant inspection and gave the garments a "100% inspection at the Depot." [107]

The pressure for more centralized control of inspection coincided with an effort being made by the ASF to improve and systematize inspection activities among the technical services. Early in the spring of 1943 it undertook a survey of inspection practices of all of the technical services. For this purpose it engaged the services of a private firm of consulting engineers—The Trundle Engineering Company of Cleveland, Ohio. The survey was initiated on 8 April 1943 and within three months the Trundle engineers submitted a comprehensive report of their findings and recommendations. [108]

The Trundle report indicated that the inspection function was not given the recognition and attention its importance warranted. In addition, there was a lack of clearly defined lines of authority and responsibility in the technical services with respect to inspection organization, methods, and practices. Specifically, Quartermaster organization charts, manuals, and directives failed to provide a clear and adequate definition of the inspection mission. Generally, the inspection function was placed within the various commodity procurement sections of the depots but there was no "standard or definite" plan for the Corps as a whole. There was a

"great need" for simplifying, standardizing, and unifying the methods, practices, and controls of all phases of inspection. In the Corps there was a tremendous duplication of effort, unnecessary travel, and wasteful utilization of manpower because its procuring depots operated on a "commodity" rather than a "geographical" basis and covered the entire United States in their respective operations. [109]

The report found the technical services engaged in an unwarranted amount of inspection which the Trundle engineers attributed to insufficient use of predetermined "scientific sampling" or quality control. The QMC, it seemed, had far to go in the reduction of the quantity and cost of its inspection. It employed various inspection methods depending on the type of product, the conditions of procurement, or the judgment of the inspector. It had no quality control in the sense of scientific sampling, and much more progress could be made in final inspection and acceptance at contractors' plants. There was also considerable room for improvement in the use of manuals to acquaint inspection personnel with the policies and practices established by higher echelons and in the recruitment and treatment of inspection personnel. [110]

Except for proposed organizational changes, the recommendations of the Trundle report

[107] (1) 2d ind, Gen Corbin, OQMG, to CG PQMD, 26 Jun 42, on ltr, same to same, 10 Jun 42, sub: Insp. (2) Ltr, Col Brady, PQMD, to TQMG, 1 Aug 42, sub: Insp of C&E, 400.163.

[108] Ltr, George T. Trundle, Jr., to Brig Gen H. C. Minton, Dir of Resources & Production Div, ASF, 2 Jul 43, atchd to *Report of Inspection Survey for Inspection Section, Facilities and Inspection Branch, Production Division, Headquarters, ASF, Washington, D. C.* (Cleveland, Ohio, July 1, 1943). Hereafter cited as Trundle Insp Rpt.

[109] Trundle Insp Rpt, Serial 2, Sec. VII, pp. 1–2, 7, 9. See also Serial 1, pp. 4–5, 6–8, 16–17, 28, 43. Note that in the report the findings common to all the technical services are summarized in Serial 1, and a brief of the findings relating to each of the technical services appears in Serial 2.

[110] Ibid., Serial 2, Sec. VII, pp. 3, 7–8, 10.

were approved.[111] To implement these approved recommendations the Trundle engineers prepared an outline of an over-all inspection manual for the ASF. Representatives of the technical services participated in meetings at which were formulated the general principles upon which the text of the inspection manual was to be based. By the winter of 1943 a draft of the manual had been prepared for the ASF and was submitted to the technical services for comment. The OQMG proposed a few changes but reported that the manual was "eminently satisfactory for its intended use insofar as the QMC is concerned."[112] This manual set forth the guiding inspection policies and procedures common to all the technical services. It was to be supplemented by inspection manuals prepared by each of the technical services.

The QMC had made many improvements prior to the Trundle survey, but its findings were a powerful stimulus to further progress in the establishment of effective controls and the formation and direction of field inspection policies. In the summer of 1943 the Inspection Section of the OQMG was promoted to a branch in the Procurement Division with primary responsibility for supervising the inspection of all material and equipment, except fuels and lubricants, for which the Corps entered into contracts. At the end of the summer a Deputy Director for Inspection was designated to assist the Director of Procurement in all inspection matters.[113]

In line with the recommendations of the Trundle report and those of the Inspection Branch, Quartermaster inspection was placed on a geographical basis in the fall of 1943. A QMC Inspection Service was created under the jurisdiction of the Director of Procurement, OQMG, with a field headquarters in New York City and ten (later eleven) inspection zones throughout the country. These zones were to handle the inspection of all Quartermaster supplies, except subsistence and fuels and lubri-

cants, produced within their geographical limits. Zone offices, established for various geographical locations to act as headquarters for field inspection of all procuring depots with contracts in these areas, serviced these contracts from receipt of the purchase orders to the completion of the final shipments.[114] Thus, decentralization was finally accomplished. In lieu of centralized control exercised by several procuring depots, one central agency, the QMC Inspection Service, controlled all inspection activities of the Corps, except those pertaining to subsistence, and fuels and lubricants.

No time was lost in setting up the field headquarters office in New York City. Measures were taken promptly to activate the inspection zones, beginning with a "trial run" for the Boston Zone, and to establish necessary controls, prepare and publish instructions and manuals, supervise and control employment and utilization of all inspection personnel, and to perform all functions incident to the transfer of supplies from manufacturing plants to receiving stations. This was not achieved without some depot opposition. Since contracts and inspectors of the Jeffersonville Depot in the Boston area were to be taken over first, initial criticism came from that depot. The Philadelphia Depot voiced its opposition, however, when new inspection zones were activated, for it felt no criterion had been set up to judge the success of the Boston experiment.[115]

[111] 1st ind, CG ASF to Dir of Material, ASF, n. d., atchd to Trundle Insp Rpt.

[112] 1st ind, Gen Corbin, OQMG, to Hq ASF, 9 Dec 43, on memo, Gen Minton, Production Div, ASF, for TQMG, 1 Dec 43, sub: Draft of Insp Manual for ASF, 461.

[113] (1) OQMG OO 25–41, 8 Jul 43, sub: Establishment of Insp Br. (2) OQMG OO 25–54, 24 Sep 43, sub: Orgn of Procurement Div.

[114] (1) OQMG Cir Ltr 149, 27 Sep 43, sub: Establishment of QMC Insp Sv, and supplements thereto. (2) See also OQMG Cir 16, 24 Apr 44, sub: QMC Insp Sv.

[115] (1) Ltr, Brig Gen A. R. Kimball, JQMD, to TQMG, 17 Nov 43, no sub. (2) Ltr, Gen Kimball

Although they registered objections, the depots did co-operate, and the Inspection Service went ahead resolutely with its mission. By the spring of 1944 it had activated all inspection zones. During its first year of operation the QMC Inspection Service made substantial progress in implementing the recommendations of the Trundle report. Subsequently, various refinements were introduced that further improved the quality of inspection and streamlined operating organizations and procedures.

The problems confronting the Inspection Service were many and varied and all demanded immediate attention. As a result of the Trundle report, plant acceptance in place of depot acceptance became the established policy of the ASF and the QMC. To complete the conversion from depot to plant acceptance, the OQMG directed that all contracts executed on or after 15 March 1944, except those for subsistence and fuels and lubricants, were to contain an article providing for determination of the place of inspection by the commanding officer of the inspection zone in which the contractor's plant was located.[116] The relative advantages of plant or destination inspection had long been the subject of heated arguments. The Philadelphia Depot remained unconvinced of the desirability of this change, but, since the die had been cast, it co-operated in furnishing any technical or contractual advice needed by inspection zone commanders in order to prevent any lowering of quality standards for the items it procured. At the same time, the depot made it a matter of record that it did not believe that the directed procedure could be successful in maintaining "the present high standards of quality."[117] Conversion of contracts was accomplished gradually. Some contracts, such as textile contracts, presented many problems. It was the summer of 1944 before plans were worked out and approved for factory inspection and acceptance of cottons, woolens, and worsteds.[118] By May 1945, however, "well over eighty percent of all plants" producing on Quartermaster contracts were operating on factory acceptance basis.[119]

The outstanding achievement in QMC inspection was this shift from nationwide administration on a commodity basis by individual procuring depots to geographical administration of all commodities under the central control of a field headquarters. This change in basic inspection policy enabled the Corps to absorb a tremendous increase in work load without a commensurate increase in personnel. Between November 1943, when the QMC Inspection Service was established, and the end of the fiscal year 1945, the number of contracts increased from 7,500 to 31,000 and the number of contractors' plants from 5,400 to over 8,500. At the same time the number of inspectors declined from about 5,000 to 4,300. In November 1943 about 60 percent of this personnel was doing depot inspection; by July 1945 less than 9 percent was so engaged.[120]

This conversion was effected without lowering the quality of inspection, a result that stemmed from a comprehensive program of quality control initiated at the same time by the Inspection Service. The program was composed of three major phases: (1) the development of

---

to same, 19 Nov 43, no sub. (3) Memo, Col A. H. Rogow, Deputy Dir for Insp, to Gen Corbin, OQMG, 23 Nov 43, no sub. (4) Ltr, Brig Gen R. Walsh, PQMD, to TQMG, 21 Dec 43, sub: Zone Orgn of QM Inspection Sv, 333.1.

[116] Ltr, Gen Corbin, OQMG, to CG PQMD, 29 Feb 44, sub: Insp of Supplies, 400.163.
[117] 1st ind, Col Jones, PQMD, to TQMG, 6 Mar 44, on above citation, 400.163.
[118] (1) Col Vere Painter, QMC Insp Sv, to TQMG, 5 Jul 44, sub: Insp of Textiles. (2) Deputy Dir for Purchases, OQMG, to QMC Insp Sv, 19 Jul 44, same sub, 400.163.
[119] QMC Manual 25–8, August 1945, sub: Proceedings: Conf of OIC's of Insp Zones, May 1945, p. 9, citing remarks of Col Painter. Hereafter cited as Conf Proceedings.
[120] Ltr, Col Painter, QMC Insp Sv, to TQMG, 16 Jun 45, sub: Additional Material for Annual Rpt FY 1945.

standard inspection procedures, (2) the utilization of time-saving gauges and other inspection devices, and (3) the institution of scientific sampling plans.

In the past the Corps had relied heavily on process inspection and final inspection at the procuring depot. Process inspection was a method of inspecting manufacturing facilities, equipment, methods of operation, and personnel in order to correct faulty operations before these led to the manufacture of defective products. Such an inspection method required experienced personnel. The decreasing number of experienced inspectors available during the war years necessitated adoption of another method of inspection, which could be used by new personnel after a minimum amount of training. Under lot-by-lot inspection, which utilized a sampling method, the contractor had to submit reasonably large lots of products for inspection and in such condition that every unit in the lot was accessible to the inspector. Acceptability of each lot was determined by sample units drawn from each part of the lot. Acceptance and rejection were on a lot basis, and since rejection involved an entire lot rather than a few defective pieces, the contractor became more aware of the need to control the quality of his product.[121]

The basis for accepting or rejecting lots, however, had to be standardized so that each producer would receive the same treatment. This was an important basic policy of the Inspection Service and was approached through two developments—by standardizing the basis for evaluating, first, the individual unit of the product and, second, the quality of the aggregate units, that is, the lot. To determine the quality of the individual unit of the product, the Inspection Service utilized a technical approach and developed the standard inspection procedure. It was an interpretation of the specification and provided the inspector with a written procedure, defining in detail the exact technique to be used by him in accepting or rejecting a particular

item.[122] The procedure was so clearly written and graphically presented that it could be understood by the least experienced inspector. To judge the quality of a lot, the Inspection Service used a statistical approach and prepared standard sampling plans based on mathematical laws of probability. The use of scientific sampling plans on a nationwide basis, permitting prompt determination of the quality of a lot with a minimum of inspection time, contributed most effectively to the ability of the Inspection Service to carry its increasing load of contracts with a decreasing inspection personnel. By June 1945 sampling plans were in use in over 2,800 plants, whereas a year earlier such procedures had barely emerged from the planning stage.[123]

At the same time that standard inspection procedures were being published for major items of Quartermaster procurement, the Inspection Service initiated an intensive program for the development of gauges and templets to further streamline and standardize inspection techniques. The use of these devices saved many man-hours of inspector time, thereby permitting maximum use of existing inspection manpower.

The QMC Inspection Service implemented other recommendations of the Trundle report. It initiated an extensive, co-ordinated training program under the direction and supervision of a special staff of training consultants at headquarters. It improved the conditions under which inspection personnel worked, and by streamlining and reducing the number of forms,

[121] (1) QMC Manual 25–5, December 1944, sub: Annual Rpt: First Year of the QMC Insp Sv, pp. 12–13. (2) QMC Insp Handbook M608–15, December 1945, sub: Sampling for Quality Control.

[122] QMC Manual 25–8, August 1945, sub: Conf Proceedings, p. 32, giving an address by Capt Lawrence R. Van Dyke, sub: The Philosophy, Logic, and Construction of SIP.

[123] (1) Ibid., p. 10. (2) Ltr, Col Painter, QMC Insp Sv, to TQMG, 16 Jun 45, sub: Additional Material for Annual Rpt FY 1945.

laboratory reports, and procedures gave the inspector greater freedom to perform his main task of quality inspection.

The Inspection Service sought to meet the criticism of the Trundle engineers on the duplication of inspection within a service and between services. Within the Corps, duplication of inspection was eliminated by the organization of the Inspection Service and its control of inspection on a geographical basis. To eliminate duplication between the services as far as possible, constant surveys of contracts at plants were made by the zone offices. As a result, the Jeffersonville Zone, for example, worked out arrangements with the Cleveland and the Cincinnati Ordnance Districts to eliminate duplication of inspection on a variety of items procured by the QMC and the Ordnance Department in its area.[124] It was the established policy of the Inspection Service to have one organization do the entire inspection job wherever possible. Usually the organization with the predominant interest in the output made the inspection, but other factors of convenience, greater knowledge, or availability of qualified inspectors were taken into consideration. Not all duplications of inspection between the services could be eliminated because there were substantial differences in methods, and some commodities required highly specialized inspection knowledge. As the Army and the Navy late in the war moved toward joint procurement of common items, questions of standardizing inspection between services were raised. The war ended before the implications of consolidated procurement could be thoroughly explored.[125]

Subsistence

The emergency and war also brought changes in the procurement and inspection of subsistence. Prior to 1941 perishable subsistence was purchased locally by Army installations. Such local procurement sufficed in time of peace but

the demands of an expanding Army in the emergency period gave rise to centralized procurement of perishables. This was effected through the establishment of the Quartermaster Market Center Program, which insured a steady and adequate flow of perishable foods to the troops and at the same time, by the distribution of buying activity, tended to cushion its impact upon the market and to stabilize production and prices.

The market center program, set up in 1941, was immediately faced with the necessity of establishing inspection procedures for the perishables it procured. Market centers began operations with the purchase of fresh fruits and vegetables. Inspection of these items was handled by both receiving station and market centers. Purchases of local home-grown fruits and vegetables made by post quartermasters had to be inspected at destination for quality, condition, and count. Market centers furnished available assistance when requested. At posts where associate market specialists or inspectors were permanently stationed, they determined final acceptance or rejection of the commodity. At all other posts served by market centers but not having permanently assigned market specialists or inspectors, a representative of the sales officer was instructed by market center personnel in the art of inspecting fruits and vegetables.

In the case of carlot shipments, the market centers encouraged contractors supplying such shipments to furnish federal certificates as evidence that the commodity met the grade requirements under which it was purchased. Final inspection, however, for condition and count was still made at destination. Where less than

---

[124] (1) Ltr, Maj Orville T. Church, JQMD, to Cleveland District Chief, Cleveland Ordnance District, 26 Jul 44, sub: Duplication of Insp. (2) Ltr, Col F. F. Taylor, JQMD, to Hq QMC Insp Sv, 2 Sep 44, same sub, 400.8.

[125] (1) QMC Manual 25–5, Dec 44, sub: Annual Rpt, p. 46. (2) QMC Manual 25–8, Aug 45, sub: Conf Proceedings, pp. 135–36, citing remarks of Col Painter.

carlot quantities were purchased from jobbers or commission men in principal markets, inspection occured, wherever possible, at point of purchase. Such inspection was made by a Quartermaster marketing specialist or by an inspector of the Department of Agriculture. Inspection certificates were forwarded with purchase orders to destination points.

In general, inspection might be accomplished at point of shipment or at destination, whichever was most feasible. Inspection at origin was encouraged in order to decrease the number of rejections at destination. Final acceptance and possession by the government was contingent upon inspection for condition and count at destination.[126]

The market center program soon extended its operations to include the purchase of dairy and poultry products and of meats and meat products. Prior to the establishment of this program, meats and meat and dairy products had been procured locally on an indefinite quantity basis for monthly periods. Whenever available, personnel of the Veterinary Corps inspected such items to determine the grade and the sanitary condition of the products, as well as of the plants in which they were produced and handled, except meat plants under the sanitary supervision of the Bureau of Animal Industry and poultry packing and canning plants operating under the supervision of the Poultry Inspection Service of the Department of Agriculture. The veterinary officer inspected these products upon delivery and, in addition, during the process of production if the product, or protection of the government's interests, made such inspection necessary. Inspection was also provided later during storage. In the process of inspection veterinary officers used the laboratory service of the local Army station or general hospital, the medical laboratories of the service commands, and the laboratory of the Army Medical Center in Washington. In some few cases they also established and maintained subsistence laboratories at Quartermaster depots. Veterinary inspection was conducted under the administrative direction of the commanding officer of the post, camp, station, depot, or procurement point and under the technical supervision of the Medical Department.[127]

In the summer of 1941 the market centers began to make purchases of butter, eggs, cheese, and poultry in definite quantities for immediate delivery. In the course of developing inspection procedures for these commodities, clashing viewpoints within the QMC were revealed. Since World War I, the Department of Agriculture had been developing a system of grading, inspection, and certification of quality and condition of fruits, vegetables, dairy and poultry products, and meats. In the case of dairy and poultry products such inspection was permissive rather than compulsory in character. It was accomplished on the basis of co-operative agreements between the Agricultural Marketing Service and the states concerned, with the contractor who made use of the inspection service paying for it on a contract basis at shipping or processing points, or on the basis of established scales of fees at terminal markets.[128]

Accustomed to the use of this inspection service, civilian personnel brought in to supervise the procurement of dairy and poultry products by the market centers favored and proposed utilizing the services of the Agricultural Marketing Service.[129] On the other hand, military

[126] (1) OQMG Cir Ltr 42, 19 Mar 41, sub: Purch of Fresh Fruits and Vegetables. (2) OQMG Cir Ltrs 263, 360, and 109, 6 Oct 41, 23 Sep 43, 15 Jul 43, respectively, sub: Purch of Perishable Subs.
[127] (1) Procurement Cir 12, Sec. IX, 1 Aug 38, sub: Changes in AR 5–360. (2) Ltr, TAG to all CA and Dept Commanders, 8 Jul 39, sub: Insp of Meat, Meat Food Products, Dairy Products and Forage. AG 431 (5–29–39) Misc D.
[128] *Agricultural Marketing Service: Organization and Functions*, Department of Agriculture, March 1940.
[129] Ltr, Maj E. F. Shepherd, OIC, Fld Hq, Chicago, to Chief of Perishable Subs Br, OQMG, 18 Aug 41, sub: Procedure for the Insp of Poultry, Eggs, Butter and Cheese, 430.

personnel were used to inspection by the Veterinary Corps and could see no reason for not extending its inspection activities. To be sure, it had long been established policy, especially in reference to eggs, butter, and hay forage for animals, for Army inspecting officers to honor a prior inspection made by any accredited official agency, unless an obvious error was plainly evident. Knowing this, some contractors, anxious to meet specifications, had used certification by the Agricultural Marketing Service. It was felt, however, that the gist of the market center proposal was that "to a large extent it completely subordinates the station veterinary officer and the station quartermaster to the action of a civil agency." This was not believed to be in the best interests of the Army.[130]

In the face of increasing Army purchases of these commodities, the QMC was confronted with the necessity of encouraging large producers and processors to bid on Quartermaster requirements. Many had refused to negotiate contracts in the past because purchases had been made to cover indefinite monthly requirements at firm prices and because rejections at Army installations had been considered unfair.[131] Complaints had arisen over differences in grading by inspectors of the Agricultural Marketing Service and the Veterinary Corps. Rejection by the veterinary officer at destination did not necessarily mean that an error had been made in grading on either side, since with perishable foods it was entirely possible for grades to change between the time of inspection at point of shipment and that made at point of receipt. It was imperative, however, that these disputes be avoided or else settled promptly.

The disagreements had to be compromised and a new inspection procedure amicably worked out with the Chief Veterinarian of the Office of The Surgeon General and with the Agricultural Marketing Service. It sought to insure, so far as possible, fair grading of the supplies upon their receipt at camp and to resolve

promptly and equitably all disagreements between inspectors. Contractors were to be encouraged to secure inspection at origin either by the Veterinary Corps or by the Agricultural Marketing Service, whichever was available. Regardless of which agency made the initial inspection, final inspection was to be accomplished at destination covering fit condition of the food for human consumption and for compliance with terms of the contract.

When any dairy or poultry products inspected at point of origin by an inspector of the Agricultural Marketing Service were found upon inspection at destination not to be of the grade contracted for, the contractor was to be notified. He might request a reinspection. In that event, at the request of the officer in charge of the market center, the Agricultural Marketing Service would send a representative to the camp, post, or station to reinspect the shipment in question. The market center also requested the commanding general of the corps area in which the post, camp, or station was located to send a veterinary officer to make a separate and independent reinspection at the same time. The two inspectors were expected to compare and discuss their findings before rendering their reports. This reinspection established the grade. If the inspectors did not agree, however, the receiving quartermaster made the final decision, "since all inspections are advisory and final acceptance or rejection rests with the Quartermaster."[132]

---

[130] Ltr, Brig Gen J. L. Frink, QM, Fourth CA, to TQMG, 5 Sep 41, same sub, 430.

[131] (1) 1st ind, Gen Corbin, OQMG, to QM, Fourth CA, 19 Sep 41, on ltr cited in n. 130. (2) Ltr, John A. Martin, QM MC Chicago, to Col Hardigg, OQMG, 10 Oct 41, sub: Veterinary Participation in Insp of Poultry, Butter, Eggs and Cheese, 400.163.

[132] (1) Ltr, C. W. Kitchen, Chief of AMS, to Col Hardigg, Chief of Subs Br, OQMG, 29 Aug 41, no sub, and reply, 8 Sep 41, no sub, 430. (2) Ltr, TAG to CGs all CAs, 12 Sep 41, sub: Insp of Butter, Eggs, Cheese and Poultry. (3) OQMG Cir Ltr 263, 6 Oct 41, sub: Purch of Perishable Subs.

The compromise established inspection procedures but did not immediately still all conflict.[133] The problem of co-ordination between inspectors of the Department of Agriculture and of the Veterinary Corps continued to be troublesome. It was emphasized anew when the Quartermaster market centers began in the summer of 1942 to purchase perishable foods for the Navy, Coast Guard, and Marine Corps. The QMC reassured the Agricultural Marketing Administration (successor to the Service) that it did not contemplate placing inspectors at Navy establishments and that it would continue to encourage vendors to use inspection by Department of Agriculture inspectors at points of origin.[134] By the summer of 1943, however, the Veterinary Corps was inspecting commodities for the Navy and Marine Corps. Actually, as the marketing centers bought food for all the armed services without reference to destination, and as Veterinary Corps officers were employed in inspecting it, there would have been considerable difficulty in restricting their activities to foods destined for any particular branch of the service, except in the case of certain types of meat which were bought only for the Navy.

The QMC believed that the prerogatives of the Veterinary Corps should be preserved, but that the activities of the inspectors of the Department of Agriculture should also be unhampered.[135] The position of the Veterinary Corps, as the inspection agency of the market center program, continued to be strengthened. In October 1941 a Veterinary Section had been established at Field Headquarters. Its functions were to provide inspection at origin of all dairy and poultry products if the purchasing section so desired and to co-ordinate all veterinary inspection at origin and destination. About the same time The Adjutant General had authorized the market center program to request the services of veterinary inspectors from the commanding generals of the corps areas in order to make inspections at origin. In November

The Quartermaster General granted permission to use veterinary inspectors assigned to Quartermaster depots for market center inspections in areas adjacent to the depots. Co-ordination of the inspection function was thereby achieved between market centers, Quartermaster depots, and corps areas. Thereafter the expansion of activities of the Veterinary Section at Field Headquarters paralleled the expansion of market center procurement. Greater effort was made to inspect at origin, and by the end of 1944 "virtually all origin inspections of dairy products and poultry, as well as other products of animal origin were being performed by veterinary inspectors."[136]

When the procurement of meat was undertaken by the market center program in the spring of 1942, the Veterinary Corps became responsible for inspection of meat at both origin and destination.[137] Although inspectors of both the Department of Agriculture and of the Veterinary Corps were in packing plants, problems of co-ordination did not arise. Congressional criticism, however, was voiced at the duplication of activities during the hearings on the 1945 appropriation bill for the Department of Agriculture. All meat packing plants supplying meats for Army consumption were required to pass federal inspection for sanitation by the Bureau of Animal Industry of the Department of Agriculture. Apart from these inspections, Department of Agriculture graders also classi-

[133] See, for example, ltr, John A. Martin, Chief of Procurement, Fld Hq, to Col Hardigg, OQMG, 10 Oct 41, sub: Veterinary Participation in the Insps of Poultry, Butter, Eggs and Cheese, and reply, 18 Oct 41, no sub, 400.163.
[134] Ltr, C. W. Kitchen, AMA, to Gen Hardigg, Chief of Subs Br, OQMG, 18 Apr 42, no sub, and reply, 28 Apr 42, no sub, 430.
[135] Memo, Maj Morrill, OQMG, for OIC, Fld Hq, Perishable Sec, OQMG, 12 Mar 43, sub: Atchd Teletype on Activities at San Francisco, 430.
[136] Rifkind, *Fresh Foods for the Armed Forces: The Quartermaster Market Center System, 1941–1948*, p. 55.
[137] OQMG Cir Ltr 360, 23 Sep 42, sub: Purch of Perishable Subs.

fied meats by grades at packing plants, but veterinary inspectors were free to accept or reject the carcasses and cuts designated for the Army. In the supervision of the curing and canning of meat products and the preparation of meat products according to specifications, the Veterinary Corps had sole inspection responsibility.

The Veterinary Corps also inspected at origin, wherever possible, and otherwise at destination all fish and sea foods procured by the market centers. Its inspection activities were extended to cover the procurement of milk, which was initiated by the market center program early in 1943.

The inspection of nonperishable subsistence involved none of the troublesome questions of conflicting prerogatives and co-ordination experienced in the case of perishable foods. Prior to 1939 canned fruits and vegetables were purchased on requisitions from military installations by depots operating on a regional basis. There was little or no depot warehousing of these items. Inspection was made at the depot, mainly through random samples drawn from destination points. During the emergency and war the vast amounts of nonperishables that had to be purchased months or a year in advance brought changes in procurement and inspection procedures.

A plan for centralized procurement was worked out by subsistence officers of the QMC, civilian business authorities such as Douglas MacKeachie, who had been a principal buyer in the purchasing service of the Atlantic and Pacific Tea Company, and his chief, Donald Nelson, co-ordinator of procurement in the National Defense Commission. Representatives of the National Canners Association were also consulted.[138] Under the plan, which went into effect in the summer of 1941, the bulk of nonperishables came to be purchased by three central procuring depots—the Jersey City Quartermaster Depot, the Chicago Quartermaster Depot, and the San Francisco General Depot

(later the California Quartermaster Depot).[139]

Inspection, normally made at origin, was the responsibility of the purchasing and contracting officer of each of these central procuring depots. Some items were procured by regional purchasing depots for all troops served by distributing depots within the regional area. In such cases, the purchasing and contracting officer of each regional purchasing depot was responsible for the inspection of all items assigned to it for purchase. Small quantities of nonperishable stores purchased locally were inspected by post, camp, and station quartermasters, who could forward samples to regional purchasing depots to determine whether the items met specification requirements.

In general, veterinary personnel were not considered competent to give proper inspection to such nonperishable subsistence as canned vegetables and fruits. Early in 1941 the OQMG made arrangements with the Agricultural Marketing Service for the use of its specialists in the inspection of canned fruits and vegetables, jams, jellies, preserves, syrup, and such other nonperishable items as they were equipped to handle. Funds to defray the expenses of such inspection were deposited with the Department of Agriculture.[140] The Agricultural Marketing Service placed a representative at each central purchasing depot to make inspections as desired by the commanding officer of the depot. He furnished an inspection certificate to the contracting and purchasing officer, and a copy was forwarded to the receiving quartermaster, who was thereupon not required to inspect for type,

[138] Marion Massen, Canned Vegetables: A Case History in Central Procurement at the Chicago Quartermaster Depot During World War I, pp. 6ff.

[139] OQMG Cir Ltr 88, 14 May 41, sub: Procurement, S&D of Nonperishable Subs Supplies.

[140] (1) Ltr, C. W. Kitchen, Chief of AMS, to Col Hardigg, OQMG, 14 Feb 41, no sub, and reply, 19 Feb 41, no sub. (2) Ltr, Gen Corbin, OQMG, to CO CQMD, 27 Feb 41, sub: Insp of Canned Fruits and Vegetables, 400.163.

class, and grade. Regional purchasing depots could call upon the services of the Agricultural Marketing Service for the inspection of carload lots of canned food items purchased by them.

Since the Agricultural Marketing Service had an extensive field organization, the practice was to call upon the nearest representative of the service to act in the depot's behalf, if the point of inspection was beyond a reasonable distance from the responsible procuring depot. Where inspections could not be furnished, the OQMG authorized depots to engage such technical services as might be required.[141] These inspection procedures were utilized throughout the war.

The prevention of losses by spoilage necessitated storage inspection of nonperishables. Some foods, like milk powder, flour, and related items, could be spoiled by moisture. Other items—evaporated milk, canned citrus products, some dehydrated foods—deteriorated with age. Nonperishable stores were therefore inspected not only at contractors' warehouses but also at depots and ports of embarkation where regular inspections and periodic sampling were made to insure their arrival at destination in sound condition.[142] Such inspection corrected defective methods of care, handling, and storage and insured issue of the oldest stocks first.

Fuels and Lubricants

Inspection of fuels and lubricants was always accomplished separately because of the terms under which these items were procured. As late as 1943 procedures established in 1939 for the inspection of these products were being followed despite the fact that no detailed written procedure for inspection was in force.[143] Quartermaster purchases of petroleum products were made largely against Treasury Procurement Schedules and Navy contracts; hence Quartermaster inspection was integrated with that of other government departmental contracts.

The Navy provided inspection on large orders at the refinery or on barge, vessel, or other transport facility. As a result of discussion in September 1942 [144] among the OQMG, the Ordnance Department, and the Bureau of Ships, Navy Department, an agreement was made with the latter whereby naval petroleum inspectors would be available for the inspection of motor fuels, diesel fuels, and lubricants in bulk shipments for overseas destinations. The Quartermaster General designated certain depots to purchase petroleum products for overseas shipment. Under this agreement these depots established liaison with the nearest Navy petroleum inspector and kept him informed of the names of contractors and prospective shipments. Upon receipt of a requisition, the depot arranged for the purchase by direct negotiation and advised the local Navy inspector, requesting copies of the inspection report. In peacetime the Navy used its own laboratories for testing purposes, but as its facilities became overtaxed during the war, much of the testing and inspection was carried out by Charles Martin and Company. The latter's report was initialed by the Navy petroleum inspector. When the problem of inspection became acute early in 1943, investigation of the files of the ANMB and of the Ordnance Department revealed that there were practically no such inspection reports covering Army shipments inspected by the Navy.

---

[141] (1) OQMG Cir Ltr 88, 14 May 41, sub: Procurement, S&D of Nonperishable Subs Supplies. (2) OQMG Cir Ltr 147, 22 Sep 43, same sub.

[142] OQMG Cir Ltr 434, 12 Dec 42, sub: Subs Stores at Depots and PE.

[143] These procedures were based on OQMG Circular 1–4, 1 March 1939, which in turn was based particularly on AR 5–360, 16 July 1937. PR 1, 14 October 1942, canceled and rescinded all procurement circulars, instructions, and directives prior to 1 July 1942. On 30 September 1942 OQMG Circular 1–4 was revised and reprinted but it made no provision for inspection of petroleum products.

[144] Ltr, AGO to TQMG, 24 Oct 42, sub: Insp of Motor Fuels, Diesel F&L for Bulk Overseas Shipmt. SPX 463.7 (10–17–42) OB-P-SPOPP.

Usually certified analyses were accepted.[145]

Inspection of petroleum products obtained under Treasury Procurement Schedules was governed by contract provisions. For example, gasoline was sampled when in the opinion of the activity concerned it was desirable to do so. Then samples were sent to and tested by the National Bureau of Standards or some other laboratory designated by the Procurement Division, Treasury Department. Such tests, however, were rarely made. The Treasury Department itself had no laboratory facilities, and it operated on the assumption that the integrity of the average petroleum oil company and the power of the government were such that certified analyses would suffice in almost every instance.

Considering the volume of petroleum products being purchased, inspection was practically nil as the year 1942 drew to a close. In many cases inspection was not in the hands of OQMG personnel because of the use of other departmental contracts. There was a small inspection unit at the Jersey City Quartermaster Depot, which inspected fuel primarily for the eastern seaboard, but its facilities were extremely limited. Most procuring depots had no petroleum inspection personnel, and existing government facilities were inadequate or overtaxed.[146] Responsibility for inspection of petroleum products was vested in the OQMG in November 1942,[147] but the petroleum organization was in the process of being centralized in the office and despite the need no attention could be given to the inspection problem.

Overseas reports on leaking containers, illegible markings, and unsatisfactory quality of materials emphasized the urgent need for inspection early in 1943. In April an Inspection Section was established in the Petroleum Branch, which put into operation during the year a nationwide inspection system. Inspection of overseas shipments was first attacked. Using the small inspection section of the Jersey City Depot as a nucleus, the Petroleum Branch directed the depot to consummate contracts with three leading commercial petroleum inspection agencies.[148] At the request of the purchasing depots these commercial agencies were to undertake complete inspection of all petroleum products and containers for offshore shipments—at refineries, storage warehouses, and at points where containers were being filled from storage tanks or tank cars. The same applied to purchases made for maneuvers. Inspection of containers by these agencies was incidental to the inspection of petroleum products. Civilian inspectors employed by the depot inspected container manufacturing plants, reclamation plants, and storage depots where empty containers were stored. In the spring of 1944 their activity came under supervision of the QMC Inspection Service.[149]

The policies initiated by the Petroleum Branch were carried to completion by the Fuels and Lubricants Division established in the OQMG in the summer of 1943. In May a program was initiated for inspection of purchases of gasoline in the zone of interior. A spot-check procedure was established for sampling gasoline at a representative cross section of posts, camps, and stations. The commanding officer was responsible for selecting competent personnel to

---

[145] (1) Irvin A. Ebaugh to Col H. E. Rounds, Chief of Petrl Br, OQMG, 3 Feb 43, sub: Rpt on Governmental Insp of Petrl Products. (2) A certified analysis was a vendor's guarantee that the product submitted was equal to the sample submitted for testing and approved at the time of establishing an approval list.

[146] Ebaugh to Rounds, OQMG, 3 Feb 43, sub: Rpt on Governmental Insp of Petrl Products.

[147] WD Cir 387, Sec. I, 28 Nov 42, sub: Responsibility for Gasoline and Lubricants.

[148] Chief of Insp Sec to Maj Wiley Butler, OQMG, 19 Apr 43, sub: Status at Present. The contracts made in April were with Charles Martin & Co., E. W. Saybolt & Co., and the Ethyl Corp. Later another agency, Phoenix Chemical Laboratory, was added to test domestic samples only.

[149] (1) Chief of Insp Sec to Chief of Tech & Plng Br, F&L Div, OQMG, 7 Jan 44, sub: Rpt of Conf. (2) See also OQMG Cir 16, 24 Apr 44, sub: QMC Insp Sv.

take and ship samples of gasoline weekly to the indicated commercial testing laboratory. In November inspection services were extended to cover other petroleum products, in particular engine oils, greases, and gear lubricants. This procedure continued in effect until the war ended.[150]

In addition, the Fuels and Lubricants Division introduced the use of field inspection supervisors. The United States was divided into four areas that were covered by these supervisors, who spot-checked the inspection of petroleum products and container manufacturing and reclamation plants, inspected container and stockpile storage at depots and storage points, and visited posts, camps, and stations to ascertain if petroleum products and containers were sampled and handled correctly.[151] Under various agreements the Fuels and Lubricants Division continued to make use of Navy inspectors.

Inspection of petroleum products was vital in the theaters, not only to analyze such products for deterioration, contamination, identification, or sabotage, but also to determine whether captured petroleum products were suitable for use by our armed forces. For this purpose the Petroleum Branch formulated plans later carried to completion by the Fuels and Lubricants Division to train technical personnel who would be able to inspect petroleum products in combat theaters. A new troop organization known as the Quartermaster Petroleum Laboratory was established. It consisted of a base laboratory stationed in a more or less permanent location and one or more mobile units which moved throughout a prescribed area. These laboratories functioned only in the theaters.[152]

---

[150] Chief of Insp Sec to Chief of Tech & Plng Br, F&L Div, OQMG, 29 Nov 43, sub: Development and Activities of the Insp Sec.

[151] Chief of Tech & Plng Br to Dir of F&L Div, OQMG, 21 Dec 43, sub: Adm and Opn of Insp Sec.

[152] (1) Chief of Petrl Br to Dir of Mil Tng Div, OQMG, 24 Apr 43, no sub. (2) Memo, Dir of Mil Tng Div, OQMG, to CG ASF, 14 Aug 43, sub: Use of Civ Institutions for Tng of Petrl Technicians.

CHAPTER IX

Quartermaster Storage Operations

The mission of the Quartermaster Corps during World War II was to supply the troops with food, clothing, equipage, fuel, and all sorts of general supplies in the proper quantity and quality at the right time and in the right place. In addition, the Corps furnished thousands of "comfort items" to promote the health and welfare of the soldier. Since the peak strength of the Army was about 8,000,000 men and the QMC also furnished various supplies to the Navy, Marine Corps, Coast Guard, and the War Shipping Administration, as well as to the lend-lease program, this supply mission constituted an enormous operation, involving the movement of millions of tons of supplies shipped or received by Quartermaster depots.

Throughout the emergency period and the months immediately following Pearl Harbor, the objectives of QMC distribution operations were the rapid expansion of the depot system and the prompt delivery of supplies. It was most important to fill supply pipelines and get supplies into the hands of the troops quickly. Toward the end of 1942, when these goals had been achieved, greater attention could be accorded the problem of balanced and equitable distribution. Improved inventory control then became increasingly important.[1]

Administrative Background

Prior to March 1942, while the OQMG was organized on a commodity basis, each of the various commodity branches of the Supply Division responsible for the procurement of particular items of supply also included among its duties the storage and distribution of these items. Problems of storage were subordinated, however, to those of distribution, and the commodity branches continued to emphasize the property accountability of supply officers rather than the control of supplies in the interest of equitable distribution and a minimum stockage in depots and stations. Even as early as the fall of 1940, however, it was recognized that the operation of the Quartermaster depot system of supply presented problems of management and administration that needed to be studied. Just as global war developed new methods and procedures of fighting, so supply problems grew more complex and modern methods of warehousing had to be adapted to the Army system of supply. Warehousing had been considered simply a matter of space control, of allocating available storage facilities among the supply services. Little or no attention had been given to the use of improved equipment for handling supplies or to the adoption of sounder methods of receiving, stacking, packing, and shipping supplies.

---

[1] Alvin P. Stauffer, *Quartermaster Depot Storage and Distribution Operations* (QMC Historical Studies 18, May 1948), pp. 4–5. The following discussion is largely based on this study, hereafter cited as *QM Depot S&D Opns.*

A study of these supply problems revealed the need for a co-ordinating unit in the OQMG, a need met by the establishment of a Depot Division in May 1941.[2] When the OQMG was later reorganized along functional lines, the Storage and Distribution Service (later Division), headed during the war years by Brig. Gen. (later Maj. Gen.) Frank F. Scowden, was established with the mission of storing, distributing, and issuing all Quartermaster supplies, as well as managing and operating Quartermaster depots. In the process the Depot Division became the Depot Operations Branch of the Storage and Distribution Service. Its responsibilities continued to be those of correlation, standardization, and management of the Quartermaster depot system.

Under the general direction of Headquarters, SOS, and later of Headquarters, ASF, the OQMG determined storage and distribution policies and procedures. It supervised the delivery of goods from the depots to ports of embarkation for oversea shipment and to posts, camps, and stations for distribution to the troops in the zone of interior. It revised and simplified depot operations; it improved the methods of receiving, storing, and shipping supplies; and it trained both civilian and military personnel in warehousing duties. Its control of supplies ceased, however, after they had been delivered by the depots to the requisitioning stations. The latter were under the supervision of the nine corps areas (later service commands). This division of authority made impossible the standardization of warehousing and distribution methods from the depots through the stations.[3]

Depot Missions

The depot storage system in World War II was based on broad principles of decentralization. The Quartermaster depots were the keystone of the Quartermaster system of supply.

Depending upon their assigned functions, they were classified as regional distributing, filler, key, or reserve depots. The mission of most Quartermaster depots included the functions of three or even all four of these classifications. The continental United States was divided into fifteen areas for the distribution of Quartermaster supplies. Each such area was served by a regional distributing depot which furnished Quartermaster supplies directly to all camps, posts, and stations within its assigned area. Among the major groups of supplies only perishable subsistence, issued through Quartermaster market centers, and fuels and lubricants, sent direct from producers to military stations under contracts made by the Procurement Division of the Treasury Department, were not normally distributed by the regional depots. Except for key items, regional depots stocked all other major items of supply in quantities sufficient to meet current demand.[4] The size of areas assigned to regional distributing depots varied greatly but was limited by such factors as the storage capacity of the depot, the density or sparsity of the military population to be served, and the time required to make deliveries. This system of regional depots permitted decentralization in the handling of zone of interior requisitions, and since a supply officer of a post, camp, or station in a particular area looked to one and only one regional depot for the supply of all Quartermaster items, the task of requisitioning officers in the zone of interior was sim-

---

[2] (1) OQMG OO 92, 14 May 41, no sub. (2) Maj Daniel Borth, "The Quartermaster Depot System of Supply," *QMR*, XXII (November–December 1942), 31. (3) See above, Ch. I, section entitled "Impact of the Emergency Period."

[3] Rpt, F. Chapin Weed, Div of Purchases, OPM, 6 Nov 41, sub: Warehousing and Distr as Found with Divided Command.

[4] (1) OQMG Cir 190, 6 May 42, sub: Asgmt of Responsibility to Depots for Distr of QM Supplies. (2) *Ibid.*, 84, 24 May 43, same sub. (3) WD SB 38–3–QM, 19 Oct 44, sub: Depot Missions.

plified. Regional depots called on reserve depots for replacement of their stocks.

Key depots handled supplies that were scarce, in limited demand, or in need of special treatment. Stockages of these commodities were relatively small, and regional depots could not conveniently or economically deal with large numbers of key items. As a consequence, certain key depots were expressly selected to handle items lacking general utility, such as war dog equipment; items required only in restricted geographical areas, such as desert, jungle, and cold-climate equipment; or items demanding unusual storage conditions, such as clothing chemically impregnated as a protection against poison gas. Because demand for these items was specialized or limited, a key depot's area of distribution might include two or more regional areas or parts of such areas. Sometimes a distribution area comprised the whole zone of interior. For example, the Jeffersonville Depot issued repair parts for tentage to all installations in the United States.[5]

To insure that ports of embarkation would receive an orderly and controlled flow of required supplies, filler depots were established, generally within 100 miles of the seaboard, to serve the port or ports they were specifically assigned to supply and to forward goods only upon the call of the port commander and only in the quantities and at the time requested. This procedure was to prevent at the ports the congestion which had developed so disastrously in World War I. In emergencies the filler depots might help meet the needs of other ports as well.

During most of the war, the New York Port of Embarkation and its outports supplied the European and Mediterranean Theaters of Operations; Boston, the American bases in the Atlantic; Charleston, the Middle East and the Persian Gulf Service Command; New Orleans, the Caribbean bases; San Francisco, the Southwest Pacific and Pacific Ocean Areas; Los Angeles, the China-Burma-India Theater; and Seattle,

Alaska. The purpose of assigning particular ports to supply specific overseas areas, and of having these overseas areas requisition directly upon the responsible ports, was to decentralize the handling of requisitions. In World War I all overseas requisitions had been sent to Washington, with consequent delay and confusion. Close co-operation had to be maintained between ports and filler depots to insure prompt movement of supplies to the ports, departure of ships on schedule, and delivery of goods at proper destinations overseas in accordance with fixed priorities.

The orderly flow of supplies to the ports was further promoted by the use of holding and reconsignment points. The need for such transit storage points had been made evident through the congestion at the ports during World War I. By the summer of 1941 such temporary storage points were required to handle lend-lease goods as well as those of the Army. Both General George Spaulding of the Division of Defense Aid (predecessor of Lend-Lease) and Col. T. H. Dillon, Chief of the Transportation Division, OQMG, were alert to the problem, and plans were made in July to begin construction of holding and reconsignment points. The first was ready for use by the time of Pearl Harbor and a second one shortly thereafter. Although the control of the holding and reconsignment points passed to the Chief of Transportation in the reorganization after March 1942, the OQMG had had a large part in their development.[6]

Reserve depots maintained reserve stocks to be used for replenishing stock levels of regional distributing and filler depots. They also stored reserve stocks which were set aside in anticipa-

---

[5] (1) OQMG cir 1-4, pars. 90–240, 25 Jan 43, sub: Distr of Supplies. (2) WD SB 38-3-QM, 19 Oct 44, sub: Depot Missions, Pt. VI, pp. 31–35.

[6] For a full discussion of the holding and reconsignment points, see Chester Wardlow, The Transportation Corps: Movements, Training, and Supply, in preparation for the series, U. S. ARMY IN WORLD WAR II.

tion of task force shortages or in preparation for specific operations, such as the alerting of a division for overseas movement, which required supplies in excess of those normally available. In addition, their reserve stocks included production on contingency reserve stocks of commodities subject to the interruption of production or unusually heavy demands. When it was necessary to accept production in excess of current needs, such excess was also classified as contingency reserves, pending redistribution.[7] In World War II, the Quartermaster General was concerned only with the replenishment of stocks in these reserve depots. This was a vast improvement over the first World War, when he had been overburdened by direct requisitions sent to him from overseas and from hundreds of posts, camps, and stations in the zone of interior.

Depending on their responsibilities, distributing depots stocked thousands of Quartermaster items, averaging about 3,500 items but ranging as high as 6,000 or more for installations with highly diverse missions.[8] Depot missions were not permanently fixed. They changed during the war as troop concentrations shifted in the zone of interior and in the theaters of operations. An installation with both filler and regional distributing functions might in the beginning be concerned mainly with delivering goods to posts, camps, and stations in the United States and subsequently, as training camp activities diminished, with forwarding supplies to ports of embarkation. Troop movements were reflected in changing stock levels, and the functions of the depots were altered with the shifts in the direction of the global conflict.[9]

Depot Storage Operations

Lessons of World War I

Depot operations in 1939 profited from the lessons learned in 1917 and 1918. During World War I the failure to provide sufficient storage facilities had resulted in an unparalleled congestion of freight along the eastern seaboard and had threatened to disorganize completely the Army's distributing system. In the absence of adequate depot storage facilities and the necessity of shipping goods promptly from manufacturers' production lines, it was the practice for each supply service to order finished items destined for Europe into eastern terminals. Piers, transit sheds, and other port facilities were soon clogged with the onrushing flood of goods, and for miles behind the terminals loaded cars were parked on railroad sidings awaiting movement to shipside. This congestion made difficult the selective loading of ships, and consequently supplies high on the priority list for movement to France could not be shipped because it was impossible to get them to the piers. Accessibility rather than the actual requirements of the American Expeditionary Forces frequently dictated the shipments made.[10]

This situation was improved early in 1918 after the government had taken over control of the railroads and the Army supply services had been reorganized with the Purchase, Storage and Traffic Division in the General Staff coordinating their activities. Storage facilities were expanded through new construction and by the lease of commercial warehouses. To prevent congestion at the ports, a new type of installation, the filler depot, was created to free ports of embarkation from the necessity of maintain-

---

[7] Ltr, Maj Gen F. F. Scowden, Dir of S&D Div, OQMG, to COs of All Depots, 14 Sep 43, sub: Definition of Sup Responsibility, 323.3.

[8] Rpt, Statistics Br, OP&C Div, OQMG, Stat Rpts to TQMG, 1944, pp. 121–22.

[9] Ltr, Gen Gregory to Col G. F. Spann, JCQMD, 8 Nov 43, sub: Change in Sup Problem.

[10] (1) Gen Scowden, "Storage and Distribution of Quartermaster Supplies," QMR, XXII (November–December 1942), 27. (2) L. H. Britten, "Storage by the Mile," QMR, I (September–October 1921), 13–16. (3) Capt J. Allen Praether, History of the Storage Division, 1917–18 (n.d., 4 vols, typescript at QM Library, Camp Lee), I, 65, 98.

ing large working stocks of overseas supplies. In addition, a zone system of supply was inaugurated on 1 July providing for the establishment of balanced inventories at depots. These installations were assigned definite geographic areas in which they would be responsible for supplying all posts, camps, and stations. This was an effort to eliminate the previous differentiation of storage activities along supply service lines. It was the goal of the Purchase, Storage and Traffic Division to unify all storage activities of the supply services in a zone under the jurisdiction of a single storage officer. When the Army reverted to peacetime conditions, however, the zone system of supply was discontinued.[11]

The experience of World War I demonstrated that adequate storage facilities were vital to an even, organized flow of supplies; that distribution was more prompt when conducted on a zonal basis; that protection of the ports of embarkation was necessary to prevent congestion resulting from the torrent of goods directed to them; and that efficient distribution was largely dependent on prior planning and close co-ordination of the activities of the supply services.

Co-ordination of Activities of Supply Services

It appeared that the unhappy experiences of 1917 were about to be repeated in 1941 in the inadequate co-ordination of the activities of the supply services. During the emergency period and until 1942, storage and distribution operations were loosely co-ordinated in the General Staff and the Office of the Assistant Secretary of War. The Secretary of War was charged with allotting all storage space owned or leased by the War Department, but in practice such allocations were based on recommendations made by the OQMG. As the service traditionally concerned with storage problems, the OQMG was charged with keeping adequate records of the

utilization of all storage space and with making recommendations as to its disposition. To enable The Quartermaster General to maintain such records, the chiefs of other supply arms and services submitted periodic reports on the amount of space in use, vacant, and needed in the near future. Twice a year The Quartermaster General sent consolidated reports to The Adjutant General.[12]

Branch depots, in which supplies belonging to a single service were stored, and general depots, consisting of supply sections of the various services, operated without any control other than that exercised by the responsible supply service.[13] The supply services were almost as autonomous as they had been in 1917, and each was procuring and distributing supplies without regard for other services. This situation was altered in March 1942 when the SOS was established as one of the three major commands of the War Department. Thereafter it directed the storage and distribution program of the Army.

Co-ordination and Control of Shipments

Efforts to co-ordinate and control the flow of supplies to depots and to ports of embarkation were made early in 1941 in order to avoid the congestion that had developed at terminals in 1917 and 1918. On the recommendation of The Quartermaster General, all shippers of goods consigned to Army installations were obliged to give notice of anticipated shipments by prepaid telegraph or teletype, specifying date, route, and size, and furnishing a brief general

---

[11] (1) Annual Report of *The Quartermaster General to the Secretary of War, 1919* (Washington, D. C., 1920), pp. 21–23, 127–28. (2) Maj Gen Peyton C. March, *The Nation at War* (Garden City, N.Y., 1932), pp. 191–95. (3) Praether, History of the Storage Division, I, 70–71.

[12] AR 700–10, Sec. II, 1 Jul 36, sub: Stor and Issue.

[13] See above, Ch. I, pp. 41–42.

description of the shipment.[14] Although this was a step in the right direction, it by no means established an adequate form of traffic control inasmuch as it merely informed the consignee of contemplated shipments without establishing a procedure by which he could regulate such shipments.

The rapid increase in the quantity of Army supplies held at ports in the weeks following Pearl Harbor made adequate control of shipments imperative. At that time operating responsibilities for inland, terminal, and overseas transportation were completely decentralized. The Quartermaster General was responsible for the maintenance and operation of the Army transport service. He operated a fleet of some 250 small vessels of all types, including 6 troop transports and 2 cargo vessels. The ports of embarkation, although a part of the transportation machinery, were under the direct control of the War Department General Staff. The situation was further complicated by the lack of control over commercial and nonmilitary shipments by the government.

A comprehensive supervisory system was urgently needed. Under the broad authority granted the Office of Defense Transportation (ODT), such a system was created in March 1942. This agency set up controls over commercial movements, while under its general direction the War and Navy Departments co-ordinated and supervised their transportation activities. The ODT authority over traffic control was delegated to and exercised by the Transportation Control Committee, consisting of representatives of the Navy, the War Department, the ODT, the War Shipping Administration, and the British Ministry of War Transport. Within the War Department the consolidation of these responsibilities in one agency was accomplished by the creation of a Transportation Division in the SOS, which some four months later became the Transportation Corps. For the duration of the war it was responsible for in-

stituting comprehensive arrangements for traffic control.[15]

The Transportation Corps prepared and disseminated information on the status of troop and freight movements; it maintained liaison with all transportation agencies operating by water, rail, truck, and air; and it acted for the War Department on the Transportation Control Committee. On the basis of daily reports covering anticipated shipments by the various government agencies for about the next forty-five days, this committee operated a block release system. By means of it all movements of goods to overseas destinations were timed and routed to prevent overcrowding either the railroads or the ports. The block releases indicated the tonnage that could be sent to each port during a given month.[16] If necessary to prevent congestion, shipments already under way could be diverted to holding and reconsignment points maintained by the Transportation Corps. Containing both covered and open storage areas, these points were located along the principal railroad lines leading to the ports. Combined with the use of filler depots at inland locations, they permitted the restriction of storage at ports for the most part to goods actually scheduled to be sent overseas in the near future. This co-ordination and control of traffic enabled the Army supply system to avoid the congestion that had occurred in 1917.

The orderly flow of shipments of supplies from the zone of interior depots to theaters of

---

[14] (1) Ltr, TQMG to ACofS G–4, 25 Feb 41, sub: Notice by Wire to Govt Consignee. (2) Ltr, TAG to TQMG, 4 Mar 41, same sub. AG 523.01 (2–28–41) M–D.

[15] Maj Gen C. P. Gross, CofT, "The Transportation Corps: Its Organization and Major Functions," *QMR*, XXIII (January–February 1944), 19ff. (2) Chester Wardlow, *The Transportation Corps: Responsibilities, Organization, and Operations* in| U. S. ARMY IN WORLD WAR II (Washington, D. C., 1951).

[16] Lecture, Maj Gen E. H. Leavey, 24 Oct 46, sub: Communications and Transportation as Essentials of Mobilization (Industrial Mobilization Course, ICAF), p. 6.

operations was further promoted by the development and use by the Army of the War Department Shipping Document. This document originated in the OQMG, growing out of a study initiated by that office in October 1942 to simplify the paper procedures covering the shipment of supplies by reducing both the number and the types of documents used. By putting all necessary information on one document, the OQMG could replace at least ten different ones used in a shipment destined for overseas, namely, the shipping ticket, the packing list, dock tallies, hatch lists, and tally-ins and tally-outs at the depot, the holding and reconsignment point, the port of embarkation, and the overseas port. The War Department Shipping Document was first used in the spring of 1943. This new procedure had the further advantage of making the shipping document, with sufficient copies for all purposes, accompany every movement of supplies, thus assuring immediate identification of the consignment and eliminating any need to recopy data at different points in transit, since all essential facts were recorded on one form.[17]

Expansion of Depot Storage Facilities

Adequacy of storage facilities was as important as efficient distribution in solving the supply problem of World War II. The QMC attacked the problem by expanding its depot system, by using commercial storage facilities, and by developing a method to assure the complete utilization of existing storage space.

Distribution of Facilities in 1940

On 31 October 1940 permanent warehouse space controlled and used by the QMC amounted to 7,700,000 square feet. This was far below the minimum space needed to supply millions of troops engaged in a global conflict,

since it was estimated that seventeen and a half square feet of floorage were necessary for each serviceman.[18] As long as the depots were engaged in the years following World War I in the routine tasks of supplying the relatively small demands of a Regular Army of less than 150,000 men and of maintaining war reserves for an armed force of 1,000,000, no great burden was imposed upon them.[19] Supply was largely a matter of issuing replacements, and stocks moved slowly as compared with initial issue to new troops. Occasionally, emergency goods to assist victims of various catastrophes were delivered to the Red Cross and other relief organizations. Such activities required neither a large labor force nor an extensive investment in materials-handling equipment. With the creation of the Civilian Conservation Corps, Quartermaster responsibility for supplying the young men enrolled in it increased enormously the activities of the depots between 1933 and 1940. In meeting this demand the depots were unconsciously preparing for the much greater expansion precipitated by World War II.

In 1940 twelve depots were engaged in handling Quartermaster supplies and of these all but two lay east of the Mississippi River.[20] Five were active storage and distributing depots. The New York General Depot was the most important of these, being responsible for the supply of nearly half the Army. It furnished practically all Quartermaster items required in Panama, Puerto Rico, and elsewhere in the

---

[17] (1) Ltr, Col J. W. G. Stephens, OQMG, to Maj Gen Orlando Ward, Office of Chief of Military History, 31 Dec 50, no sub. (2) Memo, TQMG for CG ASF, 23 Mar 43, sub: WD Shipping Document. (3) Lt Col E. B. Brownell, "Reducing Paper Work with the War Department Shipping Document," *Military Review*, XXIV (November 1944), 74–78.

[18] (1) Memo, Gen Gregory for ACofS G–4, 3 Feb 41, no sub. (2) Ltr, Gen Gregory to Gen Somervell, 27 Feb 41, sub: QMC Stor Reqmts.

[19] *Report of the Secretary of War, 1929* (Washington, D. C., 1929), pp. 7–8.

[20] Compare Charts 10 and 11.

Caribbean, and supplied installations in the huge area of New England and the Middle and South Atlantic States.[21] The Chicago Quartermaster Depot was second in importance, serving the vast interior region from Canada to the Gulf of Mexico and from eastern Alabama to western North Dakota. In 1935 a part of this area—Indiana, Kentucky, West Virginia, Tennessee, Alabama, Mississippi, and Louisiana—because of its increasing activities in supplying the Civilian Conservation Corps was transferred to the Jeffersonville Quartermaster Depot. The Eighth Corps Area Depot at Fort Sam Houston, San Antonio, Tex., supplied the southwestern area, while the San Francisco General Depot provided goods for the rest of the West as well as furnishing subsistence and certain other Quartermaster items to Hawaii, the Philippines, the garrisons in China and, through its Seattle branch, those in Alaska.[22]

This concentration of supply installations in the East followed naturally from the tendency to locate major distributing agencies in the larger commercial centers and from the necessity to build depots readily accessible to Atlantic ports during World War I. With the limited number of depots in the West, any Pacific conflict would pose difficult supply problems if this situation was not corrected. The lack of depots in the area east of the Mississippi and south of the Potomac and Ohio Rivers was another weakness of the distributing system. In this region, as in 1917, training camps and maneuver areas would inevitably be concentrated in the event of war because of the mild climate and wide stretches of open terrain.

First Phase of Expansion

The expansion of the depot system fell into three periods, paralleling the phases of the war in its impact upon the United States. The first period began in 1939 with the outbreak of war in Europe and President Roosevelt's proclama-

tion of a limited national emergency, and it ended with the fall of France in the summer of 1940. At the time of the proclamation, the President authorized an additional small increase of 17,000 men to the Regular Army. Previously, on 1 July 1939, the strength of the Army had been increased from 174,000 to 210,000.[23] These changes, together with other anticipated developments, emphasized the need for exploring the problem of depot expansion. The OQMG called upon the established depots to submit estimates of the cost for making improvements to meet the increased procurement program.[24] Before June 1940, however, little was accomplished beyond the drafting of blueprints. The country could not visualize the dangerous possibilities of the world situation, and needed appropriations were not forthcoming.

Second Phase of Expansion

The fall of France increased apprehensions as to the country's security. The second phase of the emergency, involving the passage of large appropriations to strengthen all aspects of military activity, including the supply system, lasted until the attack on Pearl Harbor. On 16 September, when the President signed the Selective

---

[21] For a general account of this depot see Col A. B. Warfield, "The Army Supply Base," *QMR*, X (March–April 1931), 19–23.

[22] For accounts of these depots see (1) Capt William J. Allen, "The Chicago Quartermaster Depot," *QMR*, VII (November–December 1927), 5–10. (2) Anon., "Jeff," *QMR*, XVI (July–August 1936), 11–15. (3) Capt Ezra Davis, "Depots of the Quartermaster Corps," *QMR*, X (November–December 1930), 24–31.

[23] *Biennial Report of the Chief of Staff of the United States Army July 1, 1939 to June 30, 1941 to the Secretary of War* (Washington, D. C., 1941), p. 2.

[24] See, for example, (1) Ltr, Col W. A. McCain, CO PQMD to TQMG, 31 Oct 39, sub: Estimates Covering Extensions and Improvements. (2) For a detailed account of the expansion at the Philadelphia Depot see Richard McCormick, The Physical Plant, 1917–42 (typescript historical report in files of Hist Sec, OQMG).

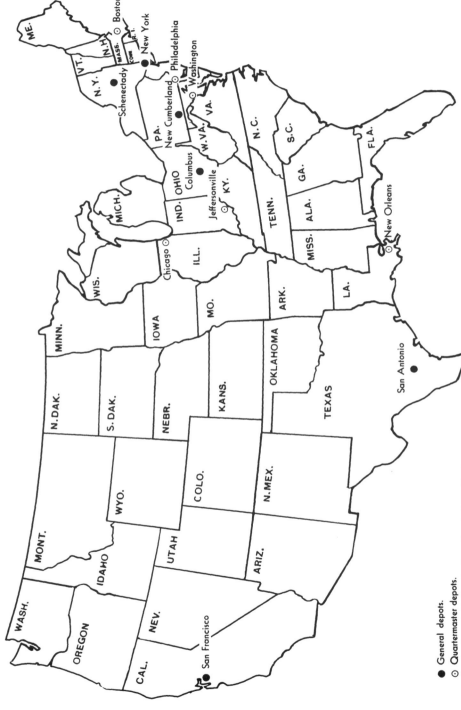

CHART 10—QUARTERMASTER CORPS DEPOT SYSTEM: 1939

● General depots.

⊙ Quartermaster depots.

Source: Compiled by author from data in OQMG files.

Service Act, the first units of the National Guard, which had been called into federal service, were inducted. The rapid expansion of the Army to about one and a half million men made urgent the need for new and larger depots to handle the vast quantities of Quartermaster supplies. Until well into 1943 the distribution problem was one of initial issue, which required relatively more storage space than issue for replacement purposes. In addition, storage was needed for stocking the reserves of critical raw materials which were essential to the prosecution of war and which had been acquired, as a precautionary measure, by the Reconstruction Finance Corporation.

During this second phase a program of expansion was inaugurated not only for enlarging old Quartermaster and general depots but for constructing new installations. When the attack on Pearl Harbor occurred, about 11,500,000 square feet of depot space were ready for Quartermaster use, approximately 50 percent more than had existed the previous year.[25] Older installations had been expanded. Two new general depots and two new Quartermaster depots were in use, while construction in some cases was about to begin and in others was well advanced on three other general depots and five additional Quartermaster depots.

Basic to the execution of this program of expansion was information on the size and distribution of the Army. In this period the OQMG began by estimating the floorage required for stocking essential items for an army of 1,400,000 men. It was thought this number would be in training by 1 July 1941. During the spring and summer the growing rate of induction into the Army and the extension of the period of service by an additional eighteen months for drafted men and National Guardsmen caused an upward revision in estimated space requirements. Calculations were then based on an army of 1,820,000.[26]

The difficulty of obtaining correct data on the distribution of troops at posts and camps created a problem in determining both the location and the size of new depots. Col. J. W. G. Stephens, Chief of the Storage Control Branch responsible for planning the expansion of the depot system, declared that, in order to secure this information, "it was necessary that we vigorously and religiously patrol the halls of the Munitions Building," then the center of War Department activities in Washington.[27] Eventually the securing of essential data made possible the determination of the distributing areas for which regional depots would have to be provided. Even then accurate estimates of storage space could not be established because unanticipated events, such as the establishment of new ports of embarkation demanding large stores of filler stocks in the interior, or the activation of new military stations with thousands of troops not included in the initial estimates, sometimes drastically increased the need for space.

In determining the locations of new installations many other complex factors in addition to troop distribution had to be studied. The governing factor in location and size was the role which the distributing depots were to play in the domestic and overseas system of supply distribution.[28] For the most part, these installations were so located that shipments could reach the stations and ports for whose supply they were responsible within twenty-four hours by rail or truck. Transportation facilities were, therefore, a prime factor for consideration. Natural commercial centers of distribution, capable of handling thousands of freight cars

[25] Rpt, Statistics Br, P&C Div, QM Depot Opns, III (November 1941), 25.

[26] Memo, TQMG for ACofS G-4, 24 Jul 41, sub: Additional Stor Reqmts.

[27] Rpt, Conf of CA QMs, Washington, D. C., 27–29 Jan 41, p. 42.

[28] Gen Scowden, "Storage and Distribution of Quartermaster Supplies," QMR, XXII (November–December 1942), 28.

daily, were obviously best suited for depot locations. The existence of favorable freight rates, an adequate labor supply, and the elimination of backhauls and crosshauls were other important factors. Backhauls and crosshauls were more widely used than is realized, and their elimination was vital because of the tremendous saving effected in transportation.

In carrying out its program of expansion, the QMC not only constructed new buildings but leased or purchased commercial warehouses for use by existing depots. It was War Department policy to restrict leasing as much as possible, but when new depots were needed in communities where real estate and building costs were exorbitant, where no great postwar need would exist for them, or where space was immediately required, most or all of the necessary structures were leased. Leasing had the advantage of quick procurement of needed space without requiring any heavy capital outlay for buying or building requisite facilities. On the other hand, leased storage space had many disadvantages. Most of the better warehouses in 1940 and 1941 were already occupied either by civilian firms or by other government agencies. Much of the remaining storage space was frequently undesirable because it was antiquated, of poor construction, and lacked adequate fire protection. Leased warehouses often had to be remodeled before they could be used for government storage. Small units, widely distributed, made impossible the use of materials-handling equipment to expedite handling and storage of supplies.[29]

In constructing warehouses the OQMG favored single-story structures so erected as to provide railroad freight sidings with loading platforms level with the car floor on one side of the warehouse and docks for truck loading and unloading on the other side. Such structures with their lofty ceilings and unlimited floor-load capacity allowed fuller utilization of space by the high tiering of supplies and permitted the efficient use of mechanical equip-

ment. They required large tracts of land, however, and consequently their construction was confined largely to the smaller urban communities or the more or less open country.

When the problems of site selection, size, and type of construction had been solved, speedy completion of building operations was most important. To expedite construction the QMC used cost-plus-fixed-fee contracts, since work often had to start before specific allotments of money could be made and before final plans could be drawn on the basis of information on the depot's intended responsibilities. The most serious delay in construction was occasioned by the shortage of building materials, particularly steel. Despite these difficulties, the Construction Division, OQMG, was able, for the most part, to carry out the expansion program as planned until late in 1941. After 15 December the Corps of Engineers became responsible for construction activities.

Third Phase of Expansion

After the attack on Pearl Harbor and during the third phase of the war, there was even greater need for speed in completing the program of depot expansion. Shortages of materials and of labor became more acute, and the construction of temporary types was substituted for permanent structures. By May 1943 Headquarters, ASF, decided not to authorize further building of any sort unless disapproval would seriously threaten the efficiency of depot operations.[30] As a result of this decision, depot construction was not expanded to keep pace with the large increase in troop strength. Originally 66,000,000 square feet of covered storage space had been estimated as necessary to supply an army of 3,200,000 men. This estimate included

---

[29] Stauffer, *QM Depot S&D Opns*, pp. 18–19.

[30] (1) Ltr, TAG to CofEngrs, 7 Mar 42, sub: Temporary Type Const. (2) Ltr, Gen Scowden, OQMG, to COs of all depots, 11 May 43, sub: Restriction on Const.

storage for Quartermaster items and those of other technical services stored in general depots administered by The Quartermaster General. In April 1945, at the peak of wartime expansion when the planned Army strength had almost trebled, the total covered space, including commercial storage, did not exceed 75,000,000 square feet—only 9,000,000 square feet more than that in the original estimate.[31]

Various factors accounted for the success of the technical services in supplying the Army of more than 8,000,000 men in World War II from warehouse facilities only slightly larger than those planned for 3,200,000 men. The wider use of materials-handling equipment and improved depot layout permitted a sharp increase in supply turnover and a better utilization of space. The pressure for storage space was alleviated by a greater use than was originally anticipated of leased and commercial storage, amounting to 11,583,000 square feet in April 1945. The greater use of open storage for selected supply items which would not deteriorate rapidly through exposure contributed to the same end. Open storage was not as valuable in Quartermaster operations as in those of some other technical services but could be used for storing such items as fuels, chemicals, and containers. On the other hand, the value of sheds was increasingly recognized by the QMC as the war progressed. This type of covered storage, consisting of sheds with roofs but no side walls and frequently no concrete floors, was easily constructed and relatively inexpensive. Such items as shovels, tent poles, and pins were among selected Quartermaster items of supply that required cover but not the degree of protection afforded by warehouses. Storage facilities were augmented by the use of holding and reconsignment points operated by the Transportation Corps to assemble supplies for overseas shipment. From the middle of 1942 congestion in depots was further relieved by the use of overseas facilities to store material shipped direct

from contractors to ports.[32]

By the beginning of 1943 the expansion program had been substantially completed. Eleven Quartermaster depots and eleven Quartermaster sections of ASF depots with a new covered storage capacity of more than 25,000,000 square feet were handling Quartermaster supplies.[33] Installations existing in 1939 had been enlarged; millions of square feet of commercial storage space had been leased; and six new ASF depots containing Quartermaster sections, six new Quartermaster depots, and seven subdepots had been established.

The pattern of geographical distribution of the depots had been greatly altered during the war years. Because of the existing concentration of depots east of the Mississippi and above the Mason and Dixon Line, the expansion program in that area had involved primarily the modernization and enlargement of these installations and the lease and construction of additional facilities to meet new demands. In contrast new depots were constructed in the South and West to provide adequate facilities for the maintenance of troops being trained below the Mason and Dixon Line and in the Southwest and to support the troops in the Pacific.[34]

Use of Commercial Storage Space

The increased storage space acquired through expansion of the depot system had to be supplemented by the use of commercial storage space. This included both dry-storage and cold-storage facilities. The huge quantities of subsistence purchased and the necessity of building adequate reserves of both perishable and non-

[31] Lecture, Brig Gen H. Feldman, 25 Oct 46, sub: Relationship of 1939 Storage Facilities to Estimated Need (Industrial Mobilization Course, ICAF), p. 4.
[32] Ibid.
[33] Statistics Br, OP&C Div, Stat Handbook of the QMC, 1943, p. 25.
[34] See Chart 11. For a more detailed discussion of the expansion of the depot system throughout the country and the changing missions of these installations, see Stauffer, QM Depot S&D Opns, pp. 27–54.

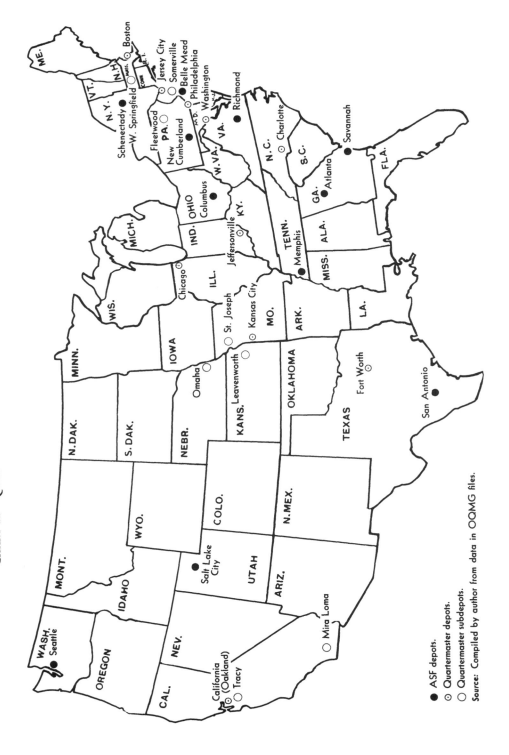

CHART 11—QUARTERMASTER CORPS DEPOT SYSTEM: 1 DECEMBER 1944

● ASF depots.
⊙ Quartermaster depots.
○ Quartermaster subdepots.

Source: Compiled by author from data in OQMG files.

perishable foods for supplying the armed forces compelled the QMC to resort extensively to the use of commercial storage.

Kansas City Plan

While commercial warehouses of the dry-storage type were not practicable for the storage of hazardous or perishable supplies or for those with a rapid turnover, nonperishable foods of a seasonal nature, especially canned fruits and vegetables, could be stored in them. From the beginning of the emergency period, the QMC had been interested in the civilian facilities that might be available for Quartermaster storage, but it was the necessity of providing storage for nonperishables that resulted in the development of a feasible plan. A review of the problem was initiated in April 1941 by a request from the Chicago Quartermaster Depot for information on contracting for commercial storage space.[35]

The problem of storage of nonperishable foods grew out of the change made in the procurement of these commodities. As the Army expanded, the peacetime practice of purchase of nonperishables by regional depots from wholesalers for direct delivery to posts, camps, and stations gave way to a new method of centralized procurement by field buyers directly from the canners before and during the producing seasons. Since such canned goods often had to be stored for as long as a year before being sent to consuming installations, valuable depot storage space would be occupied for unduly long periods. This would interfere with the fluidity of depot operations.

Under the WPB set-aside order of March 1942 canners were expected to hold government goods for as long as a year. They soon clamored for relief on storage space, particularly by the end of September when WPB Order M–237 limited to 35 percent the amount of canned goods that could be released to civilian trade before 1 December. Most processors lacked sufficient storage facilities to hold canned goods

and at the same time maintain enough space to complete the year's canning and prepare for the next season's pack. This was especially true for West Coast canners, where the wide variety of fruits and vegetables and the protracted growing season, ranging from 150 to 300 days, made the canning period longer than elsewhere.[36] The only satisfactory solution to the problem of overcrowding canners' warehouses was the prompt removal of Quartermaster supplies.

Commercial warehouses, located at widely scattered points, were well suited for the storage of fruits and vegetables which were canned in all parts of the country. The War Department had no desire to lease and operate these facilities on its own account, but it did need to know in advance what storage space would be available. It was thought that its requirements could be covered by a contract which would guarantee a definite amount of space in selected warehouses for use as needed. In June 1941 the OQMG outlined a method whereby the depots might negotiate a term contract with an association of warehousemen, thereby obtaining in a single agreement all the facilities needed for commercial storage in an entire urban community.[37]

The War Department Commercial Warehouse Pool Plan was developed to implement this method. It was popularly known as the Kansas City Plan since it grew out of an agreement devised by the Kansas City Quartermaster Depot and the Kansas City Warehouse Association.[38] By April 1942 the OQMG had ap-

---

[35] Ltr, Col H. B. Barry, CO CQMD, to TQMG, 12 Apr 41, sub: Stor, 400.24.

[36] For a more detailed treatment of the canners' storage problem see Marion Massen, *Canned Vegetables: A Case History in Central Procurement at the Chicago Quartermaster Depot During World War II* (CQMD Historical Studies 3, October 1943), pp. 75–79.

[37] OQMG Cir Ltr 107, 14 Jun 41, sub: Utilization of Pub Warehousing Fac.

[38] (1) Stauffer, *QM Depot S&D Opns*, pp. 56–61. (2) Col Stephens, "The Kansas City Plan," *QMR*, XXII (November–December 1942), 54ff.

proved a contract which provided the pattern for all future negotiations.

Briefly, under this plan the Real Estate Branch, Office of the Chief of Engineers, negotiated a contract on behalf of the War Department with a Federal Emergency Warehouse Association. This association, which included all warehousemen in a given urban area, agreed to do all the necessary handling of supplies and guaranteed that a certain proportion of the storage facilities of its members would be available on short notice. The amount of space which the association might be required to offer varied according to the length of notice given. For instance, 2½ percent might be demanded in 5 days, 5 percent in 10 days, and 10 percent in 15 days. The association posted a performance bond as a guarantee that the requested space would be made available.[39]

Eventually the Kansas City Plan operated in most of the larger urban centers where the majority of commercial warehouses were located. A large amount of storage space became available under the plan without the expense of constructing or leasing warehouses and at a cost that covered only the space actually occupied. The administrative burden on the OQMG was appreciably reduced by the establishment of a central office in each urban warehouse association, the secretary of which allocated War Department supplies among the available warehouses, and consolidated invoices for submission to the OQMG. The secretary could supply the OQMG quickly and promptly with any data concerning the storage situation in a given city.

During the spring of 1942 the group warehouse plan was employed almost entirely for Quartermaster storage under the direction of the Space Control Unit in the Depot Operations Branch. While this plan was developed mainly to establish reserves of space for the QMC, Headquarters, SOS, determined by July that it would be of advantage to all the supply services. To avoid their making separate contracts with the same associations, The Quartermaster General was given the responsibility of operating the plan for the benefit of the entire War Department.[40] So widely was the Kansas City Plan used that the number of areas in which the Federal Emergency Warehouse Association operated increased from thirteen in November 1942 to forty-two by the fall of 1944.[41]

In actual practice the QMC derived more benefit from the plan than any other supply service. About 95 percent of the space was normally consigned to it. Canned fruits and vegetables always constituted the larger part of the supplies stored under this plan. As much as 90 percent of the space allotted to the Corps at times was occupied by nonperishable foods.[42] These included not only canned fruits and vegetables but canned fish and meats, evaporated milk, and dried eggs. In addition, supplies with a slow turnover, such as cots, bedsteads, comforters, mattresses, and pillows, were also stored in commercial warehouses.

Cleveland Plan

Early in June 1943, after the Kansas City Plan had been operating for more than a year, it was criticized by the OPA, the WPB, and the Department of Justice because the rate schedules

---

[39] Ltr, Maj S. E. Beggs, OQMG, to all COs of QM Depots and QM Sup Offs of Gen Depots, 15 Apr 42. sub: Assoc of Warehousemen—Kansas City Plan.

[40] (1) SOS Cir 34, 2b, 28 Jul 42, no sub. (2) Ltr. Col Robinson E. Duff, SOS, to TQMG, 21 Jul 42, sub: Arrangements for Stor Under Kansas City Plan. (3) For the operating procedure see WD SB 10–142. 13 Oct 44, Stor: Kansas City Plan.

[41] (1) Ltr, Col J. J. O'Brien, Chief of Real Estate Br, CE, to TQMG, 21 Nov 42, sub: WD Package Plan Contracts. (2) WD SB 10–142, App. IV, 13 Oct 42, sub: Stor: Kansas City Plan.

[42] (1) Capt H. R. Pellegrino to Col Stephens, OQMG, 17 Feb 43, sub: Items Stored Commercially, 400.242. (2) During the spring and summer of 1943, 8,000 carloads of canned vegetables from the 1942 pack were stored in 246 warehouses in 39 cities by the Chicago Depot. Massen, *Canned Vegetables*, p. 78.

did not conform with maximum price regulations and because the contract arrangements did not permit normal competition between commercial warehouses. Under these circumstances there arose the issue of possible violation of the antitrust laws. Temporarily, and until 15 August 1943, the OPA exempted the contract rate schedules from the application of price ceilings. In the meantime the QMC undertook a survey to determine how these storage rates compared with those charged in March 1942, the date used by OPA in establishing permissible charges. At the same time the OQMG devised a supplementary method of obtaining commercial storage space, which became known as the Cleveland Plan since it was first tried out in that city.[43]

The new system differed from the Kansas City Plan in that separate contracts were made with individual warehousemen on the basis of competitive bids. This satisfied the Department of Justice and also the OPA because the plan expressly provided that in no instance would the government be charged more for storing an item than was permissible under maximum price regulations. This system of individual contracts made available to the War Department a wider geographical distribution of commercial warehouses, since it permitted storage in towns and small cities which lacked sufficient facilities for establishing a Federal Emergency Warehouse Association.

From an operational viewpoint the Cleveland Plan differed considerably from the Kansas City Plan. Under the new system administrative functions were decentralized to a commercial warehouse officer appointed at each of the nine regional distributing depots to serve as a liaison officer between the using services and the commercial warehouses. On behalf of the War Department he made the contracts with the warehousemen in his zone. This decentralization of procedure was completed in the summer of 1944 when the responsibility for executing contracts under the Kansas City Plan was also charged to this same officer.[44] The task of assigning space was divided between the officer and the Space Control Section, OQMG. The latter gave an assignment number to the using service while the commercial warehouse officer, out of his more detailed knowledge of the region for which he was responsible, designated the specific warehouse to which the goods of the applying service would be shipped. The Cleveland Plan insisted on no guarantee of availability of space but did require weekly reports of vacant space in warehouses operating under the plan to be transmitted to the appropriate commercial warehouse officer.[45]

Because of the objections raised to the Kansas City Plan, the OQMG developed a new method of determining rates for storage. The association plan had been adopted in the first place as a means of simplifying the rate schedule so that rate charges could be arrived at without having to refer to a complicated tariff table. If the custom of the industry had been adhered to, it would have been necessary to establish a table of tariff charges for some 800,000 different items. Under the Kansas City Plan, storage rates were established on a hundredweight basis with varying charges based on density per cubic inch of the commodity computed for six rate classes. Later in the summer of 1944 these were increased to fourteen. All warehouses within a city charged the same price. The price was arrived at by taking the average charges of

---

[43] (1) Memo, Gen Scowden, OQMG, for CG ASF, 7 Jun 43, sub: WD Commercial Warehouse Pool Plan, and appended Statement on Opns of Plan, 400.242. (2) Memo, Lt Col E. H. Foley, OQMG, for Dir of Purch Div, ASF, 2 Jul 43, sub: Approval of Proposed Warehouse Contract Form.

[44] Ltr, Gen Hardigg, OQMG, to CO JCQMD, 6 May 44, sub: Kansas City and Cleveland Plans, 400.242.

[45] (1) Memo, Gen Scowden, OQMG, for CG ASF, 7 Jun 43, sub: WD Commercial Warehouse Pool Plan. (2) Memo, Brig Gen T. L. Holland, OQMG, for CofT, 20 Aug 43, same sub, 400.242.

storage quoted by the various members of the association. This method did permit some of the warehouses to charge the government rates in excess of those which they were charging in March of 1942 and did not provide for normal competition between the various members.

Under the Cleveland Plan rates were determined by fixing a basic price per cubic foot, which, in accordance with prevailing commercial charges, varied slightly from community to community. This rate rose progressively as the density exceeded a set figure—about 31 pounds a cubic foot, which was the approximate weight required to stack goods 8 feet high in a standard warehouse with a floorload capacity of 250 pounds. Basic rates were thus determined because warehousemen desired a "specific return for each cubic foot of warehouse space" regardless of the amount of space actually occupied. The basic rate was therefore increased as the density became greater, because, other things being equal, the greater the density the lower would be the height to which goods could be stacked and the fewer the cubic feet actually filled.[46]

ASF approval of the Cleveland Plan in the fall of 1943 did not mean that the War Department was abandoning the use of the Kansas City Plan.[47] A survey of storage rates had revealed that those charged under the Kansas City Plan were only slightly in excess of OPA levels in some cities while in others they averaged about the same as the prescribed maximum rates. A further comparison of rates under the two plans showed that those under the Kansas City Plan averaged about the same as those under the Cleveland Plan. Bulky items of light density, such as comforters and mattresses, could be held more cheaply under the Cleveland Plan but the cost was about equal under the two plans for storing subsistence items weighing thirty-seven pounds a cubic foot, and the bulk of articles stored commercially weighed more than that. As a consequence, the OPA exempted the Kansas City Plan from the General Maximum Price Regulation, and during the war the two systems were used to supplement each other.[48] The scope of both plans was broadened in the autumn of 1944 by the participation of the Navy, which by that time found it necessary to relieve the pressure on its storage facilities by resorting to the use of commercial storage for its nonperishable foods.[49]

Cold Storage of Perishables

Providing cold storage for perishable subsistence became increasingly important late in 1942 and early in 1943. Until well into 1941 no problem existed, inasmuch as virtually all such foods were bought locally by military establishments in accordance with their requirements. Even after the market centers had been established in the spring of 1941, perishables continued to be sent direct, as a rule, from the producers to the requisitioning stations. The War Department had no central facilities for the storage of perishables.

In January 1941 the War Department planned to construct cold-storage units of various sizes in 46 Army installations, but early in the market center program many camps still lacked sufficient facilities to provide cold storage on the standard basis of a replenishment of fruits and vegetables at 3-day intervals and of other perish-

[46] (1) Memo, Gen Scowden, OQMG, for CG ASF, 7 Jun 43, sub: WD Commercial Warehouse Pool Plan, and appended Statement of Opn of Plan, 400.242. (2) Rpt, Col Stephens to Lt. Col Q. L. Kendall, OQMG, 16 Jan 46, sub: Control of Stor Space, OQMG.

[47] 1st ind, Hq ASF to TQMG, 28 Oct 43, on memo, TQMG for CG ASF, 30 Sep 43, sub: Cleveland Plan, 400.242.

[48] (1) Ltr, H. K. Osgood, OPA, to S. G. Spear, ODT, 24 Jan 44, no sub. (2) Ltr, S. G. Spear to Mgr, Federal Emergency Warehouse Assoc, Savannah, Ga., 17 Mar 44, no sub. (3) Col E. B. Kearns, Jr., to Dir of S&D Div, OQMG, 5 Feb 44, sub: Comparison of Rates.

[49] OQMG Daily Activity Journal, 29 Sep 44, pp. 6–7, and 16 Oct 44, p. 4.

ables at 7-day intervals.[50] To supply camps having inadequate cold-storage facilities, the market center program began in June to establish assembly and distributing points, located at conveniently situated towns and cities in which satisfactory commercial cold-storage space could be obtained at prevailing rates on a service contract basis. Some sixteen distribution points were eventually in operation.[51] In those rare instances in which suitable refrigerated space could not be found, cold-storage plants were constructed. Perishable produce stored at assembly and distribution points was not procured as a reserve but to cover specific requisitions submitted by the camps, and consequently such supplies were moved out within a short time. Storage and distribution operations of the market center program were still kept to a minimum.

Within a short time the need for developing reserve stocks of perishables became obvious. The necessity for creating a storage program developed out of the serious shortages in seasonal foods late in 1942 and the difficulty of filling requisitions for overseas movements. Requisitions were not always received sufficiently far in advance to insure delivery at the proper time, while, on the other hand, unanticipated cancellations resulted in unwieldy accumulation of supplies at market centers. Current procurement from markets in the vicinity of the ports could not be relied upon to meet the large export requirements. Reserve stocks had to be maintained for the arrival of refrigerator ships. Assembly and distribution points were therefore established in port cities, but they afforded only a temporary solution to the problem for, in accordance with their function of local redistribution of produce rather than long-range storage for overseas purposes, they maintained initially only limited stores.

Food production, although greater than in prewar years, was insufficient to meet the military requirements of the United States and its

allies, as well as the heavy civilian demand. A steady supply for the armed forces could be insured only by the adoption of a large-scale storage program of seasonal foods. The more important of these were eggs, butter, and cheese, which attained maximum production during the spring and summer. Fruit and vegetables were also seasonal, and the slaughter of cattle, hogs, and poultry followed a well-defined cycle. Military requirements, however, bore no relationship to these seasonal variations.

A co-ordinated, seasonal storage program was initiated in the spring of 1943 by the Perishable Branch of the Subsistence Division, OQMG. It proposed to schedule storage programs for shell eggs, butter, and cheese, and at a later date for other perishables when plans could be formulated. Headquarters, ASF, approved of the program "in principle" and indicated that the plans for the quantities to be stored from one flush season to another would have to be co-ordinated with the War Food Administration. By the fall, additional storage programs for apples, potatoes, boneless beef, and poultry were put into operation.[52] Similar plans were executed in 1944 and 1945.

The scope of these operations is revealed in the storage program for beef. In February 1943 about 7,900,000 pounds of beef were in storage for the armed forces. Because of the small quantities in storage, three fourths of the requisitions for beef went unfilled during the last quarter of

[50] (1) Insp rpt, John A. Hawkins to TQMG, 23 Aug 41, sub: QM Activities in Fourth CA, 7–23 Jul 41. (2) Subs Br, Sup Div, to Const Div, OQMG, 13 Sep 41, sub: Remodeling of Common Stor Bldgs for Handling Perishables.

[51] (1) Ltr, John Martin, Chief of Procurement, Fld Hq, QMMCS, to Col Hardigg, Chief of Subs Br, OQMG, 23 Jun 41, no sub. (2) Memo, F. Chapin Weed for Col Hardigg, 5 Aug 41, no sub. The first distribution point was established at Alexandria, La.

[52] (1) Memo, Gen Corbin, Actg QMG, for CG ASF, 6 Apr 43, sub: Proposed Stor Program, Perishable Subs. (2) 1st ind, Hq ASF to TQMG, 19 Apr 43, on same. (3) Memo, TQMG for CG ASF, 3 Sep 43, same sub, 430.

1942 and the first quarter of 1943. Thereafter the stores of beef gradually increased until a peak of 181,500,000 pounds was attained in July 1945 despite fluctuating stockages resulting from seasonal variations and sizable overseas shipments.[53] Butter was another commodity stocked in large quantities. Eggs, cheese, poultry, potatoes, and fresh pork were also held in large volume.

From the beginning, the lack of adequate and satisfactory refrigerated space was the chief problem of the seasonal storage program. It was further aggravated by the shortage of labor to operate these facilities.[54] At times in port cities and other large distribution centers all available space was filled to capacity. At all times, however, 10 to 25 percent of the commercial cold-storage space of the country was vacant. This did not mean that it was necessarily available to the armed forces in periods of heaviest demand. A small proportion had to be reserved for commodities in transit. The lack of operating labor made some of it unavailable. In addition, much of it was of the cooler type, whereas the Army needed freezer space, which alone was suitable for storing meat, meat products, and poultry. As the Army, in an effort to provide perishable foods for remote areas overseas, shifted from the use of chilled to frozen foods, the requirements for freezer space during the war increased rather than diminished.[55] Aside from reducing the storage period, the Army could do little to lighten the pressure on freezer space.

Generally, military foods were stored at standard commercial warehouse rates and handled by the regular employees of the warehouses. The market center program was charged with the responsibility of obtaining satisfactory refrigerated space, but since it was extremely scarce, the Storage and Distribution Division, Field Headquarters, had to co-ordinate its efforts with those of other interested agencies. The WFA, which bought perishable foods under the lend-lease program, was charged with allocating available cold-storage space among public and private users. The ODT controlled all shipments by rail, and the Interstate Commerce Commission controlled the loading and allocation of refrigerator cars. Under the auspices of the WFA, the Inter-Agency Cold-Storage Committee was formed of representatives of all the interested government agencies to discuss common problems and evolve solutions for them.[56]

Various measures were taken to relieve the shortage of cold-storage space. From the summer of 1943 until V-J Day the WFA attempted to make more of this space available by restricting civilian storage.[57] The Army tried to use to better advantage existing freezing facilities at posts, camps, and stations. It also sought to increase freezer facilities and to promote more effective employment of cold-storage space at meat packing plants, by having the plants freeze the meat prior to delivery. The post could thus store from five to seven times more of the product in space which heretofore was used for freezing.[58]

---

[53] (1) Stat Handbook of the QMC, 1943, p. 75. (2) Stat Yearbook of the QMC, 1945, p. 113. See the same tables for the storage of other subsistence items.
[54] (1) Memo, Fld Hq, QMMCS, for Maj Logan Morrill, OQMG, 8 Apr 44, sub: Cold-Stor Situation, 673. (2) Ltr, E. J. Connors, Dir of Div of Transport Pers, ODT, to Cold-Stor Warehouse Employers, 27 Jun 44, sub: Manpower Situation in Cold-Stor Warehousing, 334.
[55] Ltr, Chairman Elwood Chase, Inter-Agency Cold-Stor Committee, to Lee Marshall, WFA, 31 Jul 44, sub: Public Cold-Stor Emergency, 673.
[56] See, for example, ltr, Maj Morrill to Elwood Chase, 13 Jun 44, sub: Inter-Agency Cold-Stor Committee Mtg, 9 Jun 44, 334.
[57] (1) See WFA FO 70, Pt. 1470, 31 Jul 43, sub: Food Stor Fac. (2) Amendt 2 to same, 21 Mar 44. (3) WFA FO 90, Pt. 1470, 22 Dec 43, same sub. (4) WFA FO 111, Pt. 1470, 31 Aug 44, same sub.
[58] (1) Ltr, Gen Hardigg, OQMG, to Ashley Sellers, WFA, 1 Jan 44, no sub. (2) Ltr, Hardigg to D. D. Harde, Office of Materials and Fac, WFA, 27 May 44, no sub. (3) Ltr, J. R. Shoemaker, Asst Dir Div of Stor, ODT, to Cold-Stor Warehouses, 3 Jun 44, no sub, 673.

From time to time Army construction or acquisition of refrigerated plants was also proposed. Except for a small number of government-sponsored cold-storage facilities on the Pacific coast and an even smaller number along the Atlantic seaboard—facilities that were constructed and put into operation in the spring and summer of 1944—no significant program was undertaken. It was established ASF policy to approve as little new building with Army funds as possible.[59] Such building as was done under government sponsorship was aimed principally at alleviating storage congestion at ports of embarkation.

In the months before the landing in Normandy the difficulty of securing cold-storage space in the New York metropolitan area resulted in the development of the "back-up storage plan." It was physically impossible for the twenty-eight cold-storage warehouses in the area to store and deliver all the supplies required by the port of embarkation at a given time. The solution was to spread out the port storage reserves to neighboring areas easily accessible to New York by rail. Products were at first stored in Philadelphia, Baltimore, Boston, and Syracuse. Market centers in these cities were responsible for arranging the storage and transportation of the commodities, which could be ordered out of storage for movement to shipside only at the direction of the New York Market Center. The system was gradually expanded until earmarked supplies were stocked in seventy-two warehouses outside the New York area. In effect the basic concept of the filler depot was applied to perishable foods. The back-up storage plan solved the problem of cold-storage space at the port of embarkation and simplified the task of co-ordinating large overseas shipments without putting an undue strain upon the storage and transportation facilities in the New York metropolitan area.[60]

During the opening months of 1945 the plan was put into operation at New Orleans and also

at San Francisco, where some thirty warehouses within 200 miles of the city were in use as the war ended. Both the Army and the Navy were experiencing difficulties in co-ordinating storage, rail movement, and cargo loading of perishables at the San Francisco Port of Embarkation. A market center proposal for co-operative action resulted in the establishment of a joint Army-Navy stockpile for meat and dairy products from which requisitions for ship loadings were filled. A control board, composed of representatives of the Navy Market Office and the Quartermaster Market Center, was created to handle all requisitions, allocations to warehouses, and withdrawals from them for movement to shipside in such a way as to prevent any unmanageable congestion of available facilities.[61]

Had the Army anticipated in 1940 the huge amounts of perishables that would be procured in World War II, the problem of providing cold-storage facilities would have been better solved. It was the spring of 1943, however, before the need for a full-fledged storage and distribution plan was fully realized. By then it was too late to do more than improvise solutions. The failure to construct cold-storage plants during the emergency period and the absence of any long-range planning were the most conspicuous faults of the program for supplying the Army with perishable foods.[62]

Space Control

In still a third way the QMC attempted to provide adequate storage facilities for the dis-

[59] (1) Memo, Maj Morrill, OQMG, for OIC, Fld Hq, 15 Apr 44, sub: Cold-Stor Situation. (2) Insp rpt, John A. Hawkins to TQMG, 5 Apr 44, sub: Rpt of travel to San Francisco *et al.*, 2–25 Feb 44. (3) Insp rpt, Col Robert F. Carter to TQMG, 5 Nov 43, sub: QM Activities at Richmond *et al.*, 27–31 Oct 43, 673.
[60] For more detail see Rifkind, *Fresh Foods for the Armed Forces: the Quartermaster Market Center System, 1941–48*, pp. 123ff.
[61] *Ibid.*, pp. 124–26.
[62] Stauffer, *QM Depot S&D Opns*, p. 71.

tribution of its supplies. It developed a method to utilize completely existing storage space, since the expansion of depots and the use of commercial facilities did not mean that ample space for storing Quartermaster supplies was thereby automatically assured.

When the war began, the Corps had no clearing house definitely charged with the responsibility of controlling available space. Quartermaster procuring agencies were shipping supplies into depots without knowing what, if any, goods other agencies were shipping to the same installations, or how much space was available for the different categories of supply at these distributing points. Strategically located depots were always crowded beyond their capacity to handle supplies efficiently while other depots had a large amount of vacant space. Officers in charge of storage could not preplan for the use of space. This resulted in inefficiency in the handling of supplies and caused a considerable amount of rewarehousing to keep stock locations as consolidated as possible.[63]

Weekly depot space reports were submitted to the OQMG, but they were largely limited to statements of the total vacancy at depots plus estimates of the space situation as it would be 30, 60, and 90 days ahead. Since no standard definitions had been adopted of what constituted vacant space, each depot reported on a different basis. Such reports were inadequate for wartime, when the tempo of physical stock movements was greatly increased.[64]

Aware of the problem, The Quartermaster General in May 1942 assigned an officer to the Depot Operations Branch of the Storage and Distribution Division to develop an effective control over the utilization of storage space. A Space Control Section was established through which the commodity branches and divisions of the OQMG were to clear shipments of all supplies prior to authorizing the transfer of stocks. The section was to prevent congested storage conditions, to maintain fluid space to care for

emergencies, and to plan space assignments in advance.

These objectives could not be achieved without obtaining comprehensive information on space in the depots and a report of its use. The Space Control Section began work on a report of space utilization which would be sufficiently detailed to secure the data needed for control purposes. By the time that Headquarters, SOS, became concerned about the need for clarification and standardization of space reporting procedures, the OQMG was able to report that it had devised a new form for its report which provided clear definitions of the major terms used, such as "net usable space vacant" and "net usable space assigned." [65]

The new form proved to be complicated to fill out and a simpler method was put into effect early in January 1943 when two short forms were used instead of one.[66] The space control report, submitted semimonthly, showed space occupancy broken down by warehouse, shed, and open storage. It was further subdivided into a report of space required for (1) the storage of stock levels necessary for the completion of the depot's mission and (2) for special assignments, such as reserves, excesses of stock levels, and seasonal procurement, not directly connected with the depot's mission but for which space had to be provided. The space utilization report was submitted monthly and gave information on the use of space for nonstorage purposes— offices, bin rooms, cafeterias, and such activities as inspection, packing, crating, and shipment of supplies. Its purpose was to check the efficiency

---

[63] Rpt, Col Stephens to Col Kendall, OQMG, 16 Jan 46, sub: Control of Stor Space, OQMG, p. 1.

[64] Ibid.

[65] (1) Ltr, Col Duff, Chief of Gen Depot Sv, SOS, to TQMG et al., 1 Jul 42, sub: Standardization of Space Reporting Procedures. (2) 1st ind, Col Stephens, OQMG, to Hq SOS, 6 Jul 42, on same, 400.242.

[66] QMC Form 24 (revised 1 Jan 43) QM Space Control Rpt and QMC Form 29, QM Space Utilization Rpt.

with which space was utilized for these purposes. These reporting procedures were used throughout the war without much modification although the two reports were later combined again into one and submitted on a monthly basis.[67]

These forms furnished the data necessary for the control of depot space but provision had not been made for centralized supervision over the assignment of space. As a consequence, in many depots in the winter of 1942–43, the stock on hand and the amount due in the depots exceeded their maximum storage capacity. The gravity of the situation spurred the Depot Operations Branch to request a directive that would clarify the space assignment responsibility of the Space Control Section.[68]

Centralized control of space assignment and utilization was established on 1 February 1943.[69] A system of space assignment numbers, which constituted the depot's authority for accepting shipments, was established. Space allocations were made by the OQMG for special storage assignments as well as for supplies needed to maintain stock levels for filler and distributing purposes. When a commodity branch changed the stock level for a supply regularly handled by a depot, it had to obtain an allocation of space. Once secured, however, no further recourse to the Space Control Section was necessary as long as prescribed stock levels were maintained. When these were exceeded, a new space allocation had to be secured for the excess. Definite time limitations were placed on special space assignments, such as those obtained for supplies held for the account of other depots or for some unusual purpose. Such stock could only be replenished with the approval of the Space Control Section. In requesting space allotments, commodity branches had to indicate the nature of the supplies to be shipped, the number of square feet needed, the period of time for which space was required, and the origin and ultimate destination of the supplies. Such data enabled

the Space Control Section to prevent unnecessary backhauls and crosshauls of supplies and, if the supplies had a rapid turnover, permitted it to select storage space in a depot that was not already hard pressed because of a scarcity of labor or materials-handling equipment. All such factors had to be considered, for more was involved in making space assignments than the mere process of finding vacant space.[70]

In order to determine space requirements, the Space Control Section had to know the cubes and weights of the many Quartermaster items of supply. Unfortunately the containers in which supplies were shipped had not been completely standardized. They included a wide variety of sizes, and it was necessary to develop cubes and weights for hundreds of containers.[71] By securing from the field the measurements in inches, the weights, the type of package, and the number of units per package of each item involved, the Space Control Section was able to prepare and publish tables that simplified the depot's task of computing the space needed to store clothing and equipage, subsistence, and general supplies. Consulting these tables also enabled the Space Control Section to determine whether an installation was using its space to the maximum advantage.

The increasing demand for depot storage space that accompanied the constant expansion of overseas operations demanded the utmost efficiency and economy in its use, since relief could not be obtained through new construc-

[67] (1) QMC Form 24 (revised 6 Jun 45), QM Space Control Rpt. (2) For more detail on these forms see Stauffer, *QM Depot S&D Opns*, pp. 90–91.

[68] Depot Opns Br to Dir of S&D Div, OQMG, 27 Nov 42, sub: Control of Assgmt of Warehouse Space, 400.242.

[69] Ltr, Gen Scowden, OQMG, to COs QM Depots and QM Sup Offs, 1 Feb 43, sub: Efficient Utilization of Available Depot Stor Space, 400.242.

[70] Address, Capt Pellegrino, Chief of Space Control Sec, OQMG, 1 Apr 43, sub: Space Control.

[71] Rpt, Col Stephens to Col Kendall, OQMG, 16 Jan 46, sub: Control of Stor Space, pp. 3–4.

tion. One of the difficulties confronting the Space Control Section in its assignment of space was the discrepancy between depot reports of space and actual available square footage. This discrepancy resulted from the use by the depots of obsolete and nonstandard building plans and the failure of their reports to reflect both obstructed and unobstructed warehousing areas.

In the spring of 1943 the Storage and Distribution Division devised the controlled warehouse plan in order to provide a standard uniform method of computing the space utilized for the various activities housed within the warehouses. This plan was based on actual measurements of depot floors, excluding all obstructed and operating areas. A correct estimate of square footage was thereby furnished for storage purposes. Cubic storage capacities were indicated by noting the heights to roof beams and trusses. As a result the storage space of the depots could be determined more accurately than ever before. On the basis of these floor plans the OQMG furnished each depot with lay-out plans showing the position of operating aisles, the types of commodities to be placed in various storage areas, and the location of nonstorage activities. The intent was to provide the maximum use of warehouse space for storage purposes and the minimum for nonstorage activities. No fundamental change could be made in the lay-out plan by a depot without approval of the OQMG. As a result of placing the controlled warehouse storage plan into operation "a substantial recapture of usable storage space" was achieved.[72]

Within the limits of the general space assignments made in the lay-out plans, the depots were responsible for the detailed planning for placing particular supplies. For the sake of ready location, depots consolidated stocks of similar items as far as possible. Thus all canned peaches were placed together in one section and all canned beans in another section. But this method compelled extensive rewarehousing to re-gain space for effective utilization every time space assignments were increased or decreased because of altered stock levels. During the first half of the war the outstanding weakness of the existing lay-out system was the low operating efficiency resulting from the frequent rewarehousing of stock.

Planograph System

Early in 1944 the Space Control Section began to work out a plan that came to be known as the planograph or Quartermaster system of space utilization. Its objective was the control of the movement of supplies in and out of a depot in order to consolidate vacant space into large segments by the normal process of attrition of supplies rather than by rewarehousing.[73] The system was not new but was a consolidation and expansion of existing storage practices that had developed out of wartime experience. Its essence was the controlled physical dispersion of supplies in several different storage locations within a depot and an effective stock locator system.

The planograph system was first put into effect at the Richmond Depot on an experimental basis for foods earmarked for oversea shipment and was subsequently installed at other depots for filler subsistence. The general plan of operation called for a physical division of filler subsistence into groups, each of which contained a part of all the food articles stocked at the depot—that is, a balanced menu.[74] The number

[72] (1) Ltr, Lt Col M. J. Bradbury, OQMG, to CO RMASFD, 29 Jun 43, sub: Controlled Warehouse Plans. (2) Ltr, Gen Scowden, OQMG, to QMSO SAASFD, 18 Aug 43, same sub. (3) Ltr, Gen Scowden to CO JCQMD, 12 Oct 43, same sub, 400.242.

[73] Ltr, Brig Gen A. M. Owens, OQMG, to COs QM Depots et al., 22 Jul 44, sub: Use of Stor Space, 400.242.

[74] For the details of operation see (1) Address, Maj Pellegrino, 11 Jan 45, QMC Stor Conf, Camp Lee, Va., 11–12 Jan 45, pp. 47ff. (2) Anon., "Plan Your Warehousing by Planograph," *Quartermaster Training Service Journal*, Vol. 7, No. 10, 9 Mar 45, pp. 9–11.

of groups depended on the size of the stock level set for balanced rations.

These groups in turn were divided into five "positions" or storage locations, each of which, in the case of single-story warehouses, represented a different freight-rate classification. This method was used because the entire weight of a carload lot of assorted foods is, by railroad rule, paid for according to the highest freight-rate commodity in the car. In the case of multi-storied warehouses, it was suggested that items be combined in a single position according to their weight rather than their rate classification, with the heavier items being placed on the lower floors. Stockages of supplies within the groups were so arranged that position 1 in Group A would carry the same supplies—for example fruits and fruit juices—as position 1 in Group B, C, D, and E. Instead of having 25,000,000 balanced rations stored together, for example, under the planograph system there would be five stock levels of 5,000,000 balanced rations each. These five stock levels would be stored and operated separately.

Actually, however, provision would have to be made for an overflow group for those items which at times would exceed normal stock levels and hence could not be stored in the regular positions. This would result in a waste of space because the overflow area would always have some supplies in it while at the same time a certain amount of space would be vacant in other groups since a few stocks would always be below their established levels. To avoid this waste, space assignments for a level of 25,000,000 rations would be made on the basis of 80 percent of the level. The ration level would be planned for four groups, with the fifth, Group E, becoming the overflow area and used only for those items for which 80 percent of the level was already in existence. The overflow group was also used for storing items so small in quantity that it was not desirable to disperse them into groups. The control thus set up did

not compel rewarehousing when stock levels changed. If the authorized level of rations was reduced, all outgoing shipments would be taken from the overflow and all incoming shipments would be concentrated in the other groups. In the normal course of distribution the warehouse occupied by the overflow would soon be vacated to receive other supplies. In a group containing 5,000,000 rations, this amount could be moved by attrition within 15 days.

The success of the planograph system was dependent upon an effective stock locator system handled by specially designated clerks. This system made extensive use of locator cards, each of which indicated the position of the item, its established stock level, the stock on hand, and the date on which the item was packed. There were as many cards for an item as there were positions in which it was stored. All incoming shipments cleared through the locator clerk, who determined in what position they would be placed. The storekeeper in charge of each position selected the specific bay in which the shipment was to be stored. The locator clerk also chose the location from which an outgoing shipment was taken. His chief function was, therefore, the control of incoming and outgoing stocks so that, if necessary, space could be vacated in large segments or even entire sections of warehouses by the process of attrition.

The plan had some disadvantages. It required a high degree of accuracy in distributing the stock level at the different positions. It worked most advantageously where about 5,000,000 rations constituted the minimum stockage in any one position. The initial breakdown of the system required some major rewarehousing, and because this interrupted current depot operations at a time when they had attained their peak level for the war, no depot employed the full planograph system as it had operated at Richmond.

The proponents of the plan felt, however, that its advantages outweighed its disadvantages. The chief advantage, once the system had been installed, was the elimination of rewarehousing. It was possible to distribute workloads over wider areas in the depot. Since the same stock items were stored in at least three or perhaps five warehouses, congestion of freight cars and materials-handling equipment was reduced to a minimum because a large number of cars could be directed simultaneously to one or all of the railroad sidings of these warehouses. The system eliminated long tractor hauls if two or more items were shipped in the same freight car since complete balanced rations were stored in each group of subsistence. The plan also gave better assurance of turnover of stock because the locator clerk in ordering it out would direct movement from the section in which he had the older stock. This could be immediately determined from the locator card.

The success of the Richmond experiment resulted in a test at the Charlotte Quartermaster Depot of an application of the planograph system to clothing and equipage.[75] These supplies, however, did not lend themselves so readily to the new system as subsistence. The planograph system was therefore not extended to new fields, but the principle of dispersion of supplies continued to spread in the depots during the closing months of the war.[76] Improvements in space control did much to relieve the shortages of storage space and enabled the Corps to deliver promptly vitally needed military supplies.

Materials Handling

Handling materials, the chief activity of any supply installation, meant the removal of goods from the carrier in which they arrived; hauling them to storage areas; piling them in predetermined locations; and, conversely, the removal of supplies from storage; preparing them for shipment by packing, baling, or crating; and hauling and loading them in freight cars. Upon the speed and efficiency with which the depots executed these functions depended the successful supply of the Army.

Use of Mechanical Equipment

To achieve this end during World War II, the Army resorted to the use of mechanical equipment—fork-lift trucks and pallets, trailers, tractors, and conveyors. The Quartermaster General recognized that there would be a shortage of manpower, warehouse space, and railroad cars. He found a common solution for all three problems through development of the fork truck and pallet system.

The use of fork-lift trucks and pallets was the most significant and revolutionary storage development of the war. The fork-lift truck represented the culmination of efforts extending over half a century to combine horizontal and vertical motion in one materials-handling vehicle.[77] By far the best hoisting and stacking machine ever devised for warehouse use, this truck operated on the cantilever principle. A fork, capable of picking up and depositing packaged and strapped material, was attached at the front end. A single operator of a fork-lift truck could pick up, haul for short distances of not more than 250 feet, set down, lift, and stack a large variety of supplies. By handling supplies mechanically, the fork truck did the work of many men, thereby conserving manpower. Further savings were made by substituting women operators for men, since the lifting was entirely mechanical. By means of the fork truck, depot personnel could load and unload railroad cars much faster, even operating inside the freight cars. The freight car shortage was materially relieved by the rapidity with which cars were released. The fork truck

[75] Insp Rpt, Lt L. D. Crunkleton, 6 Feb 45, sub: Travel to CEQMD, 27–30 Jan 45.

[76] For a summary of the favorable results achieved, see Stauffer, *QM Depot S&D Opns*, p. 98.

[77] See Anon., "History of the Fork Truck," *The Palletizer*, Vol. II, No. 7 (July 1945), 8–11.

FORK-LIFT TRUCK *stacking box pallets (left) and loading a freight car (right).*

operated in narrow aisles and stacked foods to the maximum height of the warehouse, thus making the utmost use of all available space. All QMC depots were fully equipped to handle goods mechanically to take full advantage of the economies in manpower, time, and space that fork trucks made possible.[78]

Maximum economies in depot operations could be effected only by combining the use of the fork-lift truck with the palletization of depot stocks, that is, the stacking of supplies on pallets with alternate patterns for alternate tiers. Pallets were small wooden platforms with horizontal wooden strips called stringers placed underneath to give clearance for the entry of the forks. They were of various sizes and types. Those commonly employed in Quartermaster warehouses were 32 inches wide by 40 inches

long. They ordinarily were of a double-faced type, with top and bottom platforms separated by stringers. These pallets were normally used with small containers having low compression strength because, by distributing the weight of the load over a large area, they prevented the containers from being crushed. Single-faced pallets, consisting of a platform supported by under-stringers, were sometimes used to store such items as kegs of nails, pails of paint, and other solid items packed in containers strong enough to withstand pressure resting directly upon them. A third type of pallet on which a box-shaped framework equipped with upright standards and diagonal crosspieces had been

[78] Maj Reid E. Smith, "How Women and Machines Help QM Handling Problems," *Distribution and Warehousing*, XLIII (January 1944), 32.

constructed was used to store bulky or irregularly shaped goods and to furnish greater stability for items easily damaged.[79]

To speed the handling of materials, conveyors of both the belt and roller types were used to convey supplies between waiting freight car and storage points. They were also employed in a wide variety of specialized operations, such as baling, packing, overpacking, can handling, and checking size items. Gravity wheel conveyors were especially useful in multistoried warehouses where elevator service was inadequate. Various types of stackers were operated, and to handle heavy materials outside warehouses different types of cranes were employed. Tractors and trailers were formed into tractor-trailer trains which could be used to better advantage and at less cost than load-carrying trucks.

This conversion to the use of mechanical equipment was a wartime development. Handicapped by a lack of funds, the availability of a large labor supply, and the necessity of moving only a small amount of supplies for a peacetime force, the Army had relied previously on hand-operated equipment and manual labor. War reversed this situation. Then appropriations were sufficient to cover the purchase of the newest equipment, storage space was at a premium, labor became increasingly scarce, and huge quantities of supplies had to be handled at the utmost speed. By 1944 the armed forces were praised for probably having "made greater strides in the proper use of materials-handling equipment since the United States entered the war than industry had during the whole preceding decade."[80]

The QMC took a leading part in promoting the operational efficiency of the depot system.[81] When the Depot Division, OQMG, was established in May 1941, it was made responsible for procuring and distributing all warehouse equipment for Quartermaster depots and ports of embarkation and for training depot personnel in its use. During the summer, personnel of the division inspected mechanical equipment which had been locally procured and put into operation at some of the depots. They made studies of the various types and kinds of materials-handling equipment and planned for its immediate procurement in order to install it in all Quartermaster storage and distribution warehouses.[82] But appropriations for this purpose were not available until September 1941 when the first contracts for fork-lift trucks, pallets, tractors, and trailers were let.

By March 1942 when the division had become the Depot Operations Branch of the Storage and Distribution Division in the first functional reorganization of the OQMG, its responsibilities were widened to include providing equipment for the general depots, then under the control of the General Depot Division, SOS.[83] Some confusion and misunderstanding developed between the OQMG and the Transportation Service, SOS, out of the divided responsibility for equipment used in warehouses and that used on piers of ports of embarkation, but by July procurement responsibility for all such equipment had been definitely assigned to The Quartermaster General.[84] At this time the

[79] (1) Manual, Depot Opns Br, OQMG, Jul 42, sub: Warehousing and Materials Handling in QM Depot, pp. 88–90. (2) Manual, S&D Div, OQMG, Jan 44, sub: Handbook of Stor and Materials Handling Methods, *passim.*

[80] Anon., "Improved Car Plate Lifter and 4-Way Pallet," *Distribution and Warehousing,* XLIII (July 1944), 46.

[81] Address, Lt Col E. H. Ward, 10 Jan 45, QMC Stor Conf, Camp Lee, Va., 10–11 Jan 45, p. 6.

[82] (1) Chief of Standardization Br to Chief of Sup Div, OQMG, 22 Sep 41, sub: Rpt of Insp at Warehouses in 6th CA. (2) Insp Rpt, Capt S. E. Beggs and E. S. Marnon to TQMG, 15 Sep 41, sub: Rpt of Insp at Ft Wayne QMD *et al.,* 451.93.

[83] WD Cir 69, 7 Mar 42, sub: Definition of Responsibilities for Supplies.

[84] (1) Ltr, Lt Col O. G. Collins, OQMG, to Reqmts Div, SOS, 21 May 42, sub: Responsibility for Equip in PE. (2) Memo, Chairman of PAB for TQMG, 28 Jul 42, sub: Procurement of Pier and Warehouse Equip, 400.242.

OQMG was further reorganized along functional lines. A more extensive consolidation of procurement activities took place so that the Procurement Division now became responsible for purchasing pier and warehouse equipment, the Military Planning Division for estimating equipment requirements and consolidating those of the other supply services in the Army Supply Program, and the Storage and Distribution Division continued to be responsible for the storage and issue of these items.[85]

Until the fall of 1942 the QMC continued to have both procurement and purchase responsibility for warehouse and pier equipment. Procurement planning, preparation and defense of estimates, and custody of funds were included under procurement responsibility, and purchase, inspection, and distribution under purchase responsibility. By November, in the interest of fiscal procedure, procurement responsibility was reassigned to the supply services but the purchase responsibility remained with the Corps.[86]

The necessity of allocating materials-handling equipment led to a further revision of functions. Competition among the services for such equipment was keen, and the demand far exceeded the productive capacity of industry. The OQMG recommended the establishment of an allocation committee consisting of representatives from the Army, Navy, Maritime Commission, and WPB. In the fall of 1942, however, The Quartermaster General continued to allocate equipment to the supply services in proportion to their needs under the direction of the Assistant Chief of Staff for Operations, SOS.[87] By February 1943 Headquarters, SOS, took over the function of screening all requirements and allocating materials-handling equipment among the supply services and the AAF. It represented the War Department on the WPB committees which allocated such equipment among all government agencies using it. Since the supply of warehouse equipment was never sufficient to permit the normal procedure of issuing on req-

uisition, the Plans Division, SOS, and later the Storage Division, ASF, continued to exercise these functions until the war ended.[88] The broad functions originally granted the Depot Operations Branch had, by the need to allocate supplies and the functional reorganization of the OQMG, been reduced to one main function—the maintenance of stockpiles at designated distribution points against which shipments were made in accordance with allocation directives of Headquarters, ASF.

Although the Depot Operations Branch realized the importance of instituting better handling methods in depots, achievement of this end was delayed by the inability of the manufacturers to fill Army and Navy orders for equipment in the required time. Not only was the existing capacity of the manufacturers insufficient to produce fork-lift trucks in the volume needed, but critical shortages of steel and other materials and low priorities further curtailed output. The branch requested an A-1-a rating for Army warehouse equipment.[89] Efforts to secure better ratings were decidedly hampered, however, by representatives of the Army who, through the Program Determination Committee, informed the WPB that all types of industrial power trucks could be classified as luxury items. The OQMG recommended that they be classified as critical because of the growing scarcity of labor and because the necessity of

[85] OQMG OO 184, 31 Jul 42, sub: Reasgmt of QMC Functions.
[86] (1) SOS Cir 63, 18 Sep 42, sub: Pier and Warehouse Equip. (2) Memo, TAG for Chiefs of Sup Svs, et al., 15 Nov 42, sub: Reasgmt of Procurement Responsibilities, 451.93.
[87] (1) Ltr, Gen Corbin, OQMG, to ANMB, 5 Aug 42, sub: Procurement of Pier and Warehouse Equip. (2) SOS Cir 41, 13 Aug 42, sub: Allocation of MHE.
[88] (1) AGO Memo S5-39-43, 17 Feb 43, sub: MHE. (2) AGO Memo S5-82-43, 1 May 43, same sub. (3) WD Cir 33, 27 Jan 45, same sub.
[89] (1) Depot Opns Br to Priorities Br, Procurement Sv, OQMG, 14 May 42, sub: Preference Ratings. (2) Ltr, Maj R. B. McKinley, OQMG, to Priorities Div, ANMB, 12 Aug 42, sub: MHE, 451.93.

fully utilizing warehouse space made their use a vital necessity.[90] By autumn higher priorities, the allocation of larger quantities of essential materials, and the acquisition of more manufacturing facilities had appreciably relieved the stringency in the supply of this equipment.

At the beginning of the war the OQMG also found it difficult to procure pallets, since few manufacturers specialized in their production. Most of them made pallets only in small quantities and at high prices. But in July and August 1942 the OQMG ordered 1,000,000 pallets for distribution to Quartermaster depots. Production, however, was so slow in starting and shipments were so irregular that the OQMG directed depots having emergency requirements to purchase locally thousands of pallets.[91] This action resulted in a lack of uniformity and standardization which later plagued the Corps.

To reduce costs and speed production several depots in the spring of 1943 started fairly comprehensive pallet manufacturing programs.[92] The difference in the cost of pallets in different sections of the country and the desirability of using pallet pools to meet requirements emphasized the need for increased standardization by 1944. It was recognized that "central procurement would materially reduce pallet costs if shipping costs could be held at the lowest possible minimum figure."[93] Freight charges were substantially reduced by using knock-down pallets which were stored in pools at seven Quartermaster depots. To reduce pallet costs by central procurement and to provide efficient operation of pallet pools, a pallet standardization program was begun in the depots. Experiments and experience demonstrated that four sizes—32 by 40 inches, 36 by 48 inches, 48 by 48 inches, and 48 by 60 inches—were sufficient to handle efficiently the vast majority of Quartermaster supply items.[94] The pallet standardization program was well-under way by 1944.

Inadequacy of supply was only one of the handicaps impeding the installation of the pallet system in the depots. Old depot employees were reluctant to adopt new methods, and, in any case, little or nothing was known even in the commercial world about the palletization of many Quartermaster items. Subsistence, which was packed in uniformly sized, stoutly constructed containers, was easily palletized, but mattresses and items of clothing and equipage, shipped in unsubstantial cases of odd sizes, offered more difficulties. The necessity of sorting clothing according to size before it was stacked prevented the direct flow of supplies from carrier to storage that was needed to achieve maximum benefits from this new system. Palletization was therefore only partly applied at the Philadelphia Depot.[95] In 1942 most of the depots had begun to palletize supplies, and, as knowledge and availability of pallets grew, the new method was applied to an increasing proportion of supplies. By mid-1944, except for bagged and baled goods, satisfactory methods of palletizing had been developed for most Quartermaster items.[96]

Many improved storage practices contributed to increasing the efficiency of depot operations, but the most important single factor enabling the Corps to fill the unprecedented wartime demands promptly was the extensive use of pallets in conjunction with fork-lift trucks.

[90] Ltr, Gen Corbin, OQMG, to CG SOS, 30 Jan 43, sub: Shortage of Manpower in Depots.

[91] Chief of Warehouse Management Sec, Depot Opns Br, to Ex Off, S&D Div, OQMG, 9 Feb 43, sub: Long and Cross Hauls of Pallets, 451.93.

[92] Ltr, Col Bradbury, OQMG, to COs, QM Depots et al., 4 Jan 43, sub: Const of Pallets.

[93] Rpt, George W, Malloy, Stor Br, OQMG, Accomplishments of the Stor Br, OQMG, 7 Dec 41–1 Sep 45, p. 9.

[94] Ltr, Col Ward, OQMG, to COs of QM and ASF Depots, 23 Oct 44, sub: Standardization of Pallets, 451.93.

[95] Richard P. McCormick, *A History of Storage and Distribution at the Philadelphia Quartermaster Depot, 1917–43* (PQMD Historical Studies, December 1944), 491–94.

[96] For details of these developments see Stauffer, *QM Depot S&D Opns*, pp. 109–11.

Before the war, industry produced annually only 2,500 to 3,000 tractors and fork-lift trucks. In August 1945, however, the QMC alone was using 2,600 fork-lift trucks at its depots in the zone of interior. All the technical services at that time had in operation at their depots more than twice the number of fork-lift trucks produced in 1940.[97] In 1942, when fork-lift trucks were hard to procure, 24,982 persons handled a monthly average of 953,256 tons. By the first half of 1945, when the average monthly tonnage volume had increeased to 1,500,000 tons, storage personnel had been reduced to only 18,600. Between the third quarter of 1943, when the production of fork-lift trucks began to match the demand, and the second quarter of 1945, when the war reached its climax, the average number of tons handled per man a month more than doubled. The increased productivity per individual worker was estimated to have saved $80,000,000, which, under the old manual methods, would have been paid in wages.[98]

Standardization Program

In 1943 the efficiency of depot operations was further promoted by a program of standardization of mechanical equipment and of methods and practices for its use and maintenance. Although the introduction of fork-lift trucks immediately increased efficiency and operating productivity, it was not possible in 1941 and 1942 to match the proper type and size of equipment with operating conditions and needs of individual installations. It became apparent, however, that increased efficiency would result from standardizing equipment to meet the needs of specific operations. In 1943 and 1944 experts in commercial storage were employed to determine what type and capacity of equipment was best suited to the needs of each installation. In the interest of simplifying maintenance problems, training, and supervision, the aim was to standardize, as far as practicable, on one make

of equipment for an installation.[99]

Standardization was effected gradually through a planned adjustment rather than by an immediate and costly general shifting and redistribution of equipment. For example, if equipment which was nonstandard for a given depot was sent to a repair installation for maintenance, it was replaced by standard equipment. The repaired item was then sent to another installation where it did conform to the adopted standard pattern. As a result of planned adjustments, the standardization of equipment had been largely effected by 1944.

Correlating the type and capacity of equipment and the operating needs of installations increased operating efficiency and decreased maintenance costs and the loss of equipment operating hours. Standards, however, had not been established for the proper maintenance of materials-handling equipment, with the result that depot operations were impeded by the breakdown of equipment. Experience proved that a small fork-lift truck suffered as much wear and tear in 48 hours of operation as a large cargo truck in 1,000 miles of travel. The 1,000-mile maintenance service after 192 hours of operation required on every machine in connection with second echelon maintenance and the 6,000-mile service after 1,152 hours of operation provided 'inadequate protection against breakdowns. By the summer of 1944 this had been revised to a 1,000-mile check at the end of every 48 operating hours and a 6,000-mile check after 192 hours.[100] The number of trucks out of service daily at Quartermaster depots decreased

[97] (1) Anon., "Improved Car Plate Lifter and 4-Way Pallet," *Distribution and Warehousing*, XLIII (July 1944), 46. (2) Stat Yearbook of the QMC, 1945, p. 136. (3) ASF, Stat Review: World War II, p. 110.
[98] Rpt, Malloy, Accomplishments of the Stor Br, OQMG, 7 Dec 41–1 Sep 45, pp. 2–3. See Kieffer and Risch, Quartermaster Corps: Organization, Supply, and Services, Vol. II, Ch. IV.
[99] (1) *Ibid.,* pp. 4–5. (2) Stauffer, *QM Depot S&D Opns*, p. 114.
[100] WD Cir 269, 1 Jun 44, sub: Maint of MHE.

sharply from 8.5 percent in October 1943 to 2.7 percent in August 1945. The percentage for all Army Service Forces depots declined from a peak of 9.5 percent in November 1943 to 3.1 in August 1945.[101] By August 1945 the equipment standardization program had demonstrated its value in fewer deadlined machines, reduced costs of maintenance, and increased efficiency.

Apart from this effort at standardization, the initiation of a parts supply program and the education of depot maintenance personnel contributed to reducing the number of unserviceable fork-lift trucks. Because the Army had generally underestimated the important part that warehouse equipment was to play in supply movement, no provision had been made for the procurement of replacement parts. Originally, each supply service had provided parts for end items from their respective depots. The lack of parts procurement, parts lists, and maintenance manuals caused installations to develop local procurement, resort to contract repair, or to neglect maintenance. In an effort to keep equipment in operation, each of the supply services in the beginning placed large orders for replacement parts with the manufacturers of materials-handling equipment. Since they were producing to the maximum capacity of their plants, the manufacturers found it impossible to turn out complete units in the necessary volume and at the same time fill orders for replacement parts.[102]

By 1943, however, large quantities of material had been in use for a considerable period of time, and one of the most important problems facing the Army was the supply of spare parts. The necessity for co-ordinating the procurement of replacement parts led Headquarters, ASF, to centralize purchase responsibility for spare parts in the QMC to the same extent that responsibility for the procurement of materials-handling equipment was vested in it.[103] The Columbus Army Service Forces Depot became the central storage point against which all services made

their requisitions. Within the OQMG, responsibility for the maintenance of all Quartermaster equipment, because of its increasing importance, was centralized in one organizational unit—the Service Installations Division.[104] It had the primary responsibility for the supervision and co-ordination of all activities in connection with the maintenance of Quartermaster equipment, although the Procurement Division placed the contracts for parts, the Storage and Distribution Division directed storage and issue, and the Military Planning Division collaborated in the determination of requirements.

Although parts supply remained "an uphill grind" from its inception till the end of the war, the field maintenance manuals published by the Service Installations Division to effect standardization of practices and prescribe policies, the education of depot maintenance personnel, and the assistance given in programming preventative maintenance and parts supply were reflected in the progressive lowering of the quantity of deadlined equipment.[105]

The efficiency of depot operations was further increased by the standardization of methods and practices for utilizing warehouse equipment. During 1941–1942 depot personnel devised various methods for employing the new equipment in their local operations. Some of these han-

---

[101] (1) Rpt, Malloy, Accomplishments of the Stor Br, OQMG, 7 Dec 41–1 Sep 45, p. 6. (2) ASF, Stat Review: World War II, pp. 27, 110.

[102] (1) Col R. S. Brown, Chief of Maint & Equip Br, Sv Instl Div, to Gen Administrative Div, OQMG, 17 Oct 45, sub: Tour of Duty Hist Rpt. (2) Memo, Hq SOS for TQMG et al., 20 Feb 43, sub: MHE Spare Parts Program, 451.93.

[103] AGO Memo S5-82-43, 1 May 43, sub: MHE.

[104] (1) OQMG OO 25-35, 17 May 43, sub: Asgmt of Responsibilities with Respect to Maint. (2) Ltr, Gen Holland, OQMG, to COs of all depots, 6 Sep 43, sub: Procedure for Requisitioning Replacement Parts, 451.93.

[105] Rpt, Col Brown, Chief of Maint & Equip Br, Sv Instl Div, to Gen Administrative Div, OQMG, 17 Oct 45, sub: Tour of Duty Hist Rpt.

dling operations were good but others were wasteful of both personnel and equipment. Commercial storage experts in 1943 and 1944 not only evaluated the types of equipment used but also surveyed the depot methods to determine which merited general adoption by all installations. The OQMG also conducted experiments to devise standard methods for loading and unloading motor trucks, freight cars, and refrigerator cars, for blocking and bracing loaded cars to minimize or prevent damage to supplies in transit, for stacking supplies in warehouse, shed, and open storage, and for the effective and most productive use of fork-lift trucks as well as all types of conveyors, tractors and trailers, cranes, drum-handling devices, and other types of equipment.[106] The goal was to develop methods which would balance equipment and personnel so as to achieve the most effective and productive use of both. As a result of this program the tonnage of material handled per 8-hour man-day increased at the same time that the better balance achieved between personnel and equipment by improved methods decreased the manpower employed.

Palletized Unit Loads

After the use of fork-lift trucks and pallets had become a general, standard practice in all Quartermaster storage operations, an effort was made to extend the palletizing of supplies from depot warehouse operations to shipments by railroad and truck in the zone of interior as well as to those destined for overseas theaters. In initiating the palletized unit program, the Army was entering a field that had not been thoroughly explored. Industry had been making some progress before the war in shipping palletized unit loads, but after Pearl Harbor its plans were "laid aside for the duration."[107] Army experiments, made by the various supply services, were concentrated on those items which could be most easily unitized. In the

QMC these were subsistence items, and in the winter of 1942–1943 the Corps conducted experiments to determine the feasibility of using palletized unit loads to achieve greater speed and economy in the handling of subsistence.[108] The advantages of palletized unit loads were obvious in the savings that could be effected in time and manpower, in the reduced costs, the decreased pilferage, and the increased speed and efficiency in handling supplies.

The results of the early Quartermaster tests were favorable, but many technical problems had to be solved before unitized shipments could be generally applied to Army distribution operations. Palletized supplies would have to arrive undamaged at their final destination, which meant developing a means of stabilizing both the containers composing the unit load and the unit load itself. Unit loads also had to be of a size easily handled with mechanical equipment and capable of being loaded and unloaded in normal standard carriers.

The lack of fork-lift trucks and other essential equipment at all but the largest and best-equipped manufacturing plants hindered the application of the principle of palletized loads to shipments which ideally should have started at the producers' warehouses. The lack of facilities for receiving and handling such shipments overseas as well as the sizable cubical displacement of the pallet itself, which amounted to about 10 percent of an entire load, caused the Transportation Corps to oppose extensive palletization of transatlantic shipments until these aspects of the problem had been solved. Its attitude prevented any large-scale unitized movements during 1943.

---

[106] Stauffer, *QM Depot S&D Opns,* pp. 114ff.

[107] M. W. Potts, "Shipment of Palletized Unit Loads a Reality," *Distribution and Warehousing,* XLII (January 1943), 44.

[108] Ltr, M. W. Potts, Consultant, to Col Bradbury, OQMG, 4 Jan 43, sub Rpt on First Palletized Unit Load Shipments from New Cumberland QMD to NYPE.

At the beginning of 1944 the QMC initiated a new series of tests which, after many experiments with various strapping methods and with various sizes and types of pallets, achieved a satisfactory solution to the problem of developing an economical and efficient unitizing method. It was found that a pallet adhesive or glue was a more satisfactory stabilizing agent than strapping for most supply items which were to be unitized. An outstanding accomplishment was the development in the fall of 1944 of a lighter pallet which would meet the special needs of unitized loading and storage by occupying less car, ship, and warehouse space.[109]

The program had developed to the point where overseas shipments could be undertaken; however, conditions in the ETO made such movement impossible. The resources for handling palletized unit loads had improved in England, but the ports of western Europe did not have the necessary facilities. The differences, too, between American and European freight car design posed other difficulties in handling such shipments.

On the other hand, in the Pacific theaters, where the Army had built modern facilities for receiving goods, palletized shipments were welcomed. In response to requests, Headquarters, ASF, late in June 1945 directed the technical services to make such movements to the maximum extent possible.[110] The QMC speeded its preparations, but the surrender of Japan halted the program just as it was starting on a large scale. Although the abrupt termination of the program was disappointing, its value had been demonstrated, and the development of palletized unit loading of subsistence was a notable wartime achievement of the QMC.[111]

Packing Operations

The preparation of materials for shipment by proper packing, crating, or baling was an important element in the safe transport of war supplies. The shortcomings exhibited at the beginning of the war in the packing of subsistence were also evident in the packing of other Quartermaster items for overseas shipment, which were exposed to the same hazards of rough handling.[112] The packing of clothing, equipage, and general supplies also followed standard commercial practices, but these were no more suited to overseas shipment than were the packings used for food.

The need for new methods of packing was not immediately appreciated, but by mid-1941 some Quartermaster officers recognized that existing specifications did not meet wartime needs for overseas shipments.[113] In general, export packing was confined to steel-strapped wooden containers and burlap bales. Experience, however, suggested that even the prevailing specifications were not too well carried out.

The shortcomings of packing operations during the opening months of the war stemmed from the lack of a co-ordinated program for that purpose. Quartermaster packing and crating operations were not centralized in any one branch of the OQMG. The need was recognized, however, and in February 1942 responsibilities for packing and crating were vested in the Depot Division. In the functional reorganization of the OQMG that followed shortly thereafter, these responsibilities were transferred to the Storage and Distribution Division and assigned to a Packing and Crating Section of the Depot Operations Branch (later Storage Branch), where steps were taken to recruit qualified pack-

[109] (1) OQMG Daily Activity Journal, 22 Nov 44, p. 12. (2) Ibid., 26 Dec 44, p. 10.
[110] (1) Ltr, Brig Gen N. H. McKay, Actg Dir of Sup, ASF, to TQMG, 20 Jun 45, sub: Palletized Shpmt of Supplies. (2) Ltr, Gen Lutes, ASF, to TQMG, 14 Jul 45, same sub. Both in 451.93.
[111] For a detailed account of this program see Stauffer, QM Depot S&D Opns, pp. 121–35.
[112] See above, Ch. V, section on development of packaging and packing.
[113] Capt J. M. Berry to Lt Col L. O. Grice, OQMG, 31 Jul 41, sub: Packing Instructions.

ing specialists from industry. All instructions regarding packing and crating of Quartermaster supplies, either for domestic or overseas shipments, were thereafter co-ordinated and cleared by the chief of the Depot Operations Branch. All contracts for Quartermaster supplies were routed through this branch in order to check packing specifications.[114] These steps had the effect of establishing proper co-ordination of all Quartermaster packing operations and permitting the initiation of a program aimed at the continuous improvement of operating methods.

Centralization of activities was also introduced in the depot, where local packing and crating operations were centralized under a qualified packing and crating officer assigned to each depot storage division. It was his task to correlate procurement, inspection, and storage functions with respect to packing and crating. He was responsible for the proper packing, crating, and marking of all depot stock; for the training of personnel in these matters; for the inspection of incoming shipments; and for giving technical advice on packing, crating, and marking problems.[115]

It was the depot's task to select the proper specification from among the hundreds issued by the Corps and incorporate it in the contract. It determined which contractors should pack supplies for oversea shipments and assisted contractors in obtaining needed containers despite material shortages. Not all contractors could prepare supplies for oversea shipment, for many did not have the necessary personnel and equipment; hence such packing was generally confined to the largest and best-equipped plants. During the first two years of the war, when specifications had not been stabilized and contractors were lax in meeting them, one of the most important tasks, particularly of filler depots, was the repacking of supplies to insure satisfactory delivery overseas. Thus the execution of the packing program depended to a large extent upon the depots.

Formulation of Specifications

Precise definition of packing specifications for individual items was essential for successful depot packing operations, but these were nonexistent at the beginning of World War II insofar as export practices were concerned. Standard commercial practices governing domestic shipments normally met Army needs in peacetime. In war, however, overseas shipments required the development of other specifications. Problems of space, weight, protection, and conservation of materials had to be taken into consideration in their formulation.

One of the cardinal achievements of the Packing and Crating Section, OQMG, was the preparation of detailed packaging and packing specifications for the major Quartermaster items.[116] These specifications naturally depended upon the type of packaging container selected for each item of supply and, if overpacking was necessary, upon whether the container was a weatherproof fiber, nailed wood, or wirebound box. The formulation of such specifications progressed slowly, since much of 1942 and 1943 was devoted to deciding these basic developmental questions. Furthermore, few specifications could ever be firmly established inasmuch as continuous experimentation forced repeated changes.

The Packing and Crating Section began compiling overseas packing specifications in manual form. A manual for a large variety of general supplies was issued in December 1942,[117] but, because of the wide variety and the varying sizes and shapes of the items comprising gen-

---

[114] (1) See above, Ch. V, pp. 204ff. (2) Rpt, Malloy, Accomplishments of the Stor Br, OQMG, 7 Dec 41–1 Sep 45, p. 20.

[115] For a detailed account of the depot's role in the packing program see Stauffer, *QM Depot S&D Opns.*, pp. 148–52.

[116] For specifications on subsistence packing see above, Ch. V.

[117] OQMG Packing Spec GS–1, 1 Dec 42, sub: Specs for Gen Supplies.

eral supplies, no detailed specifications existed for many items even at the end of the war. Overseas packing specifications designed to insure safe delivery of nonbalable clothing and equipage—for example, tentage, raincoats, and intrenching shovels—were also written and incorporated in a manual.

Early in the war considerable confusion had resulted from the welter of individual packaging and packing specifications each using service had for its supplies. However, procurement responsibility had been delegated to the QMC for many supplies used by other services. The consequence was that contractors were bewildered by the necessity of packing the same supplies in a variety of ways. Moreover, requisitions for these items could not always be readily filled by Quartermaster depots because stocks on hand could not be used if they did not conform to the packing specification of the ordering agency.

To reduce this confusion, speed shipments, and hold packing costs to a minimum, The Quartermaster General proposed that the using services accept a single specification. A series of conferences early in 1945 resulted in an agreement that Quartermaster packing specifications would be accepted on supplies procured by the Corps for two or more services. On supplies procured by the QMC which were used by only one service, the specification of the using service was to be applied.[118]

Improvement of Methods

The solution of the problem of wartime handling hazards was also dependent on the development of improved packing materials and methods and upon better marking of supplies shipped to theaters of operations. The need for safe transport of subsistence spurred the development of the V-box, but other Quartermaster supplies also required the development of satisfactory packing. At the beginning of World War II, Quartermaster supplies on hand in depots and procured from contractors' plants, with the exception of certain heavy-type equipment and items of clothing in bales, were packed in accordance with standard commercial practice, suitable only for domestic shipment. Exported Quartermaster supplies were commonly overpacked in wood, but early in 1941 the growing scarcity of wood made any large-scale use of it impracticable.

Baling was suitable for most items of clothing and equipage, but the Philadelphia Depot objected to its extensive use for clothing because it stretched and wrinkled cloth, because modern baling facilities were not available at depots and textile plants, and because clothing manufacturers claimed it was no more economical than packing in fiber containers.[119] Since only a small percentage of clothing was being shipped overseas during the emergency period, the use of corrugated and solid fiber containers was authorized.

The growing scarcity of shipping space in 1942 and 1943, however, and the increased overseas distribution put a premium on saving space. It became the general policy early in 1942 to bale all compressible items of clothing and equipage destined for distribution abroad. Shipments within the United States continued to be made in cleated fiber and plywood boxes, heavy corrugated and solid fiber containers, and nailed wooden boxes. By the summer of 1942, however, the need to save both freight and warehouse space resulted in a move to bale all compressible clothing and equipage, whether destined for domestic or overseas shipment. Since the depots could not bale all these items, the Philadelphia Depot was directed to arrange in future procurement contracts for the baling of

---

[118] (1) Ltr, TQMG to CofEngrs *et al.*, 2 Feb 45, sub: Packing Specs. (2) Conf Rpt, E. S. Worden, 28 Apr 45, sub: Conf on Packing Specs, 25 Apr 45.

[119] (1) Insp Rpt, Capt Berry to TQMG, 11 Mar 41, sub: Rpt of Opns at PQMD. (2) Berry to TQMG, 14 May 41, sub: Baling at PQMD.

clothing, textiles, and textile equipage at contractors' plants.[120] Contractors were assisted in obtaining the necessary baling machines.

By 1943 baling productivity had to be increased if Army needs were to be filled. In part this was met by increasing the productivity per man by developing a continuous assembly line operation for baling. A second line of approach was to increase the productivity per baling machine. Early in 1943 the Philadelphia Depot developed a new method of baling based on the use of bias tubing. This tubular method replaced the flat baling method introduced during World War I. Since the ends of the tubing were closed by twisted wire ties, the need for sewing them by hand was eliminated. Although the tubular method required less cloth, it made a stronger bale capable of withstanding rougher treatment than the older type.[121] In general, one baling machine turned out as many bales a day as two had under the old method.

Cargo space was also saved through improved methods of packing Quartermaster items. Field ranges and their accessories, for example, were packed at the beginning of the war in four crates occupying 44.3 cubic feet and weighing 559 pounds. By consolidating the pots, pans, and accessory equipment and nesting them inside the oven and other open spaces, a saving of 20.2 cubic feet or 45.5 percent of the cargo space was made. The weight was cut to 480 pounds, a reduction of 14 percent. Field service shoes were packed in quantity lots instead of individual boxes with a resultant saving of 60 cubic feet of space on each 1,000 pairs of shoes.[122] Methods of packing numerous other items were improved to effect savings of space.

Whether shipped in wooden or fiber containers, Quartermaster supplies were always bound with steel strapping. Both flat and round types of strapping were used extensively. By the use of containers with steel strapping, the QMC made important savings of lumber, flatboard, and shipping space. If the steel strapping had

not been used, the thickness of the lumber used for containers would have had to be increased by about 40 percent while the use of fiber containers would have been greatly restricted.[123]

At the beginning of World War II, however, the Corps had no detailed specification for the application of steel strapping to a container of a given size and weight. Experiments were made with various types of flat and round steel strapping and by March 1943 a comprehensive specification for flat steel and round wire strappings on all types of containers was issued.[124]

During the early years of the war, the OQMG was also investigating the cause for the failure of strapping on overseas containers, a failure which resulted in damaged supplies. Study revealed that improper application, tensioning, and sealing of the strap caused the majority of the failures. Skill and experience were required to apply strapping satisfactorily but depots often had to rely on untrained personnel. Representatives of plants manufacturing steel strapping assisted in supervising and training personnel, and constant supervision caused the loss of supplies through improper strapping to decline appreciably after the spring of 1943.[125]

In December 1941 specifications did not exist for the proper marking of Quartermaster supplies to insure their arrival at the proper destination. No inadequacy of packing exasperated overseas personnel more than illegible and confusing marking which impeded easy identification of supplies. During the month of Septem-

[120] (1) Packing Sec to Chief of Depot Opns Br, S&D Div, OQMG, 2 Jul 42, sub: Baling. (2) Ltr, Gen Corbin, OQMG, to CO PQMD, 2 Dec 42, sub: Baling at Contractors' Plants.
[121] Insp Rpt, Lt Lee W. Oliver to TQMG, 25 May 43, sub: New Baling Method at PQMD.
[122] Maj F. F. Berlinger, "Packing and Crating Problems," *QMR*, XXII (January–February 1943), p. 106.
[123] Rpt, Malloy, Accomplishments of the Stor Br, OQMG, 7 Dec 41–1 Sep 45, p. 31.
[124] QMC Tentative Spec 106, 3 Mar 43, sub: Strapping.
[125] See Stauffer, *QM Depot S&D Opns*, pp. 143–45.

ber 1942, for example, more than 38,000 improperly marked packages were received at the New York Port of Embarkation alone. Three hundred men were engaged solely in the task of remarking supplies.[126] Despite these efforts to eliminate errors at the ports, defective markings continued to plague handling personnel at the ports and in the theaters to such an extent that the success of the war effort was threatened. Protests poured in from the theaters and the ports of embarkation.

In the fall of 1942, at the request of the Code Marking Policy Committee, Headquarters, SOS, directed The Quartermaster General to undertake a thorough study of marking requirements. This analysis resulted in recommendations known as the Schenectady Plan because they were first put into effect at the Schenectady Depot.[127] On one end of the container was stenciled the coded overseas destination, nomenclature and quantity of the item shipped, and the size of the container as well as its weight and cube, if the pack weighed more than 100 pounds or contained more than 8 cubic feet. In addition there was affixed to one side of the container a colored label covered with a waterproof protective lacquer. It identified the supply service and also contained data needed only in the United States, such as the consignor, consignee, requisition and shipping ticket numbers, and the coded overseas destination. Specific areas on the containers were designated for the various markings. Thus the overseas destination

was shown on a diagonal in the lower third of one end of the container. One end was left unmarked to permit necessary markings after the shipment had arrived in the theater. The objective was to simplify and clarify instructions for marking supplies destined for overseas, provide a uniform marking policy, reduce nonessential marking to a minimum, and thereby facilitate the handling of supplies in depots, ports of embarkation, and theaters of operations.

So successful was the experiment that the Schenectady Plan was adopted with a few modifications and incorporated in specifications in December 1942.[128] The general principles of the plan were established as standard marking procedures for all Army shipments. The effect was to preserve the secrecy essential in overseas shipments, facilitate identification of supplies, separate information needed for handling supplies in the United States from that required in the theaters, give prominence to the overseas address, and eliminate unnecessary markings. The faults observed during the first year of the war were thereby largely eliminated.

---

[126] Insp Rpt, Joseph Mattiello and W. R. McAdow to TQMG, 7 Oct 42, sub: QM Activities at NYPE.

[127] (1) Memo, TQMG for CG SOS, 16 Nov 42, sub: Marking of Outside Shipping Containers. (2) Ltr, Gen Scowden, OQMG, to CQM ETO, 24 Nov 42, sub: Marking of Overseas Shpmts.

[128] (1) QMC Tentative Spec 94, 15 Dec 42, sub: Specs for Marking Outside Shipping Containers by Contractors. (2) Ltr, TQMG to COs QM Depots et al., 28 Jan 43, sub: Schenectady Plan.

CHAPTER X

Stock Control Operations

The distribution phase of supply consists in getting items of issue from the point of production to the point of their final consumption, or their loss to Army use through salvage or other disposal action. In this process a number of functions are grouped under the general term "stock control." In co-ordinating and insuring the distribution and redistribution of supplies, the broad field of depot supply operations begins with the central distribution of stocks to the depots and continues with the requisitioning of material by consuming organizations, the processing of these requisitions and other documents incidental to supply, the shipment of goods, and the maintenance of stock control.[1] Handled at depots by the stock control divisions during World War II, these activities consisted mainly of "paper work," for efficient distribution was dependent upon full and accurate statistical information.

Supply Administration Prior to 1942

In the QMC, as in all other supply services, before 1939 and until well after Pearl Harbor, the keystone of the supply system was property accountability rather than equitable distribution. It was assumed, however, that equitable distribution of supplies would automatically accompany the strict enforcement of property accountability. In this system supply officers at depots and stations were pecuniarily liable for property assigned to them for formal and accurate accounting.[2] This accountability of an of-

ficer continued until the property involved had been transferred to another officer or disposed of in accordance with established procedures. As a consequence, protection of the accountable officer against possible monetary loss became the chief concern of those who handled supplies and supply records.

This system of property accountability had been introduced into the Army at the close of World War I. It had become increasingly cumbersome with the passage of time and the vast increase in the number of articles that had to be carried and accounted for in equipping and supplying the modern army. No fundamental change, however, had been made in the system until shortly before the outbreak of World War II. Then a board of officers investigating the system in the QMC made recommendations that resulted in a slight simplification of property accountability.[3]

Only gradually, under the strains imposed by war upon the resources of the United States, did the Army make effective stock control and

---

[1] (1) ASF, Statistical Review: World War II, p. 21. (2) Memo, Maj Gen LeRoy Lutes, Dir of Opns, ASF, for TQMG et al., 19 Jun 43, sub: Stock and Inventory Control.

[2] For the regulations governing property accountability and responsibility see (1) AR 35–6520 and changes thereto; (2) OQMG Cir 1–5 and changes thereto.

[3] (1) Memo, Maj Gen W. L. Reed, IG, for CofS, 5 Jul 38, sub: Prop Accountability, QMC. (2) Memo, TQMG for CofS, 21 Jul 38, same sub. (3) Ltr, TAG to TQMG et al., 16 Mar 39, sub: Proceedings of Bd Appointed to Study Prop Accountability. All in 140.2.

balanced distribution major objectives of its supply system. In peacetime the effects of any maldistribution upon military supply and the civilian economy had been negligible because of the small amount of goods involved. World War II made equitable distribution imperative. Distribution had to be co-ordinated with demand, overstocking had to be prevented, shortages and excesses avoided, and industry had to use critical materials and valuable manpower only to the extent needed to fill military requirements.

Innovations of 1940–42

By the early summer of 1940 the need to simplify the administration of supply was urgent in view of the developments at home and abroad. The increase in the strength of the Army by the federalization of the National Guard and the passage of the Selective Service Act meant that the meticulous procedures of accounting, auditing, and supply customary in a small peacetime army could not be maintained. The Supply Division of the General Staff called upon the chiefs of all supply arms and services to propose a more practical system of supply administration for the zone of interior.[4] Insofar as wartime theaters of operations were concerned, such procedures would be automatically simplified.

G–4 felt that the expansion of the Army constituted a "mobilization of major proportions," and hence it proposed extending the system of supply credit, provision for which had been made in the 1940 procurement mobilization plan.[5] The objective of the system was to insure the supply of the troops by expediting the filling of requisitions, maintaining balanced stocks, and preventing accumulation of excess stocks. Under the system, depot credits were to be established for those items which might not be equitably distributed among corps areas by the normal requisition procedures.

In the QMC this applied to clothing and equipage items. As of 1 July 1940 the stocks of clothing and equipage on hand were negligible, since the Army had been equipped for the past twenty years largely from World War I stocks. Inasmuch as it required about nine months from the time funds became available to obtain finished garments in appreciable quantities, it was apparent by the fall that production was not going to be sufficient to provide enough clothing and equipment for the large numbers of men being inducted and at the same time permit maintenance and distribution requirements. Clothing being produced was needed at precise localities where new men were being inducted, but posts and corps area quartermasters, in order to protect themselves, were submitting requisitions well in advance of troop inductions to insure having ample supplies. A centralized control of these items was desirable to provide equitable distribution.

The credit system was established in December 1940.[6] Utilizing manpower figures furnished by the Office of The Adjutant General, The Quartermaster General established depot credits each month for a specified list of clothing items. This meant that a definite allotment of these credit items was made to corps area quartermasters at designated distributing depots to cover three months' initial and maintenance requirements. Within the limits set by the size of its credits, a depot filled requisitions, but since shipments were drafts against established credits, often small in amount, both depots and corps area quartermasters had to review requisitions carefully to prevent shipment of an ex-

---

[4] (1) Ltr, TAG to Chiefs of Sup Svs *et al.*, 3 May 40, sub: Sup Admin. AG 400 (4–24–40) M-D-M. (2) Ltr, TAG to same, 8 Aug 40, same sub.

[5] (1) Memo, Brig Gen R. C. Moore, ACofS G–4, for TQMG *et al.*, 24 Jun 40, sub: Sup Under MR 4–1. (2) Memo, Moore for CofS G–4, 5 Jul 40, same sub. Both in 420.

[6] Ltr, TAG to Chiefs of Arms and Svs *et al.*, 30 Dec 40, sub: Current Sup Policies and Procedures. AG 475 (12–27–40) M-D-M.

cessive quantity to any one post. No depot could ship in excess of the credits set up for the corps area. Where credits proved inadequate, requisitions were extracted to the OQMG for action. It was also required that corps area quartermasters consider excess stocks available at other posts, camps, and stations, and fill requisitions from these supplies before applying to the depot. This procedure permitted full use of available stocks and made transshipments unnecessary. Excessive procurement was avoided and the accumulation of overstockages at certain camps, while others suffered shortages, was prevented.[7]

The credit system was ordered by the Chief of Staff, but it "was looked upon by all concerned with doubt and suspicion."[8] Various shortcomings impeded its efficient operation. Among these the most important was the failure of maintenance or replacement factors, which were based on theoretical assumptions rather than experience, to reflect actual replacement needs. Moreover, factors had been determined for only about 50 percent of the credit items of clothing. This meant that the quantities issued to stations were limited to the exact number required to equip newly inducted recruits, with no provisions made for replacements.[9]

By August 1942 the development of maximum and minimum depot stock levels, practically nonexistent up to that time, brought about the abandonment of the credit system. In the future, credit items and all other items of clothing and equipage were to be supplied within the limits set by maximum stock levels, representing the amount of an item on hand, plus the amount due in, that was deemed necessary for a depot to perform its mission, and minimum stock levels, representing the quantity below which the stock of an item could not fall without endangering the capacity of an installation to execute its supply functions.[10]

A more enduring innovation than the credit system was the direct system of supply established early in 1942 to expedite the filling of requisitions. The prewar process of requisitioning was not conducive to speed in delivery. Station requisitions were sent for review purposes first to the headquarters of the corps areas in which the stations were located, since the corps areas controlled the funds allocated by the War Department for Quartermaster supplies. They were therefore responsible for the equitable division of available money among field installations in accordance with established regulations and allowances. Requisitions then were submitted to the depots. This double review entailed days and even weeks of delay in the delivery of requisitioned goods.[11]

The abandonment after Pearl Harbor of the strict budgetary allocation of funds facilitated the adoption of the direct system of supply, which had been proposed as early as 1940. Thereafter, although corps areas retained responsibility for seeing that stations were provided with necessary supplies, they no longer reviewed requisitions. That responsibility rested with the regional distributing depots, and stations submitted their requisitions directly to them. The depots furnished supplies from their warehouses or from excess station stocks and, if

---

[7] (1) Ltr, Brig Gen C. L. Corbin, OQMG, to QMs of all CAs *et al.*, 26 Dec 40, sub: Sup Under MR 4–1, 420. (2) Maj H. R. McKenzie, "Distribution of Clothing and Equipage," *QMR*, XXI (March–April 1942), p. 30.

[8] (1) *Ibid.*, p. 29. (2) Ltr, Col H. B. Barry, CQMD, to TQMG, 11 Jan 41, sub: Sup Under MR 4–1, and 1st ind, Gen Corbin, OQMG, to CO CQMD, 15 Jan 41, 420. (3) Ltr, Col R. M. Littlejohn, OQMG, to Col T. L. Holland, ATGD, 9 May 41, no sub.

[9] (1) Ltr, Maj Gen Richard Donovan, CG Eighth CA, to TAG, 28 Apr 41, sub: Sup Under MR 4–1. (2) Memo, Col Littlejohn, OQMG, for ACofS G–4, 27 May 41, same sub. Both in 420.

[10] Ltr, Brig Gen F. F. Scowden, OQMG, for QMs of all CAs *et al.*, 9 Jul 42, sub: Sup Under MR 4–1, 420.

[11] Rpt, QM Bd to OQMG, 10 Jun 40, sub: Admin of Sup.

not available, such requisitions could be sent to another depot for action.[12]

In addition to these changes in supply procedures, the Army also introduced modifications in its accounting methods. The outstanding innovation made during 1940 and 1941 was the introduction of electric accounting machines (EAM). In the spring of 1940, in order to accelerate the production of stock reports, the Office of the Assistant Secretary of War proposed placing in all Army depots electric accounting machines made by the International Business Machines (IBM) Corporation.[13]

Bookkeeping machines then in use in Quartermaster depots were incapable of providing the variety of detailed records needed for the process of supplying the Army. In fact, a large part of the necessary accounting work had to be performed manually. The IBM Corporation tested the actual operation of its apparatus in the OQMG and at several Quartermaster depots and found it entirely applicable to the military supply system.[14] On the basis of these experiments, it developed the initial procedures for the use of these machines by the Army. Through the medium of the EAM system, reports containing data essential to the distribution of stocks were prepared, sorted, and printed within a few hours, though this work would have required days or even weeks under the old method.[15]

The installation of the new machines met with some opposition. About half of the depots were convinced that their use was a tremendous improvement whereas the other half preferred to continue under the old system. Dissatisfaction with the electric accounting machines developed out of the unfamiliarity and incompetence of the personnel handling them and from the "passive resistance on the part of some of our old time personnel to a change in methods."[16] The OQMG took steps to assign to the depots reserve officers who were familiar with IBM methods. The institution of training

courses permitted the depots to overcome the shortage of competent operators. When this had been accomplished, they were able to utilize fully the EAM system.

The electric accounting machines increased the speed with which depot personnel could prepare shipping tickets, receiving reports, accountability records, daily availability reports, due-in and due-out records, and depot stock status reports. At the same time the installation of teletype machines insured quick transmission of desired information between the depots and Washington. This transmission was an automatic process since an IBM machine had been especially developed for the Army. EAM reports made available to the OQMG the net stock status at the depot at the end of each day and consolidated figures for all depots in weekly summaries.

On the basis of this status of depot stocks, the OQMG made plans for the distribution of anticipated deliveries by contractors to central procuring depots. Until the spring of 1943, calculations as to the quantities of stocks of clothing and equipage to be shipped to depots from production points and quantities to be transferred from one depot to another were determined by manually prepared "Distribution Studies," the desired information for which was extracted from the consolidated EAM stock bal-

---

[12] (1) Ltr, TAG to CGs of all CAs *et al.,* 20 Jan 42, sub: Direct System of Sup. AG 475 (1–16–42) MO-D-M. (2) OQMG Cir Ltr 50, 31 Jan 42, same sub.

[13] Memo, ASW for TQMG, 18 Apr 40, sub: Punch-Card System, 140.2.

[14] Ltr, L. H. LaMotte to OASW, 17 Jul 40, no sub, enclosing rpt, Application of Punch-Card Equip to WD Sup Records, 140.2.

[15] For a description of the machines and how they operated see (1) Stauffer, *QM Depot S&D Opns,* pp. 159ff. (2) Maj C. C. Workman, "Electric Accounting Machines in the Quartermaster Supply Program," *QMR,* XXII (November–December 1942), 67ff.

[16] Ltr, Gen Corbin, OQMG, to All Depots Using EAM, 15 Nov 40, sub: Issuing Sups Before Receiving Rpt Prepared, 140.2.

ance reports. By that time the OQMG had developed machine distribution studies of clothing and equipage which compiled for each depot the quantities of each size of each item which were due in, due out, and on hand and also showed the stock level for each item for each depot. The machine automatically computed and printed the total assets and also the net stock position. This machine study could be prepared in three to four days in contrast to the thirty to sixty days previously required. This procedure had a material effect on better supply positions in depots. It cut down the quantities of supplies necessary in the pipeline and made possible efficient supply with smaller levels in depots. Out-of-stock conditions were reported daily by teletype and reviewed immediately by commodity sections in the OQMG which advised the depots of action to be taken so that replenishment or transfer of stock could be effected with the minimum of delay.[17]

However, unless the reports from the depots were not only prompt and frequent but accurate and uniform in character and based upon the same interpretation of the terms used, the OQMG would find it impossible to utilize the data with maximum effectiveness. As a consequence, late in 1941 the OQMG began to standardize depot procedures for processing documents.

Before such reform could be initiated, however, the OQMG had to revise completely the existing system of stock nomenclature as set forth in the Quartermaster section of the Federal Standard Stock Catalog in order to permit correct and uniform identification of the thousands of Quartermaster items. Unless the depots used the same item names, their statistical reports would have little value for determining supply requirements, allocating goods for distribution operations, or filling requisitions. During the latter part of 1940 and throughout much of 1941 the OQMG was engaged in this task of identifying and numbering stock items.

In 1941 only 12,000 items were assigned standard stock numbers. By 1944 there were over 85,000 items included in the master stock catalog file. In addition, there were over 42,000 items of spare parts for materials-handling equipment.

By the fall of 1941 the OQMG was in a position to press toward its goal of standardized depot procedures. It began to issue a series of instructions called "depot procedure directives." These new procedures were aimed at first chiefly at developing basic routines to be followed by the various branches of the depot storage and distribution divisions and at establishing improved methods of relating stock accounting and statistics to local needs. Later these procedures were more and more devised for the purpose of obtaining the information necessary to control and centralize distribution operations in the OQMG.[18] By the fall of 1942 five basic reports were being drawn from the records kept by the depots and the OQMG. According to a study made by the Control Division, SOS, at that time, these formed the basis for a "well integrated system of depot perpetual stock control." [19] Further analysis would determine whether it was being used to best advantage.

Establishment of New Methods of Stock Control

The OQMG worked constantly to expand, redesign, improve, and streamline procedures and records in order to promote efficient stock

---

[17] (1) B. J. Brown, "Merchandising Methods," *QMR*, XXII (November–December 1942), 63ff. (2) Capt Robert A. Swain, "Depot Storage and Distribution Division Organization and Procedure," *ibid.*, 59ff. (3) Ltr, Lt Col Charles C. Workman, Jr., to Maj Gen Orlando Ward, Chief of Military History, 5 Jan 51, no sub.

[18] For elaboration of these procedures see Stauffer, *QM Depot S&D Opns*, pp. 162ff.

[19] Memo, Donald K. Keith for Col J. F. Battley, Control Div, SOS, 22 Sep 42, sub: Study of Inventory Control Systems Employed by Sup Svs.

control to meet ever-changing demands. The QMC had made considerable progress toward achieving an improved stock accounting system by the adoption of uniform procedures which would enable all depots to submit reports reflecting figures derived by the same means and having the same significance. The system, however, still did not provide sufficiently complete and detailed information for the accurate determination of over-all supply requirements or for the equitable distribution of goods. This inadequacy resulted from the lack of data reflecting actual issues of supplies to troops at posts, camps, and stations, broken down by initial and replacement issue, and the failure to report regularly to depots all stocks on hand in post, camp, and station storage.[20] Realistic planning for the determination of Army supply requirements, procurement programs, and distribution plans could only be accomplished with the fullest knowledge of the location and status of stocks and the amount and purpose of issues made at stations, whether in the zone of interior or overseas.

In the OQMG, personnel responsible for stock accounting and for the computation of Army supply requirements were aware of the inadequacies of existing stock status information. So, too, were various other groups located in the OPM and later the WPB, SOS Headquarters, and in the supply services. Until mid-1942, however, the supply services were thoroughly absorbed in providing the Army with initial equipment, in filling the distribution pipeline, and in building reserves both in the United States and overseas for coming offensive operations. Until the exceptional requirements of the early stages of the war had been met and the Army was expanding at a more uniform rate, and particularly until a body of accurate statistics on replacement issues had become available, a more effective stock control system could not be established.

By the summer of 1942 the country's produc-

tive facilities had been largely converted to the manufacture of military supplies; the Army's most pressing needs for initial equipment had been met; the pipeline had been stocked sufficiently to meet the bulk of current demands; the strong pressure for immediate delivery of goods had been eased; and storage space, in many instances, was becoming congested. By this time, too, the War Department was being made increasingly aware of the hazards inherent in the accumulation of excess goods. There was a growing fear on the part of producers and consumers that the Army was holding unnecessarily large quantities of food, clothing, and other essentials. Charges of military hoarding were openly voiced. Since the Army absorbed a large part, and in a few cases virtually all, of the goods normally used by civilians, overstockages had to be scrupulously avoided in order that the civilian economy might not suffer unnecessarily in the distribution of the goods produced. The need for more effective stock control was evident.

It seemed entirely feasible to apply such control to the supply activities of the zone of interior. Here supply needs could be predicted with fairly reasonable accuracy provided improved accounting practices were adopted. The penalties of having "too little, too late" were not as drastic as in the theaters of operations, where circumstances were not so favorable for centralized management of stocks. The Commanding General, SOS, therefore urged the creation of a sounder system of inventory control applicable at first only to the zone of interior.[21]

The new system was to aim specifically at providing no more supplies to a military unit than it was officially authorized to receive. Depot and station stocks were to be kept neither

---

[20] Memo, Gen Scowden, OQMG, for ACofS for Opns, SOS, 15 Jan 43, sub: Stock Control.

[21] Address, Gen Somervell at orientation mtg of offs of Hq SOS, 30 Nov 42, no sub.

too high nor too low but properly balanced in relation to the needs of all echelons. Additional warehouse space was to be obtained through the elimination of obsolete and superfluous stores. Depot goods were to be delivered more rapidly. Information was to be collected that was essential for computing procurement requirements, scheduling purchases, and allocating supplies.[22]

Since the QMC dealt "with those supplies most closely related to the personal comfort and health of the individual," the availability of which was reduced accordingly in the civilian market, its requirements were more closely scrutinized than those of other War Department procuring agencies.[23] It was therefore extremely alert to the advantages to be gained by better inventory methods. By the summer of 1942 it felt that sufficient experience data on past issues had been accumulating during the war period to provide the basis for improved control. Initial issues to troops, replacement issues to troops, and stock on hand in posts, camps, and stations constituted the essential elements of stock status information which were not currently tabulated.[24]

While the Requirements Branch approached the problem by sending survey teams into the field to collect experience data on which to base replacement rates,[25] the Storage and Distribution Division sought to improve the stock status report. Early in the summer of 1942 the Quartermaster Board at Camp Lee was ordered to make a study of basic accounting policies and inventory conditions, as they existed at this Quartermaster post; to investigate particularly the extent of shortages and excesses; to determine the relationship between depots and the posts, camps, and stations in their distributing regions, making use in this case of the Richmond Depot; and to devise an experimental system intended to provide better methods of accounting and stock control. The board was also later directed to check the accuracy of existing records by

examining its stock reports to derive replacement factors from them for the zone of interior.[26] Since the WPB had been studying inventory control for the purpose of increasing the output of war goods by industry and had devised techniques, methods of observation, and time-saving procedures to supervise such studies, it was asked to co-operate with the Quartermaster Board in the study to be made at Camp Lee.[27]

In the meantime the Control Division, SOS, was making a survey of the stock control systems of the supply services and reporting its findings to the chief of the Distribution Division and the Assistant Chief of Staff for Operations. Emphasis was placed on standardizing methods for all the supply services, and the report recommended that regulations, aimed at uniform inventory and stock control methods and procedures throughout the distribution system, should be drawn up from "a merchandising or distribution point of view." [28] Responsibility for the supervision and execution of the regulations to insure co-ordination of the entire stock control system should be vested in the Distribution Division, SOS. The WPB report and that of the Control Division, SOS, focused attention on the problem of establishing a satisfactory stock control system throughout the supply services, and the Assistant Chief of Staff

[22] *Ibid.*

[23] Ltr, Maj Gen E. B. Gregory to Col George F. Spann, CO JCQMD, 8 Nov 43, no sub, 400.291.

[24] Ltr, Carroll Belknap to Lt Col G. P. Baker, OQMG, 8 Feb 43, sub: Fld Study of Sta Stocks.

[25] See above, Ch. VI.

[26] (1) Ltr, TQMG to Col Max R. Wainer, QM Bd, Camp Lee, Va., 26 Jun 42, sub: Study of Accounting and Inventory Practices. (2) Ltr, Col D. H. Cowles, OQMG, to same, 19 Aug 42, sub: Verification of Maint Factors. (3) Col Wainer, "The Quartermaster Board," *QMR*, XXII (March–April 1942), 106ff. (4) Dir of QM Bd to TQMG, Rpt of QM Bd, 1 Feb 42–30 Jun 44, pp. 128ff.

[27] Rpt, Accounting Br, Procurement Policy Div, WPB, 29 Dec 42, sub: Improved Control Over Distr of Supplies, USA.

[28] Memo, Donald K. Keith for Col Battley, Control Div, SOS, 2 Oct 42, sub: Summary of Findings.

for Operations, SOS, was directed to take immediate steps for this purpose.[29]

Late in 1942, when the Camp Lee study had been completed, a board of QMC officers and a consultant of the WPB was appointed to function as a Stock Control Board in the OQMG.[30] This board, as well as the Quartermaster Board, centered its attention on the management of station stock and on the strengthening of the control exercised by depots over these stocks.[31] The stock control system put into effect for all the technical services on 1 June 1943 was based primarily on the substantially similar recommendations made by these two boards. The objective was "to provide an adequate amount of supplies at the proper place and at the proper time without overstocking in any echelon of supply." [32] The system was intended to develop methods of obtaining more uniform and complete statistics of stockages in the zone of interior, to prevent the requisitioning of supplies in excess of authorized levels, to insure prompt redistribution of excess goods, to provide better use of critical materials and labor, and to assist the "civilian economy by improved distribution, proper allocation of supplies to each distributing point, and the scheduling of requirements in accordance with needs."

Stock Status Reports

One of the focal points of the new stock control system at both stations and depots was the stock status report. Prior to June 1943, such reports had been designed to meet the needs of a system of property accountability rather than of stock control. The purpose of the report was to give a record of supplies on hand, due in, due out, and issued. In the past, however, one of the many difficulties experienced in the proper stockage of depots and posts, camps, and stations, had been the lack of knowledge concerning the quantities used through initial issue and by replacement issue.

Furthermore, records had been kept with varying degrees of accuracy.[33] Among the supply services or even among the installations reporting to one service, no uniformity had existed in the accounting practices employed, in the use of nomenclature for the same item, or in the interpretation of such seemingly simple terms used in making entries as "stock on hand" and "due in." One depot, for example, listed only supplies physically in its warehouses as stock on hand, while another recorded these as well as supplies due in from contractors. Moreover, complicated paper work, rigid interpretation of regulations governing property accountability, and the necessity of formally inspecting and approving many types of supplies resulted in delays in posting incoming and outgoing supplies on depot stock status cards. It followed that discrepancies existed between the amount of stock actually on hand and that recorded. This had important consequences for Quartermaster purchasing and distribution programs.[34]

Under the new system of stock control these inadequacies were remedied. Stock status reports were now maintained primarily for the purpose of balancing supplies rather than of

[29] Memo, Maj Gen W. D. Styer, CofS, for ACofS for Opns, SOS, n. d. [circa Jan 43], sub: Stock Control.

[30] OQMG OO 30-7, 22 Dec 42, sub: Bd to Study S&D Problems.

[31] (1) Rpt, QM Bd, 31 Dec 42, sub: Stock Control. (2) Stock Control Bd, 22 Jan 43, sub: First Preliminary Rpt.

[32] WD TM 38-220, 3 May 43, sub: Stock Control Manual for Posts, Camps, and Stations, p. 1.

[33] A number of studies submitted in 1942 analyzed the weaknesses of the existing stock control systems of the supply services. (1) Dir of QM Bd to TQMG, n. d., sub: Rpt of QM Bd, Camp Lee, Va., 1 Feb 42–30 Jun 44, pp. 128–32. (2) Accounting Advisory Br, Procurement Policy Div, WPB, 29 Dec 42, sub: Rpt on Improved Control Over Distr of Supplies, USA. (3) Memo, Donald Keith for Col Battley, Control Div, SOS, 22 Sep 42, sub: Study of Inventory Control Systems Employed by Sup Svs.

[34] Memo, Gen Scowden for ACofS for Opns, SOS, 15 Jan 43, sub: Stock Control.

establishing the property accountability of the issuing officer. The new reports indicated initial and replacement issues and distinguished between issues and transfers of stocks from one depot or station to another. Memorandum receipts, which formally acknowledged the receipt of articles that were issued for temporary use but which were retained in the accountability of the supply officer, were carried on a separate stock record account in order that the figures for stock on hand would reflect only items actually available for distribution.[35]

Unless specifically exempted, stock record cards were established on each individual item of supply and equipment carried in station stock. At the end of each month or when requested by the chiefs of supply services, station supply officers prepared reports to the distributing depots on selected items which indicated the maximum stock level, the balance on hand and on memorandum receipt, the balance due in and due out, and the cumulative initial and replacement issues for the previous three months. The report also indicated the average troop strength of the station for the preceding three months, its expected strength for the coming three months, and the kind and number of organizations to be supplied.

The detailed statistical information provided in stock status reports furnished the basis for establishing more adequate and accurate depot and station stock levels. Such reports were also useful in calculating the existence and amount of excesses. They provided an experience record on which to base more accurate replacement factors that were used not only in setting stock levels but in computing over-all supply requirements. On the basis of consolidated reports by depots for their assigned areas of distribution, The Quartermaster General was provided with the data essential to improved planning of the Army Supply Program, accurate scheduling of procurement, and equitable allocation of supplies.[36]

Stock Levels

Stock levels at both stations and depots were the second focal point of the new stock control system. They were the amount of stock required to be on hand to serve as a working inventory and as a reserve. Adequate inventories were essential to provide the troops with necessary supplies and to meet any emergencies created by unanticipated demands or interruptions to the flow of supplies.

The most important phase of stock control was the correct setting of accurately determined stock levels. They helped assure equitable and balanced distribution of stocks and eliminated shortages, excesses, and surpluses. However, without accurate issue and maintenance data derived from experience, accurate stock levels could not be set. During the emergency period and the early war years sufficient reliable information about the trend of issues was not available to permit realistic determination of stock levels.[37] Furthermore, until mid-1942 the turnover of stocks was generally so rapid, the delay in production of equipment and supplies so significant, and the necessity of filling the distribution pipeline so urgent that stock levels could have had little pertinency to the immediate problem of furnishing supplies to the Army. Depots had no opportunity to acquire balanced stocks and as a consequence stock levels were not extensively used. As late as January 1943, stock levels had not been determined for many items, and even those authorized were repeatedly found inaccurate because they were based on the unsatisfactory initial and replacement factors

---

[35] (1) Stock Control Bd, 6 Feb 43, sub: Second Preliminary Rpt. (2) WD TM 38-220, 3 May 43, sub: Stock Control Manual for Posts, Camps, and Stations, *passim.*

[36] Memo, Gen Scowden for CG ASF, 27 Dec 43, sub: Sta Stock Status Rpts for QM Items.

[37] Carroll Belknap to Col Baker, Chief of Reqmts Br, Mil Plng Div, OQMG, 8 Feb 43, sub: Fld Study of Post, Camp, and Sta Stocks, Receipts and Issues.

which were then employed to compute requirements.[38]

As the production situation improved, permitting depots to be stocked in proper relation to the troops to be served, stock levels determined periodically by the commodity branches of the OQMG were authorized during 1942. Depot levels were defined as a range with a maximum and a minimum expressed in terms of a specific number of days' supply translated into definite quantities of goods. For nonperishable subsistence a 60-day supply for each man supplied within a depot's area represented the maximum level and a 20-day supply the minimum level. The maximum level for clothing, equipage, and general supplies was 120 days and the minimum a 60-day supply. Actually, however, by reason of a 30-day time lag between the initiation of action for replenishment and the receipt of such supplies, stockages normally fluctuated between a maximum of 60 days and a minimum of 30 days.[39]

According to established procedures, the maximum stock level authorized at the post, camp, and station echelon of supply was 60 days, except at stations which included reception centers. These were authorized to stock a 90-day level of those items of initial issue furnished to newly inducted soldiers at reception centers.[40]

In general, stock levels were based on maintenance factors and a consideration of the anticipated manpower in a given area of distribution. Stockages of nonperishable subsistence at depots and at posts, camps, and stations, for example, were based on "present and anticipated manpower in relation to the components of food prescribed in menus prepared for the issue of rations in kind, and upon the items authorized for sale." Published menus, however, were not infallible guides to the food actually consumed since many substitutes were repeatedly provided, and the rate of consumption in officers' messes, service clubs, post exchanges, and other

purchases at sales commissaries had never been determined.[41]

Station stock levels to provide replacement for clothing and equipage in the hands of troops were based upon tables of basic allowances and tables of allowances issued by the OQMG, which prescribed the quantity of each item on a basis of requirements for each 1,000 men for 30 days. This quantity in turn was based upon the established maintenance factor applicable to each particular item. But again, analysis of station stocks, receipts, and issues revealed that it could not be assumed that actual initial issues to troops were in accordance with prescribed tables of allowances. Nor could it be assumed that published maintenance factors measured correctly the actual rate of necessary procurement for maintenance. "All studies to date throw considerable doubt on the accuracy of the present approved maintenance factors as measurements of true maintenance needs."[42]

Stock levels for clothing and footwear items presented a special problem in that they also had to be based on established tariffs of sizes. A size tariff is a schedule listing the sizes of clothing and footwear and the proportions in which they were issued at the time the schedule was published. Distributed to field installations, they were to be used as a guide in requisition-

[38] (1) *Ibid.* (2) Ltr, TQMG to CG Seventh CA, 24 Apr 42, sub: Sup System. (3) Ltr, Gen Scowden, OQMG, to all Depots, 11 May 42, sub: Stockage Levels. Last two in 400.291.

[39] (1) Ltr, Gen Scowden, OQMG, to All Depots, 11 May 42, sub: Stockage Levels, 400.291. (2) Stock Control Bd, 22 Jan 43, sub: First Preliminary Rpt, 140.2.

[40] (1) OQMG Cir Ltr 225, 28 May 42, sub: Stock Levels and Rqn Period at Posts, Camps, and Stations. (2) Memo, ACofS for Opns, SOS, for TQMG, 22 Dec 42, sub: Distr of Sups, and 1st ind, Gen Scowden, OQMG, to ACofS for Opns, SOS, 23 Dec 42.

[41] (1) Stock Control Bd, 22 Jan 43, sub: First Preliminary Rpt. (2) Carroll Belknap to Col Baker, OQMG, 8 Feb 43, sub: Fld Study of Post, Camp, and Sta Stocks, Receipts and Issues.

[42] *Ibid.*

ing. One of the most difficult problems to solve, however, was the maintenance of stocks in proper sizes.

The national tariff of sizes in use in 1940 was based on the issue experience of World War I and the succeeding years of peace.[43] It failed, however, to provide proper stockage for the 6,000 different sizes of the various clothing and footwear items issued by the QMG because men being inducted in the Army under the Selective Service Act were in general larger than those of the peacetime Army. Furthermore, marked regional variations among enlisted men were soon observed, and the national tariff did not take these into account.

The use of this tariff in setting stock levels by sizes resulted in unbalanced inventories and the OQMG soon received complaints of shortages of particular sizes of clothing and shoes.[44] Since the national tariff lacked universal application to the heterogeneous group composing the Army in 1940 and experience data were not immediately available, the OQMG sought size information from the larger chain stores, mail-order houses, and other retail organizations whose volume of business and country-wide distribution could be expected to provide a guide to the sizes of clothing being sold to men throughout the United States. These tariffs were helpful.

By November 1941 tabulation of experience had begun after the OQMG had directed reception centers to submit weekly reports of the sizes of clothing being issued to inductees. These data provided the basis for revision of the tariff, which remained under constant study. It was frequently revised to follow the trend of personnel being inducted into the service.

When the supply system of the QMC was being analyzed during 1942, the problem of size tariffs was again emphasized. Under the stock control system inaugurated in June 1943, provision was made for the recording of issue experience for clothing in the stock status report

submitted by station quartermasters to depots. By the information obtained from them, individual station tariffs of sizes became available for computing the distribution of sized items in lieu of the national tariffs. These experience data also provided the basis for the national tariffs established by the Clothing and Equipage Branch of the Storage and Distribution Division, OQMG.[45]

Stock accounting practices that were adequate for a period when there were no reserve stocks, no filled distribution pipelines, and when industry was not rigged for war production, had to give way in the summer of 1943 to a new stock control system designed to maintain levels of supply and to assure that no more than was needed would be obtained. Stock levels became the basis of the stock control system. In translating these numbers of days of supply into actual quantities for the zone of interior, past issues as recorded in the stock status report were the primary factor used, modified by changes in troop strength, type of organization, and estimate of special conditions such as new activations which might increase issues. Control began thus with the station stock status report, which influenced the whole chain of supply. On the basis of it, requisitions were made and edited and stock levels were established. Of all the stock levels in the various echelons of supply, the station control level was the key one insofar as the zone of interior supply was concerned.[46]

[43] Address, Capt B. L. Goldstein, 3 Oct 44, sub: Proper Fitting of Clothing and Revision of Tariff Sizes, QMs' Conf, Camp Lee, Va., 2–4 Oct 44.

[44] (1) Ltr, Gen Corbin, OQMG, to QM First CA et al., 25 Apr 41, sub: Shoe Stocks. (2) Ltr, Col Littlejohn, OQMG, to Col J. P. Hasson, Eighth CA, 22 May 41, sub: Tariffs, 420.

[45] (1) Stock Control Bd, 22 Jan 43, sub: First Preliminary Rpt. (2) WD TM 38–220, 3 May 43, sub: Stock Control Manual for Posts, Camps, and Stations, p. 38.

[46] Address, Col H. W. Bobrink, 3 Oct 44, sub: Station Control Levels and Depot Levels in Relation to Supply, QMs' Conf, Camp Lee, Va., 2–4 Oct 44.

Under the system established the quantity of any item of Quartermaster supply [47] to be carried in stock at any post, camp, or station was regulated through the use of a maximum stock level, a reorder point, and a minimum stock level. The pivot of the entire system of managing inventories was the maximum stock level, that is, the greatest quantity of any item authorized to be stocked or placed on order by a stocking point. Upon its accurate calculation depended the possession of sufficient supplies by the stations and the reduction or elimination of excess stockages. The maximum distribution level authorized for posts, camps, or stations was a 90-day supply. Because of the time lag in replenishing stocks, however, this quantity was seldom, if ever, reached. Instead an average supply of 60 days was expected to be on hand. This maximum level was set by the station supply officer on the basis of issues for the previous 90 days, taking into consideration the type and strength of the organizations and the number of men to be stationed at the post. The reorder point, established at two thirds of the maximum level, designated the quantity required to insure against exhaustion of the supply during the interval between the placement of an order and delivery. The minimum stock level or danger point represented the margin of safety below which the stock on hand should not normally be reduced.[48] Station supply officers reviewed the stock record cards periodically and made necessary upward or downward adjustments of levels.

The Stock Control Board, OQMG, recommended that depot stock levels be defined in the same manner as for posts, camps, and stations, and Headquarters, ASF, directed that such levels be set for each item of supply at all depots by 14 August 1943.[49] In the QMC this meant the establishment of levels of supply in regional distributing and in filler depots commensurate with the need and demand by troops, and levels of reserve stock for contingency and utility purposes. Maximum distribution levels were established for all regional distributing depots. These levels comprised the quantity of supply, on hand and due in, necessary to maintain desired working stocks for issue to the assigned area. Included was a minimum stockage of 60 days' supply plus necessary working stock and provision to cover the in-transit and processing time needed for the replenishment of supplies.

The stock level for a filler depot was set at the quantity needed to provide an average physical stock on hand sufficient for 90 days [50] of supply to the troops assigned to the port of embarkation being supplied by a filler depot. Because accurate past issue figures for each overseas command were not available, the quantity of any item to be stocked for a filler depot was normally computed by applying to the theater of operations "maintenance factor" the estimated troop strength as of a date four months later than the effective initial date of the stock level.

The utility reserve stock level was ordinarily established only when specifically ordered by the director of the Storage and Distribution Division, OQMG, or by higher authority. It was to insure advanced preparation for a specific operation requiring supplies in addition to those

---

[47] Forage, fuel, gasoline and lubricants, laundry supplies, reclamation supplies, office furniture and machines, and warehouse equipment were excepted items subject to special procedures. Stock levels were not set for these items because of long-term blanket contracts, extreme variations in use, or the necessity of stocking far in advance, as, for example, coal in summer.

[48] (1) Stock Control Bd, 6 Feb 43, sub: Second Preliminary Rpt. (2) WD TM 38–220, 3 May 43, sub: Stock Control Manual for Posts, Camps, and Stations, pp. 18–20.

[49] (1) Stock Control Bd, 22 Jan 43, sub: First Preliminary Rpt. (2) Memo, Gen Lutes, Dir of Opns, ASF, for TQMG, 13 Jul 43, sub: Depot Stock Levels, 400.291.

[50] A 120-day supply level, which was divided between port stocks and filler stocks, was set for the San Francisco Port of Embarkation.

normally available. Contingency reserve stock levels were established when deemed essential by a commodity branch of the OQMG in order to provide against interrupted production or for unanticipated and unusual demands. Pending redistribution, necessary production beyond current needs was included in this reserve.[51]

Stock Control System in Operation

The effectiveness of the new stock control system was dependent upon the success with which the depots administered the tasks of reviewing, revising, and approving station stock levels, obtaining reasonably accurate station stock status reports, disposing of excess and obsolete stores at stations, and controlling their own inventories. More than ever the depots were the nerve centers for the entire storage and distribution function of the Army. They were hampered, however, by various difficulties. Chief of these was the necessity of substituting new concepts and procedures for those long familiar to supply personnel at a time when military activities were moving toward a climax.[52] In shifting from the first phase of supply—setting up supplies for an operation still in the planning stage—to the second of maintaining the flow of supplies necessary to support an operation, supply officers continued to be guided by the belief that a stringent management of supplies might result in the disastrous situation of having "too little, too late." The objectives of the new stock control system were misunderstood. The essentiality of records as a tool in effecting proper control was overlooked by those who voiced the sentiment: "Supply the troops, never mind the records."[53]

Limitations of Stock Status Reports

As a consequence, station stock status reports, "the focal center of stock control," were often inaccurate and out of date. Moreover, depots hesitated to point out deficiencies because they feared that criticism would embitter relations with the stations. Varying station interpretations of the terms "initial" and "replacement" issues still persisted, while the failure to distinguish between recurring and nonrecurring issues rendered more difficult the depot's task of reviewing, revising, and approving station control levels.[54] On the other hand, depot stock status cards failed to reflect accurately the amount of stock on hand. Physical inventories had to be taken repeatedly to check stock status figures with the supplies actually ready for issue. As late as June 1945 an inventory of more than 1,000 items by 12 depots revealed decided discrepancies requiring an average of 73 percent adjustments to the stock-on-hand balance.[55] Depot and station stock status reports consequently could not be used precisely as anticipated in estimating requirements. Nevertheless, information about station issues was still considered to be "the best available basis for forecasting Zone of Interior future issue requirements."[56]

More than any other technical service the QMC made use of stock status reports. Since the Corps in general supplied the individual rather than the organization, it had to be in a position to "meet changes which occur daily, in varying degrees of magnitude and with little or

---

[51] (1) Memo, Gen Lutes, Dir of Opns, ASF, for TQMG, 13 Jul 43, sub: Depot Stock Levels, 400.291. (2) S&D Div Order 73, 25 Aug 43, sub: Procedure for Establishment of Stock Levels.

[52] Col C. G. Blakeney, "The Control of Supplies," *Military Review*, XXIV (October 1944), 67–70.

[53] (1) Address, Maj Charles Workman, n. d., sub: Problems in Producing Accurate and Timely Stock Control Records. (2) ASF Cir 10, Sec. VIII, 8 Jan 44, sub: Stock Control.

[54] (1) Address, Col Bobrink, 3 Oct 44, sub: Station Control Levels and Depot Levels in Relation to Supply, QMs' Conf, Camp Lee, Va., 2–4 Oct 44. (2) Memo, Bobrink for CG ASF, 12 Apr 44, sub: Sta Control Levels, 400.291.

[55] Rpt, Stat Br, OQMG, Depot Opns, Vol. 19 · (June 1945), p. 17.

[56] Chief of C&E Sec to Ex Off, C&E Br, OQMG, 4 Feb 44, sub: Sta Stock Status Rpt.

no advance information," such as alterations in the strength and troop composition of individual stations, increases or decreases in theater strength, and changes in the allowance of an item or in the requirements of other agencies.[57] Accurate and up-to-date knowledge of "on hand" and "current issues" was required to preserve the necessary flexibility in the Quartermaster supply organization. When Headquarters, ASF, late in 1943 proposed semiannual instead of monthly station stock status reports as a means of easing the accounting burden placed on stations by the new stock control system, the OQMG protested vigorously. Prolonged discussion during the first six months of 1944 resulted in authorization for continuation of monthly reports for a selected number of Quartermaster items, but for most items the frequency of such reports was sharply curtailed.[58]

Station Stock Levels

Establishing satisfactory maximum stock levels was as troublesome for station supply officers as maintaining accurate stock status reports. ASF officer teams, visiting the major stations in the zone of interior shortly after the installation of the new stock control system, reported "a general lack of understanding among the office personnel as to the policies and instructions for reviewing levels." [59] Depot and service command supervision in the establishment, review, and adjustment of levels was inadequate. Analysis showed levels greatly in excess of past issue experience and demand. They were being revised downward slowly, but at a rate "insufficient to keep levels in line with decreasing issues and demand" as the number of troops in the zone of interior fell with the rising tempo of overseas operations. Station personnel were apt to view the determination of maximum stock levels as a mere mathematical exercise, but "neither the setting of the level nor its review can be performed by any simple

procedure such as taking past issues of an item and adjusting the quantity to the increase or decrease in expected troop strength." [60] It involved consideration and evaluation of many elements—specifically, tariff sizes, the number of men passing through a reception center if one was located within the station area, the extent of field training—and generally the strength, composition, and contemplated activities at the station.

To encourage a downward revision of maximum stock levels, the depots were directed to pursue a more vigorous supervision of station stock levels.[61] To promote the same end, station stock levels were reduced from a 90- to a 60-day level of supply. This meant, in effect, a 45-day supply since requisitions for replenishment purposes would be placed only when the quantity on hand or on order was less than three fourths of the station control level. The effectiveness with which station stock levels were administered was evident in the reduction effected in the physical stocks of clothing and equipage. The per capita value of these items at stations dropped from $45.58 on 1 June 1943, to $33.90 on 31 December 1943, and to $21.96 on 31 July 1944.[62]

[57] Memo, Gen Scowden for CG ASF, 27 Dec 43, sub: Sta Stock Status Rpts for QM Items, 400.211.

[58] (1) ASF Cir 174, Sec. VI, 9 Jun 44, sub: Sta Stock Status Rpts. (2) Ltr, Brig Gen A. M. Owens, OQMG, for COs QM Depots et al., 26 Jun 44, sub: Sta Stock Status Rpts for Selected Items, 400.219.

[59] ASF Cir 10, Sec. VIII, 8 Jan 44, sub: Stock Control.

[60] Address, Col Bobrink, 3 Oct 44, sub: Station Control Levels and Depot Levels in Relation to Supply, QMs' Conf, Camp Lee, Va., 2–4 Oct 44.

[61] (1) ASF Cir 141, Sec. II, 6 Dec 43, sub: Sta Stock Levels. (2) Ltr, TAG to Chiefs of Tech Svs, 6 Dec 43, sub: Review and Revision of Stock Levels at Posts, Camps, and Stations, 400.211 (6 Oct 43) OB-P-SPDDI-MB-A. (3) Ltr, Gen Scowden to COs QM Depots et al., 15 Dec 43, same sub.

[62] (1) Address, Col Bobrink, 3 Oct 44, sub: Station Control Levels and Depot Levels in Relation to Supply, QMs' Conf, Camp Lee, Va., 2–4 Oct 44. (2) ASF Cir 54, Sec. I, 21 Feb 44, sub: Adjustment of Sta Stock Levels.

During the winter of 1944–45 drastic reductions in station control levels were necessitated by heavy theater demands which far surpassed the requirements that had been estimated. Woolen and cotton clothing, certain items of textile equipment, and some general supplies were in urgent demand. This demand arose from the need to replace clothing and equipment items which deteriorated or were lost during the ETO campaigns of these months. The need was further augmented by the Army's responsibility for civilian supply in liberated areas and the necessity of providing clothing for prisoners of war. When the war in Europe ended, there were increased requirements for cotton clothing to outfit troops redeployed to Pacific theaters. Permissible station control levels of such critical items were lowered to a 45-day supply and in some instances to a supply of 30 days. Only by decreasing zone of interior stocks and centralizing them in depots where they could be quickly shipped to theaters could the huge overseas demands be met.[63]

The readjustment of supply levels at posts, camps, and stations early in 1944 was part of a general program initiated by Headquarters, ASF, for reviewing the logistical situation. The first and major phase of war production was ending. It had been geared to meet initial issue needs of a rapidly expanding Army of 7,700,000, to provide similar equipment for our Allies, and to furnish the operational requirements for the troops engaged in overseas operations in 1942 and 1943. In the second phase procurement would have to be scheduled to meet estimated replacements and operational requirements. A closer correlation of procurement and consumption became essential. Needed supplies had to be available on time but the accumulation of surpluses had to be avoided. To achieve these objectives a high degree of co-ordination was essential between the calculation of requirements, the scheduling of production, storage, and issue, and the disposal of surpluses.

This change in the logistical situation as it affected QMC operations was indicated initially by the establishment of a Master Production Schedule, setting an upper limit on purchasing, and controlling the rate at which required production was to take place,[64] and then by the developments which led to the supply and demand studies. These procedures became the basis for the Supply Control System established in the early spring of 1944. It achieved the desired co-ordination by integrating requirements forecasting, production scheduling, stock accounting, and disposal of excess stocks and surpluses.[65]

Headquarters, ASF, requested each technical service chief to submit a detailed operating plan for the management of supply in depots which would be in accordance with the announced levels, authorized reserves, and stock control policies.[66] By May 1944 The Quartermaster General had instructed Quartermaster depots on the stock control procedures to be put into effect.[67] Stock control furnished the basis for the Supply Control System which was to effect the best balance possible between supply and demand. That system was constructed "from the U. S. depot door,"[68] since the basic data—the records of supply on hand, issues, receipts, and dues in—were obtained from these field installations. Accuracy of such data and of inventories

---

[63] (1) OQMG Daily Activity Journal, 27 Sep 44, 25 Nov 44. (2) Ltr, Gen Corbin to COs QM Depots et al., 6 Jun 45, sub: Reduction of Sta Control Levels of Cotton Khaki Clothing, 400.291.

[64] See above, Ch. VIII.

[65] (1) ASF Cir 67, Sec. II, 7 Mar 44, sub: Stock. (2) See above, Ch. VI, for application of the system to requirements. (3) See below, pp. 384–91 for a discussion of excess stocks and surpluses.

[66] ASF Cir 67, Sec. III, 7 Mar 44, sub: Stock.

[67] (1) Stock Comptroller, OQMG, to Deputy QMG for Sup Plng et al., 15 Mar 44, sub: Implementation of WD and ASF Policies. (2) Ltr, TQMG to COs QM Depots et al., 8 May 44, sub: Stock Control Procedures Re Authorized Stock Levels and Reserves.

[68] Discussion, Brig Gen T. M. Osborne, Dir of Reqmts & Stock Control Div, ASF, ASF SvC Conf, Camp Grant, Ill., 28–30 Jun 45, p. 271.

was increasingly important. In the past errors in stock on hand could be tolerated, for there was always the chance that they could be absorbed in future procurements. As the end of the war approached, however, that possibility was eliminated.

Depot Stock Levels

Completely satisfactory stock levels were as difficult to attain at Quartermaster distributing depots as at stations. This was attributable in part to the fact that establishment and revision of maximum stock levels was accomplished by the Stock Control Branch, OQMG, which was hampered by its lack of familiarity with local conditions and by the sheer volume of work involved in computing the levels of thousands of items. Under the new procedures, the distributing depots were made responsible for establishing zone of interior maximum stock levels for every item which they had to carry to meet their assignments. Although it was anticipated that responsibility for setting levels for filler depots would be delegated to them by 1 July 1944 levels continued to be set by the commodity branches of the OQMG during the war. These levels were subject to review, revision, and approval by the OQMG.[69]

In accordance with the ASF directive, the maximum stock on hand for regional distribution by a depot was reduced from a 60 to a 45 days' supply.[70] Early in 1944 Headquarters, ASF, had suggested that depot issue experience might be used as the chief factor in setting depot stock levels. Depot issues were of questionable value, however, for they included shipments made both inside and outside the distributing area of the depot, and it was exceedingly difficult to isolate outside issues. Experience had demonstrated that station issues and control levels represented the best guide to setting a depot level, modified by changes in troop strength, type of organization, and other conditions that

might effect demand at stations. It was therefore directed that depot stock levels be computed on this basis.[71]

The task of computing so many levels on a new basis was monumental, but by the end of August most Quartermaster depots had established levels on virtually all items stocked for distribution in the zone of interior, while the commodity divisions and branches of the OQMG were expediting the establishment of levels for filler depots. The longest delay grew out of the difficulty of calculating levels for spare parts at the Columbus and Richmond Depots. The number of items for which stock levels were set by depots generally ranged between 4,000 and 5,000.[72]

The demand for certain items of Quartermaster supply, however, proved to be so unpredictable that the establishment of stock levels for them in terms of days was unrealistic. Items in sporadic demand included special force items, women's clothing, materials-handling equipment, and impermeable items. Footwear, the most highly sized item of Quartermaster supply, was often in irregular demand and hard to stock in terms of levels expressed in days of supply. As a consequence, The Quartermaster General requested and was authorized to establish at designated depots stockpiles for these items in

[69] Ltr, TQMG to COs QM Depots et al., 8 May 44, sub: Stock Control Procedures Re Authorized Stock Levels and Reserves, 400.291.

[70] There were exceptions to this rule. For supplies not stocked at stations, for example, the depot could set a maximum stock level of 90 days. On the other hand, for items stocked for assembly, manufacturing, or production, such as fabrics and findings, levels of 120 days could be established.

[71] (1) [1st ind], Brig Gen F. A. Heileman, Dir of Sup, ASF, to TQMG, 26 Jan 44. (2) Address, Col Bobrink, 3 Oct 44, sub: Station Control Levels and Depot Levels in Relation to Supply, QMs' Conf, Camp Lee, Va., 2–4 Oct 44. (3) ASF Cir 138, Sec. VII, 12 May 44, sub: Depot Stock Levels.

[72] (1) Memo, Col Bobrink, OQMG, for CG ASF, 11 Aug 44, sub: Depot Levels. (2) 2d ind, Bobrink to same, 2 Sep 44, on same. Both in 400.291.

lieu of stock levels. These were to be reviewed quarterly to determine the adequacy of each stockpile.[73]

Supply levels at filler depots were also reduced from 90 to 60 days early in 1944. However, filler depots were temporarily authorized to stock an additional "overseas contingency reserve" of 30 days for all items on which strategic reserves had not been established. In effect, the old 90-day level was thereby maintained, and was in fact re-established when the contingency reserve level on overseas stock in filler depots was discontinued in June at the time the Normandy landings occurred. In fixing filler stock levels, the commodity branches of the OQMG came more and more to rely on issue experience, modified by expected changes in strength, rather than on replacement factors.[74] Although stocks for theater requirements were normally stored in filler depots, they could upon approval of Headquarters, ASF, be stored in ports of embarkation. In any event, the entire authorized level of an item authorized for stockage at a port as well as at a filler depot was to be stored at one or the other but not at both.

The entire control of strategic, utility, and production reserves (known collectively as SUP reserves) continued to be centralized in the OQMG, where the commodity divisions and branches were responsible for establishing and replenishing such levels and directing the issue of items in these reserves in accordance with the policies and directives of the Commanding General, ASF.

Administrative Developments

Within the OQMG

The introduction of new stock control methods in 1943 necessitated administrative changes in the organization of the Storage and Distribution Division, OQMG. In order to make the new stock control procedures effective, a Stock Control Branch was established in March,[75] charged with the responsibility of supervising and co-ordinating all directives on stock control. It was to accumulate and analyze all data relative to the control of stocks, appraise performance, and recommend corrective actions. The branch was also responsible for compiling experience data and sending it to the Requirements Branch of the Military Planning Division for use in revising maintenance factors and distribution allowances. It was to prescribe the method by which stock levels at stations and depots were to be established and recommend action when these levels were unbalanced. The chief of the Stock Control Branch was also designated stock comptroller for the OQMG.

Unfortunately, these functions overlapped and frequently duplicated those which had been assigned to the Office Management and Stock Accounting Sections of the Storage Branch. In the beginning there was an informal understanding that the Stock Control Branch would handle those problems of stock record accounts at posts, camps, and stations while depot problems relating to all procedures would be handled by the Storage Branch.[76] Since the Storage Branch dealt almost entirely with depot operations, this was a natural division of work. At the same time, it was realized that the rather fine line of demarcation might be difficult to administer in practice.

Actually the problems involved in stock con-

---

[73] (1) Memo, Col A. D. Hopping, OQMG, for CG ASF, 1 Feb 45, sub: Stockpile Stock Levels. (2) 1st ind, Gen Lutes, Dir of Plans & Opns, ASF, to TQMG, 6 Feb 45, on same. Both in 400.291.

[74] (1) Ltr, TQMG to COs QM Depots, *et al.,* 8 May 44, sub: Stock Control Procedures Re Authorized Stock Levels and Reserves. (2) Ltr, same to same, 10 June 44, sub: Depot Maximum Stock Levels for T/O and ZI Reqmts.

[75] OQMG OO 25-31, 12 Mar 43, sub: Establishment of Stock Control Br, S&D Div.

[76] Chief of Stor Br to Dir of S&D Div, OQMG 9 Sep 43, sub: Clarification of Functional Duties of Stock Control and Stor Brs.

trol operations were inseparable from depot procedures. Despite co-ordinating efforts, some doubts arose at depots and in the OQMG as to whether the Storage Branch or the Stock Control Branch was responsible for handling a particular problem. The Storage Branch therefore recommended that (1) the responsibilities of the Stock Control Branch be made "merely *staff* and *advisory* so far as the Office of the Quartermaster General" was concerned with depot problems and the preparation of procedural directives placed in charge of the Storage Branch; or that (2) the Office Management and Stock Accounting Sections of the Storage Branch be absorbed into the Stock Control Branch; or that (3) the functions of each branch "be carefully and logically segregated." [77]

By the fall of 1943 the OQMG acted on these recommendations by centralizing all functions relating to office management, stock accounting, and stock control in the Office of the Stock Comptroller.[78] Two days later, however, this order was suspended by a new directive redefining the responsibilities of the Deputy The Quartermaster General for Supply Planning and Operations whose duties had originally been established on 10 October.[79] Hereafter he was to act for The Quartermaster General in directing and co-ordinating all matters concerning stock control. His recommendations on such policy matters were presented to The Quartermaster General for approval. He was responsible for carrying out established program and stock control policies.

Under his direction, the functions of the Stock Control and Storage Branches were gradually clarified during 1944. The functions of the Stock Control Branch became increasingly staff and advisory in character. In August the Office Management and Stock Accounting Sections of the Storage Branch were consolidated to form the Procedures and Stock Accounting Branch of the Storage and Distribution Division. It was responsible for designing, installing, and super-

vising clerical methods and procedures relating to the distribution and storage of Quartermaster supplies. The Stock Control Branch, on the other hand, was responsible for the formulation of general depot policies and for the supervision of their application. In general, the functions of these branches were more sharply differentiated than before.[80] This organization operated until the war ended.

Within the Depots

In the summer of 1943 changes were also effected in the administrative organizations handling stock control operations in the depots. These were an outgrowth of the general overhauling of the supply system which had been under analysis by the QMC, the Ordnance Department, and the Control Division, SOS, since the summer of 1942. By March 1943 the Control Division had evolved a new plan to standardize the organizational structure and operating methods of the depots and to provide "more efficacious supervision over their general management and warehousing policies." [81]

Headquarters, ASF, directed the chiefs of the technical services to reorganize their respective branch depots by 1 July in line with this new plan of organization. The plan was not to be applied to general depots, however, before its practicability had been determined by experimentation at a designated ASF depot.[82]

Pursuant to this directive, The Quartermaster General reorganized the Quartermaster

[77] *Ibid.*

[78] OQMG OO 25-31A, 16 Nov 43, sub: Orgn of Stock Control in OQMG.

[79] OQMG OO 25-10A, 18 Nov 43, sub: Apmt and Reasgmt of Key Pers.

[80] OQMG OO 25-74A, 4 Aug 44, sub: Establishment of Procedures & Stock Accounting Br.

[81] Control Div, SOS, Mar 43, sub: Depot Opns Rpt 67.

[82] Memo, Gen Lutes, ASF, for Chiefs of Tech Svs, 21 May 43, sub: Reorgn of Br Depots Under Rpt 67, 323.3.

depots by replacing the Storage and Distribution Division with separate Stock Control and Storage Divisions. The objective was to emphasize and correlate the various stock control activities by placing them in a division charged specifically with this responsibility. In the reassignment of functional responsibilities, the former Administrative, Editing, Incoming Property, Stock Accounting, and Service Branches of the Storage and Distribution Division were transferred to the new Stock Control Division and reorganized into four branches. The new Storage Division differed little from the former Warehouse Branch. On the other hand, all transportation functions of the depot were incorporated into a Transportation Division. At the recommendation of the OQMG, based on past operating experience, the position of Director of Supply was created in order to co-ordinate the activities of these three divisions. The director reported on behalf of the three divisions to the commanding officer of the depot, thereby relieving him of much of the burden imposed by the ASF plan of direct responsibility of the divisions to the depot commander.[83]

The application of the plan to ASF depots met with objections from The Quartermaster General, who believed that the proposed changes were "unwieldy, unworkable, and perhaps, dangerous in the effect upon the present supply system." [84] He was critical of the control vested in the commanding officer of an ASF depot, the interposition of another level of command between the chiefs of the technical services and the stock control activities of the various services occupying an ASF depot, the concentration of receiving, shipping, and storage activities in the Storage Division, and the consolidation of all stock records of the supply sections, since they had varied systems of identification and stock accounting, and reporting procedures would have to be standardized for all technical services. He questioned the advisability of embarking on this experiment at a time when the

Army was engaged in the greatest supply problem in its history.

Headquarters, ASF, defended the new plan, contending that it had been evolved out of prolonged study. It maintained that the operating viewpoint had not been neglected in the preparation. It felt that most of the objections were based on erroneous impressions; all that was necessary was a fair and impartial trial of the plan. For this purpose it requested The Quartermaster General to designate three ASF depots, one of which would be selected for the experiment.[85]

After considerable discussion the Atlanta ASF Depot was selected for the test. The depot operated under the plan for some eight months between 17 August 1943 and 1 May 1944, when the War Department directed its discontinuance. Quartermaster forebodings apparently were not realized, but no attempt was made to extend the plan to other ASF depots. Instead, even as this experiment was being initiated, Headquarters, ASF, directed the chiefs of the technical services to reorganize their supply sections in ASF depots on the same functional pattern already established in their branch depots. Accordingly, Quartermaster supply sections at ASF depots were reorganized, effective 1 September 1943.[86] This action was intended to simplify and co-ordinate stock control and storage operations throughout each technical service and thus promote efficiency of operations.

---

[83] (1) Memo, Gen Scowden for CG ASF, 7 Jun 43, sub: Recommended Orgn Stock Control Div in Br Depots, 323.3. (2) Ltr, Gen Scowden to COs QMDs, 10 Jul 43, sub: Reorgn of Br Depots.

[84] Memo, TQMG for CG ASF, 26 Jun 43, sub: Depot Opns Rpt 67 as Applied to ASFDs, 323.3.

[85] Memo, Gen Lutes, Dir of Opns, ASF, for TQMG, 8 Jul 43, sub: Depot Opns Rpt 67, 323.3.

[86] (1) Memo, Gen Lutes, ASF, for TQMG *et al.*, 29 Jul 43, sub: Orgn of Stock Control & Storage Divs at ASF Depots. (2) Ltr, Gen Scowden to QMSOs ASFDs, 23 Aug 43, sub: Reorgn of QM Sup Secs, ASFDs. Both in 323.3.

Excess Stocks

One of the most conspicuous weaknesses of the Quartermaster distribution system at the beginning of World War II was its failure to provide means of preventing the unnecessary accumulation of excess goods or, once they had been created, of redistributing overstockages to the points in greatest need. The demands of total war increasingly focused attention upon the problem of excess stocks. Any disproportionately large stocks at some depots and station warehouses, or in company, battalion, or regimental supply rooms, deprived others of sorely needed supplies. Furthermore, the redistribution of excess goods involved additional costs in rehandling at depots. Inexperienced post personnel had to be trained in the proper method of packing and marking excess goods for reshipment to the ultimate user. They also had to be instructed in salvage activities, since overstockages might consist of worn, damaged, or unserviceable goods turned in by consuming organizations, as well as of new or only slightly worn property. Classification of excess goods as new, combat serviceable, suitable for issue in the zone of interior, or fit only for limited employment had to be made before any disposal action could be taken.

The accumulation of excess goods was damaging to the war effort and to the national economy. Scarce manpower, raw materials, and transportation were thereby absorbed whereas they might better have been utilized in the production and distribution of more critical military supplies or an ampler supply of essential civilian goods. Because Quartermaster items— shoes, clothing, and foodstuffs—were especially valuable in civilian life, the Corps was particularly vulnerable insofar as the problem of excess goods was concerned. Bearing in mind the disposal problem at the end of World War I, the War Department wished to avoid the accumulation of huge excesses at the end of hostilities

in order that it might escape glutting the civilian market, lowering prices, causing unemployment, depressing industry, and burdening the government with unnecessarily heavy losses in the disposal of surplus military supplies.

Before mid-1942 the accumulation of excess stocks was not particularly alarming. Some efforts had been made during 1941 to prevent their accumulation at stations, but the inadequacy of reports handicapped any program of redistribution.[87] In any event, during the emergency period, any threat from large excesses was negligible since the expanding Army was able to absorb the military supplies produced by industry, which had not yet hit its full stride in war production.

Factors Contributing to Overstockages

By the late summer of 1942 not only were stockages at depots rising above requirements because of increased industrial output, but a number of other factors were contributing to the development of excessive station inventories. Chief of these was the "frequent movement of troops from, to, and between stations."[88] Because supply agencies were not given timely information about future troop movements and increases and decreases in station and distribution area strength, they repeatedly requisitioned supplies in quantities large enough to enable them to meet any unexpected emergencies. As a result, some military units received goods far exceeding their requirements and were forced to leave large amounts behind when they departed. In other instances, poorly informed distributing agencies failed to furnish

---

[87] (1) Ltr, Lt Col J. B. Welch, OQMG, to QMs CAs, 3 Jan 41, sub: Reporting Excess Stocks. (2) Gen Corbin, Chief of Sup Div, to TQMG, 16 Sep 41, sub: Excesses of C&E in CAs as of 1 Aug 41. (3) Corbin to TQMG, 18 Nov 41, sub: Rpt of Excess Stocks of C&E. All in 400.291.

[88] Stock Control Bd, 22 Jan 43, sub: First Preliminary Rpt.

the incoming troops with sufficient goods.

The inadequacies of the requisitioning system also contributed to the building up of excess stores. Requisitions were submitted at long intervals, often only quarterly or even semi-annually. As a result, stations requisitioned sufficient supplies to enable them to meet any unforeseen demands made before the next period of requisitioning. Excessive orders might have been scaled down if requisitions had been edited carefully, but in the months immediately after Pearl Harbor such editing was rather sketchy.

The pressure upon theater commanders and supply and transportation agencies led to a "relatively uncontrolled supply of quantities of equipment, materials, and supplies for which need was estimated rather than actual." [89] In addition, the War Department pursued an extremely liberal policy in approving special issues of equipment over and above that authorized by tables of equipment, plus replacement and operating factors. This policy resulted in many cases of overstockages or stagnation of items needed elsewhere. The prevailing laxity in editing confirmed the stations in their habit of requisitioning more supplies than were actually needed, a practice which they condoned on the ground that depots could not always make deliveries promptly or in the desired volume. There was, in fact, some justification in this explanation.

The reluctance of many stations to report excess stocks to service commands and regional depots resulted in immobilizing stocks urgently needed elsewhere merely because their existence was unknown to the agencies empowered to make transfers. The War Department repeatedly urged that action be taken to report excess property at posts, camps, and stations in order that redistribution might be effected. Such reports were important because if The Quartermaster General did not know what excess stocks were available at posts, camps, and sta-

tions, he would be compelled to continue making unnecessary purchases of these items. [90] With many items of equipment still critical, hoarding was deemed "detrimental to the successful prosecution of the war." [91] Divided responsibility, however, hindered redistribution of excess stocks. While The Quartermaster General, operating through Quartermaster depots, was given authority to move excess stocks at stations, the commanding generals of the service commands could also shift excess housekeeping properties at posts, camps, and stations within their commands. It frequently followed that neither depots nor service commands made any redistribution, each depending upon the other to take the required action. [92]

The accumulation of overstockages was also due to the time-honored custom of hoarding by supply sergeants attached to consuming military units. The War Department had proclaimed that the hoarding of excess stocks "to be used as a cushion" was unpatriotic and not to be countenanced, but even wartime exigencies had failed to uproot this ancient custom. It stemmed from the fact that commanders of companies, battalions, and regiments tended to judge supply officers mostly by their ability to have plentiful stocks constantly on hand. Hence, to impress their superiors favorably,

[89] (1) AGO Memo W700–11–43, 24 Feb 43, sub: Excess of Working Stocks. (2) Memo, Gen Scowden for ACofS for Opns, SOS, 10 Mar 43, sub: Expediting of Rqns.

[90] Address, Maj Gen C. F. Robinson, 3 Oct 44, sub: Relations of Technical Services with Service Commands, QMs' Conf, 2–4 Oct 44, Camp Lee, Va.

[91] (1) AGO Memo S700–1–42, 27 Nov 42, sub: Distr of Supplies. (2) AGO Memo W30–6–42, 12 Oct 42, sub: Collection and Redistr of Excess Prop and Equip. (3) Ltr, TAG to Chiefs of Sup Svs et al., 22 Jun 42, sub: Proper Distr of Supplies and Equip. AG 475 (6–16–42) MO–SPPD–TS–M.

[92] (1) Ibid. (2) Stock Control Bd, 22 Jan 43, sub: First Preliminary Rpt. (3) Memo, Gen Scowden for CG SOS, 2 Dec 42, sub: Distr of Supplies. (4) Memo, Gen Lutes, SOS, for TQMG, 29 Dec 44, sub: Revision of AGO Memo S700–1–42.

zealous supply officers piled up excessive stocks in the storage rooms of their military organizations.[93] Since there were thousands of companies, the ultimate result might be a dangerous unbalancing of supplies.

Unbalanced stockages also developed at depots. Nominal excesses of depot stockages were often inevitable. When industry produced supplies in excess of current requirements, it was necessary for The Quartermaster General to accumulate such supplies in reserve depots. However, he also had to consider the availability of storage space, and, in some instances, such supplies had to be divided "among the various distributing depots in relation to their normal stocks and anticipated future needs."[94] Such action frequently had the effect of raising inventories far above authorized levels. This stemmed from the failure of the Army Supply Program to base requirements on monthly schedules. Instead they were determined by calendar years, and delivery schedules were concentrated largely in the closing months of the year. A paradoxical situation resulted. On the one hand, depot commanders were required to maintain a 60-day stock level for zone of interior supply and a 90-day level for overseas supply. On the other hand, they were required to accept supplies flowing into the depots from manufacturing plants on production schedules that bore no direct relationship to established stock levels. "This," said Lt. Gen. LeRoy Lutes, who handled problems of distribution at Headquarters, ASF, during the war, "is an excellent illustration of one of the most important lessons about Army supply; that is, that the supply process is an individual entity and cannot be broken down into uncoordinated phases as production, stock control and distribution."[95]

Control Measures of 1943

Public opinion was much more impressed by overstockages than by shortages, particularly as rationing deprived civilians of accustomed goods. By the summer of 1942, with the Army aware of the dangers involved in the accumulation of excess stocks and the supply situation becoming stabilized, the War Department was able to take steps leading to the introduction of new methods of stock control.[96] One of the objectives of the new system was to insure the prompt return of excess supplies and dead stocks to depots and the disposal of unserviceable equipment and outmoded and obsolete stocks. Any stock in excess of maximum stock levels was considered excess and was to be called back to supply channels by depots. The depots were responsible for reviewing station stock status reports and issuing instructions on the disposition of excess, obsolete, and outmoded stocks. Excess stocks returned to depots were to be fully serviceable and properly packed.[97]

In the summer of 1943 the Quartermaster depots began a review of station reports to determine excesses.[98] The most urgent problems developed in connection with the steadily mounting quantities of used supplies accumulating at stations. Despite regulations requiring stations to return to depots only serviceable supplies, sizable quantities of unserviceable goods were sent. Furthermore, excess goods were not properly classified as to whether they were new, combat serviceable, suitable for issue

---

[93] (1) AGO Memo W700–7–43, 21 Jan 43, sub: Excess Supplies. (2) Rpt, Accounting Advisory Br, Procurement Policy Div, WPB, 29 Dec 42, sub: Improved Control Over Distr of Supplies, USA.

[94] Ist ind, Gen Scowden to ACofS for Opns, SOS, 23 Jan 43, on memo, Gen Lutes, SOS, for TQMG et al., 8 Jan 43, sub: Excess Stocks at Depots, 400.291.

[95] Address, 23 Sep 46, sub: The Army Supply Program (Industrial Mobilization Course, ICAF), p. 7.

[96] See above, pp. 364ff.

[97] TM 38–220, 3 May 43, sub: Stock Control Manual for Posts, Camps, and Stations, pp. 24–25.

[98] (1) Ltr, TAG to CGs of All SvCs, 23 Jun 43, sub: Sta Excesses. SPX 400 (22 Jun 43) OB–S–SPDDI–M. (2) Ltr, Gen Scowden to COs QM Depots et al., 2 Jul 43, sub: Rpt of Excess Stocks, 400.291.

in the zone of interior, or fit for use under certain conditions. In many instances, all grades of serviceable and unserviceable supplies as well as mismates of many items of clothing were found in the same containers. Returned goods were often poorly packed, sometimes because of conditions beyond the station's control, such as a lack of shipping materials, inexperienced supervision, and shortage of qualified personnel capable of packing items according to approved methods. Since depots were unable to rely upon classification of items received from posts, camps, and stations, they were compelled to build up rather large organizations to reclassify, reinspect, and repack the property received.[99]

Failure of stations to classify excess goods correctly meant that the OQMG was hampered in making extracts and transfers of supplies from one depot to another, and in setting stock levels. Furthermore, only as the degree of serviceability was known could the probable length of usability of an item be estimated. This was important to the accurate calculation of requirements for procurement purposes.[100] So flagrant had station violations of directives governing the shipment of only serviceable items become early in 1944 that the supply missions of some of the depots were being compromised by their efforts to handle the huge mass of unserviceable supplies.[101] The responsibilities of depot commanders, station commanders, and commanding generals of the service commands were consequently spelled out in detail.

Depots, too, had been remiss in following directives about excess goods. Although instructed to furnish appropriate redistribution instructions to stations on all determined excess stocks, some depots did not take action to relieve stations of further accountability. The service commands therefore complained that they could not move excess stocks despite reports made to depots according to ASF instructions. Furthermore, when the depots did send orders, they instructed stations to "excess-hold"

or "retain" such overstockages. This practice was based on insufficient depot storage space. The disposition of excess stocks was consequently a sore subject at the OQMG, at Quartermaster depots, and at service commands.[102]

As military units were shipped overseas in increasing numbers late in 1943 and 1944, the difficulties of disposing of excess stocks were augmented by the steadily growing volume of material turned in at stations by such units. A small amount of this material might be useable; much of it was fit only for salvage. In any case, it increased the vexatious burden of classification by station personnel. Early in January, Headquarters, ASF, instructed the depots to issue definite instructions to direct the return of excess serviceable equipment.[103] The OQMG was quick to point out that these instructions took no cognizance of the fact that some bulky items of Quartermaster housekeeping equipment—bedsteads and mattresses, for example—which became excess at a station should remain in storage there to ease the depot space problem.[104]

Headquarters, ASF, authorized the use of available post, camp, and station space, on the

[99] (1) Insp Rpt, Lt Col Daniel Borth, Jr., to TQMG, 9 Sep 43, sub: Rpt of Insp at CQMD et al., 1–29 Aug 43. (2) Ltr, TAG to Chiefs of Tech Svs et al., 29 Oct 43, sub: Stock Control Conf. (3) Address, Col Borth, sub: Accountability of Depots for Property Stored at Stations, QMs' Conf, 2–4 Oct 44, Camp Lee, Va.

[100] See n. 99 (3) above.

[101] ASF Cir 4, Sec. III, 4 Jan 44, sub: Return of Sta Excess Prop to Depots.

[102] (1) Ltr, Col Bobrink, OQMG, to COs QM Depots et al., 1 May 44, sub: Redistr of Sta Excess Stocks. (2) 1st ind, Gen Heileman, Dir of Sup, ASF, to TQMG, 5 Feb 44, on memo, Gen Scowden for CG ASF, 10 Jan 44, sub: ASF Cir 4. (3) Address, Gen Robinson, 3 Oct 44, sub: Relations of Tech Svs with SvCs, QMs' Conf, 2–4 Oct 44, Camp Lee, Va.

[103] ASF Cir 4, 4 Jan 44, sub: Return of Sta Excess Prop to Depots.

[104] Memo, Gen Scowden for CG ASF, 10 Jan 44, sub: ASF Cir 4, and 1st ind, Gen Heileman, Dir of Sup, ASF, to TQMG, 5 Feb 44, 400.291.

approval of the service command concerned, for bulk storage of excess stocks which could not be accommodated at depots. The reduced activity of certain stations and the inactivation of others would make a relatively large amount of space in various buildings—mess halls, classrooms, recreation buildings and barracks, as well as warehouses—available for storage purposes. Since posts, camps, and stations were not equipped to handle stocks with a rapid turnover, such storage space was to be used for slow-moving items, and, in addition, to store excess housekeeping equipment of a bulky nature which would save considerable in transportation costs. It was not intended to use station storage space as "retail distribution points" by the depot. Supplies stored there under depot control were to be shipped, except under special circumstances, only on a bulk basis to other stations.[105]

Relation to Supply Control System

As troops were shifted in ever greater numbers from the zone of interior to the United Kingdom, Headquarters, ASF, early in 1944 began a reanalysis of the logistical situation. In part this involved a downward revision of the stock levels at posts, camps, and stations and a corresponding increase in excess goods above the authorized levels. The review culminated in the establishment in March of the supply control system, which integrated requirements forecasting, production scheduling, stock accounting, and disposal of excess stocks and surpluses.

In order to accelerate the reduction of excess stocks created by these developments, Headquarters, ASF, directed the stations to prepare and submit to the depots special reports indicating all items in excess of authorized stock levels, after they had been reviewed and revised by depot personnel, and all slow-moving items that had been issued less than three times dur-

ing the preceding 90 days. Depot commanders reviewed these excess stock reports and directed disposition by (1) ordering the return of the items to supply depots; (2) directing storage under depot control at stations; or (3) requesting commanding generals of the service commands to redistribute or declare surplus those items for which such action was authorized.[106] Originally the station excess stock report was to be submitted quarterly. This was subsequently placed on a monthly basis for it was the objective of Headquarters, ASF, "to reflect as expeditiously as possible the excess stock at stations into the over-all stock picture of the Technical Services."[107]

A persistent and disturbing problem was the continued inability of most stations to inspect and classify excess stocks. By the fall of 1944 depots were authorized to send personnel to stations to inspect and classify excesses which had been reported and to furnish technical advice on packing and crating, or to order excess stocks into the depot to be inspected there for condition and classification.[108] In October The Quartermaster General appointed a committee to study the problem and recommend a course of action. The same factors of inadequate packing facilities and lack of trained personnel still hampered the stations in their classification efforts. The committee noted that various procedures had been tried to correct these difficulties but that the most satisfactory was direct depot assistance. It therefore recommended that an adequate number of "classification and pack-

---

[105] (1) ASF Cir 51, Sec. II, 17 Feb 44, sub: Sta Excess Stocks. (2) ASF Cir 63, Sec. I, 2 Mar 44, same sub. (3) ASF Manual M 416, Nov 44, sub: Stock Control Manual for Depots, pp. 10–11.

[106] ASF Cir 51, Sec. II, 17 Feb 44, sub: Reporting and Handling Sta Excess Stocks.

[107] (1) Address, Col Borth, sub: Accountability of Depots for Property Stored at Station, QMs' Conf, 2–4 Oct 44, Camp Lee, Va. (2) ASF Cir 328, Sec. I, 30 Sep 44, sub: Reporting Excess Stocks at Posts, Camps, and Stations.

[108] *Ibid.*

ing crews be organized into teams" and sent to the stations to assist them. Such teams were to be used only where the quantities involved were large or the items critical enough to warrant such action. These teams were to act in an advisory capacity for it was not intended to relieve the commanding general of the service command or the station commander of his responsibility. Although the Atlanta Depot had been experimenting with such teams and finding the method satisfactory, the OQMG did not make it mandatory for all its depots.[109]

Station inspection and classification generally remained inadequate. By the summer of 1945 The Quartermaster General recommended that all classification of excess goods at stations be discontinued and that it be accomplished only at depots. The stations were merely to segregate serviceable and unserviceable property, automatically returning the former to the depots and shipping unserviceable property to the appropriate depot for classification, packing, and storage after it had been repaired under the supervision of the service commands.[110]

At the time, ASF policies were being revised and these recommendations were not entirely adopted. The ASF instructed stations to return automatically to depots all serviceable Quartermaster excesses, except subsistence and petroleum products, if they amounted to less than a carload and were in standard depot packs. Overstockages of a carload or more were transferred to depot accountability. Unserviceable supplies were to be sent to repair installations designated as specialized shops, which repaired, classified, and packed them for storage at depots. The ASF originally directed that serviceable supplies which had been removed from depot packs were also to be sent to the repair installations for classification and packing. In the case of Quartermaster items, however, many of them would not normally be at stations in standard packs. Shipping such supplies to specialized shops would have been wasteful of transporta-

tion, and consequently within two months the ASF revised its instructions so that such Quartermaster serviceable property could be automatically shipped to the depot supplying the item to the station. Only where the serviceability of such an item was in question was it to be sent to the specialized shop.[111] Thus repair installations rather than depots became responsible for classification and packing.

Disposal of Surplus Property

The disposal of excess and surplus property, that is, goods not needed by the Army for a reasonable period of time in the future, was an important development that accompanied the efforts to promote efficient redistribution of excess stocks among Quartermaster agencies. At the beginning of World War II consideration was immediately given to the disposition of obsolete property with a view to releasing storage space in depots. Most of such property represented clothing and tools of miscellaneous types and quantities either left over from World War I or accumulated in the more than twenty years since that war.[112]

The limited objective of making storage space available soon gave way to a broader concept which was applied to the disposition of excess and surplus property. The necessity to conserve raw materials and manpower and the need to reduce, as far as possible, military de-

---

[109] (1) Committee Rpt, Brig Gen J. A. Porter, 4 Oct 44, QMs' Conf, 2–4 Oct 44, Camp Lee, Va. (2) Address, Gen Owens, 3 Oct 44, sub: Storage and Distribution Activities of QMC, *ibid.*

[110] ASF SvC Conf, Camp Grant, Ill., 28–30 Jun 45, p. 279.

[111] (1) ASF Cir 156, Sec. I, 1 May 45, sub: Material—Reclm. (2) ASF Cir 234, Sec. I, 22 Jun 45, sub: Automatic Evacuation of Excess Stock.

[112] (1) Memo, Gen Somervell for TQMG *et al.*, 24 Dec 41, sub: Bds of Officers to Make Survey of Supplies in Gen and Br Depots. (2) Memo, Col J. C. Longino, OQMG, for ACofS, G–4, 28 Jan 42, same sub. Both in 400.702.

mands upon the manufacturing and producing resources of the country during the war, made it imperative for the War Department not to accumulate serviceable property unnecessarily. Realizing that the War Department had on hand certain obsolete, outmoded, nonstandard, limited standard, substitute standard, and even standard property which was above normal requirements, the Commanding General, SOS, directed the chiefs of the supply services to make an immediate survey to expedite disposal of such property as might be surplus or obsolete.[113] Disposal of such stocks would place certain critical items in the hands of industry, where they could be used in producing other vital war products. If useless for such purposes, they could be used to replenish civilian stocks, which were being badly depleted in filling the military requirements of the expanding services.

Under existing regulations in 1942 The Quartermaster General was authorized to declare serviceable property surplus (1) when the property was in excess of the Corps' requirements; (2) when it was not desired by any other supply service; and (3) when the total current estimated value listed on the declaration did not exceed $50,000. Property evaluated over the amount was recommended to the Commanding General, SOS, for declaration as surplus to the War Department.[114] The OQMG reported its surplus property to the Procurement Division, Treasury Department, and, after clearance by that agency, it was sold by negotiation under the direction of The Quartermaster General.

Administrative Organization
Handling Disposal

In the summer of 1943 Headquarters, ASF, found that actual accomplishments in disposing of surplus property had been inadequate, although "provisions for the liquidation of obsolete, obsolescent, and outmoded property are as old as the problem."[115] There had been a cer-

tain hesitancy about declaring surplus large quantities of supplies since neither the estimating of future requirements nor the compilation of stock status data was considered sufficiently accurate to warrant such declarations.

When the basis for calculating these factors had been improved with the establishment of the new stock control system in the summer of 1943, the way was paved for the introduction of organizational and administrative changes which resulted in a more vigorous handling of the disposition of surplus property. At ASF direction The Quartermaster General created the positions of Redistribution and Salvage Officer and Property Utilization Officer for the QMC.[116] The Redistribution and Salvage Officer supervised Quartermaster salvage activities and the disposition or transfer of all Quartermaster property which had been declared surplus to the needs of the War Department. He also circularized the OQMG and Quartermaster field installations with regard to surplus property of other governmental agencies available for use. The Property Utilization Officer, on the other hand, determined the Quartermaster items and their quantities which were excess to the needs of the Corps. He circularized the other technical services and War Department agencies regarding excess Quartermaster property and arranged its transfer when requested. He notified the Redistribution and Salvage Officer of such transfers and of the declarations of surplus which had been made in reference to Quartermaster property.

---

[113] Memo, TAG for Chiefs of Sup Svs, 23 Dec 42, sub: Surplus and Obsolete Prop. SPX 400.7 (12–18–42) OP–P–SPDDS–MP–R.

[114] (1) PR 7, pars. 713.1–713.2, 14 Oct 42. (2) OQMG Cir 1–9, par. 30, 12 Dec 42, sub: Surplus Prop.

[115] 1st ind, Gen Lutes, ASF, to TQMG, 10 Jul 43, on memo, Gen Scowden, OQMG, for CG ASF, 2 Jul 43, no sub, 400.291.

[116] (1) PR 7, par. 709, as revised on 6 Jul 43. (2) OQMG OO 25–42, 20 Jul 43, sub: Redistr of Excess and Surplus Prop.

Within less than a month a Property Utilization Section was established in the Storage and Distribution Division to assist the Property Utilization Officer in carrying out his duties.[117] It was later redesignated the Redistribution and Disposal Branch. This represented the beginning of the organization within the OQMG which handled the disposition of excess and surplus Quartermaster property throughout the war years. Although a later reorganization in 1944 within the Storage and Distribution Division resulted in the establishment of a Stock Control Branch, which administered the responsibilities of the division in reference to the disposal of excess and surplus property, the basic functions of the division remained unchanged.[118] The Storage and Distribution Division continued to exercise supervision over the circularization, redistribution, and disposal of excess Quartermaster serviceable property, except in reference to subsistence and petroleum products, the responsibilities for which were vested respectively in the Subsistence and the Fuels and Lubricants Divisions.

Disposal of Nonstandard and Obsolete Items

The administrative changes initiated in the summer of 1943 were accompanied by a renewed effort to dispose of excess and surplus property. New regulations prescribed procedure for declaring serviceable military property surplus to the needs of the War Department.[119] Before military property could be declared surplus to the needs of the War Department, it had first of all to be excess to the technical services concerned, as, for example, the QMC. Obsolete and nonstandard items which were noncommon [120] and for which there existed no foreseeable requirements by another service for a converted use could be declared surplus by The Quartermaster General without circularization to other War Department components and

without reference to the Commanding General, ASF. Circularization was demanded in those instances where a requirement existed or where common items were purchased, stored, and issued by two or more technical services. All standard, substitute standard, and limited standard items that were excess to the Corps had to be referred to the Commanding General, ASF, for authority to declare such property surplus to the needs of the War Department.

The establishment of the new stock control system provided the stock status data needed for reviewing the stock position of both nonstandard and obsolete items, and standard items of Quartermaster supply. A board of officers appointed by the director of the Storage and Distribution Division, OQMG, made a study of the consolidated stock reports of the depots and prepared a master list showing an assigned stock number for each item determined by the board to be obsolete, outmoded, or not authorized for storage and issue by the QMC.[121] When such excess items were noncommon, action for disposal could be taken immediately. In the case of items common to two or more technical services, the Property Utilization Officer of the OQMG circularized lists of these items to all other technical services and to the AAF providing for a 20-day time limit within which such property could be requested for transfer within reimbursement. When he had determined that such property was surplus to the needs of the War Department, he reported

[117] OQMG OO 25–45, 9 Aug 43, sub: Orgn of Prop Utilization Sec.

[118] (1) OQMG OO 25–84, par. 3, 31 May 44, sub: Redistr and Disposal of Prop. (2) OQMG OO 25–129, 2 May 45, sub: Determination and Redistr of Excess and Disposal of Surplus Prop.

[119] WD Memo S5–140–43, 16 Jul 43, sub: Declaration of Military Prop as Surplus to WD.

[120] Noncommon items were those for which storage and issue responsibility were assigned to a particular service and were peculiar to that service.

[121] OQMG Cir Ltr 148, par. 4, 27 Sep 43, sub: Disposition of QM Prop Surplus to Needs of WD.

it by depot areas of distribution to the Redistribution and Salvage Officer of the OQMG for disposition. The latter advised the Procurement Division, Treasury Department, at Washington or the Treasury regional office having jurisdiction over the area served by the distributing depot where the property was located that such property, in specified quantities, was available for transfer or disposition. Beginning in the fall of 1943 such surplus property was disposed of by the distribution depot as directed by the Treasury Department through the Redistribution and Salvage Officer of the OQMG or by the regional Treasury office.[122] This use of the Treasury Department in the disposal of surplus relieved the Corps of many tedious details involved in the consummation of each sale of surplus property, such as mailing out invitations for bids, making abstracts of proposals and awards, depositing funds, obtaining additional payments to complete them, making refunds to unsuccessful bidders, and preparing reports.

Quartermaster depots and post quartermasters had been required to take into stock many obsolete, nonstandard, or outmoded items when such federal agencies as the CCC, the NYA, and the WPA were discontinued. In addition, large quantities of supplies pertinent to other technical services remained in Quartermaster stock at stations and depots when functions and responsibilities relating to construction, rail and water transportation, and motor transport were transferred out of the Corps early in the war. Many of these items had become obsolete, nonstandard, or outmoded.

The master list of obsolete and nonstandard items appearing on depot stock status reports prepared by the board of Quartermaster officers in the summer of 1943 included approximately 27,000 items, counting each separate stock number as an item. Of this number the depot stock status report reflected stock balances for 13,000 items, comprising approximately 34,000,000 individual units, or an average of 2,600 units per

item. Early in 1944 about 50 percent of this obsolete and nonstandard Quartermaster property had been disposed of either by transfer to other technical services or by declaration as surplus to the Procurement Division, Treasury Department.[123] Of the remaining 50 percent, 4,000 items, or 10,400,000 units, represented clothing which had not been declared surplus because it could be used for prisoners of war or for foreign relief. This quantity included CCC spruce-green clothing which had been frozen by order of the Combined Chiefs of Staff. Also included were 1,000 items which properly were the supply responsibility of other services but which had not yet been transferred. The remaining 1,600 items had not yet been processed for disposal as surplus, but the OQMG was making progress and had prepared a revised master list of nonstandard property.[124] To expedite transfer of items which were the supply responsibility of other services, Headquarters, ASF, directed the chiefs of these technical services to furnish shipping instructions to The Quartermaster General for the property which was to be transferred and to release for declaration as surplus such nonstandard and obsolete property as was not required.[125]

By way of decentralizing authority and enabling depots to dispose of excess stocks at posts, camps, and stations without consulting the OQMG, authority was delegated to depot commanders and to the representatives of the

---

[122] *Ibid.,* par. 5.

[123] 1st ind, Col Owens, OQMG, to Dir of Stock Control Div, ASF, 22 Mar 44, on memo, Dir of Sup, ASF, for TQMG, 14 Mar 44, sub: Nonstandard and Obsolete QM Property, 400.703. Other technical services received by transfer 1,200 items, while 5,200 items were processed as surplus to the Treasury Department.

[124] *Ibid.*

[125] (1) Memo, Dir of Sup, ASF, for Chief of Ordnance, 1 Apr 44, sub: Disposition of Ordnance Prop in Hands of QMC. (2) An identical letter was also sent to the CofEngrs, 400.703.

technical services in an ASF depot to declare surplus certain types of excess ASF military property. These types included serviceable obsolete items of issue as declared by The Quartermaster General; serviceable nonstandard commercial items, including articles purchased locally or secured from other government agencies, such as the CCC, the WPA, and the like; and serviceable nonstandard items of issue secured from a depot but not required by a depot for reissue under policies of The Quartermaster General.[126] This authority was granted on the assumption that the quantities involved, generally speaking, would be insignificant and scattered at various points throughout the country and that speedy action should be taken to dispose of them.[127]

An electric accounting machine listing of nonstandard and obsolete items was prepared to assist the depots in determining what items fell within these categories. About once a month the OQMG made changes in the list, which covered practically every item that could be disposed of as nonstandard property. Depot stocks were reflected in the nonstandard account, and a monthly EAM listing was furnished by all depots to the OQMG for review and circularization to other interested services and agencies. Thereafter such stocks were immediately transferred to the requisitioning office or disposed of as surplus. If subsequently any similar stocks were reported to a depot from a station, the depot had the authority to declare them surplus.[128]

Disposal of Surplus Standard Items

The OQMG also reviewed the stock position of all standard Quartermaster supplies to determine which items and what quantities of each were surplus to the needs of the War Department for a given period of time. Such stock status studies in 1943 indicated excesses for certain standard items of equipment, but disposi-

tion was deferred pending (1) a review of such studies based on a uniform procedure for estimating future requirements which was then under consideration by the Issues Forecast Committee; (2) a review of such studies based upon more recent and complete data as to actual past issues; and (3) determination of policies affecting the supply status of Table of Allowances property.[129]

It was well into 1944 before methods to determine supply requirements had become sufficiently reliable to enable surpluses of standard items to be estimated with any degree of accuracy. When the supply control system was established in the spring of 1944, progress was made because redistribution and disposal levels were defined, thereby clarifying a question that had heretofore plagued the OQMG, namely, when did excesses reach a level high enough to warrant redistribution of a part of the overstockage to other technical services, the Navy, other federal agencies, or civilian manufacturers. The purpose of procurement planning and inventory control as developed through supply and demand studies was to avoid the creation of excess stocks. The War Department recognized, however, that excesses already existed and that, because of changes in requirements and other factors, additional excesses would be unavoidable. It therefore provided that, when excess quantities were substantial and beyond the needs of the War Department for a reasonable period of time in the future, they should be re-

---

[126] ASF Cir 101, Sec. II, 13 Apr 44, sub: Delegation of Authority to Declare Prop Surplus.

[127] Address, Lt Col W. C. Strum, sub: Redistr and Disposal of Obsolete and Nonstandard Prop and Standard and Limited Standard Prop Excess to Reqmts of QMC, QMs' Conf, 2–4 Oct 44, Camp Lee, Va.

[128] (1) *Ibid.* (2) Memo, Brig Gen H. A. Barnes, OQMG, for CG ASF, 19 May 45, sub: Excess and Surplus Prop, 400.703.

[129] Memo (draft), Gen Scowden for TQMG, Jan 44, sub: Disposal of Serviceable Prop by QMC through 31 Dec 43, 400.703.

distributed, transferred to the war reserve,[130] or disposed of as surplus. To measure excesses for the purpose of disposal decisions, it was established that the United States redistribution and disposal level for purely military items having no application to civilian or war industry would be "a quantity equal to the estimated future requirements for the succeeding 24 months including the projected total authorized stock level." [131] For easily procured items which had a civilian or war industry application the calculation was made on a 12-month instead of a 24-month basis. These two groups of items were designated as classification I and II, respectively, and the chiefs of the technical services were directed to take prompt action to classify items in which significant excesses existed, in accordance with the announced policies on redistribution and disposal levels.

The chiefs of the technical services were instructed to recommend for approval to the Stock Control Division, ASF, lower United States redistribution and disposal levels than those established if the particular item was in critical civilian supply, if it could be easily procured and its retention for operational or stockage purposes above the recommended lower level was not necessary, or if it was an item that deteriorated rapidly. Only when declarations of surplus were made by The Quartermaster General in reference to items which were believed to be in short supply in civilian economy or were needed by other government agencies were such recommendations submitted to Headquarters, ASF. Transfer of redistribution and disposal quantities to the war reserve had to be approved by the director of the Stock Control Division, ASF. The Quartermaster General was responsible, however, for determining what excess Quartermaster items were suitable for redistribution to other services or to civilian industries.[132]

Because the redistribution and disposal level was calculated for the relatively long periods of 12 or 24 months, the quantity of any serviceable standard item would have had to be extremely large for the item to show a redistribution and disposal quantity. Some few items did show a balance, but, for the most part, disposal of such surplus Quartermaster items was negligible during the war and was confined to obsolete and nonstandard items. Thus during the fiscal year 1944 a total of 7,249 line items of obsolete, outmoded, and nonstandard property under Quartermaster accountability was reported by Quartermaster depots to the Procurement Division, Treasury Department, for disposal. Continued review of the supply status of standard items of Quartermaster issue made during 1944, however, resulted in the transfer to other technical services, the AAF, and the Navy Department, of excess quantities of only nine line items to the value of about $1,000,000. Other standard Quartermaster property in excess of War Department requirements, consisting of 18 items with an approximate value of $4,000,000, was reported to the Procurement Division, Treasury Department, for disposal.[133] This analysis of supply and demand studies, which had thus been initiated for the purpose of requesting disposal action where indicated, as well as the analysis of EAM records for the purpose of segregating "inactive" items to see what appropriate disposal action was taken regarding them, continued during the war under the direction of the Stock Control Branch of the Storage and Distribution Division, OQMG. Redistribution,

---

[130] The war reserve consisted of redistribution and disposal quantities of items which constituted good long-term assets against future war needs, which were not suitable for use by civilian or war industry, or for which replacement was sufficiently difficult, or involved such additional expense to the government, as to make final disposal inadvisable. ASF Cir 67, Sec. II, par. 8b (3), 7 Mar 44, sub: Procurement, Inventory, and Disposal Controls.

[131] *Ibid.*, Sec. II, par. 8b (1).

[132] *Ibid.*, Sec. II, par. 8c-f.

[133] Material submitted by S&D Div for Annual Rpt of TQMG to ASF for FY 1944, pp. 5–6.

transfers, and disposals of excess and surplus serviceable property for the 11 months of the fiscal year ending on 31 May 1945 were processed as follows: [134]

Transferred to other WD components . . .		$2,082,000
Transferred to Navy Department		714,000
Transferred to other federal agencies . . .		3,000
Sold to contractors		2,000
Other disposals		157,000
Disposal by Treasury Department	$22,498,000	
Disposal by RFC	376,000	
Disposal by WFA	102,000	
		22,976,000
Total		$25,934,000

Although the initiation of the supply control system eliminated some of the difficulties in reference to surplus disposal encountered within the OQMG, other problems quickly developed as a concomitant of relationships with disposal agencies outside the War Department. This became apparent when the Procurement Division, Treasury Department, first assumed disposal functions for the War Department. Because disposal was a new problem for this agency and it had neither the personnel nor procedure established for handling the volume of surplus goods to be disposed of, the movement of such property from Quartermaster depots tended to lag and gave rise to criticism of the Treasury Department.[135] The prompt removal of surplus declared to the Procurement Division, Treasury Department, was important because it would return idle property to use and would also relieve the Army of storage, protection, and administrative burdens. Fully aware of the importance of this program, the officials of the Treasury Department co-operated to achieve the desired ends.

But if War Department officials were critical of the delays in the removal of surpluses, Treasury Procurement officials objected to the discrepancies which appeared in the declaration forms submitted by personnel of Quartermaster depots. One of the most serious objections made was in reference to inaccurate and incorrect statements of the quantities and conditions of surplus. Such inaccuracies had resulted in situations wherein disposal agencies had sent appraisers and prospective buyers to look at property which either could not be located or was not in the described condition. Moreover, the Army was accustomed to using abbreviations of its nomenclature which were unidentifiable to anyone outside the service, and it was therefore necessary to instruct the depots to describe items so that they could be easily identified. Once property was reported to the disposal agency, it was supposed to be obligated and the property held for its disposal, but apparently Quartermaster depots assumed that, until the property was taken over by the disposal agency, the depots could do whatever they wanted with it. This assumption had to be corrected. If a need existed, it was intended that surplus property might be withdrawn, but this could not be done until the disposal agency had been notified and its approval received. Still another serious complaint had arisen over the disposition of nominal quantities of surplus property and the tendency of depots to submit declarations for insignificant quantities. This question had been raised in the spring of 1944 when the OQMG had recommended local sales for a single item or for groups of items of nonstandard or obsolete surplus property having a value of less than $50 and located at any one station.[136] As provided by amendment of PR 7,[137] no single decla-

[134] Material submitted by S&D Div for Annual Rpt of TQMG to ASF for FY 1945, p. 2.

[135] (1) Address, Col Strum, sub: Redistr and Disposal of Obsolete and Nonstandard Prop and Standard and Limited Standard Prop Excess to Reqmts of QMC, QMs' Conf, 2–4 Oct 44, Camp Lee, Va. (2) Memo, Dir of Readjustment Div, ASF, for TQMG, 18 Feb 44, sub: Transfer of surplus to Treasury Procurement, 400.703.

[136] (1) Memo, Col C. S. Hamilton, OQMG, for Hq ASF, 6 Apr 44, no sub. (2) 1st ind, Dir of Readjustment Div, ASF, to TQMG, 17 Apr 44, on same.

[137] Par. 7–701, as amended 25 May 44.

ration amounting to $100 or less could be reported to a disposal agency for disposition but was to be turned over to the local salvage officer for sale. These criticisms of the declarations being submitted were brought to the attention of the depots for correction in the fall of 1944.[138]

These problems were symptomatic of the administrative difficulties which the Corps encountered in its relationship with successive federal agencies established for the disposal of surplus property under the Surplus Property Act passed in the fall of 1944. The kaleidoscopic changes in the administration of surplus property disposal necessitated frequent reorientations in relationships. Changes in procedure under the regulations issued by the successive agencies controlling disposal compelled changes at the Quartermaster operating level and could not help but delay the rapid disposal of surplus property. The problem of excess and surplus property had been attacked by the War Department during the war years as an important aspect of its stock control operations. Unlike certain other activities, disposal of surplus property constituted a continuing responsibility after V-J Day.[139]

---

[138] (1) Ltr, Gen Owens, OQMG, to CG JQMD, 11 Sep 44, sub: Preparation of SWPA–1 Forms. (2) Address, Col Strum, sub: Redistr and Disposal of Obsolete and Nonstandard Prop and Standard and Limited Standard Prop Excess to Reqmts of QMC, QMs' Conf, 2–4 Oct 44, Camp Lee, Va.

[139] For postwar developments see Kieffer and Risch, The Quartermaster Corps: Organization, Supply, and Services, Vol. II, in preparation for this series.

Bibliographical Note

The World War II historical program of the Quartermaster Corps began officially on 11 July 1942, as an integral part of the larger War Department program, with the establishment of the Historical Section in the Office of The Quartermaster General and later of historical units at the various QMC field installations. From the first this program was envisaged as consisting of two parts: a "first narrative" phase, during which monographic studies of particular activities would be prepared as opportunity offered and as nearly concurrently with the events themselves as possible; and a "final history" phase, during which an over-all, co-ordinated, comprehensive history would be prepared in a series of volumes, based upon existing monographs and such additional research as might be necessary.

In the Historical Section, OQMG, approximately thirty monographs were projected, of which twenty-one have been published under the title, "QMC Historical Studies." They constitute the framework of research upon which are based the two volumes in the present series covering Quartermaster activities in the zone of interior. A number of unpublished studies are also on file with the Historical Section.

In addition, the historical units at the field installations prepared reports and monographs under the supervision of the Historical Section,

OQMG. Over a hundred of these are on file with the section. Only those of the Chicago Depot have been published, and they appear under the title "CQMD Historical Studies."

Late in the war, the Review Section of the Historical Division, War Department Special Staff, reviewed and approved the monographs of the Historical Section and of the field installations as meeting the standards established by the division. A considerable number of historical reports both from the section and the field installations were not submitted for approval because they were incomplete or fragmentary. Nevertheless, such reports frequently contain valuable operational information.

Although this volume makes extensive use of the approved, published monographic series, in all cases the original collection of documentary material has been reviewed and citations have been made directly from it. This has been possible because these collections of notes—largely photostatic copies—have remained on file with the Historical Section. When the present volumes are completed, these notes will be deposited with the Historical Records Section, Departmental Records Branch, Adjutant General's Office.

Since many of the monographs were written and published before the end of the war, they do not offer full coverage of Quartermaster activities for the war years. Obviously, too, the continuity required for a co-ordinated, comprehensive, final history is not provided in the individual monographs, although they are far more detailed within their respective fields than this volume can be. As a consequence, a considerable amount of fresh research had to be done to fill intervening gaps and complete the record of the war years.

This source material, as well as that used in the monographs, was located in the central files of the OQMG, maintained by the Mail and Records Branch, or in the storage files in the Technical Records Section, Departmental Records Branch, Adjutant General's Office, in Alexandria, Va. The materials include circular letters, office orders, intraoffice memoranda; correspondence with field installations, with other government agencies, and with industry; inspection reports; research and development reports, organization charts, manuals and related technical data; directives from, reports to, and correspondence with agencies exercising controls over Quartermaster operations; transcripts of conferences and interviews; and numerous other materials. In all cases, footnote citations indicate the type of document used. If such identification is not made, the document is a part of the intraoffice correspondence of the OQMG.

These records are classified according to the War Department Decimal File System, supplemented by further breakdowns originated by the Mail and Records Branch, OQMG. The central files are divided into several main groups: geographic, subject, personnel, commercial, and miscellaneous. The 400 series is probably the most important group of files since it covers supplies, services, and equipment broken down into numerous subheads on procurement, storage, and analyses and tests of items. Other files useful in the preparation of this volume are as follows:

160 series—Contracts, damages, penalties, bids
420 series—Clothing and Equipage
430 series—Subsistence
457 series—Packing Materials

In addition to the central files much use was also made of "reading files," "policy books," "diaries," and like material in the files of the operating units. Many of these were discarded and destroyed by the operating units when no longer needed for current business, but while in existence they frequently afforded the best approach for the reconstruction of any given phase of Quartermaster activity. Documents of this nature generally were duplicates of the originals filed in the Mail and Records Branch, but were less dispersed than the file copies. They therefore not only often furnished the most useful body of material on a specific subject but also offered keys to further research in the originals, though finding the latter was often a laborious task because they usually were widely dispersed under a multitude of subject headings.

In addition to documentary sources, frequent interviews with key operating personnel provided the means for filling in gaps in the documentary evidence, reconciling apparently conflicting evidence, and helping to explain abstruse technical problems.

Quartermaster source material was further supplemented by the use of similar types of materials of pertinent divisions of the Army Service Forces, particularly those of the Control Division, on file with the Historical Records Section, Departmental Records Branch, Adjutant General's Office. Historical reports and monographs, prepared within the ASF, and on file with the Office of the Chief of Military History, Department of the Army, also were used, together with a number of historical studies of the Army Ground Forces, prepared by its Historical Section.

Published materials used in the preparation of this volume include the following:

Baxter, James P., *Scientists Against Time* (Boston, 1946)

Bureau of the Budget, *The United States at War* (Washington, 1946)

CQMD Historical Studies:

> Massen, Marion, *Canned Meats Procurement for the Armed Forces During World War II* (March 1946)
>
> Massen, Marion, *Central Procurement of Dehydrated Vegetables for the Armed Forces* (March 1945)
>
> Massen, Marion, *The History of the Helmet Liner* (April 1944)
>
> Porges, Walter, *The Subsistence Research Laboratory* (May 1943)

Civilian Production Administration, *Industrial Mobilization for War—History of the War Production Board and Predecessor Agencies, 1940–1945* (Washington, 1947)

Federal Register

Industrial College of the Armed Forces, *Industrial Mobilization Course:* lectures, January 1945–April 1949

March, Peyton C., *The Nation at War* (New York, 1932)

Nelson, Otto L., Jr., *National Security and the General Staff* (Washington, 1936)

Novick, David, Melvin Anshen, and W. C. Truppner, *Wartime Production Controls* (New York, 1949)

QMC Historical Studies:

> Bradford, Donald F., *Methods of Forecasting War Requirements for Quartermaster Supplies* (May 1946)
>
> Cassidy, Elliott, *The Development of Meat, Dairy, Poultry, and Fish Products for the Army* (October 1944)
>
> Pitkin, Thomas M. and Herbert R. Rifkind, *Procurement Planning in the Quartermaster Corps, 1920–1940* (March 1943)

QMC Historical Studies—Continued

> Pitkin, Thomas M., *Quartermaster Equipment for Special Forces* (February 1944)
>
> Rifkind, Herbert R., *Fresh Foods for the Armed Forces: The Quartermaster Market Center System, 1941–1948* (1951)
>
> Risch, Erna, *Fuels for Global Conflict* (revised edition, 1952)
>
> Risch, Erna, *A Wardrobe for the Women of the Army* (October 1945)
>
> Risch, Erna and Thomas M. Pitkin, *Clothing the Soldier of World War II* (September 1946)
>
> Stauffer, Alvin P., *Quartermaster Depot Storage and Distribution Operations* (May 1948)
>
> Thatcher, Harold W., *The Development of Special Rations for the Army* (September 1944)
>
> Thatcher, Harold W., *Planning for Industrial Mobilization, 1920–1940* (August 1943)
>
> Thatcher, Harold W., *The Packaging and Packing of Subsistence for the Army* (March 1945)
>
> Yoshpe, Harry B., *Labor Problems in Quartermaster Procurement, 1939–1944* (April 1945)
>
> Yoshpe, Harry B., *Production Control in the Quartermaster Corps, 1939–1944* (December 1944)
>
> Yoshpe, Harry B., *The Small Business Man and Quartermaster Contracts, 1940–1942* (April 1943)
>
> Yoshpe, Harry B. and Marion Massen, *Procurement Policies and Procedures in the Quartermaster Corps During World War II* (June 1947)

Quartermaster Food and Container Institute for the Armed Forces, *The Subsistence Research and Development Laboratory: A Report of Wartime Problems in Subsistence Research and Development* (13 monographs, 1947——)

Quartermaster Review

United States Army in World War II:

> Wardlow, Chester C., *The Transportation Corps: Responsibilities, Organization, and Operations* (Washington, 1951)

United States Army in World War II—Continued

Watson, Mark Skinner, *Chief of Staff: Prewar Plans and Preparations* (Washington, 1950)

U. S. Congress, *Hearings of the Military Affairs Committees of the Senate and House, and sub-committees of the Appropriations Committees of the Senate and House, 1940–1944*

U. S. Congress, House, 77th Congress, First Session. *Hearings Before the Committee on Military Affairs on HR. 5630—A Bill to Make Provision for the Construction Activities of the Army* (Washington, 1941)

U. S. Congress, Senate. 77th Congress, First Session. *Additional Report of the Special Committee Investigating the National Defense Program—Camp and Cantonment Investigations* (Washington, 1941)

U. S. Congress, Senate. 77th Congress, First Session. *Hearings Before a Special Committee Investigating the National Defense Program* (Washington, 1941)

United States Statutes at Large

War Department, *Annual Reports of The Quartermaster General for 1919, 1920; Annual Reports of the Secretary of War; Biennial Report of the Chief of Staff of the United States Army July 1, 1939 to June 30, 1941*

Worsley, Thomas B., *Wartime Economic Stabilization and the Efficiency of Government Procurement* (Washington, 1949)

List of Abbreviations

AAA	Antiaircraft Artillery	CQMD	Chicago Quartermaster Depot
AAF	Army Air Forces	CRL	Climatic Research Laboratory
ACofS	Assistant Chief of Staff	CWS	Chemical Warfare Service
AG	Adjutant General	EAM	Electric accounting machine
AGF	Army Ground Forces	ETO	European Theater of Operations
AGO	Adjutant General's Office	ETOUSA	European Theater of Operations, United States Army
AIC	Army Industrial College		
AMA	Agricultural Marketing Administration	F&L	Fuels and lubricants
		FO	Food order
AMS	Agricultural Marketing Service	FY	Fiscal year
ANC	Army Nurse Corps	G–3	Operations and Training Division, General Staff
ANMB	Army and Navy Munitions Board		
ANPB	Army-Navy Petroleum Board	G–4	Supply Division, General Staff
AR	Army Regulation	GD	General depot
ASF	Army Service Forces	GFE	Government-furnished equipment and facilities
ASFD	Army Service Forces Depot		
ASP	Army Supply Program	GFM	Government-furnished material
ASW	Assistant Secretary of War	GI	General issue
ATGD	Atlanta General Depot	GMPR	General Maximum Price Regulation
BEW	Board of Economic Warfare		
BQMD	Boston Quartermaster Depot	GO	General Order
CA	Corps area	GPO	Government Printing Office
C&E	Clothing and equipage	HR	House of Representatives
CBI	China–Burma–India Theater of Operations	IBM	International Business Machines
		ICAF	Industrial College of the Armed Forces
CCC	Civilian Conservation Corps		
CE	Corps of Engineers	IG	Inspector General
CEQMD	Charlotte Quartermaster Depot	JAG	Judge Advocate General
CG	Commanding general	JCQMD	Jersey City Quartermaster Depot
CinC	Commander in chief	JQMD	Jeffersonville Quartermaster Depot
CMP	Controlled Materials Plan		
CO	Commanding officer	M Day	Mobilization Day
CofS	Chief of Staff	MHE	Materials-handling equipment
CofT	Chief of Transportation	MPS	Master production schedule
COGD	Columbus General Depot	MT	Motor transport
ComZ	Communications zone	MTO	Mediterranean Theater of Operations
CPA	Central Pacific Area		

MTOUSA	Mediterranean Theater of Operations, United States Army	PR	Procurement Regulation
MTS	Motor Transport Service	PRP	Production Requirements Plan
NATO	North African Theater of Operations	QM	Quartermaster
		QMB	Quartermaster Board
NATOUSA	North African Theater of Operations, United States Army	QMC	Quartermaster Corps
		QMCTC	Quartermaster Corps Technical Committee
NDAC	National Defense Advisory Commission	QMD	Quartermaster depot
		QMMC	Quartermaster market center
NRC	National Research Committee	QMMCS	Quartermaster market center system
NYA	National Youth Administration		
NYPE	New York Port of Embarkation	*QMR*	*The Quartermaster Review*
NYQMPO	New York Quartermaster Purchasing Office	QMSO	Quartermaster supply officer
		R&D	Research and Development
OASA	Office of the Assistant Secretary of the Army	RMASFD	Richmond Army Service Forces Depot
OASW	Office of the Assistant Secretary of War	SAASFD	San Antonio Army Service Forces Depot
OCI	Office of the Chief of Infantry	SAE	Society of Automotive Engineers
OCM	Ordnance Committee minutes	S&D	Storage and Distribution
ODT	Office of Defense Transportation	SB	Supply Bulletin
OEM	Office of Emergency Management	SFAW	Solid Fuels Administration for War
OIC	Officer in charge	SFPE	San Francisco Port of Embarkation
OO	Office order		
OPA	Office of Price Administration	SG	Surgeon General
OP&C	Organization Planning and Control	SGO	Surgeon General's Office
		SOS	Services of Supply
OPM	Office of Production Management	SP	South Pacific
		SPA	South Pacific Area
OQMG	Office of The Quartermaster General	SPAB	Supply, Priorities, and Allocations Board
OSRD	Office of Scientific Research and Development	SR&DL	Subsistence Research and Development Laboratory
OUSW	Office of the Under Secretary of War	SRL	Subsistence Research Laboratory
		SSUSA	Special Staff, United States Army
PAB	Procurement Assignment Board	SvC	Service command
P&C	Planning and Control	SW	Secretary of War
PAW	Petroleum Administration for War	SWP	Southwest Pacific
		SWPA	Southwest Pacific Area
PE	Port of embarkation	SWPC	Smaller War Plants Corporation
POA	Pacific Ocean Areas	T/A	Table of Allowances
PQMD	Philadelphia Quartermaster Depot	TAG	The Adjutant General
		T/BA	Table of Basic Allowances

TICAF	The Industrial College of the Armed Forces	USASOS	United States Army Services of Supply (in Southwest Pacific Area)
T/E	Table of Equipment		
TM	Technical Manual	USFET	United States Forces, European Theater
T/O	Table of Organization		
T/O&E	Table of Organization and Equipment	USW	Under Secretary of War
		V-J Day	Victory over Japan Day
TQMG	The Quartermaster General	WAAC	Women's Army Auxiliary Corps
UK	United Kingdom	WAC	Women's Army Corps
USAFCPA	United States Army Forces, Central Pacific Area	WD	War Department
		WDGS	War Department General Staff
USAFFE	United States Army Forces in the Far East	WFA	War Food Administration
		WPA	Work Projects Administration
USAFPOA	United States Army Forces, Pacific Ocean Areas	WPB	War Production Board

UNITED STATES ARMY IN WORLD WAR II

The following volumes have been published or are in press:

The War Department
Chief of Staff: Prewar Plans and Preparations
Washington Command Post: The Operations Division
Strategic Planning for Coalition Warfare: 1941–1942
Strategic Planning for Coalition Warfare: 1943–1944
Global Logistics and Strategy: 1940–1943
Global Logistics and Strategy: 1943–1945
The Army and Economic Mobilization
The Army and Industrial Manpower
The Army Ground Forces
The Organization of Ground Combat Troops
The Procurement and Training of Ground Combat Troops
The Army Service Forces
The Organization and Role of the Army Service Forces
The Western Hemisphere
The Framework of Hemisphere Defense
Guarding the United States and Its Outposts
The War in the Pacific
The Fall of the Philippines
Guadalcanal: The First Offensive
Victory in Papua
CARTWHEEL: The Reduction of Rabaul
Seizure of the Gilberts and Marshalls
Campaign in the Marianas
The Approach to the Philippines
Leyte: The Return to the Philippines
Triumph in the Philippines
Okinawa: The Last Battle
Strategy and Command: The First Two Years
The Mediterranean Theater of Operations
Northwest Africa: Seizing the Initiative in the West
Sicily and the Surrender of Italy
Salerno to Cassino
Cassino to the Alps
The European Theater of Operations
Cross-Channel Attack
Breakout and Pursuit
The Lorraine Campaign
The Siegfried Line Campaign
The Ardennes: Battle of the Bulge
The Last Offensive

    The Supreme Command
    Logistical Support of the Armies, Volume I
    Logistical Support of the Armies, Volume II
The Middle East Theater
    The Persian Corridor and Aid to Russia
The China-Burma-India Theater
    Stilwell's Mission to China
    Stilwell's Command Problems
    Time Runs Out in CBI
The Technical Services
    The Chemical Warfare Service: Organizing for War
    The Chemical Warfare Service: From Laboratory to Field
    The Chemical Warfare Service: Chemicals in Combat
    The Corps of Engineers: Troops and Equipment
    The Corps of Engineers: The War Against Japan
    The Corps of Engineers: The War Against Germany
    The Corps of Engineers: Military Construction in the United States
    The Medical Department: Hospitalization and Evacuation; Zone of Interior
    The Medical Department: Medical Service in the Mediterranean and Minor Theaters
    The Ordnance Department: Planning Munitions for War
    The Ordnance Department: Procurement and Supply
    The Ordnance Department: On Beachhead and Battlefront
    The Quartermaster Corps: Organization, Supply, and Services, Volume I
    The Quartermaster Corps: Organization, Supply, and Services, Volume II
    The Quartermaster Corps: Operations in the War Against Japan
    The Quartermaster Corps: Operations in the War Against Germany
    The Signal Corps: The Emergency
    The Signal Corps: The Test
    The Signal Corps: The Outcome
    The Transportation Corps: Responsibilities, Organization, and Operations
    The Transportation Corps: Movements, Training, and Supply
    The Transportation Corps: Operations Overseas
Special Studies
    Chronology: 1941–1945
    Military Relations Between the United States and Canada: 1939–1945
    Rearming the French
    Three Battles: Arnaville, Altuzzo, and Schmidt
    The Women's Army Corps
    Civil Affairs: Soldiers Become Governors
    Buying Aircraft: Materiel Procurement for the Army Air Forces
    The Employment of Negro Troops
    Manhattan: The U.S. Army and the Atomic Bomb
Pictorial Record
    The War Against Germany and Italy: Mediterranean and Adjacent Areas
    The War Against Germany: Europe and Adjacent Areas
    The War Against Japan

INDEX

Adjutant General, The, 53, 140, 181, 327
Adjutant General, Office of The, 361
Administrative Division
　nature of, 5, 6, 11
　need for reorganization of, 11, 12
　redesignation of, 12
　subdivision of, in 1940, 11
　transfer of planning functions of, 12, 210
Administrative organization. *See* Office of The Quartermaster General.
Administrator of Priorities, 58
Advisory Board, Research and Development Branch, 84
Aero Medical Research Laboratory, 177, 179
Agricultural Marketing Administration, 318
Agricultural Marketing Service, 316, 317, 318, 319, 320
Agriculture, Department of
　development of dehydration by, 199
　inspection activities of, 316, 318, 319
　priority ratings by, 299
　proposal for centralizing food procurement in, 30–31
　relations of, with Subsistence Division, 231, 232
　research by, 164, 167, 177
　use of laboratory facilities of, 84
Air Corps. *See* Army Air Corps.
Alaska Defense Command, 124
Alaskan clothing list, 75–76
Allocation System
　CMP as, 295–96
　early mandatory orders of, 292–93
　modifications of, 293
　PRP as, 293–95
　shortcomings of early, 293
American Bantam Company, 140, 141
American Can Company, 197
American Expeditionary Forces (AEF), 20, 326
American Gas Machine Company, 85, 148
Ames Baldwin Wyoming Company, 134, 136
Armored Force Board, 171
Armour and Company, 193
Army Air Corps, 70, 72
Army Air Forces, 74
Army Medical Center, 316
Army and Navy Munitions Board (ANMB)
　allocation of materials by, 294–95
　assignment of priorities by, 58, 284, 291
　commodity committees of, 56
　location of idle equipment by, 303
　petroleum inspection and, 320
　and priorities system, 290, 291
　requirements and, 223, 294
Army-Navy Petroleum Board (ANPB)
　co-ordination of petroleum requirements with, 239
　relation of Fuels and Lubricants to, 46, 240

Army-Navy Petroleum Board (ANPB)—Continued
　War Department representation on, 35
Army Nurse Corps, 110, 113, 116
Army Supply Program
　April 1942, 222
　August 1943, 217, 221, 225
　August 1944, 225
　basis for revisions of, 223
　civilian supply requirements in, 282
　definition of, 221
　evolution of, 221–25
　February 1943, 221, 237
　long-range planning of, 230
　phases of, 223
　predecessors of, 221–22
　replacement of, by Supply Control System, 227
　September 1942, 221
　shortcomings of, 226, 381
　uses of, 211, 222, 223, 224, 226, 302
Assignment of Claims Act, 305
Assistant Chief of Staff for Operations, 42, 350, 366
Assistant Secretary of War
　redesignation of, 247
　responsibility of, 247
Association of Cotton Textile Merchants of New York, 279
Atlanta ASF Depot, 378
Atlantic and Pacific Tea Company, 319
Autocar Company, 143

Back-up storage plan, 342
Bag, multiwall paper, 206
Bag, Reynolds, 204
Bag, waterproof, 204
Bag, X-crepe, 204
Bakery equipment, field
　contributions of industry to, 152, 155,
　criticism of, 153, 155
　development of mobile, 152, 155
　standardization of M-1942 field bake oven for, 152
　standardization of mobile unit, M-1945, 156
　testing of, 152, 155–56
　use of World War I, 152
Bakery Section, Subsistence Branch, 39, 40
Baling
　of clothing and equipage, 357
　increase in productivity of, 358
　new method of, 358
Barnes, Col. Harold A., 23
Barracks bag
　criticism of, 127, 130
　denim, 127
　redesign of, 127

Barracks bag—Continued
  substitution of duffel bag for, 130
Bath units, mobile
  development of lightweight model of, 166
  divided responsibility for development of, 165, 166
  inadequacy of, 165, 166
  1941 type of, 164
  twelve-shower head in, 165
  twenty-four-shower head in, 165, 166
Beef, boneless
  advantages of, 194
  development of, 192–94
  mandatory orders for, 298, 299
Blankets, wool, 69, 70
Blitz can. See Can, 5-gallon, development of:
Bobrink, Col. Henry W., 219
Boot
  Blucher, 106
  development of combat, 103–04
  development of tropical, 110
  disadvantages of jungle, 109–10
  Pershing, 102
  production difficulties in jungle, 109
  standardization of combat, 104
  standardization of jungle, 109
Boston QM Depot
  conservation program at, 103
  GFE program at, 289
  purchase of footwear at, 8, 243, 244
  research in footwear at, 77, 108, 109, 110
  shoe inspection at, 308, 310
Bramani rubber sole, 110
British Army Staff, 281
British Ministry of War Transport, 328
Browning, Brig. Gen. Albert J., 96n
Bruce, Howard, 227
Buckner, Maj. Gen. S. B., 72, 124
Budget and Accounting Division, 24
Budget Advisory Committee, 55, 57
Bureau of Animal Industry, 316, 318
Bureau of the Budget, 29, 55, 57
Bureau of Entomology and Plant Quarantine, 164
Bureau of Standards, 68, 149, 159
Butter products, 200–201
Buttons
  substitution of plastic for brass, 64
  use of brass, 63
  use of plastic, 74
Buy American Act, 257, 258

California Dried Fruit Association, 200
California QM Depot
  centralized purchase of Pacific Coast petroleum products at, 250
  experimentation with decentralized procurement at, 252
Camp Lee, 80, 95, 100
Can, 5-gallon, 144–46
Can cleaner, portable, 144

Cans, tin
  coating for, 203
  conservation of, 202–03
  labels on, 203
  use of substitutes for, 203, 204
Cantonment Division, 5
Carriers, ammunition
  development of, 127
  use of cargo pockets as, 127
Carter's spread, 201
Central Pacific Base Command, 230
Century Machine Company, 152
Charles Martin & Company, 320, 321n
Chemical Section, Research and Development Branch, 118
Chemical Warfare Service, 97, 120, 240, 261
Chevrolet Company, 143
Chicago QM Depot
  assignment of items for centralized procurement at, 250, 251
  co-operation with industry by, 85, 102
  GFE program at, 289
  prewar area served by, 330
  purchase of nonperishables by, 319
  status in 1940, 330
  subsistence procurement at, 182
  Subsistence Research Laboratory and, 35, 36, 38, 176
  use of commercial storage space by, 336
Chief of Engineers, 17, 156, 166
Chief of Staff, USA, 80, 104
Chief of Staff for Matériel, SOS, 231
Chief of Transportation, 325
Chief Veterinarian, Office of The Surgeon General, 317
Cincinnati Field Survey, 29
Cincinnati Ordnance District, 315
Civil Affairs Division, Special Staff, 281
Civilian Conservation Corps (CCC), 7, 17, 308, 329, 330, 387, 388
Civilian Personnel Affairs Division, 24
Civilian Supply
  administrative units for, 281, 282
  estimating requirements for, 211–12
  petroleum requirements for, 240
  QM participation in, 282
  QM responsibility in, 281
Civilian Supply Section, Requirements Branch, 281
Classification. See Standardization.
Clay, Maj. Gen. Lucius D., 227
Cleveland Ordnance District, 315
Cleveland Plan
  comparison of, with Kansas City Plan, 338
  determination of storage rates under, 339
  origin of, 338
Climatic Research Laboratory
  establishment of, 81
  testing program of, 81, 84, 87
Clothing
  development of specialized types of, 90, 122
  thermal protection of, 121

Clothing—Continued
  weight factor in, 121
Clothing, cold climate
  adoption of pile in, 90
  development of, 76
  use of layering pinciple in, 88
Clothing, jungle combat
  design of, 99, 100
  development of, 99–101
  improved fabrics for, 99, 100, 101
  opposition to one-piece suit in, 100
  standardization of, 100, 101
  substitution of two-piece suit in, 100
  testing of, 100
Clothing, summer combat
  camouflage patterns for, 97, 98
  development of, 97–99
  gas protection features of, 97
  simplification of design of, 97, 99
  specialized types of, 19
Clothing, winter combat
  development of, 90ff.
  pile liner in, 95, 96
  simplification of, 90, 92
  standardization of, 90
  supply of, 96, 97
  use of layering principle in, 88, 90, 92, 94, 95, 96
Clothing, women's
  for ANC, 113
  development of, 110–17
  for hospital use, 113–15
  standardization of, 115, 116
  tropical, 116
  use of layering principle in, 116
  for WAC, 110–13
  winter, 116
  for work, 115–16
Clothing and Equipage
  production lead time required for, 361
  stocks on hand in 1940 of, 361
Clothing and Equipage Branch, Storage and Distribution Division
  establishment of size tariffs by, 370
  transfer from Supply Division of, 30, 76
Clothing and Equipage Branch, Supply Division
  estimating of requirements by, 210
  in relation to developmental work, 30, 75, 76
  transfer of, 30, 76
Clothing Section, Research and Development Branch, 96, 100
Clothing and Textile Branch, 298
Coast Guard, 323
Code Marking Policy Committee, 359
Cohen, Lt. Col. Robert L., 94
Cold Climate Unit, Standardization Branch, 76
Cold Storage
  back-up storage plan for, 342
  establishment of assembly and distribution points for, 340

Cold Storage—Continued
  inadequate facilities for, 339–40, 341
  measures for relieving shortage of, 341, 342
  for reserve stocks, 340
Coleman Lamp and Stove Company, 85, 148, 149
Columbus ASF Depot, 353, 375
Combined Chiefs of Staff, 387
Combined Civil Affairs Committee, 240, 281
Combined Production Resources Board, 297
Commissary General of Purchases, 3, 4
Commissary General of Subsistence, 35
Committee on Jungle Clothing, 100
Committee on Purchases of Blind-Made Products, 245, 257, 258
Commodity Credit Corporation, 299 ,299n
Commodity Warrant Plan, 294–95
Comptroller General, 142
Compulsory Orders, 297, 298, 299
Conservation
  aluminum, 60, 61
  chromium, 62
  copper, 63–64
  cordage fiber, 68
  duck, 71–72
  food, 235
  leather, 73
  need for, of raw materials, 58, 59
  nickel, 62
  nylon, 68, 74
  QM policy on, 59–60
  and review of specifications, 60, 62, 66, 71
  rubber, 66–68
  silk, 70–71
  steel and alloy metals, 61–63
  tin, 65, 203, 203n
  wool, 68–70
  zinc, 65
Conservation Orders, 293, 300
Conservation Steering Committee
  establishment of, 60
  functions of, 60
Construction Division
  and depot expansion, 333
  re-establishment of, 6
  transfer of, 16–18
Consumption factors
  basis of, 234, 241
  definition of, 234, 241
  expression of, 215–16
  problems in theater, 235, 236
  refinement of, in Z/I, 234–35
  in theater of operations, 216
  in zone of interior, 216
Consumption and inventory records, 242
Containers, collapsible, 144
Continental Can Company, 197
Contract delinquency
  causes of, 285–87
  depot officers and, 288

Contract delinquency—Continued
  efforts of contractors to reduce, 287
  labor shortages and, 267, 268
  QM policies to reduce, 288
Contract Examination Branch, Planning and Control
    Division, 248
Contract placement
  avoidance of labor congested areas in, 267–69
  factors affecting, 265
  impact of SWPC on, 266–67
  in small plants, 266, 267
Contracting officers
  efforts to expedite deliveries, 288
  expansion of authority of, 255, 256
  pressures exerted on, 265–66
  and relief from penalties, 275
Contractors
  assistance in labor problems of, 307–08
  efforts to reduce delinquency, 287
  financial assistance to, 305–07
Contracts
  amendment of, 256
  approval of, 255
  avoidance of congested labor areas in placement of,
    267–69
  cost-plus-fixed-fee, 271, 333
  damages for delays in, 267
  depot responsibility for, 255
  development of short form of, 260–61
  deviations from standard, 255
  improvement of techniques in negotiations, 271–72
  negotiation of, 252–55
  new forms for, 256, 260
  placement policies and problems, 265ff.
  price adjustments in, 271
  and pricing policies, 269–71
  renegotiation of, 275–79
Contracts and Claims Branch, Supply Division, 12
Control Division, SOS
  and organizational developments, 23, 27, 28, 40
  and stock control, 364, 366, 377
  survey of motor transport by, 22
Control Service, OQMG, 6
Controlled Materials Plan
  announcement of, 295
  purpose of, 224, 295
  QM difficulties under, 295–96
Cooking outfit, small detachment
  development of, 151–52
  standardization of, 151
Cooking outfit, 20-man
  development of, 150
  modifications of, 150
  standardization of, 150, 151
Coordinating Research Council, 143
Corbin, Brig. Gen. Clifford L., 76, 249
Corp areas, 40
Cost analysis
  advantages of, 270

Cost analysis—Continued
  criticism of, 270
  establishment of facilities for, 270, 279
  need for, 269
Cost Analysis Branch, 270
Cotton Textile Controls, 296–97
Cowles, Col. David H., 90
Critical Tool Service, 303

Defense Aid Division, OQMG, 280, 325
Defense Aid Supply Committee, 280
Defense Plant Corporation, 248, 304, 305
Defense Special Trains, 266
Defense Supplies Rating Plan, 293
Dehydration
  advantages of, 198
  application of, to foods, 198–99, 200
  co-operative efforts of industry and QMC in,
    199–200
  of eggs and milk, 200
Depot Division
  establishment of, 15, 44
  functions of, 15, 16, 176, 349, 355
  redesignation of, 324
  weakness of, 16
Depot Operations Branch, Storage and Distribution
    Division. See also Depot Division; Storage Branch.
  co-ordination of packing instructions by, 356
  and development of space control program, 343, 344
  establishment of, 324, 349
  functions of, 350
  and responsibility for materials-handling equipment,
    349, 350
Depot Service, SOS, 43
Depots
  activities at, 38
  administrative changes in, for handling stock control
    operations, 377–78
  application of controlled warehouse plan to, 345
  autonomy of, 15, 345
  branch, definition of, 42
  centralized co-ordination of, 45
  commercial opposition to manufacturing at, 246
  control of storage space in, 343, 344
  delegation of responsibility to, 45, 255
  expansion of, 251
  function of TQMG in relation to general, 43
  general, 42
  improved procurement organization of, 249
  manufacturing operations at, 245–46
  materials handling by, 347ff.
  number of, in 1939, 38
  origin of, 4
  promotion of efficiency at, 352–53
  reassignment of items for centralized purchase at,
    251
  role of, in stock control, 372, 375
  types of, 38
  use of mechanical equipment by, 347–49

Depots (QM)
  classification of, 324
  distribution and number of, in 1940, 329
  filler, 325
  key, 325
  regional distributing, 324, 326
  reserve, 325
Deputy Director for Inspection, 312
Deputy Quartermaster General for Administration and
  Management
  establishment of, 33
  responsibilities of, 33–34
Deputy Quartermaster General for Supply Planning
  and Operations
  establishment of, 33
  redefinition of responsibilities, 377
Desert Training Center, 104
Desert Warfare Board, 99
Developmental work. *See also* Research; *individual*
  items.
  administrative organization for, 75–96
  on combat footgear, 102–10
  on combat headgear, 101–02
  industrial co-operation in, 85–86
  on jungle combat clothing, 99–101
  on leather protection, 120
  on organizational equipment, 138–72
  on packaging and packing, 201–06
  on personal equipment, 123–38
  on rations, 177–201
  standardization procedure in, 76–88
  on summer combat clothing, 97–99
  on textiles for military use, 116–20
  on winter combat clothing, 88–97
  on women's clothing, 110–17
Dillon, Col. H. T., 325
Director of Procurement, 34, 310, 312
Director of Storage and Distribution, 34
Dispenser, portable gasoline, 144
Distribution. *See also* Supply administration; Supply
  Control System.
  co-ordination of, 327
  flow of supplies in, 327, 328
  holding and reconsignment points in, 325
  lessons of World War I in, 326–27
Distribution Division, SOS, 366
Distribution factors
  application of, to requirements, 218
  rejection of, 218
Distribution requirements
  computation of, 218–21
  definition of, 218
  introduction of "carry-over" method of computing,
  219
Division of Defense Aid, 325
Doriot, Col. Georges F., 76
Duck
  centralization of QM procurement of, 264
  centralized WD procurement of, 263

Duck—Continued
  efforts to extend production of, 71, 72
  handled by pool, 263–64
  revision of specifications for, 71
  shortage of, 71, 263
Duck and Webbing Pool
  background for, 263
  operation of, 264
Duffel bag, 130
Dunn, Capt. Cecil G., 199n

E Orders, 293
EAM reports, 363, 364
Editing Branch, Storage and Distribution Division, 378
Eggs
  dehydration of, 200
  emergency order procurement of, 300
Eighth Corps Area Depot, 330
Eisenhower, Lt. Gen. Dwight D., 20, 94
Electric Accounting Machine System, 363–64
Embarkation Service, 5
Emergency Orders, 300
Emergency Price Control Act, 273, 275
Engineers, Corps of
  assumption of construction activities by, 16–17, 22,
  156, 333
  development of camouflage by, 98
  developmental work on petroleum-handling equipment by, 144
  responsibility of, for bathing equipment, 165, 166
Equipage Section, Supply Division, 264
Equipment. *See also under individual items.*
  annual surveys of, 52–54, 75
  specialized types of, 124, 172
  use of World War I, 123
Equipment Expenditure Program, 222
Equipment, organizational
  automotive, 139–43
  bakeries, field, 152–56
  bath units, mobile, 164–66
  development of, 138–71
  field range, 146–52
  laundry, 163–64
  petroleum-handling, 144–46
  refrigerator, 150-cubic foot portable, 158–60
  salvage, mobile, 160–63
  semitrailer, refrigerated, 157–58
  tentage, 166–68
  tents, 168–72
Equipment, personal. *See also under individual items.*
  development of, 123–38
Ethyl Corporation, 85, 148, 321
Excess stocks
  control measures for, initiated in 1943, 381
  difficulty of station classification of, 382, 383, 384
  disposal of, 386, 387, 388, 390
  effect of downward revision of stock levels on, 383
  effect of supply control system on, 388
  factors contributing to development of, 379–81

Excess stocks—Continued
    function of Property Utilization Officer in relation
        to, 385
    organization for handling, 385–86
    redistribution of, 384, 388, 389
Executive Order 9001, 258, 289
Expediting Production funds, 304
Export Control Act of 1940, 298

Facilities Section, Production Service, 31
Factor Control Committee, 231
Federal Company, 143
Federal Emergency Warehouse Association, 337, 338
Federal Prison Industries, Inc., 257, 258
Federal Specifications Board, 143
Federal Standard Stock Catalog, 364
Field Artillery Board, AGF, 131
Field Bag, M-1936, 124
Field baking equipment. See Bakery equipment, field.
Field Headquarters, Chicago, 39, 250
Field Pack. See Pack, field.
Field Range
    development of, M–1937, 146
    effect of materials shortages on, 61, 146–47
    maintenance problem of, 147–49
    standardization of, 146
    World War I type of, 146
Finance and Accounting Division, OQMG, 5
First War Powers Act, 254, 272
Fiscal Division, OQMG, 12, 30, 55
Fish and Wildlife Service, Department of Interior, 177
Food Distribution Administration, 299n
Food Requirements and Allocations Committee, 232
Food Service Program
    elements of, 39, 40
    establishment of, 40
    in relation to conservation, 40
    as staff agency, 41
Food Service Section, 39, 40
Footwear
    boot, combat, 104
    boot, jungle, 109, 110
    boot, tropical combat, 110
    development of, 102–10
    improvement of water-resistance in, 120
    mold-preventives for, 120–21
    overshoes, arctic, 108
    shoepacs, 106, 108
    shoes, service, Type I, 102, 103
    shoes, service, Type II, 103
    shoes, service, Type III, 104
    trenchfoot problem, 104, 106, 108
    women's, 116–17
Forbes, Dr. William, 84
Ford Motorcar Company, 143
Foreign Economic Administration, 282
Fork-lift Trucks
    advantages in using, 347
    increased production of, 352

Fork-lift Trucks—Continued
    maintenance of, 352
Forward pricing
    definition of, 270
    in relation to renegotiation, 279
Fruits
    canned, 197
    dehydrated, 197–200
    frozen, 197
    inspection of, 315, 316
    set-aside orders for, 300
Fuel and Construction Materials, Supply Division, 248
Fuel and Heavy Equipment Branch, 71
Fuel and Utilities Branch, Executive Office, 27
Fuels Branch, Resources Division, ASF, 239
Fuels and Lubricants Division
    and civilian supply, 282
    commodity organization of, 23, 34–35, 78
    co-ordination of 80-octane gasoline specification by,
        144
    development of reports by, 242
    establishment of, 211
    inspection policies of, 321–22
    predecessors of, 34
    relations with ANPB, 46
    responsibilities of, 35, 139, 144, 211, 238, 239, 240,
        250, 386
    staff responsibilities of, 240
Fuels and Petroleum Report, 242
Fumigation and bath unit
    development of, 164
    lack of need for, 165

G–3, General Staff, preparation of troop basis, 213
G–4, General Staff, 52, 53, 209, 221, 222
General Administrative Services Division, 24
General Depot Service (Division) SOS, 42, 349
General Maximum Price Regulation
    exemptions from, 274–75
    impact of, on QMC, 273, 274
    issuance of, 273
    QM protests against, 274
    in relation to food procurement, 297, 298
General Motors, 143
General Schedule of Supplies, 258
General Service Division, OQMG, 12
General Staff, 6, 222
General Supplies Branch, Supply Division, 6, 210, 248
Gloves, effect of materials shortages on design of, 73
Government-furnished equipment
    definition of, 289
    illustrations of, 289–90
    procedures for, 289
Government-furnished materials
    extension of program for, 289
    use of, to meet shortages, 288
Gregory, Maj. Gen. Edmund B., 11, 17, 21, 22, 24, 26
Grice, Lt. Col. Letcher O., 75, 110
Grove, Col. William R., 193

Hanson, Earl P., 109n
Hardigg, Brig. Gen. Carl A., 211, 231, 237
Harvard University Fatigue Laboratory, 81, 84
Haversack, 124, 125. *See also* Pack, field.
Headgear, combat
    development of, 101–02
    simplification of, 102
    standardization of, 102
Helmet liner, development of, 101–02
Herringbone twill suit
    one-piece, 97, 99, 100
    two-piece, 97, 99, 100
Herrington, Dr. Lovic P., 84
Hertz, John D., 19
Hertz committee, 19
Hertz report, 19, 19n
Hill, Dr. David B., 84
Hobby, Oveta Culp, 111
Hoffman Company, 163
Holabird Motor Transport Base, 146
Holabird Motor Transport Board, 152
Holabird QM Depot
    centralized purchase of motor transport items at, 244
    developmental work at, 141, 142, 157
    repair operations at, 245
Holding and reconsignment points, 325
Hoos, Dr. Sidney, 219
Huebsch Company, 163

Incoming Property Branch, Storage and Distribution
    Division, 378
Indefinite-quantity contracts, use of, 244, 245, 246
Indiana University, 84–85, 100
Industrial Mobilization Plan, 247
Infantry Board, 101, 126, 136
"Initial factor," 214–15
Initial issue
    definition of, 212
    difficulties of computing, 213–15
Inspection. *See also* QMC Inspection Service.
    development of, 308–22
    Trundle report on, 311
Inspection Branch, 312
Inspection of clothing and equipage
    at contractors' plants, 310, 311
    depot responsibility for prewar, 308
    plans to decentralize, 309–10
Inspection Division, 24
Inspection of petroleum products
    inadequacy of, 321
    by Navy, 320, 322
    QM policies for, 321–22
    under contract provisions, 320, 321
Inspection Section, 312, 321
Inspection of subsistence
    co-ordination problems in, 317–18
    by Department of Agriculture, 316, 317, 318, 320
    role of market center program in, 315
    Veterinary Corps and, 316, 317, 318, 319

Institute of Food Technologists, 199
Inter-Agency Cold Storage Committee, 341
Inter-Agency Food Allocations Committee, 232
Interbranch procurement system
    definition of, 244n
    establishment of, 244
    incorporation in National Defense Act, 244
    QMC participation in, 244
    slow progress of, 262
Interdepartmental procurement
    definition of, 244
    QMC participation in Treasury schedules under, 244,
        245
    supplies obtained from other federal agencies under,
        245
    use of Navy contract in, 245
International Business Machine Corporation, 363
International Division, OQMG, 33, 280
International Division, SOS (ASF), 240, 280, 281, 282
Interstate Commerce Commission, 341
Intrenching tools
    development of all-purpose, 135–36
    importance of, 133
    redesign of, 134
    standardization of combination, 136
    standardization of M–1943, 134, 135
    World War I type of, 134
Issues Forecast Committee, 388

Jacket, field, M–1943, 92, 94, 95
Jacket, field, olive-drab, 88, 97
Jacket, wool field
    classification of, 95
    design of, 94–95
    fitting problem of, 95, 96n
Jeep
    amphibious, 141
    development of, 139–41
    standardization of, 141
    testing of, 141
Jeffersonville QM Depot
    centralized purchase at, 5, 8, 244, 250, 251
    conservation efforts at, 61, 64, 68
    developmental work at, 79, 124, 138, 139, 146, 152,
        155, 159, 161, 163, 166, 167
    distribution area of, 325, 330
    GFE program at, 289, 290
    inspection at, 310, 312
    manufacturing operations at, 44, 79, 171
    procurement at, 169, 272
    role of, in Duck and Webbing Pool, 264
Jerry can. *See* Can, 5-gallon.
Jersey City QM Depot
    centralized purchase at, 250, 319
    petroleum inspection at, 321
    procurement at, 271n
Jesup, Lt. Col. Thomas S., 4
Johnson, Capt. William L., 111
Joint Army and Navy Petroleum Agency, 265

Joint Chiefs of Staff, 35, 281
Joint Procurement Committee, 265
Joint War Production Committee, 257

Kansas City Plan
    criticism of, 337
    determination of storage rates under, 330, 338, 339
    origin of, 336
    procedure under, 337
Kansas City QM Depot, 366
Kansas City Warehouse Association, 366
Kearny, Capt. Cresson H., 109, 137
Kennedy, Maj. Stephen J., 110
Keys, Dr. Ancel, 185
Kraft Cheese Company, 200, 201

Labor
    availability of, and contract replacement, 267
    efforts to overcome shortages of, 307, 308
    problems and QM assistance, 307
Labor Section
    establishment of, 47
    functions of, 47, 268, 284
Landau, Hyman G., 226n
Laundry Branch, Storage and Distribution Division,
    139, 164
Laundry equipment
    criticism of, 1941, 163
    improvement of, 163–64
Leather
    mold prevention in, 120–21
    water-resistance of, 120
Leggings
    introduction of canvas, 88
    move to eliminate, 103
Lend-lease
    accounting system for petroleum products under, 242
    administrative organization for, 280
    QM participation in, 280–81
    QM responsibility for, 279
    reverse, 281
Lend-Lease Act, 279
Letter contracts, 261
Letter purchase orders, 261
Letters of intent, 261, 262
Limitation Orders, 293
Littlejohn, Maj. Gen. Robert M., 75, 94, 95
Logan, Capt. Paul P., 178
Lutes, Lt. Gen. LeRoy, 381

M-Day, 247
M Orders, 293
MacArthur, General Douglas, 99, 109, 138
Machete, 18-inch
    camouflage of, 138
    development of, 136–38
    specification for, 138
    standardization of, 138
    testing of, 138

Machine Tabulating Branch, 229
Machine Tool Section, Resources and Production Divi-
    sion, SOS, 304
MacKeachie, Douglas, 319
Maintenance Division, ASF, 41
Mandatory measures
    in second War Powers Act, 299
    use of, in subsistence procurement, 298, 299, 300
Manpower Priorities Committee, 268
Mareng cells, 144
Marine Corps, 126, 323
Maritime Commission, 264, 276, 287, 350
Market center program
    establishment of, 38, 39, 250
    expansion of, 39
    operation of back-up storage plan under, 342
    organizational arrangements for, 39
    perishable subsistence inspection procedures under,
        315–19
    provision of cold-storage facilities under, 340, 341
Marking
    lack of specification for, 358
    Schenectady Plan for, 359
    study of requirements for, 359
Marshall, General George C., 94, 104
Massachusetts Institute of Technology Textile Labora-
    tories, 85
Master Production Schedule
    as basis of operations, 211
    evolution of, 303
    purpose of, 313, 374
    Research and Development Branch responsibility
        for, 77
    Supply and Demand Studies as basis for, 303
Materials, critical and strategic. See Conservation;
    Substitute materials.
Materials and Conservation Section, 60
Materials Controller, Military Planning Division, 296
Materials handling
    definition of, 347
    effect of shortages on, 350, 351
    increased efficiency in, by standardization of equip-
        ment, 352
    use of mechanical equipment in, 347–52
Materials-handling equipment
    allocation of, 350
    establishment of maintenance standards for, 352
    impact of shortages on production of, 350–51
    OQMG responsibility for, 349–50
    parts-supply program for, 353
    use of, 347–49
Materials shortages
    in down, 72
    in duck, 71
    effect on production of, 63–64
    end of metal, 65
    in fur, 72
    in leather, 73
    in metals, 60–64

Materials shortages—Continued
    in rubber, 66–67
    in silk, 70–71
    in wool, 68–70
Maximum Price Regulation No. 157, 274
Mayne, Alvin, 226
Meats, canned
    criticism of, 196
    developmental work on, 196–97
    types of, 196
Meats, smoked
    developmental work on, 194–95
    problem of, 195–96
Mechanical Section, Research and Development
    Branch, 134, 147, 152, 155, 157, 158, 159, 161,
    163, 165
Medical Corps, 81
Medical Department, 240, 316
Medical Nutrition Laboratory, Office of The Surgeon
    General, 177
Menus
    master, 234
    overseas, 234
Mess gear
    conservation of aluminum in, 61
    stainless steel, 61
Methods and Factors Section, Requirements Branch,
    219n
Methyl-bromide chamber
    development of, 164
    discontinuance of, 165
    improvement of, 164–65
Military Personnel and Training Division, 12, 24
Military Planning Division
    on Army research activities, 51
    and CMP, 296
    developmental work by, 165, 166, 169, 176
    efforts to centralize research in, 35, 36, 77, 117, 139
    establishment of, 29, 31, 76, 211
    functions of, 31, 156, 211
    and Master Production Schedule, 303
    in relation to OSRD, 84, 169
    representation on Food Requirements and Allocation
        Committee, 232
    and requirements, 228, 238, 353
Milk, dehydration of, 200
Milk control legislation, 259–60
Minor Findings Pool, 288
Mobile Equipment Branch, Service Installations Divi-
    sion, 161
Montgomery Ward and Company, 28
Monthly Progress Report, Section 20, 228
Motor Transport Division
    developmental work of, 139, 140, 141, 141n, 146,
        156
    establishment of, 11
    transfer of functions of, 19–22
Motor Transport School, 7, 38
Munitions Bill, 261

Munson Board, 102
Murray Committee, 302

National Association of Dyers & Cleaners, 118
National Bureau of Standards, 45, 81, 121, 309, 321
National Canners' Association, 65, 197, 319
National Defense Act, 1920
    continuation of interbureau procurement by, 244
    provisions for control of supply in, 209, 246, 247,
        283
    war planning by OQMG under, 210
National Defense Advisory Commission, 248, 252, 260,
    268, 290, 309, 319
National Defense Research Committee, OSRD, 45, 84,
    118, 120
National Guard 103, 245, 332, 361
National Research Council, 119, 169
National Youth Administration, 304, 387
Navy Department, 245, 264, 265, 265n
Navy Market Office, 342
Nelson, Donald M., 222, 319
New York Field Survey, 29
New York General Depot, 329
New York Port of Embarkation, 130, 325, 359
Nylon
    allocations of, 74
    uses of, 74

Office of the Adjutant General, 361
Office of Defense Transportation
    control of refrigerator cars by, 341
    delegation of authority over traffic control, 328
Office Management Section, Storage Branch, 376, 377
Office Order No. 84
    background for, 23–24
    issuance of, 24
    overlapping responsibilities under, 26–28
    provisions of, 24–26
Office Order No. 184
    background of, 30–31
    issuance of, 31
    modifications effected by, 31–33
    proposed transfer of subsistence responsibility, 36
Office of the Petroleum Coordinator, 239
Office of Price Administration
    criticism of Kansas City Plan by, 337–38, 339
    exemptions from rulings of, 46, 274–75, 339
    and impact on QMC, 255, 272–75
    issuance of GMPR by, 273, 298
    and QM pricing program, 270–71, 272
    and storage rates, 338, 339
Office of Price Administration and Civilian Supply, 273
Office of Production Management
    conservation by, 68
    establishment of, 58
    priorities under, 58, 59
    procurement objectives and, 222
    and production control, 283, 284, 293
    replacement of, 248, 254
    responsibilities of, 58

Office of The Quartermaster General
  administrative developments of, 1920–39, 6–7
  administrative organization of, 11–36
  commodity-type organization of, 4, 5, 6, 11, 16, 31
  continuance of commodity organization in, 34–36
  creation of supervisory posts, 33–34
  functional reorganization of, 8, 23–24, 30
  organizational surveys, 28–30
  relations of, with other agencies, 45–47
  reorganization of July 1942, 30–33
  reorganization of 1941, 12
Office of Scientific Research and Development, 45, 84
Office of the Stock Comptroller, 377
Office of The Surgeon General, 113, 115, 116, 165, 317
OQMG Allocations Planning Committee, 295
Ordnance, Chief of, 140, 143
Ordnance Department
  development of Commodity Warrant Plan by, 294–95
  loss of responsibility for helmet liner by, 85
  petroleum inspection by, 320
  and petroleum specifications, 143
  transfer of motor transport to, 22, 33, 139, 141n, 157
Ordnance Technical Committee, 144
Organization. See Office of The Quartermaster General.
Organization Planning and Control Division, 24, 26, 33, 34
Overman Act, 244
Overseas Requirements Section, Requirements Branch, 229
Overseas Requirements Tables, 229, 230, 231
Overshoes, arctic, 108
Owens-Illinois Glass Company, 197

Pack, field
  development of M–1944, 126
  M–1928, 124, 125
  M–1943, 125
  standardization of M–1945, 127
Pack, jungle
  development of, 125
  redesignation of, 125
Packaging, subsistence
  administrative responsibility for, 176, 202
  conservation of tin in, 202, 203
  definition of, 176
  developmental work by industry on, 202, 204
  establishment of testing laboratory for, 176
  impact of conservation on, 65, 202–03
  inadequacy of commercial, 201, 202
  military requirements of, 202
  use of substitute materials in, 203–04
Packing, subsistence
  administrative responsibility for, 176, 202
  definition of, 176
  development of V boxes, 205–06
  establishment of testing laboratory for, 176
  failure of commercial, 204
  military requirements of, 202

Packing, subsistence—Continued
  shortage of burlap for, 68
  specifications for, 205
  use of substitute materials in, 206
Packing and Crating Section, Storage and Distribution Division
  preparation of packing specifications by, 356
  responsibilities of, 202, 355
Packing operations. See also Marking.
  centralized depot control of, 356
  development of co-ordinated program for, 355–56
  formulation of specifications for, 356, 357
  improved methods of, 357, 358
  shortcomings of, 355
  use of steel strapping in, 358
Palletized unit program
  initiation of, 354
  problems in, 354
  progress in, 355
Pallets
  description of, 348
  difficulties in procurement of, 351
  standardization program for, 351
  use of, with fork-lift trucks, 347
Parsons, Maj. Gen. J. K., 117
Perishable Branch, Subsistence Division
  functions of, 39
  initiation of seasonal storage program by, 340
Personnel Division, OQMG, 12
Petroleum Administration for War (PAW)
  functions of, 46, 240
  relation of OQMG to, 46
Petroleum Branch
  establishment of, 238, 239
  functions of, 239
  initiation of inspection by, 321, 322
  replacement of, by Fuels and Lubricants Division, 238
Petroleum-handling equipment. See also under individual items.
  development of, 144–46
Petroleum products
  centralized purchase of, 250
  computation of requirements for, 241–42
  responsibility for estimating requirements of, 238, 239, 240
  standardization and simplification of, 143–44
  Z/I supply of, under Treasury Department contracts, 250
Philadelphia QM Depot
  baling of clothing by, 357, 358
  centralized procurement at, 5, 8, 244, 265
  developmental work at, 54, 77, 79, 99, 110, 111, 112, 113, 115, 117, 118, 119, 120, 132, 168
  GFM program at, 288
  inspection by, 309
  manufacturing at, 38, 44, 245
  opposition of, to decentralized inspection, 309, 310, 312, 313

Philadelphia QM Depot—Continued
  opposition of, to factory inspection, 310, 311
  origin of, 4
  simplification of issue by, 97, 99, 122
Phoenix Chemical Laboratory, 321n
Pierce Laboratory of Hygiene, John B., 84
Planning and Control Division
  and conservation, 60
  establishment of, 12
  friction with operating divisions, 12, 14, 15, 28
  functions of, 12, 210, 211, 248, 249, 285, 302
Planning Division, ASF, 239
Planograph System
  advantages of, 347
  disadvantages of, 346
  initiation of, 345
  method of, 345–46
  purpose of, 345
  use of stock locator system in, 346
Plastics, extensive use of, 73–74
Platt, Spencer, 29
Platt Report
  objectives of, 29
  recommendations of, 29–30, 76
Poncho
  development of, 131
  standardization of, 131
Ports of embarkation
  cold-storage facilities for, 342
  control of shipments to, 328
  designation of, for specific theater supply, 325
  flow of supplies to, 325, 327, 328
Post Office Department, 245
Poultry Inspection Service, 316
Pounder, Capt. William F., 94, 106
Preference ratings
  expediting production by, 284
  low status of QM items in, 290
  modification of, 291, 292
  scale of, 290
Price Adjustment Board, SOS, 276
Price Adjustment Section, 276, 277
Price Administrator, OQMG, 270
Price Control Act of 1942, 46
Price policies, development of, 269–71
Priorities Committee, ANMB
  establishment of, 58
  modification of ratings by, 290
Priorities Critical List, 290
Priorities Directive, 290
Priorities Division, OPM, 284
Priorities Regulation 1, 297
Priorities System
  early agencies handling, 58
  establishment of, 290
  inadequacy of initial, 290
  low rating of QMC in, 58, 290, 291
  modification of, 292
  supplements to, 292–96

Priority ratings, for food
  range of, 299
  use of, by QMC, 300
  WFA issuance of, 299–300
  WPB issuance of, 299
Procedures and Stock Accounting Branch, Storage and
    Distribution Division, 377
Procurement
  abandonment of advertising method of, 247, 252–55
  administrative organization for, 248–49
  definition of, 243
  effect of materials shortages on, 59
  expansion of centralized, 249–50, 251
  experimentation with decentralized, 251–52
  influence of other agencies on, 248
  local, and relation to estimating subsistence require-
    ments, 237
  method in 1939, 244, 246
  reduction of local, 251
  special QM responsibilities in, 279–82
  streamlining procurement methods, 252ff.
  supervision of QM, 247–48
  use of compulsory orders in, 297–98
Procurement, joint Army-Navy, 264–65
Procurement Assignment Board, 156, 262, 263
Procurement Control Branch
  establishment of, 248
  functions of, 253, 284
  replacement of, 248
Procurement districts, 247, 252
Procurement Division (Service)
  and assembly of ration components, 183
  authority of, to make supplemental agreements, 257
  civilian supply responsibility of, 282
  as control agency, 8, 44, 255, 285
  effort to transfer subsistence procurement to, 36
  establishment of, 31, 249
  failure to centralize all procurement activity in, 249
  and inspection, 312
  opposition of, on tentage simplification, 169
  and purchase of petroleum products, 34
Procurement Planning
  computation of requirements in, 209
  conflict over, 14
  for emergency procurement of critical materials, 56
  end of, 247
  failure to utilize results of, 210
  influence of, in research, 56, 57
  negotiation of contracts provided for in, 247
  prewar agencies for, 7
  proposed decentralization under, 247
  purpose of, 246–47
  responsibility for, 7
  separation of, from current procurement, 247
Procurement Regulations, 258, 260
Product Development Branch
  clarification of responsibilities of, 29, 76
  creation of, 76

Production
    alleviation of materials shortages in, 288, 289
    controls applied to, 290ff.
    earmarking orders for continuous, 302
    need for continuity in, 301
    planning of, 301–03
Production Branch
    responsibilities of, 60, 283
    transfer of, 27, 76
Production Control
    and allocation of materials, 292–300
    organization for, 283–85
    priorities and, 290–92
    use of GFM and GFE in, 288–90
Production Control Branch, Administrative Division, 11
Production Division, SOS, 223
Production expediting
    by aid in labor problems, 307–08
    by alleviation of shortages, 288ff.
    conflict over, 27
    expansion of plant facilities as a means of, 304–05
    by financial assistance, 305–07
    by location of idle equipment, 303–04
Production Expediting Section
    disintegration of, 284–85
    establishment of, 284
    functions of, 284
Production Requirements Plan
    method of allocation under, 293–94
    purpose of, 294
    QM support of, 295
    reaction to, 294
Production scheduling
    inadequacy of early, 301
    and its relation to requirements, 302–03
    in relation to surplus stocks, 303
Production Section, 285
Production Service
    absorption by Military Planning Division, 31, 211, 285
    creation of, 27
    requirements responsibility of, 211
    research responsibility of, 79
Production Urgency Committee, 268
Program Determination Committee, 350
Property accountability, 360
Property Requisitioning Act, 298
Property Utilization Officer, 385, 386
Property Utilization Section
    establishment of, 386
    redesignation of, 386
Provisional Parachute Group, 185
Purchase
    abandonment of advertising method in, 247, 252–55
    centralization of, for specialty items, 8
    by competitive bidding, 246
    decentralization of, in World War I, 5
    elimination of duplication in responsibility for, 262ff.
    open-market, 246

Purchase—Continued
    reduction of local post, 251
    removal of restrictive legislative controls on, 257–60
Purchase and Contract Branch, Planning and Control Division, 248
Purchase, Storage and Traffic Division, 6, 326, 327
Purchases Division, ASF, 298
Pyle, Ernie, 141, 150
Pyron, Brig. Gen. Walter B., 239

Quartermaster Board
    establishment of, 80
    field study of replacement factors by, 216
    study of accounting policies and inventory by, 366, 367
    tests by, 64, 80–81, 100, 125, 134, 136, 157, 158, 159, 161, 163
Quartermaster Corps (QMC)
    expansion of, 8
    field organization of, 38–45
    functions of, 3, 4, 5, 8
    impact of war on, 8
    loss of functions by, 16–22
    mission of, 3
    origin of, 3, 4
    relations of, with other agencies, 45–47
    status in 1939 of, 7
QMC Inspection Service
    achievements of, 313, 314, 315
    activation of inspection zones, 312, 313
    creation of, 312
    and implementation of Trundle report, 313
    inspection of petroleum products and containers by, 321
    items not controlled by, 312
    problems of, 313
    policy of, 313
Quartermaster Corps Technical Committee (QMCTC)
    establishment of, 54
    in relation to research program, 54, 75, 87
    standardization action by, 104, 110, 125, 134, 141, 151, 163
Quartermaster Equipment Board, 85
Quartermaster General, Office of The. See Office of The Quartermaster General.
Quartermaster Petroleum Laboratory, 322
Quartermaster Purchasing Office, NYC, 265
Quartermaster School, 7, 38, 80
Quartermaster Subsistence School, 193
Quartermaster's Department, 3, 4, 5

Ration, A, 192, 197
Ration, B, 192, 196, 197
Ration, C
    accessory kit for, 184
    beverage powders of, 183–84
    biscuit of, 180, 181, 183
    criticism of, 181, 181n, 184
    development of, 180–84

Ration, C—Continued
  improvement of, 183ff.
  M unit of, 180, 181
  standardization of, 181
Ration, D
  comparable survival types, 180
  as component of other rations, 179
  development of, 178–80
  standardization of, 179
Ration, Five-in-One, 188
Ration, Jungle, 175, 188, 189
Ration, K
  comparable assault phase types, 186, 188
  criticism of, 186
  development of, 184–86
  inclusion of, in Ten-in-One, 189, 190
  standardization of, 185–86
  theater comment on, 181n
Ration, Mountain, 188, 189
Ration, Parachute, 185
Ration, Ten-in-One
  accessory kit for, 191
  development of, 188–91
  and menu planning, 191
  modifications in 1944 of, 189, 190, 191
  predecessors of, 188
  standardization of, 189
  use of, 188
Ration system, garrison, 174
Rations
  administrative organization for development of,
    175–77
  field, in 1939, 175
  problems in development of, 175
Rations, Field
  development of, 192ff.
Rations, special
  development of, 177–92
  initial trend toward specialization of, 207
  military requirements of, 206
  need for simplification of, 189
  refinements in computing requirements for, 235–36
  significance of weight and space in, 207
  use of, 177–78
  World War I, 178
Real Estate Branch, Office of the Chief of Engineers,
  337
Rearmament and Re-equipment Program, 221
Reconstruction Finance Corporation, 276, 305, 332
Red Cross, 232, 329
Redistribution and Disposal Branch, 386
Redistribution and disposal levels, 389
Redistribution and Salvage Officer, 385, 387
"Reefer" ships, 235
Refrigerated semitrailer
  criticism of, 157
  development of, 157
  lightweight model of, 158
  standardization of, 157

Refrigeration equipment. See also under individual items.
  development of, 157–60
  responsibility for development of, 156–57
Refrigerator, 150-cubic foot portable
  development of, 158–59
  lightweight model of, 159
  standardization of, 159
Remount Branch, Supply Division, 248
Renegotiation
  background for, 275, 276
  extent of, 279
  factors considered in, 276–77
  legislative provision for, 276
  QM administrative organization for, 277
  special QM problems in, 279
Renegotiation Act, 276, 277, 278, 279
Renegotiation district offices, location of, 277
Replacement
  computation of, in requirements, 215–18
  definition of, 215
Replacement data teams, 217
Replacement factors
  improvement in accuracy of, 216–18
  percentage expression of, 215
  in theater of operations, 216, 217, 218, 225
  in zone of interior, 216
Requirements
  computation of task force, 229–30
  divided responsibility for, 209, 210, 211, 302
  elements in determination of, 212–21
  evolution of single control of, 211
  prewar method of computing, 210
  significance of accuracy in, 226
  theory of forecasting, 212
Requirements, petroleum
  administrative organization responsible for estimat-
    ing, 238–40
  development of records for computing, 242
  early efforts to improve accuracy of, 239, 240
  elements in forecasting, 241–42
  improvement in records for computing, 242
  method of computing, 232–33
  necessity for centralized control of, 238, 239
  responsibility for computation of, 238, 239, 240
Requirements, subsistence
  administrative organization responsible for estimat-
    ing, 231–32
  allowance for local procurement in estimating, 237
  basic formula in computing, 232–33
  elements in computing, 233–38
  impact of local procurement on, 237–38
  inadequacy of strength data used in estimating, 233
  method of computing, 232–33
  relations of Subsistence and Requirements Branches
    in preparation of, 231–32
  reserves and inventory data for computing, 236–37
Requirements Branch, Fuels and Lubricants Division
  development of records by, 242
  responsibilities of, 240

Requirements Branch, Military Planning Division
computation of task force requirements by, 229
development of overseas requirements tables by, 230,
231
early petroleum requirements by, 238
exceptions to control of, 211
function of, 211
improvement of accuracy in estimating techniques
by, 216, 218, 219, 221, 224, 226, 226n, 238, 366
and subsistence requirements, 231, 232, 233, 236,
238
Requirements Branch, Planning and Control Division,
27, 302
Requirements Committee, PAW, 240
Requirements Division, Production Service, 28, 211
Requirements Division, SOS (ASF), 219, 239, 240
Requisitioning of property
authority for, 298
in subsistence procurement, 299
Research. See also Developmental work.
effect of materials shortages on, 58
financial restrictions on, 55–56, 57
impact of global war on, 57–58
influence of World War I surplus property on, 52, 53
lack of integrated program for, 54–55
significance of Annual Survey of Equipment reports
for, 52–54
status of, on eve of World War II, 51–52
and substitute materials, 56–57, 58
Research and Development Branch
Advisory Board of, 84
centralization of research responsibility in, 35, 76,
77, 79, 80
and conservation, 60
developmental work of, 90, 96, 102, 103, 108, 119,
120, 131, 134, 148, 155, 157, 159, 169, 308
establishment of, 76
functions of, 77, 80, 139, 161, 176
industrial co-operation with, 85, 86, 102
and laboratories, 81, 84, 85, 176
and rations, 189
relations of, with QM Board, 80
Research Project Board, 36
Resources Division, ASF, 239
Resources Division, OQMG
creation of, 76
redesignation of, 77
Revenue Act of 1943, 259, 278
Richmond Depot, 345, 366, 375
Riddell, John T., 101
Robinson, Dr. Sid, 85
Rucksack, development of, 124

Salvage equipment, mobile
criticism of, 160–61
development of, 160, 161–63
one-ton, two-wheel cargo trailers for, 161
responsibility for development of, 161
standardization of, 160, 163
San Francisco General Depot, 250, 319, 330

San Francisco Port of Embarkation, 342
Sanitation Division, The Surgeon General's Office, 164
Saran, 109n
Saybolt, E. W., and Company, 321n
Schenectady Plan, 359
Schuylkill Arsenal, 4. See also Philadelphia Quarter-
master Depot.
Scientific Research and Development, Office of. See
Office of Scientific Research and Development.
Schwartz, Edward R., 85
Scowden, Brig. Gen. Frank F., 324
Seattle QM Depot
centralized purchase of Pacific Coast petroleum prod-
ucts at, 250
experimentation with decentralized procurement at,
252
Second War Powers Act of 1942, 299
Selective Service Act, 8, 297, 332, 361, 370
Selective Service System, 103
Service Branch, Storage and Distribution Division, 378
Service commands
redesignation of corps areas as, 40
relationship to supply agencies, 40–41
Service factor, definition of, 241
Service Installations Division, 24, 31, 157, 165, 353
Set-aside orders
for foods, 300
infractions of, 300
Shelter half
effect of duck shortage on, 131
standardization of improved, 131
use of, in combinations, 131–32
World War I, 130
Shoepac
criticism of, 106, 108
improvement of, 108
use of, 106
Shoe-rebuilding program, and conservation, 73
Shoes, service
conservation of leather in, 73
effect of materials shortages on, 103
emergence of garrison, 102–03
Type I, 102, 103
Type II, 103
Type III, 104
women's, 116
Shugg, Col. R. P., 19n
Signal Corps, 240
Simplification program
in clothing, 90, 92
conflicting factors in, 169, 170, 171, 172
in intrenching tools, 136
in relation to supply, 172
in tents, 169, 171
Siple, Dr. Paul A., 81
Size, tariffs
definition of, 369
original basis of, 370
relation to distribution requirements, 218, 219
revision of, 370

Sleeping bags
    arctic and mountain, 132
    criticism of, 133
    development of, 132–33
    shortage of down for, 72
    standardization of M-1945, 133
    wool, 132
Small Business Act, 251, 266–67
Small War Plants Division, 267
Smaller War Plant Corporation, 266, 267
Smaller War Plants Program, 265–67
Solid Fuels Administration for War (SFAW), 46
Solid Fuels Branch, OQMG, 46
Somervell, Brig. Gen. Brehon B., 19, 19n, 20, 40, 41,
    266
Space control
    centralization of, 344
    forms for obtaining data on, 343
    furthered by control warehouse plan, 345
    relief of storage space shortages by, 342–47
    study of problem of, 343
Space Control Section
    centralized control of space assignment given to, 344
    and Cleveland Plan, 338
    development of planograph system by, 345
    and development of tables for computing space re-
        quirements, 344
    function of, 343
    preparation of space control report by, 343
    space utilization report for, 343
Spaulding, Gen. George, 325
Special Forces Section, Research and Development
    Branch, 131, 134
Specifications
    responsibility of Research and Development Branch
        for, 80
    revision of, to eliminate strategic materials, 59, 60,
        61, 62
Specifications Section, Standardization Branch, 75
Standardization. See also under individual items.
    of depot procedures, 364
    of mechanical equipment, 352–54
    procedure of, 86–87
Standardization Branch
    and early developmental work, 75, 101, 110, 127,
        130, 146
    early responsibility for packing research, 176
    establishment of, 54
    relation of, to QMCTC, 54, 75
    responsibility of, in relation to research, 54, 75
    transfer of, 76
Stat report, 242
Statistical and Public Relations Branch, Administrative
    Division, 11
Steadman, Maj. Frank M., 110, 111
Stephens, Col. J. W. G., 332
Sterilization and bath unit
    criticism of, 164
    description of, 164
    reclassification of, 164

Stevens, Col. Robert T., 264
Stevens, R. R., 28
Stock Accounting Section, Storage Branch, 376, 377,
    378
Stock Comptroller, Office of the. See Office of the Stock
    Comptroller.
Stock control
    development of basic reports for purposes of, 364
    establishment of system for, 366, 367
    need for effective, 365
    stock levels in relation to, 368, 370
Stock Control Board, 366, 371
Stock Control Branch,
    clarification of responsibilities of, 377
    conflicting functions of, 376, 377
    establishment of, 376, 386
    responsibilities of, 375, 376
Stock Control Division, ASF, 225, 389
Stock Control System
    administrative organization for handling, 376–78
    establishment of, 366, 367
    misunderstanding of objectives of, 372
    and replacement issues, 217
    stock levels in relation to, 368, 370
Stock levels
    basis for establishment of, 369
    and "carry-over method" of computing, 219, 224
    definition of, 218, 368, 369
    for depots, 371, 375–76
    development of realistic, 368–69
    downward revision of station, 373, 374
    importance of station, 370–71
    in supply and demand studies, 228
    utility reserve, 371–72
Stock status reports
    improvement of, 367–68
    inadequacy of, 365, 367
    limitations of, 372
    uses of, 368
Storage Branch
    clarification of responsibilities of, 377
    conflict with Stock Control Branch, 376, 377
Storage Control Branch, 11, 15, 332
Storage and Distribution Division (Service)
    computation of short-range requirements by, 211,
        226
    conflicting functions of, 27, 28, 30, 34, 76
    controlled warehouse plan of, 345
    establishment of, 24, 211, 324
    improvement of stock status report by, 366
    1943 administrative changes in, 376
    and requisition guide, 230
    responsibilities of, 44, 176, 282, 324, 355, 386
    and subsistence, 35, 78
Storage facilities
    cold, for perishables, 339–42
    complete utilization of space in, 342–47
    construction of new, 332
    distribution of, in 1940, 329
    enlargement of old, 332

Storage facilities—Continued
  lease or purchase of commercial, 333
Storage operations. *See* Depots.
Stove, one-burner, gasoline, M–1941
  classification of, 149
  development of, 149
Stove, one-burner, gasoline, M–1942
  advantages of, 150
  development of, 149–50
  standardization of, 150
  use of, in combinations, 150
Strauss-Draper Report, 264, 264n
Subsistence. *See also* Rations; Requirements, subsistence.
  administrative organization for research in, 175–77
  cold storage of perishable, 334, 339–42
  indefinite quantity contracts for, 246
  initiation of seasonal storage program of perishable, 340
  peacetime supply of, 174
  reserve stocks of perishable, 340
  set-aside orders for, 300–01
  storage of nonperishable, 336
  supply of, in war, 174
Subsistence Branch
  commodity organization of, 23, 35, 36, 176
  early research responsibility of, 175, 176
  opposition to functional principle, 35, 36
  and preparation of requirements, 210, 211, 231, 232
  prewar location in Supply Division, 6, 35
  redesignation of, as Division, 36
  and research, 152, 175, 176, 177
  transfer to Storage and Distribution Division, 27, 35
Subsistence Department
  absorption of, by QMC, 5, 35, 176
  commodity organization of, 176
  origin of, 3
Subsistence Division. *See also* Subsistence Branch.
  efforts to functionalize, 36
  establishment of, 36
  predecessors of, 35
  in relation to research, 35–36, 176
  as War Department representative in food production and procurement matters, 231
Subsistence Research Laboratory
  and butter products, 201
  and dehydration, 199, 200
  development of special rations by, 177ff.
  developmental work on boneless beef by, 193
  establishment of, 175, 177
  functions of, 176, 177
  packaging research by, 203, 204, 205
  program of, 177
  relation of Military Planning Division to, 35, 176
  research activities of, 35
  testing by, 197
Subsistence Research Project Board, 36, 176
Subsistence School, 178, 193

Subsistence Section, Requirements Branch, 236
Subsistence Section, Research and Development Branch, 176, 177, 182
Substitute materials. *See also* Conservation.
  definition of, 59
  research in, 56, 57, 59
Supply administration
  abandonment of credit system of, 362
  direct system of, 362–63
  establishment of credit system of, 361–62
  scope of QM responsibility for, 208
  use of IBM machines in, 363
  in zone of interior, 361
Supply bureaus, reorganization in World War I, 5, 6
Supply Control Report, 228, 232, 242
Supply Control System
  administration of, in OQMG, 228–29
  advantages of, 227, 229
  co-ordination effected by, 374
  development of, 226–29
  establishment of, 227
Supply Credit System
  depot credits under, 361, 362
  establishment of, 361
  extension of, 361
  objectives of, 361
  shortcomings of, 362
Supply and demand studies
  origin of, 226, 226n, 227
  preparation of, 227–28
  use of realistic theater replacement factors in, 218
Supply Division
  abolition of, 27
  absorption of functions of, by Procurement Service, 249
  commodity organization of, 6, 11, 38, 44, 248
  estimation of current requirements by, 210, 301, 302
  friction with planners, 12, 14, 15, 16
  as procurement control agency, 8
  responsibility for research in 1939, 75, 76, 85, 139
Supply Division, G–4, 18, 42, 361
Supply, Priorities, and Allocations Board, 222
Supply services
  autonomy of, 326, 327
  SOS co-ordination of activities of, 327
Supply system
  character of peacetime, 243–46
  property accountability in, 360
  shift to balanced distribution in, 361
Surgeon General, Office of The. *See* Office of The Surgeon General.
Surgeon General, The, 117, 164
Surplus property
  disposal of, 384–91
  influence of World War I, on research, 52, 53
  nonstandard and obsolete items of, 386–88
  organization for handling, 385–86
  procedures for handling, 386, 387

Surplus property—Continued
  relations of OQMG with other agencies concerned
    with, 390–91
  standard items of, 388–91
Surplus Property Act, 391
Swift & Company, 193

Tables of Allowances, 212, 213, 214
Tables of Basic Allowances, 212, 213, 214
Tables of Equipment, 212, 214
Tables of Organization, 213
Tables of Organization and Equipment, 214
Talbott, Lt. Col. John H., 81
Tank and Combat Vehicles Division, Ordnance Depart-
    ment, 22
Tank truck, 2,500-gallon, 144
Tariff of sizes, 370, 373
Task forces, computation of requirements for, 229–30
Tent, maintenance shelter
  design of, 171
  need for, 170
  standardization of, 171
Tent, portable squad shelter
  classification of, 170
  development of, 170
Tent, sectional hospital
  design of, 171
  standardization of, 171
  use of liner in, 171
Tent, squad
  development of twelve-man, 168
  problem of procurement versus simplification in
    issue of, 393–95
  pyramidal eight-man, 168
  standardization of, 168–69
  structural modifications of, 169–70
Tentage
  color of, 167
  efforts to extend production of, 71
  fire-resistant finish for, 167
  improvements in fabric for, 168
  mildew-proofing of, 167
  shortage of duck for, 71
  weight of, 167
Test Section, 87
Testing
  field, by QM Board, 80–81
  laboratory, 81, 84, 85, 87
  by service boards, 81, 87
Textile Foundation, 84, 118, 168
Textile industry, and renegotiation, 278–79
Textile Institute, Manchester, England, 117, 168
Textile Section, Research and Development Branch,
    100, 110, 117, 131, 168
Textiles, military
  abrasion-resistant finishes for, 119
  fire-resistant treatments for, 120

Textiles, military—Continued
  improvement of, 117
  shrink-resistant treatments for, 119
  standard, in 1939, 55–56, 117
  water-repellent finishes for, 118–19
  water-resistant and wind-resistant, 117
Trailer, 2,500-gallon, 144
Transit storage points. See Holding and reconsignment
    points.
Transportation Branch, G–4, 18
Transportation Control Committee, 328
Transportation Corps
  development of mareng cells by, 144
  establishment of, 18, 328
  operation of holding and reconsignment points by,
    334
  opposition to palletization, 354
  responsibilities of, 328
Transportation Division, OQMG
  development of holding and reconsignment points
    by, 325
  re-establishment of, under National Defense Act, 6
  separation of Motor Transport from, 11
  separation of, from OQMG, 18
Transportation Division, SOS, 18, 328
Transportation Service, SOS, 349
Treasury Department
  criticism of, in handling surplus property, 390
  General Schedule of Supplies of, 245, 258, 320, 324
  objections raised by, in surplus property disposal,
    390–91
  testing of petroleum products under, 321
  use of, in surplus property disposal, 385, 387, 389
Trenchfoot, 104, 106, 108
Troop basis, 213, 222, 233
Truman Committee, 17, 18
Trundle Engineering Company of Cleveland, Ohio
  effect on QMC inspection of, 312
  inspection manual prepared by, 312
  report of, 311
  survey of inspection practices by, 311
Trucks
  industrial co-operation in development of, 141
  responsibility for development of, 139
  and specification problem, 141–42
  standardization efforts on, 142–43
  2½-ton 6x6, 141
  types of, 142, 142n

Under Secretary of War
  direct responsibility of TQMG to, 247
  and expediting production, 284
  and renegotiation, 277
  supervision of contracts by, 254
Uniform, service. See also Clothing.
  conservation of wool in, 70
  modification of World War I, 88

United States Employment Service, 47
United States Rubber Company, 108, 109
University of California, 200
University of Cincinnati, 85, 120
University of Louisville, Institute of Industrial Research, 169
University of Minnesota, 185

V boxes, 205, 206, 357
Vegetables
   canned, 197
   commercial development of, 197
   dehydrated, 197, 198, 199
   frozen, 197
   inspection of, 315, 316
   set-aside orders for, 300
   thermophilic spoilage of, 197, 198
Veterinary Corps, 316, 317, 318, 319
Veterinary Section, Field Headquarters, 318
Victory Program, 222

Wainer, Col. Max R., 80
War Contracts Price Adjustment Board, 279
War Department Commercial Warehouse Pool Plan, 336
War Department Committee on Liquid Fuels and Lubricants, 143
War Depatment Commodity Committees, 56
War Department Price Adjustment Board, 276, 279
War Department Shipping Document, 329
War Department Troop Deployment, 233
War Food Administration
   and allocation of cold-storage space, 341
   issuance of food priority ratings by, 299
   and mandatory orders, 297
   in requisitioning priority, 299
   and set-aside orders, 300–01
War Food Order, 71, 299
War Manpower Commission, 47, 268
War Munitions Program, 222
War Plans and Training Branch, Administrative Division, 11, 12, 210
War Procurenent Plans. See Procurement Planning.
War Produrement and Requirements Branch, Administrative Division, 12

War Production Board
   allocation of materials by 292, 294, 295, 296
   and ASP, 211, 223
   and conservation, 60, 65, 69, 72, 73, 109
   and contract placement, 268
   criticism of Kansas City Plan by, 337
   establishment of, 45
   and idle production equipment, 303, 304
   and labor-shortage areas, 268
   and mandatory orders, 297, 298, 299
   and negotiation of contracts, 254, 255
   OQMG relations with, 46
   priority control of, 58, 291, 292
   set-aside order of, 336
   and study of inventory control, 366
War Shipping Administration, 276, 323, 328
War Shipping Board, 264
War Shipping Document
   origin of, 329
   purpose of, 329
Warehouse Branch, 378
Washington QM Depot
   centralized purchase of offshore lubricants and greases at, 250
   laboratory facilities at, 176
Washington Package Research and Development Laboratory, 176, 202
Weight reduction, 121, 172–73
White, Dr. Jess H., 193, 195
White Company, 143
Williams, Harry, 195
Willys, 143
Women's Army Auxiliary Corps (WAAC)
   development of clothing for, 110–13, 115–16
   establishment of, 110
   redesignation of, as WAC, 110
Women's Army Corps (WAC). See WAAC.
Women's Clothing Section, Research and Development Branch, 111
Woodbury, Lt. Robert L., 109n
Work Projects Administration, 304, 387, 388

Yellow Truck and Coach, 143

Zone Inspection System, contract administration under, 252
Zone system of supply, 326

U.S. GOVERNMENT PRINTING OFFICE: 2014   385-862

PIN:073268—000